Eighth Edition

Strategies for Teaching Students with Learning and Behavior Problems

Sharon Vaughn
University of Texas–Austin

Candace S. Bos
Late of University of Texas–Austin

PEARSON

Boston   Columbus   Indianapolis   New York   San Francisco   Upper Saddle River
Amsterdam   Cape Town   Dubai   London   Madrid   Milan   Munich   Paris   Montreal   Toronto
Delhi   Mexico City   São Paulo   Sydney   Hong Kong   Seoul   Singapore   Taipei   Tokyo

Vice President and Editor in Chief: Jeffery W. Johnston
Executive Editor: Ann Castel Davis
Editorial Assistant: Penny Burleson
Senior Development Editor: Hope Madden
Vice President, Director of Marketing:
  Margaret Waples
Marketing Manager: Joanna Sabella
Marketing Coordinator: Brian Mounts
Senior Managing Editor: Pamela D. Bennett
Senior Project Manager: Sheryl Glicker Langner
Senior Operations Supervisor: Matthew Ottenweller
Senior Art Director: Diane C. Lorenzo
Cover Designer: Kellyn E. Donnelly

Photo Researcher: Lori Whitley
Coordinator, Rights and Permissions:
  Rebecca Savage
Cover image: © JLP/Jose L. Pelaez/Corbis
Full Service Project Coordinator:
  Mary Tindle/S4Carlisle Publishing Services
Media Producer: Autumn Benson
Media Project Manager: Rebecca Norsic
Composition: S4Carlisle Publishing Services
Printer/Binder: Edwards Brothers
Cover Printer: Lehigh-Phoenix Color/Hagerstown
Text Font: 10/12 Garamond

Credits and acknowledgments borrowed from other sources and reproduced, with permission, in this textbook appear on appropriate page within text.

Every effort has been made to provide accurate and current Internet information in this book. However, the Internet and information posted on it are constantly changing, so it is inevitable that some of the Internet addresses listed in this textbook will change.

Photo Credits: p. 2, iStockphoto.com; p. 30, GeoStock/Getty Images, Inc.—Photodisc/Royalty Free; p. 54, Stretch Photography/Getty Images, Inc.—Blend Images; p. 78, BananaStock/Superstock Royalty Free; p. 122, Laura Bolesta/Merrill; p. 152, Shutterstock; p. 188, David Mager/Pearson Learning Photo Studio; p. 232, Courtesy of AbleNet, Inc.; p. 284, Hope Madden/Merrill; p. 320, Shutterstock; p. 366, Scott Cunningham/Merrill

Library of Congress Cataloging-in-Publication Data
Vaughn, Sharon
  Strategies for teaching students with learning and behavior problems
/Sharon Vaughn, Candace S. Bos.—8th ed.
      p. cm.
  Sharon Vaughn listed as first author on earlier eds.
  ISBN-13: 978-0-13-703467-3
  ISBN-10: 0-13-703467-9
  1. Learning disabled children—Education—United States.   2. Problem
children—Education—United States.   3. Remedial teaching—United
States.   I. Bos, Candace S., 1950-   II. Title.
  LC4705.B67 2006 (Prev. ed.)
  371.9—dc22
                                            2010048787

10 9 8 7 6 5 4 3 2 1

www.pearsonhighered.com

ISBN-10:   0-13-703467-9
ISBN-13: 978-0-13-703467-3

To Jane Vaughn and Lucy Vaughn who practiced progress monitoring by asking me regularly how far I was and whether I would finish the book on time.

SHARON VAUGHN (Ph.D., University of Arizona) holds the H. E. Hartfelder/ Southland Corporation Regents Chair in Human Development and is the Executive Director of the Meadows Center for Preventing Educational Risk at the Univeristy of Texas. She is a recipient of the AERA Special Education SIG distinguished researcher award. She was the editor-in-chief of the Journal of Learning Disabilities and the coeditor of Learning Disabilities Research and Practice. Dr. Vaughn is the author of numerous books and research articles that address the reading and social outcomes of students with learning difficulties including Teaching Students Who Are Exceptional, Diverse, and At Risk in the General Education Classroom, with Jeanne Schumm and Candace Bos (4th ed., Allyn & Bacon). Currently she is the principal or coprincipal investigator on several Institute for Education Science, National Institute for Child Health and Human Development, and Office of Special Education Programs research grants investigating effective interventions for students with learning disabilities and behavior problems as well as students who are English language learners.

While traveling by car on a typical Arizona scorcher between Phoenix and Tucson after attending a state Association for Children and Adults with Learning Disabilities meeting, we were discussing the content and assignments for the methods courses we taught at our respective universities. The conversation inevitably drifted to what we would like to do better. Because both of us were responsible for preparing teachers and potential teachers to work effectively with students who have learning and behavior problems, we spent a considerable amount of time discussing the content of our classes. We concluded that we would like the class and the textbook for the class to provide adequate background in procedures for teaching skill and content areas such as reading, math, oral and written expression, and social and study skills. We also would like our students to understand which methods are most effective with what types of students and why.

The first edition of this book was the result of that initial lengthy discussion, which focused on the ideal content that would prepare teachers to meet the needs of elementary and secondary students with learning and behavior problems. Each new edition continues to present fresh ideas and information, always while keeping sight of our original purpose.

New to This Edition

Streamlined to better fit into a single semester, the eighth edition contains more applied teaching strategies than ever before, thoroughly revised chapters on teaching and assessing math as well as response to intervention (RTI), and an increased integration and emphasis on the topics of coteaching and working with paraprofessionals and technology.

- **Chapter 3, Response to Intervention**, is completely reconsidered, restructured, and revised.
- **Chapter 11, Assessing and Teaching Mathematics**, is completely reconsidered and revised with a dual focus on concrete classroom application and the needs of secondary students.
- All new **Tech Tips** in every chapter highlight software and other technologies that assist with instruction and student learning.

- **Evidence-Based Practice** is called out throughout chapters with classroom applications.
- **Thirty-three new Apply the Concept** features throughout chapters provide guidelines and suggestions to better prepare you to organize classroom instruction.
- **Web Resources** margin notes at points of interest throughout chapters encourage further exploration of chapter topics.

Additional Chapter Changes

CHAPTER 1: Planning and Teaching for Understanding

- Introduction rewritten to reflect current views on instructional models of learning disabilities
- The questions that educators should consider when determining the appropriate inclusion model were added with commentary on how to resolve these questions
- Prevalence and incidence data updated
- Rationale for the importance of inclusion is provided
- Progress monitoring and assessment significantly revised and updated
- Instructional adaptations revised and updated

CHAPTER 2: Approaches to Learning and Teaching

- Applied behavior analysis changed with an emphasis on classroom examples
- Tables and figures were significantly revised to provide an even clearer linkage to classroom applications
- This chapter was edited extensively to ensure clarity and brevity

CHAPTER 3: Response to Intervention

- *Entirely New!*

CHAPTER 4: Promoting Social Acceptance and Managing Behavior

- Information on cooperative learning considerably revised and updated
- Classroom-based examples of instructional practices provided

- Coordinating services revised to include RTI
- Social competence focus is shifted to social difficulties
- Social status revised
- Characteristics of social difficulties modified extensively
- New section on self-regulation
- All instructional practices updated

CHAPTER 5: Coteaching and Collaborating: Working with Professionals and Families

- New and deeper coverage of paraprofessionals
- Expanded discussion on coteaching

CHAPTER 6: Assessing and Teaching Oral Language

- Updated references, citations, and interpretations of findings related to oral language, with implications for students with learning and behavior disorders
- Revisions of school-age language development, with consideration of findings related to the target population for this book
- Section on pragmatic language completely revised to reflect current research and practice as related to target population
- Instructional and assessment practices revised to reflect current research and practice

CHAPTER 7: Assessing and Teaching Reading: Phonological Awareness, Phonics, and Word Recognition

- Updated research on and practice in phonological awareness
- Updated research on and knowledge of progress monitoring

CHAPTER 8: Assessing and Teaching Reading: Fluency and Comprehension

- Updated normative information on oral reading fluency in tables and text
- Considerably refined research on practice information on read-alouds
- Included scaffolded sustained silent reading with classroom application
- Guidelines for book accessibility considerably revised
- Provided response to intervention and reading comprehension updates
- Applications for reading comprehension revised
- Approaches to teaching reading comprehension updated, deleted, and revised

CHAPTER 9: Assessing and Teaching Writing and Spelling

- Process approach to writing revised and updated with clearer connections to students with learning disabilities and behavior disorders
- Approaches to improving writing revised and updated to reflect research-based practices
- Phonics rules for spelling revised and updated
- Instructional practices in spelling updated to reflect current research and practice
- Instructional practices in handwriting updated to reflect current research and practice

CHAPTER 10: Assessing and Teaching Content Area Learning and Vocabulary Instruction

- Updated instructional practices related to content area teaching
- Revised and updated family focus on improving language and vocabulary
- Included a section on big ideas of content learning
- Updated instructional applications

CHAPTER 11: Assessing and Teaching Mathematics

- *Entirely New!*

Text Organization and Special Features

From that conversation many years ago, we determined three important goals for this text:

1. *Foundations.* To provide information about general approaches to learning and teaching so that the foundation for the methods and procedures for teaching all learners can be better understood.
2. *Detailed methods.* To supply descriptions of methods and procedures that include sufficient detail so that teachers and other professionals know how to use them.
3. *Organization and planning.* To present information about classroom and behavior management, consultation, and collaboration with families and professionals so that beginning teachers can develop a plan of action for the school year and experienced teachers can refine these skills.

To help meet these goals, a number of special features have been developed. Apply the Concept features, Evidence Based Practice features, and Instructional Activities, for example, give special educators hands-on classroom implementations in reading, writing, content areas, and mathematics proven successful for all students, including those with learning and behavior problems.

Throughout chapters you'll find:

●●●●●● *Apply the Concept* ●●●●●●● ←

Apply the Concept features, many brand new to this edition, provide guidelines and suggestions to better prepare you to organize classroom instruction.

1-1   Adopting an RTI Model to Identify Students with Learning Disabilities

The 2004 reauthorization of IDEA recommends that states and schools abandon the IQ–achievement discrepancy to identify students with learning disabilities and instead use an

RTI approach. However, IDEA does not require that schools use RTI. Your principal asks your opinion on what your school should do to identify students with learning disabilities.

What are the pros and cons of the IQ–achievement discrepancy and RTI? Which model do you recommend that your school use in determining special education eligibility?

Evidence-Based Practice sections explicitly outline classroom applications for implementing large-scale strategies for teaching students with special needs.

●●● **EVIDENCE-BASED PRACTICE**

Phonemic Remedial Reading Lessons

PROCEDURES: The program begins by developing the readiness level for the lessons. Readiness skills include auditory discrimination and auditory sound blending. Figure 7-3 presented a simple procedure for teaching sound blending. Developing readiness also includes learning the sound–symbol associations for the short *a* sound and eleven consonant sounds (i.e., /c/, /d/, /f/, /g/, /h/, /l/, /m/, /p/, /s/, /t/, /w/).

Once these skills have been learned, the first lesson is introduced (see Figure 7-19). For each lesson, students sound out each word in each line, one letter at a time, and then give the complete word. Each lesson is organized into four parts and is based on the principle of minimal change. In the first part, only the initial consonant changes in each sequence; in the second part, only the final consonant changes; in the third part, both the initial and final consonants change; in the fourth part, the space between letters in a word is normal.

In addition to these drill lessons, high-frequency sight words are introduced and highly controlled stories are interspersed throughout the program. Frequent review lessons are also provided.

COMMENTS: This program provides a systematic and intensive approach to teaching phonic analysis skills to beginning readers. However, the approach places little emphasis on comprehension and reading for meaning and incorporates limited practice in connected text. We suggest using other books to give students the opportunity to practice their word identification and comprehension skills with other reading materials.

Instructional Activities provide a bank of step-by-step activities to bring with you into the classroom.

INSTRUCTIONAL ACTIVITIES

This section provides instructional activities related to mathematics. Some of the activities teach new skills; others are best suited for practice and reinforcement of already acquired skills. For each activity, the objective, materials, and teaching procedures are described.

▶ **Two-Digit Numbers: Focus on Reversals**

Objective: To help students understand and use two-digit numbers successfully (for use with students who write 23 for 32, 41 for 14, etc.).

Grades: Primary

Materials: Objects that can be grouped by tens (e.g., pencils, paper, chips, sticks)

2 tens   3 ones

Teaching Procedures: Four steps are recommended: First, tell the students to group objects such as Popsicle sticks or chips in tens and then to tell the number of tens and the number of ones left over. Next, the students count orally by tens and use objects to show the count (e.g., 2 tens is 20, 6 tens is 60, and so on). When multiples of ten are established, extra ones are included (e.g., 2 tens and 3 is 23). Because of naming irregularities, teens are dealt with last.

Tech Tips (*All New!*) consider software, Web sites, assistive technology, and other technologies and their implications in the classroom.

 Tech TIPS

IEP SOFTWARE PROGRAMS

The most useful IEP software programs allow teachers to select from skill sequences and author long-term and short-term objectives, freely customizing skills and objectives to meet individual needs. Often school systems or special education units adopt one particular system. You may find that to be the case in your school district. Some programs are installed in individual computers whereas others are Web based. Web-based systems are especially useful because you can access the data from any online computer while maintaining

security by the use of a password. It is also easier to move students' records along as they move from teacher to teacher and school to school.

Following is a list of IEP management software names along with their primary Web addresses:

- IEPMaker Pro, by Chalkware Education Solutions at www.iepware.com
- Class/Bridge IEP Program, by Class/Bridge at www.classplus.com
- IEP Writer Supreme II, by Super School Software at www.superschoolsoftware.com

Spotlight on Diversity
Considerations for Families Who Are Culturally and Linguistically Diverse

1. Assume that families want to help their children.
2. Consider your language when talking with parents and be thoughtful about not using language that suggests a deficit model of considering the child.
3. Provide materials in a range of formats including orally, in writing (family's language), through videotape, and through formal and informal presentations.
4. For parents who are interested, provide opportunities for families to learn the skills and activities the students are learning so they can reinforce them in the home.
5. Provide opportunities for families to influence their child's educational program.
6. Provide workshops that include role playing and rehearsing situations between families and school

personnel to increase families' confidence in working with school personnel.
7. Involve families from the community who are familiar with the culture and speak the home language of the children's families in work at the school.
8. Provide an informal meeting with families so they can exchange experiences and learn tips from each other.
9. Invite families to school and ask them to share their backgrounds or activities with other students and families.
10. Provide ongoing professional development for teachers and other educators so that they are familiar with linguistic and cultural practices and respond sensitively with this knowledge to parents and other family members.

Spotlight on Diversity features spotlight methods for teaching student populations who are culturally and linguistically diverse, including English language learners.

Visit the MyEducationLab for this course to enhance your understanding of chapter concepts with a personalized Study Plan. You'll also have the opportunity to hone your teaching skills through video-based Assignments and Activities, IRIS Center Resources, and Building Teaching Skills and Dispositions lessons.

MyEducationLab margin note and end-of-chapter feature clearly align chapter concepts with the rich media examples and applications available on the Web site that accompanies the text.

Supplements

Online Instructor's Manual with Test Items

An expanded and improved online Instructor's Manual includes numerous recommendations for presenting and extending text content. The manual consists of chapter overviews, key concepts, a lecture-discussion outline, Think and Apply sections, and suggested readings. You'll also find a complete, chapter-by-chapter bank of test items.

Online PowerPoint Lecture Slides

The PowerPoint lecture slides are available on the Instructor Resource Center at http://www.pearsonhighered.com. These lecture slides highlight key concepts and summarize key content from each chapter of the text.

The Instructor's Manual with Test Bank and the lecture slides are available on the Instructor Resource Center at http://www.pearsonhighered.com. To access the items, go to http://www.pearsonhighered.com, click on **Educators**, and then on **Download instructor resources** to get the registration page. Here you'll be able to log in or complete a one-time registration for a user name and password.

Pearson MyTest

Pearson MyTest is a powerful assessment generation program that helps instructors easily create and print quizzes and exams. Questions and tests are authored online, allowing ultimate flexibility and the ability to efficiently create

and print assessments anytime, anywhere! Instructors can access Pearson MyTest and their test bank files by going to http://www.pearsonmytest.com to log in, register, or request access. Features of Pearson MyTest include:

Premium Assessment Content

- Draw from a rich library of assessments that complement your Pearson textbook and your course's learning objectives.
- Edit questions or tests to fit your specific teaching needs.

Instructor-Friendly Resources

- Easily create and store your own questions, including images, diagrams, and charts using simple drag-and-drop and Word-like controls.
- Use additional information provided by Pearson, such as the question's difficulty level or learning objective, to help you quickly build your test.

Time-Saving Enhancements

- Add headers or footers and easily scramble questions and answer choices—all from one simple toolbar.
- Quickly create multiple versions of your test or answer key, and when ready, simply save to MS-Word or PDF format and print!
- Export your exams for import to Blackboard 6.0, CE (WebCT), or Vista (WebCT)!

New! CourseSmart eTextbook Available

CourseSmart is an exciting new choice for students looking to save money. As an alternative to purchasing the printed textbook, students can purchase an electronic version of the same content. With a CourseSmart eTextbook, students can search the text, make notes online, print out reading assignments that incorporate lecture notes, and bookmark important passages for later review. For more information, or to purchase access to the CourseSmart eTextbook, visit www.coursesmart.com.

MyEducationLab

myeducationlab *The power of classroom practice*

In *Preparing Teachers for a Changing World*, Linda Darling-Hammond and her colleagues point out that grounding teacher education in real classrooms—among real teachers and students and among actual examples of students' and teachers' work—is an important, and perhaps even an essential, part of training teachers for the complexities of teaching in today's classrooms. MyEducationLab is an on-line learning solution that provides contextualized interactive exercises, simulations, and other resources designed to help develop the knowledge and skills teachers need. All of the activities and exercises in MyEducationLab are built around essential learning outcomes for teachers and are mapped to professional teaching standards. Utilizing classroom video, authentic student and teacher artifacts, case studies, and other resources and assessments, the scaffolded learning experiences in MyEducationLab offer pre-service teachers and those who teach them a unique and valuable education tool.

For each topic covered in the course you will find the following features and resources:

Connection to National Standards

Now it is easier than ever to see how coursework is connected to national standards. Each topic on MyEducationLab lists intended learning outcomes connected to the appropriate national standards. All of the activities and exercises in MyEducationLab are mapped to the appropriate national standards and learning outcomes as well.

Assignments and Activities

Designed to enhance student understanding of concepts covered in class and save instructors preparation and grading time, these assignable exercises show concepts in action (through video, cases, and/or student and teacher artifacts). They help students deepen content knowledge and synthesize and apply concepts and strategies they read about in the book. (Correct answers for these assignments are available to the instructor only under the Instructor Resource tab.)

Building Teaching Skills and Dispositions

These learning units help students practice and strengthen skills that are essential to quality teaching. After reading the steps involved in a core teaching process, students are given an opportunity to practice applying this skill via videos, student and teacher artifacts, and/or case studies of authentic classrooms. Providing multiple opportunities to practice a single teaching concept, each activity encourages a deeper understanding and application of concepts, as well as the use of critical thinking skills.

IRIS Center Resources

The IRIS Center at Vanderbilt University (http://iris.peabody.vanderbilt.edu—funded by the U.S. Department of Education's Office of Special Education Programs (OSEP) develops training enhancement materials for pre-service and in-service teachers. The Center works with experts from across the country to create challenge-based interactive modules, case study units, and podcasts that provide research-validated information about working with students in inclusive settings. In your MyEducationLab course we have integrated this content where appropriate.

Simulations in Classroom Management

One of the most difficult challenges facing teachers today is how to balance classroom instruction with classroom management. These interactive cases focus on the classroom management issues teachers most frequently encounter on a daily basis. Each simulation presents a challenge scenario at the beginning and then offers a series of choices to solve each challenge. Along the way students receive mentor feedback on their choices and have the opportunity to make better choices if necessary. Upon exiting each simulation students will have a clear understanding of how to address these common classroom management issues and will be better equipped to handle them in the classroom.

Teacher Talk

This feature emphasizes the power of teaching through videos of master teachers, each speaker telling their own compelling stories of why they teach. These videos help teacher candidates see the bigger picture and consider why what they are learning is important to their career as a teacher. Each of these featured teachers has been awarded the Council of Chief State School Officers Teachers of the Year award, the oldest and most prestigious award for teachers.

Study Plan Specific to Your Text

A MyEducationLab Study Plan is a multiple choice assessment tied to chapter objectives, supported by study material. A well-designed Study Plan offers multiple opportunities to fully master required course content as identified by the objectives in each chapter:

- *Chapter Objectives* identify the learning outcomes for the chapter and give students targets to shoot for as they read and study.
- *Multiple Choice Assessment*s assess mastery of the content. These assessments are mapped to chapter objectives, and students can take the multiple

choice quiz as many times as they want. Not only do these quizzes provide overall scores for each objective, but they also explain why responses to particular items are correct or incorrect.

- *Study Material: Review, Practice and Enrichment* give students a deeper understanding of what they do and do not know related to chapter content. This material includes text excerpts, activities that include hints and feedback, and interactive multi-media exercises built around videos, simulations, cases, or classroom artifacts.

Course Resources The Course Resources section on MyEducationLab is designed to help students put together an effective lesson plan, prepare for and begin their career, navigate their first year of teaching, and understand key educational standards, policies, and laws. The Course Resources Tab includes the following:

- The **Lesson Plan Builder** is an effective and easy-to-use tool that students can use to create, update, and share quality lesson plans. The software also makes it easy to integrate state content standards into any lesson plan.
- The **IEP Tutorial** shows how to develop appropriate IEPs and how to conduct effective IEP conferences.
- The **Preparing a Portfolio** module provides guidelines for creating a high-quality teaching portfolio.
- **Beginning Your Career** offers tips, advice, and other valuable information on:
  - *Resume Writing and Interviewing:* Includes expert advice on how to write impressive resumes and prepare for job interviews.
  - *Your First Year of Teaching:* Provides practical tips to set up a first classroom, manage student behavior, and more easily organize for instruction and assessment.
  - *Law and Public Policies:* Details specific directives and requirements teachers need to understand under the No Child Left Behind Act and the Individuals with Disabilities Education Improvement Act of 2004.
- **Special Education Interactive Timeline** Use this tool to build your own detailed timelines based on different facets of the history and evolution of special education.

Certification and Licensure The Certification and Licensure section is designed to help students pass their licensure exam by giving them access to state test requirements, overviews of what tests cover, and sample test items.

The Certification and Licensure tab includes the following:

- **State Certification Test Requirements:** Here students can click on a state and will then be taken to a list of state certification tests.

- Students can click on the **Licensure Exams** they need to take to find:
  - Basic information about each test
  - Descriptions of what is covered on each test
  - Sample test questions with explanations of correct answers
- **National Evaluation Series™ by Pearson:** Here students can see the tests in the NES, learn what is covered on each exam, and access sample test items with descriptions and rationales of correct answers. They can also purchase interactive online tutorials developed by Pearson Evaluation Systems and the Pearson Teacher Education and Development group.
- **ETS Online Praxis Tutorials:** Here students can purchase interactive online tutorials developed by ETS and by the Pearson Teacher Education and Development group. Tutorials are available for the Praxis I exams and for select Praxis II exams.

Visit www.myeducationlab.com for a demonstration of this exciting new online teaching resource.

Acknowledgments

Candace S. Bos and I launched this book together as junior faculty 30 years ago. Since her death, I have done one of the most challenging things of my professional career, writing and revising the book without my dear friend and colleague. I knew what an outstanding writer and teacher–educator she was; I know even better now. Working on this book is a clear reminder of how much she taught me and how hard it is to work without her. Ann Davis, editor, provided more than her usual excellent support and good ideas. Hope Madden, developmental editor, provided valuable suggestions and advice. Hope is so capable and supportive that her assistance has made this the best edition yet. I would also like to thank Dr. Amory Cable for her careful and thoughtful work.

Many people deserve a great deal more acknowledgment than their names appearing here will provide. I wish to acknowledge and thank the teachers whom Candy and I have written about in this book. The time we have spent in their classrooms—observing, discussing, and teaching—has afforded us the ability to write a book that is grounded in classroom experiences and practices. These teachers include Juan Caberra, Judy Cohen, Joan Downing, Mary Lou Duffy, Joyce Duryea, Jane Eddy, Louise Fournia, Joan Gervasi, Sally Gotch, Linda Jones, Sharon Kutok, Tom Lebasseur, Tiffany Royal, Marynell Schlegel, Mary Thalgott, and Nina Zaragoza.

I also thank Janette Klingner of University of Colorado at Boulder for her support on the RTI chapter, and Terry L. Weaver of Union University for contributing and revising the math chapter. I would also like to thank several individuals whose expert support and assistance in previous editions remain in this edition: Dr. Ae-hwa Kim and Dr. Jeannie Wanzek. A special thank you to Kim Shumake for all of her support.

I especially wish to acknowledge the following individuals for their reviews of the eighth edition: Dona Bauman, University of Scranton; Cindi Nixon, Francis Marion University; Naomi Quintana, Point Loma Nazarene University; Peggy Rawn, Loyola Marymount University; and Cathy Warmack, Murray State University.

A special thank-you for the contributions of Dr. Amory Cable, Dr. Alison Gould Boardman and Katie Klingler Tackett who provided outstanding suggestions and practical ideas.

Special thanks also to my husband, Jim, and to my brother, Jim, and his wife, Meg, who provided us with a gorgeous place to write this new edition of the book in Geneva, Switzerland, and to their children Jane and Lucy who practiced progress monitoring by asking me regularly how far I was and whether I would finish the book on time.

Most important of all, we would like to thank the teacher whose observations, research, and thinking has done more to guide our development and the field of special education than any other: Samuel A. Kirk.

BRIEF CONTENTS

CONTENTS

Contents **xix**

SPECIAL FEATURES

APPLY THE CONCEPTS

EVIDENCE-BASED PRACTICE

TECH TIPS

SPOTLIGHT ON DIVERSITY

Strategies for Teaching Students with Learning and Behavior Problems

1

Planning and Teaching for Understanding

FOCUS Questions

1. Who are students with learning and behavior problems?
2. What issues relate to appropriate identification of students with learning disabilities?
3. What is an individualized education program (IEP), and what is the process for developing and updating an IEP?
4. What goes into teaching students with learning and behavior problems?

This book is about children and adolescents who have difficulty learning and interacting appropriately in school. If you saw these children in school, it is very likely that you would not be able to readily identify them until they were engaged in an academic activity that challenged them (e.g., writing, reading) or they were exhibiting extreme behaviors (e.g., screaming out of control). What are these students like? Teachers describe them this way:

Servio has a very poor self-concept. He is extremely sensitive and gets upset at the least little thing. For example, yesterday he noticed that his red crayon was broken, and he started to cry. When I told him he could have another red crayon, he continued to cry, saying that he wanted this red crayon fixed. He often says he can't do things, that he doesn't care, and that he is bad. When he has problems at home, he says he's going to be bad. He often says that he was punished at home for being bad, and he's going to be bad today at school. He used to throw things at school, but he doesn't do that anymore. He doesn't have any friends in the class, and most of the other students don't want him around them.

Dana has a great deal of difficulty with her work. She appears to have trouble remembering. Well, not always. Sometimes she remembers how to read a word; other days she looks at the same word, and it's like she has to scan all of the information in her head to try to locate the name of the word. I know she is trying, but it is very frustrating because her progress is so slow. She is also very easily distracted. Even when the instructional assistant is working with her alone, she will look up and stop working at the littlest things. Something like the air-conditioning going on and off will distract her from her work. I know she is bright enough, but she seems to have serious problems learning.

Tina is more work for me than the rest of my class put together. She has both academic problems and behavior problems. For example, after I have explained an assignment to the class, Tina always asks me several questions about the assignment. It's like I have to do everything twice, once for the class and then again for Tina. She has a terrible time with reading. She reads so slowly, and she often reads the wrong word. For example, she will say "carrot" for "circus" and "monster" for "mister." She often doesn't know what she's read after she's finished reading it. Also, she can never sit still. She is always moving around the room, sharpening her pencil, getting a book, looking out the window. It is hard for her to do the same thing for more than a few minutes. She's always bugging the other students. She's not really a bad kid, it's just that she is always doing something she's not supposed to be doing, and she takes a lot of my time.

The purpose of this book is to acquaint you with the teaching skills and strategies necessary to understand and teach students like Servio, Dana, and Tina. Throughout the chapters you will note that there will be Web sites designed to provide more information, like the one in the margin here.

This chapter provides background information on students with learning and behavior problems and an overview of the teaching–learning process. This chapter also introduces responses to intervention (RTI) as a framework for facilitating identification of students with learning and behavior problems.

As you read this book, we encourage you to reflect on how the information presented can be interwoven into your thoughts about the teaching–learning process. We encourage you to seek opportunities to work with students with learning and behavior problems and to utilize the research-based practices presented in this book in seeking supervision and feedback from well-prepared professionals. We also encourage you to use a reflective, problem-solving orientation to teaching. This model of teaching and learning serves as a framework for reflecting on what you do, consulting with others to seek better information and practices, and making adjustments to improve outcomes for students with learning and behavior problems.

Students with Learning and Behavior Problems

Who are students with learning and behavior problems? Most teaching professionals are able to recognize with little difficulty those students who have learning and behavior problems. They are students who call attention to themselves in the classroom because they have difficulty learning and interacting appropriately. Students with learning and/or behavior problems manifest one or more of the following behaviors:

- *Poor academic performance*. Students display significant problems in one or more academic areas such as spelling, reading, and mathematics. The key to understanding students with learning disabilities is that they display unexpected underachievement.

- *Attention problems*. Many students seem to have difficulty working for extended periods of time on a task. They may have trouble focusing on the teacher's directions. These students are often described by teachers as being easily distracted.

- *Hyperactivity*. Some students are overactive and have a difficult time staying in their seats and completing assigned tasks. They move from task to task, and often from location to location in the classroom. When working on an assignment, the least little noise will distract them.

- *Memory*. Many students have a hard time remembering what they were taught. Often their difficulty remembering is associated with symbols such as letters and numbers. These students may remember something one day but not the next.

- *Poor language abilities*. Many students have language difficulties that are manifested in a number of ways. As toddlers, these students may have taken longer in learning to talk. Often these language problems can be corrected through speech therapy. Many also have difficulty developing phonological awareness skills—hearing the sounds of language separately and being able to blend and segment them (e.g., hearing /b/, /a/, /t/ separately and then blending to say "bat"). Students may have difficulty with vocabulary, understanding the concept, using language to adequately express themselves orally or in writing, or developing age-appropriate math skills.

- *Aggressive behavior*. Some students are physically or verbally assaultive. They may hit, kick, get into fights, and/or verbally threaten or insult others. These children are easily upset and cope with being upset by acting out.

- *Withdrawn behavior*. Some students seldom interact with others. Unlike shy students, who may have one or two friends, these students are real loners who avoid involvement with others.

- *Bizarre behavior*. Some students display unusual patterns of behavior. They may stare for long periods of time at objects that they hold in the light, they may sit and rock, or they may display aggressive behaviors at times and withdrawn behaviors at other times.

Students with learning and/or behavior problems often exhibit more than one of these behaviors. Yet some students exhibit these behaviors and are not identified as having learning or behavior problems. There are other factors that teachers consider when determining how serious a learning and behavior problem is.

Factors to Consider in Determining How Serious a Learning or Behavior Problem Is

Fifteen to 25 percent of all students have some type of learning or behavior problem; however, students with learning disabilities and behavior problems that are identified as special education represent a much smaller percentage of the student population (typically less than 6%). Students with learning disabilities are five times more prevalent than those with behavior disorders. There are several factors to consider when you are determining how serious a problem is:

1. *Persistence of the problem.* Sometimes a student has a learning or behavior problem for a short period of time, perhaps while there is some type of crisis in the family, and then it disappears. These behaviors and feeling states are not considered problems if they occur occasionally. Other students display persistent learning and behavior problems throughout their schooling experience. These problems have more serious consequences for the students.

2. *Severity of the problem.* Is the student's learning or behavior problem mild, moderate, or severe? Is the student performing slightly below or significantly below what would normally be expected of him or her? Is the behavior slightly different or substantially different from that of the student's peers?

3. *Speed of progress.* Does the student appear to be making steady progress in the classroom despite the learning or behavior problem? We do not expect all students to learn at the same rate. In fact, in an average fourth-grade classroom, the range of performance varies from second-grade level to seventh-grade level.

4. *Motivation.* Is the student interested in learning? Does the student persist at tasks and attempt to learn? Does the student initiate and complete tasks without continual praise and encouragement?

5. *Parental response.* How do family members feel about a child's academic and/or behavioral progress? How do they think it compares with the child's progress in the past? Are they concerned about how their child's abilities compare with those of other children the same age? How have siblings performed in school?

6. *Other teachers' responses.* How did the student perform in previous classes? What do previous or other teachers say about the student's learning style, academic abilities, and behavior?

7. *Relationship with the teacher.* What type of relationship does the student have with his or her present teacher? Sometimes there is a poor interpersonal match between the student and the teacher that may interfere with the student's academic performance and/or behavior.

8. *Instructional modifications.* What attempts has the teacher made to modify the student's academic and/or behavioral program? Does the student seem responsive to attempts at intervention? If the student is not performing well in a traditional reading program, has the teacher tried other instructional approaches to reading? Has the student had opportunities to work with different students in the class? If the problem is behavior, what behavior change programs have been implemented? Have any been successful?

Is there a good match between the student and the classroom setting? Some children function best in a highly structured classroom where the rules, expectations, and assignments are very clearly stated. Other children function better in a learning environment where there is more flexibility.

9. *Adequate instruction.* Has the student had adequate exposure to the material and enough time to learn? Some students have little experience with formal learning situations before coming to school. Other students have multiple experiences, including preschool programs that teach letters and letter sounds. Students who have less exposure to school learning situations or whose parents provide few school-like learning experiences may need more time and exposure to the learning environment before they make gains. Determine what prerequisite skills are missing and how they can be acquired.

10. *Behavior–age discrepancy.* Does the student display problems that are unusual or deviant for the student's age? For example, many preschoolers will whine and withdraw to another room, but few children do so after grade 2.

11. *Other factors.* Are there other factors that might be contributing to the student's learning and/or behavior problems? For example, how closely do the student's background experiences, culture, and language match those of the teacher and other students in the class? Are there any health-related factors that may be interfering with the student's learning or behavior? Have the student's vision and hearing been adequately assessed to determine whether they might be affecting the student's learning or behavior?

Considering these factors will help you to identify the severity of the student's problems and whether the student may need additional classroom supports.

The Defining Features of Special Education

How does special education for students with learning and behavior problems differ from a good general education? Recently, individuals have addressed this issue to help teachers identify practices that promote learning for students with special needs (Florian, 2007; Landrum, Tankersley, & Kauffman, 2003; Vaughn & Linan-Thompson, 2003). Consider the following six features of instruction that, according to Heward (2003), define effective instruction for students with learning and behavior problems:

1. *Individually planned.* Instruction, materials, and setting of instruction are selected or adapted on the basis of student needs.

2. *Specialized.* Instruction and adaptations include related services and assistive technology that are not often a part of the general education curriculum.
3. *Intensive.* Precise, targeted instruction is designed to assist students in making efficient progress toward gaining necessary skills and strategies.
4. *Goal-directed.* Instruction focuses on individual goals and objectives necessary for student success.
5. *Employ research-based methods.* Selection and application of effective teaching methods are supported by research.
6. *Guided by student performance.* Student response to instruction is continually assessed for use in evaluating the effectiveness of instruction and adjusting instruction when necessary.

Heward (2003) further states that many misunderstandings about teaching and learning interfere with successful delivery of special education for students with disabilities. For example, many educators and administrators are taught that a structured curriculum including instruction and practice in individual skills is unnecessary and harmful to students' general learning. Contrary to this belief, students with learning and behavior problems often need academic tasks broken down into smaller, obtainable skills in order to progress.

Some educators also believe that student performance cannot be measured. As Heward points out, a hallmark of special education is that it is goal-directed and guided by student performance. Therefore, assessment of student outcomes is needed to guide appropriate instruction and to move students as quickly as possible through instruction to ensure student success in academics and related areas. This means that instruction must be focused and provided with a sense of urgency. Unstructured lessons and activities that are developed for the sole purpose of creativity and fun without regard for effectiveness can be detrimental to students with learning and behavior problems. These students need the very best instruction using research-supported techniques to ensure that time is not wasted and teachers are providing opportunities for students to gain the necessary abilities and obtain the motivating experience of success. Throughout this book, we will demonstrate effective instructional techniques in reading, written expression, math, and other content areas for students with learning and behavior problems.

Learning and Educational Environments for Students with Learning and Behavior Problems

Most students with learning and behavior problems are educated in the general education classroom. But students who have severe learning and behavior problems may receive a range of support services, including reading or math support, counseling, individualized instruction with a teaching assistant, and special education.

In many schools, reading or math specialists assist students with learning problems. These specialists typically provide supplemental instruction to the regular reading or math instruction the students receive in the general education classroom. Such additional instruction can help students with learning problems make sufficient progress in reaching expected performance levels. Often, specialists and classroom teachers collaborate to ensure that the instruction they provide is consistent and follows a similar sequence of skills.

Some classroom teachers have a teaching assistant who provides supplemental instruction for students with learning problems. These services are provided similarly to the services of the reading or math specialist. However, teaching assistants often do not have the instructional background that specialists do. Therefore, it is imperative that teachers provide teaching assistants with sufficient guidance. This includes planning lessons, training in effective instruction for students with learning problems, and monitoring instruction. When teaching assistants are given appropriate instructional tools for teaching students with learning problems, the supplemental help they provide often helps students to make the necessary progress to learn at expected levels.

Students with disabilities receive services through special education. PL 94-142, reauthorized in 2004 as the Individuals with Disabilities Education Act (IDEA), ensures that a continuum of placements is available for students. This continuum is conceptualized as proceeding from the least to the most restrictive. The term *restrictive*, in an educational sense, refers to the extent to which students are educated with nondisabled peers. A more restrictive setting is one in which students spend no part of their educational program with nondisabled peers. In a less restrictive setting, students may spend part of their educational day with nondisabled peers. IDEA mandates that all students should be educated in the least-restrictive educational environment possible (IDEA, 2004).

Including Students with Learning and Behavior Problems

When students with special needs are included in the general education classroom, either their specialized services are provided within the general education class, or they are pulled out of the classroom for a portion of the day to receive the services. How do schools and teachers decide if a student should be included for all or part of the school day?

The decision to include a student with special needs is made by an individual educational planning and placement committee. This committee is typically made up of one or both of the child's guardians, the special education teacher, the general education teacher, relevant professionals such as the school psychologist, and the administrator who supervises the special education program in which the student participates. At the recommendation of the special education and general education teachers and the professionals who evaluate the student's progress, the committee collectively decides whether the student's social and educational needs would best be met in the general education classroom and writes up the IEP accordingly. What types of information do special education teachers use to determine inclusion in general education? The answer varies by district and school, and several essential information sources are helpful:

- Based on classroom observations, how is the target student performing in the general education classroom?
- Based on progress monitoring and other assessment data, how effectively is the student learning in the general education classroom?
- Has the target student been provided intensive interventions? If yes, how has the student responded to these interventions?
- What types of classroom-based interventions have been provided and how effective have they been?
- What views and insights do the parents hold about the students' performance and inclusion in the general education classroom?
- What views do previous teachers and educational specialists hold about the students' performance in the general education classroom?

For students to receive special education that is outside of the general education classroom, evidence that the students' educational and social needs are better met in the special education classroom is required. Most students with emotional and learning disabilities spend at least some of their school day in general education classrooms with their nondisabled peers. Therefore, both general education and special education teachers are often responsible for the instruction and outcomes of students with disabilities.

Almost 3.3 million students with disabilities between the ages of 6 and 21, or 57% of the special education population, received instruction in general education settings for 80% of the day in the school year of 2007–2008 (U.S. Department of Education, 2007). For students between the ages of 3 and 5, 49% spent 80% or more of their time with typical achieving peers. Where were students with learning disabilities and behavior disorders educated? Almost 59% of students identified as having specific learning disabilities spent 80% of their time in general education classrooms, whereas only 37% of students identified as emotionally disturbed were in regular classrooms for that same amount of time. It is quite likely that fewer students identified as seriously emotionally disturbed are in general education because their behavior interferes significantly with the academic progress of others in the classroom. IDEA introduced the concept of a continuum of placements, including the *least restrictive environment* (LRE).

Since its passage in 1997, there has been a growing interest in educating students with disabilities with their peers who are nondisabled. IDEA contained a strong mandate to provide greater access to the general education curriculum. As more students with special needs are placed in general education classrooms, with special education teachers consulting or collaborating with classroom teachers, the emphasis on consultation/collaborative models has grown. The latest reauthorization of IDEA in 2004 puts an increased emphasis on academic performance goals and measures of accountability for students with disabilities that are consistent with standards for students without disabilities.

See Chapter 5 on coordinating instruction with families and other professionals.

Why is inclusion important for students with learning and behavior problems? Students want to be successful in the general education classroom with age-similar peers. The vast majority of students with learning disabilities and behavior problems profit from extensive time in the general education classroom when instructional and behavioral supports meet their needs. Since students with learning disabilities exhibit significant difficulties in one or more academic areas (e.g., reading, math, writing), it is likely that they will also require more intensive academic support in their areas of need. This academic support may be provided by the special education teacher within the general education classroom or at a specified time each day in a special education setting.

Students with learning disabilities and behavior problems have not always received the specific academic and behavioral supports they require in general education classrooms. Thus, inclusion may not always work as well as was intended by the law, or as was envisioned by the families of special education students (see for review, McLeskey, 2007; Schumm & Vaughn, 1991).

Lawmakers intended for students with special needs who are included in the general education classroom to receive accommodations for their learning and/or emotional needs within the classroom. The special education teacher, as consultant/collaborator with the general education classroom teacher, is to facilitate the implementation of the student's IEP and then promote effective practices and planning to ensure appropriate instruction is given. Working cooperatively with the special education teacher, the general classroom teacher is responsible for planning, monitoring, and delivering the instruction or intervention the student needs.

Most secondary-level (middle and high school) classroom teachers stated that they had not used IEPs or psychological reports to guide their planning for special education students. They had, however, gathered information from the families and former teachers of students with special needs. Some teachers said that they had very little contact with the special education teacher who monitored their students with special needs and they were not aware that the students had IEPs. A few teachers had no contact with a special education teacher and were unaware that they even had a student with special needs in their class. In such cases, there was clearly a lack of communication between the special education teacher responsible for monitoring the progress of the students with special needs and the regular classroom teacher.

▶ **WEB RESOURCES**
For further information on inclusion issues and activities that may be helpful in the classroom take a look at the following Web site:
http://www.applesfortheteacher.com.

Identifying Students with Learning Disabilities

What issues relate to appropriate identification of students with learning disabilities? Individuals with learning disabilities have typically been identified through referral by classroom teachers or families, followed by a complete battery of assessments designed to identify whether the students meet criteria as learning disabled. Typically, these assessments included an IQ and an achievement test. If students' IQ scores were a certain number of points above their achievement scores (in other words, there is a large discrepancy between the IQ and achievement scores), the students would be identified as having a learning disability because of their "unexpected underachievement." Recently, there has been considerable concern about the appropriateness of administering IQ tests to all students, particularly minority students, and the extent to which the IQ–achievement discrepancy is an appropriate measure for identification of learning disabilities (Bradley, Danielson, & Hallahan, 2002; Donovan & Cross, 2002; Stuebing et al., 2002).

What is IQ–achievement discrepancy, and what are the concerns about using it? IQ–achievement discrepancy is the common practice by which the IQ (e.g., a cognitive or intelligence test that is typically individually administered and provides an estimate of overall ability) and standardized achievement scores (e.g., an individually administered test of reading or math that typically is norm referenced) of students are compared, in the belief that a significant discrepancy (higher IQ scores than achievement scores on one or more relevant outcomes) is a strong indicator of learning disabilities. The four specific concerns about this practice are as follows:

1. The discrepancy is difficult to determine with young children and may unnecessarily postpone identification until second grade or later; this concern highlights why some refer to the IQ–achievement discrepancy as the "wait to fail" model.

2. Many young children aged 5 to 7 benefit greatly from prevention programs, particularly in reading, that could keep them from developing greater difficulties in reading or math.

3. Formal IQ and achievement tests are expensive to administer and interpret, and the money might be better used to provide instruction.

4. IQ tests provide little information to teachers to assist them in improving or modifying their instruction.

What alternatives are there to traditional IQ–achievement discrepancy approaches for identifying students with learning disabilities? The most frequently suggested alternative is RTI. Though the exact use and application of RTI varies somewhat depending on who is describing it, RTI typically involves a multitiered system of interventions, a data collection system that informs decision making, and ongoing progress monitoring. The number of tiers, what data are collected, and the measures used to determine if a child is "responding" to an intervention might differ depending on the school and content area. RTI can also be conceptualized as a systematic application of data-based decision making to enhance outcomes for all children (Burns & Ysseldyke, 2005; Haager, Klingner, & Vaughn, 2007). RTI provides a preventive approach to special education and promotes early screening and interventions so that students at risk for academic or behavior difficulties are provided with timely and appropriate services.

Further information about RTI is presented in Chapter 3.

RTI addresses concerns about the IQ–achievement discrepancy because students begin to receive help as soon as they start demonstrating academic or behavior difficulties, regardless of what grade they are in. In addition, many students, such as Carlos, need only an "extra boost" in order to be successful in the general education classroom. For students like Carlos, future reading difficulties may be prevented by early intervention. Students who respond adequately to the intervention and are able to make appropriate progress in the classroom are considered high-responders to the intervention; typically, they do not need further intervention and are unlikely to require special education. Students whose response to the intervention is low may be referred for further evaluations and considered for special education (Vaughn & Fuchs, 2006). In order to determine if a student has responded to an intervention, the measures used for screening and progress monitoring are typically quick and easy to administer and are directly related to skills needed for academic or behavior success in the classroom. Therefore, these measures help teachers pinpoint where a student is having difficulties and alter or improve their instruction accordingly (see Apply the Concept 1-1).

1-1   Adopting an RTI Model to Identify Students with Learning Disabilities

The 2004 reauthorization of IDEA recommends that states and schools abandon the IQ–achievement discrepancy to identify students with learning disabilities and instead use an RTI approach. However, IDEA does not require that schools use RTI. Your principal asks your opinion on what your school should do to identify students with learning disabilities.

What are the pros and cons of the IQ–achievement discrepancy and RTI? Which model do you recommend that your school use in determining special education eligibility?

In August 2006, regulatory guidelines for implementing RTI were published (U.S. Department of Education, 2006). Key aspects of the guidelines include the following:

- State criteria must not *require* but may *permit* that school districts utilize a severe discrepancy between intellectual ability and achievement to identify students as learning disabled.
- State criteria must permit the use of a process based on children's responses to scientific, research-based intervention, e.g., an appropriate RTI model.
- When determining specific learning disabilities (SLDs), personnel must determine whether children are making age-appropriate progress or making progress to meet state-approved grade-level standards.
- Lack of achievement may not be due to lack of appropriate instruction in reading or math. Thus, if the student has had inadequate or inappropriate instruction in the general education classroom, significant and intensive supplemental instruction is required before placement in special education.
- There are many models or frameworks for implementing RTI. To illustrate, some districts use a problem-solving model in which they implement research-based practices by using a team of professionals to make ongoing decisions, whereas other school districts use a standardized approach in which research-based interventions are provided routinely by well-trained professionals.
- Though specific procedures are not described, the importance of timelines and structured communication with family members is emphasized.
- Frequent and ongoing assessments to determine response to intervention can be determined by the state.
- RTI as a means for identifying students with learning disabilities is not a substitute for a comprehensive evaluation.
- No single procedure can be relied on to determine whether a student qualifies for special education.

The National Association of State Directors of Special Education (NASDSE) has developed a readily accessible guide to RTI that is available on its Web site (http://www.nasdse.org) entitled *Response to Intervention: Policy Considerations and Implementation* (National Association of State Directors of Special Education, 2006).

Developing an Individualized Education Program

What is an IEP, and what is the process for developing and updating an IEP? For students who have been identified as requiring special education services (including students with learning or emotional disabilities), procedures for setting goals and planning instruction are designated by law. IDEA requires that an IEP be developed for each student with special educational needs. A multidisciplinary team develops, implements, and reviews the IEP, which is both a process and a document. The process involves a group of individuals, often referred to as the IEP team, using assessment information, eligibility, and the needs of the student to establish an appropriate specialized educational program for a student with disabilities. The document is a record of the decisions that have been agreed upon by the team and a guide for improving student outcomes (Johns, Crowley, & Guetzloe, 2002). The IEP must be reviewed annually and can be revised at any time to address lack of expected progress, the results of any reevaluations, or other relevant information provided by either the school or family members. Figure 1-1 presents a sample IEP completed for John, a fifth grader with learning disabilities.

The members of the multidisciplinary team include the following people:

- A representative of the local education agency—an administrator who is qualified to supervise services to students with disabilities and who is knowledgeable about the general education curriculum as well as resources and services available
- Parent(s) or guardian(s)
- Special education teacher
- At least one general education teacher if the student is participating or is likely to participate in general education classes

Individualized Education Program

I. Demographic Information

Last	First	M.I.		Date
Smith, John E.				May 12, 2010

Student I.D.	Address		Home Phone	Work Phone
2211100	23 Lakeview St. Collier, MN 32346		(459)555-5555	(459)555-5000

Date of Birth	Grade Level	Home School	Program Eligibility
03-02-99	5	Lakeview Elementary	Learning Disabilities

Reason for Conference: ☐ Staffing ☑ Review

II. Conference

Parent Notification

Attempt #1:	Attempt #2:	Attempt #3:
Letter: 3-02-10	Phone call: 3-13-10	Notice sent home with student: 3-22-10

Parent Response: Will attend as per phone call on 3-13-10

III. Present Levels of Educational Performance

John is a 5th grade student whose disability inhibits his ability to read required material. John can read 35/100 in two minutes from a 4.0 grade level paragraph and 45/100 in two minutes from a 3.0 grade level paragraph. John can answer 8/10 literal questions and 4/10 inference questions from a 4.0 grade level passage read to him.

IV. Annual Goals and Short-Term Benchmarks

1. John will increase reading fluency to the 4.0 grade level.

   John will read orally a passage at the 4.0 grade level in 2 minutes with 50 or more words correct.

   John will use correct intonation and prosody when reading orally a passage at the 4.0 grade level 50% of the time.

2. John will improve the percentage of accuracy when responding to literal and inferential questions.

   John will answer literal questions from a 4.0 grade level passage read to him with 75% accuracy.

   John will answer inferential questions from a 4.0 grade level passage read to him with 90-100% accuracy.

Describe the extent to which the student will not participate in general education settings and explain why the student cannot be placed in general education settings.

John will not participate in general education settings for language arts, science, and social studies instruction. John requires close supervision when completing tasks, high levels of assistance, and intensive, systematic instruction.

V. Related Services

Type of Service, Aid or Modification			Location	Time per day/week
Assistive Technology:	☐ Yes	☑ No		
Adaptive PE:	☐ Yes	☑ No		
Audiology Services:	☐ Yes	☑ No		
Counseling:	☐ Yes	☑ No		
Interpreter:	☐ Yes	☑ No		
Medical Services:	☐ Yes	☑ No		
Occupational Therapy:	☐ Yes	☑ No		

(continued)

Orientation/Mobility:	❑ Yes	☑ No	
Physical Therapy:	❑ Yes	☑ No	
Psychological Services:	❑ Yes	☑ No	
Special Transportation:	❑ Yes	☑ No	
Speech/Lang. Therapy:	☑ Yes	❑ No	Self-contained class, 30 min./wk

VI. Assessment Participation

Will the student participate in state and district assessments:　☑ Yes　　❑ No

If yes, what accommodations or modifications will be provided?

❑ None　　☑ Flexible Setting　　❑ Flexible Presentation　　☑ Flexible Scheduling
❑ Flexible Responding

If no, indicate why state and district assessments are inappropriate:

VII. Transition Planning/Statement

☑ Under 14: Transition planning not needed.

❑ 14–15 years old: Statement of transition services needed that focuses on student's course of study.

❑ 16 years old: Outcome statement that describes a direction and plan for the student's post–high school years from the perspective of student, parent, and team members.

VIII. Scheduled Report to Parents/Guardians

John's parents will be informed of progress toward his annual goals via parent/teacher conferences and interim report cards (4 times per year). Parents will be notified of goals that have been met and the rate of progress toward meeting all of the annual goals.

IX. Initiation/Duration Dates

Special education and related services will initiate _September 2010_ (MM/YY), through _June 2011_ (MM/YY)

IX. Persons Attending Conference

Signature	Position	Date
Mary Smith	Parent	May 12, 2010
Jonathan Smith	Parent	May 12, 2010
Laura Jones	Special Education Teacher	May 12, 2010
Rafael Gonzalez	General Education Teacher	May 12, 2010
Larry Brick	LEA Representative	May 12, 2010
Harrison Washington	School Psychologist	May 12, 2010
John Smith	Student	May 12, 2010

- Evaluator—someone who can interpret the results from the student's educational, psychological, and/or behavioral evaluations
- Student, if the teachers and parents determine that it is appropriate for the student to attend the IEP meeting. If transition services are being discussed, the student must be invited to participate.
- Other professionals as appropriate. Parents or the school may invite others who can provide information or assistance, such as an interpreter, therapists or other personnel who work with the student, or a student advocate such as parents' friends or lawyers.

What should be included in the IEP? According to Section 514(*d*)(1)(A) of IDEA (2004), as of July 1, 2005, the IEP must include the following nine elements:

1. The student's current levels of educational performance and social-emotional functioning, including how the student's disability affects the student's involvement and progress in general education settings.
2. Measurable annual goals that address the student's individual learning needs and that, to the extent possible, enable the student to participate in and progress in the general education classroom.
3. Special education, related services, and supplementary aids and services to be provided to the student, including program modifications or supports for school personnel that will be provided for the student.
4. An explanation of the extent to which the student will not participate in general education classes.
5. A statement indicating how the student will participate in state- or districtwide assessments and outlining any modifications and accommodations to be provided during testing. If the student will not participate in state or district assessments, the IEP must include an explanation of why the student will not participate and how the student will be assessed.
6. When special education services will begin, as well as the frequency, location, and duration of services and modifications.
7. How progress toward annual goals will be measured and how the family will be regularly informed of progress toward these goals. IDEA mandates that parents/guardians be updated on their children's progress toward IEP goals and objectives at the same time as report cards are issued for all students.
8. Explanation of transition services at age 16, including measurable postsecondary goals, to help the student prepare for a job or college by taking appropriate classes and/or accessing services outside of school.
9. A list and signatures of the committee members present.

Writing Effective IEP Goals

A major part of the IEP involves the annual goals. An annual goal usually covers an entire school year. According to IDEA (2004), short-term objectives are also included for students who take alternate assessments aligned to alternate achievement standards. Short-term objectives are smaller steps that help the student reach the annual goal. Completion of related sets of short-term objectives should lead to accomplishment of the annual goals developed by the multidisciplinary team. Figure 1-2 shows an example of an annual goal and short-term objectives. Goals can address academic, social-emotional, or functional needs. The written statements of annual goals must meet certain requirements. According to Gibb and Dyches (2000), annual goals must:

- Be measurable.
- Tell what the student can reasonably achieve in a year.
- Relate to helping the student be successful in general education settings and/or address other educational needs ensuing from the disability.
- Include short-term objectives.

For IEPs that also include short-term objectives, Gibb and Dyches (2000) suggest the following:

- Describe the behavior in an observable, measurable way (e.g., "Luis will add two-digit numbers").
- Include the circumstances under which the behavior will take place (e.g., "given manipulatives and peer assistance").
- State the criterion for mastery (e.g., "with 85% accuracy").

During the IEP conference, family members and professionals work together to identify appropriate accommodations and modifications that will assist the student in learning skills in class. It is important that teachers be included in the decisions about accommodations and modifications because they are the ones responsible for implementing these in the classroom. For example, if the IEP team decides that a student needs a highlighted textbook in science, someone must be available to do the highlighting, or the accommodation cannot be carried out. Furthermore, effective communication systems must be in place so that all teachers and support personnel who will work with the student are aware of the accommodations and modifications that will be implemented. The processes involved in designing and implementing effective accommodations and modifications are discussed further in this chapter as well as in following chapters.

Writing IEPs can be challenging and many teachers use software and Web sites to facilitate their development. The most useful IEP software programs allow a teacher to select from skill sequences and write long-term and short-term objectives, freely customizing skills and objectives to meet individual needs.

Often school systems or special education units adopt one particular IEP software application for use by its entire staff. You may find that to be the case in your school district. Some programs are installed in individual

► Figure 1-2 Sample Goal and Short-Term Objectives in an IEP

Annual Goal:

Lisa McKinney will achieve a math score at the fourth-grade level or above on the Mathematics Achievement Assessment.

Short-Term Objectives

1. Lisa will demonstrate mastery of multiplication and division facts (0–10) by completing weekly one-minute timed multiplication and division fact math tests with 90% accuracy.
2. Given 10 three-digit-by-two-digit multiplication problems, Lisa will solve the problems with 90% accuracy.
3. Given 10 two-digit-by-one-digit division problems, Lisa will use long division to solve the problems with 90% accuracy.
4. Given 10 one-step word problems, Lisa will identify the operation (addition, subtraction, multiplication, or division) and solve with 90% accuracy.
5. After correctly solving five one-step word problems, Lisa will describe with 80% accuracy (either orally to the teacher or in writing) how she got her answers.
6. Given daily teacher-prepared "problem-of-the-day" assignments, Lisa will copy each problem into her math notebook and work cooperatively with a partner to solve it, showing work and the correct solution four out of five times.

computers; others are Web based. Web-based systems are especially useful because you can access the data from any online computer. It is also easier to transfer records as the child moves along in his or her education, from teacher to teacher and school to school.

Because the IEP-writing process is complicated, several software programs are available to help teachers. These programs are showcased in the Tech Tips feature.

Family Involvement

The IEP meeting is a way for family members and school personnel to communicate about the education of a student with disabilities. According to IDEA, "parents are considered equal partners with school personnel" in the IEP process. The IEP serves as a safeguard not only for students but also for families and the education team. All

 ## Tech TIPS

IEP SOFTWARE PROGRAMS

The most useful IEP software programs allow teachers to select from skill sequences and author long-term and short-term objectives, freely customizing skills and objectives to meet individual needs. Often school systems or special education units adopt one particular system. You may find that to be the case in your school district. Some programs are installed in individual computers whereas others are Web based. Web-based systems are especially useful because you can access the data from any online computer while maintaining security by the use of a password. It is also easier to move students' records along as they move from teacher to teacher and school to school.

Following is a list of IEP management software names along with their primary Web addresses:

- IEPMaker Pro, by Chalkware Education Solutions at www.iepware.com
- Class/Bridge IEP Program, by Class/Bridge at www.classplus.com
- IEP Writer Supreme II, by Super School Software at www.superschoolsoftware.com

reasonable attempts to ensure the participation of family members in the IEP process should be taken:

- Schedule IEP meetings at times that are convenient for families, checking with them in advance to determine a suitable date, time, and location.
- Notify families well in advance of the meeting. Include in the notice the purpose, time, and location of the meeting and the names and positions of the people who will be in attendance. Parents/guardians should be involved in the decision about whether the student will attend.
- If family members choose not to attend even after reasonable efforts have been made to accommodate their schedules, the school should use other methods to involve them, including telephone calls or home visits. The school must document its attempts to involve family members.
- The school must take measures to ensure that families understand IEP proceedings, including providing an interpreter if English is not their first language.
- Family involvement in the development of the IEP should be documented, and parents/guardians should receive a copy of the IEP.

Remember that often too much emphasis is placed on compliance rather than on genuine communication with family members (Harry, 2008; Harry, Allen, & McLaughlin, 1995; Seligman & Darling, 2007). Educators are more effective with they consider the following:

- Educators and parents are working as a team for a common goal—the student's success.
- Pay attention to when and why defensive behavior arises. Put your feelings aside and help others, including family members, to build positive relationships. If the team is unable to act positively, postpone interactions until the defensiveness can be handled.
- Remember that the family's values are not what is being addressed, only the needs and interests of parents/guardians and their child. Consider what the problem is, not who the person is.
- Do not waste time wishing that the people would be different. Accept them as they are. Respect a family's rights to have their own values and opinions.
- Remember that most families are doing the best that they can under the circumstances of their lives. People do not decide to be poor parents/guardians.

Student Involvement and Self-Determination

The self-directed IEP is designed to facilitate students' participation in IEP meetings (Arndt, Konrad, & Test, 2006). By law, students need to attend IEP meetings only if appropriate. In practice, many students with learning and emotional disabilities do not attend these meetings, even when the students are in secondary-level settings and are able to provide information and contribute to decision making about

their education. There are benefits to including students with disabilities in the IEP process. Involving students in this decision-making process helps them develop a commitment to learning and a sense of responsibility and control over the decisions made regarding their learning.

Chapter 5 describes strategies you can use for actively involving families in their children's education, including planning and implementing programs.

Why do many students not attend the conferences? In interviewing junior high students with learning disabilities and their parents, two major reasons are evident (Van Reusen & Bos, 1990). First, parents frequently are not aware that students can attend. Second, even when students are invited to attend, they choose not to because they feel that they do not know what to say or do, and they are afraid that the major topic of discussion will be "how bad they are doing."

To alleviate these two concerns, Van Reusen and his colleagues developed a self-advocacy strategy that is designed to inform students and prepare them to participate in educational planning or transition planning conferences (Van Reusen, Bos, Schumaker, & Deshler, 1994). Teachers can teach students this strategy in about 5 to 6 hours over a 1- to 2-week period. We have found that junior high and high school students with learning disabilities who learn this strategy provide more information during IEP conferences than do students who are only told about the IEP conference but not taught the strategy (Bos & Van Reusen, 1986; Van Reusen & Bos, 1990).

What is self-determination? It is the opportunity for individuals to make important decisions about their own lives. For individuals with disabilities, it refers to the opportunity to be actively involved in decisions about their own learning. Self-determination is important because students who engage in self-determination have improved academic performance. How can teachers improve self-determination of students in the IEP process? Teachers can actively engage students in the IEP development and the monitoring of their progress toward meeting IEP goals. This ensures that students are actively involved in the process. The following prompts and activities facilitate student engagement (Arndt, Konrad, & Test, 2006):

1. Ask students to think about their instructional and behavioral goals prior to the IEP meeting. Meet to discuss and brainstorm goals so that students are prepared for the meeting.
2. Ask students at the IEP meeting to indicate the purpose of the meeting.
3. Consider asking students the following questions:
   - What are your goals in school?
   - How successful have you been in meeting them?
   - Are you working hard to meet goals?
   - What are you doing well? What would you like to do better?

4. Prompt students to ask others at the meeting what they think of stated goals, progress, and future goals.

5. Ask students to work with the committee to develop goals for transition, academics, social, and other related areas.

6. Check frequently with students to determine if they have questions or other issues.

7. Ask students to specify the support needed to meet the agreed-upon goals.

8. Summarize and close the meeting.

Key Elements of the Transition Planning Process

The primary objectives of the transition process for individuals with disabilities is the same as it is for all of us—as seamless a transition as possible to postsecondary settings and being able to function successfully in adult life (i.e., dealing reasonably well with the demands of adulthood). All of this is within the context of knowing that each of us struggle at times with the realities of everyday life.

As the classroom teacher, how can you ensure that this happens? The vehicle for documenting transition is the IEP.

The key elements of the transition planning process include: Proactive transition education, opportunities to dream about who you want to be and how you will achieve it, assessment of critical areas to help with decision making, transition planning and opportunities to receive feedback about how you are performing and what you need to do to meet your goals. Of course, ongoing opportunities to revise and revisit dreams is also essential (Patton & Dunn, 1998). Patton and Dunn state that early on it is essential that students receive opportunities to "dream" about what they want to be, where they want to live, and how they want to live when they grow up.

The formal phase of the transition planning process begins with the comprehensive assessment of a student's transition needs. The general areas in which a transition-needs assessment should focus include a range of transition domains. The key transition areas that are identified by different states vary greatly; some of the more common transition planning areas are as follows:

- Community participation
- Daily living
- Employment
- Financial and income management
- Health
- Independent living (includes living arrangements)
- Leisure and recreation
- Postsecondary education
- Relationships and social skills
- Transportation and mobility
- Vocational training

It is important that a comprehensive transition-needs assessment consider all of these areas. If a needs assessment

is conducted effectively, the results should lead to the development of transition-related goals. In some cases, the results will lead to the recognition that more in-depth information is needed.

The actual transition planning phase comprises goal development highlighting two types of goals and a number of activities that are needed to accomplish these goals. One type of goal is *instructional,* in that it focuses on knowledge and skill needs in academic, social, behavioral, and other functional areas. Goals that are instructional should be written into a student's IEP. The other type of goal emphasizes *linkage* to needed services and supports. These goals may be quick action items (e.g., a phone call to place one's name on a waiting list), or they may be more elaborate activities (e.g., going through the process of selecting an appropriate postschool training program). Most students will not require both types of goals for every transition area that is assessed.

The reauthorization of IDEA in 2004 introduced a new component to the transition process. IDEA regulations state:

> For a child whose eligibility terminates under circumstances described in paragraph (e)(2) of this section, a public agency must provide the child with a summary of the child's academic achievement and functional performance, which shall include recommendations on how to assist the child in meeting the child's postsecondary goals. (Section 300.305(e)(3))

This new feature is designed to provide students, and their families, with a document that should be useful in a variety of adult settings (workplace, postsecondary education). The key features of the summary of performance document include generation of information on both academic and functional levels; a revisiting of "measurable" postsecondary goals; and a list of recommendations that will be helpful in settings related to the goals.

Aside from the implications that are stated in the federal definition of transition services, certain principles should guide the transition planning process. Apply the Concept 1-2 highlights the four key guiding principles, the first two of which are adapted from Patton and Dunn (1998).

Instructional goals relate to knowledge and skills needs and should be written in the IEP as academic or social goals. Linkage goals—the types of goals that are typically associated with transition planning—focus on making connections to the supports and services that will be needed in postsecondary settings and are written in the section of the IEP that deals with transition services.

In the past, some states required another document, an individual transition plan (ITP), which was a separate document from the IEP, as the principal vehicle for guiding transition activities. Most states simply included transition goals as part of the existing IEP under a section typically called "Statement of Transition Services." Historically, the focus of transition planning was primarily on

- The more that is known about the receiving settings and about the student's levels of competence to deal with these settings, the more likely a seamless transition can be achieved.
- The more comprehensive the transition-needs assessment is,

the easier it is to develop useful and meaningful transition plans.
- Effective transition assessment and plans can be achieved only when school-based transition personnel know the students or have ways to acquire this information.

- Student involvement in the transition-planning process is not only highly desirable but also required by law (i.e., based on the student's preferences and interests).

goals that we defined previously as *linkage type*. The emerging practice is to include all transition-planning information on the IEP. The critical issue is the importance of considering both instructional and linkage goal statements for areas of need.

Useful linkage-type goal statements should include the following four components, all of which contribute to development of an effective plan of action:

1. Present level of performance
2. Specific activities to be performed to accomplish the goal
3. Anticipated date of completion of activities
4. Person(s) responsible

For example, Meaghan is a high school student with significant learning disabilities and behavior disorders. Her situation illustrates why two different types of goals often need to be developed. As evident from Figure 1-3, which provides an illustration of some of the data collected to develop a better transition plan, certain areas were identified as needing attention. As an illustration of how to proceed, the following goals need to be developed for Meaghan based on numerous data sources, including findings from her transition planning inventory that indicated school personnel perceived that she could not succeed in a postsecondary program, and both the home and student agreed with that rating:

Instructional Goals (Knowledge/Skills Goals)
- Develop strategies to assist with demands of comprehending textual material.
- Improve note-taking skills.
- Improve test-taking skills.
- Develop time management skills.
- Improve various types of writing skills needed in college courses.

Linkage Goals (Transition Services Goals)
- Make Meaghan aware of the Services for Students with Disabilities Office, its services, and how to qualify.

- Identify resources that may be needed to obtain a comprehensive evaluation to document that Meaghan has a learning disability, if she chooses to disclose this and use specialized services.
- Make Meaghan aware of the general services (courses, workshops, personal assistance) provided to all students at the high school to improve study skills.
- Connect Meaghan with a contact person at the high school to whom she can go if she runs into problems with academics, managing time, and so on.
- Compile a list of names and phone numbers of private tutors whom Meaghan can contact for assistance with study skill needs.

Teaching Students with Learning and Behavior Problems

What goes into teaching students with learning and behavior problems? In the beginning of this chapter, we introduced three students, Servio, Dana, and Tina. Instruction for these students needs to be carefully orchestrated to take into account the interactive nature of their instructional needs within an effective teaching–learning process. The *teaching–learning process* is a model of teaching and learning that takes into account the complexity of the learning environment or context, the knowledge and skills of the teacher and the learner, and the instructional cycle the teacher implements to facilitate learning. An effective teaching–learning process for students with learning and/or behavior problems is based on *individual programming*. Although students may be instructed in groups, the teacher plans and designs instruction for each student's needs, realizing that students have both common and unique needs. The teaching–learning process is shown in Figure 1-4. It presents a reflective, problem-solving approach to teaching students with learning and behavior problems. Let us look first at the key players in this process: the learner and the teacher.

Section V. Profile

Planning Areas	School Rating Strongly Disagree — Strongly Agree	Home Rating Strongly Disagree — Strongly Agree	Student Rating Strongly Disagree — Strongly Agree	Knowledge/Skills Goals	Linkage Goals
Employment					
1. Knows job requirements and demands	NA 0 1 2 [3] 4 5 DK	NA 0 1 2 3 [4] 5 DK	NA 0 1 [2] 3 4 5 DK		
2. Makes informed choices	NA 0 1 2 [3] 4 5 DK	NA 0 1 2 [3] 4 5 DK	NA 0 1 2 3 [4] 5 DK		
3. Knows how to get a job	NA 0 1 2 3 [4] 5 DK	NA 0 1 2 [3] 4 5 DK	NA 0 1 2 3 [4] 5 DK		
4. Demonstrates general job skills and work attitude	NA 0 1 2 [3] 4 5 DK	NA 0 1 2 3 [4] 5 DK	NA 0 1 2 3 4 [5] DK		
5. Has specific job skills	[NA] 0 1 2 3 4 5 DK	[NA] 0 1 2 3 4 5 [DK]	[NA] 0 1 2 3 4 5 DK		
Further Education/Training					
6. Knows how to gain entry into community employment training	[NA] 0 1 2 3 4 5 DK	[NA] 0 1 2 3 4 5 DK	[NA] 0 1 2 3 4 5 DK		
7. Knows how to gain entry into GED program	[NA] 0 1 2 3 4 5 DK	[NA] 0 1 2 3 4 5 DK	[NA] 0 1 2 3 4 5 DK		
8. Knows how to gain entry into vocational/technical school	[NA] 0 1 2 3 4 5 DK	[NA] 0 1 2 3 4 5 DK	[NA] 0 1 2 3 4 5 DK		
9. Knows how to gain entry into college or university	NA 0 1 2 3 [4] 5 DK	NA 0 1 [2] 3 4 5 DK	NA 0 1 2 [3] 4 5 DK		
10. Can succeed in a postsecondary program	NA 0 [1] 2 3 4 5 DK	NA 0 1 [2] 3 4 5 DK	NA 0 [1] 2 3 4 5 DK		

Source: From *Informal Assessments in Transition Planning* (p. 156) by G. M. Clark, J. R. Patton, and R. Moulton, 2001, Austin, TX: PRO-ED. Reprinted with permission.

The Learner

The learner brings to school knowledge and experiences on which to build, and strategies to assist in the learning process. Our assessment process focuses on determining the level at which the student is functioning and what skills the student can and cannot perform. However, *knowledge, attitudes,* and *strategic learning* can also provide us with information concerning the learner and may prove to be critical features when determining how to facilitate learning. For example, if a student has little knowledge of the topic being studied, the teacher can assist the student by providing activities that build background knowledge and help the student to link this new knowledge to current knowledge.

Skills and knowledge not only play an important role in learning, but also influence the learner's attitudes and efforts toward learning. Randy and Tamara illustrate this point. In fifth grade, Randy was determined to learn how to read, although at the time he was struggling with beginning reading books. He worked all year on his reading, and at the end of the year he had grown in his reading skill by about one grade level. Still, he carried with him the attitude that reading was important and that he should continue to struggle with a process that for him was quite difficult. Tamara, on the other hand, was a sixth

Figure 1-4   The Teaching–Learning Process

TEACHING–LEARNING CONTEXT   INSTRUCTION CYCLE

Planning Instruction

Determining the Goals of Instruction and Learning

Providing, Evaluating, and Modifying Instruction

THE LEARNER AND THE TEACHER

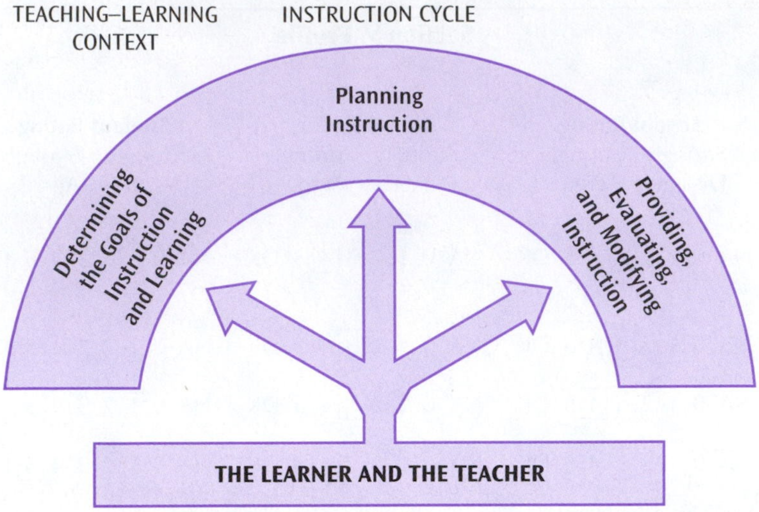

grader who was reading at about the third-grade level. For her, learning to read was a much easier process, yet she finished the year making only marginal gains. Why? She believed that reading simply was not necessary for her life and that her future goal, being a mother, just didn't require her to be a good reader. It is likely that these students' attitudes influenced their rate of learning.

A student's strategies for learning also affect the teaching–learning process. When you are told to read a chapter in a textbook and study for a test, what strategies do you employ? Do you preview the chapter before reading? Do you ask questions as you read to check your comprehension? Do you underline or take notes? Do you review your notes before the test, rehearsing the important points? These are all strategies that make you a more effective student.

The Teacher

The teacher brings to the learning situation teaching knowledge and skills; beliefs and attitudes about teaching, learning, and the world; and practices for influencing students' learning and engagement.

As you read this section, reflect on your beliefs and attitudes about teaching, learning, and students who experience learning and behavior problems. What is the nature of learning and what is the role of the teacher?

Learning can be perceived as changes in behavior that result in students demonstrating new knowledge and skills. The role of the teacher is that of an educational technician who engineers instruction or arranges the environment so that the probability of learning is increased. This is accomplished by providing students with effective instruction and rewards for learning. An effective teacher conveys knowledge and skills in a systematic, explicit manner. This perception of learning and teaching is probably best reflected in applied behavior analysis. It is also reflected in instructional strategies and materials that are based on systematic ordering and teaching of skills.

Applied behavior analysis is discussed in Chapter 2.

Learning can also be perceived as a dynamic process in which students play an active role, constantly interacting with the environment and people around them. Not only do students' notions, ideas, and skills change in the learning process, but so does the environment in which learning takes place. Thus, learning is not merely the accumulation of knowledge and skills but it is also the active construction and transformation of ideas based on observations and experiences. This perception of learning is represented in schema theory. The teacher creates an environment in which students can take risks and develop flexible learning and thinking strategies as they acquire skills and knowledge.

Schema theory is covered in Chapter 2.

For example, Ms. Kranowski, a special education teacher who works with students who have learning and behavior problems, has 11 students—fourth through sixth grade—in her self-contained class. Each day after lunch, they practice writing. Ms. Kranowski uses a process approach to teaching writing in which students select their own topics and write about them, sometimes taking several weeks to complete a piece. Students usually write multiple drafts, sharing their work with other students and the teacher.

At first, the learners in Ms. Kranowski's class needed to develop a process for writing. They needed to develop purposes for their writing other than to please the teacher or to complete the worksheets. As the students became more confident of their drafts, they needed to learn such skills as how to organize a descriptive paragraph and a story and how to use dialogue and quotation marks. Although Ms. Kranowski continues with this process approach to writing, she now also spends time teaching skills to small groups. She uses systematic skill lessons whereby she models a skill, then has the students practice it in their own writing and in published and teacher-made materials. Whereas the first approach to teaching represents an interactive model of teaching and learning, during skill lessons Ms. Kranowski serves as the conveyor of knowledge by explicitly teaching systematic skill sequences. Ms. Kranowski's instruction shifts to reflect the needs of the students in her class.

How does Ms. Kranowski explain her simultaneous use of these different approaches to the teaching—learning process?

> Well, when I first began using a process approach to teaching writing, I found that the students really learned to like writing. For me, that was a big accomplishment, since most of these kids had previously hated writing. But I also found that because these students have so many learning problems and take so much practice to learn a new skill, they just weren't getting enough opportunities to practice intensely a new writing skill when they were first trying to learn it. Consequently, they never learned the skills very well. Now, 2 days a week, we take about 20 minutes for a skill lesson. I select the skill according to the needs of the students as a group. Right now we are working on dialogue and quotation marks. I introduce the skill and show how I use it in my writing. Then several of the students demonstrate how they can use it in their writing. We use an overhead projector, and they project their writing on the screen. We talk about how to add quotation marks, and they add them right then. For the next several weeks when they are writing their pieces, I encourage them to use dialogue, and we make an effort to compliment each other when the quotation marks are right. If the students need additional practice, I provide them with stories in which they have to add quotation marks to the writing. We also take turns reading stories and books that have lots of dialogue, and the students identify the dialogue and tell where the quotes go. I realize that this is really mixing two philosophies of teaching and learning, but for me it's the best way to get the job done.

The Instructional Cycle

Within the teaching–learning process, the *instructional cycle* helps to shape and sequence teaching and learning (refer to Figure 1-4 again). Ms. Kranowski sets instructional goals; plans instruction; and provides, evaluates, and modifies instruction based on students' progress, which she monitors through ongoing assessment. She uses this cycle in a flexible way, taking into account the characteristics of the learner, her teaching beliefs and attitudes, and the context in which the teaching and learning are happening. Sometimes she changes her instructional goals on the basis of input from the students or feedback about rate of learning. Sometimes she modifies her plans and the way in which she instructs to reach her instructional goals more effectively. When Ms. Kranowski added skill lessons to the writing curriculum, she changed her plans, which resulted in changes in instruction. The features of effective instruction should be considered in developing and implementing each part of the instructional cycle.

Features of Effective Instruction

Effective instruction is tantamount to a balancing act. Some teachers appear to be magicians because they seem to effortlessly balance the various features of effective instruction. However, keeping this balance requires a clear understanding of each feature as well as knowledge about how and when to implement them. Following are some of the features of effective instruction that should be present in all teaching:

1. Assessing progress
2. Designing instruction
   - Determining goals of instruction
   - Flexible grouping
   - Adaptations
   - Scaffolding
   - Careful use of instructional time
3. Delivering instruction
   - Quick pacing
   - Sufficient opportunities for student response
   - Error feedback

These features will benefit all the students in a classroom, but they are particularly helpful for students with learning and behavior problems.

> ▶ **WEB RESOURCES**
> Two helpful resources on understanding effective instruction for students with learning disabilities are LD OnLine (http://www.ldonline.org) and Center on Instruction (http://www.centeroninstruction.org).

Assessing Progress

Assessment is an essential component of instruction for students with learning and behavior difficulties. Assessing progress means continually examining data from both formal and informal assessments to determine students' knowledge and skills. Teachers who use a variety of assessment tools to determine what students know and don't know are more likely to adjust their instruction to meet students' needs and have improved outcomes for students. You can obtain information from reading inventories, standardized tests, observations, and student work samples to assist you in monitoring students' progress and to guide planning and instruction. Monitoring students' learning will help you to determine when students require extra assistance, and you will be able to adjust instruction accordingly. Monitoring of student progress should be frequent (one to three times per week) and ongoing.

Progress Monitoring   According to the instructional cycle (Figure 1-4), instruction is implemented after learning and instructional goals have been established and instruction has been planned. However, instruction is more effective and efficient if at the same time the instruction is being implemented, it is also being evaluated and—based on the evaluation—modified.

As we evaluate, it is crucial to keep a written record of student progress. The written record provides a means for objectively reflecting on the data to determine whether progress is evident (e.g., Deno, Fuchs, Marston, & Shin, 2001; Berkeley, Bender, Peaster, & Saunders, 2009). Roehring, Duggar, Moats, Glover, and Nincey (2008) note that while progress monitoring is a useful tool, some teachers find classroom management challenges and time demands interfere with effective implementation of progress monitoring. When used effectively, progress monitoring provides a written record for communicating with others regarding student progress. Sharing progress with parents, principals, other teachers, and—most important—the student provides a sense of accomplishment and satisfaction for all involved.

Having students monitor their own progress can increase their motivation for learning and pride in their accomplishments. Self-monitoring procedures have been used successfully with students who have learning and behavior problems, using the following procedures (see for more details, Heward, 2009, pp. 428–429):

- With students, identify the academic and/or social behaviors that they will monitor. Specify them in terms that are understood by the student.
- Use procedures that make record keeping with self-monitoring easy: for example, a simple paper-pencil form, wrist counter, tally counter, or a software program (e.g., http://kidtools.missouri.edu).
- Provide prompts to remind the student to self-monitor. These prompts can be from the teacher, another student, or reminders through check marks on a paper that lists the cues for the student to monitor.
- Provide modeling to how to do the self-monitor. Show the student how to monitor and model the monitoring for them.
- Encourage the student to self-monitor. Provide frequent feedback and support to students when they self-monitor. Observe changes in their behavior and report these observations to the student as well as the parents.

Types of Evaluation Measures

Although a teacher or student can use many methods to evaluate progress, generally one or more of three basic types are used: progress graphs and charts, performance records, and process records. Progress graphs are frequently used for measuring daily progress on individual skills or knowledge. Performance records are usually used for measuring progress across time (e.g., grading period, semester, and year). Curriculum-based measurement (Fuchs & Deno, 1991) is an example of a performance record that is closely tied to the curriculum being taught. Process records not only focus on the progress that is evident in the products, but also document progress in the learning process. Portfolios, learning logs, and dialogue journals can be used for this purpose.

Progress Graphs and Charts   Progress graphs and charts are generally used to measure progress on one behavior or skill. Graphs seem particularly well suited for self-monitoring because the results are displayed in such a manner that they are easy to interpret (see Figures 1-5 and 1-6). To be suitable for a progress graph, the behavior, skill, or knowledge must be quantifiable, either by time or by occurrence. For example, Ms. Shiller, the junior high teacher for a self-contained classroom of students with emotional disabilities, uses progress graphs for the following activities:

- Silent reading rate
- Speed in completing math facts
- Percentage of questions answered correctly for the social studies assignment
- Number of times the student disrupted other students during the morning independent learning activity
- Student and teacher rating of written pieces, based on interest and readability

With a progress graph, the measurement unit is marked on the vertical axis. For example, *time* for graphing silent reading rate, *speed* for graphing math facts completed, and *percent* for graphing the percentage of social studies questions answered correctly would be marked on the vertical axis. On the horizontal axis, the occurrence unit is marked (e.g., date, teaching session, social studies assignment number). It is relatively easy to plot progress data on either a line graph, as depicted in Figure 1-5, or a bar graph, as shown in Figure 1-6.

Progress charts are usually used in the same manner as progress graphs: to measure progress on one skill or behavior. The difference between a progress chart and a progress graph is that with a chart, the score is reported but is not presented in a relational manner (see Figure 1-7). Although progress charts are generally more efficient in the use of space, they do not provide the clear visual

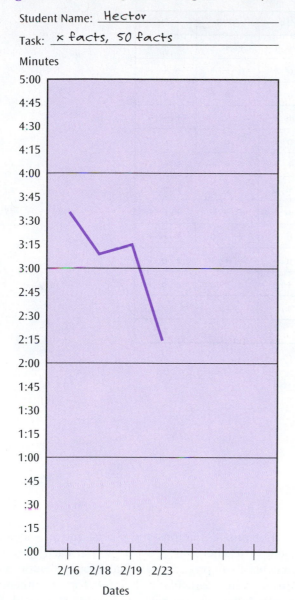

► **Figure 1-5** Timing Chart Using a Line Graph

Student Name: Hector

Task: x facts, 50 facts

Dates

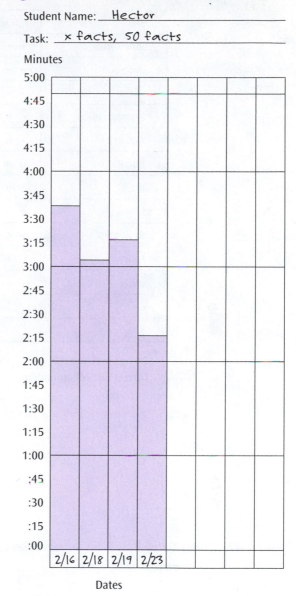

► **Figure 1-6** Timing Chart Using a Bar Graph

Student Name: Hector

Task: x facts, 50 facts

Dates

representation of student performance; therefore, student progress or lack of it is not so readily apparent. Consequently, graphing is generally recommended over charting for student self-monitoring.

Performance Records Performance records are often used to record student progress across a set of skills or knowledge and for a significant length of time. An IEP is a performance record in that annual goals and short-term objectives are written, and evaluation of the goals and objectives is recorded in the IEP (see Figure 1-1). Many school districts have developed skill and knowledge competencies or objectives that students need to attain at various grade levels. These are often arranged on an

individual student performance record so that as a student becomes proficient in a listed competency, it can be noted (see Figure 1-8). Many commercial reading, math, writing, and other content area programs publish performance records so student progress can be recorded. One caution in using such performance records is that although most of them measure proficiency, they do not measure maintenance, generalization, or application. Consequently, a teacher may receive a performance record on a student and find that the student cannot perform some of the skills that are listed as mastered.

In addition to collecting permanent products, the teacher and/or the students may want to keep a progress journal. Usually, this journal accompanies the performance

▶ Figure 1-7 Progress Chart for Sight Words

Name: Lisa

	3/12	3/14	3/15	3/18
sometimes	+ + +	+ + +	+ + +	+ + +
everyone	– – o	– o +	o + +	+ + +
when	– – –	o o +	– o +	o + +
themselves	– o +	o + +	o + +	+ + +
mystery	– o o	o o +	+ o +	+ o +
hurry	o o +	+ + +	+ + +	+ + +
their	– o –	o + o	+ o +	+ + +
friend	+ o +	+ + +	+ + +	+ + +
mountain	– o o	o o +	+ + o	+ + +
trail	– + –	– o –	– + +	+ o +
route	– – o	o + o	o + o	o o +

+ Correct and automatic

o Correct but not automatic

– Incorrect

▶ Figure 1-8 Competency-Based Performance Record

Student: Karen	
Competency Area and Skill	*Mastery*
Early Reading	
Identifies letters of alphabet	10/00
Names letters of alphabet	12/00
Holds book, turns pages one at a time	9/00
Looks first at left page, then at right	9/00
Distinguishes print from pictures	9/00
Scans left to right, top to bottom	9/00
Reads along listening to a familiar book	9/00
Rhymes words	11/00
Identifies words in a familiar book	10/00
Beginning Reading	
Reads simple stories (preprimer/primer)	3/01
Identifies consonant sounds	2/01
Identifies short vowel sounds	2/01
Identifies long vowel sounds	4/01
Identifies simple sight words in isolation	2/01
Recognizes that "s" makes words plural etc.	4/01

record or progress graphs and charts, and provides the student or teacher with space in which each can write comments about progress. Ms. Shiller found that progress journals were particularly helpful for documenting progress regarding students' behavior. She used this method in combination with graphs to evaluate several students' progress. She found that her dated journal entries provided insights into how she might modify the instructional context and the instruction.

Curriculum-based measurement (CBM) is one system of performance records that highlights the close tie between curriculum and student performance, using frequent samplings from curriculum materials to assess students' academic performance (e.g., Christ & Ardoin, 2009; Espin et al., 2008; Fuchs & Deno, 1991). CBM has been used successfully for students who have learning and behavior problems to improve reading fluency, reading comprehension, spelling, and arithmetic computation in both general education and special education classrooms (e.g., Keller-Margulis, Shapiro, & Hintze, 2008). For example, reading fluency in a third-grade class can be measured each week by having each student read 100-word passages from the reading curriculum and graphing fluency rates across time. This type of measurement provides ongoing data for making instructional decisions. Teachers can assess changes in student performance over time by considering level of performance as affected by instructional change, rate of learning (as reflected by changes in the slope of the trend line) compared to the goal or aim rate, and variability in the consistency of the performance.

Process Records: Portfolios and Learning Logs   Portfolios, learning logs, and other mechanisms for students to record their thinking and work while they are performing an academic task can facilitate learning (Murphy, 2008; Segers, Gijbels, & Thurlings, 2008). Learning logs and portfolios are particularly useful when more than one student is working on a task. In a portfolio, samples of students' work are collected across a specified period of time (e.g., month, semester, year) and then used as a reference for students' progress and as a means to encourage students to improve the quality and quantity of their work. For example, teachers may ask students to keep a portfolio of their writing as a means of documenting the improvement of the quality of their writing over time. Not only are the final products collected, but so are rough drafts, planning or brainstorming sheets, and practice sheets. For example, a student's writing portfolio might contain five stories and essays as well as the brainstorm sheets, research notes, rough drafts, revisions, and edited drafts associated with each piece of writing. Whereas reading samples (including oral reading and discussions) can be collected on audiotape, written products can be collected for writing and math. Photographs of projects in subject areas as well as the associated written work can be collected for content area work such as social studies and science. The teacher may want to set up a portfolio for each student in the class, have the students help select which pieces to place in the portfolio, and then review the portfolios with the students to identify areas of progress and assist in targeting other areas on which to work.

The teacher can also use learning logs to document students' thinking or work. Learning logs allow the students to reflect on their learning and the processes they have used in learning. For example, Mr. Briggs, a sixth-grade social studies teacher, uses learning logs for students to document the identification of the main idea and key vocabulary words as they read social studies texts. The entry of Jose (see Figure 1-9), a fifth-grade student with written expression difficulties, reflects what he is learning as a reader and author after reading the chapter entitled "Harassing Miss Harris" in the book *The Great Gilly Hopkins* (Paterson, 1978).

▶ **Figure 1-9**   Learning Log Entry for Jose and Dialogue Journal Entry for Tamara on "Harassing Miss Harris" from *The Great Gilly Hopkins* (not corrected for spelling)

Jose

I like this chapter of the book. Even thow it was hard to read, I liked it. I think that is becuase the auther lets you know just how terribl Gilly feels in her new school. I think that letting you know feelings makes writing more interesting.

Tamara

I just read the chapter on Harassing Miss Harris. I liked it a lot because sometimes I feel like Gilly. I feel so mad that I just wont to get mad and not do the work. I really like the way the author lets you kenow just how Gilly feels. I guess that is why I liked it so much. You kenow Gilly's feelings.

One of the major obstacles in evaluating student progress is planning and organizing an evaluation system. Early in the school year, the teacher should do the following:

1. Determine what is to be evaluated.
2. Determine how it is to be evaluated (e.g., progress graphs, charts, permanent product records, portfolios).
3. Determine whether and when student self-monitoring will be used (e.g., learning logs).
4. Develop the forms needed for evaluation.
5. Set up the system so that it is easy to collect, file, and retrieve progress data.

The teacher should coordinate the evaluation system with the school system and then collect and use the data to make instructional decisions.

When a teacher approaches instruction with a plan of action, it is important to remember that the plan will need to be modified. Effective instruction takes place when the instructional procedures and content match the overall teaching–learning process. Because the teaching–learning process is dynamic and flexible, the instructional process must also be dynamic and flexible.

Designing Instruction

Once objectives have been set and students' skills have been assessed, you can begin designing instruction. Designing instruction refers to using student data to plan for effective instruction (University of Texas Center for Reading and Language Arts, 2000a, 2000b). When teachers systematically adjust instruction in response to assessment information, students' rate of learning increases (Fuchs, Fuchs, Hamlett, Phillips, & Karns, 1995).

How can teachers design instruction so that the needs of all the students in a classroom are met? Many teachers find it difficult to teach the wide range of skills their students require. Because the students' deficits are so many and so varied in level, it seems impossible to cover them all. The steps to designing instruction are as follows:

1. Use the information gathered from various assessment tools. Curriculum-based measurements are particularly suited for this purpose because they are ongoing and closely aligned with curricular goals (University of Texas Center for Reading and Language Arts, 2000a, 2000b).
2. Group students with similar instructional needs.
3. Set specific instructional targets that focus on particular concepts, using curricular objectives and annual goals as a guideline.
4. Prepare a schedule, and choose and sequence appropriate activities and tasks.
5. Set up a group management system that is specifically designed to provide instruction in a variety of grouping patterns.
6. Identify students who need additional, more intensive instruction.

Determining Goals of Instruction   *Setting goals for instruction* helps a teacher know where he or she is going. Several questions a teacher may ask in setting goals for instruction and learning are as follows:

- Have I used the information I have about the characteristics of the learner?
- Have I taken into account my beliefs and attitudes?
- Have I involved the students in setting the goals?
- Have I set goals that are realistic yet challenging to both the learner and me?
- How do these goals fit within the larger teaching–learning context (e.g., goals of the school, curriculum, long-range career goals of the student)?

When Ms. Kranowski set her instructional goals for writing, she decided that she had two major objectives: to have the students experience successful writing in a variety of forms and to have the students develop writing skills that would help them in school and later in life. She wanted very much to involve the students in setting goals, believing that the students would then have a greater commitment to reaching those goals. She began the year by telling the students about "the way that writing works" in the classroom. She shared the importance of supporting each other, for she wanted students to set a goal of working together. As they worked together, shared their writing, and got to know each other better, Ms. Kranowski sat down with each one of the students and helped them select skills for improvement. By analyzing the students' written products, observing the students as they wrote, talking with the students about their writing, and using her knowledge about the scope and sequence of writing skills, she felt comfortable working with students in selecting goals. In this way, Ms. Kranowski's instructional goals were interwoven with her students' learning goals.

Flexible Grouping   Deciding what type of grouping pattern to use is also part of designing instruction. Because of the large range of abilities, interests, and background knowledge in most classrooms, it is best to use flexible grouping. Flexible grouping, another component of effective instruction, refers to the use of a variety of grouping practices that change depending on the goals and objectives for the lesson. Mixed-ability groups, same-ability groups, whole groups, pairs, and individualized instruction can be used to meet different student and instructional needs. Groups should be flexible, and students should be regrouped on a regular basis.

Adaptations   The purpose of making instructional adaptations is to ensure that students can participate in instruction, activities, homework, and assessment to the extent possible in the general education classroom. The use of adaptations enhances learning for all students, not only those with learning and behavior problems (Roller, 2002). Adaptations can be divided into three categories:

1. Instructional design (e.g., accessing resources, collaborating with other professionals, having a plan for adaptations, and integrating technology)
2. Instructional and curricular (e.g., making learning visible and explicit; using clear, simple language; breaking a task or activity into steps; and providing multiple ways of demonstrating learning)
3. Behavioral support (e.g., teaching alternative behaviors, being consistent, providing structure, and being proactive)

The use of adaptations is one way to demonstrate acceptance, respect, and interest for individual learning differences. When determining whether adaptations are necessary, consider the demands of the lesson and the skills of the learner. If there is a mismatch between the abilities required by the lesson and the student's skills, adaptations may be necessary. The adaptations that are used should create a better match between the student's skills and the task. For example, if a lesson on main ideas will require students to write the main idea of a story and a student with a reading disability has difficulty writing letters or words quickly, there may be a mismatch between the demands of the lesson and the student's abilities. If the instruction on main ideas is at the correct level for the student, adaptations to the lesson can allow the student to benefit more from the instruction. One adaptation may be to give the student extra time to write the main idea sentence. A second possible adaptation may be to have the student work with a partner to develop a main idea sentence. In this case, the student with the reading disability can be fully involved in creating the main idea sentence, but the partner can write the sentence.

Scaffolding   An essential element of effective instruction for students with learning and behavior problems is the use of scaffolding (Coyne, Kame'enui, & Simmons, 2001; Torgesen, 2002). *Scaffolding* means adjusting and extending instruction so that the student is challenged and able to develop new skills. The teacher can scaffold instruction to meet the needs of the students by manipulating the task, materials, group size, pace, presentation, and so on. The metaphor of a scaffold captures the idea of an adjustable and temporary support that can be removed when it is no longer needed. Vygotsky (1978) describes learning as occurring in the *zone of proximal development*: "the distance between the actual developmental level as described by independent problem solving and the level of potential development as determined through problem solving under adult guidance or in collaboration with more capable peers" (p. 86). Important to promoting development within the students' zones of proximal development is the teacher's ability to relinquish control of the strategies to the students (Santamaria, Fletcher, & Bos, 2002). To scaffold instruction effectively, teachers must teach new content in manageable steps; use explicit, systematic instruction for each step; and provide practice and review until students are independent and confident (see Apply the Concept 1-3).

Teaching in manageable steps involves breaking complex tasks into smaller steps to allow students to master each step of the task. Each step should be slightly more difficult than the previous one and should lead up to the full, complex skill the students are to learn. Providing specific instruction for each step of a complex task not only allows student success, but also creates a clear picture of what subskills students have mastered and what still needs further instruction or practice.

In addition to teaching in small segments, each step must be taught by using explicit, systematic instruction. Explicit instruction includes modeling, guided and independent practice, and use of consistent instructional procedures. Systematic instruction refers to sequencing instruction from easier to more difficult and teaching the easier skills to mastery before introducing more complex

● ● ● ● ● ● *Apply the Concept* ● ● ● ● ● ●

1-3	Scaffolding Instruction

Use the following guidelines to scaffold instruction for students with learning and behavior problems:

- Break the task into small steps.
- Teach easier skills first, then more difficult skills.
- Slow the pace of new skill introduction to allow for more practice of a task.

- Use a small group size.
- Make thought processes for accomplishing tasks overt by talking to students about what you are thinking when you engage in the task. Have students share what they are thinking when they practice the task.
- Teach strategies for completing complex skills.

- Model all steps involved in completing tasks.
- Provide teacher assistance during the first student attempts at skills.
- Praise the accomplishment of each small step.
- Use concrete materials during initial skill instruction.
- Vary the materials used.

skills. Many reading strategies require complex thought processes and quick decision making. Students with reading difficulties or disabilities often do not automatically infer the thought processes that good readers use. Therefore, strategies for reading words and comprehending text must be taught in an overt way. Modeling strategies and guiding students through new tasks assist them in acquiring new skills without frustration. As each step is mastered, students become more independent in their ability to perform the skill or strategy.

Scaffolding reading instruction is analogous to the process many parents use when teaching their child to ride a bike. Although most children have seen many models of other adults and children riding bikes, a model of the whole bike-riding process by itself is probably not enough for a child to understand all the tasks that go into riding a bike successfully. Consequently, many parents divide riding a bike into smaller steps and teach each step explicitly, while allowing the child sufficient opportunities to practice and master each step. For example, as a first step, a parent may model and provide guided practice for sitting on the bike. The parent may provide explicit instruction by telling the child where to place feet and hands and how to work the pedals for moving forward and braking. Second, the materials may be scaffolded by attaching training wheels. This allows the child to practice what the parent has taught about sitting and pedal movement without having to deal with balancing the bike too. After the child has mastered riding with training wheels, the next step may be for the parent to take the training wheels off and hold the bike while running with the child as the child rides the bike. This allows the child to begin getting a feel for the balance needed to ride the bike independently. Parents can also assist the child in the thought processes for bike riding—look straight ahead, don't lean to one side, and so on. This explicit instruction helps the child learn techniques for balancing on the bike. The next step may be to slowly remove the scaffold by holding the bike less and less tightly, and finally letting go while the child rides. The final step for the child is to learn to start pedaling the bike and balancing without the parent holding on to get the bike started.

Dividing bike riding into manageable steps not only helps the child learn a new, complex skill with less frustration (or in this case less injury), but also allows faster learning because the steps of the process are made explicit and practiced to mastery. Reading instruction should be similarly broken down into manageable steps, and each step should be taught explicitly and practiced to mastery. Independent reading is the ultimate result, but independent reading requires many, many steps and thought processes. For students with reading difficulties or disabilities to succeed, all of these must be taught explicitly and effectively.

Time Management One of the most powerful tools for improving learning is *careful use of instructional time*. For teachers working with students who are performing below grade level, effective time management becomes an essential part of designing and providing effective instruction. In addition to avoiding wasting time, teachers must decide how much time to give to each activity or concept. Good and Brophy (1997) found that as much as 70% of the school day is spent doing seatwork. When deciding how to sequence activities and how much time to spend on each, the teacher must think about the learner, the materials, and the task (Kame'enui & Carnine, 1998; Rosenshine, 1997). As was discussed earlier, the features of effective instruction must be balanced carefully, and their implementation must be ongoing. Assessment is a necessary step in designing instruction; similarly, instruction is an integral part of assessment and student monitoring.

Progress Monitoring Ms. Kranowski watched and listened to the students and analyzed their written products over time. She used curriculum-based measures to gauge skills in capitalization, punctuation, spelling, and grammar. All these evaluative measures led her to the same conclusion: Her students' writing skills were not improving at a rate that she considered adequate. Ms. Kranowski decided to compile all the data using a class summary sheet. She then examined the data to find similar needs among her students. Estrella, Aileen, Luther, Jacqueline, and Sally were having difficulty capitalizing proper nouns. While the rest of the class completed a first draft of a story, Ms. Kranowski spent 10 minutes with these students, providing direct and explicit instruction on the rules of capitalization. She had prepared several examples of proper nouns, which she used to monitor her students' understanding by asking them to think aloud about why the nouns were or were not capitalized.

In determining how to modify her instruction, Ms. Kranowski thought about the ideas presented in Apply the Concept 1-4. She felt that she had adequately addressed the first four questions. Student motivation, attention, encouragement, and modeling had been good. She did not feel as comfortable about her answers to the next three questions: prior knowledge, manner of presentation, and practice. Sometimes she thought she wasn't focusing enough on one or two writing skills. She tended to present too much and not allow for enough practice and feedback. Ms. Kranowski decided that her modifications had to alleviate the problems with presentation, practice, and feedback. Her solution was the skill lessons that focused on teaching specific writing skills twice a week. For Ms. Kranowski and her students, this solution was successful. Her students began acquiring and maintaining the targeted writing skills. Now she is asking questions and planning for generalization and application.

1-4   Questions for Evaluating the Instructional Process

- *Student motivation.* Am I creating a context in which learning is valued? Am I providing students appropriate choices about tasks and materials?
- *Student attention.* Am I creating an environment in which students can and are encouraged to attend to the learning task? Am I providing opportunities for students to work in settings that promote their attention?
- *Encouragement.* Am I creating a setting in which students are encouraged to take risks and be challenged by learning? Do I provide adequate feedback to each student regarding learning and social behavior?
- *Modeling.* When teaching a new task, do I first model what I want students to do? Do I use "think-alouds" to show students how I manage a task? Are the students given the opportunity to watch,

listen, and talk to others so that they can see how the knowledge or skill is learned?
- *Activating prior knowledge.* Am I getting the students to think about what they already know about a skill or topic, and are they given the opportunity to build upon that information in an organized fashion?
- *Rate, amount, and manner of presentation.* Are the new skills and knowledge being presented at a rate and amount that allows the students time to learn, and in a manner that gives them enough information yet does not overload them
- *Practice.* Are the students given ample opportunity to practice? How much time do I provide students to practice and learn from each other?
- *Feedback.* Are the students given feedback on their work so they know how and what they are learning?

- *Acquisition.* Are the students given the opportunity to learn skills and knowledge until they feel comfortable with them and to the point they do or know something almost automatically?
- *Maintenance.* Are the students given the opportunity to continue to use their skills and knowledge so that they can serve as tools for further learning?
- *Generalization.* Are the students generalizing the skills and knowledge to other tasks, settings, and situations? Are the students, other teachers, or parents seeing the learning?
- *Application.* Are the students given the opportunity to apply their skills and knowledge in new and novel situations, thereby adapting their skills to meet the new learning experiences?

Delivering Instruction

In addition to planning and designing effective instruction for students with reading problems, the delivery of the instruction must be considered. Several features occur during the delivery of effective instruction, including effective pacing, providing sufficient opportunities for students to respond, and feedback. Many of these same instructional practices are beneficial for students who are English language learners (ELLs) and also have learning problems. See Apply the Concept 1-5 for a description.

Quick Pacing   Quick pacing refers to instruction and student response that move at a manageable pace for students while taking full advantage of every minute of instruction. A quick pace eliminates unnecessary teacher talk and minimizes the amount of time between activities, allowing for more instructional time. A quick pace also keeps students alert and provide lots of opportunities for students to participate. For students who are behind in their reading skills, increased instructional time is essential. To catch up to expected levels of reading, students with reading problems have to make more progress than an average reader. A quick pace also keeps students actively engaged in the lesson. This, in turn, increases their instructional time. When the scaffolding techniques discussed earlier are used effectively,

students can be successful, and the lesson can move at a quick pace.

Sufficient Opportunities for Student Response   When delivering a lesson, teacher routines should provide for maximum opportunities for students to respond with teacher feedback. For new instruction, teachers model the expected response and then give students an opportunity to practice. For activities previously taught, students practice and review skills taught and also generalize to more difficult tasks. Therefore, lessons should be filled with opportunities for students to respond and demonstrate what they are learning. There are several ways to increase the number of opportunities to respond within a lesson:

1. *Limit teacher talk.* Limiting the length of teacher talk can be accomplished by breaking up teacher modeling or explanations of concepts with questions for the students. Students can replicate teacher models or respond to related questions as each step of a process or strategy is taught.
2. *Use choral and individual responding.* Choral responding permits all students participating in the lesson to answer at the same time. Its use, followed by individual responses of students, increases the number of opportunities a particular student has to practice skills within a lesson.

1-5 Designing Instruction for English-Language Learners (ELLs) with Learning Disabilities

Students with learning disabilities who are ELLs benefit from many of the same instructional practices associated with improved outcomes for monolingual students when teachers consider the language demands of the activities. Effective teachers adjust their instruction to consider the language and concept demands of their instruction. These teachers realize that ELLs' understanding of new concepts may be enhanced through instruction that uses routines, embeds redundancy of language use in lessons, and provides explicit discussion of vocabulary and the structure of language required to complete the task. Furthermore, teachers who are effective with ELLs present lessons that are organized to teach students to be aware of what they are learning and where they are confused. Haager and colleagues (Graves, Gersten, & Haager, 2004; Haager, Gersten, Baker, & Graves, 2003) conducted an observational study in 14 classrooms that included students who were ELLs, representing more than 10 different language groups. They identified effective teachers based on students' academic outcomes. They then looked at the instructional practices of these teachers. Effective teachers of ELLs

- used explicit teaching
- monitored student progress
- provided opportunities to practice new learning
- incorporated strategies that supported student acquisition of English language skills

Which instructional practices should you use in your teaching to ensure that English-language learners have opportunities to learn? Providing clear, specific, and easy-to-follow procedures helps students learn new skills and strategies. It is also important to provide opportunities for students to acquire the language associated with these new skills and strategies. Teaching explicitly assists students; this includes identifying and using the structural and visual cues present in words, making relationships among concepts, words, or ideas visible and connected.

---

3. *Use a variety of grouping formats.* Teaching students in small groups or using structuring lessons for pairs of students gives each student more turns to practice new skills. Students who have reading difficulties or disabilities often need extensive practice to learn new concepts. Providing additional practice opportunities within the lesson is an effective way to increase student skill levels.

Feedback   Feedback refers to the teacher assistance that is provided when students respond during a lesson, while reading a passage, or working independently. Students with academic difficulties or disabilities need teachers to assist them with errors immediately and to provide additional opportunities to practice the skill correctly after assistance (Parker, Hasbrouck, & Denton, 2002). When students read or answer questions incorrectly without immediate error feedback, they practice the skill incorrectly. The effects of inaccurate practice can add up quickly, allowing the student to learn the skill incorrectly. This means that the student will have to spend a significant amount of time relearning the skill in the future. Also, students who respond correctly benefit from positive and specific feedback about the aspects of the task they performed well. Examples of feedback include: "You added the numbers correctly in all of the problems in the first line, however there are two errors in problem #3. Can you find them?"; "I like the way you read this paragraph with expression, read the next paragraph the same way but I would like you to pause at the end of each sentence. Let me read one sentence for you to show you what I mean."

▶ FOCUS Question 1. **What is inclusion?**

Answer: In general, *inclusion* refers to full-time placement in a general education classroom with support services provided within the classroom from a special education teacher. A key element of inclusion is collaboration between the special education teacher and the general education teacher. If this collaboration is unsuccessful, the system may not work to benefit the student. Ensuring that students with disabilities receive a special education and that the IEPs of students are fulfilled is still the responsibility of teachers, even when students are fully included.

▶ FOCUS Question 2. **What issues relate to RTI and appropriate identification of students with learning disabilities?**

Answer: RTI is designed to provide early and ongoing screening to determine academic and social problems. The intention of RTI is to provide appropriate intervention services as a means to prevent later problems and to document the effectiveness of these interventions. The data resulting from documenting students' responses to interventions can be used as a data source in determining special education.

▶ FOCUS Question 3. **What is an IEP, and what is the process for developing and updating an IEP?**

Answer: The IEP is both a process and a document. The process involves a group of individuals who establish an appropriate specialized educational program. At the IEP meeting, the team determines and documents whether a student is eligible for special education services; which services will be provided, the amount of services, and where they will occur; and the goals and objectives, adaptations needed, and additional considerations as necessary, such as accommodations to statewide assessments.

▶ FOCUS Question 4. **What goes into teaching students with learning and behavior problems?**

Answer: Both the teacher and the student bring into the classroom knowledge and skills, as well as beliefs about school and about the world. Therefore, learning involves the accumulation of knowledge and skills, but it is also the active construction and transformation of ideas based on observations and experiences. Research has been conducted that supports the use of the following instructional features to meet the needs of students with learning and behavior problems: assessing progress, designing instruction, delivering instruction, and error feedback.

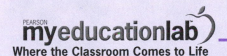

PEARSON myeducationlab
Where the Classroom Comes to Life

The MyEducationLab for this course can help you solidify your comprehension of Chapter 1 concepts.

- Gauge and further develop your understanding of chapter concepts by taking the quizzes and examining the enrichment materials in the Chapter 1 Study Plan.
- Visit Topic 8, Planning and Organization, to connect with challenge-based interactive modules, case study units, and podcasts that provide research-validated information

about working with students in inclusive settings by visiting the IRIS Center Resources.
- Explore Assignments and Activities, assignable exercises showing concepts in action through video, cases, and student and teacher artifacts.
- Practice and strengthen skills essential to quality teaching through the Building Teaching Skills and Dispositions lessons.

2

Approaches to Learning and Teaching

FOCUS Questions

1. What is applied behavioral analysis, and how can teachers use it to increase desirable behaviors or decrease undesirable behaviors?
2. How is cognitive strategy instruction (CSI) used to teach academic, cognitive, or social skills?
3. How can teachers use the features of sociocultural theory to make instruction more effective for their students?
4. How can knowledge of schema theory assist teachers in meeting the needs of students with learning and behavior problems?

Meaghan knew by the time she was a senior in college that she wanted to be a special education teacher, but was close to finishing her psychology degree and did not want to change majors. Instead, Meaghan completed her undergraduate degree in psychology and then returned to school part-time to pursue a degree with certification in special education. While going to school part-time she was also working as a teaching assistant in a middle school. Fortunately, much of what she learned in psychology was directly applicable to the work she was doing with a team of special education teachers. She had learned a great deal about various learning theories as a psychology major and, in particular, how to use applied behavior analysis. Now, much of what she was asked to implement as schoolwide behavior support was based on the applied behavior analysis she had learned as an undergraduate. She understood the importance of looking for positive behaviors and providing reinforcement to students when they exhibited them. She also understood how to be consistent in her application of rules. Furthermore, her coursework that addressed cognitive behavioral theories also assisted her in effectively implementing many of the cognitively based math and reading strategies that she was encouraged to use by the special education teachers. All in all, the longer she worked as a special education teaching assistant, the more she appreciated her strong background in learning theory.

This chapter highlights some of the critical features about how we learn that apply to delivering effective instruction and providing classroom management. Models and theories of learning can assist teachers in understanding and explaining how students learn. They also guide teachers in modifying their teaching to promote effective and efficient learning. This chapter surveys four approaches to learning and teaching: applied behavior analysis, cognitive strategy instruction, sociocultural theory of learning, and schema theory. The chapter is sequenced to move from less to more cognitively oriented models. Many of the general principles that are presented in this chapter will be applied to specific content areas in subsequent chapters. As you read this chapter, we encourage you to think about students who you know are not succeeding in school and who have learning and behavior problems. How are their learning patterns and habits explained by the various approaches to learning described in this chapter? What general teaching principles do the different approaches suggest to help such students? How can technology assist in the teaching–learning process (see this chapter's Tech Tips feature)?

PEARSON
myeducationlab

Visit the MyEducationLab for this course to enhance your understanding of chapter concepts with a personalized Study Plan. You'll also have the opportunity to hone your teaching skills through video-based Assignments and Activities, IRIS Center Resources, and Building Teaching Skills and Dispositions lessons.

Applied Behavior Analysis

What is applied behavioral analysis, and how can teachers use it to improve the behavior of their students? Teachers and other professionals who use applied behavior analysis understand that many of the behaviors of their students are learned and therefore they can be taught new behaviors. Using applied behavior analysis, the focus is on identifying observable behaviors and manipulating the antecedents and consequences of these behaviors to change behavior.

Manipulating Antecedents

An *antecedent* is an environmental event or stimulus that precedes a behavior and influences the probability that the behavior will recur in the future. For example, the students learn that when the teacher pulls the cart with the video machine on it to the front of the room, that behavior serves as an antecedent to watching a film. Antecedents influence desirable and undesirable behaviors. It is relatively easy for teachers to manipulate antecedents to change student behaviors. Teachers can do this by analyzing the environment and identifying factors that contribute to desirable and undesirable behaviors. By identifying and changing these factors, teachers can increase student learning and minimize or eliminate antecedents that interfere with successful learning. In observing antecedent behaviors, the teacher usually considers instructional content, classroom schedule, classroom rules, classroom arrangement, and peer interactions.

Instructional Content Teachers can consider a number of ways to manipulate instructional content to control behavior: make activities more interesting, incorporate student preferences, reduce task difficulties or length, provide choices, and develop functional or age-appropriate activities. By modifying educational programs, teachers can prevent students' inappropriate or undesirable behavior, and establish a pleasant classroom environment. For example, Blair (1996) found that incorporating the students' activity preferences into circle time and academic activities in a preschool/kindergarten essentially eliminated the undesirable behavior of young students who had significant behavior problems. Another example is the teacher who realized that students would begin fooling around when waiting in line to transition to recess or lunch. She decided to give students a question related to their work that they would have to solve with a partner while waiting in line.

Classroom Schedule A well-designed schedule allows everyone to predict what will occur during the school day and assist with the allocation of instructional time. Teachers can involve students in planning the daily schedule. In addition, it is important to avoid revising a schedule because changes can be disruptive, undermining students' ability to predict what will happen during the day. If there are changes to the schedule, posting them in a visible place is useful.

Classroom Rules When properly developed and stated, carefully selected rules can contribute to a positive classroom atmosphere. They help students understand what will and will not be accepted in the classroom. It is important to select a limited number of rules to make it easier for students to remember them. Seek the class's input on the rules to increase students' commitment to following them. State rules positively to help students identify the acceptable behavior, and post the rules so students can refer to them.

Classroom Arrangement Noises and crowding in a classroom sometimes increase undesirable behaviors. Arranging the furniture in the classroom to partition some areas can reduce noise levels, and limiting the number of students in any area can reduce crowding.

See Chapter 4 for additional information on classroom arrangement and sample room arrangements.

For more information on teaching prosocial skills, refer to Chapter 4.

Peer Interactions The classroom and the school are important social communities, and peer interactions play a significant role in determining the levels of desirable and undesirable behaviors. Teachers can facilitate peer interaction by pairing students who have good social skills with students who have more difficulty in prosocial skills, encouraging interaction between students with and without disabilities, and teaching prosocial skills to decrease inappropriate behaviors and to increase appropriate behaviors.

Increasing Desirable Behaviors Through Consequences

During the past few weeks, Ms. Glenn has focused on teaching Marjorie, Sheila, and Ali subtraction with regrouping. During this time, she demonstrated many of the principles by using 10 packs of sticks. The students practiced applying the principles on the chalkboard. Ms. Glenn then asked the students to practice the skills independently by completing a math sheet with 12 subtraction-with-regrouping problems. She watched them complete the first problem correctly. She then needed to teach another group, yet she wanted to be sure that these three students would continue to work on their math.

Progress Monitoring According to principles of applied behavior analysis, behavior is influenced by the consequences that follow it. Ms. Glenn needed to decide what consequences would follow appropriate math performance to maintain or increase its occurrence. She told Marjorie, Sheila, and Ali, "If you get nine or more problems correct on this math sheet, I will let you have 5 minutes of free time in the Fun Corner." Free time in the Fun Corner was a big reinforcement for all three students, and they accurately completed the math sheet while she worked with other students.

There are four principles to apply in attempting to maintain or increase behavior:

1. The behavior must already be in the student's repertoire. In the preceding example, Ms. Glenn's students knew how to perform the math task. To maintain or increase social or academic behaviors, the teacher must first be sure that the student knows how to perform the target behaviors.
2. A consequence must follow the precise behavior to be changed or must be linked to the behavior through language. For example, the teacher may say, "Because you completed all of your math assignments this week, I'll let you select a movie to watch."
3. A reinforcer is whatever follows a behavior and maintains or increases the rate of the behavior.
4. To be most powerful, reinforcement should occur immediately following the behavior.

Thus, to increase the frequency of a behavior, we can manipulate the consequence that follows the behavior.

> ▶ **WEB RESOURCES**
> See the following Web site for a historical overview of behavior analysis:
> http://genetics.biozentrum.uni-wuerzburg.de/behavior/learning/behaviorism.html.

Reinforcement Reinforcement is the most significant way to increase desirable behavior. There are two types of reinforcement: positive and negative; both increase responding. How do they differ? The major difference between positive and negative reinforcement is that *positive reinforcement* is the *presentation* of a stimulus to increase responding, whereas *negative reinforcement* is the *removal* of a stimulus to increase responding.

Positive reinforcement increases responding by following the behavior with activities, objects, food, and social rewards that are associated with increasing the behavior. Toys, games, and privileges such as helping the teacher or having extra recess time are examples of positive reinforcers. Negative reinforcement increases responding by removing a stimulus. For example, if the teacher turned off the music in the classroom and students work activity increased, then removing the noise of the music would have served as a negative reinforcement for the class.

The practice of negative reinforcement is often misused because the term *negative* is misinterpreted to mean harmful or bad, and therefore, the implication is that positive reinforcement is good and negative reinforcement is bad. Negative reinforcement simply means taking away something unpleasant if a specific behavior is exhibited. If a teacher scowls at a student until the student works, removing the scowl is negative reinforcement. The learning that takes place through negative reinforcement is avoidance learning. A common use in schools is the completion of work assignments to avoid staying after school. Students often use negative reinforcement with adults. An example is a child who throws a temper tantrum until he or she gets what he or she wants.

The effectiveness of a reinforcement program depends on selecting reinforcers that actually increase the target behavior. One way teachers can make sure that they use appropriate reinforcers for each student is to develop a reinforcer preference checklist for identifying reinforcers. Activities and events that a student selected when given a wide choice are more likely to be strongly reinforcing. To prevent students from being satiated with the reinforcer, reinforcement menus are recommended. Instead of providing one reinforcer over time, giving a choice of reinforcers increases their value and prevents satiation.

Many teachers are concerned that using reinforcers can prepare students for being "bribed" or "paid" to exhibit the behaviors that they are supposed to do. However, for students with behavior disorders, many of them have little experience using appropriate behaviors so reinforcers can serve as a means to motivate them to practice appropriate behaviors. In using reinforcers with your students, it is important to start with more *intrinsic reinforcers* such as using activities that are reinforcing to the student (e.g., listening to music, coloring) and move to more *tangible reinforcers* such as tokens and food only as necessary. For example, a hierarchy of reinforcers, ranging from internal self-reinforcement ("I did a good job") to more extrinsic or tangible reinforcers such as choosing from a toy store, are presented in Apply the Concept 2-1.

How do you decide which reinforcers you should use? Selecting reinforcers is a critical decision as it influences their effectiveness. Consider the following suggestions when selecting reinforcers:

- Observe and record behaviors and events that are reinforcing to the student. For example, some students like to have their hands or face touched with a feather, other students like verbal praise, some students like to have time with their friends.
- Consider the age and interests of the person whose behavior you want to improve and consider what is reinforcing to them.
- After you consider what you know about the person, his or her age, interests, and what he or she likes and dislikes, identify a list of potential reinforcers.
- Use the behaviors that the person likes to engage in as reinforcers for the behaviors that he or she likes less.
- Interview the person about the things that he or she likes and would be reinforcing to that person.
- Try something new as a reinforcer.
- Consider using reinforcers that occur naturally in the environment.
- Be sure to keep a record of the target behavior and the extent to which it is influenced by the reinforcers.

Secondary Reinforcers A *secondary reinforcer* is a previously neutral behavior that is paired with a reinforcer and therefore takes on reinforcing properties of its own. Thus, if the teacher always calls a student up to the teacher's desk before rewarding the student, then being called to the teacher's desk becomes a secondary reinforcer.

Sincere praise and attention are the most frequently used secondary reinforcers. Teachers are often quite skillful at using such subtle but effective secondary reinforcers as a hand on the shoulder, a pat on the head, a smile, or a wink. Many teachers position themselves carefully in the room to be near students whose behavior they want to reinforce with their attention. Apply the Concept 2-2 provides options for letting students know you value their good work and behavior.

●●●○●●●● *Apply the Concept* ●●●○●●●

2-1	Classroom Reinforcers: Intrinsic (Internal) to Extrinsic (Concrete, Tangible)

Reinforcer	Examples
Self-managed reinforcers	Checks for raising hand, stars for not fighting at lunch, charting behavior
Positive recognition by student	I did a good job; I'm working hard; I'm listening to the teacher
Positive contact from teacher or students	Standing near student, patting student's desk, providing opportunities for student's friends to sit near student
Positive feedback from teacher	"You are working hard"; "You are focusing on the lesson"; "I really like the way you cooperated."
Privileges related to the target behavior	Student who is reducing fighting at recess is given more recess time for not fighting. Student who is focusing on completing work is given less homework for completing work.
Privileges not related to target behavior	Running errands for the teacher, free time, opportunities to socialize with friends
Tangible rewards including food, tokens, materials	Raisins, crackers, school materials such as pencils or paper, tokens to exchange for toys or other items of value

2-2	33 Ways to Say "Very Good"

1. Exactly right.
2. Keep working on it, you're getting better.
3. You outdid yourself today.
4. Great!
5. You figured that out fast!
6. Good work!
7. You really make my job fun.
8. Fantastic!
9. I knew you could do it!
10. You are doing much better today.
11. Way to go!
12. Perfect!
13. That's the way to do it!
14. You are good.
15. Congratulations!
16. You got that down pat.
17. Wow!
18. That's right!
19. That's much better.
20. Wonderful!
21. That's quite an improvement!
22. That's great!
23. One more time and you will have it.
24. Tremendous!
25. You did it that time.
26. You've got your brain in gear today.
27. Nothing can stop you now.
28. Terrific!
29. Now you have it!
30. You make it look easy.
31. Sensational!
32. Good for you!
33. You are learning fast.

Recall earlier when we talked about reinforcers, we discussed that ideally teachers use the least intrusive, or intrinsic, reinforcers (e.g., teaching students to recognize their achievements). However, there are often times when special education teachers need to use more extrinsic reinforcers (e.g., toys, privileges). Sometimes teachers manage these externalizing reinforcers by initiating a token reinforcement system. A *token system* is one in which the teacher gives coupons, chips, points, or stars to students if target behaviors are exhibited. For example, the teacher may give tokens for students who are listening and not disrupting others, for doing homework, for completing work on time, for working well with others. Tokens are symbols in that they usually have little inherent value but can be exchanged for valuable things or privileges. Token systems can be simple, such as receiving stars for completing writing assignments, with each star worth 3 minutes of extra recess. Figure 2-1 presents several cards that could be used with younger students to record points. Token economies can also be quite complicated as in a level system with rewards and privileges that vary according to the level of behavioral control the student exhibits. Students are assigned to levels contingent on their behavior. Being raised or lowered to a different level occurs as points are accumulated. Points are awarded and deducted for a full range of behaviors. More complicated token systems are typically used to manage aggressive behaviors displayed by severely disturbed students.

Shaping If reinforcement increases the rate of behavior, what does a teacher do if a target behavior is occurring at a very low rate or not at all?

For example, Mr. Kladder's goal is to shape Rhonda's behavior so that she is performing multiplication facts quickly and automatically. During the initial teaching phase, Mr. Kladder rewards Rhonda for computing 3×5 by adding five 3s. After Rhonda demonstrates that she can perform this behavior with a high degree of accuracy, Mr. Kladder no longer reinforces her for adding the numbers but reinforces her only for skip-counting 5, 10, 15 and then writing the answer. After Rhonda is successfully able to skip-count, she is reinforced for computing the answer in her head and writing it down. Now Mr. Kladder begins to give Rhonda timed tests in which she is reinforced only for beating her best time. Mr. Kladder is *shaping* Rhonda's behavior by reinforcing responses that more and more closely approximate the target response.

The Premack Principle If one activity occurs more frequently than another, the more frequently occurring activity can be used as a reinforcer to increase the rate of the less frequently occurring activity (Premack, 1959). For example, Adam more frequently participates in outdoor play than in writing stories. His teacher can make outdoor play contingent on completing writing assignments. Using the Premack principle has several advantages for teachers, including ease of use, relying on events that are already occurring in the classroom. For example, a teacher might determine that a student with learning problems really likes reading, sort of likes math, and really does not like spelling. The teacher could then use reading as contingent on completing spelling. A more appropriate list for most students with learning and behavior problems might include 5 minutes of free time contingent on completing spelling. Reinforcing activities such as talking quietly with friends or listening to music can be used to increase the rate of less desirable activities such as completing a book report.

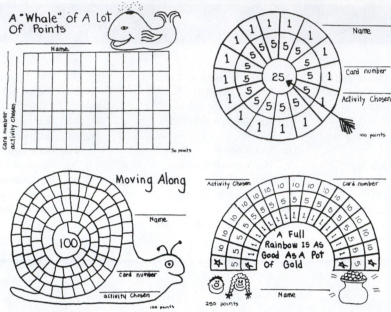

Source: P. Kaplan, J. Kohfeldt, and K. Sturla, *It's Positively Fun: Techniques for Managing the Learning Environment* (Love, 1975), pp. 15–16. Reproduced by permission of Love Publishing Company.

Group Contingencies Group contingencies can be used to increase desirable behavior or decrease undesirable behavior. When *group contingencies* are used, a group of students is either reinforced or loses reinforcement, contingent on the behavior of the entire group or of a target student in the group. For example, a teacher could establish a 20-minute block of free time at the end of the school day. Every time the noise level in the classroom exceeds the teacher's limits, she subtracts 1 minute from the allocated free time. Group contingencies can also be used to change the behavior of a particular student in the class. For instance, Carla is a 12-year-old student with behavior problems who has been mainstreamed into a sixth-grade class. During Carla's first couple of weeks in the class, she continually got into fights with her classmates during recess. The teacher told the class that she would extend their recess by 10 minutes if Carla did not get into any fights during recess. The class included Carla in their group play, and fighting was eliminated. However, there are dangers in group contingencies being dependent on the behavior of an individual. The individual could use his or her position to manipulate the behavior of others in the class. It is also possible that the individual will view himself or herself negatively because of this position.

Axelrod (1998) defines group contingencies by identifying a 10-step program for their use:

1. Select only one behavior to change.
2. Carefully specify in a written format the behavior that you want to change.
3. Determine through careful observation how often and when the behavior occurs.
4. Think about what might be reinforcing to all members of the group.
5. Decide what the group contingency will be that will cause the reinforcer to be used.
6. Be sure to identify a behavior that everyone in the group is capable of performing.
7. Provide the reinforcer contingent on a reasonable improvement in the target behavior.
8. Let each member of the group as well as the group as a whole know when they are behaving appropriately.
9. Monitor the progress of the group and each member of the group.
10. Revise the program as needed.

Contingency Contracting *Contingency contracting* is an agreement between two or more persons that specifies their behaviors and consequences. A common example of a contingency contract is the agreement between parent and child regarding an allowance. The child agrees to perform certain behaviors in return for a specified amount of money each week. The contingency contract should specify who is to do what, when, under what conditions, and for what consequences (see Figure 2-2).

I've Got An Offer You Can't Refuse

IF _____

_____ by _____

Then _____

_____

Source: P. Kaplan, J. Kohfeldt, and K. Sturla, *It's Positively Fun: Techniques for Managing the Learning Environment* (Love, 1975), p. 21. Reproduced by permission of Love Publishing Company.

Decreasing Undesirable Behaviors Through Consequences

Unfortunately, some students manifest behaviors that interfere with their learning or the learning of others. Techniques for decreasing these undesirable behaviors include extinction, differential reinforcement, response cost, punishment, and time-out.

Extinction *Extinction* is the removal of reinforcement following a behavior. For example, a teacher wants to extinguish a student's shouting out answers in class. She determines that telling the student to raise his hand is reinforcing the shouting behavior. She knows this because the shouting out continues and she recognizes that the student finds her attention (commenting on his shouting out) is reinforcing to him. To extinguish shouting out, the teacher removes the reinforcer (saying, "Raise your hand" to the student) and ignores the student's shouting out.

Extinction can be an effective means of decreasing undesirable behaviors, but it is often slow and can be impractical for many behaviors that occur within the classroom because the reinforcers for the undesirable behavior are often difficult for the teacher to control. For example, the student who continually shouted out in class was being reinforced not only by the classroom teacher's attention ("Raise your hand"), but also by other students who attended to him when he shouted out. A teacher who wants to reduce this behavior through extinction has to eliminate both the teacher's reinforcement and the reinforcement of others in the class. To compound the difficulty, slipups by a teacher or students intermittently reinforces the behavior and maintains it for a long time.

Another characteristic of extinction is its effect on the rate at which the target behavior continues to occur. During extinction, the target behavior will increase in rate or intensity before decreasing. Thus, a teacher who is attempting to eliminate tantrums through extinction will observe the tantrums occurring more frequently at first, lasting longer, and perhaps even being louder and more intense than before extinction. If the teacher continues to withhold reinforcement, usually attention, the rate and intensity will decrease, and tantrums can be eliminated. For this reason, it is extremely important to chart behavior when using extinction. To document behavior change, take *baseline data*, a record of the frequency and/or duration of the behavior before implementing the intervention, and continue to record data after intervention is implemented.

Although extinction can be an effective way to decrease undesirable behaviors, it requires patience and the ability to control all of the reinforcers. Ignoring, the most frequently applied form of extinction in the classroom, is an important skill for teachers to learn. Three points to remember about using ignoring as a means of decreasing undesirable behavior are

1. Ignoring can be effective when the behavior is being reinforced by teachers or students who are willing to discontinue reinforcement.
2. If a teacher attempts to eliminate a behavior through ignoring, the behavior must be ignored *every* time it occurs.
3. Ignoring will not be effective if the behavior is being maintained by other reinforcers, such as the attention of selected classmates.

Differential Reinforcement *Differential reinforcement* involves strengthening one set of responses in contrast to another. It is an effective procedure for developing a positive behavior management plan. The main advantage of differential reinforcement is that positive consequences are used to reduce the strength of undesirable behavior. Therefore, negative side effects associated with punishment procedures are avoided. There are several forms of differential reinforcement.

Differential Reinforcement of Incompatible Behaviors and Alternative Behaviors Differential reinforcement of incompatible behaviors (DRI) involves identifying desirable behaviors. Reinforcement is then provided contingent on the occurrence of the targeted desirable behaviors. For example, while ignoring the out-of-seat behavior of a student, the teacher targets and reinforces the desirable behavior that is incompatible with it—in this case, in-seat behavior. Therefore, when Scott is sitting in his seat, the teacher is quick to catch his appropriate behavior and reinforce it. In addition, the teacher would intermittently reinforce Scott for being in his seat. In the case of DRI, the new response (incompatible behavior) is selected because it represents an incompatible alternative to the disruptive behavior; the two behaviors cannot occur simultaneously. In differential reinforcement of alternative behaviors (DRA), the alternative behavior is not necessarily incompatible with the disruptive response, and it can occur at the same time as the undesirable behavior. The goal of using DRA is to strengthen a range of appropriate behaviors that teachers will attend to naturally, thereby reinforcing a broad repertoire of appropriate behavior. Careful planning should ensure that the reinforcers selected are sufficiently attractive and delivered with sufficient frequency to motivate student performance while removing reinforcers from the undesirable behavior. Both DRI and DRA ensure that new behaviors are fostered at the same time that undesirable behaviors are being diminished.

Differential Reinforcement of Other Behaviors Differential reinforcement of other behaviors (DRO) is the reinforcement of the nonoccurrence of target behavior during a specified time period; reinforcers are delivered following time intervals in which the target behavior does not occur. For example, a teacher may allow a student free time at the end of each 30-minute scheduled period in which no target behavior occurred. Therefore, determining the length of the reinforcement period before using DRO is important. Brief intervals of 1 to 10 minutes may be selected for high-rate behaviors, and intervals up to a day in length may be used for low-rate behaviors. DRO may be most effective when used in combination with a DRA procedure by reinforcing occurrences of alternative behavior as well as providing reinforcement for intervals in which a zero rate of the target behavior occurred. When combined with other methods, DRO can be a powerful procedure.

Regardless of the type of differential reinforcement, reinforcing behavior through consequences requires the teacher to do four things:

1. Identify the behavior that is to change (interfering behavior).
2. Identify the desirable behavior that is incompatible with the interfering behavior.
3. Stop reinforcing the interfering behavior.
4. Reinforce the desirable behavior.

Response Cost *Response cost* is a procedure in which a specified amount of a reinforcer is removed after each occurrence of the target behavior. Withdrawal of favored activities and tangible reinforcers are common response strategies for young children. For example, a student is not allowed to play during free-choice session because of his or her aggression toward peers. One of the most common response-cost strategies for older students is the withdrawal of tokens following a target behavior. For example, say students earn 20 points for completing each assignment throughout the day. Points can be exchanged for primary reinforcers at the end of the day. Engaging in a target behavior may result in a response cost of 30 points. Response cost is an aversive procedure that should be used carefully because it can inadvertently be used to punish positive behaviors. For example, teachers may be tempted to ask students to complete additional work if assignments are completed before the end of the class period, but additional work requirements may act as a response cost for early assignment completion.

Punishment *Punishment*, the opposite of reinforcement, is following a behavior with a consequence that decreases the strength of the behavior or reduces the likelihood that the behavior will continue to occur. Unfortunately, punishment does not ensure that desired behavior will occur. For example, a student who is punished for talking in class might stop talking but may not attend to his or her studies for the remainder of the day.

There are many significant arguments against the use of punishment:

- Punishment is ineffective in the long run.
- Punishment often causes undesirable emotional side effects, such as fear, aggression, and resentment.
- Punishment provides little information about what to do, teaching the individual only what not to do.
- The person who administers the punishment is often associated with it and also becomes aversive.
- Punishment frequently does not generalize across settings, thus it needs to be readministered.
- Fear of punishment often leads to escape behavior.

If there are so many arguments against using punishment, why is it so often chosen as a means for changing behavior? There are many explanations, including lack of familiarity with the consequences of punishment and the inability to effectively use a more positive approach. Also, punishment is often reinforcing to the punisher, reducing the occurrence of the undesirable behavior, therefore reinforcing its use.

The use of punishment is not suggested and instead teachers are encouraged to identify ways of reinforcing appropriate behaviors.

Time-Out *Time-out* involves removing a student from the opportunity to receive any reinforcement. For example, to impose a time-out, the teacher asks a student to sit in the hall during the remainder of a lesson, or asks a young child to leave a group, or asks a student to sit in a quiet chair until he or she is ready to join the group.

Unfortunately, time-out is frequently used inappropriately. The underlying principle behind the successful use of time-out is that the environment the student is leaving must be reinforcing and the time-out environment must be without reinforcement. This is not as easy to achieve as one might think. For example, when Elizabeth was talking and interfering with others during a science lesson, her teacher thought she would decrease Elizabeth's behavior by sending her to time-out, which was a workstation in the back of the room away from the group. The teacher became discouraged when Elizabeth's inappropriate behavior during science class increased in subsequent lessons rather than decreased. A likely explanation is that Elizabeth did not enjoy science class and found sitting in the back of the room looking at books reinforcing. The efficacy of time-out is strongly influenced by environmental factors. If the environment the student is leaving is unrewarding, then time-out is not an effective means of changing the student's behavior.

Teachers who use secluded time-out areas or contingent restraint (holding the student down plus withdrawal, exclusion, and seclusion) should be aware of the legal implications of such intervention and should obtain the necessary authorization from school administrators and from parents or guardians. A position paper on the use of behavior reduction strategies has been issued by the Council for Children with Behavior Disorders (CCBD, 2002). Recommended procedures for successfully implementing time-out are listed in Apply the Concept 2-3.

Stages of Learning

One way in which the principles of learning can be applied is through stages of learning. The *stages of learning* (see Figure 2-3) are the levels a student moves through in acquiring proficiency in learning (Bryant, Smith, & Bryant, 2007). For example, the first stage of learning, entry, is the level of performance the student is currently exhibiting. During the second stage, *acquisition*, the components of the target behavior are sequenced into teachable elements. Each teachable element is taught to mastery through a high rate of reinforcement, shaping, and consistent use of cues. When the behavior is occurring at a high level of accuracy, the focus of the learning is on proficiency. During this stage, the teacher's goal is to increase the student's accuracy and fluency in performing the behavior. At the next stage, *maintenance*, the goal is for the behavior to be maintained at the target level of accuracy and proficiency with intermittent reinforcement and a reduction in teacher assistance and cues. The next stage is *generalization*, in which the target behavior transfers across settings, persons, and materials. Generalization may be a separate skill that needs to be taught. Apply the Concept 2-4 provides further information on how to teach for generalization. At the final stage,

---

Apply the Concept

2-3   Guidelines for Implementing Time-Out

Time-out, like punishment, should be used as a last resort. Teachers should discuss this intervention with school administrators and parents before implementing it, and follow these steps:

1. Students should be told in advance which behaviors will result in time-out.
2. The amount of time students will be in time-out should be specified ahead of time.
3. The amount of time students are in time-out should be brief (1 to 5 minutes).
4. Students should be told once to go to time-out. If a student does not comply, the teacher should unemotionally place the student in time-out.
5. Time-out must occur every time an undesirable behavior occurs.

6. Contingencies should be set in advance for students who fail to comply with time-out rules.
7. The time-out area should be constantly monitored.
8. When time-out is over, a student should return to the group.
9. Positive behaviors that occur after time-out should be reinforced.

Hall and Hall (1998) provide helpful suggestions about how to handle the potential problems that occur with time-out. Several of their suggestions follow:

- Add time to a student's time-out for refusing to go to time-out or displaying other inappropriate behaviors such as screaming, yelling, and kicking.
- Students should be required to clean up any mess made during time-out before they return from time-out.

- Be sure to have a backup consequence if a student refuses to go to time-out and the amount of time added reaches 30 minutes (usually considered the maximum amount).
- Do not argue with individuals when they either try to talk you out of time-out or indicate that you have no right to put them in time-out. Ignore their comments.
- If the inappropriate behavior involves two students and it is not possible to determine the source of the problem, do not argue; put both students in time-out.
- If the student displays the behavior in a place where it is not possible to use time-out, indicate that time-out will be provided when you return to the classroom.
- Be sure to chart the effects of time-out so that you can determine whether it is working.

► **Figure 2-3** Stages of Learning

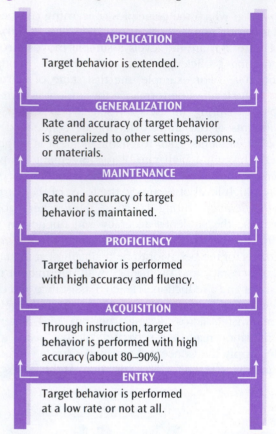

Source: Adapted from D. P. Rivera and D. D. Smith, *Teaching Students with Learning and Behavior Problems*, 3rd ed. (Boston: Allyn & Bacon, 1997).

application, the learner is required to extend and utilize the learning in new situations. Application is a difficult skill for special learners, and the teacher's role is to demonstrate and provide a range of opportunities for applying the newly acquired skill.

Cognitive Strategy Instruction

How is CSI used to teach academic, cognitive, or social skills? CSI integrates ideas from behavioral, social, and cognitive learning theories and assumes that cognitive behavior (thinking processes), like observable behaviors, can be changed. This model of instruction is based on the earlier work from social learning theory (Bandura, 1977, 1986) and cognitive behavior modification (Harris, 1985; Meichenbaum, 1977). CSI incorporates principles of behavioral learning but adds principles from social learning theory and cognitive theory that are important to consider when the goal of instruction is to change the way the student thinks. In numerous research studies, CSI has been shown to be particularly effective with students who have learning and behavior problems (Swanson, 1999a, 1999b).

Let's look at how Ms. Neal helps Marlow and his classmates better understand the science concepts and textbook she is using in her seventh-grade resource science class. Even though Marlow, a student with behavior disorders, can identify most of the words in the text, he remembers only a few details from what he reads. Ms. Neal wants to teach Marlow and his classmates how to understand and remember the major points of a reading. She decides that if she wants to teach the students this cognitive behavior, she will have to give them a consistent set of steps to use in completing the process, in much the same way that we use a consistent set of steps to tie shoes. She also knows that for the students to learn what to do, they need to observe someone else. But how can she do this?

First, she selects the steps she wants to teach Marlow and the other students to use when they read their science text. Next, she and the students discuss the strategies the students currently use and their effectiveness. They also discuss the importance of improving their skills and the payoff for improvement. Ms. Neal then tells the students about the steps she uses when she reads. To model these steps, she reads and explains what she is thinking (i.e., cognitive modeling). Then she talks them through the steps as the students try them. Finally, Ms. Neal gives the students lots of opportunities to practice the steps when reading their textbooks, encouraging them at first to say the steps aloud as they work through them. She provides feedback on how they are doing, and she teaches them how to evaluate their own performance.

Using these systematic techniques, Ms. Neal finds that in several weeks Marlow and his classmates are improving in their ability to remember the important information from their science text. In addition, they are beginning not to rely so much on the strategy she taught them. It is almost as if they are using it automatically, without having to consciously remember to use it. Ms. Neal believes that she has taught her students a good strategy for thinking about what they are reading and that she has changed their cognitive behavior (thinking processes). To promote generalization, Ms. Neal discusses with Marlow and his classmates other opportunities they have for using the strategy. The students begin keeping a list, on the board, of occasions when the strategy can be used. They also begin using the strategy on these different occasions (e.g., reading the newspaper during current events, reading other textbooks, editing each others' stories and essays) and discussing how useful the strategy was in helping them.

Common Features of Cognitive Strategy Instruction

CSI has been used to develop a range of academic and social skills. Common features of CSI include strategy steps, modeling, self-regulation, verbalization, and reflective thinking.

2-4 Generalization Strategies

Change Reinforcement

Description/Methods	Examples
Vary amount, power, and type of reinforcers.	
• Fade amount of reinforcement.	• Reduce frequency of reinforcement from completion of each assignment to completion of day's assignment.
• Decrease power of reinforcer from tangible reinforcers to verbal praise.	• Limit use of stars/stickers and add more specific statements, e.g., "Hey, you did a really good job in your math book today."
• Increase power of reinforcer when changing to mainstreamed setting.	• Give points in regular classroom although not needed in resource room.
• Use same reinforcers in different settings.	• Encourage all teachers working with a student to use the same reinforcement program.

Change Cues

Description/Methods	Examples
Vary instructions systematically.	
• Use alternate/parallel directions.	• Use variations of cue, e.g., "Find the . . ."; "Give me the . . ."; "Point to the. . . ."
• Change directions.	• Change length and vocabulary of directions to better represent the directions given in the regular classroom, e.g., "Open your book to page 42 and do the problems in set A."
	• Move from real objects to miniature objects.
• Use photograph.	• Use photograph of object or situation.
• Use picture to represent object.	• Move from object/photograph to picture of object or situation.
• Use line drawing or symbol representation.	• Use drawings from workbooks to represent objects or situations.
• Use varying print forms.	• Vary lower- and uppercase letters; vary print by using manuscript, boldface, primary type.
	• Move from manuscript to cursive.

Change Materials

Description/Methods	Examples
Vary materials within task.	
• Change medium.	• Use unlined paper, lined paper; change size of lines; change color of paper.
	• Use various writing instruments such as markers, pencil, pen, computer.
• Change media.	• Use materials such as films, microcomputers, filmstrips to present skills/concepts.
	• Provide opportunity for student to phase into mainstream.

Change Response Set

Description/Methods	Examples
Vary mode of responding.	
• Change how student is to respond.	• Ask student to write answers rather than always responding orally.
	• Teach student to respond to a variety of question types such as multiple choice, true-false, short answer.
• Change time allowed for responding.	• Decrease time allowed to complete math facts.

(continued)

2-4   Generalization Strategies   (continued)

Change Some Dimension(s) of the Stimulus

Description/Methods	Examples
Vary the stimulus systematically.	
• Use single stimulus and change size, color, and shape.	• Teach colors by changing the size, shape, and shade of "orange" objects.
• Add to number of distractors.	• Teach sight words by increasing number of words from which student is to choose.
• Use concrete (real) object.	• Introduce rhyming words by using real objects.
• Use toy or miniature representation.	• Use miniature objects when real objects are impractical.

Change Setting(s)

Description/Methods	Examples
Vary instructional work space.	
• Move from structured to less structured work arrangements.	• Move one-to-one teaching to different areas within classroom.
	• Provide opportunity for independent work.
	• Move from one-to-one instruction to small-group format.
	• Provide opportunity for student to interact in large group.

Change Teachers

Description/Methods	Examples
Vary instructors.	
• Assign student to work with different teacher.	• Select tasks so that student has opportunities to work with instructional aide, peer tutor, volunteer, regular classroom teacher, and parents.

Source: S. Vaughn, C. S. Bos, and K. A. Lund (1986, Spring). But they can do it in my room. *Teaching Exceptional Children,* pp. 177–178. Copyright © 1986 by the Council for Exceptional Children. Reprinted with permission.

Strategy Steps A series of steps are usually identified for the student to work through when solving a problem or completing a task. These steps are based on an analysis of the cognitive and observable behaviors needed to complete the task. Before Ms. Neal began teaching, she determined the steps in the reading strategy she wanted to teach Marlow and his classmates.

Modeling In CSI, modeling is used as a primary means of instruction. Modeling can be a very effective teaching technique. With CSI, students are asked not only to watch observable behaviors as the instructor performs a task, but also to listen to the teacher's self-talk. In this way, the teacher models both observable behaviors and the unobservable thinking processes associated with those behaviors. Being able to model thinking processes is an important component for teaching such cognitive skills as verbal math problem solving, finding the main idea in a paragraph, editing written work, and solving

social problems. In most instances, the person who does the modeling is the teacher or a peer, but video and puppets have also been used.

Self-Regulation Self-regulation refers to learners' monitoring their thinking and actions through language mediation. Students first use language to mediate their actions by overtly engaging in self-instruction and self-monitoring. Later, this language mediation becomes covert.

Using self-regulation, students act as their own teachers. Students are expected to take active roles in the learning process and to be responsible for their own learning. Although they work under the guidance of a teacher, students are expected to monitor their learning, change or modify strategies when difficulties arise, evaluate their performance, and in some cases provide self-reinforcement.

Peers have also been used to promote student regulation and monitoring. For example, MacArthur, Graham, and Schwartz (1991) used a peer editing strategy to increase students' knowledge about writing and revising and to increase their revising activity. The strategy was taught by special education teachers who were using a process approach to teaching writing and word processing. The steps in the peer editing strategy were as follows:

1. *Listen* and read along as the author reads.
2. *Tell* what it was about and what you like best.
3. *Read* and make *Notes*. *Clear*? Is there anything that is difficult to understand? *Details*? Where could more information be added?
4. *Discuss* your suggestions with the author.
5. The author makes revisions on the computer (MacArthur et al., 1995, p. 234).

The procedure involved peers in that steps 1 and 2 were completed by pairs of students. Then the two students worked independently to complete step 3 and then met together again for step 4 to discuss each paper and the suggested revisions. For step 5, each author worked at the computer to make the revisions that he or she thought were useful.

See Chapter 9 for a process approach to teaching writing.

Peer monitoring and support can be extremely useful in increasing appropriate behavior. For example, peers can be taught to help students monitor their behavior and record it (Anderson, Fisher, Marchant, Young, & Smith, 2006). Peers can be exceedingly helpful in group support and as reinforcers to maintain appropriate behaviors.

Progress Monitoring Aggression replacement theory (Glick & Goldstein, 1987) uses self-regulation as an effective procedure for assisting students with behavior disorders, particularly those with conduct disorders, in controlling their anger. Through aggression replacement theory, students learn to identify anger-producing situations (triggers) and to recognize their responses to these situations (cues). They then learn a number of techniques that are designed to assist them in relaxing and cognitively handling the situation. In reviewing self-regulation outcome research conducted with students with behavior disorders, Nelson, Smith, Young, and Dodd (1991) found numerous studies indicating that self-regulation procedures can be extremely effective in enhancing both the academic and social behavior of students.

Verbalization Verbalization is typically a component of self-instruction and self-monitoring in which overt verbalization is faded to covert verbalization. Many CSI programs rely on a talk-aloud or think-aloud technique (e.g., Swanson, 1999b). After listening to the teacher think aloud as he or she performs the targeted processes and task, students are encouraged to talk aloud as they initially learn the strategy. For example, Ramon might say the following as he completes a two-digit subtraction problem without regrouping: "Start at the ones place, and take the bottom number away from the top. Write the answer in the ones place. Now go to the tens

place. Do the same thing." Usually, these overt verbalizations occur only during the initial stages of learning. As the strategy becomes more automatic, students are encouraged to think to themselves instead of thinking aloud.

In addition to verbalization about the learning processes, students are also encouraged to make self-statements about their performance. For example, "That part is done. Now go to the next part" or "I'm getting much faster at this" or "I need to think about all my choices before I decide."

Meichenbaum (1977) has suggested three ways to encourage students to use self-talk:

1. Teachers can model self-talk and self-statements as they perform tasks.
2. Teachers can begin with tasks at which students are already somewhat proficient. Later, as students become comfortable with self-talk, teachers can switch to targeted tasks.
3. Students can develop and use cue cards to help them remember the steps they are to talk through.

As an example of the third method, Camp, Blom, Herbert, and Van Doorninck (1977) used the pictures in Figure 2-4 as cue cards when teaching self-control to 12 aggressive second-grade boys. The cue cards were used as reminders to self-verbalize as the boys applied these questions first to cognitive and then to interpersonal tasks.

Reflective Thinking Reflective thinking requires students to take the time to think about what they are doing. Teaching students who have learning and behavior problems to stop and think is an important skill to include in instruction (Troia, Graham, & Harris, 1999). Many of these students are impulsive and seem to act without thinking (Kauffman, 2001; Lerner, 2000). These students have limited and ineffective strategies for approaching academic tasks and social situations. They approach these tasks and situations in a disorganized, haphazard way, often without thinking about the consequence of their actions. In using cognitive strategy instruction, teachers assist students in using reflective thinking.

Let's look at how Wong, Wong, Perry, and Sawatsky (1986) encouraged reflective thinking when they taught seventh-grade students to use self-questioning when summarizing social studies texts. After teaching the students how to identify the main idea of paragraphs and how to summarize paragraphs, Wong et al. (1986) taught the students a summarization strategy. The questions the students asked themselves were as follows:

1. In this paragraph, is there anything I don't understand?
2. In this paragraph, what's the most important sentence (main-idea sentence)? Let me underline it.
3. Let me summarize the paragraph. To summarize, I rewrite the main-idea sentence and add important details.

What am I supposed to do?

What are some plans?

How is my plan working?

How did I do?

Source: B. W. Camp and M. A. S. Bash, *Think Aloud: Increasing Social and Cognitive Skills—A Problem-Solving Program for Children. Classroom Program: Grades 1–2* (Champaign, IL: Research Press, 1985), pp. 48–51. Reprinted with permission.

4. Now, does my summary statement link up with the subheading?
5. When I have written summary statements for a whole subsection:
   a. Let me review my summary statements for the whole subsection. (A subsection is one with several paragraphs under the same subheading.)
   b. Do my summary statements link up with one another?
6. At the end of an assigned reading section: Can I see all the themes here? If yes, let me predict the teacher's test question on this section. If no, let me go back to step 4. (Wong et al., 1986, pp. 25–26)

The specificity of the questions and cues can be important for success. For example, teachers can cue students about behavior before going to lunch (e.g., What are the three things we do at lunch?) or cue them about writing (e.g., remember to reread what you wrote and circle the words that you need help spelling).

Teaching Implications of Cognitive Strategy Instruction

CSI is designed to actively involve students in learning. General guidelines to consider for actively engaging students in learning include the following:

- Analyze the target behavior you want to see students using and be sure that you model or describe it carefully to students.
- Determine what strategies students are already using and encourage them to continue or describe how to apply them to the expected task.
- Select strategy steps that are as similar as possible to the strategy steps that good problem solvers use. Make them simple and easy to remember.
- Work with students to develop strategy steps that they can and will use.
- Teach prerequisite skills.
- Teach strategy steps, using modeling, self-instruction, and self-regulation.
- Give explicit feedback.
- Teach strategy generalization.
- Help students maintain the strategy.

Guidelines for monitoring the effects of instruction (see Apply the Concept 2-5) have also been suggested (Rooney & Hallahan, 1985). A growing body of research supports the use of CSI for developing academic, cognitive, and social skills (Deshler, Ellis, & Lenz, 1996; Graham, Harris, & Troia, 1998; Pressley, 1998), and reviews of research on students with learning and behavior problems consistently identify CSI as one of the most effective instructional strategies for teachers to use (Gersten, Schiller, & Vaughn, 2000; Mastropieri & Scruggs, 1997; Swanson, 1999b). As discussed in Apply the Concept 2-6, researchers at the Center for Research on Learning at the University of Kansas have developed a learning strategy curriculum as well as a number of task-specific strategies (e.g., finding the main idea, decoding unknown words, test taking, listening and taking notes) that employ CSI.

Sociocultural Theory

How can teachers use the features of sociocultural theory to make instruction more effective for students? Sociocultural theory (Vygotsky, 1978) is similar to CSI in that it highlights the importance of modeling and the use of language to facilitate learning. However, the theory assumes that learning is socially constructed and, as a social activity, is highly influenced by the funds of knowledge that learners bring to situations. Knowledge is meaningfully constructed in these social activities (Lantolf & Thorne, 2007; Moll, 1990; Tharp, Estrada, Dalton, & Yamauchi, 1999).

Vygotsky was a Russian psychologist who conducted his most important work during the 1920s and 1930s.

2-5 Guidelines for Assessing Strategy Effectiveness

Behavior	Assessment Questions
Independence	Can the student use the strategy without cues or assistance? Can the student match the appropriate strategy to the task? Can the student adapt the strategy if necessary?
Spontaneity	Does the student use the strategy without being asked or cued to do so?
Flexibility	Can the student modify and adapt the strategy to match the situation? Can the student pick out the cues in the situation to guide strategy use?
Generalization	Does the student use the strategy appropriately in various situations? Does the student use the strategy across different class periods?
Maintenance	Does the student continue to use the strategy after direct instruction of the strategy has stopped?
Reflective thinking	Does the student stop and think about how to do a task before beginning? Does the student think about which strategy to use before beginning? Does the student reflect on his or her performance and adjust the strategy if necessary?
Improved performance	Has the student's performance on the targeted task improved? Is there improvement in the student's productivity, accuracy, and task completion?
Improved self-concept	Does the student see himself or herself as an active participant in learning? Does the student see himself or herself in control of his or her learning? Does the student regard himself or herself as more successful?

Source: Adapted from K. J. Rooney and D. P. Hallahan (1985). Future direction for cognitive behavior modification research: The quest for cognitive change. *Remedial and Special Education 6* (2), p. 49. Copyright © 1985 by PRO-ED. Used with permission.

However, owing to the popularity of behavioral theories, Piaget's theory, and information-processing theory, his work did not attract great interest until the last 20 years (Byrnes, 1996). Although Vygotsky's theory of cognitive development embraces many concepts, we have highlighted three that are particularly important in using this theory for teaching students who may have special needs or are from diverse cultural and linguistic backgrounds: the use of resources, the social nature of learning (including the use of interactive dialogue), and the use of scaffolded instruction.

Use of Resources

A key concept of sociocultural theory is that teachers need to consider and use the resources that the students bring to learning (Harry & Klingner, 2006). These include such things as culture and language as well as background knowledge the learners can apply to the problem that is being solved or the knowledge being constructed. For example, in assisting Mexican American elementary students to develop literacy, Moll and Greenberg (1990) began by first exploring the *funds of knowledge* that could be gained from the community and the Hispanic and Southwestern cultures. They also examined how literacy functioned as a part of community and home life. They brought this information into the schools and used it to build a literacy program. In this way, students who are culturally diverse were given the opportunity to use sources of knowledge that are not often highlighted in traditional school curriculums. Similarly, Harry and Klingner (2006) identify ways schools can consider the home, family, language, and culture of their students and families, and to consider how to communicate and connect with them.

Social Nature of Learning and Interactive Dialogue

Another important aspect of sociocultural theory is the premise that learning occurs during social interactions; that is, learning is a social event in which language plays an important role. Applying this concept, teachers and students discuss what they are learning and how they are going about learning. Such interactive dialogue or instructional conversations between teachers and learners provide language models and tools for guiding one's inner talk about learning (Soter et al., 2008; Moll, 1990). Initially, a more expert person may model the self-talk and vocabulary related to the cognitive processes. However, this gives way to a collaborative or interactive dialogue in which the learner assumes increasing responsibility. This type of teaching allows for the instruction of cognitive and metacognitive

See Chapter 8 for more on processes students can use to check their understanding.

strategies within purposeful, meaningful discussions and provides a means for selecting, organizing, and relating the content matter being discussed. For example, in reciprocal teaching (Palincsar & Brown, 1984), a technique designed to foster comprehension and comprehension monitoring, the teacher and students take turns leading dialogues that focus on their knowledge of the information they are studying and on the processes they are using for understanding and for checking their understanding.

A synthesis of the most productive conversations (Soter et al., 2008) reveals that both teacher- and student-led discussions benefit from the following:

- Students occupying the "talk-time" for extended periods of time.
- Teachers prompting students to discuss texts by asking open-ended questions (i.e., questions that do not have a *yes* or *no* answer) that are related closely to the text and are engaging.
- Teachers asking authentic questions that are linked to the text, resulting in greater elaboration of talk by students, which results in higher-level thinking about the text.
- Promoting discussions that highlight a more analytic approach rather than providing extensive opportunities for students to express themselves in less analytic ways.

Scaffolded Instruction

Another concept of the sociocultural theory of learning relates to the role of the teacher or the expert, who encourages learners by providing temporary and adjustable support as they develop new skills, strategies, and knowledge. The instruction is referred to as *scaffolded instruction* (Tharp & Gallimore, 1988) or *mediated learning* (Kozulin & Presseisen, 1995).

> The concepts of scaffolding and zones of proximal development were explained in Chapter 1.

Actively engaging students in the process of solving problems rather than as passive members of the instructional classroom is associated with improved outcomes (Gallimore et al., 2009). For example, in a 5-year study conducted by Gallimore et al., teachers who used an inquiry-focused protocol (students were actively engaged in solving problems related to literacy and numeracy) had several key outcomes including improved student performance and greater perceptions of accountability on the part of the teachers. These outcomes were more likely to occur when teachers worked in teams with shared interests in outcomes.

In the Early Literacy Project (ELP; Englert et al., 1994, 1995; Mariage, 2000), the literacy curriculum is structured to include activities that provide opportunities for

●●●●●● *Apply the Concept* ●●●●●●

2-6 | Application of Cognitive Strategy Instruction: The Learning Strategies Curriculum

Can the principles of CSI be applied to academic tasks in such a way that adolescents with learning disabilities can be successful in performing the skills required for secondary school settings? The Strategies Intervention Model (Bulgren, Deshler, & Lenz, 2007; Deshler et al., 1996) is a comprehensive example of a series of research-based instructional practices based on CSI.

The goal of the Strategies Intervention Model is "to teach learning disabled adolescents strategies that will facilitate their acquisition, organization, storage, and retrieval of information, thus allowing them to cope with the demands of social interaction" (Alley & Deshler, 1979, p. 8). Learning strategies are

techniques, principles, or routines that enable students to learn to solve problems and complete tasks independently. Strategies include how a person thinks and acts when planning, executing, and evaluating performance on a task and its outcomes. Broadly, a learning strategy (1) includes a general approach to solving a set of problems, (2) promotes goal-directed behavior, (3) teaches selection of appropriate procedures, (4) guides implementation of a procedure, (5) shows how to monitor progress, (6) can be controlled, and (7) provides and focuses on cues to take action. Learning strategies instruction focuses on how to learn and how to use what has been learned.

The Learning Strategies Curriculum (Lenz, 2006) contains three strands of academic, task-specific strategies. The Acquisition Strand enables students to gain information from written materials and includes such strategies as the Word Identification Strategy (Lenz, Schumaker, Deshler, & Beals, 1993) and the Paraphrasing Strategy (Schumaker, Denton, & Deshler, 1993). The Storage Strand consists of strategies to assist students in organizing, storing, and retrieving information. The First-Letter Mnemonic Strategy (Nagel, Schumaker, & Deshler, 1994) is an example of a Storage Strategy. The Expression and Demonstration of Competence Strand contains strategies that enable students to complete assignments, express themselves, and take tests. The Test Taking Strategy (Hughes, Schumaker, Deshler, & Mercer, 1993), the Paragraph Writing Strategy (Lyerla, Schumaker, & Deshler, 1994), and the Error Monitoring Strategy (Schumaker, Nolan, & Deshler, 1994) are examples of strategies that assist students in taking tests, writing cohesive paragraphs, and editing written work.

Each strategy uses a teaching model that incorporates principles of cognitive behavior modification. The stages in the model are:

Acquisition

Stage 1 **Pretest and Make Commitments**
Obtain measure(s) of current functioning.
Make students aware of inefficient/ineffective habits.
Obtain students' commitments to learn.

Stage 2 **Describe the Strategy**
Ensure that students have rationales for strategy use.
Ensure that students know characteristics of situations for when and where to use the strategy.
Describe results that can be expected.
Supervise goal setting.
Describe and explain the strategy steps.
Present the remembering system.

Stage 3 **Model the Strategy**
Demonstrate the entire strategy "thinking aloud."

Involve the students in a demonstration.

Stage 4 **Elaboration and Verbal Rehearsal**
Assist students to verbally rehearse the strategy steps and what each step means.
Require students to memorize the strategy.

Stage 5 **Controlled Practice and Feedback**
Supervise practice in easy materials.
Provide positive and corrective feedback.
Move from guided practice to independent practice.
Require mastery.

Stage 6 **Advanced Practice and Feedback**
Supervise practice in materials from regular coursework.
Provide positive and corrective feedback.
Fade prompts and cues for strategy use and evaluation.
Move from guided practice to independent practice.
Require mastery.

Stage 7 **Confirm Acquisition and Make Generalization Commitments**
Obtain measure(s) of progress.
Make students aware of progress.
Obtain the students' commitment to generalize.

Phase I **Orientation**
Discuss situations, settings, and materials in which the strategy can be used.

Evaluate appropriateness of strategy in various settings and materials.
Identify helpful aspects of the strategy and adjustments.
Make students aware of cues for using the strategy.

Phase II **Activation**
Program the students' use of the strategy in a variety of situations.
Provide feedback.
Reinforce progress and success.

Phase III **Adaptation**
Identify cognitive processes.
Discuss how the strategy can be modified to meet differing demands.
Assist students in applying the modifications.

Phase IV **Maintenance**
Set goals related to long-term use.
Conduct periodic reviews.
Identify self-reinforcers and self-rewards.
Provide feedback.

This teaching model relies heavily on modeling, self-instruction, and self-regulation. It encourages students to assume an active and collaborative role in learning.

Note: The University of Kansas Center for Research on Learning requires that persons planning to implement the Learning Strategies Curriculum obtain training available through the Center for Research on Learning, 1122 West Campus Road, University of Kansas, Lawrence, KA 66045, 785-864-4780, http://www.ku-crl.org

scaffolded instruction and the teaching of strategies. Figure 2-5 provides an overview of these activities and the principles of the ELP. Important to promoting development within the students' zones of proximal development is the teacher's ability to relinquish control of the strategies to the students. To illustrate the dialogue that works within the zone of proximal development, Englert et al. (1994) describe the interactive dialogues among the teacher and students, including students at

risk for learning disabilities, during the morning news. In this lesson, the class constructed a morning news story about the information from their thematic unit on dinosaurs. Each student took responsibility for drafting a section of the story, and the class reread and edited the various sections. The teacher (T) used this opportunity to model specific writing and editing conventions and to highlight the multiple sources and classroom resources that can be employed in the literacy process.

▲ **Figure 2-5** Early Literacy Project Principles and Activities

Silent Reading

Description
Independent reading
Reading to an adult
Listening to new story at listening center

Purpose: Work on fluency for author's chair; provide experience with varied genres

Thematic Unit

Description
Teacher and students brainstorm, organize, write drafts, read texts, or interview people to get additional information about a topic or theme from multiple sources, and use reading/writing strategies flexibly to develop and communicate their knowledge
Oral/written literacy connections are made apparent

Purpose: Model learning processes; introduce literacy language, genre, and strategies; model reading/writing processes and connections; provide interrelated and meaningful contexts for acquisition and application of literacy knowledge; conventionalize and develop shared knowledge about the purpose, meaning, and self-regulation of literacy acts

Morning News

Description
Students dictate personal experience stories
Teacher acts as a scribe in recording ideas and as a coach in modeling, guiding, and prompting literacy strategies

Purpose: To model and conventionalize writing and self-monitoring strategies; demonstrate additional writing conventions; provide additional reading and comprehension experiences; promote sense of community; empower students; provide meaningful and purposeful contexts for literacy strategies

Principles of the Early Literacy Project

Using Meaningful Activities

Teaching to Self-Regulate

Apprenticing Students in the Dialogue

Empowering Students in the Community

Literature/Story Response

Description
Students read stories and respond to them in various ways (e.g. sequence stories, illustrate story events, map story events or story structure, summarize story, etc.)
Students make a personal affective response to stories
Students work with partners or small groups to develop response

Purpose: To promote students' application of literacy strategies; present varied genres to students; promote students' ownership of the discourse about texts; futher students' enjoyment of texts; make text structure visible to students

Choral and Partner Reading/Writing

Description
Choral reading & taped story reading
Partner reading & partner writing

Purpose: To provide opportunities for students to fluently read & write connected texts; to provide opportunities for students to use literacy language and knowledge; to develop reading/writing vocabulary and enjoyment of reading

Sharing Chair

Description
Read books, poems, personal writing
Students control discourse and support each other
Students ask questions, answer questions, and act as informants to peers and teacher

Purpose: Promote reading/writing connection; empower students as members of the community; allow students to make public their literacy knowledge and performance; develop shared knowledge

Author's Center

Description
Process Writing Approach (students plan, organize, draft, edit texts)
Students partner-write and work collaboratively to brainstorm ideas, gather additional information, write drafts, share drafts, receive questions, and write final draft
Students use literacy strategies modeled in thematic units

Purpose: To develop a sense of community; develop shared knowledge; provide opportunities for students to rehearse literacy strategies; empower students in appropriating and transforming strategies

Source: C. S. Englert, M. S. Roszendal, and M. Mariage (1994). Fostering the search for understanding: A teacher's strategies for leading cognitive development in "zones of proximal development." *Learning Disability Quarterly, 17,* p. 191. Reprinted by permission of Council for Learning Disabilities.

T: Lauren, you wrote this part. Would you like to read this part for us?

L: I need help with it.

T: Okay, would you like to pick somebody to read that part with you? *Lauren picks a student to help her pronounce unfamiliar words that she can't read.*

T: Does anyone have a question for Lauren about cavemen? *When no one responds, the teacher proceeds to illustrate.* Where did you get the idea about cavemen? When we were talking [referring to the time when she interacted with Lauren as she wrote this section], did we say that dinosaurs ate cavemen?

Ss: No.

T: You know what Lauren told me as she wrote that idea? She got it out of her imagination. But this paper is kind of telling true things, so I'm wondering if we should leave it in or take it out. SH, what do you think?

SH: There were cavemen. See that book right there? *Points to book.*

T: You can get it. I guess what I'm wondering is if we know for sure if they [dinosaurs] ate cavemen?

A: I saw it in a movie.

T: Was it a real movie or a cartoon movie? *Ss talks about movie and book.* All right. Do we want to leave that [part] in?

Ss: U-huh!

B: Didn't dinosaurs eat other dinosaurs?

T: We have to ask Meg because she was the writer. *B turns to Meg and repeats comment. Meg agrees that B's idea can go in the story. Then the teacher turns to ask the opinion of the class.* What do you think about adding that idea [to our story], boys and girls? "Dinosaurs eat other dinosaurs." I want you to put your thumb up if you think that is a good idea. *Surveys students.* So I'm going to put a caret here and I'm going to say, "Dinosaurs eat other dinosaurs." (Englert et al., 1994, p. 198)

This dialogue illustrates how the teacher uses interactive discussion and classroom resources to support scaffolded instruction. "For example, she encouraged Lauren to select a peer to help her read and asked students to turn to each other in making final decisions about the text. She also acknowledged the contribution of movies, texts, and students' own imagination in the writing process" (Englert et al., 1994, p. 198).

There are many instructional implications from the sociocultural theory of cognitive development. The following four are particularly important:

1. Instruction is designed to facilitate scaffolding and cooperative knowledge sharing among students and teachers within a context of mutual respect and critical acceptance of others' knowledge and experiences.

2. Learning and teaching should be meaningful, socially embedded activities.

3. Instruction should provide opportunities for mediated learning, with the teacher or expert guiding instruction within the students' zones of proximal development.

4. Students' sociocultural backgrounds should provide the basis on which learning is built.

Schema Theory

How can knowledge of schema theory assist teachers in meeting the needs of students with learning and behavior problems? Whereas applied behavior analysis focuses on observable behaviors and views learning as establishing functional relationships between a student's behavior and the stimuli in the environment, cognitive learning theory focuses on what happens in the mind, and views learning as changing the learner's cognitive structure.

Schemas

According to schema theory, our knowledge is organized into schemas. *Schemas* can be defined as organized structures of stereotypic knowledge (Schank & Abelson, 1977). They are higher-order cognitive structures that assist in understanding and recalling events and information. Researchers hypothesize that we have innumerable schemas or scripts for events and procedures and that it is our schemas that allow us to make inferences about the events that happen around us (Anderson, 1995; Rumelhart, 1980).

Read the following short passage about an event that John experienced:

> John had been waiting all week for Friday evening. He skipped lunch just to get ready for the occasion. At 6:30 P.M., he got in his car and drove to the restaurant. He planned to meet several friends. When he arrived, he got out of his car and waited outside for his friends.

At this point, you are probably using a general schema for restaurants. You could answer such questions as "Is John going to eat dinner?" and "Will John eat dinner with his friends?" However, you have not been given enough information to utilize a more specific restaurant schema. Now read on to see how your schema is sharpened:

> After a few minutes, John's friends arrived. They entered the restaurant and walked up to the counter. John placed his order first. After everyone ordered, they carried the trays of food to a booth.

How has your schema changed? You should be using a more specific schema, one for fast-food restaurants. Now you can probably answer more specific questions such as "What kind of food did John and his friends probably eat?" and "Did John leave a tip?" Utilizing schemas (e.g., our prior knowledge about stereotypic events) allows us to make inferences, thereby filling in the gaps and giving meaning to incoming information. Schemas serve a crucial role in providing an account of how old or prior knowledge interacts with new or incoming information (Anderson, 1995; Rumelhart, 1985).

Within and across schemas, concepts or ideas are organized so as to promote understanding and retrieval. Information can be stored in semantic networks composed of concepts and relationships between concepts (Ericsson & Kintsch, 1995; Rumelhart, 1980). Figure 2-6 presents a representation of the concept of *bird*. (Your network for *bird* is probably more extensive than the one presented in this figure.) The closer together the concepts are in the network, the better they serve as cues for each other's recall (Anderson, 1995; Swanson & Kim, 2007). For example, *wings* should serve as a better recall cue for *bird* than should *two*. A concept does not exist in isolation in semantic memory but is related to other concepts at higher, lower, or the same levels. In the case of *birds*, it could be filed along with *reptile* and *mammal* under the superordinate concept of animals.

Schemas and semantic networks allow us to organize our knowledge in such a way that we can retrieve information and effectively add new information to long-term memory. They also assist us in determining the relationships among ideas. However, students with learning and behavior problems may not spontaneously use their prior knowledge, and teachers must link new knowledge to existing knowledge.

Executive Functioning or Metacognition

The specific processes in the information-processing system (i.e., attention, perception, working memory, and long-term memory) are controlled or coordinated by what has been referred to as *executive functioning* (see Figure 2-7). For example, as learners, we must decide which stimuli to attend to (e.g., the book we are reading and/or the smell of the apple pie baking), whether to rely more on feature analysis or context and prior knowledge when perceiving information, what memory strategies are most effective for keeping the information active in working memory, and what is an effective and efficient way to store the information so we can retrieve it later.

▶ **Figure 2-6**   A Semantic Network for the Concept of *Bird*

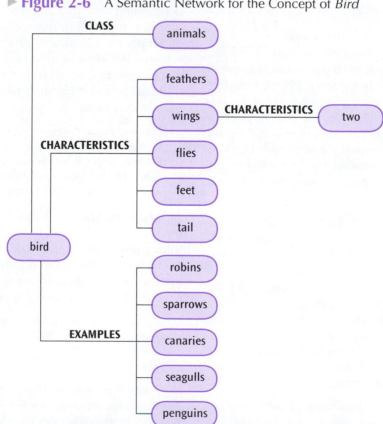

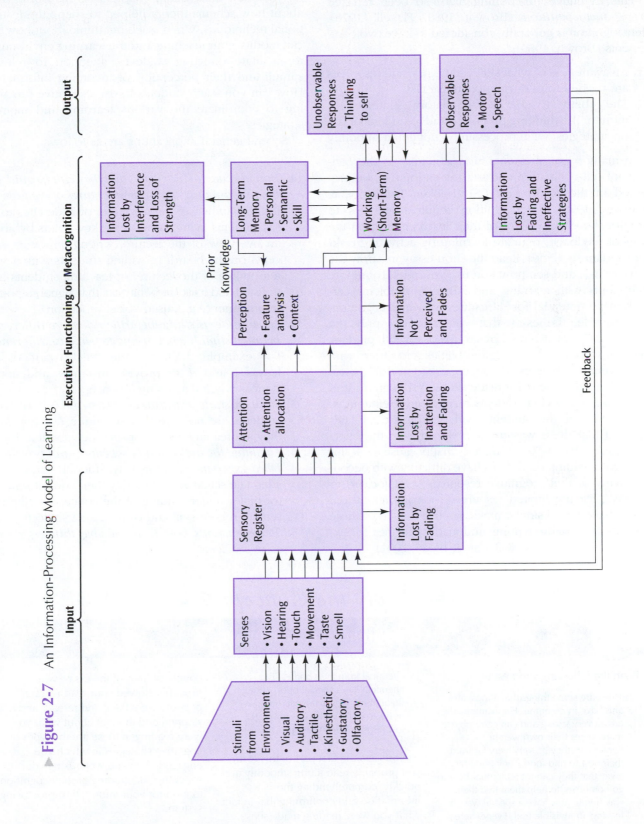

▲ **Figure 2-7** An Information-Processing Model of Learning

Making decisions allows us to control the learning process.

This executive functioning has also been referred to as *metacognition* (Brown, 1980; Flavell, 1976). Metacognition is generally considered to have two components (Brown, 1980):

1. An awareness of what skills, strategies, and resources are needed to perform a cognitive task
2. The ability to use self-regulatory strategies to monitor the thinking processes and to undertake fix-up strategies when processing is not going smoothly

In many ways, metacognition is similar to the concepts of self-evaluation and self-regulation that we presented in the section on CSI (Hacker, Dunlosky, & Graesser, 1998). Metacognition requires learners to monitor the effectiveness of their learning and, on the basis of feedback, regulate learning by activating task-appropriate strategies. Read the short essay in Apply the Concept 2-7, and see how you use your metacognition.

Students with learning and behavior problems certainly have potential for difficulties with metacognition. For example, the essay that you read in Apply the Concept 2-7 was also read by groups of seventh graders, some of whom had reading disabilities and others who were average achievers. They were asked to read the essay and decide whether it made sense. Although most of the average-achieving students recognized the inconsistency, most of the students with learning disabilities reported that there was nothing wrong with the essay (Bos & Filip, 1984). Wong suggests that because most students with reading disabilities have difficulty with decoding, many of their cognitive resources are allocated to this task, leaving limited resources for comprehension. Others have found similar metacognitive deficits in these students on reading, writing, and math tasks (see for example, Gersten, Fuchs, Williams, & Baker, 2001).

Teaching Implications of Schema Theory

As you read the content chapters in this book, think about how schema theory helped to shape the instructional techniques. When teaching, think about how you can modify your teaching and the learning environment to facilitate directing students' attention to relevant stimuli and their perception of incoming information. How can you teach students to use executive functioning to coordinate the various learning and memory strategies?

Several general implications are as follows:

1. *Provide cues to students so that they can be guided to the relevant task(s) or salient features of the task.* For instance, when giving a lecture, provide cues to assist students in attending to the key points by giving an overview of the lecture, writing important concepts on the board, providing students with a written outline of the lecture, or teaching students how to listen and look for behaviors that signal important information (e.g., raised voice, repetition).
2. *Have students study the critical feature differences between stimuli when trying to perceive differences.* For example, highlight the "stick" part of the letters *b* and *d*, or provide instances and noninstances when discussing a concept.
3. *Have the students use the context to aid in perception.* Students are not likely to substitute *bog* for *dog* if they are reading a story or sentence about a dog.
4. *Facilitate the activation of schemas, and provide labeled experiences.* In this way, students can develop adequate schemas and modify their current schemas for better understanding of the concepts being presented in both skill and content-area subjects.
5. *Teach students how to be flexible thinkers and to solve problems.*

●●●●●● *Apply the Concept* ●●●●●●

2-7   Comprehension Monitoring

Read the following short essay:

There are some things that almost all ants have in common. For example, they are all very strong and can carry objects many times their own weight. Sometimes they go very, very far from their nest to find food. They go so far away that they cannot remember how to go home. So, to help them find their way home, ants have a special way of leaving an invisible trail. Everywhere they go, they put out an invisible chemical from their bodies. This chemical has a special odor. Another thing about ants is they do not have noses to smell with. Ants never get lost. (Bos & Filip, 1984, p. 230)

As you read the first part of this essay, you probably read along smoothly and quickly, comprehending the information and confirming that in fact what you were reading made sense. However, when you read the last couple of lines of the essay, you probably slowed your reading rate, possibly went back and reread, and/or stopped and thought about what you were reading. If these are the types of cognitive strategies in which you engaged, then you were using your executive functioning or metacognition to monitor your information-processing system.

▶ FOCUS Question 1. **What is applied behavioral analysis, and how can teachers use it to increase desirable behaviors or decrease undesirable behaviors?**

Answer: Applied behavior analysis is based on the notion that behaviors are learned. In this way, individuals can either unlearn undesirable behaviors or be taught new behaviors. The first step to helping students learn and use appropriate behaviors is to manipulate antecedents, or to attend to the events or stimuli that precede certain behaviors. When undesirable behaviors do occur, using consequences can help students to unlearn or replace selected behaviors.

▶ FOCUS Question 2. **How is CSI used to teach academic, cognitive, or social skills?**

Answer: CSI is a systematic method that is used to change thinking processes by organizing the teaching and monitoring of task completion or skill development and by actively involving students in learning. Examples of strategies or skills that are taught in CSI are finding the main idea, decoding unknown words, and taking notes. In brief, the teacher selects a target strategy, works with the student to develop the strategy steps, and gives feedback.

▶ FOCUS Question 3. **How can teachers use the features of sociocultural theory to make instruction more effective for their students?**

Answer: Sociocultural theory is based on the notion that learning occurs through personal interactions. Therefore, an emphasis is placed on language as a teaching tool and the instructional conversations that occur between teachers and students (as well as between students). There is also a focus on students' resources or background knowledge, language, and culture.

▶ FOCUS Question 4. **How can knowledge of schema theory assist teachers in meeting the needs of students with learning and behavior problems?**

Answer: Schema theory posits that our knowledge is organized into schemas, or organized structures of knowledge, that assist in understanding and recalling events and information. Schema theory call our attention to various components of the brain that are activated during learning. Examples of instructional features that incorporate these theories are activating prior knowledge; relating new learning to existing schemas; and teaching and monitoring the use of metacognitive strategies to organize task completion and to check for understanding.

myeducationlab

Where the Classroom Comes to Life

The MyEducationLab for this course can help you solidify your comprehension of Chapter 2 concepts.

- Gauge and further develop your understanding of chapter concepts by taking the quizzes and examining the enrichment materials in the Chapter 2 Study Plan.
- Connect with challenge-based interactive modules, case study units, and podcasts that provide research-validated information about working with students in inclusive settings, by visiting the IRIS Center Resources.
- Explore Assignments and Activities, assignable exercises showing concepts in action through video, cases, and student and teacher artifacts.
- Practice and strengthen skills essential to quality teaching through the Building Teaching Skills and Dispositions lessons

3

Response to Intervention

1. How did we come to the response to intervention (RTI) model?
2. What are the components and implementation practices in an RTI model?
3. How does universal screening fit into RTI?
4. What is the role of the teacher in an RTI model?

As the special education teacher at Birdseye elementary school, Cathryn Cooper primarily works with students with learning disabilities, but she also serves as the special education teacher for students identified with behavior disorders. Until the last year, Cathryn's primary role at the school was as a resource teacher who provided pull-out academic support to students with identified learning disabilities, as well as an inclusion support teacher for students who were mainstreamed for most of the school day. During the last year, the school superintendent decided to transition to implementing an RTI model in their school. They were already implementing several components of an RTI model including screening for reading and math difficulties twice a year in kindergarten and first grade but decided to continue screening through fifth grade. They also were providing reading intervention support in first grade, but decided to identify appropriate interventions for students in first through fifth grades in reading and in first through third grade in math. The school principal asked Cathryn to think about how she might facilitate implementation of the RTI model schoolwide. Cathryn decided that she could assist in selecting research-based interventions in reading and math and to facilitate training of key personnel to provide these interventions. As you will see in this chapter, Cathryn and her principal provided Tier 2 interventions by hiring and training teaching assistants, and provided Tier 3 interventions using Cathryn and the reading specialist. In this chapter, you will learn more about RTI and how you might facilitate implementation in your school.

Response to Intervention

How did we come to the RTI model? Many educators perceive that although special education may be available to serve students with disabilities, there are many other students with learning needs who do not qualify for special education. What are some possible solutions to this dilemma? One solution that is recommended in the reauthorization of IDEA (IDEIA 2004) is to provide RTI as a means of preventing learning and behavior difficulties. RTI is the most current model for screening students and using their responses to intervention as a data source to facilitate identifying students who need special education services (Burns, Griffiths, Parson, Tilly, & VanDerHayden, 2007; Glover & Vaughn, 2010).

Students with learning disabilities have most often been identified by determining their potential or ability, usually with an intelligence test, and comparing that with their achievement, as measured by reading or math tests. Students who were assessed

PEARSON
myeducationlab

Visit the MyEducationLab for this course to enhance your understanding of chapter concepts with a personalized Study Plan. You'll also have the opportunity to hone your teaching skills through video-based Assignments and Activities, IRIS Center Resources, and Building Teaching Skills and Dispositions lessons.

as being low in both ability and achievement could often not qualify for special education services. This process had many difficulties, including (a) overreliance on IQ measures and (b) the requirement to wait for a discrepancy between IQ and achievement (e.g., math or reading performance), which might have meant that students would not be provided services until too late. RTI is a potential solution to these problems. Most professional organizations and experts in the field are recommending that educators use early screening and intervention as a means of determining students' success and thus subsequent needs. Students who respond well to interventions do not require subsequent support, whereas students whose response to interventions (e.g., supplemental reading instruction for 30 minutes a day) is low may be provided additional supplemental instruction. In addition, the data gathered as a result of monitoring student progress, or *progress monitoring*, might be used to assist in the referral and identification for special education.

As a result of the recommended use of RTI, eligibility and identification criteria for learning disability are described as follows (IDEIA 2004; reauthorization [614(b)(6)(A)-(B)]):

> When determining whether a child has a specific learning disability:
> - The LEA [local education agency] is not required to consider a severe discrepancy between achievement and intellectual ability.
> - The LEA may use a process that determines if a student responds to scientific, research-based intervention as part of the evaluation.

Therefore, RTI may help identify students with learning disabilities by replacing discrepancy criteria and using students' responses to intervention as data to facilitate decision making and provide instruction and learning as critical elements in the assessment process. By replacing discrepancy criteria and using students' responses to intervention as data to facilitate decision making, the RTI model may help identify students with learning disabilities while providing instruction and opportunities for learning as a critical elements in the assessment process.

Past and Present Challenges

One of the goals of RTI is to change a prevailing view related to "waiting for students to fail." Too often, when students first showed signs of struggling academically or behaviorally, the prevailing approach was to wait and hope that their progress would improve over time. The idea was that students might simply be slow to achieve academically because of normal developmental or experiential differences and that it would be a disservice to assess them prematurely and place them in special education. Yet students who struggled were provided with few avenues for extra support. Also, young students

who were evaluated for possible special education placement sometimes had not yet exhibited enough of a discrepancy between their ability and their achievement to qualify for special education services. For these reasons, this approach was often referred to as the "wait to fail" model.

RTI is different. All students are screened early, often as early as kindergarten, and their progress is assessed frequently so that those students who do not seem to be making adequate progress are provided with timely interventions, before they have a chance to fall further behind. Thus, RTI is a *prevention and intervention model*. As you read this chapter, think about what these changes mean for special educators—and for students.

Previous Identification Procedures Over the past 30 years, the field of learning disabilities has struggled with numerous challenges related to its definition and identification procedures. Vaughn and Klingner (2007) note that these challenges include

- an increase of more than 200% of students identified as having a learning disability since the category was established.
- questionable procedures for determining learning disabilities through emphasis on an IQ–achievement discrepancy and processing disorders.
- students identified using a "wait to fail" model rather than a prevention–early intervention model.
- subjectivity in student referral for services, with teachers' and others' perceptions sometimes weighing too heavily in the process.
- students' opportunities to learn not adequately considered during the referral and identification process.
- considerable variation from state to state concerning identification procedures and prevalence rates for learning disabilities.
- an identification process that provides little information to guide instructional decision making.
- problematic assessment practices, particularly for culturally and linguistically diverse students.
- disproportionate numbers of culturally and linguistically diverse students inappropriately identified for and served in special education.

These challenges to the traditional model for identifying students with learning disabilities illustrate the importance of adopting the RTI model. RTI provides early and ongoing screening of students with early intervention and uses data to facilitate decision making for identification.

Challenges to Implementing an RTI Approach Possible difficulties with implementing an RTI approach include questions about who provides the more intensive secondary and teritiary interventions (a paraprofessional, general education teacher, special education teacher, or other specialist) and the extent to which validated instructional practices exist in academic areas other than reading, such as math or writing. Nevertheless, effective implementation of RTI provides a framework for preventing academic and behavioral difficulties that will increasingly be used by school districts (Vaughn & Fuchs, 2003; Fuchs, Fuchs, & Vaughn, 2008). Another challenge involves defining RTI so that practicing school districts are able to determine (1) responders from nonresponders, (2) the necessary professional development for practicing professionals, and (3) the role of families. Ensuring family involvement in RTI can be challenging initially, as it may require adjustments to new practices. Other issues and perceived barriers to implementation of RTI include:

- Personnel may not be adequately trained to implement RTI. For example, reading specialists may not know how to provide effective interventions for nonresponders, teachers may be unfamiliar with procedures for screening and monitoring the progress of students in their classes, and special education teachers may not readily identify their roles and responsibilities within an RTI framework.
- High-quality instruction in early reading is well understood; however, research-based practices for implementing instruction in other domains (e.g., math, writing) are less well delineated. Furthermore, we know more about early reading instruction and intervention (e.g., kindergarten, first grade, second grade) than we do about reading intervention in the later grades (e.g., grades 4–8).
- Leaders at the school, district, and state levels are inadequately prepared to implement RTI practices. Many principals are learning about screening, progress monitoring, and implementation of tiers of intervention for the first time and have little experience providing the necessary leadership for effective implementation of RTI models.
- Many folks perceive RTI as a special education initiative rather than a combined general and special education initiative. Thus, classroom teachers may be disinclined to take leadership roles within the implementation of RTI if they perceive that it is really a special education initiative.
- Inadequate local- and state-level policies and resources may compromise effective implementation of RTI. School districts may not have the materials, professional development, or other resources to support implementation of RTI.
- Effective practice models for implementing RTI at the secondary level are less well developed, making it difficult for middle school and high school personnel to implement RTI models.

The overview in Table 3-1 compares identification of students with learning disabilities before IDEIA 2004 to the identification process with RTI.

Initiatives Influencing RTI

Over the past decade, three contemporary major initiatives set the stage for changes in how we think about students with disabilities and RTI. First, in August 2001, the Office of Special Education Programs brought together leading researchers to discuss numerous issues related to identifying learning disabilities (Bradley, Danielson, & Hallahan, 2002). The team reached consensus on principles related to learning disabilities and the eventual use of RTI to facilitate more appropriate identification of students with learning disabilities (Vaughn & Klingner, 2007):

- Learning disabilities is a valid construct that represents a life-span disorder.
- Individuals with learning disabilities require a special education.
- The exact prevalence of learning disabilities is unknown; however, the rate is likely between 2% and 5%.
- The use of IQ–achievement discrepancy is not adequate for identifying students with learning disabilities.
- Linking processing disabilities to learning disabilities has not been adequately established; also, most processing disabilities are difficult to measure and link to treatment.
- The use of reliable and valid data from progress monitoring is a promising addition to identifying individuals with learning disabilities.
- Much is known about effective interventions for students with learning disabilities and yet ineffective interventions continue to be used.

Second, the President's Commission on Excellence in Special Education held public hearings throughout the United States and received hundreds of written comments (President's Commission on Excellence in Special Education, 2002) about the state of special education in the nation's education system. The commission concluded that special educators were spending too much time on paperwork and not enough time teaching. The commission also noted that general education and special education seemed to be operating as two separate systems rather than as a coherent whole. In the report, the commission recommended shifting to a prevention model that takes into account the fact that students with disabilities are also part of general education and that requires special and general educators to work together more closely.

Third, the National Research Council report on the disproportionate representation of culturally and linguistically diverse students in special education provided similar recommendations to those proposed by the Office of Special Education (Donovan & Cross, 2002). The council promoted widespread use of early screening and intervention practices

Table 3-1 Identifying Students with Learning Disabilities: Prior to IDEIA 2004 and with RTI

Prior to IDEIA 2004	RTI
No universal academic screening. Little progress monitoring.	All students are screened. Progress monitoring assesses whether students are reaching goals—multiple data points are collected over an extended period of time across different tiers of intervention.
"Wait to fail" model—students frequently not provided with interventions until they have qualified for special education.	Students are provided with interventions at the first sign they are struggling; there is an increased focus on proactive responses to students' difficulties.
Focus on within-child problems or deficits.	Ecological focus. Systems approach to problem solving, focused on instruction and interventions varied in time, intensity, and focus.
Clear eligibility criteria (i.e., a child either did or did not qualify for special education services). Categorical approach—targeted, intensive interventions typically not provided unless a student was found eligible for special education.	Tiered model of service delivery with interventions provided to all students who demonstrate a need for support, regardless of whether they have a disability.
Multidisciplinary team mostly made up of special education professionals; individual students typically referred by classroom teachers with academic and/or behavioral concerns.	Problem-solving (or intervention) teams include general and special educators; teams consider progress-monitoring data and all students who are not reaching benchmarks.
Reliance on assessments, particularly standardized tests.	Collaborative educational decisions based on ongoing school, classroom, and individual student data; adjustments to instruction/intervention based on data.
Assessment data collected during a limited number of sessions.	Multiple data points collected over time and in direct relationship to the intervention provided.
"Comprehensive evaluation" consisting mainly of formal assessments conducted by individual members of the multidisciplinary team, often the same battery of tests administered to all referred children.	"Full and individualized evaluation" relies heavily on existing data collected throughout the RTI process; evaluation includes a student's response to specific validated interventions and other data gathered through observations, teacher and parent checklists, and diagnostic assessments.
Learning disability construct of "unexpected underachievement" indicated by low achievement as compared to a measure of the child's ability (i.e., IQ–achievement discrepancy).	Learning disability construct of "unexpected underachievement" indicated by low achievement and insufficient response to validated interventions that work with most students ("true peers"), even struggling ones.

Source: From Response to Intervention, by J. K. Klingner, 2009, in S. Vaughn & C. S. Bos, *Strategies for Teaching Students with Learning and Behavior Problems.* Reprinted with permission.

and RTI models. The council's premise was that if schoolwide behavior and early reading programs help culturally and linguistically diverse students receive the support they need and improve their opportunities to learn, then the number of students who exhibit ongoing problems will decrease and the students who continue to struggle will more likely be those who require a special education.

Based on these initiatives, Congress passed the Individuals with Disabilities Education Improvement Act (IDEIA 2004). The new law promoted RTI as a means for preventing learning difficulties and furthering accurate identification of students with learning disabilities. Furthermore, Congress urges the use of *early intervening services* (EIS) to provide students with support as soon as they show signs of struggling. The IDEIA 2004

- recommends using alternative approaches to identifying students with learning disabilities, but does not require abandoning use of the IQ–achievement discrepancy criterion.

- urges early screening and early intervention so that students who show signs of struggling do not fall further behind.
- recommends a multitiered intervention strategy. A *multitiered intervention strategy* is a set of layers of instruction that increase in intensity (e.g., increase amount of instruction, decrease group size) based on how well students are succeeding in a less intensive instructional format. The first tier in a multitiered intervention approach is typically the classroom instruction; the second tier is often additional instruction that is provided by the classroom teacher; and the third tier of instruction is even more instruction, often provided by a trained person or a specialist such as the special education teacher.
- asks districts to review practices to accelerate learning so that students make adequate progress in special education.
- recommends ongoing systematic progress monitoring of students' responses to high-quality, research-based

interventions. Progress monitoring provides frequent assessments of how students are learning target knowledge or skills, to determine if their response to instruction is adequate.

- requires better integration of services between general and special education.
- emphasizes the role of context when referring, identifying, and serving students in special education.

Figure 3-1 provides an overview of the practices related to RTI that are used by states.

There was a strong rationale in support of RTI practices for several reasons, not the least of which was the attempt to better integrate support and services for individuals with disabilities. For example, a student with a learning disability who is included in the general education classroom may also have a speech and language specialist, be taught in reading and math by the special education teacher, have opportunities during the day to work with the Title I reading teacher, and also meet with the school psychologist once or twice a month. One of the goals of RTI is to integrate services and to eliminate

► **Figure 3-1**   Response to Intervention (RTI) Model Recommended by State

Guidance on RTI	State Model Developed	Developing Model	No Model Specified
California	Arizona	Alabama	Alaska
Illinois	Delaware	Arkansas	New Jersey
Maine	Florida	Colorado	South Carolina
Maryland	Georgia	Connecticut	
Massachusetts	Iowa	Hawaii	
Missouri	Kansas	Idaho	
North Dakota	Louisiana	Indiana	
Tennessee	Nebraska	Kentucky	
Texas	North Carolina	Michigan	
Virginia	Ohio	Minnesota	
	Oregon	Mississippi	
	Pennsylvania	Montana	
	Utah	Nevada	
	Washington	New Hampshire	
	West Virginia	New Mexico	
		New York	
		Oklahoma	
		Rhode Island	
		South Dakota	
		Vermont	
		Wisconsin	
		Wyoming	

Source: From Implementation of Response to Intervention: A Snapshot of Progress, by S. Berkeley, W. N. Bender, L. G. Peaster, & L. Saunders, 2009, *Journal of Learning Disabilities,* 42, pp. 85–95.

settings in which general education teachers do "their thing" and special education teachers are quite separate and disconnected.

Components of Response to Intervention

What are the components and implementation practices in an RTI model? Because RTI is considered an instructional model for preventing learning and behavior problems and provides a framework for monitoring the progress of all students, particularly those with difficulties, what are the critical elements that are part of RTI? Fundamentally, there are many frameworks for implementing RTI, not just one. However, within these multiple frameworks, there are critical components that everyone agrees are essential. These are

- screening and progress monitoring.
- implementation of effective classroom instructional practices so that all students have an opportunity to learn (Tier 1).
- provision of secondary intervention (Tier 2) when students fall behind.
- provision of a more intensive individualized intervention for students for whom secondary intervention is inadequate (Tier 3). Students who are considered special education may be provided services within Tier 3 or within a fourth tier of intervention depending on the instructional framework used by the school or district.

RTI is a schoolwide model that typically starts with students in kindergarten and may continue throughout the elementary grades or even into middle school in some districts. Although no one single model is accepted as the "gold standard," RTI models commonly include four key components (Glover & Vaughn, 2010; Fuchs, Fuchs, & Vaughn, 2008; Haager, Klingner, & Vaughn, 2007; Vaughn & Fuchs, 2003):

1. They implement high-quality, research-based instruction matched to the needs of students. Only instructional practices that generally produce high learning rates for students are used, as demonstrated by scientific research. The implementation of high-quality instructional practices as interventions is intended to increase the probability of positive student responses. Whether you are teaching reading or math at the elementary or secondary level, the instructional programs, materials, and practices you use should be selected based on the best research available rather than your own ideology or perspective.

2. They provide universal screening to identify students at risk and monitor students' learning over time, to determine their level and rate of performance (for ongoing decision making). Educators assess all students' learning to determine if they are making progress toward meeting expected benchmarks at a rate commensurate with that of peers. Students who do not seem to be progressing are provided with extra assistance in the form of interventions targeted to their needs. What does this mean for you as an educator? Consider your expectations and goals for learning each week. Create a brief assessment that will help you determine what students know about what you are teaching that week. At the end of the week (or two), use the assessment again to determine how much students have learned. Use this information for reteaching and/or making decisions about additional intervention.

3. They provide interventions of increasing intensity when students continue to struggle. The intensity of instruction can be enhanced by reducing group size, increasing time, and/or making sure that interventions are even more carefully tailored to the students' instructional needs. Determine what options for providing intervention are available. Typically, schools provide additional interventions for elementary students in math and reading. It may also be possible to provide additional supports in spelling and writing. For older students, additional reading classes or after-school tutoring may be available. As another option, consider how you might restructure and regroup students so that you can provide additional instruction to those students with the highest needs.

4. They make important educational decisions based on data. Decisions about selecting instructional interventions, the intensity of the interventions (e.g., how much time each day and in what group size the intervention is provided), and the duration of the interventions (e.g., 2 weeks, 8 weeks) are based on students' responses to the interventions. As you examine students' performance based on data (e.g., weekly or biweekly assessments), consider instructional adjustments that you could make to ensure that all students have improved outcomes. Also consider whether selected students would benefit from additional instruction.

To learn about useful software and online assessment tools, see Tech Tips. These tools will help you better understand and implement an RTI model.

Screening and Progress Monitoring

Screening involves providing a reliable and valid measure that can be easily and quickly administered to large numbers of students to determine whether these students have academic difficulties. For example, in kindergarten students may be screened for reading problems by asking them to identify letters. With older students, screening may ask students to read a passage at grade level and then respond to questions. These data sources allow teachers to identify students with difficulties and then to provide them additional instruction as needed. Within an RTI model, screening is typically conducted at the beginning and middle of the year. Screening may be provided in reading, math, or for behavior.

Progress monitoring involves frequent and ongoing measurement of student knowledge and skills *and* the examination of student data to evaluate instruction. Used with a few students or the entire class, progress monitoring is essential to effective implementation of RTI because it allows key stakeholders, such as the special education and classroom teachers as well as other specialists (e.g., speech and language teacher), to determine the rate of growth students are achieving and to determine whether additional intervention is needed. To better understand why progress monitoring is used and how to use progress monitoring, see Apply the Concept 3-1.

The Three Tiers of Intervention

RTI models often discuss instruction or intervention in terms of tiers. Typically, *tiers* represent the level of intensity of instruction provided to a student or group of students (see Figure 3-2).

As students move through the tiers, the intensity of the interventions they receive increases. Some RTI models include three tiers, and others include a fourth tier. In read-

▶ **Figure 3-2** Three-Tier Model of Response to Intervention

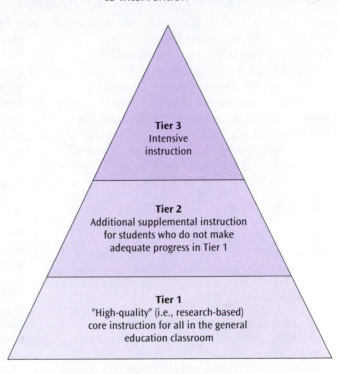

Tier 3
Intensive instruction

Tier 2
Additional supplemental instruction for students who do not make adequate progress in Tier 1

Tier 1
"High-quality" (i.e., research-based) core instruction for all in the general education classroom

ing, for example, approximately 80% of all learners make adequate progress in Tier 1, 15% to 20% may require some supplemental instruction in Tier 2, and about 5% to 6% need the intensive intervention implemented in Tier 3. As

●●○●○●● *Apply the Concept* ●●●○●●

3-1 Using Progress Monitoring in the Classroom

Why Use Progress Monitoring? ✳

- To keep track of student learning
- To identify students who need additional help
- To assist in arranging small-group instruction
- To design instruction that meets individual student needs
- To refer and identify students for special education based on data gathered during progress monitoring

How Do I Monitor Student Progress? ✳

- Assess all students at the beginning of the year in the critical areas for their grade level.
- Use assessments to identify students who need extra help and to create

goals for learning. Once you determine which students require extra help, you can plan small-group instruction.

- Monitor the progress of students in small groups more frequently (weekly or monthly) in the specific skill or area being worked on.
- Assess progress by comparing learning goals with actual student progress. Students who are making adequate progress should still be assessed approximately three times a year to ensure that they are learning and continue to achieve at grade level.

What Are the Benefits of Progress Monitoring?

According to the National Center on Monitoring Student Progress, the following are benefits of progress monitoring:

- Increased learning because instructional decisions are based on student data
- Improved accountability
- Better communication about student progress with family and other professionals
- Higher expectations for low-achieving students
- Fewer special education referrals

USING TECHNOLOGY TO IMPLEMENT RTI

A key objective of RTI is to select an instructional strategy to match a student's specific needs. Universal design, authoring software, and assessment software are aspects of technology that can facilitate RTI. Universal design is a growing movement toward designing products and environments to accommodate the diverse needs and abilities of all people.

The concept of universal design can be applied to instructional materials to meet the varied needs of all learners. We need materials that increase the usability for everyone, appealing to different learning styles, methods of input, learner backgrounds, and abilities and disabilities. Such classroom materials may have varying levels of difficulty, multiple means of input, various modes of presentation, and features to customize pace and feedback. Following are some programs that use the concept of universal design:

- *The Early Learning Series,* from Marblesoft Simtech at http://www.marblesoft.com. The programs feature multiple difficulty levels, include a built-in recordkeeping system, and allow teachers to customize the learning environment to meet the specific needs of each individual child.

- *IntelliTools, Inc.,* at http://www.intellitools.com. This company has marketed three of its most effective classroom programs with a single interface, Classroom Suite 4. The new suite includes a talking word processor and authoring program, an arithmetic authoring program, and a multimedia authoring program. Recommended for Grades PreK–8, these programs offer tremendous possibilities for customizing the curriculum for all learners.

- *The Language Arts Objective Sequence (LOSR),* by Research Press at http://www.researchpress. com. Beyond the traditional assessment software, several assessment packages may be beneficial to teachers practicing RTI. LOSR helps teachers evaluate current language arts performance levels and identify specific goals and objectives.

- *Measures of Academic Progress (MAPS),* by Northwest Evaluation Association (NWEA) at http://www.nwea.org/assessments/map.asp. This research-based, state-aligned assessment tool helps teachers monitor students' growth and progress by having students take adaptive tests in mathematics, reading, science, and language use. Teachers can then use this information to guide their instruction.

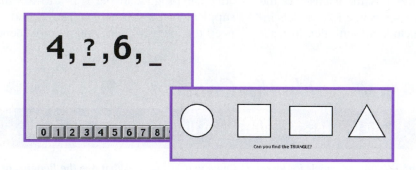

the special education teacher, your role may be to facilitate inclusion of students with disabilities in Tier 1, identifying effective treatments for Tiers 2 and 3, and perhaps training teachers and other personnel to implement interventions.

Primary Instruction, Tier 1 What distinguishes Tier 1 from all of the other tiers of instruction? The primary distinction is that Tier 1 involves all students in the classroom with an intention of providing them with the most effective instruction or behavior supports. For example, in a fourth-grade math or reading class, the math or reading instruction provided to all of the students in the class is referred to as Tier 1 instruction.

In Tier 1, general education teachers provide evidence-based instruction to all students in the class. The instruction must be evidenced-based so that when students are not making adequate progress and secondary intervention or Tier 2 instruction is provided, we know that the students have had an adequate opportunity to learn. We do not want students provided Tier 2 and Tier 3 intervention because they were not provided adequate Tier 1 instruction.

What do classroom teachers do during Tier 1 instruction? Classroom teachers or support personnel screen students using easy-to-administer screening measures that are selected for the grade level they are teaching. Typically, screening takes less than 10 minutes per student and can be done at the beginning and middle of the year. Students who are having difficulty in reading or math are administered progress-monitoring measures regularly to determine their progress. Teachers differentiate instruction as needed and strive to provide appropriate, effective instruction for their students.

Secondary Intervention, Tier 2 Secondary intervention, or Tier 2, is provided for those students who are not making adequate progress in Tier 1—in other words, those who are not responding to instruction. Tier 2 interventions are typically provided in small groups, with the intention of providing additional instruction that will allow the student to make adequate progress in Tier 1 instruction without further intervention. Tier 2 interventions supplement rather than supplant the core curriculum taught in Tier 1 general education classrooms, and are intended to reinforce the concepts and skills taught there. Yet the support that students receive in Tier 2 is still under the domain of general education. It is *not* special education. All children who appear to be struggling, as evidenced by their slow rate of progress and low assessment scores, are entitled to this support. Researchers refer to both the slow rate of progress and low levels of overall learning as a *dual discrepancy* (Fuchs, Fuchs, & Speece, 2002).

Teachers continue to monitor the progress of students while they are receiving Tier 2 support. Tier 2 interventions are provided for a fixed duration (e.g., 10 weeks). After this time, educators examine progress-monitoring and other data to answer the following questions:

- Is the student making good progress and should he or she return to Tier 1–only instruction?
- Is the student making some but not sufficient progress to move to Tier 1, thereby necessitating that he or she receive another dose of Tier 2 intervention?
- Is the student making very little progress, thereby requiring him or her to be moved to Tier 3?

Tertiary Intervention, Tier 3 Tertiary intervention, or Tier 3, is provided to those students who continue to experience difficulties and show minimal progress during secondary, or Tier 2, interventions. Typically, the majority of students who require intervention benefit from secondary intervention and do not require tertiary intervention. Tertiary intervention is typically provided for a longer time period and more frequently than secondary intervention. Depending on the number of tiers in the RTI model, this tier may or may not be special education. Tier 3 students receive explicit instruction individually or in small groups of two or three students. (See Figure 3-3 for a description of how Tiers 2 and 3 compare.)

Implementing Interventions

Not everyone agrees on who should decide which interventions to implement in an RTI model, or how these decisions should be made. Some researchers recommend a standard treatment protocol model (Fuchs & Fuchs, 2006). Others prefer a problem-solving model (Marston, Muyskens, Lau, & Canter, 2003). Still others favor a hybrid model that is a combination of these two approaches (Glover & Vaughn, 2010; Vaughn, Linan-Thompson, & Hickman, 2003). As the National Association of State Directors of Special Education noted, "Some . . . have suggested that multitier systems might use *either* a problem-solving method . . . *or* a standard treatment protocol approach. This is an artificial distinction. All RTI systems must consider implementing the best features of both approaches" (Batsche et al., 2005).

Standard Treatment Protocol Ms. Cable was a fourth-grade teacher working in a school that used an RTI framework. During her first year in the school, the principal provided training for all of the kindergarten through fifth-grade teachers on a secondary reading intervention that had been selected by the school district to be used with students who demonstrated reading difficulties. Ms. Cable was informed that because all students who were at risk for reading problems

▶ **Figure 3-3** How Do Tier 2 and Tier 3 Differ?

	Tier 2 Instruction	Tier 3 Instruction
Daily instruction	30 minutes per day **(plus Tier 1)**	50 minutes per day
Duration	10 to 12 week **(1 or 2 rounds)**	10 to 12 weeks **(possibly several rounds)**
Group size	Small group/individual	Smallest group possible/individual
Ongoing progress monitoring	Weekly	Weekly

were using the same intervention (variation within grade level), the school was using a standard protocol model.

With the *standard treatment protocol model*, the same empirically validated treatments are used for all children with similar problems (Batsche et al., 2005). The standard treatment protocol does not differ from child to child. The interventions are chosen from those that have an evidence base, and instructional decisions follow a standard protocol. Possible approaches might include explicit instruction in phonological awareness or in phonics skills, fluency or comprehension interventions, or computer programs. Specific research-based interventions for students with similar difficulties are provided in a standardized format to ensure conformity of implementation. Proponents argue that this is the most research-based of the approaches to RTI and leaves less room for error in professional judgment (Fuchs & Fuchs, 2006).

Problem-Solving Model The problem-solving model is a more individualized approach. For each child who is not progressing, a problem-solving team—composed of the classroom teacher, school psychologist, special education teacher, and any other key educational stakeholders (e.g., parent, speech and language therapist)—meets to consider all of the data available so that they can come up with an intervention plan for the child. Interventions are planned specifically for the targeted student and are provided over a reasonable period of time. The process typically follows these steps:

1. *Define the problem.* Ms. Chung, a fourth-grade teacher, indicated that Thomas was not making progress in math. He seemed easily distracted, did not complete his math work during class, did not participate in team problem-solving during math, and had incomplete math homework consistently. She was confident that Thomas was going to fail fourth-grade math. The problem-solving team suggested that the school psychologist observe Thomas during class and meet with him afterwards.
2. *Analyze the problem.* After viewing Thomas in the class, the school psychologist asked Ms. Chung to provide samples of Thomas's work over the past month. Both agreed that Thomas would benefit from small-group instruction in math for about 30 minutes every day. They thought that Thomas was making some progress but it was too slow, and they identified that when he was working in a small group he paid more attention.
3. *Develop a plan.* Several other fourth-grade students lacked progress in math, so they were assembled in a group that met every day with one of the fourth-grade teachers.

4. *Implement the plan.* Thomas started the additional math instruction the following week and received supplemental math instruction daily. His progress in math was monitored every week and this data was retained in a file.
5. *Evaluate the plan.* After 10 weeks, the problem-solving team determined that Thomas was making very good progress, and they attributed it to the additional instruction he was receiving. They projected that after about 10 more weeks of supplemental intervention he would be caught up with his classmates.

This approach maximizes problem-solving opportunities by allowing teams to be flexible. Ms. Chung appreciated that her professional expertise was valued but realized that it took considerable time to attend meetings with other professionals and design effective interventions for the students in her class who were behind in reading and math. Ms. Chung appreciated the contributions of the problem-solving team and their recommendation to involve the school psychologist. Together, she felt that they had come up with a successful strategy for Thomas.

Differences between the Standard Protocol and Problem-Solving Models Ms. Cable and Ms. Chung taught at schools that were implementing RTI frameworks, yet Ms. Cable was implementing a standard protocol intervention and Ms. Chung was implementing a problem-solving intervention for the students in her class requiring secondary (Tier 2) interventions. Research suggests that both of the models can be effective, and in fact, most sites implement a hybrid in which aspects of each model are used (Tackett, 2009).

Christ, Burns, and Ysseldyke (2005) note that the fundamental difference between the standard treatment protocol and the problem-solving model is the extent to which decision-making teams engage in analyzing individual student data before selecting and implementing interventions. With a standard treatment protocol, there is little examination of the reasons for a child's struggles. The rationale is that for secondary interventions, there is considerable evidence about what interventions are effective, and the best strategy is to implement an effective intervention. In contrast, the problem-solving model is more flexible. The emphasis is on individualized, targeted interventions based on an analysis of the learning context, environmental conditions, and instructional variables as well as on the progress-monitoring data and other assessment data for a student (Glover & Vaughn, 2010).

Decision-Making Teams How is the RTI model implemented within schools? Who takes the leadership role for directing RTI? The answers to these questions vary by school and district. It is common to have a team of professionals who work together to guide the RTI process at the school level. Schools might have one or more decision-making teams, and membership might be flexible, depending on the expertise needed for a given situation. You may be asked to be a member of the team to provide insights into curriculum expectations and suggestions for what interventions might be effective with students, or you may be asked only to attend team meetings that are relevant to students you teach.

Decision-making teams should include members with relevant expertise. One team member must have expertise in learning disabilities. Another should be an expert in the targeted area of concern (e.g., reading, mathematics, behavior). If the student is an English language learner (ELL), it is critical that someone on the team have expertise in language acquisition, and if relevant, bilingual education.

The overall purpose of the team is to ensure that the RTI model in the school is implemented effectively and that all students who need additional support are identified early, provided appropriate interventions, and monitored over time. See Apply the Concept 3-2 for more about how team members facilitate the RTI process.

Mr. Chan works in an elementary school in California. He describes how his decision-making team works:

> When the majority of a class is progressing and about 20% or fewer of the students differ from their peers in rate of progress, then the role of the team is to determine which Tier 2 interventions to implement with students who are slower to respond. When students who are receiving Tier 2 interventions continue to experience difficulty, the decision-making team convenes to determine which steps to take next. The team might decide to try different Tier 2 interventions, or perhaps more intensive Tier 3 interventions. The team might decide to initiate a more comprehensive evaluation for possible special education identification.

Mr. Chan's experience is similar to other teachers who are in schools using an RTI framework. Even within the RTI model, however, due-process safeguards apply. Families must provide permission for an evaluation to take place. As before the passage of IDEIA 2004, families may request an evaluation for their child.

Responders and Nonresponders to Intervention One of the important contributions of using a multitiered system in which students are provided primary (Tier 1), secondary (Tier 2), and tertiary (Tier 3) interventions is that it is possible to quickly identify when students are falling behind and provide additional intervention that is targeted to meet their needs. Fortunately, the majority of students respond well when provided additional intervention (Tier 2). We refer to students who respond well to intervention as *responders* or *igh responders*. These students may need additional intervention in the future but are generally able to maintain grade-level performance or near grade-level performance with occasional Tier 2 intervention. An example of a good response is when the gap narrows between a student's rate and level of progress and that of her or his peers. In other words, the student seems to be catching up. On the other hand, students who make minimal or no gains after being taught with high-quality, validated interventions are considered to be inadequately responding to intervention; in other words, they are *nonresponders*. For these students, the gap keeps growing between them and their peers. These students may need more intensive long-term interventions, most likely through special education services. See Apply the Concept 3-3 for some guidelines regarding what RTI can and cannot do.

> ▶ **WEB RESOURCES**
> Go to the National Center for Learning Disabilities (NCLD) Web site at http://www.ncld.org to expand your understanding of RTI.

Nonresponders do not seem to make adequate progress even when instructed with a research-based approach. However, teachers must realize that not all students learn in the same way. They need to understand that although one student may respond well to a given research-based intervention, another student may not. Research can only help us make educated guesses about which instructional practices are most likely to benefit

Apply the Concept

3-2 — **How Team Members Facilitate RTI**

Members of the decision-making team facilitate the RTI process in several ways, including

- reviewing progress-monitoring data of students in interventions and for grade levels and the school as a whole.

- observing classroom instruction to ensure that research-based instruction is occurring.
- providing professional development to teachers and other key educators.
- assisting with data collection and monitoring.

- facilitating instructional decision making.
- organizing intervention groups and monitoring their effectiveness.
- communicating with parents and professionals.

3-3   **What RTI Can and Cannot Do**

- RTI neither creates nor fixes learning disabilities. However, models such as 3-Tier Reading provide a safety net for students who might end up in special education simply because they have not been provided adequate instruction or appropriate

- interventions prior to being referred for special education services (see MeadowsCenter.org for a description of the 3-Tier Reading framework).

- RTI is a dynamic model that allows students to move between levels of interventions, depending on results

of ongoing progress monitoring and benchmark assessments.

- The key to the 3-Tier model and other RTI models is to provide effective instruction early to ensure that students are provided with the resources and support they need to become proficient learners.

---

the greatest number of children. But even in the best research studies, some students might actually respond better to an alternative approach. Therefore, when a child does not seem to be responding to an instructional method, it is important to try a different approach. RTI researcher Amanda VanDerHayden defines nonresponders as "students for whom we have not yet found the right intervention" (personal communication, February 2006). See Apply the Concept 3-4 for help in identifying why children may not respond to instruction.

Teachers vary a great deal in how they apply different instructional approaches. How well a teacher implements a practice affects how well students learn (Al Otaiba & Fuchs, 2006). This common sense finding has important implications for anyone implementing RTI. Determining whether a program is well implemented and appropriate for students requires observing in classrooms. The program being implemented by the classroom teacher may be appropriate, but the teacher may not be using it effectively. Maybe the teacher is struggling with classroom management and needs assistance in this area before being able to focus more on instruction. In any case, it is important to explore what can be done to improve instruction and to provide group interventions before providing individual interventions (see Apply the Concept 3-5).

Classroom observations must be part of every RTI model (Vaughn & Fuchs, 2003; Vellutino, Scanlon, Small, Fanuele, & Sweeney, 2007). Vellutino et al. (2007) note that "intervention at this level is based on the assumption that many if not most struggling readers will be able to profit from relevant modifications in classroom literacy instruction, despite the fact that they were (apparently) less well equipped than their normally achieving classmates to compensate for inadequacies in reading instruction" (p. 186). This recognition that many students struggle when their instruction is inadequate is an important one, with significant implications for culturally and linguistically diverse students who often are educated in high-poverty, high-needs schools in which teachers are sometimes not as qualified as in more affluent schools (Harry & Klingner, 2006).

RTI for Students Who Are Culturally and Linguistically Diverse

RTI has the potential to improve outcomes for students who are culturally and linguistically diverse and to more accurately determine which students need special education services (Klingner & Edwards, 2006). RTI practices that are responsive to the cultural and linguistic needs of students can assist teachers in determining whether

3-4   **Identifying Why Students May Not Respond to Instruction**

Before concluding that a student is a nonresponder who needs more intensive services, consider that there are many reasons the student may not be responding to instruction, such as:

- The method is not an effective one with this student, and a different approach would yield better results.

- The level of instruction might not be a good match for the student.

- The environment might not be conducive to learning.

To determine whether teachers should provide interventions,

- examine the program to determine whether it has been validated with students like those in the class. Some students may not be responding adequately to

instruction because the instruction is not based on empirical findings.

- determine whether instruction is at an appropriate level for students and the program is well-implemented. Students may be

low responders because they are getting inadequate amounts of instruction.

- establish whether teachers are sufficiently differentiating instruction to meet diverse student needs.

---

students' progress is related to what they are being taught, their background experiences, or how they are being taught. The quality of RTI depends on the quality of RTI team involved. Without sufficient knowledge about cultural and linguistic diversity, for example, educators implementing RTI may presume that a child who does not make progress at a certain pace must have a disability, rather than recognize that the child may need additional time and support while learning English. Educators may also equate cultural differences with cultural deficits, which may influence their interpretations of their diverse students' behaviors (Klingner & Solano-Flores, 2007).

Although the process of learning to read in a child's second language is similar to learning to read in his or her first language, there also are important differences of which teachers may not be aware (August & Shanahan, 2006). Second-language acquisition, best practices for ELLs, and cultural variations should be considered when assessing student progress, designing interventions, and interpreting ELLs' responses to interventions.

RTI approaches that respond to the cultural and linguistic diversity of students focus on, in addition to personal factors, understanding external or environmental factors that affect their opportunity to learn. For RTI to work, team members must have expertise in cultural and linguistic diversity and be knowledgeable about interventions that have been effective with culturally and linguistically diverse students with different needs.

In implementing RTI approaches with ELLs, a significant challenge is determining students' knowledge and skills in their first language and then understanding their performance in their second language. For example, there are subgroups of students whose literacy knowledge and skills in their first language (e.g., Spanish) are adequate, but whose literacy skills in their second language (e.g., English) are low. These students have demonstrated the capacity to acquire reading skills and now require instruction so they can apply those skills to the acquisition of English literacy. Other students may have low literacy

in both their first language and English because they have not received adequate instruction in either language. Still another group of students, the smallest group, demonstrates low literacy skills in both their first language and English, even after receiving adequate instruction.

Is RTI effective with ELLs? Initial research suggests that ELLs who receive scientifically based reading instruction in the early grades are likely to maintain gains, thus increasing the likelihood that they will be successful readers. Students who are ELLs and are low responders to a secondary (Tier 2) reading intervention can be identified through RTI approaches (Linan-Thompson, Cirino, & Vaughn, 2007; Linan-Thompson, Vaughn, Prater, & Cirino, 2006). For more on using RTI approaches with ELLs, see Apply the Concept 3-6.

When students demonstrate reading difficulties, providing small-group intensive interventions that target their instructional needs and then monitoring their progress ensures that instruction is modified to meet the needs of students. To meet their needs, those working with ELLs should consider the following:

- ELLs benefit from teachers who are highly interested in ensuring that their students make adequate progress in reading and that they themselves have the knowledge and skills to provide appropriate instruction.

- ELLs will be better served if teachers and school personnel do not expect or accept low performance and if they do not view students as undeserving of effective interventions.

- ELLs who exhibit learning disabilities may be underidentified and undertreated because school personnel may not have the knowledge and skills needed to identify and treat these students.

- Students benefit when school personnel are focused on meeting students' educational needs rather than on finding an external source to explain the educational needs.

3-6 Using RTI Approaches with English-Language Learners

To help determine how you can best provide instruction to your ELLs, consider the following questions:

- *What skills must educators have to effectively implement RTI for ELLs?* Having professional development provided to enhance your knowledge and skills is essential; in addition, a problem-solving team with knowledge and experience working with ELLs can be a valuable resource to facilitate decision making and to design instructional supports. The more you know about the development of oral language, early literacy, students' home languages, contextual considerations, and the cultural backgrounds of students, the better informed you will be in making appropriate decisions about interpreting screening and assessment results and in designing appropriate interventions.
- *How is screening implemented with ELLs?* ELLs can be screened on the same early reading indicators as native English-language speakers, including phonological awareness, letter knowledge, and word and text reading. Universal screenings must be conducted using native language and/or English measures that have demonstrated high validity and reliability. Provide instructional support to ELLs with low performance in reading areas even when oral language skills in English are low. Interventions should simultaneously address development of language and literacy skills in English.

- *How is progress monitoring effectively implemented with ELLs?* Monitor the progress of ELLs as frequently as you monitor the progress of all other students—a minimum of three times per year for students at grade level or above and three to six times per year for students at risk for reading problems. Consider students' accents and pronunciations when scoring English measures and provide appropriate interpretations when words are mispronounced. Do not penalize students for dialect features. Consider that students may be acquiring word meaning while acquiring word reading and, thus, oral reading fluency may proceed at an expected rate early (while students are focusing on word reading) and then proceed at a lower than expected rate later (when students are focusing more on word meaning).
- *How is primary instruction (Tier 1) provided to ELLs?* Set high but reasonable instructional expectations that provide ongoing instructional support, to ensure that these expectations are met. The core reading program for ELLs should include consideration of the foundational skills such as phonemic awareness and phonics early in the reading process, with continued emphasis on vocabulary and concept building throughout the instructional process. Reading words accurately and with prosody, as well as reading for meaning and learning, are emphasized through listening comprehension early and then later through reading

comprehension. Scaffold language and opportunities to respond. Scaffolding language includes paraphrasing key words, providing opportunities to extend answers, supporting language by using familiar synonyms (e.g., "that is also like . . .") and familiar antonyms (e.g., "that is also different from . . ."), reframing students' responses, confirming aspects of the answer that are correct, and providing language supports to further explain aspects that require refinement.
- *How are secondary (Tier 2) and tertiary (Tier 3) interventions effectively implemented for ELLs?* Provide intensive reading interventions to ELLs demonstrating low reading skills, immediately when needed. These interventions can be effectively implemented as early as first grade, as well as for more mature readers with reading difficulties. You do not need to wait for English oral language to improve before providing reading interventions. Use appropriate practices for building oracy skills and vocabulary development as well as reading skills.

Source: Adapted from *Response to Intervention in Reading for English Language Learners* by Sharon Vaughn and Alba Ortiz. The complete document is available on the NCLD Web site at http://www.ncld.org, and in *Effective Literacy and English Language Instruction for English Learners in the Elementary Grades: A Practice Guide (NCEE 2007-4011)*, by R. Gersten, S. K. Baker, T. Shanahan, S. Linan-Thompson, P. Collins, and R. Scarcella, 2007, Washington, DC: National Center for Education Evaluation and Regional Assistance, Institute of Education Sciences, U.S. Department of Education, retrieved from http://ies.ed.gov/ncee/wwc/publications/practiceguides/.

Working with Families

Family involvement has been a required part of identifying and monitoring students with disabilities since the earliest version of the IDEA. Family involvement is required in all aspects of identifying students with disabilities—regardless of the model used. If schools are using RTI models, families must be informed and involved in the process. Just as before, families can request a formal evaluation for a disability at any time. A family should also be notified early in the RTI process that a child seems to be struggling and that the school plans to try specific interventions to help. The Council for Exceptional Children (http://www.cec.sped.org) suggests that schools let families know about their child's participation in the RTI process at least by Tier 2. Schools should

- describe the RTI process.
- provide families with written intervention plans that are clearly explained.
- obtain families' consent.
- provide families with regular updates about their child's progress.

The NCLD (Cortiella, 2006) advises including the following information in written intervention plans:

- A description of the specific intervention
- The length of time (such as the number of weeks) that will be allowed for the intervention to have a positive effect
- The number of minutes per day the intervention will be implemented (such as 30 to 45 minutes)
- The persons responsible for providing the intervention
- The location where the intervention will be provided
- The factors for judging whether the student is experiencing success
- A description of the progress-monitoring strategy or approach, such as curriculum-based measurement (CBM), that will be used
- A progress-monitoring schedule
- How frequently (the parents) will receive reports about (their) child's response to the intervention

Several states have developed documents for parents, to assist them in understanding RTI.

Universal Screening

How does universal screening fit into the RTI model? *Universal screening* in reading, and sometimes in math, is an essential component of RTI models at the Tier 1 level. This process involves administering the same test to all students to determine who is likely to be at risk for academic difficulties, in the same way that schools have checked children's vision for years to screen students for potential problems. In many schools, screening is carried out three times a year: in the fall, winter, and spring. Screening instruments usually have few items and are short in duration. Screening is used to determine whether additional testing is needed. Schoolwide academic screening was rarely implemented with previous models. Instead, it was typically the classroom teacher who first noticed that students were struggling and referred them for an evaluation. Invariably some students were overlooked. With universal screening, however, everyone is tested.

What is an example of universal screening? Texas provides universal screening in reading for all students in kindergarten through second grade. The classroom teacher conducts the screening, and the most frequently used screening measure is the Texas Primary Reading Inventory (TPRI). The TPRI was developed and used to screen Texas students; this diagnostic instrument provides information on a student's reading/language arts development (from kindergarten through third grade). There is a quick screening that takes just a few minutes and is individually administered by the classroom teacher. Students' performance on the quick screen assists teachers in deciding whether a more diagnostic assessment would provide the necessary information to help teachers design instruction. The screening and assessment tool helps teachers decide in which of the critical elements of reading (e.g., phonics, fluency, and comprehension) the student needs additional instruction, and even provides lessons to facilitate decision making about what instruction should be provided.

Universal screening is also a quick way to identify general performance levels and determine whether students are on track to developing proficiency in the fundamental skills of reading and math. We know much more than we used to about how to predict future reading levels, for example, using phonological awareness and rapid naming tasks. Thus, we can determine with some accuracy which students are at risk and require additional intervention (Vellutino et al., 2007). Foorman and Ciancio (2005) point out that "the purpose of early screening could be identifying students *not* at risk so that instructional objectives can be established for students potentially at risk" (p. 494). Screening also provides valuable information about class performance and identifies teachers who might need further professional development. Once students have been identified as needing additional assistance using a screening measure, interventions are provided.

Numerous assessments can be used as screening instruments (see Table 3-2 for a list of possible reading screeners, and http://www.rtinetwork.org; http://www.centeroninstruction.org).

Some tests assess only one or two elements of reading (such as the C-TOPP, which only tests phonological processing), whereas others tap into several reading components. Some are quite quick to administer, such as the TOWRE, and others take much longer, such as the QRI-4 (Rathvon, 2004).

Using Screening to Make Educational Decisions

Screening is useful for providing quick information at the classroom or group level as well as at the student level (Fletcher, Lyon, Fuchs, & Barnes, 1997). When all of the students in a school are screened, school administrators can examine assessment results for patterns across, as well as within, classrooms. Problems that are widespread across classrooms call for schoolwide interventions.

Table 3-2 Possible Screening Measures for Reading

Assessment	Publisher and Web Site	Grades or Ages	Oral Lang.	Pa	Phon.	Word ID	Flu.	Voc.	Comp.	Comments
AIMSweb Curriculum-Based Measurement (CBM)	Edformation http://www.aimsweb.com	K–12	No	Yes	Yes	No	Yes	No	Yes	Offers Web-based data management
Basic Early Assessment of Reading (BEAR)	Riverside http://www.riverpub.com	K–3								Pencil–paper and computerized versions
Comprehensive Test of Phonological Processing (CTOPP)	PRO-ED http://www.proedinc.com	K–3								Phonological processing only
Dynamic Indicators of Basic Early Literacy Skills (DIBELS)	Sopris West/Cambium http://www.dibelsassessment.com	K–3, 4–6							Yes (4–6 only)	Grade 4–6 students assessed only in fluency and comprehension
Fox in a Box-2	CTB McGraw-Hill http://www.ctb.com	PreK–3								Includes PreK
Qualitative Reading Inventory-4 (QRI-4)	Allyn & Bacon/Longman http://www.ablongman.com	K–12								Informal assessment instrument
Scholastic Reading Inventory (SRI)	Scholastic teacher http://scholastic.com	K–12								Computer adaptive; includes data management system
Slosson Oral Reading Test (SORT-R3)	Slosson http://www.slosson.com	K–12								Word ID only
Test of Early Reading Ability (TERA-3)	Pearson http://ags.pearsonassessments.com PRO-ED http://www.proedinc.com	Ages 3.6–8.6								Assesses letter knowledge and environmental print
Test of Word Reading Efficiency (TOWRE)	Pearson http://ags.pearson.assessments.com	Ages 6.0–24.11								Pseudo-word reading and Word ID only
Texas Primary Reading Inventory (TPRI)	Texas Education Agency http://www.tpri.org	K–2	Yes							Includes screening section and inventory section

Note: Lang. = language; PA = phonological awareness; Phon. = phonics; ID = identification; Flu. = fluency; Voc. = vocabulary; Comp. = comprehension.

3-7 — Steps in Conducting Progress Monitoring

When screening students and conducting progress monitoring,

- screen all students in the fall.
- rank students by grade level and by classroom. In other words, compile assessment results so that patterns of achievement within classrooms and across classrooms at every grade level can be examined. Be sure to determine if there are normative findings to determine how students' performance compares with others outside the class, school, and district.
- identify lower achieving students in each grade or classroom.
- set goals for individual students.
- use frequent progress monitoring with students identified as low achievers. Progress monitoring might occur monthly or as often as every week, particularly with the lowest students, on targeted skills (e.g., oral reading fluency).
- students who score at adequate levels or higher on the screening instrument can be assessed less frequently, for example, three times a year (i.e., in the fall, winter, and spring).
- create graphs that provide visual displays of students' progress.
- evaluate progress-monitoring data regularly using a systematic set of decision rules to determine whether interventions seem to be effective for individual students.
- revise interventions as necessary in response to the data.

Or it could be that most of the students in the majority of classrooms do well, whereas in one or two classrooms a lot of students seem to be struggling. When this is the case, data indicate a classwide problem for which it may be most appropriate to provide interventions at the class level. When only a few students are struggling relative to their peers, then problems seem to be at an individual level, and individual interventions are warranted.

Using Progress Monitoring to Assess Students' Responses to Interventions

Whereas screening is used to assess *all* students to determine who might need additional support, progress monitoring is applied to individual students to assess their response to interventions. Like screening measures, progress-monitoring instruments are quick to administer and focus on targeted skills in the core curriculum. The purposes of progress monitoring are to closely monitor students' progress, to develop profiles of students' learning, and to assess the effectiveness of interventions so that changes can be made if necessary. These data can be quite useful if children continue to struggle and the decision is made to conduct a comprehensive evaluation of their strengths and needs. Progress-monitoring measures are administered frequently, perhaps once a month, or as often as once a week in some cases.

> ► **WEB RESOURCES**
> For more information on progress-monitoring measures and procedures specific to reading and mathematics, see the following Web sites: http://www.rtinetwork.org; http://www.centeroninstruction.org.

For a list of steps to follow in using progress monitoring, see Apply the Concept 3-7.

Role of Teachers

What is the role of the teacher within an RTI model? At a professional development session designed to improve teachers' knowledge of the RTI model at Sunset Elementary School, Mrs. Jacobs, a 20-year veteran teacher who had taught all grades from second through fifth grade, said, "I think I understand the basic principles of the RTI model, but I just don't understand what I'm supposed to do to facilitate implementation. What is my role?" Amanda VanDerHeyden (2009) indicates that teachers and other school personnel need to establish procedures to accomplish the following:

- Identify students who need intervention. This is typically done using a schoolwide screening in which students who fail the screening at their grade level are considered at risk and provided secondary or tertiary intervention.
- Provide evidence-based interventions that effectively improve learning for the vast majority of students receiving the intervention. Typically the secondary intervention (Tier 2) is provided by the classroom teacher. This may occur in small groups or individually. Sometimes teachers coordinate their Tier 2 instruction by working cooperatively with teachers in their same grade to provide intervention to a small group of students while the other teacher provides a large-class activity.

- Monitor the effects of the intervention to ensure that it positively influences learning. If the classroom teacher is providing the intervention, and if students in Tier 2 intervention are not making adequate progress, the teacher should consult with the special education teacher or school psychologist.
- Make decisions, in consultation with other key professionals, about the need for more or less intensive intervention so that monitoring students' progress through the tiers is possible.
- Meet regularly with interested stakeholders including parents, other teachers, and school psychologists to facilitate successful interventions and identification of students who need special services.

The teacher plays the most important role in implementing an RTI model. Because the primary focus of the RTI model is early identification of students who need additional assistance, the teacher is a critical link in ensuring that this happens.

> ▶ WEB RESOURCES
> Go to http://www.texasreading.org for specific research-based interventions and strategies for instruction.

Once a student has been identified as needing additional assistance, the special education teacher may be consulted. The special education teacher plays several important roles in a multitiered RTI model. These include

- collaborating with general education teachers and providing consultation services.
- helping to identify children with disabilities.
- offering intensive interventions to Tier 3 students.
- helping Tier 3 students access the general education curriculum.

Special educators may work with struggling students who have not been labeled as having disabilities. In some ways these are similar to the roles special education teachers assumed in the past, and in other ways they are quite different. These shifting roles will require some fundamental changes in the way general education and special education personnel do their work (Burns, Griffiths, Parson, Tilly, & VanDerHeyden, 2007).

Collaborating and Consulting

As with previous models, particularly coteaching and inclusion, teachers in an RTI model collaborate with other teachers (e.g., English-language development teacher, reading specialist) to provide students who have instructional or special needs with a seamless set of services. Special education teachers may still spend part of their day coteaching or meeting with general education

teachers to meet the special education students' instructional needs. The purpose of these efforts is to make sure students with disabilities receive accommodations and adaptations so that they have access to the general education curriculum and can participate in the general education program to the extent they are able.

Another way that teachers collaborate is by serving on RTI problem-solving (or intervention) teams that consider progress-monitoring data and other data and make decisions about teacher and student needs. Teachers provide their expertise when planning interventions or assessments. They are most likely the team members with the greatest expertise about learning difficulties and can offer insights about individual cases.

Using RTI Data to Identify Students with Disabilities

As you recall from the beginning of the chapter, one of the reasons Congress recommended using an RTI approach is that there was considerable concern about the validity of traditional practices for identifying students with learning disabilities (e.g., IQ–achievement discrepancy practice). For this reason, you are likely to work in a school or district that uses data from screening, progress monitoring, and other records related to students' progress in primary and secondary interventions to influence decision making about identifying students with learning disabilities.

How might this work? There is no uniform procedure used in all states; however, many states are using data they accrue during progress monitoring of students in interventions to facilitate referral and decision making about whether students do or do not have a learning disability. When students have participated in targeted interventions at the Tier 2 level and still do not seem to progress, the decision-making team may conclude that a comprehensive evaluation is needed to determine whether the students have learning disabilities. Not all researchers agree about how much and what kind of additional data are needed to make this determination. The National Association of School Psychologists emphasizes that RTI requires a "shift from a within-child deficit paradigm to an eco-behavioral perspective" (Canter, 2006). In other words, the data collected should include information about the instructional environment as well as within-child factors. For example, *within-child factors* that have traditionally been the focus of determining whether a student had special needs include cognitive functioning, which can be measured by an IQ test; academic functioning, often assessed by individually administered tests in reading, math, writing, and spelling; or functioning on such processing measures as auditory and visual tasks. The change in perspective provides less emphasis on these within-child factors and more emphasis on how students are performing in the classroom, whether students are meeting the academic and social demands of their grade level, and whether the classroom environment is conducive to learning.

Most experts agree that RTI data may not be sufficient to identify learning disabilities, but that RTI data should serve as the core of a comprehensive evaluation. It is likely that comprehensive formal and informal measures of the child's academic skills will be administered in addition to the screening measures, progress monitoring, and other assessment data already collected. The focus should be to develop a profile that includes information about the student's strengths as well as areas of need. The special education teacher and/or other members of the team would observe the child in different contexts to better understand the instructional environment and how appropriate it seems, as well as under what conditions the student seems to thrive or struggle. Observations should include a focus on how well the child is doing in comparison with similar peers.

A psychologist may or may not conduct an evaluation of the student's intellectual ability and cognitive functioning. Just how this is done depends on the state's and district's policies and what the problem-solving team decides is useful data. If the team has concerns about the child's mental and emotional health, the psychologist also conducts assessments in these areas. A social worker interviews the parents about the child's background and developmental milestones. The team collects additional information, such as about the child's attendance patterns. The family members are involved in the process as valued team members.

The teacher then works with the team to review and analyze all relevant data to make decisions about the best course of action for the child. They develop an intervention plan and set learning and, if appropriate, behavioral

goals. If the team determines that the student has a disability, then they develop an individualized education program.

See Chapter 1 to review the IEP process.

Providing Interventions

Using a research-based approach to instruction means that the vast majority of students (typically 80%) will be meeting grade-level expectations. These students will not need additional interventions. However, in some schools 20% to 40% of students will require secondary (Tier 2) or tertiary (Tier 3) interventions. What does this mean for the classroom teacher?

Depending on how your school is organized, you can expect to be involved in the delivery of the secondary interventions. This means that a subgroup of students will require additional instruction three to five times per week for 20 minutes or more. Typically this instruction is provided in small groups by the classroom teacher, a paraprofessional, a reading teacher, or other educators trained to provide interventions. Because these students may need instruction that is closely aligned with their instructional needs, the teacher providing the additional instruction uses the data from progress monitoring to guide instruction. Teachers will adjust the pacing of the lesson, provide adequate differentiation, select appropriate materials, provide students with ongoing feedback, and allow students adequate opportunities to respond with guided feedback. Providing students with appropriate feedback is essential to effective interventions. Apply the Concept 3-8 provides some examples of how to provide this feedback.

There are several helpful resources to help you with interventions. Apply the Concept 3-9 identifies considerations for implementing effective interventions.

Apply the Concept

3-8   How to Provide Appropriate Feedback

Following are examples of how to provide feedback to students that will result in an effective intervention:

- Nod, make eye contact with students, smile, and indicate approval.
- Use verbal praise providing specific feedback about what the student did well.
- Pat the student on the arm to indicate that he or she answered a question correctly.
- Repeat the students' response, adjusting it to indicate the needed

change, then ask the student to repeat the answer correctly.
- Write the student's response and then elaborate to extend or expand.
- Ask students to write a response and then give specific feedback on what aspects are correct.
- Describe why the answer or work was correct.
- Describe what the student could say or do to make the answer more correct.
- Summarize what the key ideas were.

- Summarize what students should have learned.
- Ask students to identify what they learned.
- Advise students to start the task again.
- Ask another student to build on what a different student has said.
- Show students how to make specific corrections.
- Ask students to explain how their work is correct or incorrect.
- Ask students to show you where in the text their answer was drawn.

3-9   Guidelines for Implementing Effective Tier 2 Interventions

- *Implement universal screening to identify students at risk for reading problems.* Develop procedures for screening all students at least twice a year (beginning of year and middle of year) to determine students at risk for reading or math problems. Provide students at risk with appropriate interventions.
- *Determine students' instructional needs.* Determine students' knowledge and skills related to relevant reading or math skills/knowledge expected at their grade level. For example, for reading it may be several of the following elements: phonemic awareness, alphabet knowledge, phonics, word reading, word or text fluency, vocabulary, spelling, and comprehension.
- *Form small same-ability groups.* For secondary intervention, form groups of students with similar learning needs. Group sizes should be as small as local resources will allow.
- *Provide daily, targeted instruction that is explicit, is systematic, and provides ample practice opportunities with immediate feedback.* Divide the instructional content into small instructional units (e.g., 3 to 5 minutes per unit) for each lesson.
- *Focus on the reading or math skills that have the highest impact on learning, based on students' current performance.* Provide modeled examples before student practice. Scaffold instruction and make adaptations to instruction in response to students' needs and to how quickly or slowly students are learning.
- *Follow a systematic routine.* Use clear, explicit, easy-to-follow procedures and sequence

instruction so that easier skills are introduced before more complex ones.
- *Pace instruction quickly so students are engaged and content is covered.* Maximize student engagement, including many opportunities for students to respond.
- *Provide ample opportunities for guided initial practice and independent practice.* Monitor student understanding and mastery of instruction frequently. Adapt instruction so that items are more difficult for some students and easier for other students.
- *Include frequent and cumulative reviews of previously learned material.* Reteach, when necessary.
- *Ensure that students are reading texts at the appropriate level of difficulty.* When students are reading text independently without teacher (or peer) guidance and support, levels of accuracy need to be very high. When students are reading text with teacher guidance and support, lower levels of accuracy may be appropriate. Reading accuracy levels vary from source to source. To calculate reading accuracy, divide the number of words read correctly by the total number of words read. Take into consideration:
  - *Independent level:* Texts in which no more than approximately 1 in 20 words is read incorrectly (accuracy level: 95%–100%).
  - *Instructional level:* Texts in which no more than approximately 1 in 10 words is read incorrectly. Students need instructional support from the

teacher (accuracy level: 90%–94%).
  - *Frustration level:* Texts in which more than 1 in 10 words is read incorrectly (accuracy level: less than 90%).
- *Provide many opportunities for struggling readers to apply phonics and word study learning to reading words, word lists, and connected texts.*
  - Have students practice reading words and texts at the appropriate level of difficulty (usually instructional level under the direction of the teacher).
  - Include the reading of word cards or words in phrases or sentences to increase word recognition fluency (often used with high-frequency and irregular words and words that contain previously taught letter–sound correspondences or spelling patterns).
  - Include comprehension instruction that introduces new vocabulary words, incorporates graphic organizers, and teaches comprehension strategies explicitly.
- *Include writing to support reading and spelling.* Have students apply what they are learning about letters and sounds as they write letters, sound units, words, and sentences. Involve parents so they support students' efforts by listening to them read and practice reading skills.
- *Conduct frequent progress monitoring (e.g., every 1 to 2 weeks) to track student progress and inform instruction and grouping.*

In addition to the instruction provided by the general education teacher, the special education teacher works one-on-one or with small groups of students in reading, math, or other content areas (Vaughn & Linan-Thompson, 2003). Instruction is intense, frequent, and of longer duration than at previous tiers in the RTI model. The special education teacher controls task difficulty and provides ongoing systematic and corrective feedback; progress monitoring continues. See Apply the Concept 3-10 for an example of how Marla conducts intensive interventions in her reading class.

3-10   Using Intensive Interventions

Marla is teaching a 30-minute lesson to a group of second- and third-grade students who are all reading at an upper-first- or a second-grade level. Progress-monitoring data indicate that all four students need to build their word study skills. During their first activity, the teacher asks students to review a previously taught word study component—words that end in *ide* or *ike*. She asks students to take 1 minute to write all of the words they can think of that have the -ide or -ike rime, or, in other words, are in the same word families. Marla lets them know when time is up, and they count up all of the words they have listed. The student with the most words reads them aloud, while other students check their lists to see if they have written down any words not stated by the first student, and read these aloud. This is a quick warm-up activity that also serves as a review of previously learned material.

Next Marla introduces two-syllable words that have an open vowel–silent *e* pattern: be-side, a-like, lo-cate, fe-male, e-rase, do-nate, re-tire, ro-tate, pro-vide, and mi-grate. The last two are "challenge" words because they include blends. Before the lesson began, Marla had written the words on the whiteboard at the front of the classroom, each with a hyphen between syllables. Each student also has a list of the words at his or her desk, one row with the hyphens in each word and another without them. Marla directs students to count how many syllables they see in each word. Next she has them mark vowels and consonants. She asks the students what they notice about the first syllable in each word, and then what they notice about the second syllable in each word (i.e., that all have the open vowel–silent *e* pattern). She points out that they have learned the syllables before

and probably recognize most of them. She asks them to look for syllables they know. Then together the students read the words.

Marla explains and demonstrates what the words mean. For example, for the word *erase*, she erases a word on the board, and for *retire*, she reminds the students that one of their previous teachers has retired. Students practice reading the words, first with the entire group, and then taking turns with a partner. Marla then asks students to look at the story they are reading today. She reminds them of key words previously introduced that they will see in the story. She also asks them to look at the title and the key words and pictures and to make predictions about what they will read or learn. She continues with the lesson, providing students opportunities to read silently and aloud and to ask and answer questions about what they are reading.

Using RTI Models in Middle Schools and High Schools

Because RTI was designed as a prevention approach, it is typically provided at the elementary grades. However, there are districts and school sites that are using RTI models with older students, particularly in grades 6 to 8.

Mr. Morris is one such teacher who worked at a middle school that is implementing an RTI model. As the science teacher, he was unsure what his role would be. He learned that all of the content teachers would be participating in professional development to enhance their knowledge and skills at providing vocabulary and comprehension learning to their students. This was part of the school's Tier 1 instruction and all content-area teachers (e.g., math, science, social studies, language arts) were participating.

His class consists of study groups supplemented with in-class modeling and coaching. Reading coaches, who are part of the research team, facilitate monthly study groups with content-area teachers, focus on effective practices for teaching students to read and comprehend academic (content area) text, including research-validated instructional practices targeting vocabulary (e.g., providing examples and nonexamples of words, semantic

feature analysis) and comprehension (e.g., question generation, summarization strategy instruction, strategic use of graphic organizers). Mr. Morris said, "At first I was skeptical but then I learned some very practical strategies that were actually helpful to me in teaching all of the students. The emphasis is not on preparing content area teachers to teach reading, but on giving them evidence-based instructional approaches to teach students vocabulary and comprehension in their specific content domain."

Mr. Morris went on to explain how their school uses RTI to provide secondary interventions for students identified as at risk for reading problems based on their low scores on the state assessment of reading. Selected teachers provide a standardized reading intervention to students who were at risk for reading problems but scored very close to grade-level expectations. Other teachers provided a more individualized approach to students who had more significant difficulties. Figure 3-4 compares the differences between the standardized and individualized approaches used. For a summary of reading interventions for older students with reading difficulties, see the review by Reed and Vaughn (2010).

Standardized	Individualized
Reduced instructional decision making	Increased instructional decision making based on assessment results
High control of materials used for instruction	Lower control of materials used for instruction
Highly specified curriculum	Low-to-moderate specification of curricula
Use of time specified	Flexibility in use of time to address specific student needs
High levels of fidelity to a single approach	Responsive to needs of students
Motivation results from success	Motivation considered in text selection
Systematic and explicit instruction	Systematic and explicit instruction
Fast-paced instruction	Fast-paced instruction
Ongoing progress monitoring	Ongoing progress monitoring

Source: From Response to Intervention with Older Students with Reading Difficulties, by S. Vaughn,
J. M. Fletcher, D. J. Francis, C. A. Denton, J. Wanzek, & J. Wexler et al. (2008), *Learning and Individual
Differences,* 18, pp. 338–345.

FOCUS Answers

► **FOCUS Question 1. How did we come to the RTI model?**

Answer: RTI addresses numerous challenges associated with past procedures for supporting student learning and identifying students with learning disabilities. Previous identification criteria focused on establishing a discrepancy between achievement and potential as measured with an IQ test. Yet this way of determining who qualified for special education turned out to be problematic for multiple reasons. Not all students who struggle and need special education demonstrate an IQ–achievement discrepancy. RTI provides an opportunity for schools to integrate a schoolwide approach to prevention and remediation of reading and math difficulties. As a schoolwide approach, RTI integrates school improvement. This entails coordinating screening, instruction, intervention, assessment, and progress monitoring, as well as providing ongoing professional development.

► **FOCUS Question 2. What are the components and implementation practices in an RTI model?**

Answer: RTI includes several key components. The first is high-quality, research-based instruction that is well matched to students' needs and implemented with fidelity by skilled, caring teachers. Additional components include schoolwide screening to assess the learning levels of all students and progress monitoring designed to assess individual students' learning over time. Thus, an important aspect of RTI is data-based decision making. Data are used to make decisions about which interventions to use, the intensity of interventions, and the duration of the interventions.

► **FOCUS Question 3. How does universal screening fit into RTI?**

Answer: Universal screening and progress monitoring are essential components of RTI. It is through these assessment procedures that data-based decisions can be made about which research-based instructional practices should be used to teach students. Screening is done as part of the first tier of an RTI model. All students are screened. Progress monitoring can also be part of the first tier, but it is an essential component of Tiers 2 and 3. The progress of all students who receive interventions targeted to their instructional needs is monitored frequently. The purposes of progress monitoring are to assess the effectiveness of the interventions so that changes can be made if necessary and also to develop a profile of the student's learning. These data can be quite useful when determining whether a student has a learning disability.

► **FOCUS Question 4. What is the role of the teacher in an RTI model?**

Answer: Teachers play several important roles in an RTI model. The most important role they play is to provide high-quality, research-based instruction so that when students demonstrate low reading or math skills, it is because they need additional instruction and not that their current instruction is inadequate. They may also assist with screening, progress monitoring, and providing interventions. They collaborate with other educators (e.g., special education teacher, English-language development teacher, school psychologist) and other service providers, offering consultation services and helping to identify children with disabilities. They also provide intensive interventions to special education students to help them reach learning objectives in targeted areas, such as in reading and/or math. In addition, they help special education students access the general education curriculum.

PEARSON
myeducationlab
Where the Classroom Comes to Life

The MyEducationLab for this course can help you solidify your comprehension of Chapter 3 concepts.

- Gauge and further develop your understanding of chapter concepts by taking the quizzes and examining the enrichment materials in the Chapter 3 Study Plan.
- Visit Topic 2, Inclusive Practices, to connect with challenge-based interactive modules, case study units, and podcasts that provide research-validated information about working with students in inclusive settings, by visiting the IRIS Center Resources.

- Explore Assignments and Activities, assignable exercises showing concepts in action through video, cases, and student and teacher artifacts.
- Practice and strengthen skills essential to quality teaching through the Building Teaching Skills and Dispositions lessons.

4

Promoting Social Acceptance and Managing Behavior

1. How should teachers arrange the physical and instructional environment of the classroom to promote appropriate behavior?

2. How can teachers use classroom management and positive behavioral support (PBS) to promote prosocial behavior?

3. What is the purpose of a functional behavioral assessment (FBA), and what are the procedures for developing an effective FBA?

4. What do we know about how students with behavior and learning difficulties feel about themselves, are perceived by others, and interact socially with others?

As Donna Douglas listened to her son, Jeff, playing with a classmate in his room, she closed her eyes and flinched when Jeff said, "That's not how you do it. I know how to do it. Give it to me." She hoped that the classmate would understand Jeff and not find her son's difficulty in interacting with others so disagreeable that the classmate would not return. Donna knew that Jeff was not mean or cruel, but he had a difficult time with interpersonal communication. He had trouble making and maintaining friends. He didn't seem to know how to listen and respond to others, and he often expressed himself harshly and inconsiderately.

At their weekly meeting, Malik's special education teacher's first comment to the school counselor was, "I feel let down. Malik and I had an agreement that I would give him free time at the end of the day if he brought a signed note from his regular classroom teachers that indicated his behavior was appropriate in class. After 3 days of signed notes and free time, I checked with his regular classroom teachers only to find out that Malik had his friends forge the teachers' initials. The teachers had not seen the note. Though this experience is discouraging, I remind myself that 2 years ago, Malik was incapable of spending even 30 minutes in a regular classroom without creating havoc. He has improved, and he even has a friend in the regular classroom. It is comforting to know that despite periodic setbacks, his social skills have gradually improved."

Jeff and Malik both have difficulties with social skills. Many students with learning and behavior problems have a hard time in school, at home, and at work because of how they interact with others. This chapter will help you to understand the social characteristics of students who have learning and behavior problems. It will explore how these students are perceived by others and how they respond to others. In addition, interventions that can be used to improve the social behaviors of students will be presented, along with programs and activities that can assist in teaching interpersonal social skills. First we discuss how teachers can effectively arrange the physical and instructional environment of the special education classroom to promote success.

PEARSON
myeducationlab

Visit the MyEducationLab for this course to enhance your understanding of chapter concepts with a personalized Study Plan. You'll also have the opportunity to hone your teaching skills through video-based Assignments and Activities, IRIS Center Resources, and Building Teaching Skills and Dispositions lessons.

Preparing the Physical and Instructional Environment

How should teachers arrange the physical and instructional environment of the classroom to promote appropriate behavior? As she completed her first year of teaching as a junior high special education teacher, Ms. Habib commented,

> I'm really looking forward to next year. The first year of teaching has to be the hardest. There is so much to get organized at the beginning of the year, so many decisions to be made, and so many new routines and procedures to learn. You need to determine how to arrange the room to facilitate learning, what materials to select or develop, and how to organize the materials so that the students can find them easily. You must decide how to group the students and how to schedule them into the room. In comparison to this year, next year should be a breeze. I'll be able to spend much more time refining my teaching skills, focusing on the students, and strengthening the program.

In many ways, Ms. Habib is a manager, as are all teachers. At the beginning of the year, management decisions are made at a fast and furious pace. We will explore some of the decisions that teachers have to consider in getting started, and look at some options they might consider in making those decisions. Many of the important decisions that you will be making will influence the classroom management and behavior of your students. Additionally, promoting social acceptance of students and managing the classroom to ensure positive behaviors is a critical part of every teacher's job and will be described in this chapter.

Arranging the Environment

The teaching–learning process takes place within a specific context. Making this context or environment pleasant and conducive to learning can facilitate the teaching–learning process.

For more on the teaching–learning process, see Chapter 1.

Instructional Arrangement The term *instructional arrangement* refers to the manner in which a teacher organizes instructional groups to promote learning and behavior. Inclusive settings require arranging grouping instruction with general education teachers. Generally, there are six instructional arrangements: large group instruction, small group instruction, one-to-one instruction, independent learning, cooperative learning, peer teaching, and classwide peer tutoring (Mercer & Mercer, 2005). Most teachers want to have the flexibility to provide for several different instructional arrangements within their classrooms.

Large Group Instruction In large group instruction, a teacher usually provides support or explicit instruction to a group of six or more students. Large group instruction is appropriate when the goal of instruction is similar for all students. Teachers often use this type of instructional arrangement when preteaching vocabulary, introducing reading comprehension strategies, reading aloud and asking questions, or proving information that may be useful to a large group of students. This arrangement can be used both for didactic instruction (i.e., instruction in which one person, usually the teacher, provides information) and for interactive instruction (i.e., when students and teachers discuss and share information). In large group instruction, students generally have less opportunity to get feedback about their performance and less opportunity to receive corrective feedback. Because large group instruction is the most frequently used arrangement in general education classrooms, students with reading difficulties can benefit from opportunities to learn in other grouping formats, particularly small group instruction.

Following are some activities that teachers can implement to make large group instruction as effective as possible:

- Ask all students a comprehension question, and then ask them to discuss their answer with a partner. This gives all students in the group an opportunity to reflect and comment on the question.
- Provide a whiteboard and a marker or paper and pencil to all students in the large group. Ask them to write words, sentences, letters, or answers as you instruct the group as a whole.
- Use informal member checks to determine whether students in the group agree, disagree, or have a question about an issue related to comprehension or story retelling.
- Ask selected students to provide in their own words a summary of points of view that have been expressed by several different students in the group.
- Distribute lesson reminder sheets that provide students with a structure for answering questions about what they learned from a lesson, what they liked about what they learned, and what else they would like to learn. This increases the likelihood that students will attend to lessons and learn more.

Small Group Instruction Small group instruction usually consists of groups of more than two students but fewer than six and is used when a teacher wants to provide very specific instruction, feedback, and support. Teachers form small groups of students who either are at different ability levels (heterogeneous groups) or have similar abilities in a particular curriculum area (homogeneous groups). One benefit of using small groups is that a teacher can individualize instruction to meet each group's specific needs. For example, during a cooperative learning activity in which students are grouped heterogeneously, the teacher is able to give a mini lesson to a group that is having difficulty working together.

Same-ability, or homogeneous, groups are often used for teaching specific reading skills because students can be grouped by reading level, particularly for beginning reading instruction. In using small group instruction, a teacher usually involves one group of students while the remaining students participate in independent learning, cooperative learning, or peer tutoring. Sometimes teachers who work in resource rooms schedule students so that only two to five students come at one time; thus, all the students can participate in small group instruction at once. Many teachers prefer using a horseshoe table arrangement for small group instruction because it allows them to easily reach their instructional materials and to closely interact with students.

See the section on coteaching at the end of this chapter for more ideas about how a reading specialist and/or special education teacher and general education teacher can work together to manage a variety of instructional grouping arrangements for reading in one classroom.

Following are some of the activities that teachers can implement to make small group instruction as effective as possible:

- Arrange your reading instruction schedule to allow for daily small group instruction for students who are behind in reading and several times a week for all other students.
- Provide flexible small group instruction that addresses the specific skills and instructional needs of students.
- Use student-led small groups to reteach or practice previously taught information, reread stories, develop and answer questions, and provide feedback on writing pieces.

One-to-One Instruction One-to-one instruction occurs when a teacher works individually with a student. This instructional arrangement allows the teacher to provide intensive instruction, closely monitoring student progress and modifying and adapting procedures to match the student's learning patterns. The Fernald visual-auditory-kinesthetic-tactile (VAKT) method of teaching word identification and Reading Recovery, discussed in Chapter 7, recommend a one-to-one instructional arrangement. At least some one-to-one instruction is recommended for students with learning and behavior problems because it provides them with some time each day to ask questions and receive assistance from the teacher. The major drawback of one-to-one instruction is that while one student is working with the teacher, the other students need to be actively engaged in learning. To accomplish this,

> The Fernald method and Reading Recovery are discussed in Chapter 7.

independent learning, cooperative learning, peer teaching, and classwide peer tutoring are frequently used.

Independent Learning Independent learning is one way to enable students to practice skills about which they have already received instruction and have acquired some proficiency. We frequently associate independent learning with individual worksheets, but computer activities or various assignments such as listening to an audio book, writing a story, reading a library book, or making a map for a social studies unit can also be independent learning activities. The key to successful independent learning is to ensure that the assignments and activities are ones that students have had significant practice in and have demonstrated that they can complete or initiate the assignments with little teacher guidance or feedback.

The key to effective use of independent learning is selecting activities that students can complete with minimal assistance. For example, when Miriam selects library books, Ms. Martino asks Miriam to read about 100 words to her, and then she asks Miriam several questions. If Miriam misses 5 or fewer words and can answer the questions easily, then Ms. Martino encourages her to read the book on her own. If Miriam misses 5 to 10 words, then Ms. Martino arranges for her to read the book using cooperative learning or peer tutoring. If Miriam misses more than 10 words and struggles to answer the questions, then Ms. Martino may encourage her to select another book. In fact, Ms. Martino has taught Miriam and the rest of the students in her self-contained classroom for students with behavior disorders the Five-Finger Rule: "If in reading the first couple of pages of a book, you know the words except for about five and you can ask yourself and answer five questions about what you have read, then this book is probably a good one for you to read."

Cooperative Learning Cooperative learning, sometimes considered team-based learning, occurs when students work together and use each other as a resource for learning. Four basic elements need to be included for small group learning to be cooperative: interdependence, collaborative skills, individual accountability, and group processing (Johnson, Johnson, & Smith, 2007; Michaelsen & Sweet, 2008). How can teachers establish interdependence with their students working in cooperative groups?

- Creating a learning environment in which students perceive that the goal of the group is for all members to learn, i.e., interdependence—everyone sees that it is to their advantage for all members of the group to succeed.
- Rewards are based on group performance rather than individual performance—thus better learners are motivated to support students with learning needs.

- All members of the group receive the materials needed to complete the task.
- Students have complementary roles that foster the division of labor. For example, one student may serve in the role of the group leader, another as the recorder of the ideas, and another as the team spokesperson.

Collaborative skills are required for a group to work together effectively. These collaborative skills can be taught to students explicitly by defining skills and their importance, modeling how the skills are used, allowing students to practice skills in cooperative groups, and providing students with corrective feedback (Klingner, Vaughn et al., 2004). Individual accountability ensures that each student is responsible for learning the required material and contributing to the group. Teacher evaluations (e.g., of quizzes, individual products) can help to determine whether each student has learned the material. Students can also use progress-monitoring forms to track their own behavior and progress. Progress-monitoring forms might include questions such as "How did I contribute to the learning of the group today?" and "In what way did I help or not help my group to complete our work?"

Group processing refers to giving the students the opportunity to discuss how well they are achieving their goals and working together (Johnson & Johnson, 1984a). Apply the Concept 4-1 provides additional guidelines for including students with disabilities in cooperative learning groups.

Two basic formats for cooperative learning are often used in general or special education classrooms. In a *group project,* students pool their knowledge and skills to create a project or complete an assignment. All students in the group participate in the decisions and tasks that ensure completion of the project. Using the *jigsaw format,* each student in a group is assigned a task that must be completed for the group to reach its goal. For example, in completing a fact-finding sheet on fossils, each student might be assigned to read a different source to obtain information for the different facts required on the sheet.

Johnson and Johnson (1975) suggest the following guidelines for working cooperatively:

- Each group produces one product.
- Group members assist each other.
- Group members seek assistance from other group members.
- Group members change their ideas only when logically persuaded to do so by the other members.
- Group members take responsibility for the product.

●●○●○●●● *Apply the Concept* ●●●○○●●

4-1 Guidelines for Including Students with Special Needs in Cooperative Learning Activities

When students with disabilities are included in a cooperative group lesson in the general education classroom, teachers may consider the following to facilitate their success:

- Adjust group size, and create heterogeneous groups of students who are likely to work well together. Would some students benefit from three students in a group instead of four or five? Are there target students in the class who work particularly well with students with special needs?
- Identify the strengths of the students with special needs and provide them opportunities to serve in roles in their groups that maximize what they do well and still provide them opportunities to learn. For example, if a student is a good public speaker, allow him or her to be the group spokesperson.
- Consider each student's individualized education program

(IEP) goals and academic strengths and weaknesses when assigning roles. For example, modifications in materials may be necessary if a student with below-grade-level reading skills is assigned the role of reading directions.
- Arrange the room to ensure face-to-face interaction between students and to make groups easily accessible to the teacher. Round tables work well, but chairs clustered together or open floor areas can also be used.
- Inform students of criteria for both academic and interpersonal success. Some teachers hand out a grading rubric with an outline of specific criteria for grading in each area of evaluation (e.g., creativity, neatness, group work, correct information, quiz).
- Provide mini lessons before and/or during the cooperative group activity to teach academic or

cooperative skills. Students need to know what group work "looks like," and many teachers conduct several lessons on how to work in cooperative groups before beginning the learning activities. Teachers can also provide small doses of instruction to individual groups during the activity, as needed.
- Monitor and evaluate both individual achievement and group work. Many teachers carry a clipboard with students' names and lesson objectives so that they can record student progress as they monitor groups.
- Reflect on the cooperative learning activity and note changes for future lessons. Did the lesson go as well as you would have liked? Did students learn the required material?

Cooperative learning can be used to complete group projects in content area subjects, and teachers generally consider it to have positive outcomes for students with learning and behavior problems (Jenkins, Antil, Wayne, & Vadasy, 2003). However, teachers perceive that cooperative learning has greater benefits in terms of self-concept than academic gains. The process approach to teaching writing employs aspects of cooperative learning. For example, students might share their written pieces with each other to get ideas and feedback about their writing, and in some cases, they write pieces together. Cooperative learning has also been integrated into several approaches to reading, math, writing, and even content area learning such as social studies and science. In future chapters you will learn about cooperative learning practices specifically applied to these instructional areas. Using heterogeneous cooperative learning groups in general elementary classrooms, the researchers found that these types of programs paired with cooperative learning facilitate the learning of most mainstreamed special education and remedial students.

> The process approach to teaching writing is discussed in Chapter 9.

Opportunities to participate in cooperative learning experiences are particularly important for students with learning and behavior problems. As well as supporting development of targeted academic skills, cooperative learning helps students experience positive interactions with peers and develop strategies for supporting others. In orchestrating cooperative learning, it is important to provide students with sufficient directions that they understand the purpose of the activity and the general rules for working in groups. Initially, a teacher may want to participate as a collaborator, modeling such behaviors as asking what the other people think, not ridiculing other collaborators for what they think, and helping other collaborators and accepting help from others. As students become comfortable in collaborating, they can work cooperatively in teams without the teacher's input.

Peer Teaching In this instructional arrangement, one student who has learned the targeted skills (the tutor) assists another student in learning those skills. This type of teaching takes place under a teacher's supervision. When using peer teaching, the teacher needs to plan the instruction and demonstrate the task to student pairs. The tutor then works with the learner, providing assistance and feedback. One advantage of peer teaching is that it increases opportunities for the student learning the skills to practice and get feedback (Maheady, Harper, & Malette, 2001). Peer teaching achieves this by allowing peers to supervise their classmates' responses.

One important aspect of peer teaching is preparing the students to serve as peer tutors by teaching them specific instructional and feedback routines to ensure success (Fuchs, Fuchs, Mathes, & Simmons, 1997). Students benefit from learning basic instructional procedures for providing reinforcement and corrective feedback and for knowing when to ask the teacher for assistance. For example, in Mr. Hyde's seventh-grade social studies class, students learned to work with peers to practice talking about the meaning of key concepts and terms. Each week, the key persons, places, and concepts are provided to pairs of students. As they are taught these key ideas they record them in their social studies folders. Students are then given 10 minutes to turn to their partner and review the key ideas related to these key concepts.

Remember that poor readers show academic and social gains in both the tutor and tutee roles (Elbaum, Vaughn, Hughes, & Moody, 1999). Therefore, it is important to alternate roles so that students get the chance to benefit from serving as both the tutor and the tutee. You may wonder how you might effectively integrate students with learning and behavior problems as tutors in your classroom? Research focusing on peer tutoring with special education students has most frequently been used to teach or monitor basic skills such as oral reading, answering reading comprehension questions, and practicing spelling words, math facts, and new sight-word vocabulary (Fuchs, Fuchs, Hamlett et al., 1997; Vaughn, Hughes, Moody, & Elbaum, 2001). In these cases, students with disabilities can be taught procedures for leading the peer pairing practice (e.g., reading the sight words on the card and then showing them to their partner to read), thus serving in the role of tutor. Peer tutoring improves a broad array of social and academic outcomes for students with severe disabilities, as well as increasing their access to the general education curriculum (Carter & Kennedy, 2006).

Another important type of peer teaching is cross-age tutoring, in which older students instruct younger ones. Cross-age tutoring has many advantages, including the fact that older students are supposed to know more than younger students, so there is less stigma about being tutored. Also, both the tutor and the tutee enjoy the opportunity to meet someone of a different age. Another aspect of cross-age tutoring that can be effective is allowing students with learning disabilities (LD) or behavior disorders to tutor younger students who also demonstrate learning or behavior disorders.

Classwide Peer Tutoring Classwide peer tutoring is a structured technique for improving students' reading abilities. Students of different reading levels are paired (e.g., a high or average reader is paired with a low reader) and work together on a sequence of organized activities such as oral reading, story retelling, and summarization. The reading material can be a basal reader, a trade book or magazine, or other appropriate material. The criterion is that the lower reader in each pair be able to easily read the materials assigned to his or her dyad. Peer pairing can occur within class, across classes but within grade, and across grades. This teaching takes place under a teacher's supervision. Peer teaching increases the opportunities for a student to respond by allowing peers to supervise, to model reading, ask questions, and generally support their classmates' participation in reading. When using peer teaching, the teacher needs to plan the instruction and demonstrate the task to the pair. The tutor then works with the learner, providing assistance and feedback.

Extensive research on classwide peer tutoring (e.g., Heron, Welsch, & Goddard, 2003; Topping & Ehly, 1998) and partner learning reveals that even students with disabilities as early as kindergarten (e.g., Fuchs, Fuchs, Thompson et al., 2003), as well as secondary students (Calhoon & Fuchs, 2003), benefit when the procedure is implemented consistently (e.g., 30-minute sessions conducted three times per week for at least 16 weeks). Students of all ability levels demonstrate improved reading fluency and comprehension.

Partner learning is not limited to elementary school or only as a means to enhance reading fluency. Studies have demonstrated that partner learning can also improve students' outcomes in world history, reading, math, and across academic areas (Maheady, Harper, & Mallette, 2001; Mastropieri, Scruggs, Spencer, & Fontana, 2003).

> ► **WEB RESOURCES**
> For further information on two related peer-tutoring practices view the following Web sites: Peer-Assisted Learning Strategies (PALS) (What Works Clearing House, Intervention: Peer-Assisted Learning Strategies, http://ies.ed.gov/ncee/wwc/pdf/wwc.pals); and ClassWide Peer Tutoring (CWPT) (What Works Clearing House, Intervention: ClassWide Peer Tutoring, http://ies.ed.gov/ncee/wwc/pdf/wwc_cwpt).

Physical Arrangement The physical layout of a classroom should be flexible enough to allow for different instructional arrangements. For example, the individual learning area can be reorganized into a large group instructional area by rearranging the desks. The small group instructional area can also be used for a cooperative learning project.

Following are eight ideas to keep in mind when developing the room arrangement:

1. To the extent possible, place the recreational and audiovisual/computer areas away from the teaching area. These areas will naturally be somewhat noisier than the other areas.
2. Place student materials in an area where students can easily get to the materials without bothering other students or the teacher.
3. Place your teaching materials directly behind where you teach so that you can reach materials without having to leave the instructional area.

4. If there is a time-out area, place it out of the direct line of traffic and use partitions that keep a student in the time-out area from having visual contact with other students.

> See Chapter 2 for principles governing the use of time-out.

5. Make the recreational area comfortable, with a carpet, comfortable reading chairs, pillows, and a small game table, if possible.
6. Place all the materials needed for a learning center in the learning center area. In this way, students will not be moving around the room to collect needed materials.
7. Instruct several students as to where materials and supplies are kept so that when students cannot find something, they do not ask you, but ask other students.
8. Establish procedures and settings for students who have completed tasks and/or are waiting for the teacher.

Instructional Materials and Equipment

Selecting, developing, and organizing instructional materials and equipment are important aspects of classroom management and promoting appropriate student behavior.

As a teacher, you will be making decisions about materials and curricula that you will purchase and also materials that you will develop. Some teachers tend to select published materials for their main instructional materials (e.g., sets of math materials that align with those used in the general education classroom, several reading programs each representing a different approach to reading such as linguistic and phonic approaches), then develop instructional aids and games to supplement the program (e.g., flash cards, sentence strips, recordings of the stories, board games).

Whether selecting or developing materials, there are several factors to consider:

- What evidence is there that these materials or curricula have been effective with students with learning and behavior problems?
- What curricular areas (e.g., reading, English, math, social skills) will I be responsible for teaching?
- What are the academic levels of the students I will be teaching?
- In what instructional arrangement(s) do I plan to teach each curricular area?
- How can the materials be used across the stages of learning (i.e., acquisition, proficiency, maintenance, generalization, and application)?
- Will the materials provide a means for measuring learning?
- Are the materials designed for teacher-directed learning, student-to-student learning, or individual learning?
- Will materials need to be replaced and do I have a budget to replace them?

Selecting Published Materials Besides considering the factors just mentioned, it is important to think of the cost, durability, consumability, and quality of published materials. Before materials are purchased, it is advantageous to evaluate them. Sample materials can generally be obtained from publishers or found at educational conferences or districtwide instructional centers. Teachers should read research reports that provide information about the effectiveness of materials. When research is not available, it is often useful to talk with other teachers who use materials to determine when and with whom they are effective. Sometimes it is possible to borrow the materials and have the students try them and evaluate them.

Because most teachers have restricted budgets for purchasing instructional materials, it is helpful to prioritize them according to need. Before eliminating materials from the list of materials you select, determine whether they can be obtained without purchasing them. For example, school districts often have an instructional materials library that allows teachers to check out materials for a relatively long period of time. You may be able to borrow the materials from the library rather than purchase them. Librarians are often interested in additional materials to order; it might be possible to request that they order the materials for the school library. Publishers are often interested in how their materials work with low-achieving students and students with learning and behavior problems. They may be willing to provide a set of materials if the teacher is willing to evaluate the materials and provide feedback about how the materials work with target students.

Selecting and Using Instructional Equipment In addition to selecting instructional materials, teachers will want to choose equipment to facilitate learning. Along with various software programs, such equipment is becoming an increasingly important part of a teacher's toolkit. In addition to a computer in the classroom and/or the use of a computer lab in the school, other equipment can facilitate learning in your classroom.

Recorder Tape recorders are relatively inexpensive and can be used in a variety of ways in the classroom. Headphones to accompany the tape recorder allow students to listen without disturbing others. Following are 10 instructional applications for recorders:

1. A teacher can record reading books so that students can follow along during recreational reading or use for repeated reading.
2. One way to adapt textbooks is to record them.
3. It is helpful for some students to record what they want to write before they begin writing. They can record their ideas and then listen to them as they write their first drafts.
4. Students can record their reading every 2 to 4 weeks to hear their progress. After a student records his or her reading, it is important that the teacher and the student discuss the reading, identifying strengths and areas that need improvement. This recording can also be shared with parents to demonstrate progress and document continuing needs.
5. Spelling tests can be recorded so that students can take them independently. The teacher first records the

---

Tech TIPS

USING COMPUTERS TO PROMOTE SOCIAL ACCEPTANCE

Teachers can use computers to enhance socialization skills by encouraging learners to work cooperatively at the computer. Activities that encourage students to make decisions and cooperate with other students can foster appropriate interaction whether they are playing games or doing a research project together.

Simulations, programs that require students to make real-life decisions, are popular options:

Zoo Tycoon and Zoo Tycoon 2 by Microsoft at www.microsoft.com/games/zootycoon
This program allows children to create an animal adventure together and to be part of an online community where they can ask the zookeeper questions or play mini games.

Sims 2 by Electronic Arts Inc. at http://thesims2.ea.com/
This is a current version of one of the original simulation programs. Children can create and be part of communities that they and others create. These programs continue to be creative, engaging, and highly entertaining.

Community Success by Tom Caine Associates at http://caineassociates.com/products/ community-success-p-76.html
This program is for students K–12. It allows children to practice social skills and learn about appropriate and inappropriate behaviors in different situations with the help of realistic illustrations and auditory cues. There are 45 activities that take place in a variety of settings.

words to be tested, allowing time for the students to spell the words. After the test is recorded, the teacher spells each word so that the student can self-check.

6. When working on specific social or pragmatic language skills (e.g., answering the telephone, asking for directions, introducing someone), record the students so that they can listen to and evaluate themselves.

7. At the secondary level, class lectures can be recorded. Students can then listen to review the material and complete unfinished notes.

8. Students can practice taking notes by listening to recordings of lectures. By using recordings, students can regulate the rate at which the material is presented.

9. Oral directions for independent learning activities can be recorded for students. This can be particularly helpful when a teacher is trying to conduct small group or one-to-one instruction while other students are working on independent learning activities.

10. Many instructional materials contain prerecorded resources.

Overhead or LCD Projector These excellent teaching tools allow users to display the images from a transparency or PowerPoint slide on a screen or blank wall. Transparencies or PowerPoint slides are generally teacher-made, although some come with published instructional materials. Using a projector allows a teacher to model a skill and to highlight, write, color in, and/or point to important information. For example, a teacher may use a projector to demonstrate how to add quotation marks to a story, or a student may use it to demonstrate how he or she worked a long-division problem. Using a projector can be easier than a chalkboard for presenting a lecture or leading a discussion because the overhead does not require a teacher to turn around to write.

The following are six suggestions for using an LCD or overhead projector:

1. Keep the amount of information presented relatively limited.
2. Use a different colored pen to highlight important points.
3. Have extra markers available.
4. Use the projector to develop language experience stories.
5. Use the projector to demonstrate editing and revisions in writing.
6. Use the projector along with a think-aloud procedure to demonstrate math procedures such as how to work long division.

Other Small Equipment Several other pieces of small equipment should be considered in selecting equipment for either a resource room or a self-contained classroom.

A stopwatch can serve as an instructional tool and a motivator. For some tasks, it is important that students learn to respond at an automatic level (e.g., sight words, math facts). Students can use a stopwatch to time themselves or their classmates. These times can then be recorded on a time chart (see Figure 4-1). Using these charts, students can set goals, record their times, and try to improve on previous times.

An individual writing board is an excellent tool for obtaining individual written responses during small group and large group discussions. Mr. Howell uses these boards during review sessions in his resource high school history class.

▶ **Figure 4-1** Time Chart

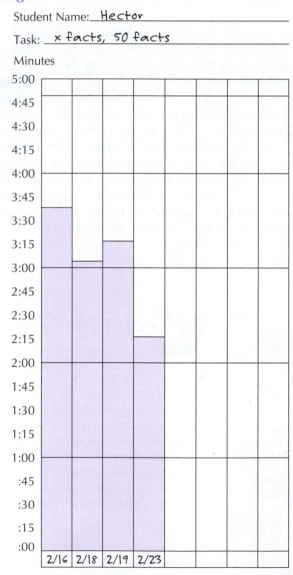

Student Name: Hector

Task: x facts, 50 facts

Dates

During the review sessions, he asks students questions, and they write their answers on the writing boards. He then asks them to display their boards. In this way, each student responds to each question in writing instead of one student orally responding to one question. Mr. Howell and the students believe that this is a better way to review because it requires them to think about and answer every question and to write the answers. Writing is important because it is generally required when the students take tests. Although small chalkboards can be used as individual writing boards, white boards and dry-erase markers are now readily available.

Developing Instructional Materials In addition to purchasing published materials and equipment, most teachers find the need to develop their own instructional materials to supplement commercial materials. For example, some teachers make sentence strips containing the sentences from each story in a beginning reader. Many teachers develop materials to provide students with additional practice in skills they are learning. Developing self-correcting materials and/or materials in a game format can be advantageous.

Self-Correcting Materials Self-correcting materials provide students with immediate feedback. Students with learning and behavior problems frequently have a history of failure and are reluctant to take risks when others are watching or listening. Self-correcting materials allow them to check themselves without sharing the information with others. Many computer programs and electronic learning games incorporate self-correction. Figure 4-2 presents an example of a self-correcting activity that teachers can easily make.

One key to self-correcting materials is immediate feedback (Mercer, Mercer, & Bott, 1984). The materials should be simple enough that students can learn to use them easily and check their answers quickly. The materials should be varied so that the interest and novelty level remain relatively high.

Another key to developing self-correcting materials is to make them durable so that they can be reused. Using heavy cardboard can increase the durability of materials. Laminating or covering the materials with clear contact paper are good ways to make materials more durable. Special markers or grease pencils can then be used.

Instructional Games Students with learning and behavior problems often need numerous opportunities to practice an academic skill. Instructional games can provide this practice in a format that is interesting to students.

▶ **Figure 4-2** Self-Correcting Activity

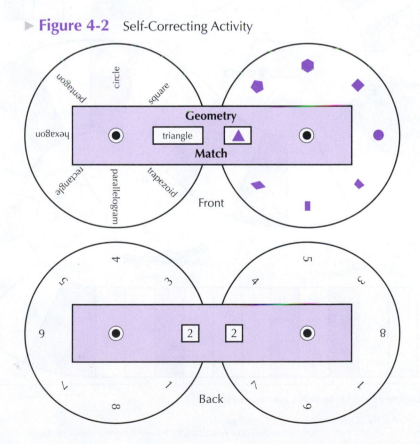

The first step in designing an instructional game is to determine the purpose of the game. For example, the purpose might be to provide practice in the following:

- Forming word families (e.g., -at: *fat, sat, cat, rat*)
- Identifying sight words associated with a specific piece of reading material being used in the classroom
- Using semantic and syntactic clues by using the cloze procedure (e.g., "For dessert Brian wanted an ice____cone.")
- Recalling multiplication facts
- Reviewing information (e.g., identifying the parts of a flower)

The second step is to select and adapt a game that can be used to practice a skill or review knowledge. For ex-ample, commercial games such as Monopoly, Chutes and Ladders, Candyland, Clue, Sorry, and Parcheesi can be adapted for classroom use. A generic game board can also be used (see Figure 4-3). Generic game boards can be purchased from some publishing companies. The key in selecting and adapting a game is to require the stu-dents to complete the instructional task as part of the turn-taking procedure. For example, when Candyland is adapted to practice sight words, students select a sight word card and a Candyland card. If they can correctly read the sight word, then they can use their Candyland card to move as indicated. When Monopoly is adapted for math facts, students first have to select and answer a math fact. If they answer it correctly, they earn the op-portunity to throw the dice and take a turn.

▶ **Figure 4-3** Generic Board Game

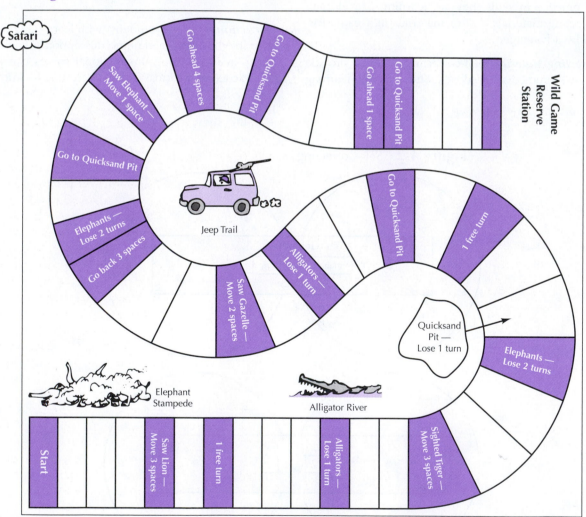

1. You are on a safari, trying to get to the Wild Game Reserve Station.
2. Begin at Start.
3. Each player rolls a die. The player with the highest number goes first.
4. Roll the die and draw a Game Card. If you answer the Game Card correctly, move the number shown on the die. If you do not answer the Game Card correctly, do not take a turn.
5. The first player to get to the Wild Game Reserve Station wins.

When the same skills are being practiced by many students in a class, the teacher may want to develop a specific game for the skill. Math Marathon is a specific game in which students move forward on a game board, depicting a race, by answering math word problems. Different sets of math word problem game cards can be developed, depending on the students' problem-solving ability levels.

The third step is to write the directions and develop the materials. MacWilliams (1978) recommends making a rough draft of the game and testing it. Posterboard glued to cardboard makes a good game board, as does a manila folder. With a manila folder, the name of the game can be written on the tab, and the board can be stored so that the students can scan the tabs to find the game. The materials for the game can be kept in an envelope inside the folder. The directions for the game and a list of materials that should be found inside can be written on the envelope.

The fourth step is to demonstrate the game to the students so that they can learn to play it independently.

Organizing and Managing Materials
Selecting and developing materials is only one part of effective materials management. Classroom materials need to be organized in such a manner that the teacher and students have easy access to the materials without bothering other students.

Ms. Beyar coteaches in a language arts classroom for 1 hour each day, during which the class is divided into either mixed-ability or same-ability groups, depending on the lesson. Ms. Beyar has several suggestions regarding managing materials in the general education classroom:

> The first thing Ms. Casey [the general education teacher] and I did was expand the student library. We purchased books that represent a wider range of reading levels. We also began to purchase small sets of books to use in reading groups. Finally, we worked together to organize a closet and a file cabinet with adapted materials and manipulatives that we both use. I find that these materials are beneficial with children of all ability levels. I didn't realize that we would benefit so much from sharing materials!

Scheduling

When teachers talk about the most difficult aspects of their jobs, they often mention scheduling. Special education teachers generally work with between 5 and 10 general education teachers (though it can be as many as 25 teachers) to coordinate pull-out, in-class, and consultation services. Special education teachers also work closely with counselors and teachers at the secondary level to ensure that students are placed in classes that will help them reach the goals and objectives of the individual education program as well as meet graduation requirements. Even special education teachers who work

in self-contained classrooms schedule students for integration into general education classroom activities for part of the day. It is essential that teachers work together to find time in the general education schedule that will be beneficial for the inclusion of students with more severe disabilities. In addition to adapting instruction, teachers need to consider whether students will have to be accompanied on their way to the general education classroom (by a student or a paraprofessional), and whether the classroom teacher or a paraprofessional will assist the students during the general education class.

When students spend most of their day in a self-contained classroom, special education teachers are responsible for their entire curriculum. Special education teachers make decisions about how to provide instruction in the various curricular areas (e.g., reading, math, writing, English, social studies, science, art, music) while still providing the students with adequate one-to-one and small group instruction so that the students can reach their educational goals in the academic areas of concern.

Scheduling within the Classroom
Whether teaching in an inclusion, resource, or self-contained classroom, it is important to use the time students spend in the classroom efficiently. There are no easy answers to scheduling problems. However, the following list presents some guidelines to use in developing a schedule:

- Schedule time to communicate with general education classroom teachers. The amount of time you schedule depends on the time your students spend in the general education classroom. Generally speaking, coteachers should schedule more time for this than resource teachers, and resource teachers should schedule more time than self-contained classroom teachers. While the frequency of such meetings will vary according to your students' needs, it is important that meeting times occur consistently. This time will prove invaluable in assisting students to be successful in regular classrooms.
- Schedule time to observe the classrooms in which your students are placed or are going to be placed. This alerts you to the class demands and schedules of the classroom, and will help you in planning for your students' learning in that classroom.
- Schedule time to meet with other professionals (e.g., speech/language pathologist, school psychologist).
- Alternate instructional arrangements. For example, do not schedule a student to participate in independent learning activities for more than 30 minutes at a time.
- Plan for time to provide the students with advance organizers, feedback, and evaluation. In this way, students will know what is going to happen, and they will have the opportunity to think about what they have accomplished.
- Allow for explicit instruction. Sometimes we have students spend the majority of their time in independent

activities, which results in little time for
them to receive direct instruction from the teacher, aide,
or tutor.

- Students who are included in general education classrooms still require specialized instruction. Organize time so that students with disabilities in general education classrooms receive the explicit instruction they need to be successful.
- Alternate preferred and less preferred activities, or make preferred activities contingent on the completion of less preferred activities.
- Let students know when the time for an activity is just about over. This gives them time to reach closure on this activity and get ready for the next activity or to ask for a time extension.
- Be consistent in scheduling, yet flexible and ready for change.
- Schedule a session with each student in which you review his or her schedule in your room and in other teachers' classrooms. Be sure that students know what is expected of them.
- Plan time to meet and talk with members of your student's family, including parents.

Figures 4-4 and 4-5 present sample schedules for a resource room and a special education program. For the resource room, the schedule for one group of students is presented, whereas the entire day's schedule is presented for the special education program.

Developing an Overall Schedule for a Resource Consultant Program Scheduling students' time while in the special education classroom is one issue, but the overall schedule for teaching in a resource or inclusion setting presents significant scheduling issues and requires that the teacher work closely with other teachers and professionals in the school. Teachers who assume roles as special education resource or inclusion teachers must first clarify and decide what their job responsibilities will be. Generally, these responsibilities can be divided into six general areas:

1. Providing direct instruction to the students, either in the general education classroom or in a separate classroom
2. Providing indirect instruction to the students by consulting with general education teachers and parents
3. Assessing current and referred students
4. Serving as an instructional resource for other teachers and professionals within the school
5. Planning, coteaching, and modifying instructional materials and/or assessments for students
6. Facilitating implementation of response to intervention (RTI) models in their schools

▶ **Figure 4-4** Schedule for Fourth- Through Sixth-Grade Students

Date: 4/15

Time	José	Amelia	Scott	Todd	Carmen	Frank
10:00	Small Group Instruction Reading ↓	Comprehension Computer Activity ↓	Small Group Instruction Reading ↓	Social Studies Text Using Request Procedure with Carmen ↓	Social Studies Text Using Request Procedure with Todd ↓	Small Group Instruction Reading ↓
10:20	Inferential Comprehension Activity on Computer	Small Group Instruction Reading ↓	Social Studies Text with Self-Questioning	Small Group Instruction Reading ↓	Small Group Instruction Reading ↓	Word Drill Social Studies Text with Self-Questioning
10:40	Writing Process ↓	Writing Process ↓	Writing Process (Computer)	Writing Process ↓	Writing Process ↓	Writing Process (Computer)
	Spelling	Spelling	Spelling	Spelling	Spelling	Spelling
11:15	Practice Computer	Practice Game	Practice Game	Practice Tape Recorder Test	Practice Game	Practice Game

Figure 4-5 Sample Schedule for Intermediate-Level Special Education Program

		Activity		
Time	Group 1	Group 2	Group 3	Group 4
8:15	Writing Process Students working on reports			
9:15	Reading: Small group instruction (teacher)	Reading: Independent learning activities	Learning center: Map reading	Reading: Small group instruction (aide)
9:45	Reading: Independent learning activities	Reading: Small group instruction (aide)	Reading: Small group instruction (teacher)	Learning center: Map reading
10:15	Announcements			
10:20	Recess			
10:45	Math: Group instruction (teacher)		Computer lab for Math practice (aide)	
11:15	Computer lab (aide)		Group instruction (teacher)	
11:50	Lunch			
12:40	Recreational Reading/Writing			
1:00	Social Studies: Large group instruction			
1:45	Science: Cooperative learning activities			
2:15	Recess			
2:40	Health—Mon./Art—Tues./P.E.—Wed./Special Activity—Thurs., Fri. (Current: Producing a play)			
3:10	Earned "fun time" or time to complete work			
3:30	Dismissal			

The time a teacher spends in each of these roles will directly influence the schedule he or she develops. For example, if the teacher's major roles are to provide instructional services indirectly to students, to assess current and referred students, and to serve as an instructional resource, then little time will be spent in scheduling groups of students in the resource room. Instead, the teacher will serve primarily as a consultant to others. A sample schedule for a teacher who provides direct and indirect support is presented in Figure 4-6.

By contrast, Ms. Beyar provides explicit instruction to most of the students she teaches for an average of 60 minutes per day, 4 days per week. Because she serves 22 students, she has developed a schedule that allows her some time to consult with general education teachers on a consistent basis, but she has also allocated time to teach and assess current and referred students. To facilitate her scheduling, she has for the most part grouped students according to grade level, with the older students attending in the morning and the younger students in the afternoon.

She explains her schedule as follows:

I have arranged for the older students to come in the morning because I feel that I can take over the responsibility for teaching these students reading and writing—the content that is usually taught in the morning in many general education classrooms. I have developed a strong program in teaching reading comprehension, and I am using a process approach to teaching writing. Currently I am using content area textbooks, trade books, and literature for teaching reading comprehension, and the students are working on writing reports, literature critiques, and short stories on topics of their choice. Because I am responsible for these students' reading and writing, I am accountable for grading the students in these areas. Using this schedule, these students for the most part are in the general education classroom for content area subjects and math. I feel that this is important. When they go to junior high, they will probably be taking general math, science, social studies, and other content area classes. If they have been missing these classes in the general education classroom during the fourth through sixth grades, they will really have trouble catching up. It's hard enough for these students—we want to give them every advantage possible.

I often provide their reading instruction in content areas such as social studies and science. Thus, while the emphasis is on reading rather than knowledge acquisition, I feel that I am extending their background knowledge of concepts they will be taught in social studies and science.

I have the younger students come after lunch, because I feel that many of these students need two doses of reading, writing, and math. These students get instruction in these areas in the morning in the general education

Week of: ___April 15___

Time	Monday	Tuesday	Wednesday	Thursday	Friday
7:30	IEP Meeting	Instructional Review Meeting (2nd grade)	Child Study Team Meeting	IEP Meeting	Instructional Review Meeting (4th grade)
8:15	Work with 5th-grade low-reading group →				→
9:00	Observe and assist LD/EH students in classroom (1st-grade)	Assessment	Observe and assist (2nd grade, kindergarten)	3rd grade 4th grade	5th grade 6th grade
11:30	Meet with individual teachers	Planning and material development →	→	Meet with individual teachers	Planning and material development
12:30	Lunch →				→
1:00	Work with 2nd-grade low-reading group →				→
1:30	Conduct study skills class for selected 4th–6th graders	Conduct social skills class for group of EH students	Conduct study skills class	Conduct social skills class	Conduct study skills class
2:00	Work with Ms. Jones on implementing writing process →		→	Work with Mr. Peters on using semantic feature analysis for teaching vocabulary	Assessment
2:30	Provide direct instruction in reading to 5 students with learning disabilities →			→	↓
3:30	Dismissal (check with teachers as needed) →				→
3:45	End of day				

classroom, and then I give them additional instruction in the afternoon. With this arrangement, it is important that I communicate with the general education classroom teachers so that we each know what the other is doing. We don't want to confuse the students by giving them conflicting information or approaches to reading.

I also have one day a week that I use for assessment, consulting with classroom teachers, checking on the students in the general education classroom, and meeting and planning with my teaching assistant. I feel that this time is very important. All of my students spend most of the school day in the regular classroom. If they are really struggling in those settings, I need to know so that I can provide additional support.

There are always some exceptions to the general guidelines I use for scheduling. I have three students whom I monitor only in the general classroom. These students see me as a group on my assessment/consulting day. We talk about how it is going and discuss what is working for them and what frustrates them. I feel that this time is critical for their successful inclusion. I also have 2 fifth-grade students who have good oral language skills but are reading on the first-grade level. They come for an additional 30 minutes late in the day, and we use the Fernald (VAKT) method to learn sight words.

I also developed a special schedule for my teachers' aide. She works directly with students to supplement and enhance skills they have initiated with me. She also provides supports to students with learning and behavior problems in the general education classroom by providing modified assignments, homework, and assessments.

Coordinating Services for Students with Learning and Behavior Problems Prior to Identification

Students with learning and behavior problems are more likely to be successful in general education classrooms both academically and socially when special and general education teachers work together. The practices that follow can be incorporated into a resource room model, inclusion model, or RTI model:

- Work closely with parents and key educational leaders to be sure you integrate their ideas about effective instruction and management.
- Observe students in all of the settings in which they are learning to determine their academic and social demands.
- Assist teachers in adapting materials, instruction, assessments, and the instructional environment to facilitate students' needs.
- Monitor the students once they are in general education classes.
- Meet regularly with the students to discuss progress and concerns.
- Communicate frequently with teachers to discuss progress and concerns.
- Suggest that classroom teachers use a buddy system in which a student with special needs is paired with a "veteran" to help the special needs student learn the rules, procedures, and routines of the classroom.
- Coteach to support the integration of students with special needs during instruction.

Special Considerations for Scheduling in Secondary Settings Scheduling in resource and consultant programs in secondary settings generally is less flexible than in elementary-level programs. Teachers must work within the confines of the instructional periods and the curricular units that students must complete for high school graduation. One of the major responsibilities for resource/consultant teachers in secondary settings is to determine subject areas in which students need special classes and areas in which they can succeed in general education classes without instructional support. These decisions about scheduling must be made on an individual basis and should be made with the involvement and commitment of the student as well as the teachers involved.

With the greater use of learning and study strategies in secondary special education programs, secondary special education teachers may want to consider their role as that of learning and behavior specialists. As learning and behavior specialists at the secondary level, teachers spend part of their day consulting with the content area teachers/specialists, coteaching, discussing progress-monitoring measures and how to administer and use data, and approaches to successfully transit. dents to postsecondary experiences (e.g., 2- college, work, or other professional training).

Classroom Management

How can teachers use classroom management and PBS to promote prosocial behavior? When someone mentions classroom management, most teachers think of discipline and classroom management rules. In fact, many special education teachers most dread the part of their job that addresses students' behaviors, largely because teachers think of classroom management as what one does *after* a student has a behavior problem. Another way to think about classroom management is to consider what one can do to establish a classroom climate that promotes desirable behaviors and reduces inappropriate behaviors. Thus, the majority of a teacher's classroom management efforts take place *before* any behavior problems. Students are taught to have expectations for the behaviors and routines of the classroom. Take a look at the Web site Positive Behavioral Interventions & Supports, designed to assist teachers in preventing behavior problems as well as solving them (http://www.pbis.org).

It is important to establish processes and procedures early in the year that provide students with a clear understanding of the class routines and the behaviors that are acceptable within these routines. Organizing these acceptable practices as a group and establishing them early is a critical first step for successful classroom management (Rogers, 2002). One way to inform students of the classroom rules is to discuss the rules with them. The more specifically a teacher defines what he or she wants students to do and not do, the more likely the teacher is to see those behaviors. For example, teachers should consider providing clear expectations about the following:

- When it is acceptable to talk with peers and when it is not
- When it is acceptable to move around the classroom and when it is not
- How students are expected to move from the classroom to other settings in the school
- Behaviors expected during typical class routines such as group work, whole-class instruction, and individual study time
- When and how assignments should be submitted
- What students should do when they have a conflict with another student

> *Rely on your mentors*

As new children enter the class during the year, assigning a veteran student as a guide or mentor can help the new student to understand the rule system of the classroom.

classroom rules is to regulate stu-
...ikely to disrupt learning and
...mage or injury to property or
... conduct rules, most class-
...les under which they func-
...1981). Sharing the explicit conduct
...ating the rewards of working within the
...particularly important for students with be-
...oblems. Making rewards contingent on full class
...cipation can also assist a teacher because students will
encourage each other to work within the rule system.

Ms. Schiller works with junior high students with emotional disorders in a self-contained setting. Establishing
conduct rules early in the year and setting up a reward
system for "good behavior" is an important part of her
program. Ms. Schiller comments:

> As far as I know, all of the students in this class are here
> primarily because they cannot cope with the rule systems
> in regular classrooms. This happens for a variety of rea-
> sons, and as a part of our social skills program, we dis-
> cuss some of the reasons and how to cope with them. But
> the majority of the day is focused on academic learning.
> To accomplish effective learning, we have a set of writ-
> ten and unwritten rules that the students and I are will-
> ing to operate under. We establish these rules at the
> beginning of the year during class meetings. In these
> meetings, we talk about how the school operates and the
> rules under which it operates, and then we decide what
> rules we want the classroom to function under. Usually it
> takes several days to establish these rules. The rules we
> generally decide on are these:
>
> - During discussions, one person talks at a time.
> - When a person is talking, it is the responsibility of
>   the rest of us to listen.
> - Work quietly so you won't bother others.
> - No hitting, shoving, kicking, etc.
> - No screaming.
> - Do not take other people's possessions without
>   asking.
> - Treat classmates and teachers with respect and
>   consideration.
> - When outside the classroom, follow the rules of
>   the school or those established by the supervisor.
>
> Each day when we have a class meeting, we discuss
> the rules, our success with using these rules, and how the
> rules have operated. Sometimes we add new rules based
> on our discussions. I involve the students in this evalua-
> tion and decision making. Eventually, we begin to decide
> when the rules can be made more flexible. In this way,
> I hope that I am helping the students assume more
> responsibility for their own behavior while at the same
> time maintaining a learning environment that is con-
> ducive to academic as well as social growth.
>
> I think there are three main reasons this rule system
> works in my classroom. First, the students feel like they
> own the system and have a responsibility to make it
> work. We have opportunities to discuss the system and
> to make changes. Second, we also establish a token

system for appropriate behavior
and learning. Third, I communicate regularly with the parents,
letting them know how their
child is performing.

See Chapter 2 for more
on token systems.

The classroom rules that a teacher establishes depend
on the social context of the school and the classroom and
the teaching–learning process. Some guidelines to use in
developing and implementing classroom rules and management systems follow:

- Have the students help in selecting rules for the
  classroom.
- Select the fewest number of rules possible.
- Check with the principal or appropriate administra-
  tive personnel to determine whether the rules are
  within the school guidelines.
- Select rules that are enforceable.
- Select rules that are reasonable.
- Determine consistent consequences for rule infrac-
  tions.
- Have students evaluate their behavior in relation to
  the rules.
- Modify rules only when necessary.
- Have frequent group meetings in which students
  provide self-feedback as well as feedback to others
  about their behavior.
- Allow students to provide solutions to nagging class
  or school issues through problem solving.
- Consider rules that are consistently broken and determine ways to provide time each day for students
  to appropriately break the rule. For example, if students are talking during class, tell them that if they
  are respectful to others for
  45 minutes you will provide
  them 5 minutes at the end of
  class to talk with each other.

The teaching–learning
process is described in
Chapter 1.

Classroom Management and Student Behavior

Lisa Rosario is a first-year, middle school resource-room
teacher in a suburban school district. She is not happy
with the behavior of the students who come to the resource room. She told an experienced special education
teacher in her school, "I feel like I know what to teach
and how to teach, but I just can't seem to get the students
to behave so that they can learn. What can I do to make
the students change?" The experienced teacher suggested that Ms. Rosario first look at her own behavior in
order to change the behavior of the students in her classroom. Figure 4-7 provides a checklist for teachers to evaluate the effectiveness of their interventions.

Ms. Rosario is not alone. Teachers identify classroom
management as a cause of stress and frequently cite it as
the reason they leave the teaching profession (Cangelosi,
2004; Elam & Gallup, 1989). Following are some guidelines

► Figure 4-7 Implementation Checklist

If your intervention is not working, consider the following:

- Have you adequately identified and defined the target behavior?
- Have you selected the right kind of reinforcer? (What you decided on may not be reinforcing to the student.)
- Are you providing reinforcement soon enough?
- Are you providing too much reinforcement?
- Are you giving too little reinforcement?
- Are you being consistent in your implementation of the intervention program?
- Have you made the intervention program more complicated than it needs to be?
- Are others involved following through (e.g., principal, parent, "buddy")?
- Is the social reinforcement by peers outweighing your contracted reinforcement?
- Did you fail to give reinforcers promised or earned?

for Ms. Rosario to consider to assist in facilitating more appropriate behavior on the part of her students:

1. *Look for the positive behavior, and let students know you recognize it.* Most teachers indicate that they provide a lot of positive reinforcement to their students. However, observations in special and general education teachers' classes indicate relatively low levels of positive reinforcement (McIntosh, Vaughn, Schumm, Haager, & Lee, 1993). Teachers need to provide a lot more positive feedback than they think is necessary.

One of the fundamental rules about positive feedback is that it needs to be both specific and immediate. "Carla's homework is completed exactly the way I asked for it to be done. She has numbered the problems, left space between answers so that they are easy to read, and written the appropriate heading at the top of the paper." A second fundamental rule about positive feedback is that teachers need to be clear about what behaviors are desirable and undesirable.

A clear list of class rules and consequences is an important step in making classroom management expectations understandable. Rules and procedures form the structure of classroom management (Brophy, 1988; Cangelosi, 2004). Procedures that are part of the classroom routines need to be taught to students. Rules outline the behaviors that are acceptable and unacceptable. Teachers' criteria for what constitutes a behavior problem is the basis for classroom rules (Emmer, Evertson, Sanford, Clements, & Worsham, 1989). Think back to Lisa Rosario, who indicated that she had difficulty with classroom management. In further discussion with the

experienced teacher, Ms. Rosario realized difficulty establishing and enforcing classroom p. Once the experienced teacher observed in her c. and assisted her in establishing routines, Ms. experienced significantly fewer difficulties with room management.

Positive reinforcement is more effective at the elementary level than in middle school, and least effective with high school students (Forness, 1973; Stallings, 1975). This does not mean that positive reinforcement should be avoided with older students, but merely that it should be handled in a different way. Elementary students find public recognition in front of the entire class more rewarding than do older students, who prefer to receive individual feedback.

2. *Reinforcers can be used to encourage positive behavior.* Both positive reinforcement and negative reinforcement increase behavior. Most people think that negative reinforcement means something harmful or "negative," but that is not the case. Positive reinforcement is the presentation of a stimulus (verbal response, physical response such as touching, or a tangible response such as a reward) following the target behavior, intended to increase a target behavior. Figure 4-8 lists reinforcers that teachers may want to consider for use in their classrooms.

See Chapter 2 for more on reinforcement.

3. *Use a token economy.* A token economy is a structured plan for delivering reinforcers (tokens) following the display of target students' behaviors and/or the absence of undesirable student behaviors. Token economies can be adapted for use in a variety of settings, and have been used extensively in special education. For example, teachers can post in the classroom a list of desirable behaviors (e.g., raising a hand and waiting to be called on by the teacher before talking) as well as undesirable behaviors (e.g., hitting classmates). Posted along with the behaviors are the corresponding number of tokens (e.g., points, chips, tickets) that students can earn for exhibiting target behaviors and eliminating noxious behaviors. Teachers can award tokens as target behaviors occur and/or deliver tokens after a specific period of time has elapsed (e.g., Terrell receives one token at the start of each hour provided that he has not hit a peer during the previous 60 minutes). Teachers can award tokens to individuals as in the previous example, or award the entire class. Either way, the underlying principle is that students will be motivated to earn tokens that are collected and exchanged for previously determined privileges (e.g., a class pizza party or first choice of equipment at recess).

4. *Change inappropriate behavior.* Behaviors that are interfering are the ones that teachers can most easily identify. It is much easier for teachers to list the behaviors they would like to see reduced than to identify behaviors that they would like to see increased. Morgan

...for behaving well.
...mselves, "I'm working hard and

...wn behavior.

...gnition from the teacher that a student is behaving
...priately, "Juan you are following directions on this assign-
...ent."

- Physical recognition from the teacher that students are behaving appropriately. Teacher moves around the classroom and touches students on the shoulder who are behaving appropriately.
- Teacher informs family or other professionals of the appropriate behavior of a student. This can be accomplished with "good news notes" or verbally.

Peer Recognition
- Teacher informs other students of the appropriate behavior of a student. "The award for Student of the Day goes to the outstanding improvement in behavior demonstrated by [student's name]."
- Peers can put the names of students who have demonstrated appropriate behavior into a designated box. These names can be read at the end of the week.
- A designated period of time is allocated at the end of the class period (high school) or day (elementary school) to ask students to recognize their fellow classmates who have demonstrated outstanding behavior.

Privileges
- Students are awarded free time after displaying appropriate behavior.
- Students are allowed to serve in key classroom roles after demonstrating outstanding behavior.

- Students are awarded passes that they can trade in for a night without homework.

Activities
- Students can perform an activity they like (e.g., drawing) after they complete the desired activity (e.g., the activity during that class period).
- Students can perform their tasks on the computer.
- Students can perform their tasks with a partner they select.

Tokens
- Tokens are items (e.g., chips, play money, points) that can be exchanged for something of value.
- Use tokens to reward groups or teams who are behaving appropriately.
- Allow groups of individuals to accumulate tokens that they can "spend" on privileges such as no homework, or free time.

Tangibles
- Tangibles are rewards that are desirable objects to students but usually not objects that they can consume (e.g., toys, pencils, erasers, paper, crayons).
- Tokens can be exchanged for tangible reinforcers.
- Tangible reinforcers can be used to reward the class for meeting a class goal.
- Tangible reinforcers may be needed to maintain the behavior of a student with severe behavior problems.

Consumables
- Consumables are rewards that are desirable objects to students that they consume (e.g., raisins, pieces of cereal, candy).
- Tokens can be exchanged for consumable reinforcers.
- Consumable reinforcers can be used to reward the class for meeting a class goal.
- Consumable reinforcers may be needed to maintain the behavior of a student with severe behavior problems.

Source: Adapted from S. Vaughn, C. S. Bos, & J. S. Schumm, *Teaching Students Who Are Exceptional, Diverse, and at Risk* (Boston: Allyn & Bacon, 2011).

and Reinhart (1991) identified the following guiding principles to assist in changing inappropriate behavior of students:

- Do not use threats. Consider carefully the consequences that you intend to use. Do not threaten students with a consequence that you are actually unwilling to use or that will force you to back down.
- Follow through consistently on the rules you make with the consequences you have predetermined.
- Do not establish so many rules that you spend too much time applying consequences. You will find yourself continually at war with the students.
- Do not establish consequences that are punishing to you. If you are stressed or inconvenienced by the consequence, you may eventually begin to resent the student, which would interfere with your relationship.
- Listen and talk to the student, but avoid disagreements or arguments. If you are tempted to argue, set another time to continue the discussion.

- Use logic, principles, and effective guidelines to make decisions. Avoid using your power to make students do something without connecting it to a logical principle.
- Do not focus on minor or personal peeves. Focus on the problems that are the most interfering.
- Treat each student as an individual with unique problems and abilities. Avoid comparing students' behaviors or abilities, as this does not assist students in self-understanding or in better understanding the problems and abilities of others.
- Remember that students' problems belong to them. Although their problems may interfere with your work, they are not *your* problems. Students with behavior or emotional problems are often successful at transferring their problems to others. Students need to learn to resolve their own conflicts.
- Students often say or do things that are upsetting to teachers. Recognize your feelings, and do not let them control your behavior. Do not respond to the

upsetting behavior of a student by striking back, humiliating, embarrassing, or berating the student.

- Solicit the assistance of families and students in putting any problem in writing to ensure that everyone agrees on what needs to be changed.
- Get student and family input on the behavior problem and suggestions for what might reduce it.
- Set up a plan that identifies the problem, consequence, and/or rewards for changes in behavior. See Figure 4-9 and Figure 4-10 for a sample behavior contract and a self-management plan, respectively.

Positive Behavioral Support

In recent years, the principles of behavior management have been applied in various community settings (e.g., school, family) with supports to reduce problem behaviors and develop appropriate behaviors that lead to

▶ **Figure 4-9** Sample Behavior Contract

Date: _____

Mr. Wangiri will give one point to Joleen when she exhibits any of the following in his classroom:

1. She raises her hand appropriately and waits for the teacher to call on her before responding to a question or seeking information.
2. She sits appropriately (in chair with all four legs on the ground).
3. When annoyed by other students, she ignores them or informs the teacher instead of yelling at and/or hitting others.

After Joleen has earned 10 points, she may select one of the following:

1. She may obtain a 20-minute coupon to be used at any time to work on the computer.
2. She may serve as the teacher's assistant for a day.
3. She may obtain a 15-minute coupon for free time.
4. She may have lunch with the teacher and brought by the teacher.

Joleen may continue to select awards for every 10 points earned. New awards may be decided upon by the teacher and Joleen, and added to the list. I, Joleen Moore, agree to the conditions stated above, and understand that I will not be allowed any of the rewards until I have earned 10 points following the above stated guidelines.

_____
(student's signature)

I, Mr. Wangiri, agree to the conditions stated above. I will give Joleen one of the aforementioned rewards only after she has earned 10 points.

_____
(teacher's signature)

▶ **Figure 4-10** Self-Management Plan

Name: Kiernen Smathers

Target Behavior: Submit completed homework to the teacher on time or meet with teacher before the assignment is due to agree on an alternative date and time.

Where Behavior Occurs: Mathematics and Science

Goals:

1. Kiernen will use an assignment book and write down the assignments, guidelines, and due dates. The teacher will initial these to ensure that he understands them and has written them correctly.
2. Kiernen will interpret what he needs to do for each assignment and ask questions as needed.
3. Kiernen will discuss any assignments with the teacher ahead of time if he anticipates not having them ready on time.

Time Line: Meet each Friday to review progress and assignments. Revise plan as needed.

Reinforcer: Kiernen will receive 15 minutes of extra time to work on the computer each day his assignments are completed.

Evaluation: Kiernen will write a brief description of the program's success.

enhanced social relations. This modification of behavior management principles is called *positive behavioral support* (PBS). Many schools find that they are coping with increasing numbers of behavior problems, fighting, bullying, discontent among students, and general lack of discipline. This situation does not exist because teachers or administrators are not caring or lack concern about the issue. It occurs because a schoolwide adoption of a consistent and fluent model needs to occur. PBS is a proven model for establishing a positive schoolwide community (Horner, Sugai et al., 2009).

The focus of PBS is to develop individualized interventions that stress prevention of problem behaviors through effective educational programming to improve an individual's quality of life (Janney & Snell, 2000). Because behavior is a form of communication and is often related to the context, PBS involves careful observation of circumstances and the purpose of a problem behavior. A significant number of negative behaviors can be dealt with by modifying the environment (e.g., altering seating arrangements). PBS also emphasizes teaching appropriate behaviors to replace the inappropriate behavior in a normalized setting (Janney & Snell, 2000).

Recall from Chapter 2 that applied behavior analysis is based on identifying observable behaviors and manipulating antecedents and consequences of these behaviors to change behavior. The application of these principles to change maladaptive behaviors is referred to as behavioral therapy. The three major components of applied behavior analysis are as follows:

1. *Target behaviors are defined operationally.* For example, a teacher described a behaviorally disturbed child in her classroom as "emotional." Although most of us know what *emotional* means, each of us probably imagines a somewhat different behavioral repertoire when we think of a student as behaving in an emotional way. In the same way, if asked to chart the emotional behavior of a student, it is unlikely that any two observers will offer the same observations. For this reason, teachers are asked to describe the behaviors that they observe when a student is acting emotionally. "*When I ask her to turn in her work, she puts her head down on her desk, sighs, and then crumples her paper.*" Identifying specific behaviors students exhibit assists teachers in clarifying what is disturbing them, and it also assists in the second step, measurement.

2. *Target behaviors are measured.* To determine a student's present level of functioning and to determine if a selected intervention is effective, target behaviors must be measured before and during intervention. Some behaviors are easy to identify and measure. For example, the number of times Val completes his arithmetic assignment is relatively easy to tabulate. However, behaviors such as "out of seat" and "off task" require more elaborate measurement procedures.

The three types of measurement procedures most frequently used are event, duration, and interval sampling. *Event sampling* measures the number of times a behavior occurs in a designated amount of time. Sample behaviors include the number of times the bus driver reports a student's misconduct, the number of times a student is late for class, or the number of times a student does not turn in a homework assignment. *Duration sampling* measures the length of time a behavior occurs, for example, the amount of time a student is out of seat, how long a student cries, or the amount of time a student is off task. It is possible to use event and duration samplings for the same behavior. The teacher might want to use both measurements or select the measurement procedure that will give the most information about the behavior. *Interval sampling* explores whether a behavior occurs during a specific interval of time. For example, a teacher may record whether a student is reported for fighting during recess periods. Interval sampling is used when it is difficult to tell when a behavior begins or ends and when a behavior occurs very frequently.

In addition to the measurement of the target behavior, it is helpful to identify the antecedents and consequences of the target behavior. Knowing what occurs before a problem behavior and what occurs immediately after gives important information that assists in developing an intervention. If every time a student cries, the teacher talks to the student for a few minutes, it could be the teacher's attention that is maintaining the behavior. Listing antecedents can provide information about the environment, events, or people who trigger the target behavior. An analysis of antecedents and consequences facilitates the establishment of a successful intervention procedure.

3. *Goals and treatment intervention are established.* On the basis of observation and measurement data and an analysis of antecedents and consequences, goals for changing behavior and intervention strategies are established. The purpose of establishing goals is to specify the desired frequency or duration of the behavior. Goal setting is most effective when the person exhibiting the target behavior is involved in establishing the goals. For example, Dukas is aware that he gets into too many fights and wants to reduce this behavior. After the target behavior has been identified and measured, the teacher and student examine the data and identify that the only time Dukas gets into fights is during the lunchtime recess. They set up a contract in which the teacher agrees to give Dukas 10 minutes of free time at the end of each day in which he does not get into a fight. The student agrees with the contract. The teacher continues to measure the student's behavior to determine whether the suggested treatment plan is effective.

Using time-out can help reduce problem behaviors, but it can also be misused. What is time-out? Time-out is when students are informed of the negative behaviors for which they will be denied access to opportunities for positive reinforcement (Alberto & Troutman, 2006). Some examples of time-out practices outlined by Ryan, Sanders, Katsiyannis, and Yell (2007) include the following:

- *Planned Ignoring*—This occurs when the teacher allows the student to remain in the setting, however, all attention from the teacher and peers is removed for a designated period of time.
- *Withdrawal of Materials*—All materials related to the behavior are removed for a specified period of time. For example, if a student throws a ball at another student in an aggressive manner, he or she is not allowed access to the ball for a specified period of time.
- *Contingent Observation*—Students are removed from the setting but are able to observe. For example, on the playground a student who exhibits inappropriate behavior watches from the sidelines for a specified period of time.
- *Seclusion Time-Out*—The student is removed from the setting and placed in isolation for a specified period of time.

When using time-out practices, remember the following guidelines:

- Use time-out as a last resort.
- Discuss time-out procedures with school administrators and parents before implementation.
- Put time-out procedures in writing, and file them with school rules.
- Provide students with information in advance about what behaviors will result in time-out.
- Place students in time-out only for brief time periods (15–20 minutes).
- Before placing the student in time-out, specify the amount of time he or she will be in time-out.
- Tell the student to go to time-out. If the student does not comply, the teacher should unemotionally place the student in time-out.
- Use time-out *immediately* following the inappropriate behavior.
- Establish contingencies in advance for the student who fails to comply with time-out rules.
- Always monitor the time-out area.
- When the time specified for time-out is over, the student should join his or her classmates.
- Provide reinforcement for appropriate behavior after time-out.

There are many treatment strategies in behavior support that teachers can use to effect change. For example, teachers can use reinforcers to shape new behaviors, reinforce incompatible behaviors, or maintain or increase desired behavior. Teachers can use extinction, punishment, or time-out to eliminate undesired behaviors. Figure 4-11 presents guidelines for using time-out. Teachers may use contracts or token economies to change behavior. These strategies are discussed in the section on applied behavior analysis in Chapter 2. With these intervention strategies, consequences are controlled by another (e.g., the teacher). Self-management is a procedure in which the individual controls the consequences. Self-management is particularly effective with older children, adolescents, and adults because the control and responsibility for change are placed in their hands. With assistance from a teacher, counselor, or other influential adult, the adolescent implements a self-management program by following three steps:

1. Identify the behavior the person wants to change (e.g., being late for school).
2. Identify the antecedents and consequences associated with the behavior. For example, Kamala says, "When the alarm rings, I continue to lie in bed. I also wait until the last minute to run to the bus stop, and I frequently miss the bus."
3. Develop a plan that alters the antecedents and provides consequences that will maintain the desired behavior. For example, Kamala decides to get up as soon as the alarm rings and to leave for the bus stop without waiting until the last minute. She arranges with her parents to have the car on Friday nights if she has arrived at school on time every day that week.

An obvious disadvantage of a self-control model of behavior change is that it relies on the student's motivation for success. Students who are not interested in changing behaviors and who are not willing to analyze antecedents and consequences and develop potentially successful intervention strategies will be unsuccessful with self-determined behavior-change plans.

Rick is a fourth-grade student who has LD, poor social skills, and difficulty interacting with peers. He was seen hitting other students and is known to get into fights for no apparent reason. A careful observation of Rick's interactions with peers and his behaviors suggested that hitting was Rick's way of saying, "Get off my back." Rick was taught to say, "Get off my back" and walk away instead of hitting. All the teachers in the school reminded Rick to "use his words instead of his hands" to communicate. He was taught other specific skills necessary for successful social interactions such as joining a group and initiating and maintaining a conversation. Teachers tried to pair Rick with other students during classroom activities to provide him with opportunities to practice his new skills.

In this case, Rick's behavior and the environment in which target behaviors occurred were observed. Once the causes, circumstances, and purposes of the behaviors had been identified, the classroom teacher met with other teachers to discuss and enlist their help in providing Rick with the support he would need. The teachers also developed a list of specific social skills to teach Rick. Over time, Rick's problem behaviors decreased, his social skills improved, and he made friends with a few students.

Kasim is a first-grade student with behavior problems. He gets in trouble for taking materials from his neighbors without requesting their permission. His teacher moved Kasim's desk closer to the end of the row so that he would have only three neighbors. She also taught Kasim to think and take out all the materials he needed to do a particular assignment—for example, completing a worksheet requires the worksheet, pencil, and eraser. She even placed a small box labeled "materials needed" on his table so that Kasim could place all the materials he needed for a particular task in his box and not have to borrow from his neighbors. The teacher also taught Kasim appropriate ways of asking others to lend him their materials.

In this case, Kasim's target behaviors and the environment in which they occurred were observed, and then the causes, circumstances, and purposes of the behavior were determined. The teacher then decided to alter the physical environment (by moving Kasim's desk) to reduce the circumstances in which Kasim could intrude on his neighbors. She also taught him alternative behaviors (organizing his materials) to replace his inappropriate behaviors (taking materials from neighbors).

Schoolwide Positive Behavior Support Models What does a schoolwide PBS model look like? The first step is to establish a primary prevention model in which the focus is on preventing behavior problems schoolwide (OSEP Technical Assistance Center on Positive Behavioral Interventions and Supports, 2009; Sugai, Horner, & Gresham, 2002). This requires ensuring that most school goals (80% or more) are stated in positive terms. The use of punishment is severely restricted to only emergency and very severe cases. This means that all school personnel know the positive rules that are established and that a concerted effort is made to ensure that all students are aware of positive school behavior and rules. School administrators are also actively involved in knowing and supporting implementation of the rules. This requires establishing contracts with students who have ongoing behavior problems to identify their needs and establish peer and adult support for changing their behaviors. Thus, ongoing progress monitoring is also an important feature. Though initially time-consuming to establish, PBS yields significant results over time, reduces behavior problems, and improves the school climate. For students with disabilities whose behavior problems are so profound that they interfere with their learning or that of their classmates, an FBA is required.

Considerable evidence shows that PBS can be taught to and used by parents/guardians very effectively (Lucyshyn, Dunlap, & Albin, 2002). Parents and other family members have successfully engaged students with severe problem behaviors in alternative behaviors and modified contexts that no longer support their behavior problems. How can this be done? Much like the procedures used by general and special education teachers with students with extreme behavior problems, family members can identify the behavior problems through assessment and then alter their feedback so that the child's behavior problems are no longer supported and thus become ineffective (Janney & Snell, 2008; Lucyshyn, Horner, Dunlap, Albin, & Ben, 2002). This yields more positive and constructive parent–child interactions.

Developing a Functional Behavioral Assessment

What is the purpose of an FBA, and what are the procedures for developing an effective FBA? According to the Individuals with Disabilities Education Act (IDEA), students with disabilities who have significant behavior problems that interfere with their own learning or with the learning of other students must have an FBA. An FBA and a behavioral improvement plan (BIP) are designed to identify behavior problems of students and to develop an intervention plan to treat these behavior problems. The procedures and practices for developing a BIP are not nearly as well defined as are those for an IEP, and many school personnel still are unclear about how and when to conduct FBAs and design BIPs. Because it is much more likely that an FBA and BIP will assist a student than it will interfere, it is always a good idea to conduct a FBA and develop BIP.

According to Shippen, Simpson, and Crites (2003) and the Positive Behavioral Interventions and Support Technical Assistance Center (PBIS@oregon.uoregon.edu), there are several critical steps in conducting an effective FBA:

1. Define the target behavior in behavioral terms. Clearly specify the behavior(s) you would like to see the student perform in observational terms that can be recorded and monitored.
2. Collect and monitor the target behaviors through ongoing data collection that considers frequency, intensity, and rate.
3. Record the events and behaviors that precede and follow the target behavior. In this way, the antecedent, behavior, and consequences are noted.
4. Develop a hypothesis of the conditions under which the target behavior occurs. This hypothesis guides the intervention plan.
5. Develop an intervention plan that considers the antecedents and reinforcers and is built to test the hypothesis.

Figure 4-12 provides an example of an FBA.

Response to Intervention and Classroom Behavioral Support

Many of the fundamental principles of RTI have been used to support appropriate schoolwide behavior. For example, Sugai and colleagues (Fairbanks, Sugai, Guardino, & Lathrop, 2007; Sugai et al., 2000) emphasized graduated levels of social support as a means of improving schoolwide behavior as well as for addressing the social and behavioral problems of individual students. What does RTI mean with respect to social behavior issues?

- *Tier I:* As part of a schoolwide behavioral support program, a school might screen for behavior problems and introduce increasingly intensive interventions to meet school, teacher, and student needs. Schoolwide expectations establish appropriate consequences and procedures for reviewing progress toward schoolwide goals. Practices at the classroom level include opportunities for students to participate and be engaged in classroom activities; positive support for appropriate behavior; minimizing transition time between activities; and ongoing feedback and support for academics and social behavior.
- *Tier II:* In a behavioral support model, students who display similar behavior problems might be provided

with an intervention that provides additional supports, prompts, feedback, and acknowledgment to ensure that behavioral changes occur.
- *Tier III:* If the combination of a schoolwide behavioral support model and group interventions is not associated with improved behavioral outcomes, then more specific and intensive interventions focused at the student level are introduced and monitored.

Social Difficulties

What do we know about how students with behavior and learning difficulties feel about themselves, are perceived by others, and interact socially with others? Students with behavior problems often have social difficulties. More than 75% of students with behavior problems have problems significant enough for the students to be classified as in need of clinical intervention (Nelson, Babyak, Gonzalez, & Benner, 2003). But what about students with LD? This section discusses the social characteristics of students with LD and describes the social problems associated with adolescents.

Perceptions of Students with Social Difficulties

The social interaction of students with behavior disorders is often described as having two dimensions: externalizing and internalizing (Cooper & Bilton, 2002). Externalizing behaviors are those that are extremely disturbing or intolerable to others (e.g., aggression, hyperactivity, delinquency). Conversely, internalizing behaviors are those that are more likely to adversely affect the student who displays them than other people (e.g., depression, immaturity, obsessive–compulsive behavior, shyness).

Students with behavior disorders who exhibit externalizing behaviors appear to be experts at identifying and performing the behaviors that are most disturbing to others. Donald, in the following example, is a student who exhibits externalizing behaviors.

When Mr. Kline discovered that Donald was to be placed in his fourth-grade class next year, his stomach did a flip-flop. "Any student but Donald," thought Mr. Kline, "he's the terror of the school." Every teacher who had had Donald in class had come to the teachers' lounge at the end of the day exhausted and discouraged. The real catastrophe was the effect Donald seemed to have on the rest of the class. Mild behavior problems in other students seemed to worsen with Donald's encouragement. Donald's hot temper and foul language left him continually fighting with other students. This year, he had hit his teacher in the chest when she had tried to prevent him from running out of the classroom. While escaping, he shouted, "I'll sue you if you touch me." Mr. Kline had once seen Donald running at full speed down the hall, knocking over students along the way, and screeching as though he were putting on brakes

► **Figure 4-12**   A Sample Functional Behavioral Assessment

Target Behavior I: _____

Baseline Assessment Method:
    parent interview
    teacher interview
    checklists
    systematic observation
    frequency counts of target behaviors
    sequence analysis (required)
    norm-referenced assessments

Baseline Frequency of Target Behavior:
_____
_____
_____
_____
_____
_____
_____

Target Behavior II: _____

Baseline Assessment Method:
    parent interview
    teacher interview
    checklists
    systematic observation
    frequency counts of target behaviors
    sequence analysis (required)
    norm-referenced assessments

Baseline Frequency of Target Behavior:
_____
_____
_____
_____
_____
_____
_____

Target Behavior III: _____

Baseline Assessment Method:
    parent interview
    teacher interview
    checklists
    systematic observation
    frequency counts of target behaviors
    sequence analysis (required)
    norm-referenced assessments

Baseline Frequency of Target Behavior:
_____
_____
_____
_____
_____
_____
_____

Purpose of target Behavior I:

1. To obtain something?   yes   no   what? _____
2. To escape/avoid something? yes no what? _____
3. Other factors?   yes   no   what? _____
Hypothesis: _____
Replacement Behavioral Goal: _____
Necessary Skills?   yes   no, needs additional instruction in _____

Purpose of target Behavior II:

1. To obtain something?   yes   no   what? _____
2. To escape/avoid something? yes no what? _____
3. Other factors?   yes   no   what? _____
Hypothesis: _____
Replacement Behavioral Goal: _____
Necessary Skills?   yes   no, needs additional instruction in _____

Purpose of target Behavior III:

1. To obtain something?   yes   no   what? _____
2. To escape/avoid something? yes no what? _____
3. Other factors?   yes   no   what? _____
Hypothesis: _____
Replacement Behavioral Goal: _____
Necessary Skills?   yes   no,   needs additional instruction in _____

as he swerved into his classroom. Mr. Kline knew that next year was going to be a difficult one.

Students like Donald are frequently avoided by more socially competent students in class and are disliked and feared by other class members. They are loners who move from one group to the next after alienating group members, or they develop friendships with other students whose behavior is also disturbing to others. These students present extremely difficult classroom management problems.

Students with behavior disorders who exhibit internalizing behaviors are often less disturbing to others but

Student Name: _____   School: _____   Meeting Date: _____

Submitting Teacher: _____   Beginning Date: _____   Review/End Date: _____

Functional Behavioral Assessment Worksheet
(Sequence Analysis)

Antecedent	Behavior of Concern	Consequence

I. Committee Determined Target Behaviors

1. _____

2. _____

3. _____

The following persons attended and participated in the FBA meeting:

Name:	Position:	Date:
_____	Parent	_____
_____	LEA Represintative	_____
_____	Special Education Teacher	
_____	Student	
_____	General Education Teacher	
_____	_____	_____
_____	_____	_____
_____	_____	_____

Method for Reporting Progress to Parent: **Frequency for Reporting Progress to Parent:**

☐ progress report   _____

☐ parent confernce   _____

☐ other   _____

Source: M. E. Shippen, R. G. Simpson, & S. A. Crites (2003, May/June), A practical guide to functional behavioral assessment, *Teaching Exceptional Children, 35,* pp. 43–44. Copyright © 2003 by the Council for Exceptional Children. Reprinted with permission.

frequently create concern because of their bizarre behavior. Elisa, in the following example, is a student who exhibits internalizing behaviors.

Elisa, a fifth grader, had just moved to the area. Her mother brought Elisa to register for school but refused to speak with the school secretary. Instead, she demanded that she be allowed to register Elisa with the school principal. Elisa's mother told the school principal that Elisa would sometimes act "funny" to get attention and should be told to stop as soon as she tried it. The principal noted that Elisa had not said one word. In fact, she had sat in a chair next to her mother looking down and rocking gently. Elisa's mother said that Elisa had been receiving special education services during part of the day and was in a regular classroom most of the day. In the regular classroom, Elisa was a loner. She spoke to no one. When another student approached her, Elisa reared back and scratched into the air with her long fingernails, imitating a cat. If other children said something to her, Elisa would "hiss" at them. She would sit in the room, usually completing her assignments and, whenever possible, practicing writing elaborate cursive letters with her multicolored pen. She spent most of the day rocking. She even rocked while she worked.

Problems like Elisa's are usually thought of as being internal and resulting from a unique pathology. Other classmates, recognizing that these children are very different, may attempt to interact, but they are usually rebuffed. Students with internalizing behaviors are easy victims for students whose problem behaviors are more externalizing.

It is important to note that not all youngsters with behavior problems demonstrate either externalizing or internalizing problems. Many youngsters with behavior disorders display both externalizing and internalizing problems. This is not difficult to understand if one imagines a child who is often shy and withdrawn who, when frustrated or forced to interact with others, becomes aggressive and acts out.

Externalizing and internalizing behaviors are more frequently characteristics of students with behavior problems than of students with LD. Students with LD typically display less severe emotional and behavior difficulties. However, many students with LD have difficulties in making and maintaining positive interpersonal relationships with others. When compared with their peers without LD, students with LD are

- inconsistent and less effective in displaying appropriate conversational skills, and exhibit difficulties in developing these skills (Hartas & Donahue, 1997; Westwood, 2003).
- identified as being more poorly accepted by their peers even as early as kindergarten (Tur-Kaspa, 2004; Vaughn, Elbaum, & Schumm, 1996; Vaughn, McIntosh, & Spencer-Rowe, 1991; Wiener & Tardif, 2004).
- at greater risk for social alienation and rejection by teachers and classmates (Montague & Rinaldi, 2001; Seidel & Vaughn, 1991).
- more likely to be rejected, neglected, and unaccepted by peers (Kuhne & Wiener, 2000; Wiener, 2002).
- perceived as having lower social status and social skills (Le Mare & de la Ronde, 2000; Stone & LaGreca, 1990).
- less accepted by peers even before being identified as having LD (Vaughn, Hogan, Kouzekanani, & Shapiro, 1990).

- more willing to conform to peer pressure to engage in antisocial activities (Bryan, Pearl, & Fallon, 1989; Farmer, Pearl, & Van Acker, 1996).
- less likely than other students to interact with teachers and classmates (Greenham, 1999; McIntosh et al., 1993).
- more likely to demonstrate higher levels of depression than general education students (Heath & Wiener, 1996; Howard & Tryon, 2002).
- more likely to report higher rates of loneliness and more concern and worry about their close personal relationships (Al-Yagon & Mikulincer, 2004).

Unfortunately, the lower social status of students with LD reflects not only the perceptions of peers but also of teachers. Teachers perceive these students as less socially competent and less desirable to have in the classroom (Juvonen & Bear, 1992; Vaughn, Schumm, Jallad, Slusher, & Saumell, 1996). However, findings indicate that teachers' perceptions of these students may be influenced by students' academic self-perceptions and that a cyclical relationship may exist between the two. Meltzer et al. (2004) found that students with LD who exhibited positive academic self-perceptions were more likely to work hard and use strategies in their schoolwork than those who exhibited negative academic self-perceptions. Students with LD with positive academic self-perceptions were rated by their teachers as working as hard as, and academically performing similar to, their peers without LD. However, teachers rated students with LD with negative academic self-perceptions as achieving at below average level in comparison to their peers, and as making limited efforts.

In general education classrooms where youngsters with LD are accepted by their teachers, they are also accepted by their peers (Vaughn, McIntosh, Schumm, Haager, & Callwood, 1993). In such classrooms, these students are as well accepted and have as many friends as other students. It can be speculated that teachers in inclusive settings spend more time with students with LD and therefore have different views toward these students. Wiener and Tardif (2004) found that children in more inclusive settings were better accepted by their peers and had fewer teacher-rated problem behaviors. Thus, an important role of special education teachers is to assist general education teachers in seeing the many positive outcomes of treating students with special needs as accepted members of the classroom.

The educational setting in which students are placed can affect the number of reciprocal friendships that students make and maintain. Reciprocal friends are two students who independently nominate each other as friends. For example, both Marta and Indira write down each other's names on a list of friends. Low-achieving students, average-achieving students, and those with LD demonstrated an increased number of reciprocal friendships in inclusive settings. In these settings, the special and general education teachers coplanned, and the special education teacher provided a range of services in the classroom, such as working individually or with small groups of students with LD and leading lessons and demonstrating adaptations. Students in classrooms where the special education teacher cotaught with the general education teacher for the entire day did not make similar gains (Vaughn, Elbaum, Schumm, & Hughes, 1998). However, a recent study found that although students in self-contained special education classes reported a similar number of friends as students in inclusive settings, these children also reported a lower quality of friendship and more loneliness than their peers in inclusive settings (Wiener & Tardif, 2004). These studies suggest that a classroom climate of high acceptance and expectations can enhance mutual regard and acceptance of students with LD and low-achieving students, and may actually contribute to the quality of their friendships. Apply the Concept 4-2 describes a study examining the social outcomes of students with LD in four different classroom types.

In discussing the social skills of students with LD and how others perceive them, it is important to realize that we are talking generally about students with LD. Not all students with LD have social difficulties. Many of them are socially competent, making and maintaining friends and struggling to please their teachers and parents. Many adults with LD who are participating in postsecondary education programs identify their social skills as their strengths.

Characteristics of Students with Social Disabilities

We expect students with behavior disorders to have difficulty in successfully interacting with others. Students with behavior disorders are identified and placed in special programs because their social problems are so interfering that these students are unable to function adequately with only the services provided within the general education classroom.

Social Interaction The type and quality of interactions that students with LD engage in are different from those of their peers.

In one of the few studies that have been conducted to examine general education teachers' behavior toward middle and high school students with LD (McIntosh et al., 1993), the findings indicated that middle and high school teachers do not treat students with LD differently from other students in the classroom. There are, of course, positive and negative sides to this finding. From a positive

● ● ● ● ● ● *Apply the Concept* ● ● ● ● ● ●

4-2 Does Inclusion Improve the Social and Emotional Functioning of Students with Learning Disabilities?

A primary rationale for placing students with LD in more inclusive settings is that these settings are expected to reduce students' social difficulties and promote peer acceptance and social adjustment. A recent study examined the social acceptance, number of friends, quality of relationships, self-concept, loneliness, and social skills of students with LD and their peers without LD across four educational settings related to the level of intensity of academic support required by the student (Wiener & Tardif, 2004):

High-Intensity Support of Student with LD

- Special education placement for at least 50% of the school day

- Inclusion in general education setting all day. Classes were co-taught by a special education and a general education teacher

Low-Intensity Support of Student with LD

- Resource-room setting for 30 to 90 minutes per day
- Inclusion in general education setting all day with in-class support from the special education teacher for 30 to 90 minutes a day

Overall, the largest and greatest number of findings were differences in social functioning between students with LD and their classmates without LD, regardless of setting.

Regardless of the type of program a student attended (resource, inclusion, self-contained), students with LD scored lower on all aspects of social functioning (e.g., social skills, loneliness, social acceptance, number of friends) than did their classmates without LD.

The social skills of students in more inclusive settings were better than those of students in resource or self-contained settings. For example, students with LD in inclusive classrooms perceived their classmates as better companions, and they were less lonely. Teachers also perceived these students' behavior as less problematic.

perspective, teachers treated all students fairly and impartially, and although praise was given infrequently, it was given at the same rate both to students with LD and to students without LD. From a negative perspective, youngsters with LD interacted infrequently with the teacher, other students, and classroom activities, and teachers made few, if any, adaptations to increase the involvement or ensure the learning of these students.

However, students with LD can be taught specific behaviors to increase positive teacher and peer attention (Alber, Heward, & Hippler, 1999; Wolford, Heward, & Alber, 2001). In one study, students with LD were taught to show their work to the teacher and ask questions such as "How am I doing?" The results indicated that students who asked questions received more positive teacher attention and instructional feedback. These students also completed their workbook assignments with increased accuracy (Alber et al., 1999). A second study found that when students with LD were taught how to recruit positive peer assistance, they were found to decrease the number of inappropriate recruiting responses, to decrease negative statements from peers and increase positive statements, and to increase their academic performance. Positive recruitment was done by training students on how and when to ask for help (Wolford et al., 2001). These studies suggest that although students with LD often play a passive role in the classroom, they can be taught specific behaviors to actively solicit positive teacher and peer attention. This is a simple but valuable tool that special education teachers can use to ensure that their students display behaviors in general education classrooms that increase their likelihood for teacher acceptance and feedback.

Communication Difficulties Expressing one's ideas and feelings and understanding the ideas and feelings of others are integral parts of socialization. Adults and children who have good social skills can communicate effectively with others, whereas students with learning and behavior problems frequently have trouble in this area, known as *pragmatic communication*. Children with LD often have poor pragmatic skills, such as eye contact, turn-taking, initiative, interaction, sharing, requesting, and responding (Abudarham, 2002).

The student with LD is often a difficult communication partner. For example, verbal disagreements during a learning task between students with mild intellectual disabilities and normal-achieving students were examined in one study (Okrainec & Hughes, 1996). Students with mild intellectual disabilities initiated conflicts less often, thus taking on a respondent/opposee role, and used higher-level conflict-initiating strategies, such as justification, delay/distractions, and question/challenges, less often. Initiating conflicts less often can prevent the exchanges of ideas that promote intellectual development as well as moral development and social development for students with mild intellectual disabilities. In addition, justifications can be a useful verbal skill for averting conflicts that may result in aggressive or violent acts. It is interesting to note that familiarity with one's partner positively affects the performance on communication tasks of students with LD but has no impact for children without LD (Mathinos, 1987). Perhaps knowledge of one's partners serves as a motivator for students with LD to use the communication skills they have.

Aggression Perhaps the behavior with which teachers are least able to cope is aggression (Hart, 2002). Aggressive behaviors include assaulting others, fighting, bullying, having temper tantrums, quarreling, ignoring the rights of others, using a negative tone of voice, threatening, and demanding immediate compliance. Many students with behavior problems display these types of aggressive behaviors.

> ▶ *WEB RESOURCES*
> For more information about meeting the needs of students with destructive behaviors, consider viewing the Web site from the Institution on Violence and Destructive Behavior (http://www.uoregon.edu/-ivdb/).

In a study conducted by Lancelotta and Vaughn (1989), five types of aggressive behaviors and their relation to peer social acceptance were examined:

1. *Provoked physical aggression:* Attacks or fights back following provocation from another.
2. *Outburst aggression:* Has uncontrollable outbursts without apparent provocation that may or may not be directed at another person. An example is a student who gets angry and throws a fit for no apparent reason.
3. *Unprovoked physical aggression:* Attacks or acts aggressively toward another person without provocation. An example is a student who starts a fight for no reason.
4. *Verbal aggression:* Says aggressive things to another person to attack or intimidate him or her. An example is a student who threatens to beat up another.
5. *Indirect aggression:* Attacks or attempts to hurt another indirectly so that it is not likely to be obvious who did it. An example is a student who tells the teacher that another student does bad things.

The study demonstrated that girls are less tolerant of all types of aggression than are boys. Also, all types of aggression resulted in lower peer ratings by their fellow students, with the exception of provoked aggression for boys. This means that boys who fight back when they are attacked first by other boys are not any more likely to be poorly accepted. This, however, is not true for girls who fight back when they are attacked. All of the other subtypes of aggression are related to poor peer acceptance.

Aggression does not go away without treatment and is correlated with such negative outcomes as alcoholism, unpopularity, aggressive responses from others, academic failure, and adult antisocial behaviors. Specific skills for teaching students to deal more effectively with their aggressive responses are an important component of social skills programs for students with behavior disorders.

Following are some ways in which teachers can address aggression and bullying in the classroom:

- All students must understand what types of behaviors are considered aggressive. Teachers can hold class discussions about which examples of aggressive behavior are identified and listed to ensure that all students know what is meant by *aggression*.
- Teachers can establish a no-tolerance rule regarding aggressive behavior and have a schoolwide plan for how every adult and child will handle aggression from others. *No tolerance* means that the school has a policy (other than expulsion) for responding to aggressive behavior.
- The teacher can inform students that they will be protected, and demonstrate this (Shore, 2003).
- The teacher can provide preemptive techniques to prevent fights. This can include stopping heated arguments and monitoring students who do not usually get along.

- The teacher and other school staff can stop fighting immediately and firmly (Shore, 2003).
- The teacher can identify when and where the student is aggressive and attempt to eliminate those situations.
- The teacher can teach students to resolve their own conflicts and mediate difficulties between other students.
- The teacher can ask students to describe what happened before and during an aggressive act (Shore, 2003).
- As a schoolwide model, the school staff can establish a caring and supportive environment for students and adults.

Apply the Concept 4-3 discusses the problem of bullying and teasing students with disabilities.

Attention Problems/Hyperactivity Attention deficits and hyperactivity are characteristics that are often observed in students with learning and behavior disorders. Families report that 3.7% of children have both attention deficit/hyperactivity disorder (ADHD) and LD (Smith & Adams, 2006). Students with attention deficits frequently display a pattern of inattention, and students with hyperactivity often exhibit patterns of impulsivity; these patterns are evident in a variety of contexts, including home and school.

In the classroom, inattention is manifested in a failure to pay attention to details, careless mistakes, misplacing needed items, messy work, and difficulty in persisting with a task until completion (American Psychiatric Association, 2000). Hyperactivity may be exhibited through fidgetiness, inability to engage in quiet activities, difficulty staying seated, blurting out answers, flitting from one task to another, and excessive talking (American

Apply the Concept

| 4-3 | **Preventing Bullying and Teasing of Individuals with Disabilities** |

Have you ever worried about a school bully or excessive teasing? If you have, you are not alone. Schools and educators have reported that bullying and excessive teasing are a serious school problem, one that is exacerbated when students are perceived as different. Thus, students with learning and behavior problems may be particularly susceptible to harassment and bullying. When students are isolated from their peers or do not participate in

mainstream programs, they are at increased risk for bullying (Hoover & Salk, 2003).

Following are some facts about bullying (Hoover & Stenhjem, 2003):

- Bullying is the most common form of aggression among youths.
- Many teachers (as many as 25%) do not perceive that bullying is wrong and therefore rarely intervene. Be sure you work to change this view

and stop bullying as soon as you see it.

- Most students perceive that schools do little to respond to bullying.
- Physical bullying peaks in middle school.

Olweus (1993) has designed a schoolwide intervention program to prevent or reduce bullying. For information on implementing the model, visit the program Web site at http://www.secondstep.org.

Psychiatric Association, 2000; U.S. Department of Education, 2006).

Students with attention deficits and/or hyperactivity may be treated with medication. Several stimulant medications (e.g., Dexedrine, Ritalin) are available that help students to focus by adjusting the parts of the brain that regulate attention, impulse control, and mood (Cooper & Bilton, 2002; Hallowell & Ratey, 1995). The Food and Drug Administration approved atomoxetine, a new type of nonstimulant medication for the treatment of ADHD (U.S. Department of Education, 2003). As with any medication, unwanted side effects can occur. Some of the side effects of stimulant medications include facial tics, loss of appetite, headaches, and difficulty sleeping (Cooper & Bilton, 2002; Swanson et al., 1993). Some children experience unpleasant physical symptoms and are affected by the drugs in some settings but not in others. Most children who receive medication for hyperactivity are under the care of a physician whom they see infrequently. Thus, monitoring the effectiveness of the drug is often the responsibility of family members and teachers. Perhaps the most effective technique for monitoring the effects of drugs is observing the student's behavior and determining whether there have been significant changes, either positive or negative.

Similarly, educational evaluations can be used to assess the degree to which children's ADHD symptoms affect their academic performance. The teacher identifies and defines specific behaviors that are indicative of hyperactivity and then charts the occurrence of these behaviors (U.S. Department of Education, 2003). Whereas medication may be necessary for some children, even successful use of medication does not make the LD disappear (Routh, 1979; Silver & Hagin, 2002).

When students demonstrate attention problems, teachers can do the following:

- Use clear ways of cueing students to obtain their attention (Shore, 2003). For example, say, "I'm counting backward to one, and then I want all eyes on me. Five, four, three, two, one." Some teachers use chimes or other instruments to obtain students' attention. Another idea is to tell students that you are going to clap a pattern and then you want them to "clap the same pattern and then look at me."
- Develop a signaling system with a student or selected students to cue them to pay attention. The signal could be a slight touch on the shoulder or passing the student a colored card to indicate that he or she is not paying attention.
- Look for times when students are attending and focusing, and also establish a system for cueing them when they are doing well.
- Consider where in the classroom and near whom students work, and make adjustments to promote better focus on assignments.

- Shorten the work periods and assignments. Focus on understanding and getting a few items right rather than completing all aspects of tasks.
- Provide clear and limited directions that are easier to follow.
- Assist students in making effective transitions.
- If a student is taking medication, monitor his or her behavior to note the effects of the medication and possible changes in behavior (Shore, 2003).
- Use computer-assisted learning (Westwood, 2003).
- Check out the following organizations and their Web sites for additional information: Attention Deficit Disorder Association (http://www.add.org), and Children and Adults with Attention-Deficit/Hyperactivity Disorder (http://www.chadd.org).

Self-Concept Ask parents what they most want for their children and many of them will mention that they want their children to be happy and to be successful—they want them to be proud of themselves. In many ways, they are hoping that their children have a healthy and positive self-concept, or self-perception. How we view ourselves is highly related to our comparison group. Therefore, it is not surprising that students with learning and behavior difficulties often have poor self-concepts. These students are aware of how their learning performance compares with that of others. Morrison (1985) demonstrated that two factors significantly influence self-perception of students with LD: type of classroom placement (e.g., self-contained, general education classroom) and what aspect of self-perception is being evaluated (e.g., academic, social, behavioral).

The self-perceptions of students with LD can be surprisingly accurate. In general, they rate themselves as low on academic ability (Chapman & Boersman, 1980) and like other children on overall feelings of self-worth (Bear, Clever, & Proctor, 1991; Bryan, 1986). They identify reading and spelling as the academic areas in which they are lower than other children and yet perceive themselves as being relatively intelligent (Kloomok & Cosden, 1994; Renik, 1987). A longitudinal study of students with LD suggests that they may differ from low-achieving students in that they do not become more negative about themselves as they grow older (Kistner & Osborne, 1987).

What can teachers do to improve the self-concept of students with LD or behavior problems? A summary of research on self-concept and students with LD reveals that younger students do not benefit from counseling as an intervention, whereas middle and high school students do (Elbaum & Vaughn, 2001). It may be useful to involve students in extracurricular activities such as sports or music, as students with LD who participate in these activities have a similar self-concept as average-achieving students (Kloomok & Cosden, 1994). Teachers and parents can provide opportunities for students to demonstrate what they do well and provide encouragement in the areas of difficulty. One parent described it this way:

> The best thing that happened to my son is swimming. We knew from the time Kevin was an infant that he was different from our other two children. We were not surprised when he had difficulties in school and was later identified as learning-disabled. His visual/motor problems made it difficult for him to play ball sports, so we encouraged his interest in swimming. He joined a swim team when he was six, and all his friends know he has won many swimming awards. No matter how discouraged he feels about school, he has one area in which he is successful.

Apply the Concept 4-4 describes what teachers might do to support self-regulation in students.

Social Difficulties That Are Prevalent During Adolescence

In addition to the characteristics of students with learning and behavior disorders that we discussed earlier, several difficulties are prevalent during adolescence that can affect students with special needs. These are the mental health issues of social alienation, suicide, anorexia nervosa, and alcohol and other drug abuse. Why might special education

teachers need to consider these difficulties as well as other variables related to social adjustment in adolescents with learning and behavior problems? Perhaps the most important reason is that teachers are often the first to be aware of mental health problems and can be valuable resources for identification and support. The majority of youth and adolescents with self-reported mental health problems were provided special education services (Talbott & Fleming, 2003).

Social Alienation Social alienation arises from the extent to which youngsters feel that they are not part of or do not have an affinity for the school or the people in the school. Social alienation has been interpreted to refer to alienation from teachers or peers (Seidel & Vaughn, 1991). Not surprisingly, social alienation begins early in a youngster's school career but is most obvious during adolescence. In a study by Seidel and Vaughn (1991), students with LD who dropped out of school differed from those who did not when they rated how they felt about teachers and classmates. Not surprisingly, students with LD who drop out do not perceive their teachers as friends. Furthermore, these students are more likely to state, "The thing I hated most about school was my teachers." Students with LD who dropped out also felt that their

Apply the Concept

4-4	How Teachers Can Promote Students' Self-Regulation

To promote students' self-regulation, or monitoring of their own behavior without adult supervision or direction, teachers may want to do the following:

1. Offer process-directed praise or criticism (Dweck & Kamins, 1999) such as, "This paper is clearly written," or, "You really concentrated and finished this biology assignment." Focus on the activity the students are engaged in, such as reading, writing, or art, and avoid person-directed praise or comments such as, "You are good in biology." This will help reduce the amount of external reinforcement needed and instead reinforce student performance.

2. Reduce the amount of external reinforcement and focus on reinforcing student performance. Rather than saying, "Good work" or "Excellent job," focus on the behaviors, such as, "You really

concentrated and finished this biology assignment. You needed to ask for help, but you got it done. How do you feel about it?"

3. Link students' behaviors to outcomes. "You spent 10 minutes working hard on this worksheet, and you finished it."

4. Provide encouragement. Because they experience continued failure, many students are discouraged from attempting tasks they are capable of performing.

5. Discuss academic tasks and social activities in which the student experiences success.

6. Discuss your own failures or difficulties, and express what you do to cope with these. Be sure to provide examples of when you persist and examples of when you give up.

7. Encourage students to take responsibility for their successes. "You received a B on your biology

test. How do you think you got such a good grade?" Encourage students to describe what they did (e.g., how they studied). Discourage students from saying, "I was lucky" or "It was an easy test."

8. Encourage students to take responsibility for their failures. For example, in response to the question "Why do you think you are staying after school?" encourage students to take responsibility for what got them there. "Yes, I am sure Jason's behavior was hard to ignore. I am aware that you did some things to get you here. What did you do?"

9. Structure learning and social activities to reduce failure.

10. Teach students how to learn information and how to demonstrate their control of their learning task.

11. Teach students to use procedures and techniques to monitor their own gains in academic areas.

classmates "would not have missed them if they moved away," and they did not look forward to seeing their friends at school. Interestingly, these students did not differ on their academic achievement scores but did differ on the extent to which they felt that they were socially accepted and liked by their teachers and classmates.

Different school environments trigger feelings of loneliness in students depending on the individual student's temperament. Thus, it is important for teachers to realize that students who are more withdrawn need additional support to be comfortable in less structured settings. It may be useful to rehearse with them what they can do or to assist them in establishing routines with which they are comfortable in these settings. Pavri and Monda-Amaya (2000) interviewed fourth- and fifth-grade students with LD to determine their experience with school-related loneliness, which coping strategies the students used, and which intervention strategies the students perceived as useful. Students indicated self-initiated and peer-initiated strategies to be most helpful, followed closely by teacher-initiated strategies.

To help students feel less socially alienated, teachers can do the following:

- Provide opportunities for students to work in small groups that encourage all students to participate.
- Set the tone in the class that all students are valuable and have something important to contribute.
- Take a moment between classes to ask about students and demonstrate that you care.
- Allow students to participate in decision making regarding class rules and management.
- Identify youngsters who are uninvolved and/or detached, and refer them to the counselor.
- Encourage students to participate in school-related extracurricular activities.
- Ask students who are lonely whether there is a person in the class they like, and seat them nearby.
- Try grouping students into small groups or pairing students during activities.
- Provide students with activities to engage in with peers (e.g., hide and go seek) during less structured times such as recess and lunch. Encourage students to play together.

Suicide Two Leominster, Massachusetts, teenagers died in a shotgun suicide pact next to an empty bottle of champagne after writing farewell notes that included "I love to die I'd be happier I know it! So please let me go. No hard feelings" (*Boston Herald,* November 10, 1984, p. 1). Although the autopsy showed high levels of alcohol in the girls' bloodstreams, there were no indications that either girl was involved with other drugs or was pregnant. It appeared as though both girls willingly participated in the suicide act. In another note, one of the girls wrote, "I know it was for the best. I can't handle this sucky world

any longer" (*Boston Herald,* November 10, 1984, p. 7). The cause of the suicide pact is unknown.

After being forbidden to see each other, a 14-year-old boy and a 13-year-old girl ran away. Shortly thereafter, they leaped into a river and drowned (*Miami Herald,* November 9, 1995, p. 10).

Any suicide is shocking, but the suicide of a child or adolescent is particularly tragic. Suicides between birth and the age of 15 are termed *childhood suicides.* Between ages 15 and 19, they are referred to as *adolescent suicides.* Many deaths of adolescents are viewed as accidents and not reported as suicide; therefore, the statistics on adolescent suicide are probably woefully underreported (Toolan, 1981). However, suicide is one of the top three causes of death for people under 24 years of age; 5,000 adolescents each year take their own lives in the United States. And there is agreement that the rate of adolescent suicide is on the rise (Cimbolic & Jobes, 1990; Henry, Stephenson, Hanson, & Hargett, 1993; Popenhagen & Qualley, 1998). Female attempts at suicide greatly outnumber those of males (Hawton, 1982); however, male attempts are more frequently successful.

Suicide attempts by adolescents are frequently made to accomplish one or more of the following four goals:

1. To escape stress or stressful situations
2. To demonstrate to others how desperate they are
3. To hurt or get back at others
4. To get others to change (Wicks-Nelson & Israel, 1984)

Suicide attempts most frequently occur after interpersonal problems with boyfriends or girlfriends, parents, or teachers (Wannan & Fombonne, 1998). Often, these relationships have had prolonged difficulties. Disturbed peer relationships are a significant contributing factor to suicide attempts. Adolescents feel unique, as if there are no solutions to their particular problems. In addition, adolescents often feel responsible for their problems and are unlikely to seek assistance, thus leaving them feeling isolated (Culp, Clyman, & Culp, 1995). "Life is a chronic problem. There appears no way out. Solutions previously tried have failed. To end the chronic problem, death appears to be the only way left" (Teicher, 1973, p. 137, in Sheras, 1983).

"Suicidal patients are often very difficult because they so frequently deny the seriousness of their attempts" (Toolan, 1981, p. 320). They often make comments such as, "It was all a mistake. I am much better now." Even if they attempt to discount the attempt, it should be treated with extreme seriousness.

Early detection of students who are at risk for suicide can help in providing services and reducing that risk. Students who are contemplating suicide may provide subtle verbal clues such as: "Don't bother grading my test, because by tomorrow it really won't matter what I got on it" (American Foundation for Suicide Prevention,

2009; American Academy of Child and Adolescent Psychology, 2009). Signs that may be related to suicide include depression, flat affect, an emotion-laden event (e.g., parental divorce), and isolation. Teachers of students with learning and behavior problems should be particularly knowledgeable about these symptoms since these students, particularly those in special education classrooms, are considered by their counselors to be more at risk for depression (Howard & Tryon, 2002). Also, students with severe reading problems are significantly more likely to experience suicidal ideation or suicide attempts and are also more likely to drop out of school (Daniel et al., 2007). Apply the Concept 4-5 presents some warning signs of suicide.

Sheras (1983) offers six general considerations for dealing with adolescent suicide attempts:

1. All suicide attempts must be taken seriously. Do not interpret the behavior as merely a plea for attention. Do not try to decide whether the attempt is real. The National Mental Health Association (2003) indicates that four out of five suicidal adolescents provide clear signs that they are considering suicide, including the following:
- Direct and indirect threat
- Obsession with death
- Writing that refers to death
- Dramatic changes in appearance or personality (e.g., changes in eating and/or sleeping habits)
- Giving away possessions
- Change in school behavior

2. Develop or reestablish communication with the person. Suicide is a form of communication from a person who feels that he or she has no other way to communicate.

3. Reestablish emotional or interpersonal support. Suicide is an expression of alienation, and the person needs to be reconnected with significant others.

4. Involve the adolescent in individual and/or family therapy. Often, the adolescent feels unable to establish communication with a significant person (e.g., a parent) and needs assistance from another to do so.

5. Work with the youngster to identify the problem or problems and to provide realistic practical solutions to the problems.

6. Devise a "no-kill" contract that requires a student to promise in writing not to inflict harm on himself or herself. Students who have agreed to such a contract tend to find it more difficult to follow through with plans of suicide (Pfeffer, 1986).

Rourke, Young, and Leenaars (1989) have identified a specific subtype of LD that put students at risk for

●●●●●●● *Apply the Concept* ●●●●●●●

4-5   What Are Some of the Suicide Warning Signs?

These warning signs should be taken very seriously and never ignored. Teach adolescents and young adults these signs so that they can respond appropriately to their peers.

- *Suicide Notes*—If you find, read, or are told about a suicide note that has been written do not consider it silly or funny. Take it very seriously and report it.
- *Threats*—All threats to do harm to oneself should be taken very seriously.
- *Previous Attempts*—Pay particular attention to students who have attempted suicide in the past.
- *Depression*—When depression includes signs of helplessness or hopelessness be very concerned about risk for suicide.
- *Final Arrangements*—Consider efforts to make final arrangements such as giving away valuable

objects and preparing goodbyes as serious risk signs for suicide.
- *Self-Injurious Behavior*—Treat attempts at injuring oneself such as jumping out of a car and cutting as risk signs for suicide.
- *Sudden Changes in Appearance, Personality, Friends, and Behavior*—Observe dramatic changes in appearance (neat to sloppy), excessive changes in personality, and other significant changes as potential signs for risk of suicide.
- *Death and Suicide Themes*—Students may exhibit unusual and peculiar preoccupation with death themes that they demonstrate in their drawings and writings.

There are a variety of online resources that you can access for more information:
American Academy for Child and Adolescent Psychiatry, http://www.aacap.org;

American Association of Suicidology, http://www.suicidology.org;
Depression and Bipolar Support Alliance (DBSA), http://www.dbsalliance.org;
Light for Life Program, http://www.yellowribbon.org;
National Institute of Mental Health Suicide Prevention Resources, http://www.nimh.nih.gov/suicideprevention/index.cfm;
National Mental Health Association, http://www.nmha.org;
U.S. Department of Health and Human Services, National Strategy on Suicide Prevention, http://www.mentalhealth.samhsa.gov/suicideprevention.

Source: R. Lieberman & K. C. Cowan, *Save a Friend: Tips for Teens to Prevent Suicide* (Bethesda, MD: National Association of School Psychologists, 2006), http://www.nasponline.org.

depression and suicide. This *nonverbal LD* subtype includes such characteristics as bilateral tactile-perceptual deficits, bilateral psychomotor coordination problems, severe difficulties in visual–spatial–organizational abilities, difficulty with nonverbal problem solving, good rote verbal capacities, and difficulty adapting to novel and complex situations. Fletcher (1989) urges that students with nonverbal LD be identified early and treated promptly. Because verbal skills are highly valued, particularly in school settings, it is likely that many students with nonverbal LD go unnoticed.

Intervention Strategies

Understanding and using different interventions to affect the social skills of students with LD and behavior disorders is extremely important. Using a particular intervention may be effective with one student but considerably less effective with another student or another problem. By understanding many approaches, teachers increase the likelihood of success with all students. The real challenge is knowing when to use which approach with which student. The best way to determine whether an intervention is working is to target specific social skills and to measure their progress over time. Though immediate improvement is unlikely, there should be some improvement in 4 to 6 weeks; if there is no improvement, the teacher may consider trying another intervention.

There is a range of intervention strategies to assist in teaching appropriate social skills to students with LD and behavior disorders. The purpose of social skills training is to teach the students a complex response set that allows them to adapt to the numerous problems that occur in social situations. Common goals of social skills training programs include the ability to do the following:

- Solve problems and make decisions quickly.
- Adapt to situations that are new or unexpected.
- Use coping strategies for responding to emotional upsets.
- Communicate effectively with others.
- Make and maintain friends.
- Reduce anxiety.
- Reduce problem behaviors.

Working with Families of Students with Social Difficulties

Working with families and engaging them in resolving social and behavioral issues at school and at home is an essential part of a successful intervention program. This is true regardless of the age of the student. Many teachers find it easier to engage families when they are teaching very young children. However, families of older students are critical links to effective social and behavioral outcomes for their children.

Interpersonal Problem Solving

Most people spend an extraordinary amount of time preventing and solving interpersonal problems. Whether we are concerned about what to say to our neighbor whose dog barks loudly in the middle of the night, how to handle an irate customer at work, or our relationships with our parents and siblings, interpersonal problems are an ongoing part of life. Some people seem to acquire the skills necessary for interpersonal problem solving easily and with little or no direct instruction; others, particularly students with learning and behavior disorders, need more direct instruction in how to prevent and resolve difficulties with others.

The goal of interpersonal problem-solving (IPS) training is to empower students with a wide range of strategies that allow them to develop and maintain positive relationships with others, cope effectively with others, solve their own problems, and resolve conflict with others. The problem-solving approach attempts to provide the student with a process for solving conflicts.

Four skills appear to be particularly important for successful problem resolution (Bell & D'Zurilla, 2009; Vaughn, Levine, & Ridley, 1986). First, the student must be able to identify and define the problem. Second, the student must be able to generate a variety of alternative solutions to any given problem. Third, the student must be able to identify and evaluate the possible consequences of each alternative. Finally, the student must be able to implement the solution and determine the effects of the solution implementation. This may require rehearsal and modeling.

Whereas these four components are characteristic of most interpersonal problem-solving programs, programs often incorporate additional components and procedures. For example, a social problem-solving intervention was conducted with 50 students with serious emotional disturbances by Amish, Gesten, Smith, Clark, and Stark (1988). The intervention consisted of 15 structured lessons that occurred for 40 minutes once each week. The following problem-solving steps were taught:

1. Say what the problem is and how you feel.
2. Decide on a goal.
3. Stop and think before you decide what to do.
4. Think of many possible solutions to the problem.
5. Think about what will happen next after each possible solution.
6. When you find a good solution, try it.

The results of the intervention indicated that students with serious emotional disturbances who participated in the intervention improved their social problem-solving skills and were able to generate more alternatives to interviewing and role-playing measures.

The following sections describe several IPS programs that have been developed, implemented, and evaluated with students who have learning and behavior disorders.

FAST and SLAM

FAST is a strategy that is taught as part of an IPS program to second-, third-, and fourth-grade students with LD who have been identified as having social skills problems (Vaughn & Lancelotta, 1990; Vaughn, Lancelotta, & Minnis 1988; Vaughn et al., 1991). The purpose of FAST is to teach students to consider problems carefully before responding to them and to consider alternatives and their consequences. Figure 4-13 presents the FAST strategy. In step 1, Freeze and Think, students are taught to identify the problem. In step 2, Alternatives, students are taught to consider possible ways of solving the problem. In step 3, Solution Evaluation, students are asked to prepare a solution or course of action for solving the problem that is both safe and fair. The idea is to get students to consider solutions that will be effective in the long run. Step 4, Try It, asks students to rehearse and implement the solution. If they are unsuccessful at implementing the solution, students are taught to go back to alternatives. Students with LD practiced this strategy by using real problems generated by themselves and their peers. Following is a description of the procedures used in the problem-solving study.

1. In each classroom, ask students to rate all same-sex classmates on the extent to which they would like to be friends with them. Students who receive few friendship votes and many no-friendship votes are identified as not well accepted. Students who receive many friendship votes and few no-friendship votes are identified as very well accepted.

2. Students with LD who are not well accepted are paired with a same-sex popular classmate, and the pairs become the IPS skills trainers for the class and school.

3. Children who are selected as IPS skills trainers are removed from the classroom two to three times a week and are taught problem-solving strategies for approximately 30 minutes each session.

4. These students who are the "class trainers" are taught the FAST strategy (see above) such as accepting negative feedback, receiving positive feedback, and making friendship overtures.

5. Classmates record problems they have at home and at school and place their lists in the classroom problem-solving box. Trainers use these lists as they learn the strategies outside of class as well as for in-class discussion.

6. After the IPS trainers have learned a strategy, such as FAST, they teach it to the entire class, with backup and support from the classroom teacher.

7. During subsequent weeks, the trainers leave the room for only one session per week and practice the FAST strategy as well as other strategies with classmates at least one time per week. These reviews include large group explanations and small group problem-solving exercises.

8. Students who are selected as trainers are recognized by their teacher for their special skills. Other students are asked to consult the problem-solving trainer when they have difficulties.

Apply the Concept 4-6 shows an activity sheet used as part of a homework assignment for students participating in the training.

Based on principles similar to those of the FAST strategy, SLAM is a technique that can be used to assist students in accepting and assimilating negative feedback and comments from others (McIntosh, Vaughn, & Bennerson, 1995). The SLAM strategy is practiced in small groups and presented to the class. The components of the SLAM strategy are as follows:

1. *Stop* —Stop whatever you are doing.
2. *Look* —Look the person in the eye.
3. *Ask* —Ask the person a question to clarify what he or she means.
4. *Make* —Make an appropriate response to the person.

Figure 4-14 presents the lyrics to the SLAM Strategy Song.

ASSET: A Social Skills Program for Adolescents

The purpose of ASSET is to teach adolescents the social skills they need to interact successfully with peers and adults (Hazel, Schumaker, Sherman, & Sheldon-Wildgen, 1981). Eight social skills are considered fundamental to successful relationships:

1. *Giving positive feedback.* This skill teaches students how to thank someone and how to give a compliment.

▶ **Figure 4-13**   FAST: An Interpersonal Problem-Solving Strategy

> **Freeze and think!**
>   What is the problem?
>
> **Alternatives?**
>   What are my possible solutions?
>
> **Solution evaluation**
>   Choose the best solution:
>   safe?
>   fair?
>
> **Try it!**
>   Slowly and carefully
>   Does it work?

4-6 Activity Sheet for FAST

This activity sheet can be used to give children written practice in using the FAST strategy. You are in the cafeteria. Another student keeps bugging you. He hits you, pokes you, tries to steal your food, and will not stop bullying you. You start to get angry. What would you do? Use FAST to help you solve the problem.

1. *Freeze and think.* What is the problem?

   _____
   _____

2. *Alternatives.* What are your possible solutions?

   _____
   _____
   _____

3. *Solution evaluation.* Choose the best one. Remember: Safe and fair works in the long run.

   _____
   _____

4. *Try it.* Do you think this will work?

   _____
   _____

   A friend of yours is upset. She is teased a lot, especially by a boy named Kenny. She told you that she wants to run away from school. What could you tell your friend to help her solve the problem? Use FAST to help you.

1. _____
   _____
   _____
   _____

2. _____
   _____
   _____

3. _____
   _____
   _____

4. _____
   _____
   _____

▶ **Figure 4-14** Lyrics to the SLAM Strategy Song

> Accepting negative feedback, feedback, feedback.
> Accepting negative feedback, feedback, feedback.
> Stop what you're doing. Look them in the eye.
> Fix your face. We'll tell you why.
> Accepting negative feedback, feedback, feedback.
> Accepting negative feedback, feedback, feedback.
> Listen with your ears to what they say.
> This is no time for you to play.
> Accepting negative feedback, feedback, feedback.
> Accepting negative feedback, feedback, feedback.
> Ask a question if you don't understand.
> Don't stand there in wonderland.
> Accepting negative feedback, feedback, feedback.
> Accepting negative feedback, feedback, feedback.
> Make a response to their concerns.
> Accepting negative feedback is the way to learn.

2. *Giving negative feedback.* This skill teaches students to give correction and feedback in a way that is not threatening.

3. *Accepting negative feedback.* This skill teaches students the all-important ability to receive negative feedback without walking away, showing hostility, or other inappropriate emotional reactions.

4. *Resisting peer pressure.* This skill teaches students to refuse their friends who are trying to seduce them into some form of delinquent behavior.

5. *Problem solving.* This skill teaches students a process for solving their own interpersonal difficulties.

6. *Negotiation.* This skill teaches students to use their problem-solving skills with another person to come to a mutually acceptable resolution.

7. *Following instructions.* This skill teaches students to listen and respond to instructions.

8. *Conversation.* This skill teaches students to initiate and maintain a conversation.

The Leader's Guide (Hazel et al., 1981) that comes with the ASSET program provides instructions for running the groups and teaching the skills. Eight teaching sessions are provided on videotapes that demonstrate the skills. Program materials include skill sheets, home notes, and criterion checklists. See Apply the Concept 4-7 for a description of the procedures for implementing ASSET.

Circle of Friends Circle of Friends is a friendship enhancement program that has been evaluated with 6- to 12-year-old students with emotional and behavioral disorders (Frederickson & Turner, 2003). The primary purpose of Circle of Friends is to establish a supportive meeting each week (for about 1 hour) to provide opportunities for peers to learn to interact and support their fellow students with emotional or behavior problems.

4-7

ASSET—A Social Skills Program for Adolescents

Procedures

Each lesson is taught to a small group of adolescents. There are nine basic steps to each lesson:

1. Review homework and previously learned social skills.
2. Explain the new skill for the day's lesson.
3. Explain why the skill is important and should be learned and practiced.
4. Give a realistic and specific example to illustrate the use of the skill.
5. Examine each of the skill steps that are necessary to carry out the new social skill.

6. Model the skill, and provide opportunities for students and others to demonstrate correct and incorrect use of the skills.
7. Use verbal rehearsal to familiarize the students with the sequence of steps in each social skill, and provide a procedure for students to be automatic with their knowledge of the skill steps.
8. Use behavioral rehearsal to allow each student to practice and demonstrate the skill steps until they reach criterion.
9. Assign homework that provides opportunities for the students to practice the skills in other settings.

These nine steps are followed for each of the eight specific social skills listed above.

Comments

The ASSET program has been evaluated with eight students with LD (Hazel, Schumaker, Sherman, & Sheldon, 1982). That evaluation demonstrated that the students with LD involved in the intervention increased in the use of social skills in role-play settings. The curriculum guide provides specific teaching procedures and is particularly relevant to teachers working with adolescents.

  EVIDENCE-BASED PRACTICE

Circle of Friends

PROCEDURES: Circles of Friends are run by the counselor or school psychologist with the classroom teacher as a participant. The focus child is a student whom the teacher has identified as having significant behavior problems and peer interaction difficulties that would improve if peers in the classroom provided the appropriate interactions and supports. An outside leader (usually school psychologist or counselor) conducts the Circle of Friends group. Students from the target student's class are included in the Circle of Friends. Typically, the target student is not present during the meetings.

Following are the main features in using Circle of Friends in the classroom:

1. During the first meeting, the leader explains to the group why the target student is not present and solicits the cooperation and support of the peers. Students who are participating are first asked to identify only the strengths and positive behaviors of the target student.
2. After the target student's positive behaviors have been identified, the leader asks students to identify the challenging behaviors that the target student exhibits. The leader makes links between the target student's difficult behaviors and the types of responses and supports that students could provide. Then the leader requests that six to eight students volunteer to

serve as the Circle of Friends. The rest of the students are dismissed.
3. The Circle of Friends meet approximately eight times with the leader and the target student. During these meetings, students are reminded to follow the basic ground rules of confidentiality, seeking adult help if they are worried, and listening carefully to each person.
4. The leader and students identify a target behavior and roles that each of them will play to ensure that the target student is able to maintain the target behavior. Students' role-play and set goals for the forthcoming week. Each week, they review and describe their success and establish new behavioral goals.

COMMENTS: Students with emotional and behavior disorders who participated in the Circle of Friends (Frederickson & Turner, 2003) were better accepted by their peers in the classroom after participation than were similar students who had not participated in such a program. Although the Circle of Friends did not influence students' overall perceptions of the climate of the classroom, it did (positively) influence their perceptions of the target student.

Skillstreaming: Structured Learning Structured learning is a psychoeducational and behavioral approach to teaching prosocial skills to students both with and without disabilities (Goldstein, Sprafkin, Gershaw, & Klein, 1980). Skillstreaming can be implemented by teachers, social workers, psychologists, or school counselors. The program is available for young children (McGinnis & Goldstein, 2003), elementary-age children (McGinnis & Goldstein), as well as adolescents (Goldstein, McGinnis, Sprafkin, Gershaw, & Klein, 1995). A related program, the Stop and Think Social Skills Program (Knoff, 2003), provides a manual for teachers, a classroom set of materials for teachers and students, and specific lessons for all grade levels from kindergarten through eighth grade.

The first component, *modeling,* involves a verbal and behavioral description of the target skill as well as the steps that comprise the target skill. At this point, the teacher might role-play the steps in the skill, and other models may also role-play, exhibiting the target skill itself. During the second step, students are encouraged to enact role plays based on actual life experiences. These role plays are facilitated by coaching and cues from the teacher. Next, the teacher and other observers provide feedback. Specific attention is paid to elements of each role play that were effective and appropriate. Skills that were not role-played effectively are modeled by the teacher. In the final step, students are provided with opportunities to practice the steps and skills in the real world (e.g., outside the classroom).

The structured learning procedure for elementary students offers 60 prosocial skills and their constituent steps, arranged into five groups: classroom survival skills, friendship-making skills, skills for dealing with feelings, skill alternatives to aggression, and skills for dealing with stress. The structured learning procedure for adolescents also has 60 prosocial skills. It differs from the program for elementary students by including skills related to planning and decision making.

Principles for Teaching Social Skills

There are a number of points that teachers need to consider, no matter what social skills program they utilize:

1. *Develop cooperative learning.* Classrooms can be structured so that there is a win–lose atmosphere in which children compete with each other for grades and teacher attention, or structured so that children work on their own with little interaction among classmates, or structured for cooperative learning so children work alone, with pairs, and with groups, helping each other master the assigned material. Cooperative learning techniques in the classroom result in increases in self-esteem, social skills, and learning (Johnson & Johnson, 1986). Teachers can structure learning activities so that they involve cooperative learning and teach students techniques for working with pairs or in a group. The following four elements need to be present for cooperative learning to occur in small groups (Johnson & Johnson, 1986):

a. Students must perceive that they cannot succeed at the required task unless all members of the group succeed. This may require appropriate division of labor and giving a single grade for the entire group's performance.

b. There must be individual accountability so that each member of the group is assessed and realizes that his or her performance is critical for group success.

c. Students must have the necessary collaborative skills to function effectively in a group. This may include managing conflicts, active listening, leadership skill, and problem solving.

d. Sufficient time for group process must be allowed, including discussing how well the group is performing, developing a plan of action, and identifying what needs to happen.

2. *Involve peers in the training program for low-social-status students.* An important function of social skills training is to alter the way in which peers perceive students who are identified as low in social status. Including popular peers in the social skills training program increases the likelihood that they will have opportunities to observe the changes in target students and to cue and reinforce appropriate behavior in the classroom. For example, a study conducted by Vaughn, McIntosh, and Spencer-Rowe (1991) found that popular students who were involved in the social skills training with low-social-status students were more likely to increase the social status ratings of the low-social-status students than were popular students who were not involved in the training.

Involving students with high social status with those with lower social status improves the way in which the low-social-status students are perceived by others (Frederickson & Turner, 2003).

Students benefit from working with peers in supportive and academically structured activities. Students not only benefit academically when interventions focus on reading and math outcomes, but there is also a small effect for social, self-concept, and behavioral outcomes as well (Ginsburg-Block, Rohrbeck, & Fantuzzo, 2006). Thus, there are benefits academically as well as socially.

3. *Use principles of effective instruction.* Many teachers claim that they do not know how to teach social skills. Considering the social skills difficulties of special education students, methods of teaching social skills to students may need to become part of teacher training programs.

Teaching social skills requires implementing principles of effective instruction. These are used and explained throughout this text and include obtaining student commitment, identifying target behavior, pretesting, teaching, modeling, rehearsing, role playing, providing feedback, practicing in controlled settings, practicing in other settings, posttesting, and follow-up. Following are social skills that learning- and behavior-disordered students frequently need to be taught:

- *Body language.* This includes how students walk, where they stand during a conversation, what their body language "says," gestures, eye contact, and appropriate facial reactions.

- *Greetings.* This may include expanding students' repertoire of greetings, selecting appropriate greetings for different people, and interpreting and responding to the greetings of others.
- *Initiating and maintaining a conversation.* This includes a wide range of behaviors such as knowing when to approach someone; knowing how to ask inviting, open questions; knowing how to respond to comments made by others; and maintaining a conversation with a range of people, including those who are too talkative and those who volunteer little conversation.
- *Giving positive feedback.* Knowing how and when to give sincere, genuine, positive feedback and comments.
- *Accepting positive feedback.* Knowing how to accept positive feedback from others.
- *Giving negative feedback.* Knowing how and when to give specific negative feedback.
- *Accepting negative feedback.* Knowing how to accept negative feedback from others.
- *Identifying feelings in self and others.* Being able to recognize feelings in both self and others is how students are able to predict how they will feel in a given situation and prepare for responding appropriately to one's own and others' feelings.
- *Problem solving and conflict resolution.* Knowing and using problem-solving skills to prevent and solve difficulties.

4. *Teach needed skills.* Many social skills training programs fail because youngsters are trained to do things that they already know how to do. For example, in a social skills training group with students with LD, the trainer was teaching the students to initiate conversations with others. Through role playing, the trainer soon learned that the students already knew how to initiate conversations but did not know how to sustain them. In addition to being taught appropriate skills, students need to learn when and with whom to use the skills. One student put it this way: "I would never try problem solving like this with my father, but I know it would work with my mom."

5. *Teach for transfer of learning.* For social skills to transfer or generalize to other settings, the program must require the rehearsal and implementation of target skills across settings. Social skills training programs need to ensure that learned skills are systematically demonstrated in the classroom, on the playground, and at home.

6. *Empower students.* Many students with learning difficulties feel discouraged and unable to influence their learning. They turn the responsibility for learning over to the teacher and become passive learners. How can we empower students?

- *Choice.* Students need to feel that they are actively involved in their learning.

- *Consequences.* Students will learn from the natural and logical consequences of their choices.
- *Documented progress.* In addition to teacher documentation of progress made, students need to learn procedures for monitoring and assessing their progress.
- *Control.* Students need to feel as though they can exercise control over what happens to them. Some students feel as though their learning is in someone else's hands and therefore is someone else's responsibility.

7. *Identify strengths.* When developing social skills interventions for students with special needs, be sure to consider their strengths as well as their needs. Because appearance and athletic ability relate to social acceptance, these areas need to be considered when determining the type of social intervention needed. For example, if a youngster's physical appearance is a strength, the teacher can compliment the student on his or her hair, what the student is wearing, or how neat and sharp the student looks. Also, knowing something about the students' areas of strength can be helpful in identifying social contexts that may be promising for promoting positive peer interactions (Vaughn & LaGreca, 1992). For example, a student with LD who is a particularly good swimmer and a member of a swim team may find it easier to make friends on the swim team than in the academic setting. Students with LD who acquire strengths in appearance and athletic activities may have areas of strength from which to build their social skills. However, many children with LD do not have the motor ability or eye–hand coordination to succeed in the athletic area. Other areas, such as hobbies or special interests, can be presented in the classroom so that the student with LD has an opportunity to be perceived as one who is knowledgeable. Students with learning and behavior disorders who are not well accepted by their classmates may have friends in the neighborhood or within their families (e.g., cousins). Perhaps the most important point to remember is that if a child is not well accepted by peers at school, this does not necessarily mean that the child does not have effective social relationships outside of the school setting.

8. *Reciprocal friendships.* Reciprocal friendship is the mutual identification as "best friend" by two students; that is, a student who identifies another student as his or her best friend is also identified by that same youngster as a best friend. It has been hypothesized that reciprocal friendships play an important role in reducing the negative effects of low peer acceptance (Vaughn, McIntosh et al., 1993). From this perspective, it may be less important to increase the overall acceptance of a student in the classroom and more effective to concentrate on the development of a mutual best friend. Because it is quite unlikely that all students in the classroom are going to like all of the other youngsters equally, development of a reciprocal friendship is a more realistic goal for most youngsters with learning and behavior problems.

INSTRUCTIONAL ACTIVITIES

This section provides instructional activities related to developing socialization skills. Some of the activities teach new skills; others are best suited for practice and reinforcement of already acquired skills. For each activity, the objective, materials, and teaching procedures are described.

▶ Please Help

Objective: To teach students a process for asking for help when needed and yet continuing to work until assistance is given; to have a record-keeping system that allows the teacher to monitor how many times each day he or she assists each student.

Grades: Primary and intermediate

Materials: A 6- to 8-inch card that states "Please Help _____ [student's name]" and provides a place to list the date and comments

PLEASE HELP JENNIFER		
DATE	TIME	COMMENTS

Teaching Procedures: Construct the Please Help card for each student, including a place to mark the date and comments. Give all the students a card, and inform them that they are to place the card on their desks when they need help. They are to continue working until the teacher or someone else is able to provide assistance.

When you or your assistant is able to provide help, mark the date and time on the card and any appropriate comments such as "We needed to review the rules for long division," or "She could not remember the difference between long and short vowels," or "He solved the problem himself before I arrived."

▶ Problem Box

Objective: To give students an opportunity to identify problems they are having with others and to feel that their problems will be heard and attended to.

Grades: All grades

Materials: Shoebox decorated and labeled as "Problem Box"

Teaching Procedures: Show the students the box that is decorated and identified as the Problem Box. Place the box in a prominent location in the classroom. Tell the students that when they have problems with other students, teachers, or even at home, they can write the problems down and put them in the box. At the end of every day, you and the students will spend a designated amount of time (e.g., 15 minutes) reading problems and trying to solve them as a class. Be sure to tell students that they do not need to identify themselves or their notes.

During the designated time, open the Problem Box and read a selected note. Solicit assistance from the class in solving the note. Direct students' attention to identifying the problem, suggesting solutions, evaluating the consequences of the solutions, identifying a solution, and describing how it might be implemented.

▶ A Date by Telephone

Objective: To give students structured skills for obtaining a date by telephone.

Grades: Secondary

Materials: Two nonworking telephones

Teaching Procedures: Discuss with the students why preplanning a telephone call with a prospective date might be advantageous. Tell them that you are going to teach them some points to remember when calling to ask for a date. After you describe each of the following points, role-play them so that the students can observe their appropriate use:

1. Telephone at an *appropriate time.*
2. Use an *icebreaker,* such as recalling a mutually shared experience or a recent event in school.
3. *State what you would like to do and ask him or her to do it.* Ask the person whether he or she likes to go to the movies. When there is an initial lull in the conversation, mention a particular movie that you would like to take her or him to, and state when you would like to go. Then ask the person whether he or she would like to go with you.
4. If yes, *make appropriate arrangements* for day, time, and transportation. If no, ask whether you can call again.

Be sure that each student has an opportunity to role-play.

▶ Making and Keeping Friends

Objective: To have students identify the characteristics of peers who are successful at making and keeping friends and, after identifying these characteristics, to evaluate themselves in how well they perform.

Grades: Intermediate and secondary

Materials: Writing materials

Teaching Procedures: Ask the students to think of children they know who are good at making and keeping friends. Brainstorm what these children do that makes them successful at making and keeping friends. On an overhead projector or chalkboard, write the student-generated responses about the characteristics of children good at making and keeping friends. Then select the most agreed-on characteristics, and write them on a sheet of paper with smiley faces, neutral faces, and frowning faces so that students can circle the face that is most like them in response to that characteristic. Finally, ask students to identify one characteristic that they would like to target to improve their skills at making and maintaining friends.

How Good Are You at Making and Keeping Friends?

Next to each item, circle the face that best describes how well you do.

1. I tell friends the truth.

   ☺   😐   ☹

2. I call friends on the phone.

   ☺   😐   ☹

3. I share my favorite toys and games with friends.

   ☺   😐   ☹

▶ Identifying Feelings

Objective: To identify the feelings of others and self and to respond better to those feelings.

Grades: Primary and intermediate

Materials: Cards with pictures of people in situations in which their feelings can be observed or deduced

Teaching Procedures: Select pictures that elicit feeling words such as *happy, angry, jealous, hurt, sad,* and *mad.* Show the pictures to the students, and ask them to identify the feelings of the people in the pictures. Discuss what information in the picture cued them to the emotional states of the people. Then ask the students to draw a picture of a time when they felt as the person in the picture feels. Conclude by asking students to discuss their pictures.

▶ I'm New Here (and Scared)

By Sandra Stroud*

Objective: To help students who are new to your community and school make a positive adjustment. For many students, moving to a new school can be an especially traumatic experience.

Grades: K–12

Materials: The *goodwill* of a group of socially competent student volunteers and their adult leader—a teacher, guidance counselor, or school administrator

Teaching Procedures: The adult in charge organizes a school service club whose purpose is to take new students under its wing and help them feel welcome at their school. Students in this organization can be given sensitivity training to help them understand how new students feel when they move to a new area of the country and enter a new school. The group can discuss and decide on the many strategies they can use to help new students feel at home. One of their functions could be to speak to whole classes about how it feels to be a new student at a school and to suggest how each student at this school can help new students when they arrive.

For a new student, nothing is quite as traumatic when entering a new school as having no friend or group with whom to sit when the students go to the cafeteria for lunch. Therefore, one of a new student's greatest needs is for someone to invite him or her to have lunch with them. This should be the number-one priority of the members of the welcoming club. New students may eventually become members of this club, joining in the effort of welcoming and helping the new students who follow them.

▶ I'm in My Own Little House

By Sandra Stroud

Objective: To help young children acquire a sense of personal space as well as an understanding of other people's space. Many young children have not acquired an inner sense of space—of their own space and of space that belongs to others. As a result, the more active of these youngsters, usually little boys, tend to intrude on other children's space and, in the process, annoy the other children. As a result, they may not be well liked by their classmates. The problem is made worse by the fact that

---

*Note: This instructional activity was written by a mother who would have been so grateful if her son's middle school had had such a program when he entered the eighth grade there. As it was, things were pretty rough for him until his band teacher realized that he was skipping lunch. She paved the way for him to begin eating lunch with a group of boys who became his best friends.

many primary school children sit at long tables where the space of one student often overlaps the space of others.

Grades: Primary

Materials: Individual student desks, and colored masking tape

Teaching Procedures: The teacher arranges the room so that each student desk sits in a 3-square-foot area. The desks are just close enough to each other to make it possible for students to pass materials from one student to another without leaving their seats. On the floor around each desk, the teacher outlines the 3-square-foot block with colored masking tape.

The teacher explains the taped areas, or blocks, by telling a story about a child who wanted a little house that was all her own where no one would bother her or her belongings. This was "her" house. Just as her house was hers, she knew that the other children needed their houses and that she shouldn't bother them or their houses either. (The teacher makes up the story according to his or her imagination or to fit the situation in the classroom.)

▶ Introducing People

By Dheepa Sridhar

Objective: To teach students to introduce friends to one another appropriately.

Grades: Intermediate and secondary

Materials: None required

Teaching Procedures: Discuss the importance of introducing people. Allow students to share experiences such as when they were with a friend who was either good at or had difficulty in introducing them to his or her other friends. Tell students that you are going to teach them some points to remember when they introduce people to each other. After describing each of the following points, ask students to role-play to demonstrate their use:

- Provide additional information about the person being introduced such as "This is R. J.; he's new to our town," or "This is R. J.; he's good at baseball."
- Provide additional information about people in the group who have common interests with the new person such as "Steve plays basketball."
- Talk about those common interests.

▶ Invitation to Play

By Dheepa Sridhar

Objective: To teach students to invite a classmate to play with them.

Grades: Primary

Materials: Toys

Teaching Procedures: Tell students that they should take the following steps when requesting a classmate to join them in play:

1. Decide what you want to play (e.g., jump rope, building with Legos).
2. Check to see whether you have the materials (rope or Legos).
3. Check to see what the person you want to play with is doing.
4. Wait for a lull in the activity that the person is engaging in.
5. Ask the person whether he or she would like to play (rope or Legos).
6. If the person refuses, ask what else he or she would like to play.
7. Have students role-play and provide feedback.

▶ In Your Shoes

By Dheepa Sridhar

Objective: To facilitate students in taking a different perspective.

Grades: Intermediate and high school

Materials: Cardboard cutouts of two pairs of shoes of different colors, masking tape, index cards with social problems written on them (e.g., "Jake was supposed to go to a baseball game with Ashraf over the weekend. He has been looking forward to this event all week. On Friday, Ashraf says that he would rather go to a movie instead of the game.")

Teaching Procedures: Discuss the importance of taking the other person's perspective. Tell the students this activity will help them see a different perspective.

1. Tape a line on the floor with the masking tape. Write the name of a character (e.g., Jake and Ashraf) on each pair of shoes. Place each pair of shoes on either side of the line.
2. Have two students volunteer to be Jake or Ashraf.
3. Ask one student to stand on Jake's shoes and the other student to stand on Ashraf's shoes.
4. Let them talk about the problem.
5. Ask the students to exchange places and discuss the problem.
6. Help the students to reach a solution that is acceptable to both parties.

This activity can also be used with students who are experiencing problems with each other instead of hypothetical situations. Although only two students can participate at a time, the rest of the class can help by generating solutions and discussing the consequences of those solutions.

▶ FOCUS Question 1. How should teachers arrange the physical and instructional environment of the classroom to promote appropriate behavior?

Answer: Teachers must pay attention to the physical space in which they teach. They should keep books and resources organized and clearly marked, and they should use a variety of instructional arrangements depending on student needs and learning activities.

▶ FOCUS Question 2. How can teachers use classroom management and PBS to promote prosocial behavior?

Answer: The use of classroom management strategies is important because it creates an environment with structure and routine so that learning can occur. Teachers should develop procedures, rules, consequences, and reinforcers so that both they and the students know how to navigate the classroom and what to expect if something goes wrong. Teachers who implement effective classroom management recognize and reinforce positive behavior as well as identify and change inappropriate behaviors. PBS is a classroom management system that focuses on prevention of problem behaviors through attention to the learning environment.

▶ FOCUS Question 3. What is the purpose of an FBA, and what are the procedures for developing an effective FBA?

Answer: An FBA is designed to identify behavior problems of students, and a BIP is used to develop an intervention plan to treat these behavior problems. An FBA is required if students' behavior is interfering with their learning or the learning of other students.

▶ FOCUS Question 4. What do we know about how students with behavior and learning difficulties feel about themselves, are perceived by others, and interact socially with others?

Answer: Students with behavior and learning difficulties often lack the social competence necessary to engage in effective interactions with others. Although students with behavior disorders by definition lack social competence and generally have severe emotional and behavioral difficulties, many individuals with LD also struggle to make and maintain positive interpersonal relationships with others. Individuals with LD often (but not always) have poor conversational skills; may have difficulty perceiving, interpreting, and processing social information; may exhibit aggressive behaviors or attention problems; and may display atypical appearance.

PEARSON
myeducationlab
Where the Classroom Comes to Life

The MyEducationLab for this course can help you solidify your comprehension of Chapter 4 concepts.

- Gauge and further develop your understanding of chapter concepts by taking the quizzes and examining the enrichment materials in the Chapter 4 Study Plan.
- Visit Topic 10, Classroom Behavior Management, to connect with challenge-based interactive modules, case study units, and podcasts that provide research-validated information about working with students in inclusive settings, by visiting the IRIS Center Resources.
- Explore Assignments and Activities, assignable exercises showing concepts in action through video, cases, and student and teacher artifacts.
- Practice and strengthen skills essential to quality teaching through the Building Teaching Skills and Dispositions lessons.

Coteaching and Collaborating: Working with Professionals and Families

1. What are some of the challenges of working in an inclusive classroom and working with general education teachers?
2. What are three major models for consultation and collaboration?
3. What are the principles of communication, and how can teachers communicate with parents and professionals?
4. What is the teacher's role in addressing the needs of the entire family?

Mrs. Tupa works in a hospital emergency room, so she is accustomed to talking to people who are grieving. Mrs. Tupa states:

I often speak to parents about the recovery of their children. Fortunately, most of the children have injuries or illnesses from which they will recover completely. I've been trained in the importance of telling the parents as quickly and completely as possible all we know about their child's condition. The only reason I'm telling you this is that I want you to understand that I am accustomed to dealing with difficulties. But I was unprepared for the inconsistent information I would receive about our son.

When our third child, Chad, was born, my husband and I couldn't have been happier. Our first two children were girls, whom we enjoy immensely, but both of us were hoping for a boy. Chad walked and talked later than the girls, but I knew that boys are often developmentally slower than girls, so we were not concerned. Even when he was a preschooler, we knew Chad was different. He often had difficulty thinking of the right word for an object, and he was clumsier than other children his age. When we spoke with his pediatrician, the doctor informed us that this was not uncommon.

When Chad entered kindergarten, he did not know all of his colors and showed little ability to remember the names of the letters in the alphabet. His kindergarten teacher said that she had seen a number of students like Chad, often boys, and suggested that we keep Chad in kindergarten another year. Our neighbor, who is a teacher, thought this might not be a good idea, since Chad was already large for his age. We spoke with the principal, who seemed very busy and thought we should take the advice of the kindergarten teacher. We retained Chad. Spending another year in kindergarten seemed to do little good, however. Chad was still unable to identify letters, though he was very popular because of his size and knowledge of the kindergarten routine.

First grade was worse yet. Chad showed no signs of reading and was confusing letters. His writing resembled that of a much younger child. By now we were very concerned and made several appointments with his first-grade teacher. She was very responsive and suggested that we have Chad tutored during the summer. The tutor said that Chad had an attention problem and was having trouble with letter and word reversals. She suggested that we have him tested for learning disabilities. The school psychologist agreed to do the testing, and it was late in the fall before we were called and given the results.

Though both my husband and I are professionals, we felt somewhat intimidated by the number of school personnel at the meeting. On our way home, as we tried to reconstruct what we heard, we realized that we had misunderstood and missed a lot of information. I heard the school personnel say Chad's intelligence was normal, but my husband thought that it couldn't be normal because his verbal intelligence was low. We decided to make a list of questions to ask at our next meeting. We felt that we had made a major stride forward, since Chad would now be receiving special instruction for 1 hour each day from a learning disabilities specialist; however, we still felt we understood very little about his problems. I only wish we had been told more completely and quickly about Chad's problem.

Many parents have had similar experiences. They have noticed that their child is different in some areas from other children of the same age. These parents seek advice from friends, medical professionals, and school professionals and often feel confused and frustrated. When the child is identified as having learning disabilities or emotional disorders, many parents at first feel relieved, hoping that this identification will lead to solutions that will eliminate the child's learning or behavior problem. The difficult adjustments are that the child will probably always have learning or behavior problems and that the special education teacher will be unable to provide any magic cures, and certainly no quick solutions.

Learning disabilities and emotional disorders are complex phenomena, and knowledge of all the factors that they involve is incomplete. Special education teachers must be sensitive to parental concerns about identification and intervention, yet speak honestly about what they know and do not know. Teachers must provide families with encouragement without giving false hopes. Families need to know what educators' best knowledge of their child's learning and behavior problem is and to be informed of what educators are less sure of.

This chapter focuses on the special education teacher as a coteacher and an effective communicator. One of the essential roles of the special education teachers is coteaching and working with other professional (e.g., general education teacher, school psychologist), as well as communicating with family members and between special education teachers and other school-related professionals. In the same way that management and communication are the cornerstones of business, they are the cornerstones of effective teaching. Whether working in a coteaching setting, as a consultant, as a resource, or as a self-contained teacher, the special education teacher makes thousands of management decisions each day regarding the teaching–learning process and the instructional cycle. This chapter deals with the issue of the special education teacher as a manager, communicator, and collaborator.

Challenges to Successful Inclusion and Coteaching

What are some of the challenges of working in an inclusive classroom and working with general education teachers? There has probably never been a time in history when educators faced greater challenges and opportunities than those we face in the United States today. Classroom teachers are required to provide instruction for increasingly diverse student populations and are still held accountable for covering the prescribed curriculum in a manner that ensures most students learn that content. Classroom teachers sometimes feel that they must choose between covering the full content of the curriculum or spending sufficient instructional time on curriculum components to ensure that students with special needs learn. Many teachers make the choice to "go on,"

even when students with disabilities and other low-achieving students have not learned very much.

Many special education students need more time to master new concepts and skills, and they master those concepts and skills only if instruction is presented to them in a manner that enables them to grasp the new material. Teachers must know and use a variety of instructional strategies to ensure that all students have an opportunity to learn. This takes time and planning. The first priority must be to ensure that students succeed in learning the content that is covered.

In general, teachers at the middle and high school levels indicate that it is often not feasible for them to plan specifically for students with special needs (Isherwood & Barger-Anderson, 2007; Schumm, Vaughn et al., 1995). Furthermore, when coteaching has been compared to other models such as resource-room settings, the findings for students are mixed (Zigmond & Magiera, 2002). This suggests that the model of service delivery may not be the issue; rather, the quality of instruction provided to students is what makes the difference (Zigmond, 2003). General education teachers are willing to work with special education professionals to make accommodations for students with special needs as they teach—particularly when those accommodations are useful to other learners in the classroom. There are many opportunities for special and general education teachers to align their knowledge and skills and improve outcomes for students with disabilities.

Challenges to Special Education Teachers

Two special education teachers at different schools had very different points of view about their experiences working as coteachers with general education teachers to improve learning for students with disabilities. One teacher said, "It was the best year of my teaching career. Ms. Walberg was terrific and taught me so much about what to expect from regular education. I think all of the students benefited because we worked so well together and shared so much of the teaching." Another teacher at a different school said, "This year was enough to get me to leave education. I never really felt like I was an equal partner in the classroom. I always felt like I was the teaching assistant. Furthermore, it was so painful to watch how practices were implemented for students who needed help and weren't getting it. Yet I never really felt anyone was listening to me."

Ms. Peres, a special education teacher, states it this way:

I am convinced that students with disabilities need to be in general education classrooms if at all possible. However, I have learned that we need to prepare them both socially and academically. Much of what we do in special education classrooms does not prepare them for general education. They are used to individual and small group instruction, receiving lots of feedback and lots of reinforcement, and being relatively free to ask for and receive assistance. This does not reflect what happens in the general education classrooms in this school. Although the teachers are great, they have 28 to 32 students in each class. Large group instruction and cooperative and independent learning are the most frequently used instructional arrangements.

The first key to making inclusion work is to cooperate with the general classroom teacher and to observe that classroom to determine the learning and social demands.

The second key is to gain a commitment from the student. He or she has to want to work toward the goal. I always describe the classroom demands to the student, and sometimes he or she goes to observe. Then we plan how we're going to get ready for "going to Mrs. Fereira's class for math."

The third key is to begin simulating those learning and social demands in my classroom. I start gradually. Usually, I begin by decreasing the feedback and reinforcement. Next I focus on the academic demands. I get the lessons and textbooks from the classroom teacher, and I begin to assign the lessons. At first, the rate of learning is matched

to the student's learning rate. But once the student is succeeding with the assignments, I begin to increase the rate until it matches that of the general education classroom. As this procedure continues, I gradually reduce the amount of reinforcement and feedback and work with the student to become a more independent learner.

The fourth key is to monitor the student and to continue to work with the classroom teacher to modify and adapt materials, methods, and the teaching–learning environment as needed.

I have developed this strategy through experience. Many times, I have found that my test scores, informal assessments, and student progress data indicate that the student is reading at grade level. In the past, I would jump to the conclusion that the student was ready to perform without assistance in the general education classroom. Yet too often I would find the student in difficulties within 3 weeks. I was really setting the students up for failure. I had attended only to their reading level, not to the social and academic demands.

I've been very successful with this strategy. I have all but 4 of my 14 students included for most of the school day.

Ms. Peres's discussion of how she provides effective instruction and behavioral support for her students in the general education classroom demonstrates that she values communication, collaboration, and consultation with the general education classroom teachers.

> ▶ WEB RESOURCES
> What You Need to Know About Special Education
> http://specialed.about.com/education/specialed/library/
> weekly/blswchwaub2.htm?terms=collaboration.

Understanding the Challenges of General Education Classrooms

Special education teachers need to understand what students with special needs can reasonably expect in general education classrooms so that they can provide the support and skills necessary for success. Although expectations vary considerably between elementary and secondary teachers (Isherwood & Barger-Anderson, 2007; Salend, Gordon, & Lopez-Vona, 2002; Schumm & Vaughn, 1992a, 1992b) and obviously from teacher to teacher, there are some common expectations:

• General education teachers are willing to make adaptations and accommodations that require little preplanning. These adaptations and accommodations are more likely to occur if they can be done during the instructional process. If instructional modifications to assignments or tests are required, the special education teacher can assist in providing them. See Apply the Concept 5-1 for a list of feasible adaptations.
• Teachers treat students with special needs in much the same way that they treat other students (Friend, Hurley-Chamberlain, & Cook, 2006; McIntosh, Vaughn,

5-1

Adaptations General Education Teachers Are Willing to Make

Teachers identified the following as *highly* feasible to implement:

1. Provide reinforcement and encouragement to assist students with learning.
2. Establish a personal relationship with included students.
3. Involve included students in whole-class activities.
4. Establish routines that are appropriate for included students.

5. Establish expectations for learning and behavior.

Teachers identified the following as *not* likely to be implemented:

1. Adapt long-range plans to meet the needs of included students.
2. Adjust the physical arrangement of the room to meet the needs of included students.

3. Use alternative materials or adapt current materials for students with special needs.
4. Adapt scoring and grading criteria for students with special needs.
5. Provide individualizing instruction to meet students' special needs.

Source: Adapted from J. S. Schumm & S. Vaughn (1991), Making adaptations for mainstreamed students: General classroom teachers' perspectives. *Remedial and Special Education, 12* (4), pp. 18–27.

Schumm, Haager, & Lee, 1993). This is, of course, both good and bad news. Teachers treat students with special needs with the same respect and consideration they give to other students. However, they provide few accommodations (particularly at the middle and high school levels) to meet the students' individual learning needs.

- Students with special needs participate infrequently in class activities, ask fewer questions than other students do, and rarely respond to teachers' questions (McIntosh et al., 1993). Students with special needs display a passive learning style that does little to increase the likelihood that general education teachers will meet their learning needs.

- Whole-class activity is by far the primary mode of instruction at the middle and high school levels and for social studies and science at the elementary level (McIntosh et al., 1993; Schumm et al., 1995a). Thus, students with special needs who are accustomed to working in small groups and receiving extensive teacher direction are unlikely to receive these same considerations in the general education classroom.

- Undifferentiated large group instruction is representative of what occurs in general education classrooms; yet one-on-one instruction is a better predictor of students' success (Soukup, Wehmeyer, Bashinski, & Bovaird, 2007). Teachers largely follow the sequence of activities provided in the teacher's manual and do not consider the learning needs of groups or individual students.

▶ **WEB RESOURCES**

For more information about meeting the needs of all students in inclusive classrooms, see the Web site on inclusive education resources from the J. P. Das Developmental Disabilities Centre http://www.ualberta.ca/~jpdasddc/index.html.

Consultation and Collaboration

What are three major models for consultation and collaboration? Although both terms—*consultation* and *collaboration*—are often used to describe the role of many special education teachers, teachers prefer the term *collaboration*. Why? Teachers indicate that they prefer collaborative modes of working on student problems rather than handing over problems to experts or working on them independently (Arguelles, Vaughn, & Schumm, 1996; Morrison, Walker, Wakefield, & Solberg, 1994). Teachers perceive that the term *collaboration* more accurately describes the nature of their relationships. As one special education teacher noted, "We actually work together to solve problems. It's not like I have all of the answers or she has all of the problems. We really help each other come up with ideas that work." We have found that general education teachers feel much the same way.

What is collaboration? Collaboration refers to the interaction that occurs between two professionals, often between special education teachers and general education teachers, and to the roles that they play as equal partners in problem-solving endeavors. When teachers collaborate, they

- work together to solve problems and generate feasible solutions that they implement and evaluate.
- reflect on their own instructional practices and are eager to make changes that improve outcomes for students.

What are some of the ways in which special education teachers might expect to collaborate with other professionals? A significant part of their role is to collaborate with parents and any other specialist who is associated with the special needs students with whom the teacher works. Whether working as a resource room teacher, a self-contained special education teacher, or a coteacher, special education teachers also have considerable opportunities to collaborate with general education teachers. They may also work in a program in which most of the workday involves collaboration with other teachers. At the elementary, middle, and secondary school levels, teachers are increasingly working in more collaborative ways with other professionals (Idol, Nevin, & Paolucci-Whitcomb, 2000).

One important way in which special education teachers collaborate with general education professionals is in developing ways to make curricula more accessible to students with special needs. Curriculum planning can address such important issues as identifying changes in curriculum that are forecast by national boards and professional groups, identifying the ways in which these new trends will affect the curriculum and students with special needs, examining the scope and sequence of the present curriculum and determining where changes best fit, identifying new goals and discussing the prerequisite skills needed for students with special needs, and identifying areas of mismatch or in which new curriculum is inappropriate for target students.

Additional ways in which special education teachers collaborate with general education teachers include:

- *Coteaching*—Working with classroom teachers to provide instruction together in general education classrooms. For example, a special education teacher might coteach with an English teacher at the secondary level who has several students with disabilities in his class. The goal would be for the special education teacher to provide access to the general education curriculum for the students with disabilities. The special education teacher might provide small group instruction within the classroom, modify homework assignments, and assist with test preparation and other accommodations for students with disabilities as needed.
- *Consultant teaching*—Working with classroom teachers to solve problems for students with disabilities who will be included in general education classrooms. For example, the special education teacher may be asked to observe the student with disabilities in the general education classroom as a means to identifying behavioral or instructional practices that might facilitate success for the target student. Another example may be that the special education teacher modifies particular tests or assignments to promote access to the general education curriculum for the student with disabilities. Consultant teaching differs from coteaching in that the special education teacher observes, assesses, and helps plan for instruction but typically does not provide direct instruction in the general education classroom.
- *Coordination of paraprofessionals*—Working with classroom teachers to coordinate and support the activities of paraprofessionals who assist students with disabilities in the general education classroom. For example, the special education teacher may have a paraprofessional assigned to a student with severe behavior problems during science and math in the general education classroom. The student may have the knowledge and skills to benefit from the general education classroom but may not have the appropriate behaviors. The special education teacher could provide the paraprofessional with the guidelines for positive behavioral support to enhance student's success in the classroom.
- *Teacher assistance teams (TATs)*—Participating in school-based teams of professionals, classroom teachers, and administrators that assist classroom teachers in meeting the instructional and behavior needs of individual students. For example, the special education teacher might organize grade-level meetings at the elementary level (e.g., all fourth-grade teachers meet at the same time) or content area meetings at the middle school level (e.g., all social studies teachers meet at the same time) to discuss ways to promote successful learning and behavior for students with learning and behavior problems.

Procedures for Collaboration Within a Response to Intervention (RTI) Framework

What is the role of the special education teacher within an RTI framework? RTI has provided new opportunities and expectations for cooperation between special education teachers and general education teachers. Special education teachers may meet and plan with general education teachers about the Tier 2 interventions provided in math and reading, and may also play a significant role in providing interventions for students in Tier 3. What are some of the collaborative activities that special education teachers may engage in within an RTI framework? A few considerations follow (Haager & Mahdavi, 2007; Hoover & Patton, 2008):

- Organizing screening and progress-monitoring measures and determining cut points for which students will be provided reading and math intervention
- Determining how interventions should be implemented and organized
- Developing a checklist for high-quality implementation of interventions
- Developing training for teachers and paraprofessionals to provide high-quality intervention
- How to adjust interventions to meet the needs of students performing at a range of grade levels and with varying instructional needs
- How to adjust instruction when students make minimal progress in interventions

In summary, the critical role for the special education teacher is to collaborate with all key stakeholders in the school, including school psychologists, speech and language specialists, general education teachers, and school leaders, to make critical decisions about (1) determining and implementing research-based practices, (2) collecting and using ongoing data to make effective decisions for students with learning and behavioral problems, (3) identifying appropriate practices for differentiating instruction within the classroom and interventions, and (4) communicating effectively with all key stakeholders so that appropriate instruction is provided to all students with learning and behavior problems.

Resources Needed for Collaboration

No resource impedes successful collaboration more than time. Special and general education teachers confirm the difficulties of finding adequate time to effectively collaborate during the work day (Friend, 2000; Stivers, 2008). If time is not built into teachers' schedules, collaboration is unlikely to occur on a regular basis. Furthermore, if it is not part of the schedule, then teachers come to resent having to collaborate because it means taking time from their personal schedules. Another critical aspect of time management for special education teachers is finding mutually available time when they can collaborate with the many teachers with whom they work. Time management is especially challenging at the secondary level. Following are some ways in which collaborative time can be arranged (Vaughn, Bos, & Schumm, 2010):

- Administrators designate a common time for collaborating professionals (e.g., all fifth-grade team members) to work together.
- School boards pay professionals for one extra time period each week that can be used to collaborate or meet with families.
- School districts provide early dismissal for students one day a week so that team members have a common planning time.
- Teachers meet for brief but focused planning periods on a regularly scheduled basis.
- Resources such as administrators, families, volunteers, and university students are used to help cover classes. For example, short planning sessions may be scheduled during recess when larger groups of students can be monitored by a teacher and a volunteer.

Space for meeting is another necessary resource. Special education teachers are often fortunate because they have an office or a small classroom for their materials. But finding a quiet place to meet is particularly challenging in schools where overcrowding is the norm.

Additionally, participants in collaborative models need to be familiar with procedures for successful collaboration. An orientation that addresses basic questions about their roles and responsibilities is helpful to all personnel who are involved in collaboration. Administrative support can be crucial to ensuring that teachers are given appropriate time, space, and knowledge of procedures to implement an effective collaborative model.

Like other educational approaches, consultation and collaboration models have the potential for benefit as well as misuse and misunderstanding. Apply the Concept 5-2 describes potential benefits and misuses.

Collaboration Issues and Dilemmas

All special education teachers work collaboratively with general education teachers and many special education teachers work with general education teachers at least 50% of the time. Consequently, special education teachers need to recognize several issues and dilemmas in order to perform their job effectively.

1. *Student ownership.* Traditionally, special education students have been the responsibility of the special education teacher, even if they were placed in a general education classroom for part of the day. This perspective is no longer feasible or desirable. The new perspective is one of shared ownership whereby all educators feel responsible for the success of the student with special needs.

2. *Individual versus class focus.* General education teachers have the responsibility for all students in their class. Particularly at the upper elementary and secondary grade levels, general education teachers focus on teaching the content and less on teaching individual students. This contrasts with the focus of special education teachers, whose planning and instruction is aimed at the needs of individual students. These differing perspectives may mean that general and special education teachers need to develop solutions that promote content support within a model that provides the necessary instructional support for students with special needs. Mrs. Vermillion put it this way: "I am a special education teacher and so the direction of my interest is always with the individual student and how the educational setting can be altered to meet his or her needs. During the last few years I realize that I've needed to adjust my perspective if I am to work effectively with classroom teachers. When they think about planning for students, they think about the class as a whole." What are some of the changes Mrs. Vermillion has instituted so that she can have a more successful connection with the general education teacher?

- Develop materials including assessments and homework that are content appropriate, enhance learning for all students, and meet the needs of students with disabilities.
- Spend additional time learning the content so that she can provide appropriate accommodations for students.
- Look for resources for the general education teacher (e.g., books, charts, videos) that provide content instruction but also support learning of students with disabilities.

5-2   Benefits and Misuses of Consultation and Collaboration

Consultation and collaboration models have several potential benefits and misuses (Zigmond, 2003).

Potential Benefits

1. Reduction of stigma
2. Better understanding across education disciplines
3. On-the-job training for general education teachers in skills for effectively meeting the needs of special education students
4. Reduced mislabeling of students as disabled
5. Suitability in meeting the needs of secondary school students
6. Spillover benefits to general education students from working cooperatively with special education teacher

Potential Misuses/Problems

1. Excessive caseload management for special education teachers
2. Unrealistic expectations from viewing the consulting model as a panacea and/or undertraining and overloading the special education teacher
3. Inadequate support and cooperation from classroom teachers
4. Converting the model to a tutoring or aide approach
5. Providing inadequate funding
6. Faulty assumptions about cost savings
7. Faulty assumptions about program effectiveness
8. Unrealistic expectations for changes in academic success and social acceptance
9. Inadequate preparation for vocational experiences after school
10. Inadequate time to plan, communicate, and effectively instruct target students

Overall, the most important question to address is whether students with learning and behavior problems are having their needs met through a consultation and collaborative model. The model may be highly effective for some students and less so for others.

---

3. *Content versus accommodation*. When classroom teachers discuss their planning and instruction, one of the most consistent themes is content coverage (Kloo & Zigmond, 2008; Schumm et al., 1995). Classroom teachers recognize that state and national laws pressure them to cover more content. Jon Lau, a ninth-grade science teacher, says, "Waiting until the students understand would result in lack of adequate coverage of material. It is my responsibility to cover the content in the time I am allocated."

This notion of content coverage as the horse leading the instructional wagon is a consistent and pervasive problem in general education and now directly influences the instruction of students with special needs. There is some consensus that "less is more" and that a reduced focus on content coverage would enhance the quality of instruction for all learners.

You can imagine the difficulty for classroom teachers who feel pressured to cover extensive amounts of content when special education teachers make suggestions that slow down the pace or require them to make adaptations for students' special learning needs. This issue is not insolvable. Teachers are willing to make adaptations and accommodations they believe will help students and do not require extensive amounts of preparation.

4. *New roles for special education teachers*. Perhaps one of the greatest challenges for teachers who are learning to work collaboratively with other teachers is that they assume different roles than those they previously had. These roles can include supporting special education students in the general education classroom; teaching with another teacher in a content area in which they have little or no background knowledge, particularly at the secondary level; helping students with assignments; and engaging in disciplining and classroom management of a range of students (Weiss & Lloyd, 2002). A veteran special education teacher tells of the changing roles and responsibilities of moving from her own classroom to coteaching with other teachers. She discusses this role shift with the kind of nostalgia that shows that she misses many of the comforts of her own classroom and routines, yet realizes that many students are benefiting from her engagement in the general education classroom (Klingner & Vaughn, 2002).

What are some of the activities of special education teachers who are working more collaboratively with general education teachers? They spend the majority of their time in general education classrooms either monitoring the learning and behavior of target students or teaching a large group of students (six or more but not the entire class) (Harbort et al., 2007). Less frequently occurring activities include responding to students comments or questions, small group instruction (fewer than six students), extended individual student interaction, and managing behavior.

5. *Real world versus the student's world*. Another dichotomy between general and special education teachers is the purpose of education. Classroom teachers feel that they are preparing students for the "real world." From their perspective, people in the real world do not make accommodations for different learning styles. Fundamentally, they view the real world as expecting the same thing from everybody and therefore, to best prepare youngsters, their role as teachers is to expect the same thing from every student.

Ms. McDowell, a secondary special education teacher, handles the problem this way: "When classroom teachers talk to me about the real world, I'm prepared. First, I present them with the idea that students are never going to be successful in the real world if they do not have an opportunity to learn and experience success in their present world. Their present world is that teacher's classroom. Second, I present them with the fact that employers are required by law to make reasonable accommodations for individuals with disabilities. Also, I never ask general education teachers to make adaptations or accommodations that aren't useful to most students in the classroom." In fact, instructional interventions that are used to improve learning for students with disabilities are at least as effective—and sometimes more effective—for students without disabilities (Vaughn, Gersten, & Chard, 2000).

Problem-Solving Models Problem-solving models are ways in which teams of educators (e.g., special education teacher, general education teacher, speech and language therapist, school counselor, reading specialist) at each school implement a prevention approach to meeting the needs of students at risk for special needs and with special needs. These approaches provide instructional, behavioral, and assessment support to teachers at the school-building level so that early services can be provided to students to ensure their needs are met. Problem-solving approaches have as goals early prevention of learning and behavior problems, use of student data to influence decision making about placement in special education, and replacing more traditional approaches to assessing and identifying students with disabilities.

How do you implement a problem-solving approach in your school? The problem-solving model is systematic and involves frequent and ongoing student-data collection. In most cases, students are screened using relatively easy to administer reading and/or math screening measures.

When students are identified as having difficulties, they are provided evidence-based interventions using ongoing student-progress-monitoring measures to ensure that students are closing the gap between their current performance and expected performance. Students who make adequate progress are no longer provided intervention and those who need additional supports may be provided more extensive interventions. These interventions can be provided by personnel trained by the special education teacher or other educational personnel, or in some schools certified teachers provide the instructional support.

Problem-solving models are considered necessary because there are many students whose needs are not met early and who fall behind academically. In a traditional special education model, students are often not referred for special education support until third or fourth grade, when their learning needs are significant and are not readily remediated. The intention of problem-solving models is that students' needs will be met early and that based on students' responses to these early interventions, better information about which students have special needs can be determined.

Problem-solving approaches are used in several states, including Minnesota, Iowa, and North Carolina to name a few, and typically involve variations on the following four-step process:

- Define the problem—in other words specifically designate what the student's need is academically or behaviorally (e.g., Marcus is reading two grade levels behind his peers and is reading 40 words correctly per minute when the school average for his grade is 97 words per minute.
- Plan an intervention—the team decides what the appropriate intervention for Marcus would be. In this case, Marcus is provided 30 minutes daily of additional instruction in a small group that is instructed by the reading specialist.
- Implement the intervention—the team decides that Marcus would continue in the intervention for 12 weeks with progress monitoring using oral reading fluency obtained every other week.
- Evaluate the student's progress—based on student progress after 12 weeks the team would decide if Marcus is making adequate progress but needs to continue in the intervention, is making adequate progress and can discontinue participation in the intervention, or is making inadequate progress and another more intensive intervention is required.

Interventions are usually selected from a bank of research-based interventions that have been identified by the school or district (Berkley, Bender, Peaster, & Saunders, 2009).

Another example of a problem-solving model is the teacher assistance team (TAT) model (Chalfant & Pysh, 1989, 1992; http://www.emstac.org/registered/topics/disproportionality/models/tat.htm, downloaded 12/1/2009) designed to provide a teacher support system for classroom teachers. The TAT is a school-based problem-solving unit that assists teachers in generating intervention strategies. The TAT model provides a forum wherein classroom teachers can engage in a collaborative problem-solving process. The model is based on four assumptions related to teacher empowerment:

1. Considerable knowledge and talent exist among classroom teachers.
2. Classroom teachers can and do help many students with learning and behavior problems. Every effort should be made in the general classroom before a referral for special education services is made.
3. Teachers can resolve more problems by working together than by working alone.
4. Teachers learn best by solving immediate and relevant classroom problems.

Under the TAT approach, a team of professionals works cooperatively with classroom teachers to develop successful programs and strategies in the general education classroom for students with learning and behavior problems. Often, these teams are established to eliminate unnecessary testing and referral for special education. Whereas the original purpose was to work with students who have learning and behavior problems who were not currently placed in special education, it is possible to establish teams that focus on students already identified as special-needs students.

 EVIDENCE-BASED PRACTICE

Teacher Assistance Team (TAT)

PROCEDURES: The core team in the TAT model is generally composed of three elected members (primarily classroom teachers rather than special education teachers) with the requesting teacher also participating as a team member. The team may ask other teachers, specialists, or the principal to join the team as they deem necessary or to serve as permanent members. One person serves as coordinator and is charged with such responsibilities as alerting the team members to the time and place of the meetings and distributing information so that the members are briefed before coming to the problem-solving meeting.

When teachers refer classroom problems to the team, they complete a request for assistance in which they address four areas:

1. Describing what they would like students *to be able to do* that they do not currently do
2. Describing what students *do* (assets) and what they *do not do* (deficits)
3. Describing what they have done to help students cope with their problems
4. Providing background information and/or previous assessment data that are relevant to the problem

At the TAT meeting, team members complete a 30-minute problem-solving process for each request. The process consists of the following steps:

1. Reviewing the summary information, providing the opportunity for the teacher to clarify or provide additional information, and reaching consensus on what the problem is
2. Identifying the primary concern and establishing an objective for solving the problem
3. Brainstorming ideas for solving the problem and reaching the objective
4. Having the teacher requesting assistance select intervention strategies, which the teacher and team refine into a classroom intervention plan
5. Developing a means of measuring the success of the intervention plan
6. Establishing a date and time for a 15-minute follow-up meeting

Using this format, a TAT generally handles two new requests, or one new request and two follow-ups, during a 1-hour meeting.

COMMENTS: The TAT model has been used widely throughout the United States and Canada. It has been shown to be effective in helping teachers cope with the learning and behavior problems of students in the general school population. It is also may empower teachers to meet the needs of students with disabilities in their classrooms and reduce the number of students who are inappropriately referred for special education. Due to its success in reducing the number of inappropriate referrals to special education, the TAT model is identified in the literature as a prereferral intervention. However, the original intent of the process was to serve as a resource for all students at a school. This process has also been used with students previously identified as having special needs, with the children's special education and general education teachers serving as team members and participating in the problem-solving process.

Several factors seem particularly relevant to the success of this model within a school. First, it is important that the school administration support such a program by providing teachers with time for meetings and some type of incentive for serving as team members. Second, schoolwide staff training in effective and efficient problem-solving strategies and the TAT process facilitates the success of the model (Bay, Bryan, & O'Connor, 1994; Chalfant & Pysh, 1989).

Coteaching

Coteaching, or cooperative teaching, occurs when general and special education teachers coordinate their efforts and jointly teach special and general education students, sharing planning, presentation, assessment, and classroom management to promote successful outcomes for all students (Gately & Gately, 2001). Villa, Thousand, and Nevin (2008) also remind us what coteaching is not. Coteaching is not one person teaching while another prepares materials, not one person's views dominating

5-3 Coteaching Perceptions

Consider asking and answering these questions with your coteacher as a means for determining areas of strength and potential areas to focus on within your coteaching setting:

1. We both have equal access to all information about general education students in the class?
2. We both have equal access to all information about special education students in the class?
3. We both are perceived by key administrators as appropriate contacts for issues about the class?
4. We both are perceived by parents as appropriate contacts for issues about the class?
5. If a problem with a student arises, we are both comfortable addressing it and communicating with each other about it?
6. We have adequate time to plan?
7. We both have access to materials in the classroom?
8. The desks and chairs for both teachers are equivalent?
9. Decisions about what to teach are shared?
10. Decisions about how to teach are discussed and agreed upon?
11. Decisions about adaptations to meet the special learning needs of students are discussed and agreed upon?
12. Decisions about adaptations to tests and other evaluations are discussed and agreed upon?
13. We provide each other with feedback that is useful and improves our instruction?
14. We coteach effectively and with few difficulties?
15. We respect the contributions of our coteacher?
16. We communicate and problem solve problems effectively?

---

instructional decision making, not tutoring, and not one person watching while another teaches. See Apply the Concept 5-3 for a description of questions to ask to promote a successful co-teaching experience.

Although there is some debate over the effectiveness of coteaching as a way to meet the needs of students with disabilities (Isherwood & Barger-Anderson, 2007; Zigmond, 2001), limited data indicate that coteaching can have a positive impact on student achievement (Scruggs, Mastropieri, & McDuffie, 2007). Of course, the effectiveness of coteaching is related to what students need to learn and whether they can learn it well within a coteaching setting. Generally, teachers report that they benefited professionally from coteaching. They also report increased cooperation among students within their class and additional time and attention for students with disabilities. Teachers did consistently express concerns that many of the students with disabilities demonstrated significantly low academic skills with learning needs that were difficult to meet in the general education classroom (Scruggs, Mastropieri, & McDuffie, 2007).

Villa, Thousand, and Nevin (2008) indicate that coteaching is likely to be beneficial when:

- Teacher use of collaborative skills increases teacher responsiveness. When teachers share ideas, work together, and promote each others' successes in the classroom, all students are provided improved instruction. When collaboration is effective, there is a broader range of students who have access to the curriculum.
- Teachers support and identify the use of research-based practices. In coteaching settings, teachers can structure classrooms to use various grouping practices, reducing the prevailing use of whole class instruction and increasing small group and peer teaching. Coteaching also provides opportunities for teachers to identify research-based practices and inform each other of ways to more effectively implement these practices.
- Teachers use problem solving to provide individualized learning and meet all students' needs. Teachers who identify learning and behavior problems in their class and solve problems to more effectively meet the needs of students are likely to yield beneficial learning outcomes.
- Teachers empower each other through coteaching. Teachers who effectively coteach can empower each other through collaborative decision making, confirming effective practices, and sharing difficult situations.

How Coteaching Works When coteaching, special and general education teachers plan broad, overall goals and desired outcomes for the class as a whole as well as for specific students in the class. Both special and general classroom teachers lead instruction during the same instructional period. Although one teacher may provide some instruction to the group as a whole, most of the instructional time involves both teachers working with small groups or with individual students. Because students are frequently grouped heterogeneously, the special education teacher works with many students, including those who are identified as benefiting from special education. Complementary instruction and supportive learning activities are part of the teachers' coplanning and instruction.

Coteaching Models Coteaching involves much more than just putting a special and a general education teacher in the same classroom. For example, Weiss and Lloyd (2002, 2003) found that in coteaching situations it was often difficult for special education teachers to provide the type of focused, explicit instruction that they used in special education classrooms. Therefore, to be successful, both teachers must carefully plan what role each will take and the type of instruction they will each provide.

Teachers can implement a variety of coteaching models. Many teachers select a coteaching model based on both overall instructional goals and the individual needs of students in the classroom. Before choosing a coteaching model, the general and special education teachers need to decide what lesson or unit will be taught, being careful to consider general education curriculum requirements as well as the individual needs of students with disabilities specified on their individualized education program (IEP). Most teachers find that they use more than one model during a week and even during a day. Following are several coteaching models that teachers have found useful (Conderman, Bresnahan, & Pedersen, 2009; Vaughn, Schumm, & Arguelles, 1997).

Model A: One Group. One Lead Teacher, One Teacher "Teaching on Purpose" Many teachers in coteaching situations end up spending their time grazing, that is, going from student to student, to make sure they are following along, but without a specific plan or goal in mind. "Teaching on purpose" is a method of checking for understanding and providing short installments of explicit instruction that are related to key ideas, concepts, or vocabulary from the main lesson. When teaching on purpose, one of the teachers gives short lessons to individuals, pairs, or small groups of students during or as a follow-up to whole group instruction. In 1 or 2 minutes, the teacher who is teaching on purpose might approach a student after instruction by the lead teacher to follow up on key ideas and concepts, encourage participation, answer questions, or review directions. In about 5 minutes, the teacher can review concepts and vocabulary or check for understanding. If further instruction is needed, the teacher can take a bit longer to provide a mini lesson that is related to the main lesson (e.g., how to find the main idea). When coteaching is used effectively, the teacher has a specific objective in mind and targets particular students to ensure that they are learning specified material. Some examples of what coteachers can do when they teach on purpose include:

- Reinforce big ideas of the lesson to one or two students.
- Ask a student a question related to the overall instruction to see if they are learning.
- Ask student to write the key word or words about what they are learning.

- Connect what students are currently learning to previous learning.
- Check written work and provide specific feedback and suggestions.

Model B: Two Mixed-Ability Groups. Two Teachers Teach the Same Content In Model B, the class is divided into two mixed-ability groups, and each teacher instructs one group. The purpose of this coteaching model is to reduce the group size so as to increase the number of opportunities for students to participate and interact with one another, and to have their responses and knowledge monitored by a teacher. This format is often used when difficult new content is introduced or when smaller groups are beneficial for certain instructional activities, such as discussion. For example, the coteachers may divide the class into two heterogeneous groups during the discussion of a book that has been read as a whole group. At the end of the lesson, the two groups come together to summarize what they learned and to integrate information between groups. Some other examples of when you might use this grouping format include:

- One teacher is doing a science lab experiment with half of the class while the other teacher is reviewing key ideas related to learning from the experiment.
- One teacher is teaching about a controversial issue in social studies (e.g., socialism versus capitalism) and the other teacher is teaching the same content, but the small groups allow students more opportunities for discussion.
- One teacher is reviewing key grammatical functions related to paragraph writing with half of the students who need the lesson, while the other teacher is working on composing 5 paragraph essays.

Model C: Two Same-Ability Groups. Teachers Teach Different Content Students are divided into two groups on the basis of their skill level in the topic area. One teacher reteaches while the other teacher provides alternative information or extension activities to the second group. For example, during a unit on fractions, one teacher can lead a reteaching activity on dividing the parts of a whole, while the other teacher facilitates an activity on creating story problems using fractions. In effective coteaching, the general education teacher does not always assume the role of lead teacher, nor does the special education teacher always reteach. Teachers share responsibilities and alter roles from one lesson to the next.

Model D: Multiple Groups. Teachers Monitor/Teach Model D is often used during cooperative learning activities and in reading groups and learning centers. One option for Model D is to have several heterogeneous groups and one or two homogeneous groups based on skill level. One or both teachers work with groups for the entire period. For example, during reading in Ms. Chamber's fifth-grade class the special education teacher, Mrs. Scholar, provides reading instruction to a group of students with low reading ability that includes several students with disabilities. The classroom teacher has two other groups who rotate between working in centers and working with her in a group. Another example is Mr. Young's third-grade math class in which Mrs. Scholar and he arrange for four groups of students to rotate between them and two centers during a 50-minute period. This allows each teacher to work with a relatively small group of students (approximate 5–7) for 25 minutes every day. Another possibility during social studies or science is to have students move in small groups through four or five centers. Two centers are teacher-assisted, and the remaining centers have activities that can be done independently by groups. Students might also work in cooperative groups or pairs while both teachers provide mini lessons and monitor progress.

Model E: Whole Class. Two Teachers Teach Together In this model, teachers work cooperatively to teach a lesson. One teacher may lead the whole class lesson while the other teacher interjects to clarify the material. Often the general education teacher provides curriculum material, and the special education teacher adds strategies to help students with disabilities remember key ideas and organize information. For example, teachers might spend 10 minutes modeling problem-solving techniques and explaining directions for a science lesson on observation in which students will work cooperatively to record observations and make predictions about a "mystery matter." One teacher lists the steps of the activity, while the other points to a flowchart indicating the correct sequence to follow. In the next section on coteaching with secondary students, there is a description of activities that Mr. Prudhi (a special education teacher) might use to support instruction. These examples are very relevant for the model of two teachers teaching together.

Coteaching with Secondary Students Coteaching varies necessarily between elementary and secondary levels. At the elementary level it is not uncommon for coteaching to occur for as much as half of the day. In these settings, the special education teacher may have as many as six to eight students in two target classrooms for most or all of the day. The special education teacher could then spend several hours a day in each of those classrooms coteaching with the general education teacher. For example, the special education teacher Ms. Gentry coteaches with the fourth-grade teacher Mr. Marcus and the fifth-grade teacher Ms. Lau. She teaches reading and math in the morning with Mr. Marcus and then again with Ms. Lau in the afternoon. The special education teacher coplans reading and

math activities with the general education teacher, and both decide how to target and support the learning of the students with disabilities.

At the secondary level, coteaching is different for the special education teacher Mr. Prudhi. He would describe his role as more of a supportive teacher (Villa, Thousand, & Nevin, 2008), meaning that the content area teacher for math, social studies, and science take primary responsibility for designing and delivering the lesson and his role is to support instruction for students with disabilities. What are some of the activities that Mr. Prudhi might perform within the supportive teaching role?

He might

- determine the big idea of the instructional unit that week and make it clear to the students with special needs.
- identify the key academic vocabulary and concepts related to learning the unit, and teach those to students with special needs to ensure that they can learn the content.
- identify resources that would facilitate learning for students with special needs, such as supportive texts written at levels the student can read, technology that would provide access to visual images or other information to promote learning, and/or a video that would make some of the key concepts more accessible.
- conduct a pretest on the material to be taught that week to determine what students know and what they need to know to successfully master the information that week.
- provide modifications to assignments, homework, or assessments so that they are accessible to students with disabilities.
- communicate with key personnel at the school to facilitate learning for target students.
- communicate with parents to facilitate learning for target students.
- develop resources, such as overheads, PowerPoint slides, graphs, and other learning devices, to facilitate learning for all students.
- provide 60-second lessons to key students to reinforce ideas taught and ensure learning.
- provide small group lessons to key students as needed.
- follow up with students to ensure learning is sustained and connected to previous learning.

Apply the Concept 5-4 provides guidelines for effective coteaching in elementary school classes for students with learning and behavior problems.

Coplanning Special education teachers often coplan with general education teachers for the students with special needs who are in their classrooms. Sometimes

5-4 Guidelines for Effective Coteaching

Effective coteaching involves the following:

1. *Voluntary participants.* Teachers should choose to work together and should not be forced into a collaborative teaching situation (Scruggs, Mastropieri, & McDuffie, 2007). Ms. Andrews is a special education teacher who has been coteaching in three fourth-grade classrooms for several years to assist children with learning and behavior problems. She began collaborating after attending a workshop on coteaching with the fourth-grade team from her school. She says the reason she and her team are successful is because "we enjoy working together, have compatible teaching styles, and feel comfortable discussing differences."

2. *Shared responsibility.* Teachers combine their knowledge and resources to plan instruction. Therefore, they also share the accountability for the outcomes of those decisions.

3. *Reciprocity of ideas.* While the amount and nature of input will vary by teacher, both teachers must accept each other's contributions as integral to the collaborative process.

4. *Problem solving.* Not only must teachers collaborate to identify and find solutions to meet student needs, they also must accept that problems will arise when two professionals work together to coordinate instruction. Dealing with problems that arise during collaboration is not so different from finding solutions to student problems. To solve a problem it is helpful to identify concerns, share

information regarding the problem, brainstorm possible solutions, evaluate the ideas and create a solution plan, try the solution, and evaluate its success (Villa, Thousand, & Nevin, 2008).

5. *Interactive communication.* Effective communication occurs when teachers trust each other and are not afraid to voice either their agreement or disagreement, when they communicate accurately and directly, and when they remain sensitive to differences (Villa, Thousand, & Nevin, 2008).

6. *Conflict resolution.* Disagreements and even arguments are inevitable in any collaborative process. Implementing a plan to resolve conflicts can lead to better solutions than if the problem is ignored (Idol et al., 2000).

special education teachers also coteach in those classrooms; at other times, they assist the teacher in planning and making adaptations for students with special needs to lessons that will be taught without their assistance or facilitate development of appropriate evaluations or homework assignments.

In long-range coplanning, special education and general education teachers plan broad overall goals and outcomes for a class and the specific students with disabilities who are in that class. This coplanning of broad goals occurs quarterly or more frequently as needed, and accommodates the IEPs of students with disabilities.

Special education and general education teachers may also coplan specific lessons and outcomes for a unit of study or for a designated period of time (e.g., weekly). The planning pyramid (Schumm, Vaughn, & Harris, 1997) provides a process for coplanning by special and general education teachers to meet the needs of students with disabilities in general education classrooms. As can be seen in Figure 5-1, a form for unit planning, and in Figures 5-2 and 5-3, forms for lesson planning, forms can be used to facilitate the process. Working together, teachers complete the forms to identify their objectives, materials needed, and their

roles and responsibilities in delivering the instruction. While planning, the special education teacher can provide ideas for adaptations, clarification, scaffolding, and use of materials to facilitate learning. Essential to the success of the planning pyramid is the identification of core ideas, concepts, vocabulary, and/or principles that the teachers determine to be essential for all students to learn. This information is entered at the base of the pyramid. Information that the teacher deems important for most students to learn is written in the middle of the pyramid. Information for a few students to learn is written at the top of the pyramid. Teachers who implement the planning pyramid find that it not only facilitates the organization of the material they intend to teach, but also provides guidelines for instruction (Schumm et al., 1997).

Successful Coteaching Joyce Duryea is an elementary special education teacher who has worked as a resource room teacher for 9 years (Klingner & Vaughn, 2002, provide a case study of Joyce if you would like to read more about her). She was asked to work collaboratively with three general education teachers who had approximately five students with disabilities in each of their classrooms. Joyce said, "When I was preparing to be a special

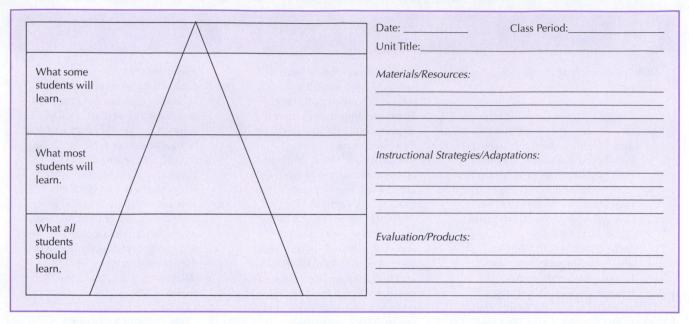

education teacher, it never occurred to me that I would need to know how to coteach in a general education classroom. I always thought I would have my group of students with special needs and that is the way it would be." However, she has found her new role exciting and challenging. Joyce puts it this way: "I think I'm a better teacher now, and I definitely have a much better understanding of what goes on in the general education classroom and what kinds of expectations I need to have for my students."

► **Figure 5-2** Weekly Coplanning Form

Time Period: _____	Week Of: _____		Content Area: _____
Goals:	GE		SE
	_____		_____
Activities:	GE		SE
Monday	_____		_____
Tuesday	_____		_____
Wednesday	_____		_____
Thursday	_____		_____
Friday	_____		_____
Material(s):	GE		SE
Monday	_____		_____
Tuesday	_____		_____
Wednesday	_____		_____
Thursday	_____		_____
Friday	_____		_____
Groups/Students:	GE		SE
Monday	_____		_____
Tuesday	_____		_____
Wednesday	_____		_____
Thursday	_____		_____
Friday	_____		_____
Evaluation:	_____	**Other:**	_____

General Educator: ___Ms. Marco___   Special Educator: ___Ms. Sanders___   Grade: _____5_____

Date	Coteaching Technique	Specific Teacher Tasks	Materials	Evaluation	Individual Student Needs
2/8	Model B: Two mixed-ability groups	Literary Discussion: Both teachers lead discussions on the class reading of *The Cay*. In each group, teacher and students write comprehension questions. Students call on volunteers to respond to their questions. Teacher interjects throughout the discussion, making sure all students have a chance to ask and answer questions.	Student copies of *The Cay* Discussion journals	Evaluate discussion journals Monitor participation	Assist Roger in formulating a response to share with class; remind Sam to pause first to organize thoughts before responding; Joe completes journal on computer
2/9	Model D: Five same-ability groups	Literacy Groups: Teachers each work with one of the two lower groups to provide explicit instruction in word analysis. The other three student groups work independently to complete reading and literacy assignments.	Student books Reading log	Chart number of words decoded correctly Evaluate reading logs	Ms. M: Mini lesson on *r*-controlled vowels Ms. S: Reteach syllabication strategy for decoding
2/10	Model D: Six mixed-ability groups	Survival Centers: Ms. S works at the Vocabulary center with Roger's group. She then follows his group to the Survival Word Game station and provides a word building mini lesson. Ms. S remains at the Word Building station and provides a building words mini lesson to Sandy's group. Ms. M monitors the remaining groups.	Center activities	Monitor group work Evaluate student work in word building	Roger works in a pair instead of in a foursome; Sandy brings behavior contract to stations
2/11	Model A: One group: Teaching on purpose	Research Reports: Ms. S gives directions for research report. Ms. M monitors work while Ms. S sees three small skill level groups (10–12 minutes each) to work on fluency/decoding.	Step-by-step research planners	Record fluency progress on student charts Evaluate planners	Roger uses modified research planner; Joe and Pedro complete work on computer
2/12	Model C: Two groups: One reteach	Research Reports: Ms. S works with students who are ready to begin research while Ms. M reteaches students who need assistance to develop a plan for their individual research projects.	Step-by-step research planners Research materials	Evaluate planners	Julie and Sam paraphrase steps before writing; Joe and Pedro complete work on computer

Several core issues must be addressed if coteaching partnerships are likely to be successful (Scruggs, Mastropieri, & McDuffie, 2007; Vaughn & Schumm, 1996):

• *Who gives grades, and how do we grade?* Perhaps the issue that warrants the most discussion before coteaching is grading. Special education teachers are accustomed to grading based on the effort, motivation, and abilities of their students. General education teachers consider grades from the perspective of a uniform set of expectations. Communicating about

grading procedures for in-class assignments, tests, and homework will reduce the friction that is frequently associated with grading students with disabilities in the general education classroom. Grading can be particularly challenging at the secondary level where grades can be used to make high-stakes decisions about access to postsecondary education, rank in class, and graduation.

• *Whose classroom management rules do we use, and who enforces them?* Most general and special education teachers know the types of academic and social behaviors they find acceptable and unacceptable. Rarely is there disagreement between teachers about the more extreme behaviors; however, the subtle classroom management issues that are part of the ongoing routines of running a classroom can cause concerns for teachers. It is beneficial for teachers to discuss their classroom management styles and their expectations for each other in maintaining a smoothly running classroom. Critical to success is determining when and with whom the special education teacher should intervene for discipline purposes.

- *What space do I get?* When a special education teacher spends part of his or her day instructing in another teacher's classroom, it is extremely useful to have a designated area for the special education teacher to keep materials. Special education teachers who coteach for part of the school day in another teacher's classroom feel more at home and are better accepted by the students when they have a legitimate claim on space, including a designated desk and chair.

- *What do we tell the students?* Teachers often wonder whether students should be told that they have two teachers or whether they should reveal that one of the teachers is a special education teacher. We think that it is a good idea to inform the students that they will be having two teachers and to introduce the special teacher as a "learning abilities" specialist. Students both accept and like the idea of having two teachers. In interviews with elementary students who had two teachers (special education and general education), the students revealed that they very much liked having two teachers in the classroom (Klingner, Vaughn, & Schumm, 1998). Similarly, early in the school year, inform parents that their child will have two teachers and that both will be responsible for their child's learning.

- *How can we find time to coplan and coordinate?* The most pervasive concern of both general and special education teachers who coteach is finding enough time during the school day to plan and discuss their instruction and the learning of their students. This is of particular concern for special education teachers who are working with more than one general education teacher. Teachers need a minimum of 45 minutes of uninterrupted planning time each week if they are to have a successful coteaching experience. One suggestion that has been made by several of the teacher teams with whom we have worked is to designate a day or a half-day every 6 to 8 weeks when teachers meet exclusively to plan and discuss the progress of students as well as changes in their instructional practices.

  - *How do we ensure that there is parity between teachers?* Teachers consistently report that having equal footing in the classroom is the preferred working arrangement for successful coteaching. There may be occasional examples of a teacher

having considerable more knowledge and expertise and thus serving as the mentor for the coteacher, but typically when teachers view themselves and each other as having skills and knowledge to benefit the coteaching situation, success is more likely.

- *How do we know if it's working?* Many teachers work so hard to make coteaching work that they overlook the most important goal: ensuring that students learn. Teachers must collect and evaluate student data to determine whether instruction is effective. A general rule to follow if students are not making adequate progress is to increase the intensity of instruction and decrease the teacher–student ratio. In addition to student learning, it is important that coteachers take time to evaluate the coteaching process. Dieker (2001) found that effective coteachers discussed their roles and responsibilities on an ongoing basis and made adjustments as needed.

Collaboration with Paraprofessionals and Families

In addition to working closely with general educators, special education teachers must also collaborate frequently with paraprofessionals and families. While some of the same principles for collaborating with general educators apply when collaborating with paraprofessionals and families, it is important to keep in mind that the differences in roles and expertise between you and the paraprofessionals and families will influence how you communicate and collaborate. However, you all should share a common goal: student success.

Collaborating with Paraprofessionals Schools often rely on paraprofessionals to provide support to general and special education teachers and students. Often, the special education teacher is in charge of supervising paraprofessionals. Many exceptional education specialists work closely with paraprofessional teaching assistants. Although teaching assistants never have complete responsibility for planning, implementing, or evaluating a student's program, they often participate in all of these areas. It is important that paraprofessionals not be assigned to students whom the teacher then spends little time seeing. Paraprofessionals need to have their teaching responsibilities rotated among many students so that the teacher spends frequent intervals teaching and evaluating all students. Because paraprofessionals are often responsible for implementing class rules, they need to be completely familiar with class and school rules and their consequences. Many paraprofessionals comment that they are successful in their roles when they have confidence that they understand what is expected of them. Suggestions for working with paraprofessionals are provided in Apply the Concept 5-5.

Working with Paraprofessionals

Jamie DeFraites is a first-grade teacher in New Orleans. Her multicultural classroom of 22 students includes 11 Vietnamese children and 2 Hispanic students who are English-language learners. Jamie explains, "I love my class and was actually asked to loop to second grade—so I'll have the same students next year!"

Jamie is fortunate enough to work with two paraprofessionals, who join her classroom at different times during the day. Here are Jamie's tips for working with paraprofessionals:

1. It's important to have mutual respect and trust. I let the paraprofessionals know how fortunate I feel to have additional adults in the classroom and how important their job is in helping all students learn. I also thank them every chance I get—in the presence of the principal, parents, and students.

2. At the beginning of the year, I talk with the paraprofessionals individually about their interests and skills and try to match their duties with their strengths. Both paraprofessionals are bilingual (one in Vietnamese and one in Spanish), so assisting me with parent communication is very important. One of the paraprofessionals is very creative and helps me design learning centers. The other is very interested in math and helps me with review and extra practice for students with challenges in that area.

3. Each of the paraprofessionals is eager to learn new skills and strategies. It is worth my time to explain instructional strategies to them so that they can do more than grade papers—they can actually interact with children in small groups or individually. It took me a long time to learn to teach—I'm still learning. I don't assume that the paraprofessionals automatically know how to teach. If I can share some of my training, the payoff is big for my students.

4. At the beginning of the year, we also clarify roles, responsibilities, classroom routines, and expectations for student learning and behavior. Spending that time in planning and communicating is time well spent. We're on the same page.

5. The paraprofessionals both work with several other teachers, so their time in my class is very limited. We have to make each minute count. Their tasks have to be well defined. I also plan a backup—what to do when there is nothing to do.

6. Finally, I encourage the paraprofessionals to get additional professional training. I let them know about workshops and other opportunities to learn. The more they learn, the more my students benefit!

Jamie admits that she would like to have a regular planning time with the paraprofessionals. As she says, "Often, we have to plan on the run." Also, her school district does not require periodic feedback or performance review sessions. This is something Jamie definitely recommends. "Fortunately, I have not run into problems with either paraprofessional, but if I did, it would be a good idea to have a system for giving feedback in a systematic way."

Source: Sharon Vaughn, Candace S. Bos, & Jeanne Shay Schumm, *Teaching Exceptional, Diverse, and At-Risk Students in the General Education Classroom,* 5th ed. (Boston: Allyn & Bacon, 2010). Copyright © by Pearson Education. Reprinted by permission of the publisher.

What skills are important in working with paraprofessionals? Several competencies that administrators, teachers, and paraprofessionals identified as important for teachers to have when working with paraprofessionals (Ashbaker & Morgan, 2006; Wallace, Shin, Bartholomay, & Stahl 2001) include:

- *Open communication.* Teachers should share student-related information as well as explain the role of the paraprofessional to the paraprofessional as well as to all other personnel.
- *Planning and scheduling.* Coordinating the paraprofessionals' schedules is the responsibility of the special education teacher at most schools. It may be helpful to have a written schedule that is evaluated and revised based on students' needs and observation of effective practices.

- *Instructional support.* Teachers should provide regular feedback to paraprofessionals about their instruction. Schedule time frequently initially, and then less often as paraprofessionals' skills are established, to observe instruction, provide feedback, and then model the instructional practices you are hoping to see implemented by the paraprofessional.
- *Modeling for paraprofessionals.* Modeling instructional strategies and a professional manner of interacting with students are part of a teacher's responsibility when supervising paraprofessionals.
- *Training.* Special education teachers are often responsible for providing on-the-job training for paraprofessionals. This includes expectations about communicating with others, communicating with students, managing student behavior, and completing appropriate paperwork.

- *Providing support for RTI.* Many paraprofessionals are asked to serve key roles in the implementation of RTI models. These roles include screening students, scoring screening and progress-monitoring measures, and providing interventions to individual students or small groups. Paraprofessionals work much more successfully when they are fully and adequately prepared for these roles and provided ongoing support and feedback from the special education teacher.

- *Responding to students, teachers, and families in ethically responsible ways.* One of the critical roles of the special education teacher is to adequately prepare paraprofessionals for their ethical responsibilities related to confidential student and family information as well as grades and student behavior. The Council for Exceptional Children (CEC) provides guidelines for paraprofessionals on ethical practices (http://www.cec.sped.org). Ethical practice skills recommended by CEC for paraprofessionals include (a) responding to professionals, students, and family members in ways that are consistent with laws and policies, (b) demonstrating problem solving, flexible thinking, conflict management techniques, and analysis of personal strengths and preferences, (c) acting as a role model for students with disabilities, (d) demonstrating a commitment to supporting learners in achieving their potential, (e) demonstrating that they are able to separate personal and professional issues as a paraeducator, (f) maintaining a high level of competence and integrity, (g) using prudent judgement, (h) demonstrating proficiency in oral and written communication as well as other academic skills as needed, (i) engaging in activities to increase one's own knowledge and skills, (j) engaging in self-assessment, and (k) accepting and using constructive feedback.

- *Management.* Teachers need to maintain regular and positive interactions with paraprofessionals and support their skill improvements.

Collaborating with Families Family involvement and collaboration is fundamental to students success. What can you do to help increase family and school collaboration? Dettmer, Thurston, and Selberg (2004) provided some key ideas:

- Place the focus of any discussion on the needs and wants of the family and the students, not on their values.
- Accept the family and the student as they are. Stop wishing that they were different.

- Remember that most family members are not trying to provide poor parenting. Rather, they are often doing the best they can in their given circumstances.
- Respect the family's right to have different values than you do. That does not make them poor parents.

In addition, remember that family members are often experts on their child. In most circumstances, they know their child much better than you do. Approach them with this knowledge in mind. Do your best not to talk down to parents; treat them as you would like to be treated if your roles were reversed. By establishing a collaborative relationship with parents, you may obtain insights about your students that you would not be able to get in any other manner.

When working with families from diverse cultural and linguistic backgrounds, it is important to learn as much as you can about your students' backgrounds. A minimal but important step is to learn the correct pronunciation of the family's name and a few words in their native language. Enlist the support of a translator, if possible. Ideally, the translator should be trained in special education.

Matuszny, Banda, and Coleman (2007) developed a four-step plan for collaborating with culturally and linguistically diverse families. The plan is designed to aid teachers in better understanding a particular family's needs as well as to strengthen the trust between the family and the teacher. The first phase is *initiation*. During this phase, which preferably occurs prior to start of the school year, the family members and teacher get to know each other. This contact should be informal and fun. True collaboration is difficult if the relationship between a family and teacher remains impersonal and/or uncomfortable. During *building the foundation*, the second phase, teachers establish trust with families by providing them with choices (such as how they would like to be involved in the classroom or how they would like to receive information from the teacher) and asking for input on certain classroom routines or behavioral procedures. The third phase, *maintenance and support,* involves positive communication, which is delivered according to the families' preferences about how they would like to be contacted. *Wrap-up and reflection* is the last phase of collaboration. In this phase, the teacher and the family reflect on what worked and did not work in terms of their collaboration. This information can be used to plan for the next year or passed on to the next teacher.

Collaboration in an RTI Model Collaboration among the various personnel involved in a school's RTI model is essential for a number of reasons. First, remember that using an RTI framework can help a school identify what supplemental instruction or intervention students may need to "catch up" to their grade-level peers. In order to ensure that a student is receiving appropriate intervention, communication among the classroom teacher, intervention provider, and other school personnel (such as the reading coach, special education teacher, or school psychologist) needs to be consistent and frequent. Many schools implementing RTI set aside regular weekly or monthly meeting times and space for teachers and specialists to discuss student data and make instructional changes, if necessary.

Collaboration between professionals also helps schools address what several administrators have identified as the number-one challenge to successful implementation of RTI: scheduling. By having teachers work collaboratively in creating schedules conducive to providing interventions, schools are better able to offer interventions on a consistent basis. Mrs. Middlestock, an elementary special education teacher, works with teachers at each grade level prior to the beginning of the school year to help teachers identify a common time across grade levels when students can be pulled out for interventions. By working collaboratively with her colleagues to identify intervention times, Mrs. Middlestock feels that she achieves greater teacher buy-in in terms of support for RTI and that teachers are more likely not to forget to send their students to her for Tier II interventions.

In some schools, particularly at the middle school level, Tier II interventions are used to preteach or reteach concepts from the general education curriculum. Therefore, it is crucial that classroom teachers and intervention teachers collaborate on pacing and content so that students are pretaught vocabulary and concepts and/or given additional practice on concepts or skills in a timely and appropriate manner. In addition, collaboration can be used to ensure that intervention teachers are delivering interventions with fidelity. In schools using RTI to identify students with learning disabilities, it is necessary to ensure that the interventions the students receive are delivered as they were designed to be taught. Mrs. Middlestock collaborates frequently with the other intervention providers and when possible observes them to make certain that all of the interventions are being delivered with fidelity.

Communication with Other Professionals

What are the principles of communication, and how can teachers communicate with parents and professionals? In addition to assessment, intervention, curriculum development, and classroom management, a major role for the teacher of students with learning and behavior problems is communication. Effective special education teachers communicate regularly with general education and other special education teachers school administrators, and other educational and psychological professionals such as the school psychologist, speech/language therapist, and so on. Ability to communicate effectively is a skill that significantly affects an educator's job success. Despite the importance of this skill, most teachers finish school with no formal training in communication.

Principles of Communication

Successful communication with parents, teachers, and other professionals is built on certain principles. Particularly within inclusion models and frameworks that emphasize RTI, teachers' success with communication influences positively their success as professionals and the learning outcomes of their students.

Mutual Respect and Trust Building mutual respect and trust is essential for successful communication. As a special education teacher, you are likely to work cooperatively with the school psychologist in several important ways including screening students and evaluating students who are referred for special education or who have been placed in special education for several years and require another evaluation. You may also work with the speech and language specialist as many of the students with disabilities also demonstrate speech or language problems currently, or have done so previously. It is very likely you will be coteaching, coplanning, or cooperating on an ongoing basis with several general education teachers. All of these individuals will have more confidence in you and be more willing to work with you to benefit students with disabilities if you establish a relationship of respect and trust with them.

Acceptance People know if you do not accept them or do not value what they have to say. Parents/guardians are aware when teachers do not really want to see them during conferences but are merely fulfilling a responsibility. Acceptance is communicated by how you listen, look, respond, and interact with others.

Pointers for communicating acceptance include the following:

- Demonstrate respect for the knowledge and needs of each of the professionals with whom you work. Often special education teachers assume that general education teachers do not "understand" the needs of the target student with disabilities.
- Demonstrate respect for the diverse languages and cultures that families and their children represent.
- Introduce professionals to other members of the education team in a way that sets the tone for acceptance.
- Give each professional working with the student an opportunity to speak and be heard.
- Ensure that a language of acceptance is used by all professionals and families.

Listening Effective listening is more than waiting politely for the person to finish. It requires hearing the message the person is sending. Effective listeners listen for the real content of the message as well as for the feelings in the message. Often this requires restating the message to ensure understanding.

Mrs. Garcia, the mother of 12-year-old Felipe, telephoned his special education resource room teacher, Mr. Sanchez.

> *Mrs. Garcia:* Felipe has been complaining for the past couple of weeks that he has too much work to do in his biology and math classes and that he is falling behind. He says he is flunking biology.
>
> *Mr. Sanchez:* How much would you say he is studying each night?
>
> *Mrs. Garcia:* It's hard to say. He stays out with his friends until dinner, and then after dinner, he starts talking about all his homework. Sometimes he sits in front of the TV with his books, and sometimes he goes to his room.
>
> *Mr. Sanchez:* He has mentioned in my class how much work he has to do. I wonder if he is feeling a lot of pressure from different teachers, including me?
>
> *Mrs. Garcia:* Well, he has said he thinks you are working him too hard. I know sometimes he is lazy, but maybe you could talk to him.
>
> *Mr. Sanchez:* Felipe works very hard in my class, and I expect a great deal from him. I will talk with him after school and arrange a meeting with his other teachers as well.
>
> *Mrs. Garcia:* Thank you, and please do not tell Felipe I called. He would be very upset with me.

Questioning Knowing what type of questions to ask can help individuals to obtain the information they need. Questions can be open or closed. An *open question* is a question that allows the respondent a full range of responses and discourages short, yes-or-no answers. Open questions begin with *how, what, tell me about*, and similar phrases.

Mrs. Lishenko suspected that Matt, one of her students, was staying up very late at night, because he was coming to school very tired and seemed to drag all day. He was also resting his head on his desk in the afternoon. She decided to call Matt's father to discuss the problem. She started the conversation by giving Matt's father some information about a meeting of family members that was going to be held in the school district that she thought would be of particular interest to him. She then proceeded to describe Matt's behavior in class. Finally, Mrs. Lishenko asked, "What do you think might be happening?" Matt's father began to confide that he was not paying much attention to Matt's bedtime and that Matt was staying up late watching movies on the new DVD player. Mrs. Lishenko's question gave Matt's father the opportunity to explain what he thought was happening. Rather than posing several possibilities or telling Matt's father that Matt was staying up too late at night, Mrs. Lishenko asked an open question, which allowed Matt's father to interpret the situation. Matt's father suggested that he would establish a firm bedtime. In

this situation, asking an open question allowed Matt's father both to indicate how he felt and to offer a solution.

Involving people in identifying problems increases the likelihood that they will not feel threatened and that they will be willing to make necessary changes.

Staying Directed Follow the lead of professionals, paraprofessionals, and parents whenever they are talking about a student. A skillful consultant is able to respond to others and still keep the discussion focused. It is not uncommon for families to mention other related home factors that may be influencing their child's progress in school, such as marital difficulties, financial problems, or other personal problems. When professionals or parents discuss serious problems that are beyond our reach as educators, we need to assist them in finding other resources to help them with their problems. Ms. Lopez, a special education teacher at the middle school keeps the name and telephone number of the school counselor as well as other community outreach resources near her telephone. She is ready to refer parents and other professionals for assistance when needed.

Apply the Concept 5-6 provides a list of tips for effective communication with professionals and families.

Developing Interviewing Skills

Interviews are the key to open communication and effective intervention. Special education teachers often work as consultants to paraprofessionals, regular classroom teachers, to other educational and psychological specialists, and to families. These interviewing skills help to meet the need to ask questions that inform and to follow up appropriately on information provided. There are five steps to good interviewing:

1. *Ask open questions.* Open questions permit respondents a full range of answers, allowing them to bring up a topic or problem they have on their mind. Open questions are generally followed by questions that require more specificity. Mr. Schwab, the special education resource room teacher, began his interview with Mrs. Francosa, the fourth-grade teacher, by asking an open question: "How is Yusuf's behavior lately?"

2. *Obtain specificity.* This requires asking questions or making restatements that identify or document the problem. After Mrs. Francosa describes Yusuf's behavior in the regular classroom, Mr. Schwab attempts to identify key points and to obtain specificity in describing the behavior: "You said Yusuf's behavior is better in the classroom but worse on the playground. Can you identify which behaviors in the classroom are better and which behaviors on the playground are worse?" Without drilling the interviewee, an attempt is made to identify the problem and provide documentation for its occurrence so that an appropriate intervention can be constructed.

3. *Identify the problem.* Problem identification can be based on information obtained, or it can be decided by

5-6   Facilitating Effective Communication with Professionals and Families

1. Indicate respect for their knowledge and understanding of the child.
2. Demonstrate respect for the diverse languages and cultures families and their children represent.
3. Introduce them to other members of the education team in a way that sets the tone for acceptance.
4. Give each person an opportunity to speak and be heard.
5. Ensure that a language of acceptance is used by all professionals and family members.
6. Even when you are busy, take the time to let professionals and family members know that you value them, and that you are just unable to meet with them at this time.
7. Avoid giving advice unless it is requested. This does not mean that you can never give suggestions; however, the suggestions should be given with the expectation that the person may or may not choose to implement them.
8. Avoid providing false reassurances to colleagues or families. False reassurances may make them and you feel better in the short run but in the long run are harmful. When things do not work out as you predicted, everyone can become disappointed and potentially lose trust.
9. Ask specific questions. Using unfocused questions makes it difficult to conduct a consistent, purposeful conversation.
10. Avoid changing topics too often; this requires that you monitor the topic and direct others to return to the topic.
11. Avoid interrupting others or being interrupted, which disturbs the conversation and makes effective collaboration difficult.
12. Avoid using clichés. A cliché as a response to a problem situation makes the other person feel as though you are trivializing the problem.
13. Respond to colleagues and family members in ways that attend to both the content of their message and their feelings.
14. Avoid jumping too quickly to a solution. Listening carefully and fully to the message will help you get at the root of the problem.

Source: S. Vaughn, C. S. Bos, & J. S. Schumm, *Teaching Students Who Are Exceptional, Diverse, and At-Risk in the General Education Classroom* (Boston: Allyn & Bacon, 2010). Reprinted with permission.

---

the person being interviewed, often in the process of answering questions: "It seems like there is good progress in terms of completing classroom work. Let's figure out a way of reinforcing that behavior. There's a problem with Yusuf's responding to teasing on the playground. His response has been to fight, which is getting him in more trouble. Any thoughts about how we might change that behavior?"

After listening to suggestions from the teacher, Mr. Schwab might add, "Let me provide some suggestions that have been effective in the past with other students."

4. *Solve problems.* Suggestions for solving identified problems and implementing the solutions are generated. Both the professional being interviewed and the consultant contribute suggestions to solving the problem. Often, other professionals are included in the suggestions: "Perhaps we could discuss Yusuf's problem with his counselor and ask her to teach him some strategies for coping with teasing. We could also identify the students who are teasing him and reinforce them for not teasing."

The tone for problem solving should be one of flexibility. There are often many possible solutions but only a few that will work with a particular student. The goal is to find a solution the teacher is willing to implement that is effective for the student.

5. *Summarize and give feedback.* Summarize the problem and the plan of action. Be sure to indicate who is responsible for what. Whenever possible, establish a timeline for completing the tasks: "You will send home notes to Yusuf's parents, informing them of his progress in seatwork in the classroom. I will meet with the counselor about his problem on the playground, and you will talk with his peers and arrange a system for reinforcing them for not teasing. I'll check back with you during lunch this week to see how things are going. I'm very pleased with this progress, and I am sure much of it is due to your hard work and follow-up."

Working with Other Professionals

What is the role of the special education teacher as a consultant to general education teachers, and what are the considerations and barriers for successful inclusion? Consulting and communicating with professionals is an important task for teachers of students with learning and behavior problems. Teachers need to develop and maintain contact with the school psychologist, counselor, speech/language therapist, physical therapist, occupational therapist, principal, and other related professionals. Because 90% of all students with learning and behavior disorders are included for all or part of the day, a positive, cooperative working relationship with general classroom teachers may be most important of all.

Communication with General Education Teachers

When a student with a learning or behavior problem is placed in the regular classroom, there are several steps the special education teacher can take to communicate effectively with the general education teacher:

1. Describe the type of learning or behavior problem the child has and some general guidelines for how to deal with it in the regular classroom.
2. Provide a copy of the child's IEP to the classroom teacher, and discuss the goals, objectives, special materials, and procedures needed.
3. Describe the progress reports you will be providing to the home and putting in your files.
4. Develop a schedule for regular meetings, and discuss other times that both the classroom teacher and special teacher are available for meetings.
5. Ask the classroom teacher how you can help, and describe the special accommodations that are needed.

Even when special education teachers develop and maintain an effective communication program with general education teachers, there are still a number of potential barriers to successful inclusion:

1. *The general education teacher may feel unable to meet the needs of the included student with disabilities.* Ms. Huang has been teaching second grade for 2 years. When she was informed that Omar, a student who has been identified as having an emotional disorder, was going to be included in her general education classroom for several hours each morning, she panicked. She explained to the principal that she had not taken any coursework in special education and did not feel able to meet the needs of the new student. The special education teacher met with Ms. Huang to describe Omar's behavior and explain the progress he was making. She assured Ms. Huang that Omar would be carefully monitored and that she would check with Omar and Ms. Huang daily at first and then less frequently as he adapted to the new setting and schedule. She asked Ms. Huang to explain what types of activities usually occurred during the time Omar would be in her room, and she identified ways for Ms. Huang to be successful with Omar. The special education teacher took careful notes and asked many questions about Ms. Huang's expectations so that she could prepare Omar before his transition to the regular classroom. In this situation, communication that provided specific information about the student's learning problems and what the classroom teacher could do to ensure a successful learning environment proved most helpful. In addition, the special education teacher obtained expectations about the general education classroom so that she could best prepare the student for the transition.

2. *The general education classroom teacher may not want to work with the included student with disabilities.*

Mr. Caruffe, a seventh-grade science teacher, expected all students to perform the same work at the same time, with no exceptions. He was particularly opposed to having special education students in his classroom because he felt that they required modifications to his core program. His philosophy was, "If students need modifications, they don't belong in the general education classroom, they belong in special education." Dealing with teachers like Mr. Caruffe can be particularly challenging for special education teachers. Despite continuous attempts to work out a collaborative effort, educational philosophies can be sufficiently different that special education teachers feel it is hopeless to attempt inclusion in certain classrooms. Problems arise when alternative classrooms are not available without reducing the content areas available to special students. If there are multiple teachers for each content area, students may be included into classes where teachers are more accepting. Principals can help by setting a school policy that rewards teachers for working appropriately with pupils who have learning and behavior problems.

In a survey of elementary, middle, and high school teachers (Schumm & Vaughn, 1992a, 1992b), the majority of teachers indicated that they felt unprepared to meet the needs of special education students but were willing to have them in their classrooms. This suggests that special education teachers need to work closely with other teachers to improve their knowledge, skills, and confidence.

3. *Finding time to meet regularly with all classroom teachers is difficult.* At the elementary level, special education teachers meet regularly with all classroom teachers who have students included for all or part of the day. This consultation includes discussing students' progress, planning students' programs, adapting instruction in the general classroom, and solving immediate academic and social problems with students. It is better to meet weekly with classroom teachers for a short period of time (10 to 15 minutes) than to meet less often for longer periods of time. When classroom teachers and their students perceive the special education room as a resource rather than a closed room for special students, they have positive perceptions of the teacher and of the students who attend (Vaughn & Bos, 1987).

At the secondary level, continued involvement with all classroom teachers is a challenge. In large schools, the exceptional students' general education classroom teachers vary within content area and by year. It is possible for special education teachers to have over 25 teachers with whom they consult. Special education teachers manage this by meeting with teachers in small groups. Sometimes they organize these groups by content area to discuss successful adaptations made within a common content. Sometimes meetings are organized to focus on the needs of a particular student, and all teachers who work with this student meet at the same time. Finding time and maintaining contact with general education teachers requires creativity and persistence.

4. *Students may not be accepted socially by peers in the general education classroom.* This problem occurs not just with students who have behavior problems, but also with students who have learning disabilities. Placing students in classrooms where their peers are displaying appropriate social behaviors does not mean that students with learning and behavior disorders will internalize and display these appropriate behaviors (Gresham, 1982). According to both general education and special classroom teachers, the skills most essential to success in the general education classroom are interacting positively with others, following class rules, and exhibiting proper work habits (Salend & Lutz, 1984). Following is a list of behaviors that are considered important by both general education and special educators for success in the general education classrooms:

- Follows directions
- Asks for help when appropriate
- Begins an assignment after the teacher gives the assignment to the class
- Demonstrates adequate attention
- Obeys class rules
- Tries to complete a task before giving up
- Doesn't speak when others are talking
- Works well with others
- Respects the feelings of others
- Refrains from cursing and swearing
- Avoids getting in fights with other students
- Plays cooperatively with others
- Respects the property of others
- Shares materials and property with others
- Refrains from stealing the property of others
- Tells the truth

Special education teachers may want to focus on teaching these behaviors before and during a student's transition to inclusion.

Working with Families

This section of the chapter highlights the teacher's interaction with families. Family adjustment to a child with learning and behavior problems is discussed first. Within this section, family adjustment, sibling adjustment, and family-centered practice are described. We also explore families' involvement with the schools and their role in the planning of the child's educational program.
What is the teacher's role in addressing the needs of the entire family?

Family Adjustment

The family is an important force in a child's learning and development. From a systems perspective, many mental health professionals recommend an integrated approach to working with students with learning disabilities and behavior disorders. This integrated approach typically involves all or part of the family in the program, including an initial meeting with the entire family; involvement of selected family members; or ongoing clinical help that involves the family at certain times. Not all families who have children with learning and behavior problems need therapeutic assistance. For example, a family-centered approach to positive behavioral supports has been heralded for families of children with severe behavior and emotional difficulties (Carr et al., 2002).

Adjusting to a child with learning and behavior disorders is often difficult resulting in stress (Lessenberry & Rehfeldt, 2004), with greater stress for those families who have children with signification social and behavioral disabilities, particularly those that are disruptive (Hastings, Daley, Burns, & Beck, 2006; Orsmond, Seltzer, Greenberg, & Krauss, 2006). Understanding how families adjust and interact with the child on the basis of their interpretation of the child's needs is an important role for the special education teacher. However, several key findings about families of children with disabilities have positive implications in working with these families (Ferguson, 2002):

- Overall patterns of adjustment and well-being are similar across families with children with and without disabilities. Thus, families who have a child with a disability are probably more like other families than they are different.
- Significant numbers of parents and siblings report that there are perceived benefits and positive outcomes from having a child or sibling with disabilities. This does not suggest that all aspects are easy but that many aspects are viewed positively.
- Having a family member with disabilities is stressful to all members of the family, but engaging the family in meaningful and functional ways is beneficial.

Siblings In addition to how parents respond to a child with learning or behavior problems, the responses of other siblings is important. Lardieri, Blacher, and Swanson (2000) conducted a study to determine whether the presence of a child with learning disabilities, with or without reported behavior problems, affects the psychological well-being and self-concept of the child's siblings. Although sibling relationships in families of children with and without learning disabilities differed in their perception of the quality of their sibling relationships and self-reports of their own behavior, the difference was not significant enough to render a clinical diagnosis of sibling maladjustment. Not surprisingly, some siblings appear to be affected very little, whereas others are affected more seriously. Some siblings may have concerns about causes of the difficulty; explanations for the unusual behaviors of their sibling; adjustments in parenting that may be interpreted as more time, attention, or leniency toward their sibling (Gallagher, Powell, & Rhodes, 2006).

Many families are concerned because their child with learning disabilities or behavior disorders takes more of their time and consideration than do the other children in the family. Siblings may feel as though the child with special needs is getting all of the family's attention and special privileges. It is important for parents/guardians to develop schedules in which they assign special time for each of their children. A sibling of a child with learning disabilities commented:

> Everything always seems to center around Scott. He always seems to be the focus of the conversation and whom my parents are concerned about. I do pretty well in school and don't seem to have many problems, so sometimes I feel left out. It really meant a lot to me when my mother and father both scheduled time during the week for me to be alone with them. Usually my dad and I would go to the park, and sometimes we would go on an errand. Often my mom and I would work together in the kitchen, making my favorite dessert, chocolate chip cookies. The best part was that it was just me and them. I really think it helped me be more understanding of Scott. Somehow, I just didn't resent him so much anymore.

Family-Centered Practice

Teachers who consider the family and students' needs as the center of their decision making, involving them in the process of designing and refining educational plans, programs, and goals, are using family-centered practice.

What does this mean to a teacher? How could the teacher design each student's program with consideration of the family's strengths and needs? There are two essential things for teachers to keep in mind: The family should be viewed as the director of the service delivery process and as the ultimate decision maker; and teachers should focus on a family's strengths, not its deficiencies. Important components of family-centered practice include:

- The concept of family as the unit of attention or concern
- The importance of a collaboration between families and professionals
- An understanding of family needs and its strengths or capabilities
- Family choice or decision making and the uniqueness or culture of families
- The provision of specific types of services
- Maintenance of children in their own homes
- Empowerment of families

It may be useful to consider that schools perceive that they are more "family-centered" than they actually are. In addition, family-centered practices are more likely to occur at the preschool level and then occur less frequently as students move through the grades (Dunst, 2002).

Figure 5-4 shows a worksheet to use in family-centered practice in gathering feedback from families.

Family Involvement with Schools

By the time children reach school, families have already spent 5 years observing them. Many families are aware from the day their child enters school that the child is different from other children. Often the child spends 2 to 3 difficult years in school before being referred for learning disabilities or behavior disorders. During this time, many families have spent hours communicating with school counselors, psychologists, and teachers. Some of these contacts were initiated by the family members. Often, family members feel frustrated and alone. They are unsure what to do, and because of the complexity of their child's condition, professionals are often unable to provide the precise answers parents need. Apply the Concept 5-7 describes what families generally want from professionals.

> ▶ **WEB RESOURCES**
> Parental Involvement http://www.ed.gov/legislation/ESEA/Title_I/parinv.html.

Family Involvement in Planning and Placement Conferences Families provide consent for evaluation, participate in the program and educational plan, and are kept involved in all decisions regarding a child's educational program. Why are families so involved in special education?

First, it ensures cooperation between home and school. Families can provide information about the child to which the schools may not have access, and family members can follow up on educational goals in the home. Second, it ensures that families will have access to information about student evaluations and records and can better monitor appropriate placement and programming by the school. One area that holds significant potential benefits is involving family members in the planning and placement conference for the child. The information that is obtained about the child's learning and behavior problems can increase family members' understanding, which in turn can lead to changes in family behavior toward the child. In addition, family members learn about the focus of the child's school program and can reinforce those learning and behavior efforts in the home. Unfortunately, this is more the ideal than a description of the real world. Despite the best intentions of school personnel and parents, cooperative and extensive family involvement in the placement and planning process is minimal.

There are many explanations for lack of family involvement in educational planning. One is that school personnel do not have adequate time to meet with families and fully explain the child's program or do not know how to take advantage of family members' knowledge and preferences (Harry, 2008). In a recent review of research on parent involvement for students with disabilities from different cultural groups, Harry's (2008) review of the literature concludes that there are several

► **Figure 5-4**   Parent–Teacher Collaboration Review and Reflection Worksheet

Directions: Please answer the following questions. Where you see the word *Other*, if desired, please write in any information that you want to add.

1. **What helped you feel more comfortable working with your child's teacher? (Check the events/activities that you believe were most helpful to you):**

   ___ The beginning of the year celebration that gave parents and teachers the chance to meet each other as people first (event held before school started)

   ___ Being asked about what I needed and how I wanted to receive information (The Parent Needs and Preferences Information Worksheet)

   ___ The information that was provided

   ___ The way information was provided (Tell how info. was provided: _____)

   ___ The frequency with which I received information (How often? _____)

   ___ Adjusting meeting times to meet my schedule

   ___ Other: _____

2. **What was *not* helpful in making you feel more comfortable working with your child's teacher? (Check the events/activities that you believe were not helpful to you):**

   ___ The beginning of the year celebration that gave parents and teachers the chance to meet each other as people first (event held before school started)

   ___ Being asked about what I needed and how I wanted to receive information (such as The Parent Needs and Preferences Information Worksheet that you may have completed earlier this year)

   ___ The information that was provided

   ___ The way information was provided (Tell how info. was provided: _____)

   ___ The frequency with which I received information (How often? _____)

   ___ Adjusting meeting times to meet my schedule

   ___ Other: _____

3. **Please write down any supports that you want to see more of and any additional ideas you have for how the school/teacher can help you maintain your connection and comfort in working collaboratively with them in the upcoming year. If more space is needed, please feel free to use the back of this page to provide your thoughts and ideas.**

Source: Adapted from R. M. Matuszny, D. R. Banda, & T. J. Coleman (2007), A progressive plan for building collaborative relationships with parents from diverse backgrounds, *Teaching Exceptional Children* (Mar./Apr.), pp. 24–31. Copyright 2007 by the Council for Exceptional Children. Reprinted with permission.

barriers to widespread use of ideal practices, including a deficit view of families, cross-cultural misunderstandings related to the meanings of disability, and culturally different views of the roles of parents and caregivers.

Often families can attend meetings only early in the morning before going to work or in the evening on their way home. These times usually conflict with the schedules of school personnel and require them to meet with

●●●●●●● *Apply the Concept* ●●●●●●●

5-7   What Families of Students with Learning Disabilities Want from Professionals

In a survey of over 200 families of children with learning disabilities, families indicated what they really wanted from professionals (Dembinski & Mauser, 1977). A summary of the findings follows:

1. Families want professionals to communicate without the use of jargon. When technical terms are necessary, they would like to have the terms explained so that they can understand.

2. Whenever possible, they would like conferences to be held so that all family members can attend.

3. They would like to receive written materials that provide information that will assist them in understanding their child's problem.

4. They would like to receive a copy of a written report about their child.

5. They would like specific advice on how to manage specific behavior problems of their child or how to teach needed skills.

6. They would like information on their child's social as well as academic behavior.

Coteaching and Collaborating: Working with Professionals and Families   **147** families outside of their required work time. Because of their dedication and interest in children, professionals are often willing to meet at these times, but they are not motivated to meet for extended periods of time.

Families may perceive the professionals as responsible for appropriate decisions in their child's best interest and do not want to be coparticipants in the educational program. Rather than a lack of interest in the child's program, this may actually indicate less confidence in their own ability to participate effectively.

It could be that families would like to be more involved but feel intimidated by the number of professionals and the uncommon terminology:

> No matter how well we might know our own children, we are not prepared to talk to teachers, principals, psychologists, or counselors, much less participate in the educational decision-making process. Although parents do have a lot of information, it is not the "right" kind. When we go to speak to administrators at school we hear about IEP's, MA's, criteria, auditory processing, regulations, and sometimes, due process. At first, there seems to be no correspondence between what we know and what the people in schools are talking about. (*Exceptional Parent*, 1984, p. 41)

During conferences, special education teachers need to be sensitive to family members' feelings and needs. They can serve as advocates for the parents, asking questions of the classroom teacher or other professionals that he or she feels the family member may have wanted to ask but did not.

The Spotlight on Diversity feature provides considerations for working with families from culturally and linguistically diverse groups.

Conferences with Family Members: Planned and Unplanned Planned conferences with family members occur frequently and include multidisciplinary team meetings, annual parent–student meetings, or regularly scheduled meetings to report on academic and behavioral progress.

Conferences provide teachers with the opportunity to do the following:

- Review the student's materials, grades, and work progress.
- Meet with other professionals to provide an overall review and report on student progress.
- Review the student's portfolio, assessment information, and progress reports.
- Provide samples of the student's most recent work.
- Establish and review goals and criteria for academic and behavioral work.

Sometimes conferences with families are unplanned (Turnbull & Turnbull, 1990). Family members may phone, stop by the school, or schedule a conference with little notice. When this occurs, there are several procedures for the teacher to remember: Listen carefully until the family members have expressed the purpose of their visit, paraphrase what you understand to be their question or issues, and respond to the question and issue as completely as possible. Often family members stop by with a simple question or concern that is a disguise for a larger issue; that is why it is important to listen carefully and wait until family members are finished.

Individuals with Disabilities Education Act and Family Involvement

The (IDEA) was passed in 1990 and was most recently amended in 2004. This law ensures that all youngsters with disabilities receive a free, appropriate public education, which emphasizes special education and related services designed to meet their unique needs. All students between the ages of 3 and 21 are eligible for a program of special education and related services under Part B of the IDEA; children with disabilities from birth to age 3 are eligible for special education and related services under Part C. Part C, which is a subchapter of the IDEA, is about infants and toddlers with disabilities.

 Tech TIPS

HELPFUL RESOURCES FOR PARENTS OF CHILDREN WITH SPECIAL NEEDS

There are a number of online resources that you can provide to parents to alert them to suggestions for how they can best advocate for their children. These sites also provide helpful tools and recommendations to parents of children with special needs.

The Parent Teacher Association,
 www.pta.org/parentinvolvement
This organization provides parents a voice in advocating for the safety and success of other children as well.

National Education Association,
 www.nea.org/parents
This Web site provides valuable resources for parents and for teachers in their collaborative efforts with parents.

Exceptional Parent Magazine,
 www.eparent.com
This Web site offers vast online resources for parents of students with disabilities.

Spotlight on Diversity
Considerations for Families Who Are Culturally and Linguistically Diverse

1. Assume that families want to help their children.
2. Consider your language when talking with parents and be thoughtful about not using language that suggests a deficit model of considering the child.
3. Provide materials in a range of formats including orally, in writing (family's language), through videotape, and through formal and informal presentations.
4. For parents who are interested, provide opportunities for families to learn the skills and activities the students are learning so they can reinforce them in the home.
5. Provide opportunities for families to influence their child's educational program.
6. Provide workshops that include role playing and rehearsing situations between families and school

personnel to increase families' confidence in working with school personnel.

7. Involve families from the community who are familiar with the culture and speak the home language of the children's families in work at the school.
8. Provide an informal meeting with families so they can exchange experiences and learn tips from each other.
9. Invite families to school and ask them to share their backgrounds or activities with other students and families.
10. Provide ongoing professional development for teachers and other educators so that they are familiar with linguistic and cultural practices and respond sensitively with this knowledge to parents and other family members.

The law provides for early intervention services that meet the developmental needs of children from birth to the age of 3 and their families, including physical development, cognition, language, social, and self-help skills. Parents and families play an important role, and an individualized program plan must be designed to meet their needs. This program plan, called the Individualized Family Service Plan (IFSP), should provide a coordinated array of services, including the following:

- Screening and assessment
- Psychological assessment and intervention
- Occupational and physical therapy
- Speech, language, and audiology
- Family involvement, training, and home visits
- Specialized instruction for parents and the target student
- Case management
- Health services that may be needed to allow the student to benefit from the intervention service

See Apply the Concept 5-8 for an overview of family involvement in special education.

Criteria for Establishing an IFSP

The IFSP is a family-oriented approach to designing an effective management plan for the infants and toddlers with disabilities (birth to age 3). The IFSP must be developed by a multidisciplinary team and should include the following elements:

- A description of the child's level of functioning across the developmental areas: physical, cognitive, communication, social or emotional, and adaptive
- An assessment of the family, including a description of the family's strengths and needs as they

relate to enhancing the development of the child with disabilities
- A description of the major goals or outcomes expected for the child with disabilities and the family (as they relate to providing opportunities for the student)
- Procedures for measuring progress, including a timeline, objectives, and evaluation procedures
- A description of natural environments in which the early intervention services will be provided
- A description of the early intervention services needed to provide appropriate help for the child and family
- Specifically when the specialized intervention will begin and how long it will last
- A designated case manager
- A specific transition plan from the birth-to-three program into the preschool program

Response to Intervention and Family Involvement

Families have an important role to play when schools implement RTI. This model provides new challenges and opportunities for engaging and communicating with families about their children's progress. Technically, most of what occurs within an RTI model occurs within general education, so questions can arise about when and how to communicate effectively with families.

First, many families may neither know what RTI is nor understand why their child is being screened for learning difficulties. Second, families value knowing if their child is receiving secondary or tertiary interventions and having access to the findings from progress monitoring. Third, teachers can assist families by providing them with a list of sample questions they might want to ask about RTI. An excellent source of information for parents about RTI is the National Center for Learning Disabilities (http://www.LD.org).

5-8 **Family Involvement in the Special Education Process**

The chart presents an overview of the special education process for families of school-aged children. It covers issues from the time a child is referred for evaluation through the development of the IEP for the child. It shows how to share information between schools and families or how families can participate in the process.

```
┌─────────────────────────────────────────────────────────┐
│ Families or school district staff or others request an   │
│ evaluation: In this stage, written consent from parents  │
│ or guardians is needed.                                  │
└─────────────────────────────────────────────────────────┘
                          ↓
┌─────────────────────────────────────────────────────────┐         ┌──────────────┐
│ Evaluation and eligibility decision: Families are        │   →     │ Not eligible │
│ introduced to the team process at this point. It is      │         └──────────────┘
│ important to provide evaluation information thoroughly    │
│ because this information is the basis for developing the  │
│ IEP.                                                      │
└─────────────────────────────────────────────────────────┘
                          ↓
        ┌──────────────────────────────────┐
        │ Eligible for special education   │
        └──────────────────────────────────┘
                          ↓
┌─────────────────────────────────────────────────────────┐         ┌──────────────────┐
│ IEP is developed and placement is determined: Not only   │   →     │ Parents/guardians│
│ recommendations by professionals but also the family's   │         │ disagree         │
│ willingness are important in this process. Parents/       │         └──────────────────┘
│ guardians have a right to attend IEP meetings and         │
│ participate in the development of the IEP. Their          │
│ agreement is needed.                                      │
└─────────────────────────────────────────────────────────┘
                          ↓
        ┌──────────────────────────────────┐
        │ Parents/guardians agree          │
        └──────────────────────────────────┘
                          ↓
┌─────────────────────────────────────────────────────────┐
│ Annual IEP meeting: Families and professionals need to   │
│ meet regularly to share information about progress.      │
│ There is an annual IEP meeting to examine the process    │
│ and revise the IEP if necessary. Families may require    │
│ certain services.                                        │
└─────────────────────────────────────────────────────────┘
```

Response to Intervention: Ten Questions Parents Should Ask As states and school districts work to implement an RTI process that provides early help to struggling students, families need to understand the components essential to the appropriate implementation of RTI. Here are 10 questions to ask about RTI to help guide you through the process:

1. Is the school district currently using an RTI process to provide additional support to struggling students? If not, do they plan to?
2. What screening procedures are used to identify students in need of intervention?
3. What are the interventions and instructional programs being used? What research supports their effectiveness?
4. What process is used to determine the intervention that will be provided?
5. What length of time is allowed for an intervention before determining if the student is making adequate progress?
6. What strategy is being used to monitor student progress? What are the types of data that will be collected and how will student progress be conveyed to parents?
7. Is a written intervention plan provided to parents as part of the RTI process?
8. Is the teacher or other person responsible for providing the interventions trained in using them?
9. When and how will information about a student's performance and progress be provided?
10. At what point in the RTI process are students who are suspected of having a learning disability referred for formal evaluation?

► **FOCUS Question 1. What are some of the challenges of working in an inclusive classroom and working with general education teachers?**

Answer: General education teachers have different levels of experience in working with other teachers and students with learning and behavioral problems. Furthermore, many students are not prepared for general education classrooms. Potential problems can be avoided if general education teachers know and use a variety of instructional strategies. This effort takes time and planning, and it can result in less content coverage within a given time frame. Special education teachers can facilitate inclusion by working closely with general education teachers; observing general education classrooms; simulating the academic and social demands of general education classrooms in the special education classroom; and assisting classroom teachers in adapting materials, instruction, and the instructional environment.

► **FOCUS Question 2. What are three major models for consultation and collaboration?**

Answer: Special education teachers work with other professionals to develop systems that meet the needs of students with learning and behavioral problems within an individual school setting. Coteaching occurs when special education and classroom teachers provide instruction together in the general education classroom. Consultant teaching occurs when the special educator works with the classroom teacher to solve problems for students with disabilities in the general education classroom. Special education teachers also coordinate paraprofessionals who assist students with disabilities in the general education classroom. TATs are school-based teams (including support professionals, classroom teachers, and administrators) that assist the classroom teacher in meeting individual students' instructional and behavior needs.

► **FOCUS Question 3. What are the principles of communication, and how can teachers communicate with parents and professionals?**

Answer: Teachers should take the time to build mutual trust, to accept others' points of view, to really listen to what families and other professionals say, to provide encouragement to family members and personnel who work with students with special needs, and to use straightforward language to explain information. In addition, teachers can learn more from personal communication by asking open-ended questions that solicit thorough responses. Teachers must also balance listening and responding to others with focusing the conversation or meeting. In this way, teachers develop a working alliance in which all members of the group have a common goal of developing an appropriate program for the student.

► **FOCUS Question 4. What is the teacher's role in addressing the needs of the entire family?**

Answer: Families have different issues and concerns; identifying and addressing the needs of the entire family is essential to assisting a student. Teachers can also assist families by attending to students even when they are not in school, such as providing resources for summer activities, guidelines for assisting students with homework or academic skills, and accessing support systems with other parents or organizations. By valuing the parents' role in their child's education and by using the knowledge parents have about their child, teachers and families can work together to develop an appropriate educational program. RTI practices provide a unique opportunity for schools and families to communicate and collaborate prior to referral, during screening and assessment, when secondary interventions are provided, and through examining data collected.

myeducationlab

Where the Classroom Comes to Life

The MyEducationLab for this course can help you solidify your comprehension of Chapter 5 concepts.

- Gauge and further develop your understanding of chapter concepts by taking the quizzes and examining the enrichment materials in the Chapter 5 Study Plan.
- Visit Topic 3, Collaboration, to connect with challenge-based interactive modules, case study units, and podcasts that provide research-validated information about

working with students in inclusive settings, by visiting the IRIS Center Resources.

- explore Assignments and Activities, assignable exercises showing concepts in action through video, cases, and student and teacher artifacts.
- practice and strengthen skills essential to quality teaching through the Building Teaching Skills and Dispositions lessons.

6

Assessing and Teaching Oral Language

FOCUS Questions

1. What are the two main areas of language delays, and how do they manifest themselves in the development of content, form, and use of language?
2. What guidelines can assist in teaching oral language, content, form, and use?
3. What are the strategies and considerations on which teachers should focus when teaching culturally and linguistically diverse learners?
4. How can teachers work with families to develop students' language skills?
5. How can special education teachers work with language specialists to implement RTI?

Malik is a second grader who is good at sports—especially soccer. He seems like such a capable young boy until he talks. Whether he is having a conversation or trying to read, he has difficulty thinking of the right words. Yesterday he was trying to describe the work that he and his dad had done on his go-cart. He could not think of the words *screwdriver, hammer, sandpaper, wheels, axle, steering wheel*, and *engine*. Sometimes he tried to describe what he wanted to say; for example, when he could not think of *screwdriver,* he said, "It's the thing you use to put in things that are kind of like nails." Sometimes he can only think of a word that is similar to the word he is trying to say; for example, he said, "I was using the hitter to hit some nails." Malik also has trouble remembering words when he reads. He does not remember simple sight words and consequently has to resort to attempting to sound out the words. Often, the words he cannot remember are not phonetic (e.g., *come, are, was, very*), so his strategy is only somewhat useful. Malik is in a second-grade classroom, but he receives speech and language therapy for his language problems, and in addition to his core reading program, he receives tutoring support for his reading difficulties.

Monica is in fifth grade. If you just listen to her, you would not necessarily recognize that she has a language problem. Her vocabulary is adequate for a student her age, and she uses fairly sophisticated sentences. But Monica's language frequently seems to get her in trouble. Monica is growing up in a tough neighborhood, but she goes to school in a middle-class neighborhood across town. She has difficulty switching her language style to match the new context of the school. She continues to use the language she uses with friends, resulting in the interpretation that she is both arrogant and disrespectful to teachers. Monica also has other problems using language effectively. She has difficulty determining when a listener is not understanding what she is trying to explain. Instead of restating her point in another way, she continues with her description or explanation. When the listener asks her to clarify a point, Monica implies that the listener is stupid. She also does not take turns easily during conversations. She either monopolizes the conversation or expects the other person to do all the talking while she gives little feedback to indicate that she is listening. Consequently, Monica is perceived as a student with behavior problems, although there is no indication of any serious emotional problems. She sees her counselor once a week. However, this is really not enough. She has difficulty with reading and writing, and this influences her learning in social studies and science as well. In the last several months, the speech/language pathologist has been consulting with the counselor and Monica's teachers. They are working with Monica to help her use language more effectively and to vary it across contexts. Perhaps with all professionals working together, they will be able to eliminate some of the learning and behavior problems Monica is currently experiencing.

Antoine is a third grader with language delays. He started talking at age 3 1/2, and his language now seems more like that of a first grader. He began receiving speech and language therapy at age 4. Although he is currently in a class for students with mild-to-moderate disabilities, he receives speech and language therapy for 30 minutes, 4 days a week. Antoine is delayed in all aspects of language. His vocabulary is limited, he uses simple sentence patterns, and he uses language primarily to obtain information and attention and to inform others of his needs. He rarely initiates a conversation, but he will carry on a conversation if the other person takes the lead. Mrs. Borman, his teacher, works closely with the speech/language pathologist to help ensure that Antoine is receiving the structured language programming he needs throughout the school day. One of Mrs. Borman's roles in this programming is to provide Antoine with many opportunities to practice and receive feedback on the skills he is learning in speech/language therapy.

As teachers, we will undoubtedly work with students like Malik, Monica, and Antoine. To assist these students in developing effective language and communication skills, we need to understand the *content of language instruction* and *strategies for teaching language*.

Content of Language Instruction

What are the two main areas of language delays, and how do they manifest themselves in the development of content, form, and use of language? Language is a vehicle for communicating our ideas, beliefs, and needs. Language is an arbitrary system, or code, by which we communicate. Language allows us to share our knowledge with others and organize the knowledge in our long-term memory so that we can retrieve it and use it to communicate.

The major purpose of language is communication. Both in school and in our society, language is a powerful resource. We use language to do the following:

- Maintain contact with others
- Facilitate learning to read
- Gain information
- Give information
- Persuade
- Accomplish goals
- Monitor our own behavior when we talk to ourselves

Language functions as an integral part of the communication process because it allows us to represent ideas by using a conventional code.

A person's ability to understand what is being communicated is referred to as *comprehension* or *receptive* language, whereas a person's ability to convey an intended message is referred to as *production* or *expressive* language. It is assumed that for the communication process to be effective a speaker and a listener will use the same code and know the same rules of language. You have probably had the experience of trying to explain a need to someone who speaks a different language. You probably found yourself using many more gestures than usual. This is because although your listener could not understand your verbal communication code, he or she could understand your nonverbal code (gestures).

Some students with learning or language problems also experience developmental delays in comprehension or receptive language. They frequently ask for information to be repeated or clarified. In school, these students have difficulties with the following:

- Following directions
- Hearing the sounds in words (phonemes)
- Blending and segmenting the sounds in words
- Understanding the meaning of concepts (particularly temporal and spatial concepts and technical or abstract concepts)
- Seeing relationships among concepts
- Understanding humor and figurative language
- Understanding multiple meanings
- Understanding questions (particularly *how* and *why* questions)
- Understanding less common and irregular verb tenses
- Understanding compound and complex sentences
- Realizing they do not understand what is being said

Students with language problems may also have delays in production or expressive language. Students with delays in expressive language have difficulty with the following:

- Using correct grammar
- Using compound and complex sentences
- Thinking of the right word to convey the concept (word finding)
- Discussing abstract, temporal, or spatial concepts
- Changing the communication style to fit various social contexts

- Providing enough information to the listener (e.g., starting a conversation with "He took it to the fair," when *he* and *it* have not been previously identified)
- Maintaining the topic during a conversation
- Retelling narratives and past events
- Repairing communication breakdowns

Although some students with learning or language problems have difficulty with both receptive and expressive language, other students experience difficulty primarily with expressive language. Students who have only expressive language difficulties generally understand much more than they are able to communicate.

Relationship of Oral and Written Communication

We use language when we read, write, and communicate orally. In written communication, the writer is similar to the speaker in that the writer is responsible for sending a message. The reader is similar to a listener, whose job it is to interpret or construct the message. The relationship of speaking and listening to writing and reading is presented in Figure 6-1. Because both oral and written communication are language based, a student who is having difficulty in oral communication (e.g., understanding figurative language) will also have difficulty in written communication. For example, research consistently tells us that vocabulary knowledge is one of the best predictors of reading achievement (Cromley & Azevedo, 2007; Ellemann, Lindo, Morphy, & Compton, 2009). Furthermore, youngsters who have oral language difficulties in general or difficulties with grammatical knowledge are also at risk for reading disabilities (Catts, Fey, Tomblin, & Zhang, 2002). However, there are important differences between oral and written communication. For example, in oral communication there is a dynamic shifting between the roles of speaker and listener. A speaker can obtain immediate feedback from a listener. Consequently, the speaker can adjust the way in which a message is expressed (e.g., lower the vocabulary level, re-explain, or restate) more easily than the author can. This chapter presents methods for teaching students who have difficulty with oral communication; the next three chapters describe methods for teaching students who have difficulty with written communication (reading and writing). Some of the instructional ideas will be similar because of the underlying language base of both oral and written communication. In some instances, an instructional strategy that is suggested as a reading comprehension strategy can also be used as a listening or writing strategy (e.g., teaching students to ask themselves the questions Who? What? When? Where? Why? and How? as they read, write, speak, or listen). We encourage you to keep in mind the close relationship of oral and written communication as you read the next four chapters.

Components of Language

The content of language instruction for students with learning or language problems focuses on teaching the language code, the rules of the code, and how to use the code to communicate. To help us understand language so that we can more effectively plan the content of language instruction, we will consider several components of language.

Content Content, also called *semantics,* refers to the ideas or concepts we are communicating. Keiko can communicate her desire for two chocolate-chip cookies in numerous ways. For example, she can say, "I want two chocolate-chip cookies," or "Me want choc-chip cookies" (while pointing to the cookie jar and then holding up two fingers). In both cases, the content or ideas are the same.

When we teach content, we are teaching concepts and helping students to learn the labels (vocabulary) for those concepts. When a young child asks such questions as What's that? or What are you doing? we often respond by giving the label for the object (e.g., spoon, blanket, shirt) or the action (i.e., stirring, making the bed, ironing). In this way, we are teaching the labels for the ideas or concepts.

We are also teaching content when we help students see the relationships among the ideas or concepts. The semantic network diagram of the concept of *bird,* depicted in Figure 2-6, is one way to demonstrate how ideas are related. In that case, we used a network that represented the concept of *bird* in terms of its class, properties, and

▶ **Figure 6-1** Relationship of Oral and Written Communication

A Model of the Communication Process

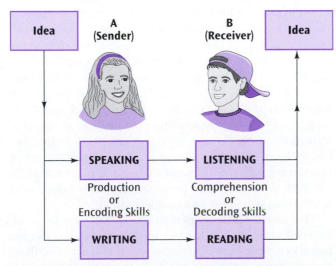

Source: Adapted from J. Lerner, *Learning Disabilities: Theories, Diagnosis, and Teaching Strategies,* 8th ed. (Boston: Houghton Mifflin, 2000), p. 344.

examples. Much of education, whether teaching about fruits and vegetables in primary grades or the characteristics of capitalism and communism in high school, centers on teaching about ideas, the relationships among the ideas, and the vocabulary that labels the ideas (Beck, McKeown, & Kucan, 2002; Bulgren, Deshler, & Lenz, 2007).

Form *Form* refers to the structure and sound of language. In the example of Keiko wanting two chocolate-chip cookies, two different forms were presented for the underlying meaning of the message. Form is usually further divided into phonology, morphology, and syntax.

Phonology Phonemes are the actual sounds produced by speakers. Phonemes are the smallest linguistic units of sound that can signal a meaning difference. In the English language, there are approximately 45 phonemes, or speech sounds, that are classified as either vowels or consonants (e.g., /a/, /k/, /ch/). Learning speech sounds and their relationships to the written letters can help students to identify unknown words when they read and spell (Blachman, 2000; Foorman, 2007).

Phonology refers to the rules for combining and patterning phonemes within the language. Phonology also includes the control of vocal features (timing, frequency, duration) that influence the meaning we express when talking. Without changing any words, we can vary the underlying meaning of a sentence simply by the way we change our voice (e.g., intonation, pitch, and stress). For example, try saying, "I like that?" and "I like that." Depending on the intonation, stress, and pitch, the first statement can mean "I don't like that," and the second one can mean "I do like that."

Morphology Whereas phonology focuses on sounds, morphology focuses on the rule system that governs the structure of words and word forms. Whereas phonemes are the smallest sound units, morphemes are the smallest unit of language that conveys meaning. There are two different kinds of morphemes: root words or words that can stand alone (e.g., *cat, run, pretty, small, form*), and affixes (prefixes, suffixes, and inflectional endings) that are added to words and change the meaning of the words (e.g., *cats, rerun, smallest, transformation*).

Helping elementary and secondary students learn the various affixes and their meanings can assist them in decoding words, determining the meaning of words, and spelling. For example, students who do not recognize or know the meaning of the word *predetermination* can break it into the root word *determine* (to decide), the prefix *pre-* (before), and the suffix *-tion* (denoting action in a noun). Then the students can decode or spell the word and generate the meaning of *predetermination* as a decision made in advance.

Developmentally, inflectional endings are the easiest to learn, followed by suffixes and then prefixes (Owens, 2007).

Inflectional endings can be taught through structured conversation; suffixes and prefixes usually require more formal instruction in both oral and written form (Moats, 1995). The most frequently used prefixes in American English are un-, in-, dis-, and non-. Table 6-1 presents some common prefixes, suffixes, and inflectional endings, along with their meanings and several examples. As you can see from the table, definitions of prefixes and suffixes are sometimes vague. Although only one or two definitions are provided in the table, some affixes have four or more definitions (Gunning, 2010). Teaching this information (or a simplified list for elementary-age students) can assist students in understanding and learning new vocabulary and in decoding unknown words. To give students a sense of the meanings, provide experiences with several examples.

Syntax *Syntax* refers to the order of words in sentences and the rules for determining that order. Just as phonemes combine to form words, words combine to form phrases and sentences. In the same way that rules determine how phonemes can be combined, rules also determine how words can be combined. The basic syntactical structure for English is subject + verb + object (e.g., "Mike eats cereal").

The rules for combining words vary across languages. For example, in English, adjectives almost always precede the noun they modify (e.g., a delicious apple), whereas in Spanish, adjectives generally follow the noun they modify (e.g., *una manzana deliciosa*—an apple delicious).

Use *Pragmatics* refers to the purposes or functions of communication or how we use language to communicate (Owens, 2007). Language use, or pragmatics, grows significantly during the school years (Owens, 2007). During the later school years, students use language proficiently with multiple meanings, employing figurative language, sarcasm, and jokes (Bernstein, 1986). This is also true for individuals with communication difficulties (Hengst, Frame, Neuman-Stritzel, & Gannaway, 2005). Students also learn to vary their communication style, or *register*, on the basis of a listener's characteristics and knowledge concerning the topic. By the age of 13, students can switch from peer register to adult register, depending on the person with whom they are talking, and from formal register to an informal register, depending on the setting and circumstances (Nippold & Sun, 2008; Owens, 2007). Pragmatics for students in middle school is an important aspect of functioning within the classroom, because pragmatic skills are critical to academic progress and in building peer relationships (Brice & Montgomery, 1996).

The way a speaker uses language will also be influenced by the knowledge the speaker thinks the listener has about the topic being discussed. If you are describing how to hang a picture on a wall, the language you use will depend on whether you think the listener is familiar

Table 6-1 Common Inflectional Endings, Prefixes, and Suffixes

Common Forms	Meanings	Examples
Inflectional Endings		
-ed	notes past tense on verbs	helped, studied
-ing	notes present progressive on verbs	helping, studying
-s/-es	notes third person singular on verbs	he helps, she studies
-s/-es	notes plurals on nouns	cats, parties
-'s	notes possessive	Juan's, cat's
Prefixes		
ante-	before, front	antecedent, anterior
anti-	against	antifreeze, antitoxin
bi-	two	bicycle, bisect
co-	with, together	coworker, cooperate
de-	down, remove, reduce, do the opposite	descent, dethrone, devalue, deactivate
dis-	opposite	distrust, distaste
en-	to cover, to cause to be	encompass, enslave
ex-	former, from	expatriate, explain
hyper-	above, more, excessive	hyperactive, hyperventilate
hypo-	below, less	hypoactive, hypodermic
il-	not	illogical
im-	not, in, into	impatient
in-	not, in, into	incomplete, inclusion
inter-	between, together	interact, intervene
ir-	not, into	irreversible
mis-	wrong	miscalculate
non-	not	nonstop
out-	beyond, exceeds	outlast, outside
pre-	before, in front of	preface, precaution
pro-	before, in front of, in favor of	proceed, proactive
re-	again, backward motion	repeat, rewind
semi-	half	semifinalist
sub-	under, less than	subordinate, subtitle
super-	above, superior	superordinate
trans-	across, beyond	transportation
un-	not	unlucky, unclear
Suffixes		
-able	capable of, tendency to	dependable
-age	result of action or place	breakage, orphanage
-al	pertaining to	personal
-ance	changing an action to a state	hindrance
-ation	changing an action to a state	determination
-ant	one who (occupation)	accountant, attendant
-en	noting action from an adjective	harden, loosen
-ence	changing an action to a state	dependence, reference
-er/or	notes occupation or type of person	lawyer, writer, sculptor
-er	notes comparative (between two)	larger, younger
-est	notes superlative (among more than two)	largest, youngest
-ful	full of	bountiful, joyful
-fy	to make	magnify, identify

(*continued*)

Table 6-1 Continued

Common Forms	Meanings	Examples
-ible	capable of, tendency to	credible, collectible
-ion/-tion	changing an action to a state	confusion, transformation
-ish	belonging to, characteristic of	Finnish, greenish
-ist	one who (occupation)	artist, biologist
-ive	changes action to characteristic or tendency	creative, active
-less	unable to, without	harmless, thoughtless
-ly	denotes adverbs	loudly, friendly
-ment	result of an action (noun)	entertainment, excitement
-ness	quality, state of being	happiness, deafness
-ous	full of, having	victorious, harmonious
-some	quality or state	handsome, bothersome
-ward	turning to	homeward, wayward
-y	characterized by, inclined to	dirty, sleepy

with a plastic anchor and screw. The manner in which a topic is introduced, maintained, and changes, as well as how we reference topics, is governed by rules of pragmatics. Students who are learning English as a second language and bilingual students with communication disorders may need explicit instruction in pragmatics.

Formalist views of language have assumed that language is a composite of various rule systems consisting of semantics, phonology, morphology, syntax, and pragmatics. However, more recent views of language and language intervention have highlighted language as a social tool; in this view, pragmatics is viewed as the overall organizing aspect of language (Owens, 2007). This model (see Figure 6-2) has direct implications for language intervention in terms of both targets for intervention and methods of intervention. An approach in which

pragmatics is the overall organizing aspect calls for an interactive, conversational approach to teaching and one that reflects the context in which language is used (Owens, 2007). This has been referred to as a *functional* or *holistic approach* to language intervention (Ellis, 2005).

School-Age Language Development and Difficulties

Knowing how language develops during the school years and what difficulties students with learning or language problems demonstrate during these years will help us make decisions concerning the content and focus of language instruction.

> **WEB RESOURCES**
> For a helpful Web site, see Net Connections for Communication Disorders and Sciences (http://www.mnsu.edu/dept/comdis/kuster2/welcome.html).

There is growing evidence to suggest that many students with reading problems have mild to moderate language problems; the largest subgroup of students with learning disabilities are those who experience language difficulties (Catts & Kahmi, 2005).

Although more research would be valuable to support a comprehensive scope and sequence for school-age language development, there is enough information to assist us in planning the content of language instruction. Let's examine the development of content, form, and use at the school-age level and the difficulties that students with learning or language problems demonstrate.

Content During the school years, children increase the size of their vocabularies and their ability to understand and talk about abstract concepts.

▶ **Figure 6-2** Components of Language from a Functionalist Perspective

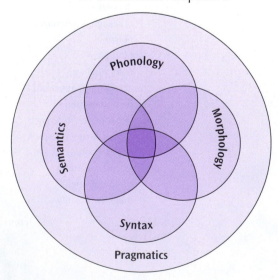

Vocabulary Growth During the school years, one of the areas in which students demonstrate the greatest amount of growth is vocabulary. When students enter school, their estimated speaking vocabulary is about 2,500 words (Owens, 2007). In comparison, when technical words are not counted, average adult speakers converse in everyday conversation using about 10,000 words, and the average high school graduate knows and uses an estimated 60,000 to 80,000 words (Carroll, 1964). School provides students with opportunities to listen, read, and learn, thus increasing their vocabularies. Even math, which is often considered less language-based than social studies and science, contains a significant number of concepts and words to learn (e.g., *subtract, estimate, rational number, trapezoid*).

There is also an increase in the breadth and specificity of meanings. For example, for a preschooler, the word *bird* may refer to any animal that flies. However, most children later learn a whole set of specific vocabulary that defines different types of birds and their characteristics. The semantic network that was depicted in Figure 2-6 becomes increasingly complex and more interrelated as a student's knowledge of birds increases.

During the school years, students improve considerably in their understanding and organization of abstract concepts. Some examples of this include students' organization of words and ability to group them by such features as animate or inanimate, spatial (location) or temporal (time) relationships, and real or imaginary. For example, in learning about fossils, students learn to simultaneously classify different types of fossils (e.g., trilobites, crinoids, brachiopods) according to plant/animal, extinct/not extinct, and location (e.g., sea, lake, or land).

As students become more proficient word and concept learners, they also learn the multiple meanings of many common words. For example, the word *bank* has several meanings and can function as a noun or a verb:

Lou sat on the *bank* fishing.
You can *bank* on him to be there.
Put your money in the *bank* for now.
He was able to *bank* the ball to make the basket.

Students with language problems generally have vocabularies that are more limited than average, and their word meanings are generally more concrete and less flexible (Catts & Kahmi, 2005; Owens, 2010). For example, fifth-grade students with reading disabilities sometimes had difficulty considering three different characteristics of fossils simultaneously (Bos & Anders, 1990a). Questions such as "Which fossils are extinct sea animals?" required the students to juggle too much information. In comparison, they could easily answer questions for which they had to deal with only one characteristic at a time, for example, "Which fossils live in the sea?" "Which fossils are animals?" and "Which fossils are extinct?"

Many students with reading and language disabilities have greater difficulty understanding that words can have multiple meanings and knowing which meaning to apply. For example, in the question "Was the *fare* that you paid for your taxi ride to the *fair* a *fair* price?" students are required to know and use three different meanings for the word *fair/fare*.

Figurative Language During the school years, students also develop greater understanding and ability to use figurative language. Figurative language represents abstract concepts and usually requires an inferential rather than literal interpretation. Figurative language allows students to use language in truly creative ways (Owens, 2007). The primary types of figurative language include the following:

- Idioms (e.g., "It's raining cats and dogs.")
- Metaphors (e.g., "She had her eagle-eye watching for him.")
- Similes (e.g., "He ran like a frightened rabbit.")
- Proverbs (e.g., "The early bird catches the worm.")

Students with language disorders and other disabilities and students who are from other cultures or who have English as their second language tend to have difficulty with figurative language. Yet figurative language, particularly idioms, is used frequently in the classroom. Classroom research has shown that teachers use idioms in approximately 11% of their utterances and that third- to eighth-grade reading programs contain idioms in approximately 6.7% of their sentences (Lazar, Warr-Leeper, Nicholson, & Johnson, 1989). Table 6-2 presents some common American English idioms. Discussing and using these idioms and adding to the list can assist students with language disorders and second-language learners in improving their understanding and use of the English language.

Word Retrieval Some students with learning or language problems also experience difficulties with word retrieval or word finding (Owens, 2010; Nippold, 1998). A word retrieval problem is like having the word on the tip of your tongue but not quite being able to think of it. The following dialogue presents a conversation between two third-grade students—one with normal language and the other with word-retrieval problems:

> ▶ **WEB RESOURCES**
> For additional information on word-finding difficulties, check out the following Web site: http://www.wordfinding.com.

Setting: Third-grade classroom
Topic: Discussion about how to make an Easter basket

Susan: Are you going to make, uh, make, uh . . . one of these things [pointing to the Easter basket on the bookshelf]?
Cori: Oh, you mean an Easter basket?
Susan: Yeah, an Easter basket.
Cori: Sure, I'd like to, but I'm not sure how to do it. Can you help me?

Table 6-2 Common American English Idioms

Animals	red-letter day	Tools and Work
a bull in a china shop	true blue	bury the hatchet
as stubborn as a mule		has an axe to grind
going to the dogs	**Games and Sports**	hit the nail on the head
playing possum	ace up my sleeve	throw a monkey wrench into it
a fly in the ointment	cards are stacked against me	doctor the books
clinging like a leech	got lost in the shuffle	has a screw loose
grinning like a Cheshire cat	keep your head above water	hit the roof
	paddle your own canoe	nursing his wounds
Body Parts	ballpark figure	sober as a judge
on the tip of my tongue	get to first base	
raised eyebrows	keep the ball rolling	**Vehicles**
turn the other cheek	on the rebound	fix your wagon
put your best foot forward	jockey for position	like ships passing in the night
turn heads		on the wagon
	Foods	don't rock the boat
Clothing	eat crow	missed the boat
dressed to kill	humble pie	take a back seat
hot under the collar	that takes the cake	
wear the pants in the	a finger in every pie	**Weather**
family	in a jam	calm before the storm
fit like a glove		haven't the foggiest
straitlaced	**Plants**	steal her thunder
	heard it through the grapevine	come rain or shine
Colors	resting on his laurels	right as rain
gray area	shrinking violet	throw caution to the wind
once in a blue moon	no bed of roses	
tickled pink	shaking like a leaf	
has a yellow streak	withered on the vine	

Source: R. E. Owens, Jr., Language Disorders: A Functional Approach to Assessment and Intervention, 2nd ed. (Boston: Allyn & Bacon, 1995), p. 347. Copyright © 1995 by Allyn and Bacon. Reprinted with permission. Compiled from Boatner, Gates, & Makkai (1975); Clark (1990); Gibbs (1987); Gulland & Hinds-Howell (1986); Kirkpatrick & Schwarz (1982); Palmatier & Ray (1989).

Susan: Yeah, first you'll need some, uh, some, uh, the things you cut with, you know . . .

Cori: Scissors.

Susan: Yeah, and some paper and the thing you use to stick things together with.

Cori: Tape?

Susan: No, uh, uh, sticky stuff.

Cori: Oh, well let's get the stuff we need.

Susan: Let's go to, uh, uh, the shelf, uh, where you get, you know, the stuff to cut up.

Cori: Yeah, the paper, and let's also get the glue.

It is obvious from the conversation that both students were frustrated by the communication process. Susan's language is filled with indefinite words (*thing, stuff*), circumlocutions ("The things you cut with"), and fillers ("Let's go to, uh, the shelf, um, where you get, you know, the stuff to cut up"). At first, students like Susan may seem very talkative because of their overuse of descriptions, circumlocutions, and fillers (Swafford & Reed, 1986); however, after one listens to them for a while, their language seems empty of information.

Word retrieval or word-finding problems can result from two possible sources (Kail and Leonard, 1986). One source is with the storage, in that the student's understanding is not

elaborate; in other words, the semantic network is not well developed, and the meaning is shallow (German, 1992). For example, when a student's semantic network for the concept *bird* (see Figure 2-6) is well developed, it will be easier to retrieve the word than if the semantic network is limited and the word has been learned in isolation. Therefore, in assisting students, it is important to help them develop more elaborate understandings of concepts. A second source of word-finding problems is with the retrieval or search and recovery of the word. In this case, teaching and providing cues (e.g., it's something you ride; peanut butter and _____; it's a type of bird) can assist in retrieval (Nippold, 1992, 1998; Wiig & Semel, 1984). Students with learning or language problems may have difficulty with word-storage problems, word-retrieval problems, or both (German, 1992; Johnson et al., 1999).

Form During the school years, students continue to learn more complex sentence structures (Nippold, 1993, 1998; Owens, 2010). Although by age 5 most students understand and generate basic sentences, first graders produce neither sentences that are completely grammatical ("He'll might go to jail") nor sentences that reflect the syntactical complexities of the English language. Table 6-3 presents the sequence for selected syntactical structures. Some of

Table 6-3 Developmental Sequence for Comprehension of Sentence Types

Syntactic Structure	Sentence	Age of Comprehension By 75%		By 90%
Simple imperative	Go!	4–6*	to	6–0 years
Negative imperative	Don't cross!	5–6	to	7–0+ years
Active declarative				
Regular noun and present progressive	The girl is jumping.	3–0	to	3–0 years
Irregular noun and present progressive	The sheep is eating.	6–6	to	7–0 years
Past tense	The man painted the house.	5–6	to	7–0+ years
Past participle	The lion has eaten.	6–0	to	7–0+ years
Future	He will hit the ball.	7–0	to	7–0+ years
Reversible	The car bumps the train.	6–6	to	7–0+ years
Perfective	The man has been cutting trees.	7–0+	to	7–0+ years
Interrogative				
Who . . .	Who is by the table?	3–0	to	3–0 years
What . . .	What do we eat?	3–6	to	5–0 years
When . . .	When do you sleep?	3–6	to	5–6 years
Negation				
Explicit	The girl isn't running.	5–6	to	7–0+ years
Inherent	These two are different.	6–6	to	7–0+ years
Reversible passive	The boy is chased by the dog.	5–6	to	6–0 years
Conjunction				
If . . .	If you're the teacher, point to the dog; if not, point to the bear.	7–0+	to	7–0+ years
. . . then	Look at the third picture; then point to the baby of his animal.	7–0+	to	7–0+ years
neither . . . nor	Find the one that is neither the ball nor the table.	7–0+	to	7–0+ years

Source: E. H. Wiig & E. Semel, *Language Assessment & Intervention for the Learning Disabled,* 2nd ed. (Columbus, OH: C. E. Merrill, 1984). Reprinted with permission of the senior author, Elizabeth H. Wiig, Ph.D., Knowledge Research Institute, Inc.
*4–6 = 4 years, 6 months

the most difficult structures require the use of complex sentences and cohesive devices such as causals (*because*), conditionals (*if*), and enabling relationships (*so that*).

Another later-developing sentence structure involves passive construction ("The boy is chased by the dog"), which is usually not established until ages 5 to 7 (Chomsky, 1969; Owens, 2007). What makes older students' language different from that of younger students in terms of form is the new arrangements and increasingly complex combinations of basic forms (Scott & Stokes, 1995).

As sentence complexity increases, so does the average length of sentences. Yet it is important to know that mature language still has some grammatical errors, false starts, hesitations, and revisions. Table 6-4 demonstrates the growth in the number of words per sentence or communication unit. As is evident in Table 6-4, spoken sentence length matches chronological age (i.e., an 8-year-old student's sentences are, on the average, eight words long) until the age of approximately 9 years, when the growth curve begins to slow. By high school, adolescents' conversational utterances average 10 to 12 words. Average sentence length, however, is consistently shorter in conversational discourse than in narrative discourse

(Leadholm & Miller, 1992; Nelson, 1998). Youngsters also continue to increase use of inflectional endings, suffixes, prefixes, and irregular verbs. Students with language problems are slower to develop advanced syntactic structures; these delays are most evident in the elementary grades (Owens, 2007). Table 6-5 lists the age ranges for when various word formations and irregular verb usages are developed.

Use The area of most important linguistic growth during the school years is language use or pragmatics, as discussed earlier in this chapter. Throughout the school years, students become more empathetic toward the listener and able to understand a variety of perspectives. Older children can vary their communication style, or register, as we discussed earlier.

Young school-age children use language to, for example,

- gain and hold attention in a socially acceptable manner.
- use others, when appropriate, as resources for assistance or information.
- express affection or hostility and anger appropriately.
- direct and follow peers.
- compete with peers in storytelling and boasts.

Assessing and Teaching Oral Language

Table 6-4 Average Number of Words per Communication Unit (mean)

Grade	High Group	Random Group	Low Group
1	7.91	6.88	5.91
2	8.10	7.56	6.65
3	8.38	7.62	7.08
4	9.28	9.00	7.55
5	9.59	8.82	7.90
6	10.32	9.82	8.57
7	11.14	9.75	9.01
8	11.59	10.71	9.52
9	11.73	10.96	9.26
10	12.34	10.68	9.41
11	13.00	11.17	10.18
12	12.84	11.70	10.65

Source: W. Loban, *Language Development: Kindergarten through Grade Twelve,* Res. Report #18 (Urbana, IL: National Council of Teachers of English, 1976), p. 27. Reprinted by permission of the publisher.

Table 6-5 Development of Word Formation Rules and Irregular Verbs

Word Formation Rules and Irregular Verbs	Age Range (In Years–Months)
Regular noun plurals (balls, chairs)	3–6 to 7–0+
Present progressive tense (running)	3–0 to 3–6
Present progressive tense (going)	3–6 to 5–6
Adjective forms	
Comparative (smaller, taller)	4–0 to 5–0
Superlative (shortest, tallest)	3–0 to 3–6
Noun derivation	
-er (hitter, painter, farmer)	3–6 to 6–6
-man (fisherman)	5–6 to 6–0
-ist (artist, bicyclist)	6–6 to 7–0+
Adverbial derivation (easily, gently)	7–0+
Irregular verbs	
went	4–6 to 5–0
broke, fell, took, came, made, sat, threw	5–0 to 6–0
bit, cut, drive, fed, ran, wrote, read, rode	6–0 to 7–0
drank, drew, hid, rang, slept, swam	7–0 to 8–0
caught, hung, left, built, sent, shook	8–0 to 9–0

Source: Adapted from E. Carrow, *Test of Auditory Comprehension of Language* (San Antonio, TX: Pearson, 2009); K. Shipley, M. Maddox, & J. Driver (1991), Children's development of irregular past tense verb forms, *Language, Speech, and Hearing Services in Schools, 22*, pp. 115–112; E. H. Wiig & E. Semel, *Language Assessment and Intervention for the Learning Disabled*, 2nd ed. (Columbus, OH: C. E. Merrill, 1984).

- express pride in themselves and in personal accomplishments.
- role-play.

By adolescence, students reflect communicative competence (Fujiki, Brinton, & Todd, 1996; Owens, 2005; Wiig & Semel, 1984) in that they can do the following:

- Express positive and negative feelings and reactions to others.
- Present, understand, and respond to information in spoken messages related to persons, objects, events, or processes that are not immediately visible.
- Take the role of another person.
- Understand and present complex messages.
- Adapt messages to the needs of others.
- On the basis of prior experience, approach verbal interactions with expectations of what to say and how to say it.
- Select different forms for their messages on the basis of the age, status, and reactions of the listeners.
- Use sarcasm and double meanings.
- Make deliberate use of metaphors.

Some students with learning or language problems also experience difficulties with language *use,* or pragmatics (Brinton, Fujiki, & McKee, 1998; Owens, 2007). The following dialogue demonstrates how Brice, an adolescent with behavior disorders and subsequent learning problems, has difficulty using language effectively in a conversation with a peer. He tends to switch topics (lack of topic maintenance), does not provide enough context for his listener, does not provide adequate referents for his pronouns, and does not respond to his listener's requests for clarification. In addition, Brice is unaware of his failure to communicate effectively and blames his conversational partner for communication breakdowns.

Setting: Computer lab

Topic: Brice is explaining to Reid how to play a computer game.

Brice: Did you get in trouble for last night?

Reid: What do you mean for last night?

Brice: You know, for what you did.

Reid: I'm not sure what you're talking about.

Brice: Want to learn how to play Chopperlifter?

Reid: Yeah, I guess, but what about last night?

Brice: Well, one thing you do is put it in the slot and turn on the computer.

Reid: What thing? Do you mean the CD?

Brice: Sure I do. Now watch. *Brice boots the CD and selects Chopperlifter from a game menu.* You got to take it and go pick up the men.

Reid: You mean the helicopter?

Brice: Yeah, aren't you listening?

Reid: Yeah, but you're not telling me enough about the game.

Brice: Yes I am. You're just like my brother, you don't listen.

Reid: I'm not going to put up with this. I'll see you around.

Although this is not reflected in the language sample, Brice also has difficulty varying his language for different audiences. He sometimes sounds disrespectful to adults because he does not vary his language to suit different speakers or contexts. Finally, Brice and other students with pragmatic language difficulties, including students with behavior disorders, tend to misinterpret emotions or meanings indicated by nonverbal communication, including facial expressions and body language, more frequently than their normal peers do. These students may not be classified as having speech and language problems because they have fluent, complex, and clear articulation. Challenging for these students is complex language in which they do not understand some of the subtle messages (Bishop & Norbury, 2002).

It is important to remember that content, form, and use are related. Sometimes students who appear to have difficulties with language use have them because of limited content and form. For these students, it is important to focus instruction in the areas of content and form and find out whether language use automatically improves.

Guidelines for Teaching Language

What guidelines can assist in teaching oral language, content, form, and use? In teaching students with learning or language problems, teachers have traditionally focused on teaching academic skills and have placed less emphasis on the development of oral language skills. However, it is clear that language continues to develop during the school years and that students with reading problems show difficulties in oral language that affect oral as well as written communication (Cooper, Roth, Schatschneider, & Speece, 2002). Let's look at some general principles and procedures for teaching oral language skills to these students.

General Guidelines for Teaching Oral Language

Opportunities for teaching oral language abound in the school setting. When we teach students new concepts and vocabulary in content area subjects, we are teaching oral language. When students learn how to give oral reports or retell a story, how to introduce themselves, or how to use irregular verbs, they are learning language. A list of general procedures or guidelines for teaching language is presented in Apply the Concept 6-1 and discussed in this section. These principles are not only important for students with learning problems but can also be beneficial for other students in the classroom. The speech/language pathologist is a good source for additional guidelines, techniques, and teaching ideas.

Teach Language in Purposeful Contexts Whether a teacher is teaching a student to use causal relationships (form), to categorize fossils (content), or how to use the telephone to request information (use), it is important to teach language in context. It is difficult to imagine teaching someone how to use a hammer, drill, or saw without using nails, boards, and probably the goal of making a simple wood project. The same should apply in teaching students to use language. Rote practice of sentence structures or rehearsal of word definitions will teach the student little unless this is paired with how to use language.

To foster teaching language in context, the teacher should plan activities that highlight the language skill being taught. For example, Mr. Cardoni used the contexts of following a recipe for chocolate-chip cookies and of building bird feeders to teach the vocabulary related to fractions (e.g., half, one quarter, two thirds, part, whole, fraction). During the activities, the students measured and compared the different fractional parts (e.g., determining what fraction one teaspoon is of one tablespoon). This allowed Mr. Cardoni and his students to talk about the

●●●●●● *Apply the Concept* ●●●●●●

6-1	General Principles for Teaching Language

- Teach language in purposeful contexts.
- In most cases, follow the sequence of normal language development.
- Teach comprehension and production.
- Use conversations to promote language development.
- Adjust pacing, chunk information, and check for understanding to promote comprehension.

- Increase wait time to promote production.
- Use effective teaching strategies when presenting a new concept or skill.
- Use self-talk and parallel talk to describe what you and others are doing or thinking.
- Use modeling to demonstrate language.
- Use expansion and elaboration.

- Use structured language programs to provide intensive practice and feedback.
- Use language as an intrinsic motivator.
- Systematically plan and instruct for generalization.

concepts of fractions in a situation in which fractions played an important role in the project and to demonstrate with concrete examples the differences between fractions.

In Most Cases, Follow the Sequence of Normal Language Development Determining the content of instruction is a major part of the teaching–learning process, whether it be in language, academics, content areas, or social areas. Students with language difficulties may need additional instruction in one of the areas of language development, such as, content, form, or use. For example, Monica, the fifth grader with word-finding problems has difficulty primarily in the area of content. On the other hand, Brice appears to have adequate content and form in his language but has difficulty with use. Therefore, in planning a language program, begin by determining what knowledge and skills a student has already acquired in the areas of content, form, and use, and then target the subsequent areas in the development process. For instance, if the student is already using past tense ("The boy ate the cake"), you might next focus on past participle ("The boy has eaten the cake") (see Table 6-3). A speech/language pathologist can be an excellent resource for helping to determine what to teach next.

Teach Comprehension and Production Give students opportunities to develop both their understanding (comprehension) and their ability to express (production) the new knowledge or skill you are teaching. For example, when teaching students to comprehend the past participle, a teacher should label examples of events that have already happened (e.g., "Juan has sharpened his pencil" or "Kim has finished her math assignment"). When providing intensive practice and feedback, the teacher shows students picture-sequence cards (see Figure 6-3) and asks students to identify the picture that demonstrates that something "has happened." To teach production, ask students to explain what has happened by using the past participle form. For example, the teacher could ask, "What have you just done?" When teaching the concepts and vocabulary associated with

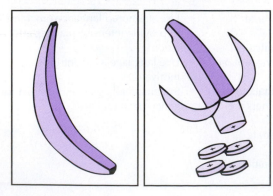

▶ **Figure 6-3** Sequence Cards to Help Students Comprehend and Produce Tenses

a new unit or piece of literature, the teacher provides students with opportunities not only to listen to explanations but also to discuss their knowledge of the concepts. Using the pause procedure (Ruhl, Hughes, & Gajar, 1990), whereby the teacher pauses at logical breaks in the lecture so students can discuss what they are learning with a partner, provides such opportunities. Vaughn and colleagues used the pause procedure of asking students to turn and discuss key concepts and ideas during social studies instruction to enhance vocabulary and comprehension (Vaughn et al., 2009).

Use Conversations to Promote Language Development Students with language problems need opportunities to engage in conversations. Observational research has shown that teachers, in general, are not as responsive to students with language problems as they are to average- and high-achieving students (Pecyna-Rhyner, Lehr, & Pudlas, 1990). Plan opportunities for students to engage in conversations with you and other students as they work, think, and play. Using discussion groups or promoting "turning and talking" with a peer rather than a question–answer format for reviewing a book or current event is an example of how conversations can be integrated into the classroom. These conversations need not be long, and in secondary settings, they can be accomplished as students enter the room. Apply the Concept 6-2 provides more ideas that you can use and share with teachers and parents about how to promote language through the use of conversations.

Adjust Pacing, Chunk Information, and Check for Understanding to Promote Comprehension Second-language learners and students with language problems often have difficulty comprehending what is being said during class, particularly in content area classes. To promote language comprehension, adjust your pacing so that these students have time to process the language input. The flow of instruction need not suffer, but when you are discussing new or difficult concepts or ideas, slow the pace and highlight the key ideas by writing them, demonstrating their meaning, and/or repeating them. It is not unusual for teachers to privately identify several students whom they use to gauge the pacing of their instruction and determine when to move on. Be sure to include the students with language and learning problems in this group.

It is also helpful if the amount of information that is provided in each segment is reduced. Consequently, information can be chunked or segmented into smaller amounts. For example, observing his students in Mr. Hunt's fifth-grade science class, Mr. Fong noticed that his students usually listened to Mr. Hunt present the first 5 of 15 vocabulary words for a new chapter and recorded about 3 of the words in their science notebooks. After Mr. Fong shared this information with Mr. Hunt, Mr. Hunt decided to chunk the vocabulary into groups of 3 to 5 words and introduce each group only when they were needed rather than all of them at the beginning of a new chapter.

6-2   Promoting Language Through Conversations

- Talk about things in which the child/adolescent is interested.
- Follow their lead in the conversation. Reply to their initiations and comments. Share their excitement.
- Don't ask too many questions. If you must, use questions such as *how did/do . . .*, *why did/do . . .*, and *what happened . . .* that result in longer explanatory answers.
- Encourage the child/adolescent to ask questions. Respond by using information the student has provided as well as integrating new information.

- Use a pleasant tone of voice. You can be light and humorous. Children love it when adults are a little silly.
- Don't be judgmental or make fun of a child's language. If you try to catch and correct all errors, the child will stop talking to you. Rather than correct language or state what is wrong, repeat their statements using correct language.
- Allow enough time for the child to respond.
- Treat the child with courtesy by not interrupting when the child is talking.

- Provide opportunities for the child to use language and to have that language work to accomplish his or her goals.
- Include the child in family and classroom discussions. Encourage participation and listen to his/her ideas.
- Be accepting of the child and of the child's language. Hugs and acceptance go a long way.

Source: Adapted from R. E. Owens, Jr., *Language Disorders: A Functional Approach to Assessment and Intervention* (Boston: Allyn & Bacon, 2010).

Checking for understanding is also important for facilitating language comprehension. Having a student repeat directions or tell another student what was just discussed are ways to check for understanding other than asking questions.

Increase Wait Time to Promote Production When Marilyn Fantell, a speech/language pathologist, talks about the most important principles for teachers to use when teaching students with language and learning problems, the first one she mentions is wait time. Some students need time to understand what has just been said and to construct a response. These students may have particular difficulty with form (e.g., syntax) and need the extra time to think about the form they should use in constructing their response. Therefore, when a response is required from these students, a teacher should give students extra time to formulate their answer before giving an additional prompt or calling on another student.

Use Effective Teaching Strategies in Presenting a New Concept or Skill As students progress in school, the demands to learn new content and concepts increase exponentially. Particularly for older students, concept knowledge in math, science, and social studies represents a lot of their growth in concept development. Using effective teaching strategies helps students with language difficulties to gain the concepts and content that they need for success in content area classes. Based on the teaching–learning process, there are a number of effective teaching strategies that should be incorporated into language instruction. Apply the Concept 6-3 lists key strategies that can be used in teaching a new concept.

Use Self-Talk and Parallel Talk to Describe What You and Others Are Doing or Thinking Using self-talk and parallel talk demonstrates how language is connected to activities. Self-talk describes what the teacher is doing or thinking; parallel talk describes what the student is doing or thinking. Ms. Baraka, a special education teacher who is coteaching in a first-grade classroom, uses parallel talk and self-talk when she joins the students at the different learning centers. She explains, "When I join a center, I try to sit down and join in the activities rather than asking students questions. I describe what I am doing and what other students in the group are doing. For example, I might say, 'Voytek is making a clay animal. It's blue, and right now he is putting a ferocious snarl on the animal's face. I wonder what kind of animal it is. I think I'll ask Voytek.'" In this way, the students get to hear how words can describe what someone is doing and thinking, and it focuses the attention on the student and the ongoing activities.

Use Modeling to Demonstrate Language Modeling plays an important role in learning language. Whether for learning a new sentence structure, new vocabulary, or a new function or use for language, modeling is a powerful tool. For example, Ms. Simons and her eighth-grade students in resource English class were working on improving discussion skills during literature discussion groups. Ms. Simon was concerned about the number of students who did not clarify what they were saying when it was obvious that other students were not understanding.

To teach clarification skills, Ms. Simons initiated a discussion about clarifying ideas and then modeled how not clarifying ideas and not asking for clarification can lead to confusion. She exaggerated the examples, and the

6-3   Effective Teaching Strategies for Language Intervention

Gillam and Loeb (2010) identify principles for proving language intervention to school-age children:

1. *Intensity.* Intensive remediation is essential to progress for students with language impairments. If there is not adequate time during the day for highly focused language intervention, then summers and afterschool time is needed.

2. *Active Attention.* Students are more likely to benefit from language interventions when they are interested and engaged in what they are being presented. Signaling students to make sure that they are attending and ready to learn, cueing them when they are paying attention, and providing them with feedback that is engaging about their learning will help ensure that the language intervention is effective.

3. *Feedback.* Receiving feedback about whether responses are correct and then elaborating on this feedback to enhance learning is essential to remediating language difficulties. Direct and not indirect feedback is needed. "That's right, you remembered to sequence your story" is an example of direct feedback.

4. *Rewards.* Supporting internal motivation and recognizing learning and achievement through rewards is an essential feature of effective language intervention programs.

Source: From "Insights from a Randomized Controlled Trial," by R. B. Gillam & D. F. Loeb, January 19, 2010. *American Speech-Language Association Leader.*

---

students seemed to enjoy this. Next, Ms. Simons modeled clarification skills as she participated with the students in their literature discussions. As individual students used effective clarifying skills, she commented on this, so that peers were also serving as models. Use of computers with speech recognition and synthetic speech capability also provides for language models and systematic practice (see Tech Tips).

Use Expansion and Elaboration Language expansion is a technique that is used to facilitate the development of more complex language form and content. By repeating what students say in a slightly more complex manner, the teacher demonstrates how their thoughts can be more fully expressed. For example, Ms. Lee, an elementary teacher, is working to get Rob to connect his ideas and to use adverbs to describe his actions. As he finished several math problems, Rob reported, "I got the first one easy. The second one was hard." Ms. Lee replied, "Oh, you got the first one easily, but the second one was hard." The teacher does not want to imply that she is correcting the student; she is simply showing him a more complex way of expressing the thought. Also, the teacher should expand only one or two elements at once, or the expansion will be too complex for the student to profit from it.

Language elaboration is used to build on the content of a student's language and provide additional information on the topic. For example, Chris, a fourth-grade student with language disabilities, was explaining that snakes have smooth skin. Mr. Anderson elaborated on Chris's idea by commenting, "Snakes have smooth skin and so do lizards. Are there other animals in the desert that have smooth skin?"

Use Structured Language Programs to Provide Intensive Practice and Feedback Teaching in context is critical for learning and generalization. However, sometimes by teaching in context, we do not provide the students with adequate opportunities to practice a new skill. Students who have learning problems need the practice and feedback provided in many language programs and activities to gain mastery of the skill. For example, *Language for Learning* (Engelmann & Osborn, 2008), designed primarily for early elementary students, and *Figurative Language: A Comprehensive Program* (2nd ed.; Gorman-Gard, retrieved from Web site April 12, 2010; http://www.superduperinc.com), designed for older students, provide intensive practice in different language content and forms. However, these programs should not serve as the students' entire language program. Although they provide practice and feedback, they generally do not teach the skill within the relevant contexts that are needed for purposeful learning and generalization.

Use Language as an Intrinsic Motivator Because language is such an enabling tool, it carries a great deal of intrinsic reinforcement for most children. Rather than using praise ("I like the way you said that" or "Good talking"), we can capitalize on the naturally reinforcing nature of language. For example, during a cooking activity, Mr. Shapiro asks the students, "How can we figure out how much two thirds of a cup plus three fourths of a cup of flour is?" After Nikki explains, Mr. Shapiro comments, "Now we know how to figure that out. Shall we give it a try?" Later, the teacher asks how to sift flour. After Rona explains, Mr. Shapiro says, "I've got it. Do you think we can sift it just the way Rona explained to us?" Rather than

USING SOFTWARE TO IMPROVE ORAL LANGUAGE SKILLS

Laureate Learning Systems (http://www.laureatelearning.com) is a software company that markets research-based language development software for infants and preschoolers; learners with developmental disabilities, autism, and visual impairments; adolescents and adults with developmental disabilities, aphasia, and traumatic brain injury; and instructional programs for elementary reading and English as a second language. Laureate describes seven stages of language functioning: interpreted communication, intentional communication, single words, word combinations, early syntax, syntax mastery, and complete generative grammar. The language acquisition ages described with the stages range from 0–4 months to 5 years and up.

Talk Time with Tucker and Tiger's Tale are software programs requiring the learner to speak to the computer, thus encouraging expressive language and stimulating speech. In Talk Time with Tucker, a voice-activated program, Tucker, an animated character, talks and moves with the learner's vocalizations. Clear articulation is not required. In Tiger's Tale an animated tiger has lost his voice. The learners speak to help the tiger and can play back the completed movie, listening to their own recorded voices speaking for the tiger.

Additional software programs from Laureate Learning Systems that help to teach critical oral language skills are Following Directions, First Categories, Twenty Categories, and Micro-LADS. These programs teach learners to follow instructions, categorize objects, and learn language syntax.

The Thinkology series from Heartsoft, Inc. (http://www.heartsoft.com) is another useful software option for oral language improvement. This series offers carefully crafted instruction in Volume I: Clarity, Volume II: Accuracy, and Volume III: Logic and is appropriate for learners from kindergarten through grade 4. These titles track learners' progress and provide superb handouts and worksheets to help orient learners to the material as well as paper-and-pencil follow-up to the computer instruction.

Two additional programs are available from Tool Factory (http://www.toolfactory.com). Sound Beginnings—Making Sounds is a set of voice-activated games designed for students who are at the early stages of acquiring spoken language. Idiom Track is a program using fun graphics that illustrate the literal and real meanings of idiomatic phrases. Activities gradually build up the learners' understanding and confidence in the social skills of communication.

I WANT IT: Activity 6

commenting on how good their language was and disrupting the flow of communication, Mr. Shapiro complimented Nikki and Rona by letting them know how useful the information was. When a student's purposes and intents are fulfilled because of the language the student uses, those language behaviors are naturally reinforced. The student learns that appropriate language use is a powerful tool in controlling the environment (Paul & Norbury, 2007; Owens, 2007).

Systematically Plan and Instruct for Generalization As is the case in teaching other skills, language instruction must incorporate into the instructional sequence a variety of contexts, settings, and people with which students interact if they are to generalize the language skills (Beck et al., 2002).

Since language is part of all of our instruction, generalizing principles of language development across settings is possible. Ms. McDonald, a special education resource teacher; Mrs. Kim, the second-grade teacher; and Ms. Cortez, the speech/language pathologist, are working with Julie, a second-grade child with learning disabilities, on sequencing events and using sequence markers (e.g., first, second, next, last). When Julie goes to language and resource classes, Mrs. Kim sends a note that lists, in order, the activities Julie has participated in so far during the day. When Julie returns from language and resource class, Ms. Cortez sends back a note that lists her language activities. Each teacher then converses with Julie about what she did in the other teachers' classes, emphasizing sequence and sequence markers. Other activities also build generalization for Julie. Whenever the teachers or Julie's mother reads Julie a story, Julie retells the story and is asked sequence questions. During the weekly cooking activity, Julie and the other students tell the steps in making the food for the day, and these steps are written on large chart paper with numbers listed beside them. Julie also arranges picture sequence cards and

is then asked to describe them. With these activities, Julie receives numerous opportunities to generalize this language skill to a variety of contexts, persons, and settings.

Teaching Content

We teach language content throughout the day. For example, one of the major goals in teaching a new unit in social studies and science is for the students to understand and use the new vocabulary. What are some of the basic vocabulary categories that we may want to teach? Table 6-6 lists some general categories of words and word relationships. Let us look at some strategies for teaching content or vocabulary, whether it be the more

Table 6-6 Categories of Words and Word Relationships

Categories	School-Related Examples
Existence/nouns	science, math, reading, vowels, consonants, sentences, paragraphs
Actions/verbs	verbs often used in instruction—draw, write, circle, underline, discuss, compare, critique, defend
Attributes/adjectives	words that describe such attributes as size, shape, texture, weight, position (high/low, first/last), color, age, speed, affect, attractiveness
Attributes/adverbs	words that describe actions, such as easily, hurriedly, busily, willingly
Prepositions	locative (in, on, under, beside, in front of, ahead of, behind), directional (off, out of, away from, toward, around, through), temporal (before, after, between), for, from, at, of, to, with, without

Personal pronouns	*Subjective*	*Objective*	*Possessive*
	I	me	my, mine
	you	you	your
	she, he, it	her, him, it	her, his, its
	we	us	our
	they	them	their

Categories	School-Related Examples
Demonstrative pronouns	this, that, these, those
Indefinite and negative pronouns	a/an, someone, somebody, something, somewhere, anyone, anybody, anything, anywhere, no one, nobody, nothing, nowhere, the
Antonyms	full/empty, boiling/freezing, easy/hard, soft/hard
Synonyms	pants/slacks/trousers/britches
	laugh/giggle/chuckle
	happy/glad/pleased/elated/tickled pink
Homonyms	sail/sale, bear/bare
Multiple-meaning words	run fast, run in your stockings, go for a run, in the long run
Comparative relationships	taller than, shorter than
Spatial relationships	*see* Prepositions
Temporal-sequential relationships	words connoting measurement, time (days of the week, minutes, seasons), temporal prepositions (first, last, next, then)
Conditional relationships	if . . . then
Causal relationships	because, therefore, since
Conjunctive relationships	and
Disjunctive relationships	either . . . or
Contrastive relationships	but, although
Enabling relationships	in order that, so that
Figurative language	*Idioms:* catch a plane; hit the road
	Metaphors: her eagle eye
	Similes: her eyes twinkled like stars; busy as a beaver
	Proverbs: The early bird catches the worm.

general vocabulary listed in Table 6-6 or the specific vocabulary found in content area instruction.

Emphasize Critical Features When teaching new concepts, emphasize the features that are important to the meaning. For example, in teaching the concepts of *mountains* and *hills*, the distinguishing or critical features to emphasize are *size* and *height*. In comparison, the *texture of the land* is not important, since it is not a feature that usually helps us to distinguish between hills and mountains. Comparing and contrasting two concepts using a Venn diagram can help students to see the important characteristics (see Figure 6-4). Students remember vocabulary better if they think about how they can use it. Figure 6-5 presents one way in which students can think about a concept in multiple ways.

▶ **Figure 6-4** Venn Diagram for Comparing Concepts

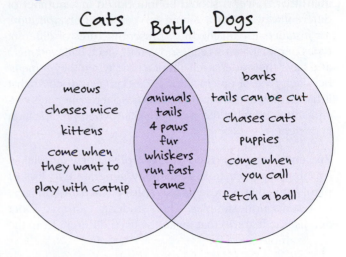

Cats   Both   Dogs

Cats: meows / chases mice / kittens / come when they want to / play with catnip

Both: animals / tails / 4 paws / fur / whiskers / run fast / tame

Dogs: barks / tails can be cut / chases cats / puppies / come when you call / fetch a ball

▶ **Figure 6-5** Thinking About a Concept in Multiple Ways

Definition	Sentence	Illustration
An oven or furnace for hardening or drying something	a kiln is for rapid drying of lumber.	
Synonym	**Word**	**Antonym**
Microwave	Kiln	Freezer
Create an original sentence using the vocabulary word.	Create an analogy using the vocabulary word.	Where might you hear this word used?
I used a kiln to dry my lumber for a house.	Kiln is to microwave as icebox is to freezer.	You might find this in a glass blower's shop.

Vary Concept Introductions Teachers need to keep in mind that concepts should be introduced in a number of different ways. When teaching the concept of *precipitation,* for instance, the teacher may present pictures of different types of precipitation (e.g., snow, rain, sleet, hail, and mist) and have the students tell about a time when they remember each type of precipitation. The class can discuss what is happening to the water in the atmosphere when it is precipitating and what the weather is like when precipitation is present.

Present Examples and Nonexamples For example, in learning about cacti, students may generate two lists of plants: one that represents examples of cacti and one that represents nonexamples. Then students can talk about and list the features that make the cacti different from the nonexamples.

Categorize New Concepts This is a valuable strategy to ensure students understand how the concepts relate to other concepts. If the concept of *melancholy* is being taught, the students should learn that this is an example of a feeling or emotion. Other feelings are gladness, relief, and hurt. Characteristics of people who are melancholy are "not happy," "quiet," "not talkative," and "somber." These ideas can be depicted in a visual diagram, such as a semantic map, which shows how the different concepts relate to one another (see Figure 6-6).

Present New Vocabulary Simply To help students understand the new material they are learning, present new vocabulary in simple sentences or phrases. It is harder to learn a new concept or idea if the teacher is using difficult language to explain what it means. The rule of thumb is to use simple sentences or phrases to introduce new concepts (i.e., four- to seven-word sentences and two- to four-word phrases).

Reinforce with Games Use games and other activities to reinforce newly introduced concepts. For example, Twenty Questions is a good game to use to get students to think about the characteristics of a concept and the categories in which the concept falls.

Name That Category is a game that can be played similarly to Name That Tune, except that the object of the game is to earn points by naming the category when examples of a category are given. The sooner the category is named, the more points the player receives.

Oral or written *cloze* passages, like that shown in Figure 6-7, can be used to highlight a particular set of concepts being taught.

Additional ideas for teaching new concepts and the relationships among those concepts, particularly as they relate to teaching content area subjects (i.e., science, social studies, vocational areas), are discussed in Chapter 10.

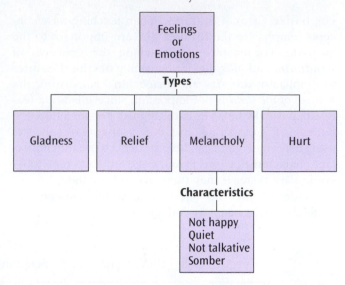

► **Figure 6-6** Semantic Map of the Concept of *Melancholy*

Idioms, metaphors, similes, and proverbs can be used when playing Charades, with the students acting out the literal meanings of the phrases (e.g., *catch a plane, blow your stack*).

A number of language materials and programs are available for teaching concepts to school-age students. The Instructional Activities feature below provides selected programs and materials.

Increase Word-Finding Ability Another difficulty that some students with learning disabilities encounter involves word finding. These students know words but are unable to recall them automatically. Most frequently, these words are nouns. Several techniques can be used to assist students in increasing their ability to recall words, thereby increasing the accuracy and fluency of their expressive language (Owens, 2010; Paul & Norbury, 2007).

Teach Students to Classify and Categorize Words Teaching students to classify and categorize words should improve their long-term memory and thus help them to recall and retrieve specific words. When learning new concepts, students should be encouraged to name the category and then rapidly name the vocabulary in the category. Pictures, written words, and graphic representations such as a semantic map (see Figure 6-6) may help with this activity. When students are having difficulty retrieving a word, provide information about the word to help them retrieve it. For example, if a student is having trouble thinking of the word *eraser,* say to them "it has 3 syllables and begins with this sound, 'e'."

Teach Students to Use Visual Imagery Getting students to "see" in their minds the objects they are trying to retrieve can sometimes help them think of words. To help

Figure 6-7 Sample Cloze Emphasizing Prepositions

Cloze passages can be used either as an oral or written activity, or combined with the oral activity reinforcing the written.

More than anything else, Robert wanted _____ climb _____ the top _____ the mountain. Every day _____ his way home _____ school he looked up _____ the mountain. It was so high that the few trees _____ the top looked very small. He had heard that it would take a day _____ climb _____ the summit, and a day to get back _____ the mountain. One evening when he was looking _____ his window, he saw a campfire burning _____ the top of the mountain. He knew _____ only he practiced hiking, he could make it.

Well, this spring he would start practicing. He and his friend Jim could join the Young Hikers' Club and _____ early summer they would be ready _____ the climb. Robert could hardly wait _____ spring _____ come.

Figure 6-8 Associative Tasks for Improving Word Retrieval and Developing Vocabulary

Free Association Tasks
Name as many things as you can in a specified amount of time (usually one to three minutes).

Controlled Association Tasks
Name as many foods, animals, things you take hiking, kinds of fish, etc., as you can think of in a specified amount of time (usually one to three minutes).

Antonym Association Tasks
Listen to each word and tell me the word that means the exact opposite.

    girl
    man
    hot
    inside
    happy

Synonym Association Tasks
Listen to each word and tell me the word that means about the same thing.

    small
    giggle
    mad
    rapid

Categorization Tasks
Listen to these words and tell me what they are.

    dog, cat, fish, alligator
    bread, fruit, vegetables, chicken
    robin, sparrow, eagle

Temporal Relationship Tasks
Listen to each word and tell me what you think of.

    winter   (ice skating, skiing, sledding)
    evening   (watching TV, supper, homework)
    Christmas   (gifts, Santa Claus, carols)

Agent–Action Relationship Tasks
Listen to the names of these animals and objects. Each of them goes with a special action. Tell me what special thing each one of these does.

    plane   (flies)
    lion   (roars)
    doorbell   (rings)

Action–Object Relationship Tasks
Listen to these actions. Each one goes with special objects. Tell me what the objects are.

    fly   (planes, helicopters, kites)
    run   (animals, insects)
    button   (shirts, jackets)

Source: E. H. Wiig & E. Semel, *Language Assessment & Intervention for the Learning Disabled*, 2nd ed. (Columbus, OH: C. E. Merrill, 1984). Reprinted with permission of the senior author, Elizabeth H. Wiig, Ph.D., Knowledge Research Institute, Inc.

students develop these mental images, encourage them to picture new words in their minds. For example, when students are trying to learn the parts of a flower, have them picture a flower in their minds, with the labels for the parts written on the different parts. Have them talk about the kind of flower they pictured, discussing the parts as they describe the flower.

Teach Students to Use Word Association Clues to Help in Retrieving Words Activities in which students learn and practice word associations (e.g., peanut butter and _____;

red, white, and _____) can facilitate word retrieval. These activities may be as broad as asking students to name as many things as they can think of in a given amount of time. But generally, the teacher will want to focus the associations. Figure 6-8 presents a variety of association tasks that are more focused. In using these focused activities, keep the pace rapid and the total time for the activity short (one to three minutes). If students have established strong word associations, then when they cannot think of the correct word, providing an associative clue can assist them in retrieving the correct word.

Teach Students to Use Synonyms and Antonyms When students cannot recall the precise word they want, an alternative word can be used. Students may be taught to state that the desired word "is the opposite of _____" or "is almost like _____." For example, when struggling to find the word *joyful,* a student can be encouraged to say "It's when you're really happy" or "It's the opposite of feeling sad."

Use Sound, Semantic, or Multiple-Choice Cues to Assist Students in Recalling Words Providing students with cues can assist them in retrieving words. For example, teachers might cue, "It starts with a /k/" (sound cue), "It's not a peach, it's a _____" (semantic cue), or "It's either a banana, a cat, or a bowl" (multiple-choice cue).

Increase Elaboration in Language

Some students with learning disabilities use language that is not very elaborate. When asked to retell stories or events or to give descriptions, these students provide only the most basic information. Teachers can:

1. *Model elaboration by introducing familiar objects or pictured objects and by demonstrating verbal descriptions of their attributes and functions.* In this step, the teacher describes the object, noting its attributes and functions. In some instances, the teacher may want to contrast it to similar or related objects—for example, describing a cactus and comparing it to a rosebush.

2. *Have students elaborate in response to direct questions.* After modeling, the teacher asks students direct questions about the object that require them to focus on its attributes and functions. For example, the teacher may ask, "What kind of stem does a cactus have? Why does it have such a chunky stem?"

3. *Have students spontaneously describe the object or pictured object.* The teacher asks students to describe the object, using such cues as "Tell me about the cactus. What else can you tell me about it? Are there any other things about it that are important? In what way is a cactus like a rosebush?"

Teaching Form

Form refers to the structure of language. Tables 6-3 and 6-4 present syntactical and morphological forms that are relevant in teaching school-age students with language and learning problems. This section presents some procedures and activities for teaching these language forms.

Utilize Developmental Sequences

An effective approach to instruction is to teach new sentence structures or prefixes, suffixes, and inflectional endings according to developmental sequences or the order of difficulty. Tables 6-3 and 6-5, as well as language programs and activities designed to teach form (see Instructional Activities later in this chapter), can assist teachers in deciding the order in which to teach the various sentence and morphological forms.

Use Familiar Examples

When teaching a new structure or form, use familiar, concrete examples and vocabulary. For example, Mrs. Ogbu wants to have her students work on passive sentences. She begins by having her students act out simple events (e.g., Julio tagged Maria during a relay race). Then she asks the students to tell her a sentence about the event. She writes it on the board ("Julio tagged Maria"). Next she shows the students how she can say what had happened in a different way ("Maria was tagged by Julio"). Then the students act out other events and give sentences in the passive voice. In this way, Mrs. Ogbu starts with concrete experiences and uses familiar, simple vocabulary to teach the new sentence structure.

Use Simple Sentences

Simplify your language when teaching a new sentence or morphological form. When Mrs. Ogbu initially taught her students passive voice sentences, she used very simple sentences. She could have said, "Julio chased Maria while playing tag," but this sentence would have been much more difficult for the students to put in the passive voice.

Encourage Extension

Once the students have learned the new form, have them extend it to situations that need more elaborated and complex sentences and less familiar vocabulary. For example, when teaching the morphological ending -er, move from familiar vocabulary such as *teacher, reader,* and *writer* to less familiar vocabulary such as *painter, plumber, framer,* and *landscaper* in the context of house construction and to the exceptions in this area, such as *mason* and *electrician.*

Use Concrete Objects

To make lessons more concrete for learners, use actual objects and events or pictures of them when initially teaching a new structure or form, and pair oral communication with written. Mrs. Ogbu uses the event of playing tag to teach passive voice sentences. She also pairs the oral sentences with the written sentences by writing them on the board. Word and sentence boundaries are clarified by written language, and pictures or actual experiences can assist the students in focusing on the target language pattern. Figure 6-9 demonstrates how pictures and written words can demonstrate possessives.

Vary Introductions

New sentence or word forms should be introduced in a variety of ways. For example, when teaching comparative and superlative forms of adjectives

Figure 6-9 Visual Representation Depicting Possessive Marker

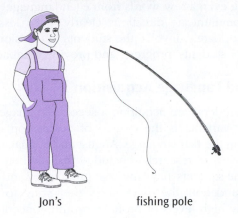

Jon's   fishing pole

Table 6-7 Comparison Chart

Item	Long	Longer	Longest
red pencils	Susan	Kim	Danny
blue pencils	Susan	Cori	Ken
yellow pencils	Kim	Danny	Ken
white shoelaces	Kim	Danny	Ken
black shoelaces	Cori	Susan	Kim
brown hair	Cori	Kim	Susan
blond hair	Danny	Ken	Stefan

during a measuring activity, Ms. Kamulu has the students determine who has the "long/longer/longest" pencils, pens, scissors, shoelaces, hair, and so on. Numerous comparisons can be made by using items found in a classroom, and the various comparisons may be depicted on a chart such as the one shown in Table 6-7. Students can then use the examples and the chart to discuss the comparisons and to practice the targeted language skills.

Teaching Use

According to the American Speech-Language-Hearing Association (ASHA, http://www.asha.org/public/speech/development/pragmatics.htm; retrieved April 14, 2010), pragmatics involves three major communication skills:

1. Using language for different *purposes*
   - Greetings (e.g., hello)
   - Informing (e.g., I am going to school now)
   - Demanding (e.g., I won't go to school)
   - Promising (e.g., I am going to school in 10 minutes)
   - Requesting (e.g., Would you take me to school?)
2. Using language *responsively* to *adjust* to the needs of the listener or situation
   - Using different language with friends and parents
   - Providing appropriate background information so listeners can understand what you are saying
3. *Using the rules* for conversations and storytelling that are appropriate for the context and culture
   - Being an effective conversational partner by taking turns, listening, asking questions
   - Interpreting the expressions and facial signals of the other person
   - Providing appropriate cues verbally and nonverbally so your communication is understandable

What do students do who have difficulties with pragmatics and what can you do to assist them? Students who have pragmatic problems are likely to say inappropriate or unrelated things. For example, another student may be telling a story about a movie they saw and the student with pragmatic problems may interrupt with an unrelated comment. Sometimes students with pragmatic difficulties do not pick up on social cues and are perceived as inappropriate, making these students less popular and perhaps isolated by peers.

What are some of the things you can do as a teacher to improve language development of students with difficulties with pragmatics?

Use Role Play Consider role playing to simulate different situations in which the targeted pragmatic skills are required. Ms. Peterson uses role playing in her class so that students will have some idea what it will feel like when they are in a situation that requires them to communicate in a certain way or for a specific purpose. Last week the students had to ask each other for directions to their houses during pretend telephone conversations. This week students are practicing how to ask questions during a simulated science lesson.

Use Pictures or Simulations Some students have difficulty discriminating different nonverbal and verbal communication that accompanies various feelings. By using pantomime or pictures, students can determine what feelings are being expressed and can discuss the cues that helped them determine the feelings. Encourage students to attend to other students' feelings by using such statements as "You look like you're feeling . . ." or "I bet you feel really . . ." or "I can't tell how you're feeling."

Use Conversations Conversations work well as a framework for teaching functional language. Conversations about topics that are familiar to the students or about common experiences can serve as ideal situations for building students' pragmatic skills. Teachers can serve as facilitators by assisting students in using the following conversational skills (http://www.asha.org/public/speech/development/PragmaticLanguageTips.htm; retrieved from ASHA Web site, April, 14, 2010):

Desired Language Function	Suggested Question or Comment
Comment	"What did you do?" "Tell me about . . ."
Request	"Tell your friend . . ." "What do you want?"
Question	"Ask me"

Planning Instruction for Students Who Are Culturally and Linguistically Diverse

What are the strategies and considerations on which teachers should focus when teaching culturally and linguistically diverse learners? As a teacher, you will have students from many different cultures and students who are in the process of acquiring English as a second language or second dialect. You may or may not be familiar with the culture and language of these students. Still, it will be important for these students to feel comfortable in your class.

Diversity

Francisco is a good example of such a student. He emigrated from Costa Rica to Nebraska at the age of 4 with his parents and siblings. Francisco and his family now live in a Spanish-speaking community within Omaha. Francisco entered school at age 5 with Spanish as his first language and only limited knowledge of English. This situation is common for children who emigrate from countries in Central and South America, Asia and the Pacific Islands, and Eastern Europe. Teachers' knowledge of second-language acquisition and general instructional guidelines can help to make school a success for students like Francisco by helping them view their home language and culture as assets while also learning English (Goldenberg, 2008). Effective teachers do the following:

- Have high expectations of their students and believe that all students are capable of academic success
- See themselves as members of the community and see teaching as a way to give back to the community
- Believe in diversity, meeting individual student needs, and interacting with other teachers to support shared decision making
- Display a sense of confidence in their ability to be successful with students who are culturally and linguistically diverse

- Honor the languages of the students in their class by recognizing these languages as valuable and acquiring even a few words from each language
- Communicate directions clearly, pace lessons appropriately, involve the students in decisions, monitor students' progress, and provide feedback

Second Language Acquisition

When students are acquiring a second language, an important variable is the degree of acquisition or proficiency in the first language. August and Shanahan (2008) in a review of research concluded that the better developed the students' first language proficiency and conceptual foundation, the more likely they were to develop similarly high levels of proficiency and conceptual ability in the second language.

As can be seen in Figure 6-10, both languages have separate surface features, represented by two different icebergs. However, less visible below the surface is the underlying proficiency that is common to both languages. For example, Table 6-8 compares the phonological, morphological, and syntactical features in Spanish and English, and Table 6-9 highlights some of the grammatical contrasts in African American Vernacular English and Standard American English (SAE). Regardless of the language a person is using, the thoughts that accompany the talking, reading, writing, and listening come from the same language core.

Teachers may assume that students who can converse easily in their second language are ready to learn new concepts, strategies, and skills in that language, but this is not necessarily the case. For example, when Jong Hoon entered Ms. Dembrow's third-grade class, she immediately noticed that he conversed easily with the other

▶ **Figure 6-10** Iceberg Analogy of Language Proficiency

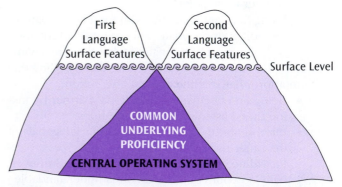

Source: Adapted from J. Cummins, *Bilingualism and Minority Language Children* (Toronto: Ontario Institute for Studies in Education, 1980). Reprinted with permission of University of Toronto Press. For more information, see Jim Cummins' Second Language Learning and Literacy Development Web (http://www.iteachilearn.com/cummins).

Table 6-8 Comparison of Spanish and English Languages

Phonological	Morphological	Syntactical
Fewer vowel sounds: no short *a* (hat), short *i* (fish), short *u* (up), short double *o* (took), or schwa (sofa) *Fewer consonant sounds:* no /j/ (jump), /v/ (vase), /z/ (zipper), /sh/ (shoe), /ŋ/ (sing), /hw/ (when), /zh/ (beige) Some possible confusions: /b/ pronounced /p/: *cab* becomes *cap* /j/ pronounced /y/: *jet* becomes *yet* /ŋ/ pronounced as /n/: *thing* becomes *thin* /v/ pronounced as /b/: *vote* becomes *boat* /y/ pronounced as /j/: *yes* becomes *jes* /sk/, /sp/, /st/ pronounced as /esk/, /esp/, /est/: *speak* becomes *espeak* /a/ pronounced as /e/: *bat* becomes *bet* /i/ pronounced as /ē/: *hit* becomes *heat* /ē/ pronounced as /i/: *heal* becomes *hill* /u/ pronounced as /o/: *hut* becomes *hot* /ŏŏ/ pronounced as /o͞o/: *look* becomes *Luke*	*de* (of) used to show possession: *Joe's pen* becomes *the pen of Joe* *más* (more) used to show comparison: *faster* becomes *more fast*	use of *no* for *not:* He no do his homework. no auxiliary verbs: She no play soccer. adjectives after nouns: the car blue agreement of adjectives: the elephants bigs no inversion of question: Anna is here? articles with professional titles: I went to the Dr. Rodriguez.

Source: Adapted from C. A. O'Brien, *Teaching the Language-Different Child to Read* (Columbus, OH: C. E. Merrill, 1973).

Table 6-9 Grammatical Contrasts Between African American English and Standard American English

African American English Grammatical Structure	SAE Grammatical Structure
Possessive -'s	

Nonobligatory word where word position expresses possession
  Get *mother* coat.
  It be mother's.
	Obligatory regardless of position
	  Get *mother's* coat
	  It's mother's.

Plural -s	

Nonobligatory with numerical quantifier
  He got ten *dollar.*
  Look at the cat.
	Obligatory regardless of numerical quantifier
	  He has ten *dollars.*
	  Look at the cats.

Regular past -ed	

Nonobligatory; reduced as consonant cluster
  Yesterday, I *walk* to school.
	Obligatory
	  Yesterday, I *walked* to school.

Irregular past	

Case by case, some verbs inflected, others not
  I *see* him last week.
	All irregular verbs inflected
	  I *saw* him last week.

Regular present tense third person singular -s	

Nonobligatory
  She *eat* too much.
	Obligatory
	  She *eats* too much.

Irregular present tense third person singular -s	

Nonobligatory
  He *do* my job.
	Obligatory
	  He *does* my job.

Indefinite an	

Use of indefinite a
  He ride in a airplane.
	Use of *an* before nouns beginning with a vowel
	  He rode in *an* airplane.

(continued)

Table 6-9 Continued

African American English Grammatical Structure	SAE Grammatical Structure
Pronouns	
Pronominal apposition: pronoun immediately follows noun	Pronoun used elsewhere in sentence or in other sentence; not in apposition
Momma *she* mad. She . . .	Momma is mad. *She* . . .
Future tense	
More frequent use of *be going to* (gonna)	More frequent use of *will*
I *be going to* dance tonight.	I *will* dance tonight.
I *gonna* dance tonight.	I *am going to* dance tonight.
Omit *will* preceding *be*	Obligatory use of *will*
I *be* home late*r*.	I *will* (I'll) *be* home later.
Negation	
Triple negative	Absence of triple negative
Nobody don't never like me.	*No* one ever likes me.
Use of *ain't*.	*Ain't* is unacceptable form
I *ain't* going.	*I'm not* going.
Modals	
Double modals for such forms as *might, could,* and *should*	Single modal use
I *might could* go.	I *might be able to* go.
Questions	
Same form for direct and indirect	Different forms for direct and indirect
What *it is?*	What *is it?*
Do you know what *it is?*	*Do you* know what *it is?*
Relative pronouns	
Nonobligatory in most cases	Nonobligatory with *that* only
He the one stole it.	He's the one *who* stole it.
It the one you like.	It's the one (that) you like.
Conditional if	
Use of *do* for conditional *if*	Use of *if*
I ask *did* she go.	I asked *if* she went.
Perfect construction	
Been used for action in the distant past	*Been* not used
He *been* gone.	He left a long time ago.
Copula	
Nonobligatory when contractible	Obligatory in contractible and noncontractible forms
He sick.	He's sick.
Habitual or *general state*	
Marked with uninflected *be*	Nonuse of *be;* verb inflected
She *be* workin'.	She's *working* now.

Source: Robert E. Owens, Jr., *Language Disorders: A Functional Approach to Assessment and Intervention* (Boston: Allyn & Bacon, 2010). Copyright © 2010 by Pearson Education. Reprinted by permission of the publisher. Data drawn from Baratz (1968); Fasold & Wolfram (1970); R. Williams & Wolfram (1977).

students in the class and with her. Jong Hoon had emigrated from Korea 2 years earlier and had begun learning English through the school's ESL (English as a Second Language) program. His parents are also studying English in a night course and feel that learning English is important for their economic and personal success in America. Still, Korean is the language that the family speaks primarily in the home. Jong Hoon's language acquisition experiences illustrate the four components described by Ovander and Collier (1998): language development, academic development, cognitive development, and sociocultural processes.

For example, as Ms. Dembrow became familiar with Jong Hoon, she realized that while his conversational skills made him a comfortable member of the classroom community (*language development*), he was not proficient in academic tasks such as reading and writing in English (*academic development*). She also found that in social studies and science, it was important for her to provide lots of context for teaching new concepts (*cognitive development*). When Ms. Dembrow referred Jong Hoon for possible special education services because of his difficulty with academics, she was not aware of typical patterns of second-language acquisition difficulties. But in problem-solving discussions with the bilingual speech/language pathologist and ESL teacher, she learned that different timelines for developing academic knowledge and skills are to be expected and should not be confused with reading disabilities (*sociocultural processes*).

Strategies for Teaching Culturally and Linguistically Diverse Learners

For Jong Hoon and the other students who were in the process of acquiring English as a second language, providing the link to their cultures helped to give them a context in which they could build both their language and cognitive skills.

Other teaching strategies and accommodations include the following:

- Simplify your language but continue to use more complex language as the students' understanding progresses.
- Repeat important phrases and emphasize key vocabulary.
- Demonstrate concepts; use manipulatives.
- Adapt the materials, don't water down the content.
- Include both language development and content vocabulary development.
- Brainstorm with the whole group.

- Provide direct experiences (e.g., read sources, watch videos).
- Increase wait time.
- Respond to the *message,* not to the correctness of the pronunciation or grammar.
- Don't force reluctant students to speak.
- Pair or group native speakers together.
- Use cooperative learning and peer-group strategies.
- Learn as much as you can about your students' languages and cultures.
- Build on the students' prior knowledge.
- Bring the students' home languages and cultures into the classroom and curriculum.
- Use photos, pictures, and videos to illustrate key ideas and concepts.
- Provide advanced organizers of the "big ideas" of what you are teaching—review these ideas.
- Provide language objectives for every lesson.
- Provide students with opportunities to turn and talk with a partner to express their ideas with one other student.
- Allow students to provide key word answers rather than complete sentences.
- Teach key vocabulary and concepts.
- Monitor students' progress to ensure success.

(Echevarria, Vogt, & Short, 2009; Francis et al., 2007; Gersten et al., 2007)

At some time, most teachers will work with students who are culturally and linguistically diverse. Making accommodations and using strategies that promote second language acquisition while fostering an understanding of the students' first languages and cultures will assist the students in becoming successful learners.

Working with Families to Extend Language Concepts

How can teachers work with families to develop students' language skills? Children are more likely to learn new vocabulary and language structures when they are active participants in their learning and can practice new concepts in different contexts (home and school). Keep all language activities short and fun so that parents/guardians do not view communication as homework. In planning language activities, it is also important to be aware of cultural and linguistic differences in the home. If a family does not speak English, encourage the student to complete these activities in the language used at home. The following are some suggestions for using newly learned language concepts in a variety of environments:

- Send home a short description or picture of a recent classroom activity or field trip. Encourage parents/guardians to ask open-ended rather than closed questions about the activity. For example, a parent might say, "I understand that you made a papier-mâché vase today. How did you do that?"

- Inform parents/guardians of new vocabulary that children are learning. Have children write a note to their families about what they learned. A child might say, "I learned the word *notorious* today."
- Have children bring new words to class that they have heard at home. Create a word "treasure chest" and encourage the children to be vocabulary "hunters."
- Inform parents of new social language concepts that their children have practiced in class. Have children describe the concept to their families. For instance, a child might say, "I learned what to say if someone is bullying me." Encourage families to practice similar role plays with the child at home.
- When possible, have students ask their parents questions about topics that they are learning in class. For example, if the class is discussing the food pyramid, have the children ask their families about favorite foods, and set aside a time for them to report to the class on their findings.
- To practice figurative language, have children tell jokes or word puns to their families at home.
- To practice asking questions and listening skills, have students ask their families about hypothetical situations discussed in class. Themes may come from journal topics such as "What would you do if you had a million dollars?"
- Encourage families to discuss books that they read with their children. Send home some tips to encourage discussion around a book (e.g., talk about the pictures, relate the story to the child's own experiences).

Response to Intervention: Working with the Speech/Language Teacher

How can special education teachers work with language specialists to implement RTI? The role of the school-based speech/language teacher has changed significantly in the past decades because of legislative changes in special education. Traditionally, the speech/language teacher has used a clinical/medical model of assessment and intervention, treating students individually or in small groups in a separate resource room. However, educational reforms have increased participation of students with disabilities in the general education classroom. In particular, RTI has provided opportunities for increasing interaction among classroom teachers, special education teachers, and speech/language personnel.

RTI models have provided many speech/language teachers opportunities to work closely with other school professionals and parents in a team model, using a combination of direct and indirect service methods to promote language development and assist students with communication disorders. In addition to providing individual or group therapy, these teachers may also collaborate with classroom teachers to develop modifications and strategies for students within the classroom. The role of the speech/language teacher may vary owing to differences in caseload, state or district regulations, and staffing needs. ASHA (*http://www.asha.org/slp/schools/prof-consult/NewRolesSLP.htm*; downloaded April 9, 2010) recognizes that RTI provides interesting and valuable new roles and responsibilities for the speech/language educator and also new challenges. With respect to assessment, as districts move from more formal models of assessment to ongoing assessments, speech language therapists will need to shift their assessment procedures as well so that they think about assessment as it contributes to decision making about student progress. This will require that more instructionally relevant assessments are administered more frequently.

Assessment and Intervention

Speech/language therapists may also engage in expanded roles related to prevention and intervention. For example, they may assist in schoolwide screening to identify students with early literacy and oral language problems, may assist in developing and/or delivering appropriate prevention practices schoolwide, and may provide interventions to students with communication difficulties.

There are a variety of ways in which speech/language teachers may help students with language difficulties within the school setting. For students with literacy and language difficulties, they may

- collaborate with classroom teachers to implement developmentally appropriate language arts and literacy programs.
- assist in modifying and selecting language and instructional strategies that integrate oral and written communication skills.
- provide information and training to school personnel regarding the linguistic bases of reading and writing.
- provide information and support for parents of at-risk children regarding language and literacy activities in the home environment.

- collaborate with reading professionals and classroom teachers to augment the success of students with language and reading impairments.

For students with difficulties with social–emotional communication skills, they may

- provide information regarding the link between social–emotional problems and social communication skills (pragmatics).
- assist in training school staff to use effective verbal and nonverbal communication strategies in conflict resolution.
- demonstrate lessons to enhance pragmatic communication skills (problem solving, social communication).

Ehren, Montgomery, Rudebusch, and Whitmire (2006) provide suggestions to speech/language therapists about how they might expand their role to facilitate RTI in the schools. They indicate that with respect to program design, speech/language therapists can

- explain the role of language in curriculum and instruction.
- provide research-based knowledge on language screening and assessment.
- provide research-based knowledge on effective language interventions.
- assist in identifying screening measures.
- provide professional development on language.
- interpret the school-level progress in addressing intervention needs of students.
- participate in the development and implementation of progress monitoring.
- consult with teachers on issues related to RTI and intervention.
- help families understand the language basis of literacy and learning.

Involving speech/language therapists in the RTI model implemented schoolwide involves communication and collaboration, but the benefits for teachers, students, and parents are significant.

INSTRUCTIONAL ACTIVITIES

This section provides instructional activities related to oral language. Some of the activities teach new skills; others are best suited for practice and reinforcement of already acquired skills. For each activity, the objective, materials, and teaching procedures are described. When possible, use these activities to reinforce the oral language within the curriculum content (current vocabulary or class topic). See Figure 6-11 for a description of selected materials addressing critical components of language development.

▶ Partner Talk

Objective: To provide students with opportunities to produce and orally share ideas and thoughts about a topic (including responses to comprehension questions).

Grades: Primary

Materials: Two or three questions prepared beforehand by the teacher for discussion. These may be comprehension questions (literal and interpretive) or any type of questions for discussion.

Teaching Procedures: Have all students find a partner and sit knee to knee, facing each other. Tell the students you would like them to respond to the question you are going to ask. Ask the question, then allow 2 to 3 minutes for students to think of their individual responses. Instruct each member of the pair to take a turn responding to the question, and then to discuss their responses together. For example, if using story comprehension questions, students might discuss what each thinks will happen next in the story, what each thinks is the story problem, or what each might have done differently if he or she were the main character. After 3 to 5 minutes, ask students to return to the larger group, and invite them to share their responses.

Adaptations: This activity can be adapted for older students by having them write responses or new endings to stories together.

▶ Chef for a Day

Objective: To provide students with opportunities to provide a detailed explanation while using ordinal words (*first, second, next,* etc.).

Grades: Primary

Materials: 8″ × 11″ card stock, about five sheets per student

Teaching Procedures: Tell students that they will be explaining to their classmates how to make their favorite meal or snack. Students should draw pictures of the ingredients and steps in the process on separate sheets of card stock (ingredients on one sheet, each step in the process on a separate, additional sheet) and should number their sheets of paper to correspond with the order of steps in the process. Students then share their recipes with their classmates.

Younger students may only provide two or three steps in the process, whereas older students may have more than five steps. Monitor student progress, and suggest adding or combining steps on the sheets of paper as needed. Encourage the students to use specific vocabulary (e.g., *mix, stir, pour, combine,* and *spread*) rather than general vocabulary (e.g., *put*) in their explanations. The recipes should not be too simple (with too few steps to adequately create the snack) or too complicated (so many details that the process is not well understood).

► **Figure 6-11** Selected Materials for Teaching Language

Programs and Games for Global Language Development

HELP (2004) by Andrea M. Lazzari and Patricia M. Peters. East Moline, IL: LinguiSystems, Inc.

Activities include practice on linguistic concepts, paraphrasing activities, thinking and problem-solving tasks, and pragmatic skills as well as language in daily life. Exercises include describing objects and defining words, reading and listening, and applying language skills.

Language Lessons in the Classroom (2003) by Susan Diamond. Phoenix, AZ: ECL Publications.

This book contains over 140 reproducible language activities designed for use in the classroom or by parents at home and designed to stimulate language development and facilitate effective communication skills.

Each language lesson includes: language objectives, materials needed (if any), appropriate grade levels, activity procedure, and consultation ideas. Focuses primarily on students in grades K–5.

Peabody Language Development Kits (copyright 2009) by L. M. Dunn, J. O. Smith, K. B. Horton, and D. D. Smith. San Antonio, TX: Pearson.

This program consists of lessons and materials in a kit that includes lesson manuals, picture cards grouped by categories, puppets to demonstrate concepts, posters depicting scenes and stories, sound books of sound and song activities, and colored chips for manipulation activities such as counting, sequencing, and grouping.

Programs for Auditory Processing

Listen My Children, and You Shall Hear (3rd ed.; 2008) by Betty Lou Kratoville. Austin, TX: Pro-Ed.

This revision of classic stories addresses listening comprehension, vocabulary development, and auditory memory. The third edition improves on the previous edition by combining all of the activities into a single, comprehensive volume. Stories have been updated and a reproducible tracking form for tracking progress is provided at the end of the book.

50 Quick-Play Listening Games (2005) by Kelly Malone, Karen Stontz, and Paul F. Johnson. East Moline, IL: LinguiSystems, Inc.

This book contains ready-to-copy games that reflect classroom listening demands, including phonological awareness, identifying the main idea and details, and following directions. The games are easy to play and may be used individually or in small groups. Intended for grades K–5.

100% Listening 2-Book Set (2002) by LinguiSystems, Inc. East Moline, IL: LinguiSystems, Inc.

This two-book set targets classroom listening skills necessary at both the primary and intermediate levels. Skills are presented sequentially and mirror daily classroom situations. The books are also sold separately. Targets grades K–5.

Programs and Games for Vocabulary Development and Word Retrieval

Library of Vocabulary Photographs (2010). Austin, TX: Pro-Ed.

One of the essential tools for building vocabulary is to have a collection of pictures to use to demonstrate key words. The complete kit contains more than 600 photographs with the key words on the back. These photographs represent clothing items, community members, appliances, fruits and nuts, parts of the house and the body, tools, toys, recreation, sports, etc. Kits representing each of the areas, e.g., community members, can be purchased separately.

50 Quick-Play Vocabulary Games (2004) by Paul F. Johnson and Patti Halfman. East Moline, IL: LinguiSystems, Inc.

The games included in this resource target thematic vocabulary (such as animals, transportation, and space) and vocabulary skills (such as figurative language, context clues, and abbreviations). The path and card games will help engage your students target vocabulary needs. Intended for grades 1–6.

125 Vocabulary Builders (2000) by Linda Bowers, Rosemary Huisingh, Carolyn LoGiudice, Jane Orman, and Paul F. Johnson. East Moline, IL: LinguiSystems, Inc.

A book of paper-and-pencil tasks for students aged 10–15. These tasks are designed to provide practice with newly acquired vocabulary words.

Concept Builders (2008) by C. Weiner, J. Creighton, and T.S. Lyons. Pearson, Oxford, UK.

These materials are designed to help children explore 43 basic language concepts through active participation in fun activities and conversations. A concept board and pictures for each language concept (e.g., wet/dry) can be copied. Students respond to your questions, such as "Water is ___?" The child chooses which side of the board to place the pictures by asking questions for each picture, for example, "Is this object wet or dry?" Materials are designed to provide interactive dialogue and questioning in conversations with parents, teachers, and/or speech-language teachers.

10 Quick-Play Folder Games: Associations (2005) by Lauri Whiskeyman and Barb Truman. East Moline, IL: LinguiSystems, Inc.

One in a series of folder games (targeting skills such as categories, rhyming, and concepts), this kit contains five double-sided game boards that are ready to play. Targeted skills include describing functions, assigning categories, and reviewing words with multiple meanings. Also available in Spanish. Intended for grades PreK–4.

The Word Book (2010) by E.H.Wiig and E. Freedman. Knowledge Research Institute.

A book of activities designed for teachers or other personnel interested in promoting word and concept learning with youngsters.

Rocky's Mountain: A Word-Finding Game (1999) by Gina V. Williamson and Susan S. Shields. East Moline, IL: LinguiSystems, Inc.

A board game that assists children ages 4–9 with acquiring one of four word-finding strategies. The four strategies are visual imagery, word association, sound/letter cueing, and categorization.

10 Quick-Play Folder Games: Vocabulary (2007) by LinguiSystems. East Moline, IL: LinguiSystems, Inc.

The games in the set address many skills necessary for vocabulary acquisition. Stimulus items are presented in both Spanish and English. Intended for ages 9–13.

▶ **Figure 6-11** Continued

Programs and Games for Grammar

Connect-A-Card (2008). Austin, TX: Pro-Ed.

Students use cards to build oral sentences, including complex and compound sentences. Using two picture phrase cards and a conjunction card representing 15 of the most commonly used conjunctions including *and, but, although, because.* Designed for all ages; primarily used for ages 6–12.

Teaching Morphology Developmentally (Revised) (2008) by Kenneth G. Shipley and Carolyn J. Banis. Austin, TX: Pro-Ed.

This program is designed for students aged 2½ to 10. Activities for teaching bound morphemes include present progressive, plurals, possessives, past tenses, third-person singulars, and superlatives. Includes 552 stimulus cards, a manual, and a reproducible worksheet manual.

Grammar Scramble: A Grammar and Sentence-Building Game (1998) by Rick and Linda Bowers. East Moline, IL: LinguiSystems, Inc.

A board game with a crossword puzzle format in which students have to intersect sentences. Appropriate for students ages 8 to adulted, this program is useful for developing carryover skills for grammar.

100% Grammar (1997) by Mike and Carolyn LoGiudice. East Moline, IL: LinguiSystems, Inc.

A series of paper-and-pencil activities designed to teach essential grammar components for students aged 9–14. The program includes pretests and posttests for each concept, making it helpful for charting progress. Also available in a "LITE" edition with practice items that have fewer contextual demands than the items in the regular edition.

Scissors, Glue, and Grammar, Too! (1996) by Susan Boegler and Debbie Abruzzini. East Moline, IL: LinguiSystems, Inc.

Cut-and-paste activities for students aged 4–9. Engaging activities to reinforce regular and irregular verbs, comparatives and superlatives, possessive pronouns, "wh-" questions, and more.

Gram's Cracker: A Grammar Game (2000) by Julie Cole. East Moline, IL: LinguiSystems, Inc.

Students "help" the mouse get to his hole by practicing grammar concepts such as use of pronouns, possessives, past-tense verbs, comparatives, superlatives, copulas, present progressive verbs, and negatives. This game has four levels of difficulty (identification, multiple choice, sentence completion, and sentence formulation). It is designed for students aged 4–9.

Programs for Pragmatics

Exploring Pragmatic Language (2008) by M.B. Bernarding. Austin, TX: Pro-Ed.

Two game boards provide opportunities to develop and use pragmatic-language skills with thematic game activities. More than 50 activity-barrier games addressing inferences, guessing, storytelling, and question-and-answer. Designed for students aged 6–14.

Pragmatic Activities for Language Intervention (2008) by Rhea Paul. Austin, TX: Pro-Ed.

Lessons involve conversational language in a variety of activities including crafts, role playing, and puppetry. Lessons address developing early words, semantic relations, and word combinations with young children; teaching preschoolers syntax, vocabulary, and concepts needed for communication and school readiness; and assisting older children make the transition from oral language to literacy with metalinguistic activities and complex language forms and concepts.

Conversations: A Framework for Language Intervention (1996) by Barbara Hoskins. Eau Claire, WI: Thinking Publications.

Offers professionals a framework for facilitating conversational interaction with individuals aged 9 and up who are having difficulty with communication skills. This resource provides the facilitator with plans for helping groups of individuals work together to become more effective conversational partners. Conversations provide many specific activities and suggestions. Professionals may also use them to generate, adapt, and develop other productive ways of working with these varying age groups.

Who? What? When? . . . And More (1999) by Pro-Ed, Inc. Austin, TX: Pro-Ed, Inc.

This board game requires players to answer a mix of "wh-" questions. Intended for ages 6–12.

Adaptations: Have students work in pairs or groups to create the recipe. Have students write some or all of the words in their recipe (this is a good activity for practicing the command form of verbs). If more than one student chooses the same snack, have them compare their recipes to notice similarities and differences in the ways each makes the same snack. Try to make the food item following one of the student's directions.

▶ **Creature from Outer Space**

Objective: To provide students with opportunities for elaboration in response to "wh-" questions regarding concrete, everyday objects and actions (not in response to a story).

Grades: 2–5

Materials: Everyday classroom objects

Teaching Procedures: Tell the class that you are a space creature who has just landed on planet Earth. You are trying to gather information about life on Earth to take back to share with scientists on your planet. Then ask about anything in the room, and follow up student responses with additional questions that require further elaboration or definition. For example:

Teacher: "What is this?"
Student: "It's a pair of scissors."
Teacher: "What are scissors?"

Assessing and Teaching Oral Language   **181**

Student: "You use them to cut paper."
Teacher: "What is paper?"
Student: "It's something you write on."
Teacher: "What is writing?"
Student: "It's making words on paper."
Teacher: "Why do you make words on paper?"

At some point (before students become frustrated) you can tell them you understand and then move on to the next object (or continue the next day).

Adaptations: For younger children, use a puppet to represent the alien creature. This activity can be made more difficult by asking more *how* and *why* questions and by selecting things in the classroom that will require higher levels of thought and explanation (e.g., asking about a poem on the wall or about a science experiment). This is also a great activity to check understanding of new vocabulary.

▶ What Did You Say?

Objective: To provide students with opportunities to practice saying things in different ways for different purposes.

Grades: 1–5

Materials: None

Teaching Procedures: This activity helps students understand how the same thing can be said in very different ways (intonation and wording), depending on the context of the situation and the person being spoken to. Have students say the following words, phrases, and sentences using different intonations, given the contexts that follow each:

"Hello"
- To the principal
- To their best friend
- To a baby
- To a person they don't like
- When answering the phone

"Good-bye"
- To their best friend at the end of the day
- To their teacher
- To a friend who is moving away
- To their mom on the phone
- To someone they don't know on the phone

"How are you?"
- As if they were a teacher asking a student at the beginning of the day
- To a friend who is sick
- To a classmate who seems sad
- To someone they just met

Adaptations: Have students think of different words or expressions they could use instead of the words in quotations above. For example, a student may say "Hi!" or "Hey!" to his or her best friend instead of "Hello." Use simple puppets (e.g., pictures on popsicle sticks) to assist

the students in adopting different roles. For older students, have them practice more complex language tasks in different contexts (making requests, asking for advice, describing a past event).

▶ Which One Doesn't Belong?

Objective: To have students identify specific relationships among vocabulary words that they have learned.

Grades: 1–5

Materials: Weekly vocabulary words as a foundation for a list of four words, of which three of the four words are related according to a specific dimension, and one is not. (They do not necessarily need to be written for students.) You may need to use other, related words in the activity to provide relationships to your target vocabulary words. This will vary according to the idea or concept and the students' ability level.

Teaching Procedures: Tell students that you are going to play a game that will help them think about the main idea you are stressing, for example, colors, animal groups, or important events in state history. You will tell them four words or phrases, and they are to tell you which one of the four does not belong with the others and why. Tell the students the four items. Then have the students tell you which are related and why. Then have them tell you why the fourth is not related to the other three. For example, if one of the weekly vocabulary words is *valley*, the teacher may write *valley, mountain, river*, and *desert* on the board. Students explain why *valley, mountain*, and *desert* are similar and why *river* is different. You may also ask them to generate other words in the same category.

Adaptations: Have younger students choose from items that can be visualized, such as colors, animals, or objects. The difficulty of the task can be ameliorated by having the actual objects or pictures of the objects for the students to see or by having the students visualize the objects. Older students can choose more successfully from the idea and concept level, although visuals to trigger knowledge may be helpful.

▶ It's for Sale!

Objective: To have students use language to elaborate and persuade.

Grades: 3–6 or above (maybe grade 2 at a much simpler level)

Materials: Slips of paper with various products on each one, either written or as pictures from a magazine (e.g., camera, soccer ball, car, perfume or makeup, specific shoes, etc.)

Teaching Procedures: This can be done in small or large group format on one day or with a few students a day across many days. Students should be familiar with skills used in persuasion before undertaking this activity.

Ask students to draw a slip of paper or item from a jar or hat. Allow them a short but sufficient amount of time to gather their initial thoughts about the item, then give each student 5 minutes to try to "sell" their product to the class or small group. The goal is for students to convince their classmates that they really need or want this product.

After the student is finished, allow classmates 5 minutes to ask him or her questions about the product; the "salesperson" will have to come up with answers to support his or her case and/or further descriptions of the product (these, of course, may be invented).

Adaptations: Students can be given extra points for including recent idioms or vocabulary in their presentation. After students ask questions of the "salesperson," have them raise their hands to show whether they would want to buy the product. Whoever "sells" the most wins. Students can also work in groups rather than individually to present the product. Have older students try to sell an idea rather than a product. For example, if you have been studying the food pyramid and nutrition, you could write on a piece of paper: "It's important to eat vegetables." The student who draws this paper has to give a persuasive argument to eat vegetables.

▶ Scavenger Hunt

Objective: To provide students with opportunities to consider and state relationships between two objects.

Grades: K–2 (see the "Adaptations" section for similar activity for students in grades 3–5)

Materials: Different items from around the classroom or ones typically found in a house (e.g., envelope, ruler, paintbrush, book, spatula, sponge, cookie cutter)

Teaching Procedure: Prepare a list of pairs of seemingly unrelated items in advance (e.g., book and paintbrush). Tell each student the pair of items they are to find (or have pictures of the items for younger students; for older students, write the names of the objects). Direct students to look for the items. When they find them, have students talk about the two objects—how they are alike, how they are different, how they are used, and how they might go together. In the example of book and paintbrush, a child might be able to relate the two objects by saying that the illustrator used a paintbrush to make the pictures in the book. For an example such as pencil and paintbrush, they are alike because both are used to write or draw, but they are different because a paintbrush also needs paint in order to write or draw. For kindergarten students, the comparisons will need to be simpler and more concrete than for older students.

Adaptations: Adapt this game for students in grades 3–5 by having them compare two nouns (or any other types of words or parts of grammar that are being studied). Prepare 30–40 word cards with nouns on them (this is great for reviewing and practicing new vocabulary). Divide the class into two groups. Give the first two students in each group a word card each. Direct the two students from each group to work together to create a sentence comparing the two nouns; the first pair to create a sentence wins a point for their team. Continue until one of the teams reaches a predetermined goal and wins the game.

▶ Daydream Chair

Objective: To provide students with opportunities to generate ideas about and elaborate on concepts or future story events.

Grades: 1–4

Materials: A special chair in the classroom (e.g., a rocking chair or a director's chair)

Teaching Procedures: Ask a few students each day to take turns sitting in the "Daydream Chair," describing what each would do if he or she were a certain person or object (or, for older students, in a certain situation).

Adaptations: For younger students, ask them what they would do if they were a famous person, a tree, a book, a paintbrush, or a similar object. Vary the object or person by student so that each is describing something different. This can also be done in relation to occupations, by having students discuss what people in different occupations do as part of their jobs. To assist the students in portraying their character, have them hold a picture of the person or object in front of them as they are speaking in the first person (e.g., "I am an astronaut . . ."). Older students can be asked similar questions about what they would do, would have done, or might do in the future if they were a particular character from a story. Vary characters by student.

▶ Find the Way

Objective: To provide students with practice in giving and interpreting directions.

Grades: All grades

Materials: (1) Maps of different areas. For example, use a map of the school for younger students, and use a map of the local area, the state, or the area you are studying in social studies for older students. The map should be labeled. (2) Put the names of places on the map and on small cards so that the cards can be drawn during the game.

Teaching Procedures: One student is designated as "It." This student is given a map and draws a card that gives the name of the place he or she is to find. The student draws the route on his or her map. The other students are given the same map, but they do not know the destination or the route. Without showing the map to the other students, the student who is "It" must describe, by using words only, how to get to the destination. The other students are allowed to ask three questions to help clarify the directions.

To modify this exercise into a game format, each student can receive a point for each time he or she is successful in directing the other students to the location. After a student has finished, discuss how he or she was effective in giving directions, and make recommendations to improve his or her language abilities.

Adaptations: A similar format can be used with one student directing the other students on a treasure hunt.

▶ Many Meanings

Objective: To give students practice with using homonyms and words with multiple meanings.

Grades: Intermediate and secondary

Materials: (1) Any generic game board with a die or spinner and pieces to serve as players. (2) A variety of meaning cards and homonyms or words that have multiple meanings (e.g., *heal/heel, meet/meat*) written on one side.

Teaching Procedures: Have the students set up the game and clarify the rules. For each turn, a student rolls the die or spins the spinner. The student then picks a card and uses each homonym in a separate sentence to show the difference between the meanings of the words or the multiple meanings. If the student's sentences reflect correct meanings, he or she moves the marker the number of spaces shown on the die or spinner. If the student is unable to make a sentence, other students may help him or her, but the student cannot move the marker. The first student to reach the finish line wins.

Adaptations: Have the students work in teams, or have the students give definitions of the words rather than using them in sentences.

▶ Surprise Pouches

Objective: To give students practice in describing objects.

Grades: Primary

Materials: (1) A cloth pouch with a drawstring. (2) Small objects that will fit in the pouch.

Teaching Procedures: Place a small object in the pouch, and have one student in the group feel the object without looking in the pouch. The student cannot give the name of the object but must describe it. The student describes what he or she feels while the rest of the students in the group try to guess what is in the pouch. When the student who is feeling the object thinks the other students have guessed correctly, he or she takes the object out to see whether the students are right. Have the students discuss how the descriptive words helped them guess the object. For example, "Smooth and round made me think it was a ball."

Put a new object in the pouch, and have another student describe the object. Each student should get several turns at describing the objects.

▶ I Spy

Objective: To provide students with opportunities to practice and develop descriptive vocabulary.

Grades: Elementary

Materials: Objects in the surrounding environment or vocabulary words

Teaching Procedures: Locate an object in the environment. Provide the students with clues that describe the object using the stem "I spy. . . ." For example, "I spy something that has green, narrow leaves." "I spy something that has rough bark." After each clue, the students try to guess what you are spying. The first person to identify the object becomes the next person to select an object and describe it.

Adaptations: For some students, you may need to assist in picking an object and giving "I spy" clues. If your weekly vocabulary list includes adjectives, give the students extra points for using those words in their descriptions. For older children, place a written list of vocabulary words on the board and ask them to describe words from that list in the game.

▶ The Add-On Game

Objective: To provide students with practice in listening to each other while categorizing and making associations between words within a topic.

Grades: Primary

Materials: Starter phrases that allow students to develop a list. For example:

- I went to the desert and I saw . . .
- I went up in space and I saw . . .
- I went back in time and I saw . . .

Teaching Procedures: The students and teacher sit in a circle. Use a topic from social studies, language arts, or science to start your discussion. For example, if you have been studying animals in the rain forest, a student can begin the game by saying, "I went to the rain forest and saw. . . ." This student names one thing that he or she might see in the rain forest. The next student in the circle then repeats the sentence, listing the first item and adding another item. The next student repeats both items and adds a third, and so on. This game can be played in two ways. To play competitively, the student is eliminated from the game when he or she cannot list all the items. The last student to remain in the game wins. To play cooperatively, the object of the game is for the group to beat the number of items remembered in previous games. To keep all students in the game, each student may be allowed two assists from a friend during the game (students are not "out" when incorrect). If a student has already used the two assists, then the number of items the group has correctly remembered is determined and compared to see whether the group beat previous scores.

Adaptations: This can be adapted to current events or holidays (e.g., gifts for Christmas or treats you got for Halloween).

▶ Round-Robin Stories

Objective: To provide students with opportunities to develop story grammar.

Grades: Elementary

Materials: None required, though a picture of a scene or setting may help students to start the story

Teaching Procedures: To get students ready to start round-robin stories, tell them that they are going to be telling a story as a group and that each student is to build on the story. Using a picture (if available and needed), tell what the story is going to be about. For example, "This story is about a group of friends who want to earn money to buy something." Have the students identify basic components of the story (names of the characters, setting) and begin telling the story. After several sentences, start a sentence, and have one student in the group finish the sentence. Model a variety of sentence starters. For example:

Subordinate Clauses
- When Jimmy went into the store, he . . .
- After Rita saw the dog in the window, she . . .

Direct Quotations
- Then the father said, ". . ."
- Suddenly, Raul screamed, ". . ."

Causal and Conditional Complex Sentences
- She didn't want to buy the brown dog because . . .
- He felt sad because . . .
- If she spent all of her money, she . . .

On the basis of their ending, start another sentence, and have another student finish it. As students become accustomed to this storytelling process, they should be able to build directly on each other's sentences without your having to start each sentence.

Adaptations: Use the same procedure, but use wordless picture books to guide students in telling the story.

▶ Barrier Game

Objective: To provide students with practice in describing how to make something and to provide practice in listening to directions.

Grades: Elementary

Materials: (1) Colored blocks for building objects or crayons for drawing objects. (2) Some type of barrier to block the view between the two students or the student and the teacher.

Teaching Procedures: Divide class into pairs, and explain the directions to the students. Have the students sit so that the barrier is between them. One student draws a simple picture or builds a simple block design. During or after the building or drawing, the student describes to the other student how to make the design. The other student attempts to duplicate the work and can ask questions to get help. When the second student has finished, remove the barrier and have the students compare their work.

Adaptations: After the students become successful at the activity, the number of questions that can be asked can be limited.

▶ Category Sort

Objective: To provide students with practice in sorting objects or word cards by categories.

Grades: Primary

Materials: (1) Objects or word cards that can be sorted by one or more categories (e.g., colored bears, colored blocks, colored buttons, colored marbles, types of animals, types of food). (2) Word cards that represent categories. (3) Sorting boxes (i.e., small boxes in which the students can sort objects or cards).

Teaching Procedures: Put a category word card next to each box. Demonstrate how to name each object or word card, and then put all the like objects or cards in the same box. Once the student has sorted the objects or cards, he or she names each category and the objects or cards in each category. The student then talks about what is alike about all the objects or cards in one category. Give older students vocabulary or spelling words to sort. Model how to sort the words in different ways (by meaning, spelling, part of speech, etc.)

▶ Create a Comic

Objective: To provide students with practice in using dialogue and telling stories.

Grades: Intermediate and junior high

Materials: Familiar comic strips or sequences in comic books. Blank out the words in the balloons.

Teaching Procedures: Present the comic strip to the students, and discuss with them what they know about the comic-strip characters, what is happening, and what could be written in each of the balloons. Have the students write in the different balloons. Take turns reading the comic strip, with different students reading what different characters say. The different comic strips can be put into a comic book that can be shared with other students.

Adaptations: After students are comfortable with this activity, they can illustrate and dictate their own comic strips.

▶ Play the Part

Objective: To provide students with practice in using language during simulations of typical interactions.

Grades: Intermediate and secondary

Materials: Simulation cards. Each card should describe the situation, the characters, and the goal of the language interaction. Some examples are given below.

Situation 1: Two friends meet a third person who is an old friend and known to only one of them. *Characters:* New friend, old friend, person making the introductions. *Goal:* Introduce new friend to old friend and get a conversation started among the three of you.

Situation 2: One person approaches another asking how to find a store about 10 blocks away. *Characters:* Stranger, person giving directions. *Goal:* Give directions that will allow the stranger to find the store.

Situation 3: Two friends are in a store. One tells the other that he or she intends to steal a small item from the store. *Characters:* Friend, person persuading. *Goal:* Convince the friend not to shoplift.

Teaching Procedures: Explain that each person is to assume the described role and participate as if this were a real situation.

Have the students assume the various characters and discuss what they are going to say in their roles. The students then carry out the role play. Have the students discuss how effective each person was in using language to accomplish the goal.

▶ Fun with Figurative Language

Objective: To provide students with opportunities to enhance proverb and/or idiom understanding.

Grades: Intermediate and junior high

Materials: Text from class that contains proverbs (e.g., "The early bird catches the worm") or idioms (e.g., "Keep your head above water")

Teaching Procedures: Select a proverb or idiom that is easily explained (e.g., "One rotten apple spoils the barrel"), and model how to interpret the meaning. First, examine the literal meaning, and draw a rough picture if necessary. Then examine the context of the proverb, and consider the character's motivations and feelings. Divide students into small groups. Each group may discuss one or two proverbs within the story using the modeled techniques. In addition, relate the proverb to students' lives and experiences. Discuss when and why a person may use a particular proverb or idiom.

FOCUS Answers

▶ **FOCUS Question 1. What are the two main areas of language delays, and how do they manifest themselves in the development of content, form, and use of language?**

Answer: Language delays occur either in receptive language (e.g., following directions) or in expressive language (e.g., word finding). Difficulties in either area commonly influence the production and understanding of the *content* aspect of language, which may lead to difficulty with creative aspects of language, such as understanding and using figurative language. The *form* of language refers to its structure and sound, so for students with language delays, sentences are often shorter and do not progress to contain the same complexity as do the sentences of their peers. *Use*, or pragmatics, is perhaps the most important aspect of language growth. Some students with language difficulties tend to misinterpret meanings and emotions expressed by others and may not be able to express themselves effectively.

▶ **FOCUS Question 2. What guidelines can assist in teaching oral language, content, form, and use?**

Answer: One strategy that promotes *oral* language development includes providing opportunities for students to engage in meaningful conversations. *Content* teaching involves vocabulary development and understanding and applying new concepts. Teaching *form* requires teaching and practicing specific language structures such as prefixes and suffixes. To develop pragmatics, use role plays or pictures to simulate situations such as greetings, question asking, and expressing emotions.

► FOCUS Question 3. What are the strategies and considerations on which teachers should focus when teaching culturally and linguistically diverse learners?

Answer: Effective instruction for culturally and linguistically diverse learners incorporates two key components. Teachers must both develop the student's English-language acquisition and incorporate the student's first language and culture into learning experiences.

► FOCUS Question 4. How can teachers work with families to develop students' language skills?

Answer: Children are more likely to learn new vocabulary and language structures when they can practice new concepts in different contexts (home and school). Examples of home activities include informing families of the vocabulary that is being learned at school and encouraging them to discuss these new words with their children; having families ask open-ended questions about activities, books that they are reading at home, or current events; and inviting families and children to play with language by telling jokes or making puns.

► FOCUS Question 5. How can special education teachers work with language specialists to implement RTI?

Answer: Within RTI frameworks, special education teachers can work with language specialists to promote language and literacy development with at-risk students as well as students with special needs by (a) collaborating and coteaching with the general education teacher to promote appropriate language and literacy activities including modifying and adjusting typical instruction, (b) providing professional development to school personnel regarding the linguistic bases of reading and writing, (c) providing information and support for parents of at-risk children regarding language and literacy activities in the home environment, and (d) demonstrating lessons that promote language and literacy outcomes for at-risk students and students with disabilities.

PEARSON
myeducationlab
Where the Classroom Comes to Life

The MyEducationLab for this course can help you solidify your comprehension of Chapter 6 concepts.

- Gauge and further develop your understanding of chapter concepts by taking the quizzes and examining the enrichment materials in the Chapter 6 Study Plan.
- Visit Topic 4, Assessing and Teaching Literacy and Language, to connect with challenge-based interactive modules, case study units, and podcasts that provide research-validated information about working with students in inclusive settings, by visiting the IRIS Center Resources.
- Explore Assignments and Activities, assignable exercises showing concepts in action through video, cases, and student and teacher artifacts.
- Practice and strengthen skills essential to quality teaching through the Building Teaching Skills and Dispositions lessons.

7

Assessing and Teaching Reading: Phonological Awareness, Phonics, and Word Recognition

1. How can teachers address the two overarching concepts that guide reading instruction?
2. What are the definitions and examples of instruction of phonological awareness, letter–sound correspondence, and phonics?
3. What are the definitions of the six main decoding strategies, and how does each contribute to successful word identification?
4. How can the use of explicit and implicit code instruction be compared?

Special education teachers teach many students who have difficulties in learning to read. Whether working as a coteacher with a kindergarten or first-grade teacher; working with a group of students and providing intensive, small group instruction in an elementary school; or teaching reading through the content area in a middle or high school, special education teachers spend a great deal of their time teaching reading. Why is this the case? First, reading is often considered to be the most important area of education (Glover & Vaughn, 2010). Reading for understanding and learning is necessary for content-area classes such as social studies, science, and vocational education and for successful employment. Second, students with learning and behavior disabilities have reading targeted as an area of need and have individualized education program (IEP) goals related to reading, more than any other academic area. Third, longitudinal research indicates that if students with learning and behavior problems do not learn to read by the end of third grade, their chances of having reading difficulties throughout their schooling and into adulthood are about 50% (Fletcher, Lyon, Fuchs, & Barnes, 2007). Therefore, developing successful readers early is essential.

Students have a variety of strengths and needs in the area of reading, thus targeted reading instruction is often beneficial. Let's look at two students and see what targeted instruction might be for these students. Kyle is a second grader who is receiving special education services for his learning disability in the area of reading. He reads at a beginning level and can recognize only about 30 words. When he comes to a word he does not recognize, he sometimes attempts to sound out the word. However, he has difficulty remembering common letter–sound correspondences. This means that when he sees letters, he does not automatically know the sound that letter makes. He also struggles with blending the sounds so that he can generate a word that is close enough to the correct word that he can figure it out. For Kyle, reading instruction will focus primarily on building phonological awareness, letter–sound correspondences, decoding strategies, and fluent word identification. The methods for teaching these components of reading that are presented in this chapter could assist in developing the automatic word recognition that would allow him to focus more of his attention on understanding what he reads. However, though the emphasis is placed on these more basic skills, his instructional program should also include repeated reading of independent and instructional-level decodable books (i.e., books that primarily use words that reflect the phonic and word patterns he has already learned) to build fluency. It should also include the listening, supported reading, and

PEARSON
myeducationlab

Visit the MyEducationLab for this course to enhance your understanding of chapter concepts with a personalized Study Plan. You'll also have the opportunity to hone your teaching skills through video-based Assignments and Activities, IRIS Center Resources, and Building Teaching Skills and Dispositions lessons.

Chapters 8 and 10 discuss reading comprehension and vocabulary development. Chapter 9 provides information on skill building for writing.

discussion of a wide variety of literature and content area materials to support his development of vocabulary and comprehension. Finally, it will be important for Kyle to have writing activities that related directly to his reading skills. For example, as he is learning the sounds to read *at* he can also learn to write words that end in -at such as *hat, mat, fat,* and *cat.* Similarly, as he develops his understanding of different types of text and genres (e.g., narratives such as folktales, adventure stories, and mysteries; expositions such as descriptions, comparisons/contrasts, persuasions), he can build skills at writing).

Manuel, the other student, is an eighth grader who is reading at approximately the fourth-grade level. He entered school speaking both Spanish and English. He struggled with learning to read in Spanish because of his limited vocabulary knowledge and comprehension skills (e.g., getting the main idea, comprehension monitoring). He began reading in English during second grade and continued to struggle with vocabulary knowledge and comprehension, and also had difficulty with decoding in English, because its letter–sound relationships are not as regular as those in Spanish. As an eighth grader, he is taking English/language arts from Ms. Gonzalez, the special education teacher. Ms. Gonzalez described Manuel's instructional reading program as follows:

Manuel and the other students in his group are working on building their vocabulary, comprehension, and advanced decoding skills. Currently, they are learning to decode multisyllabic words (e.g., *construction, reconsider*) in which they learn to identify and separate the prefixes, suffixes, and endings. Then if they don't recognize the root word, they use the information they know about open and closed syllables to decode the root word. One of the benefits of this strategy is that the students learn the meanings of the prefixes and suffixes, so it really helps them in learning what the word means. They also use the context by rereading the sentence or the surrounding sentences. For Manuel, this helps him build his decoding skills and vocabulary knowledge at the same time. We also take the time to learn related words. For example, if the word is *construction*, we make a "struct" web with words such as *destruction, construct, reconstruction,* and *deconstruct.* For teaching comprehension, Manuel and his classmates are learning to use collaborative strategic reading. It teaches the comprehension strategies previewing, questioning, summarizing, clarifying, and comprehension monitoring. The students work in collaborative learning groups, and we have been focusing on the eighth-grade social studies content, since Manuel and his fellow students are in general education social studies classes. Next semester, the social studies teacher and I are planning to coteach, and we'll use collaborative strategic reading 2 to 3 days a week to build comprehension skills while learning social studies content knowledge.

Like Kyle's, Manuel's reading program contains various components of reading depending on his needs: word identification [this chapter], vocabulary development, and comprehension.

In this chapter, we present specific methods, techniques, and approaches for teaching phonological awareness, letter–sound relationships, and the alphabetic principle as well as strategies for teaching word identification and word study.

Think about how the oral language strategies and instructional techniques that were discussed in Chapter 6 are related to reading and writing and could be incorporated into your teaching.

Although we have divided our discussion of reading and writing instruction into four chapters (Chapters 7 through 10), we stress the importance of the relationships between reading and writing. Critical to successful reading instruction for students with learning and behavior problems are opportunities for them to spell the words they are learning to read, write about what they are reading, and write stories and essays using structures and conventions similar to the ones they are reading. As you read these four chapters, think about how reading and writing are reciprocal processes and how they can be taught in such a way that each complements and supports the other.

Reading and Reading Instruction

How can teachers address the two overarching concepts that guide reading instruction? The goal of reading instruction is to give students the skills, strategies, and knowledge to read fluently and understand various texts for purposes of enjoyment and learning, whether reading a book, magazine, sign, pamphlet, e-mail message, or Internet site. To accomplish this goal, it is important to think about two overarching concepts.

1. *Reading is a skilled and strategic process in which learning to decode and read words accurately and rapidly is essential.* The average student entering school has a broad command of oral language. However, reading requires students to be able to distinguish the individual sounds that make up words and understand that letters represent sounds in language. Reading entails using the attentional, perceptual, memory, and retrieval processes necessary to automatically identify or decode words.

The process of recognizing words is called *decoding* or *word recognition*. As students become proficient readers, they recognize most words with little effort. But as students are learning to read or when readers encounter an unknown word, they use decoding to segment and then blend the word by sounds and patterns (e.g., individual sounds; spelling patterns such as -at, -ight; prefixes; suffixes; syllables) and use syntax and context (e.g., semantics) to assist in decoding. In developing decoding skills, students develop metalinguistics, that is, knowledge and skills focused on how language operates.

Knowing and demonstrating how to blend and segment words into sounds or phonemes is a key phonological or metalinguistic skill for decoding and one for which students with learning/reading disabilities have particular difficulty (e.g., Torgesen, 2000). When decoding is fluent, effort can be focused on comprehension. Thus, a goal of reading and reading instruction is to decode effortlessly so that attention is on comprehension.

As emergent readers encounter print in their environment, they ask questions and learn about how language is represented in its written form. They engage in the following:

- Pretending to read favorite print (e.g., books, poems, songs, chants)
- Reading what they have drawn or written, even when no one else can
- Pointing to just one word, the first word in a sentence, one letter, the first letter in the word, the longest word, etc.
- Recognizing some concrete words (e.g., their names, friends' names, words in the environment such as McDonald's)
- Recognizing and generating rhyming words
- Naming many letters and telling you words that begin with the common initial sound

As beginning readers proceed with learning to read, they learn to

- Identify letters by name.
- Say the common sounds of letters.
- Blend the sounds represented by letters into decodable words.
- Read irregular words.
- Read words, then sentences, and then longer text.

2. *Reading entails understanding the text and depends on active engagement and interpretation by the reader.* Understanding is influenced by both the text and the readers' prior knowledge (Cromley & Azevedo, 2007). When readers read, the author does not simply convey ideas to the readers but stimulates readers to actively engage in such strategies as *predicting* to make hypotheses about the meaning, *summarizing* to put in their own words the major points in the text, *questioning* to promote and check for understanding, and *clarifying* when concepts are not clear. Furthermore, effective readers *make connections* between their prior knowledge (background knowledge) and what they are reading while *monitoring* their comprehension to determine whether they understand what they are reading. When they are not sure, they may decide to employ fix-up strategies such as rereading or reading on for further clarification, or they may decide not to worry about the confusion depending on the purpose for reading. Knowing about these strategies and in which situations to apply different strategies is called *metacognition.*

For more on metacognition, see Chapter 2.

Students who have reading difficulties frequently have difficulty with efficient memory processing. Memory processes play an integral role in reading comprehension (van den Broek, Rapp, & Kendeou, 2005) because it facilitates a coherent construction of the text. If memory processes are inadequate, then more active strategic processes come into play to maintain or repair understanding. This is why monitoring your reading comprehension while you read is so important. It allows the reader to stop and activate strategies to repair understanding. Studies with good and poor readers suggest that the poor readers do not automatically monitor their comprehension or engage in strategic behavior to restore meaning when there is a comprehension breakdown (Bos & Filip, 1984).

These two overarching concepts can assist in organizing reading instruction into components or areas as depicted in Figure 7-1. These components and their integration are important in learning how to read effectively and in using reading as a vehicle for learning and entertainment. Because it is important to emphasize certain components or aspects of reading based on the student's level of development and needs, particularly for students with learning/reading disabilities, instruction should integrate these components. For example, while Kyle's reading program emphasized developing phonological awareness, letter–sound correspondences, and word recognition skills, he also engaged in activities to promote fluency and listening/reading comprehension. In contrast, Manuel's reading program focused on advanced decoding skills, fluency, and comprehension. In this chapter, we turn our attention to the first two components of reading and reading instruction.

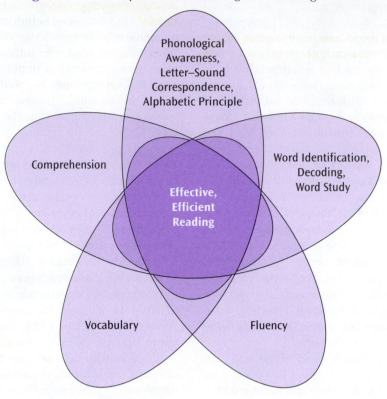

Phonological Awareness, Letter–Sound Correspondence, and Phonics

What are the definitions and examples of instruction of phonological awareness, letter–sound correspondence, and phonics? What is phonological awareness? *Phonological awareness* is knowing and demonstrating that spoken language can be broken down into smaller units (words, syllables, phonemes), which can be manipulated within the alphabetic system or orthography (Vaughn, Bos, & Schumm, 2011). Phonological awareness encompasses the discrimination, counting, rhyming, alliteration, blending, segmentation, and manipulating of syllables, onset-rimes, and phonemes. Examples of activities that support these skills are presented in Apply the Concept 7-1.

Phonemic awareness is the most complex part of a phonological awareness continuum that includes rhyming and segmenting words and sentences. Phonemic awareness is the ability to recognize the smallest sound units of spoken language and how these units of sound, or phonemes, can be separated (pulled apart or segmented), blended (put back together), and manipulated (added, deleted, and substituted). The phoneme is the smallest sound in spoken language that makes a difference in words. For instructional purposes related to reading, a phoneme is a single sound that maps to print—sometimes to one letter and sometimes to more than one letter.

Phonological awareness engages students in oral language activities. However, before students can apply these skills to reading, they need to understand phonics. *Phonics* is the way in which the sounds of our language (not the letters) map to print. It is knowing how letter names and sounds relate to each other (i.e., *letter–sound correspondence*). Let's see how a teacher applies these concepts.

Ms. Hernandez, the special education teacher, works for 30 minutes, three times a week in Ms. Harry's kindergarten class. She works with a small group of students who have the most difficulty learning to make letter–sound correspondences and who have difficulty separating words into their individual phonemes and blending and segmenting phonemes. With these kindergartners, Ms. Hernandez reinforces the key words that Ms. Harry is teaching with each letter–sound, (e.g., *b*, *ball*, /b/), and has students participate in listening activities in which they have to count the number of syllables in words and sounds in simple words (e.g., *me* and *sit*) and create word families (e.g., *it, sit, mitt, bit, fit, hit*). At first, she has the students listen when working on these activities. Then she uses letters to demonstrate how the syllables and sounds are related to print.

Ms. Hernandez also works with a small group of six students in Ms. Yu's first-grade class who have difficulty learning to read. Ms. Hernandez engages these students in such activities as listening and clapping the number of sounds in words to help them segment the sounds; saying each sound in a word slowly and then saying them fast to practice blending. When writing the sound, she has them say the word, then say the sounds, then say the first sound and write it, then say the first two sounds and write the second sound, and so on until they have written the word. She consistently pairs speech and print.

Ms. Hernandez is directly teaching phonological awareness, letter–sound relationships, and phonics, all of which are associated with successful reading and spelling. Evidence from research provides consistent support for the important role that phonological awareness and processing play in learning to read (Adams, 1990; Blachman, 2000; Ehri, 2004; National Reading Panel, 2000). The skills associated with phonological processing, particularly blending and segmenting individual phonemes, have been one of the most consistent predictors of difficulties in learning to read. Children who lack this metalinguistic insight are likely to be among the poorest readers and, because of their poor reading, to be identified as having a learning or reading disability (e.g., Blachman, 2000; Schatschneider, Fletcher, Francis, Carlson, & Foorman, 2004). Hence, Ms. Hernandez is working with students in kindergarten and first grade to help prevent or lessen later reading disabilities.

Development of Phonological Awareness and Phonics

In general, children's awareness of the phonological structure of the English language develops from larger units of sounds (e.g., words in a sentence, syllables in a word) to smaller units (e.g., onset-rimes, phonemes). Skills such as rhyming and alliteration develop earlier, and skills such as sound blending, segmenting, and manipulation of phonemes develop later. Activities related to blending, segmenting, and manipulating phonemes are the most important for improving reading. Table 7-1 presents a

●●●●●● *Apply the Concept* ●●●●●●

7-1 Phonological Skills and Example Activities

- *Discrimination:* students listen to determine whether two words begin or end with the same sound.
- *Counting:* students clap the number word in a sentence, syllables in a word (e.g., *cowboy, carrot*), sounds in a word (e.g., *me, jump*).
- *Rhyming:* students create word families with rhyming words (e.g., *all, call, fall, ball*).
- *Alliteration:* students create tongue twisters (e.g., Sally's silly shoe sank slowly in the slime).

- *Blending:* students say the sounds in a word and then say them fast while the teacher pushes blocks or letters together to demonstrate blending.
- *Segmenting:* students say the word and then clap and say each syllable or sound (e.g., *running* is /run/ /ing/ or /r/ /u/ /n/ /i/ /ng/).
- *Manipulating:* deleting, adding, substituting, and transposing.
- *Deleting:* students listen to words and say them without the

first sound (e.g., *bat* becomes *at*).
- *Adding:* students listen to words and add syllables (e.g., *run* becomes *running, come* becomes *coming*).
- *Substituting:* students listen and change sounds (e.g., change /r/ in *run* to /b/ and make *bun*).
- *Transposing:* students reverse the sounds (e.g., *nat* becomes *tan*).

Table 7-1 Phonological Awareness Continuum

Later Developing	
Skill	**Example**
Phoneme blending, segmentation, and manipulations	Blending phonemes into words, segmenting words into individual phonemes, and manipulating phonemes (e.g., deleting, adding, substituting, transposing) in spoken words
Onset-rime blending and segmentation	Blending/segmenting the initial consonant or consonant cluster (onset) from the vowel and consonant sounds spoken after it (rime)
Syllable blending and segmentation	Blending syllables to say words or segmenting spoken words into syllables
Sentence segmentation	Segmenting sentences into spoken words
Rhyme/alliteration	Matching the ending sounds of words/producing groups of words that begin with the same initial sound
Early Developing	

Source: Adapted from *First Grade Teacher Reading Academy* (Austin: University of Texas, Texas Center for Reading and Language Arts, 2009).

continuum for the development of phonological awareness with definitions. While phonological awareness encompasses the entire continuum, activities that focus on individual sounds in words describe *phonemic awareness*.

The more advanced skills of phoneme blending, segmenting, and manipulation are most related to success in learning to read (Cavanaugh, Kim, Wanzek, & Vaughn, 2004; Manyak, 2008; Torgesen, Wagner, & Rashotte, 1994). This is an important point for teachers to remember because it should guide their instruction. The primary focus of phonemic awareness with young children is not rhyming; rather, the focus should be on increasing their awareness of the individual sounds in language and how each of these sounds can be represented by a letter or combination of letters. Remember, linking sounds to print is the most immediate goal.

The sequence for teaching phonemic awareness usually starts with teaching segmenting and blending words and syllables before teaching segmenting and blending onset-rimes and phonemes. However, some children vary in the acquisition of these skills. Therefore, instruction at the phoneme level should never be delayed until students understand rhyme or any other phonological awareness skill on the continuum.

Teaching Phonological Awareness and Phonics

The majority of students at risk for reading difficulties have poor phonological awareness and can profit from explicit instruction in blending, segmenting, and manipulating sounds and mapping these sounds to letters as early as possible. As students learn the letter–sound correspondences, phonological tasks such as oral blending and segmenting of onset-rimes and phonemes can be paired with graphemes (letters), thereby explicitly teaching the relationship of speech to print—the alphabetic principle (Goswami, 1998).

Teaching phonological awareness includes such activities as the following:

- Listening for words that begin with the same sound (e.g., having all the students whose name begins with /b/ line up)
- Clapping the number of syllables in words and phonemes in words
- Blending and segmenting words by syllables and sounds
- Segmenting and manipulating sounds and syllables

To build blending and segmenting skills, a frequently used technique that assists students in learning to separate and blend sounds is the use of the Elkonin procedure, often referred to as Elkonin boxes (Elkonin, 1973). As a phonological task, students listen to a word and push a marker, block, or other small object into a printed square for each sound they hear (see Figure 7-2). As students gain knowledge about the letter–sound relationships, they can

▶ **Figure 7-2** Using the Elkonin Procedure to Support Phonemic Awareness

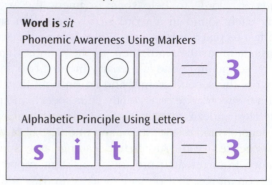

push or write letters in the boxes. It is one way in which an oral language activity can be made more visible and kinesthetic. Other ways are tapping one finger to the thumb for each sound or watching your mouth in a mirror and feeling the facial movements by placing your fingers on your cheeks and concentrating on how your mouth changes when different sounds are made (Lindamood & Lindamood, 1998).

In teaching phonological awareness to students who are having difficulty learning to read, it is important to determine the tasks that are difficult for the student and then to focus instruction according to the students' level of development and needs. For example, Emilia is a second-semester first grader who can segment and blend syllables and onset-rimes (e.g., s-it, f-at, r-un) but has great difficulty segmenting and blending individual phonemes. She has been using manipulatives and counting on her fingers to assist herself, but she is still having difficulty hearing the individual sounds. Emilia may benefit from instruction that demonstrates how the rime is further divided into individual sounds. Emilia could also watch and feel her mouth as she says each sound to see how it changes as when saying the /a/ and then /t/, the sounds in the word *at*. For Emilia, who has learned the letter–sound correspondences for about six consonant sounds and the short vowel /a/, using letters in the boxes can help her understand how speech maps to print and to read words.

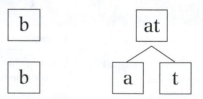

Students may also need assistance in learning how to blend sounds. Figure 7-3 presents a simple procedure for teaching sound blending. The same procedure can be used for teaching how to segment words, except that the teacher would begin with the sounds separated and then gradually present them closer together until they are blended into a word.

> ► **Figure 7-3** Procedure for Teaching Sound Blending

To train a child in sound blending, use the following procedure.

Teacher:	Say *shoe*.
Child:	Shoe.
Teacher:	Now, what am I saying? **/sh-sh-sh/oo-oo-oo/.** [Say it with prolonged sounds, but no break between the sounds. If the child responds correctly, say:] Good. Now what am I saying? [Give a little break between the sounds.] **/Sh/oe/.** [Then say it with the child.] Shoe. Now what am I saying? [Give a quarter-second break between the sounds.] **/Sh/oe/.**
Child:	Shoe.
Teacher:	Shoe. Good. What am I saying now? [with a half-second break between the sounds] **/Sh/oe/.**
Child:	Shoe.
Teacher:	Now what am I saying? [Give a one-second break between the sounds.] **/Sh/oe/.**

At each step, if the child does not respond with "shoe," repeat the previous step and then again stretch out the sounds, confirming or prompting at each step. Proceed by increasing the duration until the child can say "shoe" in response to the sounds with approximately one second between them.

Repeat this experience with the word *me*.

The main task for the teacher is to give a word with two sounds, increasing the duration of time between them until the child gets the idea of putting the sounds together. Then the child is presented with three-sound words such as **/f/a/t/,** and then with four-sound words such as **/s/a/n/d/.** It is important to recognize that the number of sounds in a word may not correspond to the number of letters in a word. For example, the word *shoe* has four letters, but only two sounds. The teacher must be careful to present the sounds correctly and use the correct timing.

Source: S. A. Kirk, W. D. Kirk, & E. H. Minskoff, *Phonic Remedial Reading Lessons* (Novato, CA: Academic Therapy Publications, 1985), pp. 12–13. Reprinted by permission.

> ► **Figure 7-4** Selected Programs and Resources for Teaching Phonological Awareness and Phonics

A Basic Guide to Understanding, Assessing, and Teaching Phonological Awareness by Torgesen, J. K., and Mathes, P. G., 2000, Austin, TX: PRO-ED.

Interventions for Reading Success by Haager, D., Domino, J. A., and Windmueller, M. P., 2006, Baltimore: Brookes.

Ladders to Literacy: A Kindergarten Activity Book, 2nd ed., by O'Connor, R. E., Notari-Syverson, A., and Vadasy, P. F., 2005, Baltimore: Brookes.

The Lindamood Phoneme Sequencing Program for Reading, Spelling, and Speech by Lindamood, P. A., and Lindamood, P., 1998, Austin, TX: PRO-ED.

Phonemic Awareness in Young Children: A Classroom Curriculum by Adams, M. J., Foorman, B. G., Lundberg, I., and Beeler, T., 1998, Baltimore: Brookes.

Phonological Awareness and Primary Phonics by Gunning, T. G., 2000, Boston: Allyn & Bacon.

Phonological Awareness Assessment and Instruction: A Sound Beginning by Lane, H. B., and Pullen, P. C., 2004, Boston: Allyn & Bacon.

The Phonological Awareness Book by Robertson, C., and Salter, W., 1995, East Moline, IL: LinguiSystems.

Phonological Awareness Training for Reading by Torgesen, J. K., and Bryant, B. R., 1994, Austin, TX: PRO-ED.

Road to the Code: A Program of Early Literacy Activities to Develop Phonological Awareness by Blachman, B. A., Ball, E. W., Black, R., and Tangel, D. M., 2000, Baltimore: Brookes.

Sounds Abound by Catts, H., and Olsen, T., 1993, East Moline, IL: LinguiSystems.

The Sounds Abound Program: Teaching Phonological Awareness in the Classroom (formerly Sounds Start) by Lechner, O., and Podhajski, B., 1998, East Moline, IL: LinguiSystems.

General guidelines for teaching phonological awareness activities include the following:

- Consider the students' levels of development and tasks that need to be mastered.
- Model each activity.
- Use manipulatives and movement to make auditory or oral tasks more visible.
- Move from easier to more difficult tasks, considering level of development (syllables, onset-rimes, phonemes), phoneme position (initial, final, medial), number of sounds in a word (*cat* is easier than

split), and phonological features of the words (e.g., continuant consonants /m/, /n/, /s/ are easier than stops or clipped sounds /t/, /b/, /d/).
- Provide feedback and opportunities for practice and review.
- Make learning fun.

A number of programs and resources are available for teaching phonological awareness and phonics (see Figure 7-4 for a selected list), and a number of sources provide lists of children's books focused on different aspects of phonological awareness (Strickland &

Schickedanz, 2009; Yopp & Yopp, 2009). Tech Tips highlights information about using computer software to teach phonological awareness and word recognition skills.

Response to Intervention and Progress Monitoring: Phonological Awareness and Phonics

Successfully preventing reading disabilities and appropriately serving students with reading disabilities requires an understanding of how response to intervention (RTI) and progress monitoring can be coordinated at the early grades to address phonological awareness and phonics.

Response to Intervention How do we know if students are responding to instruction in phonemic awareness and phonics? The answers to several questions can provide valuable information for determining students' responses to instruction:

- Have students received scientifically based reading instruction in phonemic awareness and phonics from their classroom teacher?
- Have students received adequate opportunities to respond, obtain feedback, and see modeling to scaffold their learning?
- How does the performance of students with low response compare to the performance of other students in the class?
- Have students with low phonemic awareness received instructional opportunities in small groups to acquire phonemic awareness and phonics?
- Is progress monitoring data available to show the scope of the student's progress?

Tech TIPS

USING TECHNOLOGY TO BUILD PHONOLOGICAL AWARENESS AND WORD RECOGNITION

Its multimedia capabilities make the computer an ideal tool for building phonological awareness and word recognition—tirelessly repeating sounds, words, and phrases for students who need reinforcement of these concepts.

Don Johnston Incorporated (http://www.donjohnston.com) offers *Simon S. I. O.*, a program that can help students to learn sounds, build words, and learn word families. They can read words aloud into a microphone and hear them repeated back. The software reinforces correct responses and keeps an accurate accounting of learner progress. It also encourages comprehension in addition to pronunciation.

The *Earobics* series is another software offering from Don Johnston Incorporated. In *Earobics Step 1*, *Earobics Step 2*, and *Earobics for Adolescents and Adults*, learners can practice sound blending, rhyming, and sound discrimination. These programs concentrate on phonological awareness skills for learners who are struggling to improve reading and spelling skills. Other tutorial software from this publisher that provide structured literacy activities are *WordMaker* and *All My Words*.

Balanced Literacy, from IntelliTools, Inc. (http://www.intellitools.com), provides a full-year reading program for beginning readers. Using sequential presentation of skills, the program includes guided reading, comprehension, phonics instruction, and beginning writing. Also from IntelliTools, Inc.,

are *Phonemic Awareness Activities*, which are add-ons to the *Classroom Suite* software.

Word Munchers from The Learning Company (http://www.learningcompany.com) is an arcade-like game in which the learner must "munch" words with specific vowel sounds. Unlike the previous software that were tutorials, this game is obviously reinforced practice—learners are practicing skills taught prior to playing the game. *Word Muncher Deluxe* includes games using vocabulary, sentence structure, and grammar, in addition to vowel sounds.

A Screenshot from *Simon S.I.O.*
(Copyright © 2005 Don Johnston Incorporated)

Answering these questions can help us determine whether students have received adequate instruction and thus whether their low response is a function of exceptional needs in the target area. Knowing the opportunities students have to learn helps us discern the severity of the problem.

How do we know when students are responding adequately to instruction in phonics and word study? If students are receiving scientifically based reading instruction in phonics and word study, we can determine whether they are low or high responders based on two essential criteria: (1) How do they respond relative to others in their class and others in the same grade in other classes in the school? and (2) What is the slope of their progress based on progress-monitoring measures acquired at least every 2 weeks? If a student's progress is significantly below other students in the class and/or his slope for his progress based on progress monitoring of phonics and word study is lower than expected, then the student may not be responding adequately to phonics and word-study instruction.

Progress Monitoring Determining students' performance in each of the building blocks of reading (e.g., phonemic awareness, phonics, word reading) is an essential first step in designing an effective intervention program. Teachers using progress monitoring can determine what students can do and what they need to learn. Thus, teachers can design an instructional program that is targeted to the needs of the students. Assessments that tell the teacher specifically how a student is performing and what else the student needs to know are referred to as *diagnostic assessments*. Using appropriate assessments, teachers can determine how the student's performance compares with those of other students of that same age or in that grade. These assessments are referred to as *norm-based assessments*. Appropriate assessments allow the teacher to monitor the progress of students and determine whether their progress is on track or whether the teacher needs to alter instruction to improve their performance. These assessments are referred to as *progress-monitoring assessment* or *curriculum-based measures*.

Progress monitoring of students' knowledge and skills in phonological awareness and the alphabetic principle provides teachers with necessary data to inform decision making about grouping and instruction. A good progress-monitoring system will also allow teachers to determine whether any of the three important aspects of phonemic awareness are problematic: deletion, segmenting, and/or blending.

Progress monitoring in phonemic awareness assists teachers in identifying students who are at risk for failing to acquire phonemic awareness skills, and in monitoring the progress that students make in response to phonemic awareness instruction. There are two important aspects

of phonemic progress-monitoring measures: They should be predictive of later reading ability, and they need to guide instruction. The following brief descriptions of tests and progress-monitoring measures may be useful for teachers as they make decisions about what methods they will use to monitor students' progress in phonemic awareness:

- *STAR: Early Literacy (SEL)*. SEL is a computer-adaptive procedure that provides for ongoing assessment of early literacy skills including general readiness to read, graphophonemic knowledge, phonemic awareness, phonics, comprehension, structural analysis, and vocabulary. The test takes approximately 10 minutes and can be used with students in grades K through 3. The program is available through Renaissance Learning (http://www.renlearn.com).

- *AIMSweb Systems*. These systems offer progress-monitoring tools for letter-naming fluency, letter–sound fluency, phoneme segmentation fluency, and nonsense-word fluency. There are 23–33 alternative forms available for each grade and ongoing technical support is provided. The program is available from Edformation, Inc. (http://www.aimsweb.com).

- *Yopp–Singer Test of Phoneme Segmentation*. Students are asked to segment each phoneme separately in a list of 22 presented words. Students receive credit if they say all of the sounds in the word correctly. For example, if students are asked to identify the phonemes in *fit*, they would receive no credit for getting the first phoneme correct if they missed the following two phonemes. Students also receive feedback after each response. For responses that are correct, students are told that they are right. For responses that are incorrect, students are told the correct response by the test administrator. Like most phonemic awareness measures, this one is administered individually to children (Yopp, 1995).

- *Phoneme Segmentation Fluency*. There are 20 forms of this measure with 20 words for each form. All forms have two to five phonemes for each of the 20 words. This measure is also individually administered; however, unlike the Yopp–Singer Test of Phoneme Segmentation, this measure is timed. Students are given 60 seconds to get as many phonemes correct as possible. Students receive points for each phoneme (word part) correct even if the entire word is not correct. Also, students are not provided corrective feedback for errors (Kaminski & Good, 1996).

> ▶ **WEB RESOURCES**
>
> For a complete description of this phoneme segmentation fluency measure as well as information on technical adequacy, video clip on administration and scoring, and examples of how to administer and score, see the following Web site: https://dibels.uoregon.edu/measures/psf.php.

- *Comprehensive Test of Phonological Processing (CTOPP).* The CTOPP is administered individually to students to determine their skill in phonological awareness and to guide the teacher in designing appropriate instruction. The test is designed for individuals between the ages of 5 and 24 and assesses three areas: phonological awareness, phonological memory, and rapid naming ability. If teachers are interested in assessing more specific areas of phonological awareness, additional subtests are available.

> ▶ **WEB RESOURCES**
> For further information on the CTOPP see
> http://www.proedinc.com.

When selecting a measure, teachers consider the following:

- Does it accurately predict which students will have later difficulties in reading?
- Does it differentiate current high, average, and low performers?
- Does it determine which phonemic awareness skills they need to teach?
- Does it provide multiple forms so that they can administer it multiple times per year?
- Is it matched with the needs of the population of students they teach?

If the teacher can answer yes to all of the above, the measure will serve well.

Teaching Letter–Sound Correspondences

As students learn letter–sound correspondences and move to higher phonological awareness skills such as blending, segmenting, and manipulating sounds, it is important that they associate speech with print (Shaywitz, Morris, & Shaywitz, 2008; Simmons, Kame'enui, Stoolmiller, Coyne, & Harn, 2003), thereby teaching the alphabetic principle or understanding that the sequence of letters in written words represents the sequence of sounds in spoken words. In Figure 7-2, while the task in the first row involves asking the students to segment words into sounds by moving a marker into a box for each sound (phonemic awareness), in the second row the students pair the sounds with letters by writing the letters in the boxes (alphabetic principle). Sometimes a phoneme is represented by more than one letter (e.g., consonant digraphs such as /sh/, /ch/, /ph/). One way to note this is by using a dotted line between the letters in the digraphs.

| f | i | s | h |

Knowledge of individual speech sounds is not particularly important when using oral language to converse. However, in learning to read and write and in developing a second language, this knowledge can be quite valuable and is accentuated by these tasks. Expert estimates of the number of speech sounds or phonemes in English vary from 40 to 52. For purposes of teaching students, most estimates are about 44 (Fromkin & Rodman, 1998; Owens, 2010). In learning to read and write, students learn more than 100 spellings (graphemes) for these phonemes.

The largest division of phonemes is consonants (C) or vowels (V). Table 7-2 presents the 25 consonant sounds with their typical spellings and representative words that use these sounds. The table groups the sounds according to the manner in which they are articulated and highlights how the sounds are related. For example, there are eight sound pairs in which the only difference between the two sounds in each pair is whether the sounds are produced with a resonance in the throat (voiced) or without resonance (voiceless):

Voiced	Voiceless
/b/ bat	/p/ pat
/d/ dig	/t/ tack
/g/ gate	/k/ kite
/v/ vase	/f/ fit
/th/ this	/th/ think
/z/ zip	/s/ sat
/zh/ buzz	/sh/ ship
/j/ jump	/ch/ chip

For students who consistently confuse voiced or voiceless sounds, it is helpful to teach whether the sounds are voiced or unvoiced. They can distinguish the difference by placing their fingers on their throat to feel the vibrations in their larynxes or by covering both their ears and listening as they say the sound pairs. Having students check whether they can feel the sound may help them to decode or spell a word.

Consonant sounds can also be distinguished by the flow of air as stops or continuants. Stops are aptly named because they are of short duration and the airflow is stopped completely for a short time (Moats, 2000). Stops (or clipped sounds) include /b/, /d/, /g/, /j/, /k/, /p/, /t/, and /ch/. In contrast, continuant sounds can be blended smoothly with the next sound without a break in the air flow (e.g., /f/, /s/, /v/, /w/, /z/, /sh/, /zh/, and /th/). The following are important points to remember when teaching consonants:

- CVC words that begin with continuants and end with stops are generally the easiest for blending the sounds (e.g., *fat, sap*).
- In some programs, when blending stops it is suggested to "bounce the stop sounds," such as /b-b-b-b-a-t-t-t/ for *bat* (Slavin, Madden, Karweit, Dolan, & Wasik,

Table 7-2 Consonant Sounds, Typical Spellings, and Manner of Articulation

Consonant Sounds	Typical Spellings	Initial	Middle, Final	Manner of Articulation
/p/	p	pot, pick	stop	voiceless stop @ lips
/b/	b	bat, barn	cab, robe	voiced stop @ lips
/t/	t, -ed	time, tap	pot, messed	voiceless stop @ tongue behind teeth
/d/	d, -ed	deer, dinner	bad, ride, cried	voiced stop @ tongue behind teeth
/k/	c, k, ck, qu	kiss, can, quick	back, critique	voiceless stop @ back of mouth
/g/	g	gate, girl	rag	voiced stop @ back of mouth
/f/	f, ph	first, fit	graph, off, rough	voiceless fricative @ lip/teeth
/v/	v	very, vase	love	voiced fricative @ lip/teeth
/th/	th	think, thin	mother, either	voiceless fricative @ tongue between teeth
/th/	th	the, then	both, ether	voiced fricative @ tongue between teeth
/s/	s, c	sap, cent, psychology	less, piece	voiceless fricative @ tongue behind teeth
/z/	z, -es, -s, x	zip, Xerox	has, dogs, messes, lazy	voiced fricative @ tongue behind teeth
/sh/	sh	ship, sure, chef	push, mission, ration	voiceless fricative @ roof of mouth
/zh/	z, s		azure, measure, beige	voiced fricative @ roof of mouth
/ch/	ch, tch	chip, chase	much, hatch	voiceless affricate @ roof of mouth
/j/	j, g	jump, gist	judge, soldier	voiced affricate @ roof of mouth
/m/	m	me, mom	him, autumn, comb	nasal @ lips
/n/	n, kn, gn, pn, mn	now, know, gnat, pneumonia, mnemonics	pan, sign	nasal @ tongue behind teeth
/ng/	ng		sing, English	nasal @ back of mouth
/y/	y	you, use	feud	voiced glide @ roof of mouth
/wh/	wh	where, whale		voiceless glide @ back of mouth with rounding of lips
/w/	w	we, witch	sewer	voiced glide @ back of mouth with rounding of lips
/h/	h	happy, who		voiceless glide @ throat
/l/	l	lady, lion	mail, babble	liquid @ tongue behind teeth
/r/	r	ride, write		liquid @ tongue behind teeth

Source: Adapted from V. Fromkin & R. Rodman, *Introduction to Language*, 6th ed. (Orlando, FL: Harcourt Brace, 2004); and L. C. Moats, *Spelling: Development, Disability and Instruction* (Baltimore: York Press, 1995).

1992), so that students do not attach a "schwa" sound to the stop consonants (e.g., /buh/ and /tuh/).

- Nasal sounds are difficult to hear, sound different in the middle of words (e.g., *wet* or *went*), and are often omitted or substituted by emergent readers and writers. One strategy that students can use to check for a nasal is to gently touch their noses while saying the word and feel whether the nose vibrates.
- Students may have problems hearing the difference between /wh/ and /w/ because many Americans pronounce them in the same manner—for example, *witch* and *which* (Moats, 2000).
- The sounds /r/ and /l/ can be difficult for some students because they are some of the last sounds that students learn to articulate and because their pronunciation varies considerably across languages (e.g., in Spanish, they may be trilled or rolled; in Japanese and Cantonese, the sounds of these two phonemes are not differentiated).

This information about consonant sounds is helpful when teachers analyze students' oral reading and spelling. Students who know the letter–sound correspondences are more likely to substitute similar sounds. For example, it is more likely that students would substitute /n/ or /m/ for /ng/ than other sounds because they are nasals. Similarly, substitutions of /d/ for /b/ and /p/ for /b/ could well be related to the similar manner in which the sounds are articulated (i.e., /d/ and /b/—similar formation of the mouth; /p/ and /b/—same formation of mouth but voiceless and voiced) rather then to visual processing.

The English language also makes use of consonant digraphs and consonant blends. A *consonant digraph* is two consonants that represent one sound (*ph* for /f/). A *consonant blend*, or *consonant cluster*, combines the sounds of two or more consonants so that they are clustered together. Table 7-3 provides a listing of the consonant digraphs and blends. When students omit a letter in

Table 7-3 Common Consonant Digraphs and Clusters

Common Consonant Digraphs		Common Initial Consonant Clusters			
Correspondence	**Example Words**	**With *l***	**Example Words**	**With *s***	**Example Words**
ch = /ch/	chair, church	bl	blanket, black	sc	score, scale
gh = /f/	rough, tough	cl	clock, clothes	sch	school, schedule
kn = /n/	knot, knob	fl	flag, fly	scr	scream, scrub
ng = /˜/	thing, sing	gl	glove, glue	sk	sky, skin
ph = /f/	phone, photograph	pl	plum, place	sl	sled, sleep
sc = /s/	scissors, scientist	sl	slide, show	sm	smoke, smile
sh = /sh/	shoe, shop			sn	snake, sneakers
th = /th/	there, them	**With *r***	**Example Words**	sp	spider, spot
th = /th/	thumb, thunder	br	broom, bread	st	star, stop
wh = /w/	wheel, where	cr	crow, crash	str	street, stream
wr = /r/	wrench, wrestle	dr	dress, drink	sw	sweater, swim
		fr	frog, from		
		gr	green, ground		
		pr	prince, prepare		

Common Final Consonant Clusters			
With *n*	**Example Words**	**With *l***	**Example Words**
nce	prince, chance	ld	field, old
nch	lunch, bunch	lf	wolf, self
nd	hand, wind	lk	milk, silk
nk	tank, wink	lm	film
nt	tent, sent	lp	help
		lt	salt, belt
Other	**Example Words**	lve	twelve, solve
ct	fact, effect		
mp	jump, camp		
sp	wasp, grasp		
st	nest, best		

Source: Adapted from T. G. Gunning, *Creating Literacy Instruction for All Students,* 7th ed. (Boston: Allyn & Bacon, 2010).

a cluster, such as reading *fog* for *frog*, ask questions that lead them to see that the second sound in the blend is missing (e.g., "Listen, what sound do you hear after the /f/ in *frog*, /f-r-o-g/?" "What two sounds does the word *frog* begin with?"). It may also be helpful to have the students compare the words in written form or use boxes to assist students in seeing the missing letter.

The second category of sounds is vowels. In general, there must be a vowel in every English syllable, and consonants are formed around the vowel. Vowel sounds can be ordered on the basis of the open or closed position of the mouth, as shown in the vowel circle in Figure 7-5. Say each of the vowels in the vowel circle, and note how your mouth moves from a closed, smiling position (e) to an open position (oo).

As with the consonants, we can analyze students' oral reading and spelling to learn about their knowledge of vowels sounds. For example, substituting an /e/ for /a/ would be more likely than substituting an /e/ for /o/ because of the closeness of the sounds. It is also obvious why students often confuse /ir/, /er/, and /ur/ in spelling, since these three spellings represent the same sound. Thus, *bird* can be spelled *bird, burd,* and *berd,* and the student must use visual memory to remember that it is *bird*. The vowel sounds have different spelling patterns as demonstrated in Table 7-4. Sometimes the same spelling pattern has different sounds (e.g., the "ea" in *beat* and *bread* or the "ou" in *soup, could,* and *shout*). For students with severe difficulties in decoding, it may be helpful to systematically teach the frequency of the sounds for a

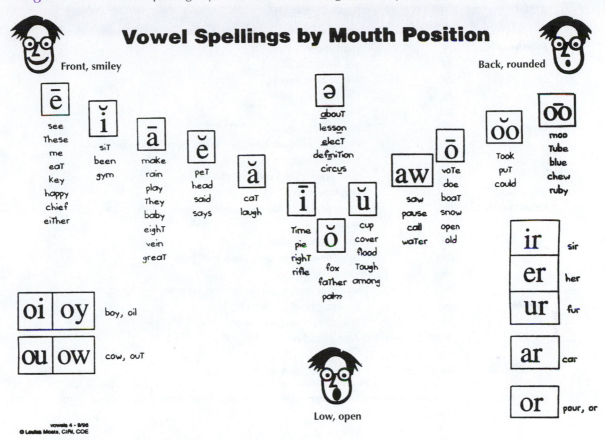

Source: L. C. Moats, *Speech to Print: Language Essentials for Teachers* (Baltimore: Brookes, 2000), p. 94. Copyright © 2000 by Paul H. Brookes Publishing Co. Inc. Reprinted with permission. (www.brookespublishing.com/store/books/moats-3874/index.htm.)

vowel combination so that when decoding an unknown word, they can try the various sounds in a systematic manner and use syntax and semantics (i.e., context of the text) to determine the word. Vowel combinations with order of frequency for the different sounds (Herzog, 1998) are as follows:

Vowel Combination	Order of Frequency for Different Sounds
ea	/e/ as in *eat*, /e/ as in *bread*, /a/ as in *great*
ei	/e/ as in *ceiling*, /a/ as in *vein*
ey	/e/ as in *key*, /a/ as in *grey*
ie	/e/ as in *piece*, /i/ as in *pie*
oo	/oo/ as in *moon*, /oo/ as in *book*
ou	/ou/ as in *house*, /oo/ as in *soup*
ow	/ou/ as in *owl*, /o/ as in *snow*

Students who are acquiring English and speak another language may not have developed fluency in all the English sounds. This is because different languages use different speech sounds, and students are most comfortable using the speech sounds of their native language. Chapter 6 (Oral Language) Table 6.7 provides a comparison of the phonological as well as the morphological and syntactical features of Spanish and English. Common phonological confusions include the following:

/b/ pronounced as /p/
/v/ pronounced as /b/
/ch/ pronounced as /sh/
/j/ pronounced as /h/
/l/ pronounced as /y/
a number of differences in vowel pronunciations

Consequently, students may have difficulty not only pronouncing these sounds but also hearing them. Do not be surprised if *chin* is read and spelled as *shin* or *vase* is read and spelled as *base*.

Guidelines for Teaching Letter–Sound Correspondences

Students use letter–sound correspondences to decode words. Struggling readers benefit from learning to blend and segment sounds so that they can decode and spell words.

Table 7-4 Vowel Spellings

	Vowel Sound	Major Spellings
Short Vowels	/a/	rag, happen
	/e/	get, letter, thread
	/i/	wig, middle, event
	/o/	fox, problem, father
	/u/	bus
Long Vowels	/ā/	name, favor, say, sail
	/ē/	he, even, eat, seed, bean, key, these, either, funny, serious
	/ī/	hide, tiny, high, lie, sky
	/ō/	vote, open, coat, bowl, old, though
	/ū/	use, human, few
Other Vowels	/aw/	daughter, law, walk, off, bought
	/oi/	noise, toy
	/ŏŏ/	wood, should, push
	/ōō/	soon, new, prove, group, two, fruit, truth
	/ow/	tower, south
	/@/	above, operation, similar, opinion, suppose
r Vowels	/ar/	far, large, heart
	/air/	hair, care, where, stair, bear
	/i(@)r/	dear, steer, here
	/@r/	her, sir, fur, earth
	/or/	horse, door, tour, more

Source: Adapted from T. G. Gunning, *Creating Literacy Instruction for All Students*, 7th ed. (Boston: Allyn & Bacon, 2010).

A number of programs have been developed using systematic approaches to introduce the letter–sound relationships and how to blend sounds to read words (e.g., *Word Detectives: Benchmark Word Identification Program for Beginning Readers* [Gaskins, Cress, O'Hara, & Donnelly, 1998]; *Corrective Reading* [Engelmann et al., 1999]; *Lindamood Phoneme Sequencing Program for Reading, Spelling, and Speech* [Lindamood & Lindamood, 1998]; *Phonic Remedial Reading Lessons* [Kirk, Kirk, & Minskoff, 1985]; *Alphabet Phonics* [Cox, 1992]; *Kindergarten Peer Assisted Learning*, or *KPALS* [Mathes, Torgeson, & Howard, 2001]). These programs have similar features of instruction that include

- teaching a core set of frequently used consonants and short vowel sounds that represent clear sounds and nonreversible letter forms (e.g., /a/, /i/, /d/, /f/, /g/, /h/, /l/, /n/, /p/, /s/, and /t/). (See Figure 7-6 for a list of 120 words that can be made using these 11 letter–sound correspondences.)
- beginning immediately to blend and segment the sounds to read and spell the words and read the words in decodable text (i.e., text in which most of the words are composed of letter–sound correspondences that have been taught).
- separating the introduction of letter sounds with similar auditory or visual features (e.g., /e/ and /i/, /m/ and /n/, /b and /d/).

- using a consistent key word to assist students in hearing and remembering the sound (e.g., *a apple* /a/, *b boy* /b/).
- teaching that some letters can represent more than one sound. For each letter, first teach the most frequent sound, and then teach other sounds (e.g., in English, /c/ in *cat* then /s/ in *city*, and /g/ in *gate* then /j/ in *Jim*; in Spanish, /g/ in *gato* [cat] then /h/ in *gemelo* [twin]).
- teaching that different letters can make the same sound, such as the /s/ in *sit* and *city*.
- teaching that sounds can be represented by a single letter or a combination of letters (e.g., /e/ in *me* and *meet*).
- adding a kinesthetic component by having students trace or write the letter as they say the sound.
- having students use mirrors and feel their mouths to see and feel how sounds are different.
- color-coding consonants and vowels so that the two categories of sounds are highlighted.

Knowing letter–sound correspondences is a key element in understanding the alphabetic principle and learning to decode and spell unknown words. However, programs that focus too heavily on teaching letter–sound relationships and not on putting them to use in reading

► **Figure 7-6** Words Using 11 Common Letter–Sound Correspondences

i, t, p, n, s, a, d, l, f, h, g

1. it	16. sin	31. tan	46. tap	61. slat	76. lint	91. pass	106. pits
2. if	17. fin	32. pan	47. nap	62. flat	77. hint	92. lass	107. sits
3. in	18. lid	33. Dan	48. sap	63. flap	78. past	93. glass	108. fits
4. tip	19. did	34. fan	49. lap	64. flag	79. fast	94. pill	109. hits
5. nip	20. hid	35. pad	50. gap	65. span	80. last	95. hill	110. pats
6. sip	21. dig	36. sad	51. gas	66. snap	81. list	96. gill	111. hats
7. pip	22. fig	37. dad	52. snip	67. plan	82. lisp	97. still	112. taps
8. lip	23. pig	38. lad	53. slip	68. glad	83. gasp	98. stiff	113. naps
9. pit	24. gig	39. fad	54. spit	69. snag	84. stand	99. sniff	114. gaps
10. sit	25. at	40. had	55. slit	70. and	85. gland	100. staff	115. slips
11. fit	26. an	41. tag	56. flit	71. sand	86. plant	101. add	116. slits
12. lit	27. pat	42. nag	57. tilt	72. hand	87. slant	102. tips	117. flips
13. hit	28. sat	43. lag	58. flip	73. land	88. split	103. nips	118. flaps
14. tin	29. fat	44. sag	59. spin	74. sift	89. splat	104. sips	119. snaps
15. pin	30. hat	45. pal	60. slid	75. lift	90. splint	105. lips	120. lifts

Source: Neuhas Education Center, Bellaire, Texas. Based on A. R. Cox, *Foundations for Literacy: Structures and Techniques for Multisensory Teaching of Written English Skills* (Cambridge, MA: Educators Publishing Services, 1992).

connected text are likely to be ineffective. Through modeling and discussion, students need to understand that the purpose for learning these relationships is to apply them to their reading and writing activities (National Reading Panel, 2000).

Family Participation in Beginning Reading

Parents/guardians are very interested in having information that will allow them to provide the best support possible to their children as they acquire the important early skills related to reading. Consider demonstrating some of the activities that family members can do at home and encouraging them to engage children in fun and meaningful activities that are associated with improved outcomes in reading. The following are some inexpensive or free materials available to families:

• *A Child Becomes a Reader: Birth to Preschool* (2002). This 31-page guide is written for parents/guardians and provides excellent ideas to build early language and sound awareness skills in young children. To order copies of this booklet, contact the National Institute for Literacy at EdPubs, P.O. Box 1398, Jessup, MD 20794–1398. Call 800-228-8813, or e-mail edpuborders@edpubs.org.

• *A Child Becomes a Reader: Kindergarten to Grade 3* (2002). This 63-page guide is written for parents/guardians and provides valuable and exciting ideas and activities that parents can use at home to enhance reading outcomes for their children in kindergarten through third grade. To order copies of this booklet, contact the National Institute for Literacy at EdPubs, P.O. Box 1398, Jessup, MD 20794–1398. Call 800-228-8813, or e-mail edpuborders@edpubs.org.

► **WEB RESOURCES**

Many Web sites also contain valuable information for parents on how to teach young children to read. Some useful sites include the following:

• The Partnership for Reading
  http://www.nifl.gov/partnershipforreading;
• National Institute for Literacy (NIFL)
  http://www.nifl.gov;
• No Child Left Behind Especially for Parents
  http://www.nochildleftbehind.gov/parents;
• The National Association for the Education of Young Children
  http://www.NAEYC.org.

Word Identification, Decoding, and Word Study

What are the definitions of the seven main decoding strategies, and how does each contribute to successful word identification? Being able to quickly and easily recognize words is the key to successful reading (Ehri, 2004; Fletcher et al., 2007). Successful readers identify words automatically, and if a word is unknown, have effective decoding strategies to decipher the word. Successful reading requires students to develop a sight word vocabulary (i.e., words that students recognize without conscious effort) and decoding strategies to support them when they encounter an unknown word (Ehri, 2004; National Reading Panel, 2000).

What Is a Sight Word?

A *sight word* is one students can read quickly and automatically with little delay. When reading words by sight, the words are accessed from information in memory, that is, from one's storehouse of words. For emergent readers, visual cues assist in recognizing familiar words when they are highly contextualized (e.g., a child recognizes *McDonald's* when it is presented with the golden arches but not when the word is presented without that context). Knowledge of letter–sound relationships serves as a powerful system that ties the written forms of specific words to their pronunciations and allows children to recognize words (e.g., *McDonald's* as an individual word). Students more efficiently store words in memory when they group or consolidate words by multiletter units such as onset-rimes, syllables, suffixes, prefixes, and base words. For example, if readers know -tion, in-, and -ing as multiletter units, then learning longer sight words such as *questioning* and *interesting* is easier. Thus, ==teaching key spelling patterns, prefixes and suffixes, and major syllable types can assist students in learning to automatically recognize words and read more fluently== (Juel & Deffes, 2004; Juel & Minden-Cupp, 2000).

You can tell when readers are reading words by sight because they read the words as whole units, with no pauses between smaller units (syllables, sounds), and they read the words within one second of seeing them. To experience how powerful automatic word recognition is, look at Figure 7-7. Say the name of each picture as quickly as you can, and ignore the words printed on the pictures. Was it almost impossible to ignore the words? This occurs because you are processing the words automatically, in this case despite your intention to ignore them. It is particularly important that readers have multiple opportunities to practice reading and spelling words until they become automatic and have word identification or decoding strategies to assist them in decoding a word when it is not automatically recognized.

Decoding Strategies for Identifying Words

What decoding or word identification strategies do readers employ to decode words they do not know automatically? Research on teaching struggling readers, including those with specific reading disabilities, would suggest that seven strategies are helpful in teaching these students to decode words (see Apply the Concept 7-2).

Phonic Analysis

Identify and Blend Letter-Sound Correspondences into Words This is referred to as *phonic analysis* or ==*phonics.*== This strategy builds on the alphabetic principle and assumes that the students have basic levels of phonological awareness and knowledge of some letter–sound correspondences. It entails the process of converting letters into sounds, blending the sounds to form a word, and searching memory to find a known word that resembles those blended sounds. Teachers use many cues to assist students in using phonic analysis to decode words:

- Cue the students to say each sound, and then have them say it fast.

▶ **Figure 7-7** Picture-Naming Task Demonstrating How Words Are Processed Automatically

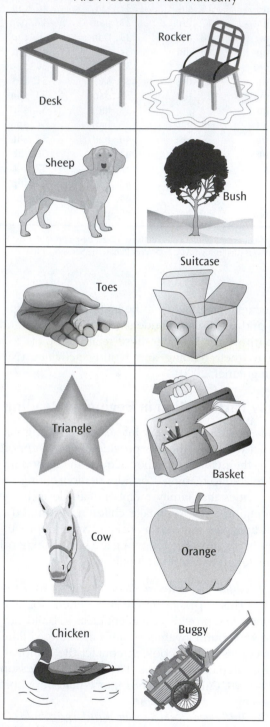

Source: Adapted from L. Ehri (1987), Learning to read and spell words, *Journal of Reading Behavior, 19,* pp. 5–11.

- Demonstrate and have the students point to each letter sound as they say the sound, and then have the students sweep their fingers under the word when they say it fast.
- Place letters apart when saying the sounds, and then push the letters together when you say it fast.

- Begin with simple familiar VC (*in*) and CVC (*him*) words and then move to more complex sound patterns (e.g., CCVC (*slim*), CVCC (*duck*), CVCe (*make*)).

Figure 7-8 provides a scope and sequence for teaching phonics.

▶ **Figure 7-8** Scope and Sequence for Teaching Phonics

Level	Categories	Correspondence	Model Word	Correspondence	Model Word
Preparatory	Letter names, phonemic awareness, rhyming, segmentation, perception of initial consonants				
1	High-frequency initial consonants	s = /s/	sea	r = /r/	rug
		f = /f/	fish	l = /l/	lamp
		m = /m/	men	g = /g/	game
		t = /t/	toy	n = /n/	nine
		d = /d/	dog	h = /h/	hit
	Long vowels: word-ending single-letter vowels and digraphs	e = /ē/	he, me	ee = /ē/	bee, see
		o = /ō/	no, so		
	Lower-frequency initial consonants and x	c = /k/	can	c = /s/	city
		b = /b/	boy	g = /j/	gym
		v = /v/	vase	y = /y/	yo-yo
		j = /j/	jacket	z = /z/	zebra
		p = /p/	pot	x = /ks/	box
		w = /w/	wagon	x = /gs/	example
		k = /k/	kite		
	High-frequency initial consonant digraphs	ch = /ch/	church	th = /th/	thumb
		sh = /sh/	ship	wh = /wh/	wheel
		th = /th/	this		
	Short vowels	a = /a/	hat	u = /u/	pup
		i = /i/	fish	o = /o/	pot
		e = /e/	net		
2	Initial consonant clusters	st = /st/	stop	fr = /fr/	free
		pl = /pl/	play	fl = /fl/	flood
		pr = /pr/	print	str = /str/	street
		gr = /gr/	green	cr = /kr/	cry
		tr = /tr/	tree	sm = /sm/	small
		cl = /kl/	clean	sp = /sp/	speak
		br = /br/	bring	bl = /bl/	blur
		dr = /dr/	drive		
	Final consonant clusters	ld = /ld/	cold	mp = /mp	lamp
		lf = /lf/	shelf	nd = /nd/	hand
		sk = /sk/	mask	nt = /nt/	ant
		st = /st/	best	nk = /dk/	think
	Less frequent digraphs and other consonant elements	ck = /k/	lock	ng = /ng/	hang
		dge = /j/	bridge		
	Long vowels: final e marker	a-e = /a&/	save	e-e = /e&/	these
		i-e = /&&/	five	u-e = /u&/	use	o-e =
/o&/	hope				
	Digraphs and trigraphs	ee = /e&/	green	ow = /o&/	show
		ai/ay = /a&/	aim, play	igh = /&&/	light	oa =

(*continued*)

Level	Categories	Correspondence	Model Word	Correspondence	Model Word
/o&/	boat	ea = /e&/	bread		ea =
/e&/	bean				
	Other vowels	ou/ow = /ow/	out, owl	oo = /oo&/	book
	oi/oy = /oi/	oil, toy		oo = /oo&&/	tool	au/aw =
/aw/	author, paw				
	r vowels	ar = /ar/	car	are = /air/	care
	er = /&r/	her		air = /air/	hair	ir =
/&r/	sir	ear = /i(&)r/	fear		ur =
/&r/	burn	eer = /i(&)r/	steer		or = /or/
	for				
3	Consonants mission	ti = /sh/	action		ssi =
/sh/		t, ti = /ch/		future question	
	Consonant digraphs	ch = /k/	choir	kn = /n/	knee
	ch = /sh/	chef		wr = /r/	wrap	gh =/g/
	ghost	ph = /f/	photo		
	Vowels	y = /e&/	city	o = /aw/	off
	y = /&&/	why		al = /aw/	ball	y = /i/
	gym	ew = /u&/	few		a = /o/
	father	e = /i/	remain		

Source: Thomas G. Gunning, *Creating Literacy Instruction for All Students*, 8th ed. (Boston: Allyn & Bacon, 2010). Copyright © 2010 by Pearson Education. Reprinted by permission of the publisher.

Apply the Concept

7-2	Strategies for Decoding Unknown Words

- *Phonic Analysis:* Identify and blend letter–sound correspondences into words.
- *Onset-Rime:* Use common spelling patterns (onset-rimes) to decode words by blending the initial sound(s) with the spelling pattern or by using analogy.
- *Synthetic and Analytic Phonics.*
- *Structural Analysis:* Use knowledge of word structures such as compound words, root words, suffixes, prefixes, and inflectional endings to decode words and assist with meaning.
- *Syllabication:* Use common syllable types to decode multisyllabic words.
- *Automatic Word Recognition:* Recognize high-frequency and less predictable words and practice to automaticity.
- *Syntax and Semantics:* Use knowledge of word order (syntax) and context (semantics) to support pronunciation and confirm word meaning.
- *Use Other Resources:* Use other resources such as asking someone or using a dictionary.

Onset-Rime

Use Common Spelling Patterns to Decode Words by Blending One salient feature of the English language is the use of spelling patterns, also referred to as onset-rimes, phonograms, or word families. When using spelling patterns to decode an unknown word, students can segment the word between the onset (/bl/ in the word *blend*) and the rime (end) and then blend the onset and rime to make the word (*blend*). Figure 7-9 presents a list of 37 common rimes that make almost 500 words (Wylie & Durrell, 1970) and a more complete list of rimes is presented in Figure 7-10. Guidelines

► **Figure 7-9** Thirty-Seven Common Rime Patterns from Primary-Grade Texts

-ack	-ail	-ain	-ake	-ale
-ame	-an	-ank	-ap	-ash
-at	-ate	-aw	-ay	
	-ell	-est		
-eat				
-ice	-ick	-ide	-ight	-ill
-in	-ine	-ing	-ink	-ip
-ir				
-ock	-oke	-op	-ore	-or
-uck	-ug	-ump	-unk	

	Vowel Sound	Major Spellings	Model Word
Short Vowels	/a/	rag, happen, have	cat
	/e/	get, letter, thread	bed
	/i/	wig, middle, event	fish
	/o/	fox, problem, father	mop
	/u/	bus	cup
Long Vowels	/ā/	name, favor, say, sail	rake
	/ē/	he, even, eat, seed, bean, key, these, either, funny, serious	wheel
	/ī/	hide, tiny, high, lie, sky	nine
	/ō/	vote, open, coat, bowl, old, though	nose
	/ū/	use, human	cube
Other Vowels	/aw/	daughter, law, walk, off, bought	saw
	/oi/	noise, toy	boy
	/o͝o/	wood, should, push	foot
	/o͞o/	soon, new, prove, group, two, fruit, truth	school
	/ow/	tower, south	cow
	/ə/	above, operation, similar, opinion, suppose	banana
r Vowels	/ar/	far, large, heart	car
	/air/	hair, care, where, stair, bear	chair
	/i(ə)r/	dear, steer, here	deer
	/ər/	her, sir, fur, earth	bird
	/i(ə)r/	fire, wire	tire
	/or/	horse, door, tour, more	four

Source: Thomas G. Gunning, *Creating Literacy Instruction for All Students,* 8th ed. (Boston: Allyn & Bacon, 2010). Copyright © 2000 by Pearson Education. Reprinted by permission of the publisher.

for teaching onset-rimes follow the same guidelines as those suggested for teaching phonic analysis except that the word is segmented at the level of onset-rime rather than at the phoneme level. In contrast, Spanish does not use onset-rime to the extent that English does and, consequently, it is generally not taught. However, words that contain rhyming syllables can form word families, such as /sa/ in *masa* (flour), *tasa* (cup), and *casa* (home).

Synthetic and Analytic Phonics Teaching word analysis by having students learn individual letter–sound correspondences or rime patterns and then blending the sounds together to make the word is referred to as a *synthetic method* for teaching word analysis. For example, if the word is *pan*, then the students would say each sound individually (/p/ /a/ /n/) or the onset-rime (/p/ /an/) and then blend them together to make the word *pan*. Using this method, the students are saying the individual sounds or onset-rime and then *synthesizing* or combining them to make the word.

Teachers can also use an *analogy method* for teaching word analysis, thereby providing students with a means of decoding a word other than sounding it out or blending the sounds into a word. When teaching onset-rime, teachers would cue the students to look at the unknown word to determine the spelling pattern (e.g., /an/). Then they think of the key word (e.g., *pan*) or other words with the same spelling pattern (*ran, than, tan*). The students then substitute the initial sound(s) of the unknown word for the initial sound(s) of the key word (*fat*). Cues that students can use to promote decoding by analogy are as follows:

"What words do I know that look the same?"
"What words do I know that end (or begin) with the same letters?"

Structural Analysis
Use Knowledge of Word Structures Such as Compound Words, Root Words, Suffixes, Prefixes, and Inflectional Endings to Decode Words and Assist with Meaning Between the third and seventh grades, children learn from 3,000 to 26,000 words. Most of these words are encountered through reading and learning to be aware of words you don't know the meaning of (word consciousness), and only a limited number are taught directly (Graves, 2006; Nagy & Scott, 2000). Teach students, including secondary students, to analyze words for compound words, root words, prefixes, suffixes, and inflectional endings (Reed, 2008) for the following reasons:

- It provides students with ways to segment longer, multisyllabic words into decodable (and meaningful) parts.
- It assists students in determining the meaning of words.

Assessing and Teaching Reading: Phonological Awareness, Phonics, and Word Recognition

For example, the word *unbelievable* can be segmented into three parts, un-believe-able. Not only does chunking make the word easier to decode, it also tells us about the meaning. In the case of *unbelievable*, *un-* means "not," and *-able* means "is or can be." Hence, *unbelievable* means "something that is not to be believed."

Teaching students to divide words into meaning parts (morphemes) is often first begun by analyzing compound words. Then high-frequency prefixes (e.g., dis-, re-, in-, un-), suffixes (e.g., -er/-or, -ly, -tion/-ion, -ness), and inflectional endings (e.g., -s, -es, -ing, -ed) can be taught. See Apply the Concept 7-3 to learn more about what prefixes, suffixes, and inflectional endings to teach. Table 6-1 provides a list of common prefixes, suffixes, and inflectional endings and their meanings.

Ideas and guidelines for teaching and reinforcing structural analysis include the following:

- Teach meanings along with recognition of the meaning parts.
- Explain and demonstrate how many big words are just smaller words with prefixes, suffixes, and endings.
- Write words on word cards, and cut the cards by meaning parts. Have students say each part and then put the word together and blend the parts together to say the word. Discuss the meaning of each part.
- Ask students to sort or generate words by meaning parts. Following is an example:

Pre- (Before)	In (Not)	Re- (Again)	Super- (Superior)
precaution	incomplete	replace	supermarket
prevent	incompatible	return	superintendent
precede	insignificant	redo	superman

- Present words that have the same prefix or suffix but in which the prefix or suffix has different meanings. Ask students to sort words by their meanings. If students are sorting, leave space so that they can add more words. Following is an example:

People Who Do	Things That Do	More	Words That Have -er
reporter	computer	fatter	cover
geographer	heater	greater	master
runner	dishwasher	shorter	never

- Ask students to decode words they do not know, by covering all but one part of the word and having them identify it, then uncovering the next part and identifying it, and so on. Then have them blend the parts together to read the word.
- Make a class or student dictionary that has each word part, its meaning, and several example words.
- Develop word webs or maps that demonstrate how one root word can make a cadre of related words (see Figure 7-11).

Syllabication

Use Common Syllable Types Many students with reading disabilities have particular difficulty decoding multisyllabic words. This skill becomes critical by about third grade. Six basic syllable configurations or types can be identified in English spelling; these are presented in Table 7-5. The syllable types are useful because they encourage students to look for and recognize print patterns across words.

When teaching syllable types, emphasize that each syllable has one vowel sound. However, the vowel sound may be represented by one or more letters (e.g., CVCe, vowel team). Ideas for teaching include dialogues that promote discovering the generalization, word sorts by syllable types, and games to provide practice. For example, in teaching the CVCe (e.g., *cake, lime, pole, tube*), the following dialogue encourages students to induce the generalization:

Teacher: How many vowel sounds do you hear in each of these words? [Say "five, rope, cape, cube, kite, these."]
Students: One.

Apply the Concept

7-3 Which Prefixes, Suffixes, and Inflectional Endings Should You Teach?

How many prefixes do you need to teach? Four prefixes, un-, re-, in- (and im-, ir-, il- meaning *not*), and dis- account for 58% of all prefixed words. If you add 14 more prefixes (en-/em-, non-, in-/im- (meaning *in*), mis-, sub-, pre-, inter-, fore-, de-, trans-, super-, semi-, anti-, and mid-) you will have accounted for about 95% of words with prefixes (White, Sowell, & Yanagihara, 1989). The inflectional endings of -s/-es, -ed, and -ing account for about 65% of words that have inflectional endings and suffixes. If you add the suffixes -ly, -er/or, -ion/-tion, -ible/-able, -al, -y, -ness, -ity, and -ment, you have accounted for over 85%. Other suffixes that are used frequently include -er/est (comparative), -ic, -ous, -en, -ive, -ful, and -less (White et al., 1989). Remember, it is important to teach the meanings along with how to decode them.

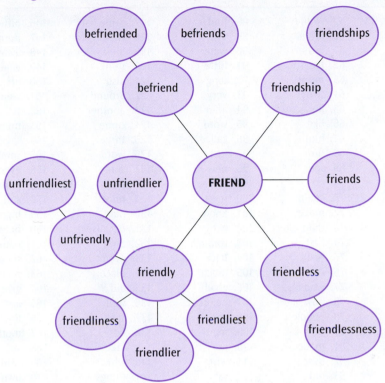

Source: Adapted from C. S. Bos, N. Mather, H. Silver-Pacuilla, & R. Friedmann Narr (2000), Learning to teach early literacy skills—collaboratively, *Teaching Exceptional Children, 32* (5), pp. 38–45.

Teacher: [Write "five, rope, cape, cube, kite, these."] How many vowels do you see?

Students: Two.

Teacher: Which vowel sound do you hear? Tell me what is happening with the *e?*

Students: The first vowel is long, and you do not hear the *e.*

Demonstrate how adding the *e* to the end of CVC words makes the short vowel change to a long sound (*cap* becomes *cape, kit* becomes *kite*). For younger students, teachers may want to generate a story about how the *e* bosses the vowel and makes it a long vowel sound—hence, "The Bossy E." Books such as *Market Day for Mrs. Wordy* also demonstrate the concept.

Automatic Word Recognition

Automatically Recognize High-Frequency and Less Phonetically Regular Words Regardless of their letter–sound predictability, words need to be taught so that they are automatically recognized. Furthermore, it is not practical to teach students to analyze all words in the English language because the patterns they follow may not occur frequently enough to teach. Figure 7-12 presents a list of

Table 7-5 Six Syllable Types

Type	Description/Examples
Closed (CVC)	Ends in at least one consonant; vowel is short: *bed, lost,* and *magnet,* dap- in *dapple,* hos- in *hostel*
Open (CV)	Ends in one vowel; vowel is long: mo- in *moment,* ti- in *tiger,* ta- in *table,* me
Consonant-Vowel-Consonant-e (CVCe)	Ends in one vowel, one consonant, and a final *e;* vowel is long, the final *e* is silent: *name, slope, five,* -pite in *despite,* -pete in *compete*
Vowel Team (CVVC)	Uses two adjacent vowels; sounds of vowel teams vary: *rain, sweet,* -geal in *congeal,* train- in *trainer,* bea- in *beagle*
R-controlled (CV+r)	Vowel is followed by /r/ and vowel pronunciation is affected by /r/: *fern, burn, car, forge, charter*
Consonant-le (-C+le)	Unaccented final syllable with a consonant plus /l/ and silent *e:* -dle in *candle,* -tle in *little,* -zle in *puzzle*

1. the	30. had	59. would	88. find	117. same	146. different	175. am
2. of	31. but	60. other	89. use	118. right	147. numbers	176. us
3. and	32. what	61. into	90. water	119. look	148. away	177. left
4. a	33. all	62. has	91. little	120. think	149. again	178. end
5. to	34. were	63. more	92. long	121. also	150. off	179. along
6. in	35. when	64. two	93. very	122. around	151. went	180. while
7. as	36. we	65. her	94. after	123. another	152. tell	181. sound
8. you	37. there	66. like	95. word	124. came	153. men	182. house
9. that	38. can	67. him	96. called	125. three	154. say	183. might
10. it	39. an	68. time	97. just	126. word	155. small	184. next
11. he	40. your	69. see	98. new	127. come	156. every	185. below
12. for	41. which	70. no	99. where	128. work	157. found	186. saw
13. was	42. their	71. could	100. most	129. must	158. still	187. something
14. on	43. said	72. make	101. know	130. part	159. big	188. thought
15. are	44. if	73. than	102. get	131. because	160. between	189. both
16. as	45. will	74. first	103. through	132. does	161. name	190. few
17. with	46. do	75. been	104. back	133. even	162. should	191. those
18. his	47. each	76. its	105. much	134. place	163. home	192. school
19. they	48. about	77. who	106. good	135. old	164. give	193. show
20. at	49. how	78. now	107. before	136. well	165. air	194. always
21. be	50. up	79. people	108. go	137. such	166. line	195. looked
22. this	51. our	80. my	109. man	138. here	167. mother	196. large
23. from	52. then	81. made	110. our	139. take	168. set	197. often
24. I	53. them	82. over	111. write	140. why	169. world	198. together
25. have	54. she	83. did	112. sat	141. things	170. own	199. ask
26. not	55. many	84. down	113. me	142. great	171. under	200. turn
27. or	56. some	85. way	114. day	143. help	172. last	
28. by	57. so	86. only	115. too	144. put	173. read	
29. one	58. these	87. may	116. any	145. years	174. never	

Source: Thomas G. Gunning, *Creating Literacy Instruction for All Children,* 7th ed. (Boston: Allyn & Bacon, 2010). Copyright © 2010 by Pearson Education. Reprinted by permission of the publisher. Adapted from S. M. Zeno, S. H. Ivens, R. T. Millard, & R. Duvvuri, *The Educator's Word Frequency Guide* (Brewster, NY: Touchstone Applied Science Associates, 1995).

200 high-frequency words in order of their frequency of occurrence. This list is drawn from a compilation of words that occur in books and other materials read by school children and make up about 60% of the words found in these texts (Zeno, Ivens, Millard, & Duvvuri, 1995). For example, the most frequently occurring word, *the*, makes up about 2% of words.

Two factors should be considered in deciding what words to teach as high-frequency words: utility and ease of learning (Gunning, 2010). The biggest payoff for students will be learning words that occur most frequently. The words *the, of, and, a, to, in, is, you, that,* and *it* account for more than 20% of the words that students will encounter. In considering the ease of learning, nouns and words with a distinctive shape are generally easier to learn. With struggling readers, teachers should first teach the words that the students will encounter most frequently.

The following guidelines can be used for teaching less predictable words (Cunningham, 2008; Gunning, 2010):

- Teach the most frequently occurring words.
- Check to make sure that students understand word meaning, particularly if they have limited language, a specific language disability, or are English-language learners (ELLs).
- Introduce new words before students encounter them in text.
- Limit the number of words that are introduced in a single lesson.
- Reinforce associations by adding a kinesthetic component such as tracing, copying, and writing from memory.
- Introduce visually similar words (e.g., *where* and *were, was* and *saw*) in separate lessons to avoid confusion.
- Ask students to compare visually similar words (e.g., *what* with *when*) and highlight the differences between the two words.
- Provide multiple opportunities for students to read words in text and as single words until they automatically recognize the words.
- Review words that have been taught previously, particularly if the students miscall them when reading text.
- Provide opportunities for students to get automatic at recognizing words, such as with games that require quick word recognition or power writing (i.e., writing the words multiple times in a short length of time).

Syntax and Semantics

Use Knowledge of Word Order (Syntax) and Context (Semantics) to Support Pronunciation and Confirm Word Meaning Although students with reading difficulties often rely too heavily on syntax and context to decode unknown words (Briggs, Austin, & Underwood, 1984), good readers use syntax and context to cross-check their pronunciation and monitor comprehension (Share & Stanovich, 1995; Torgesen, 1999). Key questions that students can ask are as follows:

"Does that sound right here?"
"Does that make sense?"

Students should first be taught to decode unknown words using phonics, structural analysis, and syllabication. Then teach them to cross-check pronunciation by asking whether words "make sense."

In looking at these seven word-decoding strategies, instruction for students who are having difficulty learning provides systematic instruction in letter–sound correspondences, phonic and structural analysis, and syllabication because they are the powerful strategies for reading text in alphabetic writing systems. In addition, reading instruction should provide numerous and varied opportunities to read and write with most of the reader's attention focusing on comprehension.

Teaching Phonics, Word Recognition, and Word Study

How can the use of explicit and implicit code instruction be compared? Jamal, a third grader, has the lowest reading level in his class, and he is not making progress in reading. When he reads first-grade-level texts out loud, the teacher assists him in pronouncing about 30% of the words. He reads slowly and cannot remember previously known words. He knows fewer than 30 sight words, and he applies inconsistent strategies to decode words. Sometimes he attempts to sound out a word letter by letter, but he has difficulty with the letter–sound relationships beyond the first several letters, particularly the vowel sounds, as well as difficulty in accurately blending the sounds together. Hence, this strategy rarely results in his pronouncing the words correctly. Even though Jamal struggles in decoding the individual words, he can generally get the meaning of these simple texts. He has good oral language skills, and his life experiences result in his being familiar with much of the content of what he reads (he has adequate background knowledge). His math skills are at a third-grade level, although he has not yet learned his math facts to the automatic level.

Lupita, another third grader, is also struggling to learn to read. Like Jamal, she is reading at the first-grade level, and she has a sight vocabulary of about 40 words in Spanish and 25 in English. When she entered kindergarten, she had limited oral language proficiency in both Spanish and English. She is in a bilingual program that initially taught reading in Spanish but began transitioning her to English in second grade. This year, much of the reading instruction is in English. Like Jamal, she has difficulty remembering words automatically, and her reading, even of very easy text, is slow and laborious. Her decoding strategies rely primarily on sounding out words, but she does not know many of the letter–sound correspondences and has difficulty blending. When she does not recognize a word, her most consistent strategy is to look to the teacher for assistance. Lupita's oral language in both Spanish and English is low. Although she communicates with her friends, she is shy about responding in class and appears to have limited background experiences to assist her understanding what she is reading or learning. Lupita does well in basic math but has difficulty with word problems.

In beginning to work with students who have limited sight words and word identification strategies, like Jamal and Lupita, it is helpful not only to determine the students' current strategies, but also to determine what instructional approaches have been used previously, how consistently, for how long, and with what success. It is also helpful to use the intervention research to inform the teacher's decision making. If the school the student is attending is using an RTI model, data about previous interventions may be available.

Beginning reading approaches that emphasize explicit, direct teaching of phonological awareness and word identification strategies that rely on using phonics, onset-rime, and structural analysis result in greater gains in word recognition and comprehension than approaches in which phonological awareness and phonics are more implicitly taught (National Reading Panel, 2000). Consequently, explicit code instruction approaches should be a part of a balanced reading approach for most students with special needs.

> ▶ **WEB RESOURCES**
> For helpful Web sites on learning more about explicit code instruction see:
> - Reading Rockets
>   http://www.readingrockets.org;
> - International Dyslexia Association
>   http://www.interdys.org;
> - International Reading Association
>   http://www.reading.org;
> - Vaughn Gross Center for Reading at the University of Texas
>   http://www.texasreading.org;
> - Florida Center for Reading at the Florida State University
>   http://www.fcrr.org;
> - LD Online
>   http://www.ldonline.org.

Explicit Code Instruction

Explicit code approaches teach phonological awareness; letter–sound correspondences; the alphabetic principle; and the use of phonic analysis, structural analysis, and syllabication to decode unknown words. They emphasize three instructional features:

1. Systematic instruction of letter–sound correspondences and teaching students to blend the sounds to make words and segment sounds to spell words
2. Scaffolded instruction so that modeling, guidance, and positive and corrective feedback are integral features of instruction
3. Multiple opportunities for practice and review in various contexts (e.g., games with words cards, constructing sentences, reading texts)

Typically, the beginning reading materials that are associated with these approaches are controlled for the phonic and structural patterns they use; hence, they are referred to as *decodable text*. See Apply the Concept 7-4 for information about different text types and their purposes related to teaching students beginning reading.

Linguistic Approach: Onset-Rime and Word Families

The linguistic approach uses controlled text and word families (onset-rimes, phonograms, or spelling patterns) such as -at, -ight, and -ent to teach word recognition. This approach is particularly useful for students with reading problems.

Beck (2006) describes word-building sequences in which word types are organized into four categories.

- The A category addresses CVC words and short vowels with blends and digraphs. Students learn to read simple word combinations with a minimal number of variations in letter–sound combinations and then increasingly more complex letter combinations. Words like *sat, lit, sand* are learned first progressing to more complex letter combinations such as pitch, right, and fling.
- The B category addresses instruction in CVCe words (e.g., *rate, bike, tone*). The words are organized based on the complexity of their patterns and thus teachers can readily determine where students are having difficulty and what to reteach.
- The C category addresses instruction in long-vowel digraphs and vowel pairs that have the same vowel phoneme (e.g., *pail, day*).
- The D category focuses on r-controlled vowels such as *car, turn*, and *fern*.

 *Apply the Concept*

| 7-4 | **Text Types and How They Facilitate Learning to Read** |

For students with learning and behavior problems, matching the text type with the level and purpose for instruction provides a scaffold that supports students as they learn to read as well as providing them with opportunities to practice what they are learning (Palincsar & Duke, 2004).

Beginning text can be classified into five general categories, each of which serves a different but complementary purpose for teaching students to read.

Type of Text and Characteristics

Predictable/Pattern Language

- Repeated language patterns with accompanying pictures that make it easy to predict what the rest of the text says
- Control of language pattern, rhyme, rhythm, sentence structure with difficulty increasing gradually across levels of text
- Example of text: "I have a soccer ball (picture of soccer ball). I have a basketball (picture). I have a baseball (picture). I have a kick ball (picture). I like to play ball."

Types

- Patterned text with picture/text match
- Cumulative pattern with information added on each page (e.g., "I ate an apple. I ate an apple and some grapes. I ate an apple, some grapes, and three bananas. I have a stomachache.")
- Familiar poems and songs

Support for Beginning Reading

Emphasizes Student Use of

- Memory
- Context and picture clues
- Repeating language patterns
- Repeating reading of text

Emphasizes Teacher Use of

- Modeling the concept that print has meaning
- Modeling how books work (e.g., concept of a sentence, word; directionality)
- Developing oral reading fluency and expression

Decodable Text

- Text that introduces sound–symbol relationships, onset-rimes, and sight words in a controlled sequence so that difficulty level increases across levels
- Text that provides opportunities to apply the alphabetic principle and begin reading using the letter–sound correspondences and onset-rimes that have been taught
- Control for words, sound–symbol relationships, onset-rimes, sentence structure
- Example: "Peg had a pet pup. The pup was sad. The pup wanted to get fed, but Peg was in bed. The pup ran to Peg's bed."

Types

- Emphasizes onset-rimes such as "The fat cat sat on the hat." Sometimes called *linguistic readers*.
- Emphasizes systematic introduction of sound/symbol relationships, usually starting with a few consonants and short vowels in CVC words. Sometimes called *phonic readers*.

Emphasizes Student Use of

- Blending sounds and sounding out words to decode them
- Using onset-rimes to make words and using analogy to decode words (e.g., "If I know *pit*, then this word must be *lit*.")
- Learning to recognize less predictable words by sight as whole words (e.g., *was, come*)

Emphasizes Teacher Use of

- Modeling how to blend and segment sounds and providing independent practice in these skills
- Developing students' letter–sound and simple spelling pattern knowledge
- Sounding out words when unknown
- Using onset-rime or word chunks to decode words
- Developing independent, fluent reading of words, sentences, and connected text

Transitional Text

- Integrates predictable and decodable text so that across levels predictability decreases and decodability increases
- Example: "So she said to Grandpa, 'Can you rock Nick for a little while? Maybe you can get him to stop.' 'Sure,' Grandpa said. 'Now I can try.' But Grandpa had no luck. So he said to me. 'Can you play with Nick for a little while? Maybe you can get him to stop.' 'Sure,' I said. 'I will pick him up. It's my turn to try!'" (*Pick Up Nick* by Kate McGroven, pp. 10–14).

Emphasizes Student Use of

- Diminishing use of memory and context clues to identify words
- Increasing use of blending sounds, sounding out words, and onset-rime to decode unknown words
- Learning to recognize less predictable words by sight

Emphasizes Teacher Use of

- Modeling how to blend and segment sounds
- Modeling how to sound out and use onset-rime to decode unknown words
- Developing independent, fluent reading of words, sentences, and connected text

Easy Reader Text

- Series of books that gradually increase in difficulty across levels but are less controlled than predictable, decodable, or transitional texts
- Less control of words with more difficult high-frequency words, more polysyllabic words, and more complex sentences
- More complex plot and information and more text per page
- Some use of short chapters
- Example: "'And it means that we can begin a whole new year together, Toad. Think of it,' said Frog. 'We will skip through the meadows and run through the woods and swim in the river?'" (*Frog and Toad Are Friends* by Arnold Lobel, p. 8).

Emphasizes Student Use of

- Using simple syllabication, prefixes/suffixes, and chunking with polysyllabic words (e.g., *unprepared*) and using more complex spelling patterns (e.g., *fright*)
- Using sight word knowledge and working on automaticity and fluency

Emphasizes Teacher Use of

- Modeling more complex decoding strategies using more difficult words
- Developing student's oral reading fluency and expression
- Modeling comprehension strategies while reading aloud

Authentic Literature and Nonfiction

- Text that is written with limited regard for word or sentence difficulty and provides more complex plots and information
- Varies widely in style and genre

Examples:

- *Peter Rabbit* by Beatrix Potter
- *Owl Moon* by Jane Yolen
- *Bearman: Exploring the World of Black Bears* by Laurence Pringle

Emphasizes Student Use of

- Listening and reading comprehension strategies
- Developing knowledge of different writing styles and genres
- Applying advanced decoding strategies in less controlled texts

Emphasizes Teacher Use of

- Reading for enjoyment and modeling fluency when reading aloud
- Motivating students and creating interest in reading
- Discussing literature and teaching listening/reading/comprehension strategies

Linguistic Approach—Onset-Rime and Word Families

PROCEDURES: The linguistic approach is built on a salient feature of the English language, that is, onset-rime. Figure 7-9 presents a list of 37 common rimes and an even more complete list is found in Figure 7-10. In teaching onset-rime, words are segmented and blended at the onset-rime level rather than the phoneme level, and words are taught in related groups that are often referred to as *word families* (e.g., -at: *cat, fat, bat, sat, rat;* -ight: *right, might, fight*). Sight or less phonetically regular words are kept to a minimum. Figure 7-13 provides an example of a beginning text from a typical linguistic reader. These readers give the students extensive practice with the word families and systematically introduce onset-rime patterns. Figure 7-14 presents a list of selected linguistic reading programs and linguistic readers.

When students cannot identify a word-family word, one strategy is to use a synthetic method of decoding by having them segment the word at the onset-rime level (e.g., for the word *flat*, cover the /fl/ and have the student read the /at/, then cover the /at/ and have the student give the sound /fl/, and then expose the whole word and have the student blend the two segments together to make the word *flat*). Another strategy is to use an analogy method in which the students think of another word, or the key word, they know with the same rime pattern (e.g., *cat*) and then substitute the initial sound(s) to make the word *flat*. Activities such as word sorts in which students sort words by word families, constructing word walls using onset-rime patterns, making word family houses (see Figure 7-15), and playing games such as Word Family Concentration and Can You Write a Word That Rimes With are all ways of reinforcing onset-rime patterns.

COMMENTS: Teaching students about onset-rime and word families gives them another context for understanding the alphabetic principle and how English sounds map to print. It also reinforces the phonological awareness skill of rhyming. The use of a linguistic approach and linguistic readers provides struggling readers with multiple opportunities to learn and practice onset-rime patterns. Some students benefit from decoding at the phoneme level (e.g., /c-a-t/) in addition to learning decoding at the onset-rime level (e.g., /c-at/). Students with reading problems who are instructed in both these decoding methods make the greatest gains in reading (Lovett, Lacerenza, Borden, Frijters, Steinbach, & De Palma, 2000). Several cautions should be mentioned in regard to this approach. First, like other explicit code instruction, the texts often provide limited opportunities

▶ **Figure 7-13** Sample Linguistic Reading Story

Nat and the Rat

Nat is a cat.
She is a fat cat.
She likes to sit on her mat.
Dad likes to pat Nat.
One day Nat sat on Dad's lap for a pat.
Nat saw a rat.
She jumped off Dad's lap and ran after the rat.
That made Nat tired.
So Nat sat on her mat.

▶ **Figure 7-14** Selected Linguistic Reading Programs and Readers

---

The Basic Reading Series, Rasmussen, D., and Goldberg, L., 2000, Columbus, OH: SRA/McGraw-Hill.

Foundations, 2004, Bothell, WA: The Wright Group/McGraw-Hill.

Let's Read: A Linguistic Reading Program, Bloomfield, L., and Barnhart, R. K., 1965, 1994–1997, Cambridge, MA: Educators Publishing Service.

Merrill Reading Program, Bertin, P. et al., 1999, Columbus, OH: SRA/McGraw-Hill.

Preventing Academic Failure, Bertin, P., and Perlman, E., 1999, Columbus, OH: SRA/McGraw-Hill.

Ready Readers, 2004, Parsippany, NJ: Modern Curriculum Press/Pearson.

Sullivan's Programmed Reading (3rd ed.), Buchanan, C., 1988, Honesdale, PA: Phoenix Learning Resources.

Sundance Phonic Letters, Sounds, Readers, 1998–1999, Northborough, MA: Sundance.

▶ **Figure 7-15** Word Family House

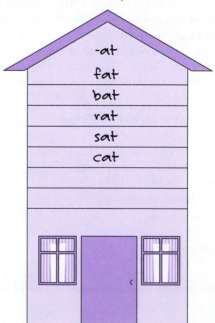

-at
fat
bat
rat
sat
cat

for the development of comprehension. Therefore, the use of children's narrative and expository literature should be incorporated into the reading program to develop listening comprehension. To demonstrate this point, reread the text given in Figure 7-13, and then try to generate five comprehension questions. Second, some words that are introduced in a family may represent unfamiliar or abstract concepts. For example, when learning the -og family, a student may be asked to read about "the fog in the bog."

Reading Mastery and Corrective Reading *Reading Mastery: Rainbow Edition* (Engelmann et al., 1995) and *Corrective Reading* (Engelmann et al., 1999) are highly structured, systematic reading programs that use a direct instruction model for teaching (Carnine, Silbert, & Kame'enui, 1997) and a synthetic method for teaching phonics and structural analysis. These programs directly teach individual sound–symbol relationships, blending of sounds, and how to build these sounds into words. The programs include components in decoding and comprehension, with comprehension focusing on the systematic development of logical reasoning skills and the use of questioning to promote comprehension. Whereas *Reading Mastery* is designed for elementary-level students, *Corrective Reading* is designed for students in grades 4 through 12 who have not mastered decoding and comprehension skills. Both programs are best taught in small- to medium-sized groups.

 ● **EVIDENCE-BASED PRACTICE**

Reading Mastery and Corrective Reading

PROCEDURES: *Reading Mastery* and *Corrective Reading* are built on principles of direct instruction (Carnine et al., 1997), which for reading include the following:

- Design instruction to maximize the amount of time students are engaged (e.g., students work in small groups with teacher; students give responses in unison after adequate wait time so that all students have time to think).
- Teach students to rely on strategies rather than require them to memorize information (e.g., teach several letter sounds such as /m/, /t/, /s/, /f/, /a/, and /i/ and the sounding-out strategy to decode words).
- Teach procedures to generalize knowledge (e.g., have students apply the sounding-out strategy to new sounds to build additional words).
- Use a teaching format that includes an introduction stage, followed by guided practice, independent practice, and review.
- Teach to mastery (specific criterion level).
- Teach one skill or strategy at a time.
- Systematically teach skills and strategies in a cumulative manner.

- Prerequisite knowledge or skills are taught first (e.g., sounds of letters before words).
- Instances that are consistent with the strategy are introduced before exceptions (e.g., teach consistent CVCe words such as *gave* and *made* before exceptions such as *have*).
- High-utility knowledge is introduced before less useful knowledge (e.g., teach frequent irregular words such as *of* and *was* before less frequent ones such as *heir* and *neon*).
- Easy skills are taught before more difficult ones.
- Information and strategies that are likely to be confused are introduced separately (e.g., letters *b* and *d* and words *were* and *where*).
- Systematic review and practice are provided.
- Monitor student performance and provide corrective feedback.
- Use a reinforcement system that promotes student engagement and learning.

In both programs, students are taught a consistent method of responding to sounds and sounding out words. Using the guide in Figure 7-16, teachers touch the first ball of the arrow and cue as follows:

"Say it with me or sound it out. Get ready."

They touch quickly under each sound, saying each sound: /rrreeed/. They repeat until students are consistent and then cue as follows:

"Say it fast. What sound or what word?"

They repeat until students consistently respond with the sound or word.

In both programs, the teacher is given specific procedures to follow, including scripted lessons. These scripted lessons specify what the teacher is to say and include hand signals. Part of an early lesson from *Corrective Reading: Word Attack Basics—Decoding A* is presented in Figure 7-17. Each lesson contains multiple exercises that focus on word attack skills such as sound identification, pronunciations, say the sounds, word reading, sentence reading, story reading, and spelling from dictation. Lessons are designed to last from 30 to 50 minutes with time provided for direct teaching, group reading, individual reading practice, and monitoring of progress with feedback. Both programs have placement tests.

Whereas *Corrective Reading* uses standard print, the initial levels of *Reading Mastery* employ modified print that includes marking the long vowel sounds and reducing

▶ **Figure 7-16** Guide for Sounding Out a Word

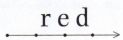

Exercise 2
Pronunciations

Note: Do not write the words on the board. This is an oral exercise.

Task A

1. Listen. He was mad. [Pause.] **Mad.** Say it. [Signal.] *Mad.*
2. Next word. Listen. They wrestled on a mat. [Pause.] **Mat.** Say it. [Signal.] *Mat.*
3. Next word: **ram.** Say it. [Signal.] *Ram.*
4. [Repeat step 3 for *sat, reem, seem.*]
5. [Repeat all the words until firm.]

Task B Sit, rim, fin

1. I'll say words that have the sound iii. What sound? [Signal.] *iii.* Yes, *iii.*
2. [Repeat step 1 until firm.]
3. Listen: **sit, rim, fin.** Your turn: **sit.** Say it. [Signal.] *Sit.* Yes, *sit.*
4. Next word: **rim.** Say it. [Signal.] *Rim.* Yes, *rim.*
5. Next word: **fin.** Say it. [Signal.] *Fin.* Yes, *fin.*
6. [Repeat steps 3–5 until firm.]
7. What's the middle sound in the word rrriiimmm? [Signal.] *iii.* Yes, *iii.*
8. [Repeat step 7 until firm.]

Exercise 3
Say The Sounds

Note: Do not write the words on the board. This is an oral exercise.

1. First you're going to say a word slowly without stopping between the sounds. Then you're going to say the word fast.
2. Listen: *ssseee.* [Hold up a finger for each sound.]
3. Say the sounds in [pause] *ssseee.* Get ready. [Hold up a finger for each sound.] *ssseee.* [Repeat until the students say the sounds without stopping.]
4. Say it fast. [Signal.] *See.*
5. What word? [Signal.] *See.* Yes, *see.*
6. [Repeat steps 2–5 for *sad, mad, mat, me, seed, in, if, sat, ran, rat.*]

Exercise 4
Sound Introduction

1. [Point to *i.*] One sound this letter makes is *iii.* What sound? [Touch.] *iii.*
2. [Point to *d.*] This letter makes the sound *d.* What sound? [Touch.] *d.*
3. Say each sound when I touch it.
4. [Point to 1.] What sound? [Touch under] i. *iii.*
5. [Repeat step 4 for d, e, d, r, t, s, ă, m.]

To correct:
   a. [Say the sound loudly as soon as you hear an error.]
   b. [Point to the sound.] This sound is _____. What sound? [Touch.]

c. [Repeat the series of letters until all the students can correctly identify all the sounds in order.]
6. [Point to the circled letters.] The sound for one of these letters is the same as the letter name. That's the name you say when you say the alphabet.
7. [Point to *i.*] Listen: iii. Is that a letter name? [Signal.] *No.* Right, it isn't.
8. [Point to *a.*] Listen: **ăăă.** Is that a letter name? [Signal.] *No.* Right, it isn't.
9. [Point to *e.*] Listen: **eee.** Is that a letter name? [Signal.] *Yes.* Yes, it is. Remember, the sound you're learning for eee is the same as the letter name.

$$\boxed{i} \quad d \quad \boxed{e}$$
$$d \quad r \quad t$$
$$s \quad \boxed{a} \quad m$$

Individual Test

I'll call on different students to say all the sounds. If everybody I call on can say all the sounds without making a mistake, we'll go on to the next exercise. [Call on two or three students. Touch under each sound. Each student says all the sounds.]

Exercise 6
Word Reading

Task A Sat

1. Say each sound when I touch it
   [Point to *a.*] What sound?
   [Touch under *s.*] *sss.*
   [Point to *a.*] What sound?
   [Touch under *a*] **ăăă.**
   [Point to *t.*] What sound?
   [Touch under *t.*] *t.*
2. [Touch the ball of the arrow for *sat.*]
   Now I'm going to sound out the word. I won't stop between the sounds.
   [Touch under *s, a, t* as you say.] **sssăăă.t.**
   [Point to *t.*] What sound?
3. [Touch the ball of the arrow.] Do it with me. Sound it out. Get ready.
   [Touch under *s, a, t.*] **sssaaat.** [Repeat until the students say the sounds without pausing]
4. Again. Sound it out. Get ready. [Touch under *s, a, t.*] **sssaaat.** [Repeat until firm.]
5. All by yourselves. Sound it out. Get ready. [Touch under *s, a, t.*] **sssaaat.** [Repeat until firm.]
6. [Touch the ball of the arrow.] Say it fast. [Slash right, along the arrow. *Sat.*] Yes, you read the word *sat.*

s a t

Source: S. Engelmann, L. Carnine, & G. Johnson, *Corrective Reading: Word-Attack Basics, Teacher Presentation Book I—Decoding A* (Columbus, OH: SRA/McGraw-Hill, 1999), pp. 26–29. Reprinted by permission of the McGraw-Hill Companies.

► **Figure 7-18**   Sample from a Story from *Reading Mastery: Rainbow Edition*

thē fat man and his dog had

a car. thē car did not run.

Source: S. Engelmann & E. C. Bruner, *Reading Mastery I: Rainbow Edition—Storybook I* (Columbus, OH: SRA/McGraw-Hill, 1995), pp. 53–54. Reprinted by permission of the McGraw-Hill Companies.

the size of silent letters (see Figure 7-18). Both programs provide for reading of decodable text; though *Corrective Reading* emphasizes reading expository texts.

Corrective Reading teaches skills in word identification including word attack, decoding strategies, and skill application and skills in comprehension including thinking basics, comprehension skills, and concept applications. The program provides daily feedback and has a built-in reinforcement system.

COMMENTS: Research has demonstrated that these programs are effective for improving the reading skills of students with reading difficulties and students from disadvantaged backgrounds (Becker, 1977; Gersten, Carnine, & Woodward, 1987; Gregory, Hackney, & Gregory, 1982; Grossen, 1999; Kame'enui et al., 1998; Polloway, Epstein, Polloway, Patton, & Ball, 1986; Thorne, 1978; Vitale, Medland, Romance, & Weaver, 1993). Much of the teaching of phonic analysis skills is conducted in an explicit manner, which has been demonstrated to be advantageous for students with learning and behavior problems (Swanson, 1999b). Several cautions should be noted. First, these programs rely heavily on oral presentation by the teacher and oral responses and reading by the students. Second, the programs are highly scripted, making modifications difficult. Third, the nonstandard print used with Levels I and II of *Reading Mastery* may limit some students' access to other decodable books. Although other books with the nonstandard print are available, the number is limited.

Phonic Remedial Reading Lessons The *Phonic Remedial Reading Lessons* (Kirk et al., 1985) were developed in the 1930s to teach phonic analysis skills to students who had mild mental retardation. The lessons follow principles of systematic direct instruction in that they utilize such principles as minimal change, one response to one symbol, progress from easy to hard, frequent review and overlearning, corrective feedback, verbal mediation, and multisensory learning. The lessons are designed as an intensive phonics program to be used individually or in groups of no more than two or three students. They are not recommended as a general technique for teaching

beginning reading; rather, they are a technique to use with students who have not yet learned an efficient method of identifying unknown words (Kirk et al., 1985).

⬤ ⬤ ⬤ **EVIDENCE-BASED PRACTICE**

Phonemic Remedial Reading Lessons

PROCEDURES: The program begins by developing the readiness level for the lessons. Readiness skills include auditory discrimination and auditory sound blending. Figure 7-3 presented a simple procedure for teaching sound blending. Developing readiness also includes learning the sound–symbol associations for the short *a* sound and eleven consonant sounds (i.e., /c/, /d/, /f/, /g/, /h/, /l/, /m/, /p/, /s/, /t/, /w/).

Once these skills have been learned, the first lesson is introduced (see Figure 7-19). For each lesson, students sound out each word in each line, one letter at a time, and then give the complete word. Each lesson is organized into four parts and is based on the principle of minimal change. In the first part, only the initial consonant changes in each sequence; in the second part, only the final consonant changes; in the third part, both the initial and final consonants change; in the fourth part, the space between letters in a word is normal.

In addition to these drill lessons, high-frequency sight words are introduced and highly controlled stories are interspersed throughout the program. Frequent review lessons are also provided.

COMMENTS: This program provides a systematic and intensive approach to teaching phonic analysis skills to beginning readers. However, the approach places little emphasis on comprehension and reading for meaning and incorporates limited practice in connected text. We suggest using other books to give students the opportunity to practice their word identification and comprehension skills with other reading materials.

English-Language Learners and Reading Difficulties To what extent are the practices identified for phonological awareness and phonics appropriate for students who are

Assessing and Teaching Reading: Phonological Awareness, Phonics, and Word Recognition   **217**

► **Figure 7-19** First Lesson from Phonic Remedial Reading Lessons

a

at	sat	mat	hat	fat
am	ham	Sam	Pam	tam
sad	mad	had	lad	dad
wag	sag	tag	lag	hag

sat	sap	Sam	sad	
map	mam	mad	mat	
hag	ham	hat	had	
cat	cap	cad	cam	

sat	am	sad	pat	mad
had	mat	tag	fat	ham
lag	ham	wag	hat	sap
sad	tap	cap	dad	at

map	hag	cat	sat	ham	tap
sap	map	hat	sad	tag	am
Pam	mat	had	tap	hat	dad
fat	mad	at	wag	cap	sag

Source: S. A. Kirk, W. D. Kirk, & E. H. Minskoff, *Phonic Remedial Reading Lessons* (Novato, CA: Academic Therapy Publications, 1985), p. 22. Reprinted by permission.

ELLs? If they are appropriate, how can teachers facilitate their acquisition of these skills in English? Unfortunately, we know substantially more about teaching students with reading difficulties who are monolingual English students than about teaching students who are ELLs. However, there is a growing knowledge base to inform our instruction in early reading with ELLs (Denton, Anthony, Parker, & Hasbrouck, 2004; Gunn, Biglan, Smoklowski, & Ary, 2000; Vaughn, Cirino et al., 2006; Vaughn & Ortiz, 2009). A summary of findings reveals:

- ELLs who were given direct instruction in early reading in English benefited in the number of words read correctly per minute (Gunn et al., 2000).
- Bilingual students with significant reading problems who participated in 22 tutoring sessions in a systematic and explicit approach to phonics and word and sentence reading significantly improved on word identification when compared with controls (Denton et al., 2004).
- Moderate-to-high effect sizes were reported for word attack, passage comprehension, phoneme segmentation, and oral reading fluency among second-grade ELLs at risk for reading disabilities participating in 58 sessions (35 minutes each) of supplemental intervention in group sizes of one to three students (Linan-Thompson, Vaughn, Hickman-Davis, & Kouzekanani, 2003). Only three students made less than 6 months' growth during the 3-month intervention.
- In a study of young children with problems learning to read in English but who spoke Sylheti (a dialect from Bangladesh), students who participated in Jolly Phonics rather than Big Books made significant gains on phonics recognition and recall and writing sounds, as well as on reading words and reading nonwords (Stuart, 1999). Findings indicate that a more structured, systematic approach that includes phonics resulted in better outcomes for ELLs than interventions without these elements.
- Young bilingual students (Spanish/English) with low literacy and oral language skills taught to read in English made considerable gains over their first-grade year and maintained these advantages into second grade (Vaughn, Cirino et al., 2006; Vaughn, Mathes et al., 2006). Similarly, young bilingual students (Spanish/English) with low literacy and oral language skills taught to read in Spanish also made considerable gains and outperformed comparison students and maintained these gains into second grade (Vaughn, Cirino et al., 2006; Vaughn, Linan-Thompson et al., 2006).

Good readers—whether they are monolingual English or ELLs—rely primarily on decoding words (understanding the sound-to-print correspondence, or alphabetic principle). They do not rely primarily on context or pictures to identify words. When they use context, it is to confirm word reading or to better understand text meaning. Well-developed phonics instruction helps ELLs develop the skills and strategies they need to effectively and efficiently establish a map for making sense of how English language works in print. As with monolingual students, phonics instruction is a piece of the reading instruction, not the entire program. Good phonics instruction is well integrated into language activities, story time, and small group support to create a balanced reading program. Learning to read in languages in which the print is less consistently connected to sounds (like English) takes longer than learning to read in languages that have more consistent orthographies, such as Spanish (Seymour, 2006).

Multisensory Structured Language Instruction Multisensory structured language programs combine systematic explicit teaching of phonemic awareness, the alphabetic principle, phonics and structural analysis, syllabication, and decoding with activities that incorporate the visual, auditory, kinesthetic (movement), and tactile (touch) (VAKT) modalities. Multisensory structured language instruction was developed in the 1930s by Samuel Orton, a neuropathologist, and Anne Gillingham, a school psychologist. They developed reading remediation methods that built associations between the modalities such as "having the child trace [the letter] over a pattern drawn by the teacher, at the same time giving its sound or phonetic equivalent" (Orton, 1937, p. 159) or teaching spelling through analysis and writing of the sequence of sounds in words. The content of multisensory structured language programs includes teaching phonology and phonological awareness; sound–symbol associations that must be mastered in two directions: visual to auditory and auditory to visual; syllable instruction; morphology syntax; and semantics. These programs use the following instructional features or principles (McIntyre & Pickering, 1995):

- Multisensory presentation of VAKT modalities are used simultaneously to enhance memory and learning
- Systematic and cumulative progression that follows the logical order of the language, moves from easy to difficult, and provides systematic review to strengthen memory
- Direct instruction that entails the explicit teaching of all concepts, skills, and strategies
- Systematic practice of decoding and spelling skills at the word, sentence, and text levels in controlled, decodable text
- Diagnostic teaching that requires teachers to be adept at individualizing instruction on the basis of careful and continual assessment of students' learning
- Instruction that incorporates synthetic methods (teaching the parts and how they work together to make a whole) and analytic methods (teaching the whole and how it can be broken down into its component parts)

These programs are designed for students with dyslexia or those who are experiencing substantial difficulty learning to read. Examples of multisensory structured language programs in addition to other structured reading programs are presented in Figure 7-20. The Gillingham-Stillman method (Gillingham & Stillman, 1973) is described in more detail. It is designed for third- through sixth-grade students

▶ **Figure 7-20**   Selected Phonics Reading Programs

Alphabetic Phonics and *Foundations for Literacy*, Cox, A. R., Cambridge, MA: Educators Publishing Service.

Fundations: Wilson Language Basics for K–3, Wilson, B. A., 2005, Millbury, MA: Wilson Language Training Corporation.

The Herman Method for Reversing Reading Failure, Herman, R. D., 1993, Sherman Oaks, CA: Herman Method Institute.

Language! The Comprehensive Literacy Curriculum, Greene, J. F., Longmont, CO: Sopris West.

Lindamood Phoneme Sequencing Program for Reading, Spelling, and Speech: The LiPS Program, Lindamood, P., and Lindamood, P., Austin, TX: PRO-ED.

Project Read, Enfield, M. L., and Greene, V., 2006, Bloomington, MN: Language Circle Enterprise.

Read Well, Sprick, M., Longmont, CO: Sopris West.

Recipe for Reading: A Structured Approach to Linguistics, Traub, N., Bloom, F. et al., 2000, Cambridge, MA: Educators Publishing Service.

Wilson Reading System, Wilson, B. A., 2004, Millbury, MA: Wilson Language Training Corporation.

The Writing Road to Reading, 5th ed., Spalding, R. B. and North, M. E., 2003, Phoenix, AZ: Spalding Educational International.

of average or above-average ability and normal sensory acuity who are having difficulty learning to read. With some adaptations, it can be modified to work with both older and younger students.

   EVIDENCE-BASED PRACTICE

Teaching Phonic Generalizations

PROCEDURES: This method teaches students how to identify words by teaching phonic generalizations and how to apply these generalizations in reading and spelling. It is designed to be used as the exclusive method for teaching reading, spelling, and penmanship for a two-year period at minimum.

The method is introduced by discussing the importance of reading and writing, how some children have difficulty learning to read and spell using whole-word methods, and how this method has helped other students. Thereafter, a sequence of lessons is completed, beginning with learning the names of the letters and the letter sounds, learning words through blending sounds, and reading sentences and stories.

Teaching Letters and Sounds. The teaching of letter names and letter sounds employs associations between visual, auditory, and kinesthetic inputs. Each new sound–symbol relationship or phonogram is taught by having the students make three associations:

1. *Association I (reading).* Students learn to associate the written letter with the letter name and then with the letter sound. The teacher shows the students the letter. The students repeat the name. The letter sound is learned by using the same procedure.

2. *Association II (oral spelling).* Students learn to associate the oral sound with the name of the letter. To do this, the teacher says the sound and asks the students to give its corresponding letter.

3. *Association III (written spelling).* The students learn to write the letter through teacher modeling, tracing, copying, and writing the letter from memory. The students then associate the letter sound with the written letter by the teacher directing them to write the letter that has the _____ sound.

The following six features are important to note in teaching these associations:

1. Cursive writing is preferred and suggested over manuscript.
2. Letters are always introduced by a key word.
3. Vowels and consonants are differentiated by different-colored drill cards (e.g., white for consonants, salmon for vowels).
4. The first letters introduced (i.e., *a, b, f, h, i, j, k, m, p,* and *t*) represent clear sounds and nonreversible letter forms.
5. Drill cards are used to introduce each letter and to provide practice in sound and letter identification.
6. The writing procedure is applied to learning all new letters. The procedure for writing is as follows:
   a. The teacher makes the letter.
   b. The students trace the letter.
   c. The students copy it.
   d. The students write it from memory.

Teaching Words. After the first 10 letters and sounds have been learned by using the associations, students begin blending them together into words. Words that can be made from the 10 letters are written on yellow word cards and are kept in student word boxes (jewel cases). Students are taught to read and spell words.

To teach blending and reading, the letter drill cards that form a word (e.g., *b—a—t*) are laid out on the table or put in a pocket chart. The students are asked to give the sounds of the letters in succession, repeating the series of sounds again and again with increasing speed and smoothness until they are saying the word. This procedure is used to learn new words. Timed activities are used to give the students practice reading the words.

To teach spelling, the analysis of words into their component sounds should begin a few days after blending is started. To teach this method of spelling, the teacher pronounces a word the students can read, first quickly and then slowly. The teacher then asks the students, "What sound did you hear first?" and then asks, "What letter says /b/?" The students then find the *b* card. When all cards have been found, the students write the word. Gillingham and Stillman (1973) stress the importance of using this procedure for spelling. After the teacher pronounces /bat/:

1. Students repeat.
2. Students name letters *b-a-t.*
3. Student write, naming each letter while forming it /b-a-t/.
4. Students read *bat.*

This procedure is referred to as simultaneous oral spelling, or SOS. Gillingham and Stillman comment that after a few days of practice in blending and SOS, it should be an almost invariable routine to have students check their own errors. When a word is read wrong, students should be asked to spell what they have just said and match it against the original word. When a word is misspelled orally, the teacher may write the offered spelling and say, "Read this [e.g., *bit*]." The students would respond, "Bit." The teacher would say, "Correct, but I dictated the word /bat/."

As the students continue to learn and practice new words, they also continue to learn new sound–symbol associations or phonograms. As new phonograms are introduced, more and more words are practiced and added to the word boxes. An example of a daily lesson might be the following:

1. Practice Association I with learned phonograms.
2. Practice Association II with learned phonograms.
3. Practice Association III with learned phonograms.
4. Practice timed word reading for automaticity and accuracy.
5. Practice timed spelling and writing words for automaticity and accuracy.

Sentences and Stories. When students can read and write three-letter phonetic words, sentence and story reading is begun. This begins with reading simple, highly structured stories called "Little Stories." These stories are first practiced silently until the students think they can read them perfectly. Students may ask the teacher for assistance. The teacher pronounces nonphonetic words and cues the student to sound out phonetically regular words. Then the students read the sentence or story orally. The story is to be read perfectly with proper inflection. Later, the stories are dictated to the students. An example of a story is as follows:

Sam hit Ann.
Then Ann hit Sam.
Sam ran and Ann ran.
Ann had a tan mitten.
This is Ann's tan mitten.
Ann lost it.
Sam got the mitten.
Sam sent the mitten to Ann.

Multisensory Structured Language Instruction

COMMENTS: For the most part, multisensory structured language programs have been designed and used as remedial programs for students who have not learned to read successfully. Much of the original research that supports their use was clinical case studies summarized in a review by McIntyre and Pickering (1995) and more recently analyzed by Ritchey and Goeke (2006). Studies of older students with reading disabilities, although limited, do indicate that these students make substantial gains when the principles and content of multisensory structure language are employed (Greene, 1996; Torgesen, Wagner, & Rashotte, 1997; Torgesen, Wagner, Rashotte, Alexander, & Conway, 1997). Several considerations are worth keeping in mind when deciding to use structured language programs. First, they are best employed by teachers who have been trained in multisensory procedures. A list of institutions and organizations that offer training can be obtained from the International Dyslexia Association (800-222-3123), Academic Language Therapy Association (972-907-3924), Academy of Orton-Gillingham Practitioners and Educators (914-373-8919), and International Multisensory Structured Language Education Council (972-774-1772). Second, in general, these programs emphasize decoding skills and strategies and use text with such controlled vocabulary that it can be difficult to build comprehension skills. Hence, a number of the programs suggest simultaneously building listening comprehension until students are able to read more conventional text.

Word Study: Making Words, Word Building, and Word Walls Both reading and special educators have stressed the importance of word study as a way of learning the relationships between speech sounds and print, of building word recognition and spelling skills, and of developing vocabulary (Bear, Invernizzi, Templeton, & Johnston, 2000; Cunningham, 2008; Gunning, 2010; Henry, 1997). For students with learning and behavior problems, opportunities to construct words using magnetic letters, letter tiles, or laminated letters provide experience in manipulating sounds to find out how the words are affected. For example, the teacher might start with the sounds /s/, /t/, /r/, /n/, and /a/ and ask, "What two sounds make the word *at*?" The teacher would then ask the students to add a letter sound to the beginning to make the word *sat*. Then the students would be directed to remove the /s/. The teacher would then say, "What sound would you add to the beginning to make the word *rat*? Now listen. We're going to make a three-letter word. Take off the /t/ sound at the end of the word. Now add the sound that will make the word *ran*."

Word Study

PROCEDURES: There are many activities that can be developed around word sorts, building words, and word walls. A number of resource books are available, including the following:

- *Building Words: A Resource Manual for Teaching Word Analysis and Spelling Strategies* (2001) by T. Gunning, Boston: Allyn and Bacon.
- *Making Words* (1994a) and *Making Big Words* (1994b) by P. Cunningham and D. Hall, Parsippany, NJ: Good Apple.
- *Patterns for Success in Reading and Spelling: A Multisensory Approach to Teaching Phonics and Word Analysis* (1996) by M. Henry, Austin, TX: Pro-Ed.
- *Phonics They Use: Words for Reading and Writing* (5th ed.) (2008) by P. Cunningham, New York: Longman.
- *Word Journeys: Assessment-Guided Phonics, Spelling, and Vocabulary Instruction* (2000) by K. Ganske, New York: Guilford Press.
- *Words Their Way: Word Study for Phonics, Vocabulary, and Spelling Instruction* (3rd ed.) (2004) by D. Bear, M., Upper Saddle River, NJ: Pearson.

Making Words (Cunningham & Hall, 1994a) is one method that has been used and adapted for students with learning and behavior problems (Schumm & Vaughn, 1995). Using a specific set of letters (e.g., *a, c, h, r, s, t*), students make approximately 15 words beginning with two-letter words (e.g., *at*) and progressing to three-, four-, and five-letter words (e.g., *tar, cart, star, cash*) until the final "mystery word" is made (e.g., *scratch*). To use *Making Words*, each student needs a set of letters, and the teacher needs a large set of letters and a sentence strip chart to hold the cards and words that are constructed. Before the lesson, the teacher puts the letters the students will need during the lesson in plastic bags and gives a bag to each student. The three steps in the activity are as follows:

1. *Making words.* After the students have identified their letters, the teacher writes the numeral on the board for the number of letters the students are to put in their words. Next, the teacher cues the students to make different two-letter words. For example, with the word *scratch*, the teacher might ask the students to construct the word *at*. When working with a class of students, after each word has been constructed, the teacher selects one student who was correct to use the set of large letters and the chart to spell the word for the other students to check their work. Then the teacher might ask the students to add /c/ to the word *at* to make *cat*, or to make the word *art* and then rearrange the letters to make the word *tar*. The teacher continues to guide students through the

lesson by directing them to make words with their letters. The last word includes all the letters a student has been given for the lesson.

2. *Word sorting.* The teacher puts up on the sentence strip chart all the words the students have constructed. The teacher then asks the students how some of the words are alike, and students sort the words by spelling patterns. For example, the teacher would take the word *car* and have the students find the other words that begin with c—*cars, cash, cart;* or the teacher would take the word *art* and have the students find the other art words—*cart, chart.* Other students hypothesize why the words are alike, which assists the students in seeing the spelling patterns.

3. *Making words quickly.* Students write as many words as they can using the day's letters, writing the words in a Making Words Log. Students first write the letters from the lesson, and when the teacher says, "Go," they write words for 2 minutes.

COMMENTS: Both special education and general education teachers have found this practice an effective and efficient way to organize word identification instruction. Students report that they enjoy the activity and manipulating the letters (Cunningham, 1991; Schumm & Vaughn, 1995). However, Schumm and Vaughn (1995) found it necessary to develop simpler lessons and to focus more on teaching word families with less able readers.

Implicit Code Instruction

In comparison to explicit code instruction approaches, implicit code instruction in general does the following:

- Places more emphasis on using context clues, including picture clues, in decoding unknown words
- Begins by teaching an initial set of sight words
- Uses known words to discover word patterns and phonic generalizations
- Teaches onset-rime and phonic and structural analysis within the context of meaningful stories and books
- Puts less emphasis on systematically controlling the introduction of letter–sound relationships and spelling patterns
- Uses text in which the language patterns are at the sentence level (e.g., "I see a dog," "I see a cat," "I see a bear") rather than the word family or phoneme level (e.g., "The fat cat sat on a mat")

This section presents two implicit code instruction approaches that have been used with students who experience difficulties in developing fluent word recognition and effective word identification strategies: modified language experience and the Fernald (VAKT) method.

Modified Language Experience Approach This approach to teaching early reading facilitates the transfer from oral language to written language by capitalizing on children's linguistic, cognitive, social, and cultural knowledge and abilities (Stauffer, 1970; Wanzek & Vaughn, 2009). These approaches use the students' own language, repeated reading, visual configuration, and context clues to identify words. Several methods for teaching language experience approaches have been developed: Allen's Language Experience Approach in Communication (Allen, 1976; Allen & Allen, 1966–68, 1982); Ashton-Warner's Organic Reading (Ashton-Warner, 1958, 1963, 1972); and Stauffer's Language-Experience Approach (Stauffer, 1970). The modified language experience approach that we describe is designed for students who have limited experience or success with reading and little or no sight vocabularies. The six objectives are as follows:

1. To teach the concept that text is talk written down
2. To teach the metalinguistic skills of sentence and word segmentation
3. To teach left-to-right progression
4. To teach use of semantic and syntactic clues
5. To teach recognition of words both within the context of the experience story and in isolation
6. To teach phonic and structural analysis by discovering patterns in known words

The approach is built on the idea that oral and written language are interdependent and that oral language can serve as the base for the development of written language.

 **EVIDENCE-BASED PRACTICE**

Modified Language Experience Approach

PROCEDURES: The procedures for this modified language experience approach are similar to those suggested by Stauffer (1970). However, more structure and practice have been incorporated into this modification to provide for the needs of students who experience difficulties in learning to read. It is designed to be used individually or with groups of two to five students. At the heart of this approach is the language experience story, a story the students write about events, persons, or things of their choice (see Figure 7-21).

First Day. For the first day of instruction, guidelines for developing a language experience story are:

1. *Provide or select an experience.* Provide or have the students select an experience that is of interest to them. Sometimes a picture can help to stimulate ideas, but be sure the students have experiences related to the picture. Remember—you are relying on the students' memory of the experience and their memory for the language used to describe the experience.

2. *Explain the procedure to the students.* Explain that the students are going to be dictating a story about the selected experience. This story will then become their reading text or book.

► Figure 7-21 Dictated Language Experience Story

Woody Woodpecker was driving a jet to outer space and saw some aliens. And he got on his jet and went to Jupiter and saw some people from outer space and they were driving jets, too.

3. *Discuss the experience.* Discuss the experience with students so that they can begin to think about what they want to put in the dictated story. Students with learning and behavior problems sometimes have difficulty organizing their thoughts. The discussion can serve as time for the students to plan what they want to say. To facilitate the planning process, you may want to write notes or construct a map or web.

4. *Write the dictated story.* Have the students tell the story while you write it. Students should watch as you write or type it. If you are working with several students you may want to write the story on large chart paper. Have each of the students contribute to the story. If you are working with an individual, sit next to the student so that he or she can see what you write. Encourage the students to use natural voices. The language experience story presented in Figure 7-21 was dictated by Sam, a third grader reading at the primer level.

5. *Read the story to the students.* Ask the students to listen to the story to determine whether they want to make any changes. Make changes accordingly.

6. *Have students read the story.* First have the students read the story together with you (choral reading) until they seem comfortable with the story. When you are choral reading, point to the words so that the students focus on the text as they read. Next have the students read individually and pronounce words that they cannot identify. In some cases, a student may give you a lengthy story, yet his or her memory for text is limited. When this occurs, you may work on the story in parts, beginning with only the first several sentences or first paragraph.

7. *Encourage the students to read the story to others.* This is often a very intrinsically reinforcing activity.

8. *Type the story.* If the story has not already been typed, type it and make one copy for each student. Also make a second copy for each student to keep and use for record keeping.

Second Day. For the second day of instruction, guidelines for reading the story are as follows:

1. *Practice reading the story.* Have the students practice reading the story using choral reading, individual reading, and reading to one another. When the students are reading individually and they come to a word they do not recognize, encourage them to look at the word and think of what word would make sense. Having the students read to the end of the sentence can also help them to think of a word that makes sense. If students cannot recall the word, pronounce it.

2. *Focus on individual words and sentences.* Have the students match, locate, and read individual sentences and words in the story. Discuss what markers are used to denote sentences and words. Finally, have the students read the story to themselves and underline the words they think they know.

3. *Check on known words.* Have each student read the story orally. On your copy of the story, record the words the student knows.

4. *Type the words from the story on word cards.* Type the words each student knows from the story on word cards.

Third Day. Guidelines for the third day are as follows:

1. *Practice reading the story.* Repeat the type of activities described in step 1 of the second day.

2. *Focus on individual sentences and words.* Repeat the type of activities described in step 2 of the second day.

3. *Check on known words.* With the word cards in the *same order* as the words in the text, have each student read the word cards, and record the words the student knows.

4. *Practice reading the story.* Repeat the type of activities described in step 1 of the second day.

5. *Focus on sentences and words.* Repeat the type of activities described in step 2 of the second day.

6. *Check on known words.* With the cards in *random order*, have each student read the words, and record the words each student knows.

Fourth Day. Guidelines for the fourth day are as follows:

1. *Check on known words.* Repeat step 3 from the third day, using only the words the student knows from the previous day.

2. *Enter known words in word bank.* Each student should make word cards (3 × 5 index cards or scraps of posterboard work well) for the words that he or she can identify in step 1. These words should be filed by the student in his or her word bank (index card box). Words that the student cannot identify should not be included.

3. *Read, illustrate, and publish the story.* Have the students read the story and decide whether they want to illustrate it and/or put it into a language experience book. Books can be developed for individual students, or one book can be made for the group. Students can then share these books with each other and with other interested people and place them in the library.

Once the students have completed at least one story and have developed 15 to 20 words in their word banks, they can begin to use the banks for a variety of activities, such as generating new sentences, locating words with similar parts (i.e., inflectional endings, beginning sounds, shapes), and categorizing words by use (e.g., action words, naming words, describing words).

As the number of sight words continues to increase, students can write their own stories, using the words from the word bank to assist them. More suggestions for developing activities based on the word bank are given in Apply the Concept 7-5.

COMMENTS: The modified language experience approach provides a method for teaching children initial skills in reading, including the recognition of sight words. The approach utilizes the students' memory, oral language, and background experiences (Robertson, 1999; Wanzek & Vaughn, 2009), as well as visual configuration and context clues. Once the initial sight vocabulary has been built to between 30 and 100 words, students should be encouraged to read other books and stories. Having students record their stories during initial reading and reading on the fourth day allows the teacher to monitor growth.

This approach lends itself to the use of computer technology (Duling, 1999), particularly with the use of word processing, desktop publishing, and multimedia software that incorporates voice and graphics, such as *Children's Writing and Publishing Center* (Learning Company), *Kidwriter II* (Davidson and Associates), and *Kid Pix* (Broderbund), or language experience–based software programs such as *Writing to Read* (Martin & Friedburg, 1986). For example, Stratton, Grindler, and Postell (1992) integrated word processing and photography into a language experience for middle school students.

Activities are incorporated into the approach to encourage the development of the metalinguistic skills of sentence and word segmentation. However, this approach does not present a systematic method for teaching phonic and structural analysis. For students who have difficulty with these skills, a more structured method of teaching phonic and structural analysis may be needed after they have developed an initial sight vocabulary. This approach may not provide some students with enough drill and practice to develop a sight vocabulary. In those cases, it will be necessary to supplement this approach with activities presented in the section on techniques for building sight words.

●●●●●●● *Apply the Concept* ●●●●●●●

7-5

Suggested Activities for Word Bank Cards

1. Alphabetize words in word banks.
2. Match the word with the same word as it occurs in newspapers, magazines, etc.
3. Make a poster of the words known.
4. Complete sentences using word banks. Provide students with a stem or incomplete sentences and have students fill slots with as many different words as possible. Example:

   He ran to the _____. The _____ and _____ ran into the park.

5. Find or categorize words in word banks:

naming words	science words
action words	color words
descriptive words	animal words
words with more than one meaning	names of people
words with the same meaning	interesting words
opposites	funny words
people words	exciting words

6. Locate words beginning the same, ending the same, or meaning the same.
7. Locate words with various endings.
8. Match sentences in stories with words from word bank.
9. Use word bank cards for matching-card games, such as grab and bingo.
10. Organize words into a story. Students might need to borrow words for this use and may wish to illustrate or make a permanent record of it.
11. Delete words from a story. Have students use words from their word banks to complete the story.
12. Scramble the sentences in the story or words in a sentence.
13. Establish class word banks for different classroom centers, such as science words, number words, weather words, house words, family words.

Source: Adapted from R. J. Tierney, J. E. Readence, & E. K. Dishner, *Reading Strategies and Practices: Guide for Improving Instruction* (Boston: Allyn & Bacon, 2005).

Fernald (VAKT) Method The Fernald method (Fernald, 1943, 1988) uses a multisensory or visual-auditory-kinesthetic-tactile (VAKT) approach to teach students to read and write words. This method was used by Grace Fernald and her associates in the clinic school at the University of California at Los Angeles in the 1920s. It is designed for students who have severe difficulties learning and remembering words when reading, who have a limited sight vocabulary, and for whom other methods have not been successful. It is usually taught on an individual basis.

  EVIDENCE-BASED PRACTICE

Fernald Method (VAKT)

PROCEDURES: The Fernald method consists of four stages through which students progress as they learn to identify unknown words more effectively. The first stage, which is the most laborious, requires a multisensory approach and utilizes a language experience format. By the final stage, students are reading books and are able to identify unknown words from the context and their similarity to words or word parts already learned. At this stage, the students are no longer tracing or writing a word to learn it.

Stage One. Guidelines for Stage One are as follows:

1. *Solicit the student's commitment to learn.* Tell the student that you are going to be showing him or her a technique for learning to read unknown words that has been successful with many students who have not learned in other ways. Inform the student that this method will take concentration and effort on his or her part, but it should be successful.

2. *Select a word to learn.* Have the student select a word (regardless of length) that he or she cannot read but would like to learn to read. Discuss the meaning of the word, and listen for the number of syllables.

3. *Write the word.* Sit beside the student, and have him or her watch and listen while you:
   a. Say the word.
   b. Using a broad-tipped marker on a piece of unlined paper approximately 4″ × 11″, write the word in blackboard-size script, or in print if the student does not write in cursive. Say the word as you write it.
   c. Say the word again as you smoothly move your finger underneath the word. See Figure 7-22 for a model.

4. *Model tracing the word.* Model how the student is to trace the word so that he or she might learn it. Do not explain the process, but simply say to the student, "Watch what I do and listen to what I say."
   a. Say the word.
   b. Trace the word using one or two fingers. The fingers should touch the paper in order to receive the tactile stimulation. As you trace the word, say the

▶ **Figure 7-22** Sample Word Using Fernald Technique

word. Fernald (1943) stresses that the student must say each part of the word as he or she traces it. This is necessary to establish the connection between the sound of the word and its form so that the student will eventually recognize the word from the visual stimulus alone. It is important that this vocalization of the word be natural; that is, it should be a repetition of the word as it actually sounds—not stilted or distorted sounding—out of letters or syllables in such a way that the word is lost in the process. The sound for each letter is never given separately or overemphasized. In a longer word, such as *important*, the student says *im* while tracing the first syllable, *por* while tracing the second syllable, and *tant* as he or she traces the last syllable.
   c. Say the word again while moving the tracing finger(s) underneath the word in a sweeping motion.

Model this process several times, and then have the student practice the process. If the student does not complete the process correctly, stop the student when he or she makes an error and cue, "Not quite. Watch me do it again." Continue this procedure until the student is completing the three-stage process correctly.

5. *Trace until learned.* Have the student continue tracing the word until the student thinks that he or she can write the word from memory.

6. *Write from memory.* When the student feels ready, remove the model, and have the student write the word from memory, saying the word as he or she writes. Fernald (1943) stresses that the student should always write the word without looking at the copy. She comments:

> When the child copies the word, looking back and forth from the word he is writing to the copy, he breaks the word up into small and meaningless units. The flow of the hand in writing the word is interrupted and the eye movements are back and forth from the word to the copy instead of those which the eye would make in adjusting to the word as it is being written. This writing of the word without the copy is important at all stages of learning to write and spell. The copying of words is a most serious block to learning to write them correctly and to recognize them after they have been written (p. 37).

7. *File the word.* After the word has been written three times correctly, the student should place it in his or her word bank.

8. *Type the word.* Within an interval of 24 hours, the student should type and read each word learned by using this process. This helps to establish the link between the written and typed word.

The number of words learned per session using this VAKT process depends on the number of tracings a student needs to learn a new word. This number varies greatly among students. We have worked with students who need fewer than five tracings to learn a new word, whereas other students required over 50 tracings when first beginning this approach.

Fernald (1943) reports, "As soon as a child has discovered that he can learn to write words, we let him start 'story writing'" (p. 33). As the student writes a story and comes to a word he or she cannot spell, the tracing process is repeated. These stories should be typed within 24 hours so that the student can read the newly learned words in typed form within the context of the story.

Stage Two. When the student no longer needs to trace words to learn them, he or she moves to Stage Two. In this stage, the teacher writes the requested word in cursive (or manuscript) for the student. The student then simply looks at the word, saying it while looking at it, and then writes it without looking at the copy, saying each part of the word as he or she writes it from memory. As with Stage One, words to be learned are obtained from words the student requests while writing stories. The word bank continues to function as a resource for the student, but a smaller word box can be used, since the teacher is writing the words in ordinary script size.

Stage Three. The student progresses to the third stage when he or she is able to learn directly from the printed word without having it written. In this stage, the student looks at the unknown printed word, and the teacher pronounces it. The student then says the word while looking at it and then writes it from memory. Fernald reports that during this stage, students still read poorly but are able to recognize quite difficult words almost without exception after having written them.

During this stage, the student is encouraged to read as much as and whatever he or she wants. Unknown words are pronounced, and when the passage is finished, the unknown words are learned by using the technique described in the preceding paragraph.

Stage Four. The student is able to recognize new words from their similarity to words or parts of words he or she has already learned. At first, a student may need to pronounce the word and write it on a scrap of paper to assist in remembering it, but later this becomes unnecessary. The student continues to read books that interest him or her. When reading scientific or other difficult material, the student is encouraged to scan the paragraph and lightly underline each word he or she does not know. These words are then discussed for recognition and meaning before reading.

COMMENTS: Empirical evidence lends support to this approach for teaching word identification to students with severe reading disabilities (Berres & Eyer, 1970; Coterell, 1972; Fernald, 1943; Kress & Johnson, 1970; Thorpe & Borden, 1985). Although this approach tends to be successful with such readers, the first several stages are very time consuming for both the teacher and the student, and this approach is appropriate only when other approaches have not been successful.

Techniques for Building Sight Words

Students who read fluently recognize individual words automatically or when they are reading text. Students with reading disabilities struggle with automatic word recognition, which is important not only for words that are decodable (e.g., *and, then, it*), but especially for high-frequency words that are less phonetically regular (e.g., *the, you, was, have*). See Figure 7-12 for a list of high-frequency words. This section presents several techniques that teachers can use to assist students in remembering words.

Sight Word Association Procedure The sight word association procedure (SWAP; Bradley, 1975) uses corrective feedback and drill and practice to assist students in associating spoken words with written form. The procedure is appropriate to use with students who are beginning to learn to identify words across various contexts or texts, or with students who require more practice of new words than their current reading program provides. It is designed to be used individually or with small groups.

 EVIDENCE-BASED PRACTICE

Sight Word Association Procedure

PROCEDURES: Begin by selecting words from the text that the students consistently miscall or do not identify at an automatic level. Write each word on a word card. The procedure for teaching these words (usually three to seven words at a time) is as follows:

1. Discuss the words with students to ensure that they understand the meanings of the words as the words are being used in the text.

2. Present the words to the students one word at a time. Each word is exposed for 5 seconds, and the teacher says the word twice.

3. Shuffle the cards, and ask students to identify the word on each card. Provide corrective feedback by verifying the correctly identified words, giving the correct word for any word that is miscalled, and saying the word if students do not respond in 5 seconds.

4. Present all the words again, using the format given in step 2.

5. Have students identify each word, using the format given in step 3. Repeat this step at least two more times or until they can automatically recognize all the words.

If students continue to have difficulty recognizing a word after the seventh exposure to the word, switch from a recall task to a recognition task. To do this, place several word cards on the table, and have the learners point to each word as you say it. If the students still continue to have difficulty learning the words, use a different technique to teach the words, such as picture association techniques, sentence/word association techniques, or a cloze procedure. A record sheet for keeping track of individual student responses is presented in Figure 7-23. Be sure to review words every several days to determine whether the words are being retained; reteach if necessary.

COMMENTS: This procedure provides a technique for systematically practicing unknown words. It utilizes principles of corrective feedback and mass and distributed practice to teach words. However, there are several important cautions: (1) use in conjunction with an approach to reading that stresses reading text and utilizing other decoding strategies, (2) ensure students know the meanings of the words being taught, (3) give students ample opportunity to read these words in context.

Picture Association Technique Using a key picture to aid in identifying a word can be beneficial (Mastropieri & Scruggs, 1998). This method allows the readers to associate the word with a visual image. It is on this premise that picture association techniques use key pictures to help students associate a spoken word with its written form.

Picture Association Technique

PROCEDURES: Select words that the students are having difficulty identifying when reading. At first, choose words that are easily imaged, such as nouns, verbs, and adjectives. Write each word on a card (usually three to seven words). On a separate card, draw a simple picture, or find a picture and attach it to the card. In some cases, the students may want to draw their own pictures. Use the following procedure to teach the picture–word association:

1. Place each picture in front of the students, labeling each one as you present it. Have the students practice repeating the names of the pictures.

2. Place next to each picture the word it represents, again saying the name of the word. Have students practice saying the names of the words.

3. Have students match the words to the pictures and say the name of the word while matching it. Repeat this process until students easily match the pictures and words.

4. Place the words in front of the students, and have them identify the words as you say them. If they cannot identify the correct word, have them think of the picture to aid in their recognition. If they still cannot point to the word, show them the picture that goes with the word.

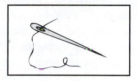 

5. Have students recall the words by showing the word cards one at a time. Again, if students cannot recall a word, have them think of the picture. If they still cannot think of the word, tell them to look at the picture that goes with the word.

6. Continue this procedure until the students can identify all the words at an automatic level. The same

▶ **Figure 7-23** Sight Word Association Procedure (SWAP) Record Sheet

Words	Inital Teaching					Retention			√ Correct 0 Incorrect Comments
	1	2	3	4	5	1	2	3	

Assessing and Teaching Reading: Phonological Awareness, Phonics, and Word Recognition   **227** record sheet as the one used for SWAP (Figure 7-23) can be used for this procedure.

7. Have students review the words on subsequent days and, most important, give them plenty of opportunities to read the words in text. When a student is reading and cannot identify a word, encourage the student to think of the picture.

COMMENTS: This picture association technique assists students in forming visual images that facilitate their identification of words. As with the SWAP, this procedure should be used only as a supplemental technique, and students should be given ample opportunities to read the words in text.

 EVIDENCE-BASED PRACTICE

Sentence–Word Association Technique

This technique encourages students to associate unknown words with a familiar spoken word, phrase, or sentence.

PROCEDURES: Select three to seven words that students are consistently having difficulty recognizing. Discuss these words with the students, and ask them to find the words in the text and read them in a sentence. Tell the students to decide on a key word, phrase, or sentence that will help them to remember the word. For example, for the word *was* a sentence might be "Today he is, yesterday he _____." For the word *there* the sentence might be "Are you _____?" Put the words to be taught on word cards, and put the associated word, phrase, or sentence on separate cards. Teach the associations between the key word, phrase, or sentence and the unknown word, using the same procedures as were described for the picture association technique. After teaching, when a student is reading and comes to one of the new words and cannot remember it, have the student think of the associated clue. If the student cannot think of the associated clue orally, tell them the clue.

INSTRUCTIONAL ACTIVITIES

This section provides instructional activities that are related to phonological awareness, phonics, and word identification. Some of the activities teach new skills; others are best suited for practice and reinforcement of already acquired skills. For each activity, the objective, materials, and teaching procedures are described.

▶ My Sound Book

Objective: To provide students with practice in finding pictures that start with a specific consonant or vowel sound.

Grades: Primary

Materials: (1) A three-ring binder or folder into which "sound pages" can be inserted. (2) Magazines, old books, or workbooks that can be cut up. (3) Stickers, scissors, and glue.

Teaching Procedures: Explain to the students that each of them will be making a book where they can collect and keep pictures and stickers that start with various sounds. Select one sound that the students are learning, and have them write the letter representing the sound on the top of the page. Then have them look through magazines, old books, and workbooks to find pictures starting with the sound. Once they have selected the pictures, have them say the names to you so that you both can determine whether the pictures represent the designated sound. Then have students glue the pictures on the sound pages, leaving room to add other pictures they find while looking for pictures representing other sounds. Have students put the sound page in the notebook and share their pictures with other students. Continue until the book is complete. As students collect stickers, you may want to encourage them to put them in the sound book.

▶ Vowel Match

Objective: To provide students with practice in decoding words that have various vowel sounds.

Grades: Primary and intermediate

Materials: (1) One file folder that is divided into two playing areas that consist of 10 boxes for each player. In each box, paste a picture that illustrates a vowel sound. (2) Thirty to 40 playing cards with pictures illustrating vowel sounds.

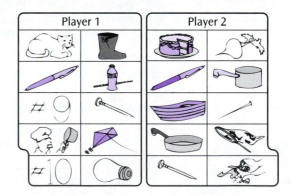

Teaching Procedures: Explain the game to the students. Shuffle the cards and place them face down near the players. Each student draws a card and checks to see whether the vowel sound illustrated on the card matches one of the pictures on his or her side of the game folder. If it does, the player places the card over the picture on the game folder. If the picture does not match, the card is discarded. The first player to cover all the boxes wins the game.

Adaptations: This game is easily adapted to teaching rhyming words and other sounds such as consonant digraphs or blends.

▶ Sight Word Bingo

Objective: To provide students with practice in recognizing words.

Grades: Primary and intermediate

Materials: (1) Posterboard cut into 10″ × 8″ pieces to use for bingo cards. (2) A list of new words students have encountered in their reading. Such lists can be found in the back of basal readers or in books of lists such as *The New Reading Teacher's Book of Lists* (Fry, Fountoukidis, & Polk, 1985). To make the bingo cards, randomly select words from the list, and write them on the card as illustrated. (3) Colored markers.

Word Bingo			
happen	should	night	enough
below	never	complete	thought
grow	where	while	building
every	through	include	were
country	even	important	between

Teaching Procedures: One student (or the teacher) is designated as the caller. Each of the remaining students gets a bingo card. The caller randomly selects a word from the list and says the word. The students place a colored marker on the square in which the word is written. The first person to cover all the squares in a horizontal, vertical, or diagonal row calls, "Bingo." The caller and the student then verify the words. If they are verified, that student wins.

Adaptations: Bingo is a generic game that can be adapted to provide practice for a variety of skills. Following are some examples:

- *Consonant bingo:* Put pictures of objects that start with initial consonants, blends, or digraphs on the bingo cards. The caller says the letters, and the students mark the pictures that have the same consonant, blend, or digraph. This can also be adapted for final consonants.
- *Prefix bingo:* Write prefixes on the bingo cards. The caller says a word with a prefix or gives the definition of a prefix, and the students mark the prefix on their cards.

- *Math fact bingo:* Write the answers to math facts on the bingo cards. The caller says a math fact, and the students mark the answer.

▶ Compound Concentration

Objective: To give students practice in identifying compound words and to illustrate how words may be combined to form compound words.

Grades: Intermediate and secondary

Materials: Thirty-six index cards (3″ × 5″) on which the two parts of 18 compound words have been written. Make sure that each part can only be joined with one other part.

Teaching Procedure: Have a student shuffle the cards and place the cards face down in six rows with six cards each. Each player takes a turn at turning over two cards. The student then decides whether the two words make a compound word. If the words do not make a compound word, then the cards are again turned face down, and the next player takes a turn. If the words make a compound word, then the player gets those two cards and turns over two more cards. The student continues playing until two cards are turned over that do not make a compound word. The game is over when all the cards are matched. The winner is the player with the most cards.

Adaptations: Concentration can be adapted for many skills. Students can match synonyms, antonyms, prefixes, suffixes, initial or final consonants, categories, and math facts.

▶ Go Fish for Rimes

Objective: To give the students practice in identifying and reading words with rimes.

Grades: Intermediate and secondary

Materials: Twenty to 30 index cards (3″ × 5″) on which words with a particular rime pattern (e.g., -ake, -ail, -ime, -ight) are written. Make sure that each word is written on two cards so that students can match them.

Teaching Procedures: Have students shuffle the cards and deal five cards to each player. The rest of the cards are placed face down in a pile on the table. Each player reads his or her own cards. Any player who has two cards that contain the same word reads the word and places the pair of cards face up in front of himself or herself (provide assistance as necessary). After everyone has laid out their pairs, the first student asks one other student whether he or she has a specific word (e.g., "Do you have *rake*?"). The student who was asked looks at his or her cards. If that student has the card, he or she reads the card and hands it to the first student. That student puts the pair face up in front of him or her and takes another turn. If the student who is being asked for a card does not have the card, he or she says, "Go fish," the first student takes a card from the pile, and the next student takes his or her turn. When a student has laid down all of his or her cards, the game is over. The person with the most pairs wins.

Adaptations: Go Fish can be adapted for many skills. Students can match synonyms, antonyms, prefixes, suffixes, or compound words.

FOCUS Answers

▶ **FOCUS Question 1. How can teachers address the two over-arching concepts that guide reading instruction?**

Answer: Reading instruction involves teaching the basic skills necessary to read words accurately and rapidly. Reading instruction also incorporates strategies to assist readers in understanding what they read by expanding vocabulary and using comprehension strategies. There is a general progression of skills, and instruction should be organized into the essential components, the focus of which is based on individual student needs.

▶ **FOCUS Question 2. What are the definitions and examples of instruction of phonological awareness, letter–sound correspondence, and phonics?**

Answer: Phonological awareness is knowing and demonstrating that spoken language can be broken down into smaller units (words, syllables, phonemes). Activities in phonological awareness are conducted orally. For example, a teacher says the word *that*, and students clap the number of sounds they hear (three claps). Letter–sound correspondence is knowing how letter names and sounds relate to each other. Phonics is the idea that words are composed of letters that represent sounds, that those sounds are related to each other (letter–sound correspondence), and that they can be used to pronounce or spell words. Activities involving phonics relate sounds to print and may involve direct teaching of letter sounds, phonemes, and activities to practice the letter–sound relationships. For example, a teacher gives students the phoneme /at/, and students add letters to make additional words (e.g., *cat, that, mat, splat*).

▶ **FOCUS Question 3. What are the definitions of the seven main decoding strategies, and how does each contribute to successful word identification?**

Answer:

1. Phonic analysis involves identifying and blending letter–sound correspondences into words.

2. Onset-rime consists of using common spelling patterns to decode words by blending either individual sounds/patterns or using an analogy method to think of a word with similar sounds/patterns. Knowledge of common rimes assists readers in recognizing a large number of words that contain the core patterns.

3. Synthetic and analytic phonics

4. Structural analysis involves analyzing words to assist with decoding and determining the meanings of words. Structural analysis is particularly effective for decoding longer, multisyllabic words.

5. Knowledge of syllabication assists readers in recognizing similar chunks of print across words.

6. Automatic word recognition is knowing a word without having to decode it. Because certain words are repeated so often (e.g., *the*), reading is made easier when one can automatically recognize high-frequency words that are less phonetically regular.

7. A knowledge of syntax (word order) and semantics (word meaning) can assist readers in cross-checking pronunciation and monitoring comprehension.

▶ **FOCUS Question 4. How can the use of explicit and implicit code instruction be compared?**

Answer: Explicit code approaches teach phonological awareness; letter–sound correspondences; the alphabetic principle; and the use of phonic analysis, structural analysis, and syllabication to decode unknown words. Reading materials associated with this technique generally use decodable texts that highlight specific phonic or structural patterns. Implicit code instruction emphasizes the use of context clues, including picture cues, to decode unknown words. Texts are chosen that will be meaningful to readers and not for particular letter–sound relationships or spelling patterns. Implicit code instruction is often used with emergent readers who have had difficulties developing sight vocabulary and word analysis skills.

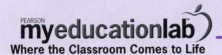

Where the Classroom Comes to Life

The MyEducationLab for this course can help you solidify your comprehension of Chapter 7 concepts.

- Gauge and further develop your understanding of chapter concepts by taking the quizzes and examining the enrichment materials in the Chapters 7 Study Plan.
- Visit Topic 4, Assessing and Teaching Literacy and Language, to connect with challenge-based interactive modules, case study units, and podcasts that provide research-validated information about working with students in inclusive settings, by visiting the IRIS Center Resources.

- Explore Assignments and Activities, assignable exercises showing concepts in action through video, cases, and student and teacher artifacts.
- Practice and strengthen skills essential to quality teaching through the Building Teaching Skills and Dispositions lessons.

8

Assessing and Teaching Reading: Fluency and Comprehension

1. What is reading fluency, and how is progress in fluency monitored?
2. What are effective instructional practices for increasing reading fluency?
3. What assessments and instructional components should be present in a reading comprehension program?
4. What is the purpose of comprehension instruction?

Jeff is a second grader who continues to sound out many words. Consequently, his reading is very slow. Because Jeff uses so much of his cognitive effort reading each word, he has little remaining to concentrate on understanding what he reads.

Shoshanna, a fourth grader, had great difficulty learning to read. After several years of failure, she was taught using a multisensory structured language approach and her word reading improved. However, Shoshanna's reading rate is slow, which interferes with her understanding. When asked to define reading, she places emphasis on reading words correctly rather than on understanding what she reads. Though Jeff and Shoshanna have developed systems for identifying words, they are having difficulties reading fluently—that is, quickly and easily with accuracy and expression.

Why is poor fluency performance a problem? Research indicates that students with significant reading disabilities have difficulty developing fluency and continue to be slow readers into adolescence and adulthood (Chard, Vaughn, & Tyler, 2002; Wexler, Vaughn, Edmonds, & Reutebuch, 2008). Students who are slow and labored readers (low fluency) may benefit from fluency instruction aimed at improving their automatic word recognition and practices focused on assisting them in allocating more effort to constructing meaning from what they are reading.

This chapter addresses reading-related constructs of fluency and comprehension for students with reading problems. One key to becoming a good reader is to engage in reading for learning and enjoyment. Yet students with reading difficulties often do not have as many opportunities to engage in reading during school and do not choose reading as a leisure-time activity.

Teachers can assist students in becoming fluent readers and provide them with a wide choice of literature and other materials to read and discuss so that reading becomes a source of learning, enjoyment, and satisfaction. To reach this goal, it is important to plan instruction that focuses on strategies for building fluency and promoting active reading comprehension as presented in this chapter.

> Chapter 7 addressed the building blocks of reading: foundational skills, such as phonemic awareness, phonics, and word recognition, that serve as a necessary base for acquiring more proficiency in reading.

PEARSON myeducationlab

Visit the MyEducationLab for this course to enhance your understanding of chapter concepts with a personalized Study Plan. You'll also have the opportunity to hone your teaching skills through video-based Assignments and Activities, IRIS Center Resources, and Building Teaching Skills and Dispositions lessons.

Assessing Fluency and Monitoring Student Progress

What is reading fluency, and how is progress in fluency monitored? Fluency is the ability to read a text at an appropriate rate, accurately, and with expression (i.e., *prosody*). We often refer to *fluent readers* as individuals who read with automaticity. By *automaticity* we mean the quick, effortless, and accurate reading of words. It is important to note that although there is emphasis on speed of reading, we do not mean that students should race through what they read without enjoyment or without monitoring their understanding. We are referring to a rate of reading that occurs with little focus or emphasis on decoding individual words. In addition to reading accurately and with appropriate speed, fluency also includes prosody, or reading with phrasing, expression, and in a way that communicates understanding.

Of all of the elements of reading (e.g., phonemic awareness, phonics, word study, comprehension), fluency is the one that is most readily assessed and monitored. That is because in relatively little time, teachers can determine whether students are making adequate progress in fluency and how their progress compares to other students in the same grade at that time of year. Fluency has three parts: rate of reading, accuracy of word reading, and prosody. We typically assess rate and accuracy of reading to determine progress in fluency because prosody is not a particularly strong predictor of reading fluency or comprehension, whereas rate and accuracy of word reading are very good predictors of fluency and comprehension (Stahl & Kuhn, 2002).

Remember that the goal of improving children's rate of reading is not that they read faster, but that they read with such automaticity that they can free up their thinking to understand and enjoy text. With the increased emphasis on oral reading fluency as a progress-monitoring measure, there is concern that some teachers may lose touch with the most important aspect of reading: reading to learn and enjoy text.

Monitoring Student Progress in Fluency

Fluency is most frequently measured by the number of words read correctly per minute (WCPM) and through observations of phrasing, smoothness, and pace. An important reference for teachers to know is the number of WCPM in a specified grade-level passage. For example, Michael reads 50 words per minute in mid-first-grade-level passages. Because Michael is a third-grade student, his fluency indicates that he is considerably behind expectations both in the number of words he reads correctly as well as the level of text he reads. Table 8-1 provides an overview of fluency norms and rates by grade level.

How do you measure WCPM? A teacher selects two to three passages that are unfamiliar to a student and are at

Table 8-1 Reading Fluency Guidelines for Grades 1–8

Grade	Fall	Winter	Spring
1	–	23–47	53–82
2	51–79	72–100	89–117
3	71–99	92–120	107–137
4	94–119	112–139	123–152
5	110–139	127–156	139–168
6	127–153	140–167	150–177
7	128–156	136–165	150–177
8	133–161	146–173	151–177

Source: Adapted from Behavioral Research and Reading, 2005.

a student's instructional reading level, the level at which the student can read with the teacher's support, or independent reading level. Word recognition is around 90% at the instructional level and at or near 100% at the independent level. After selecting the passages, the teacher makes two copies of each passage of text to be used with the targeted student: one for recording errors and one for the student to read. A stopwatch can be used for timing, and it is often helpful to tape-record the student's reading on a monthly basis so that the student can hear as well as see his or her progress.

> ▶ **WEB RESOURCES**
> Many fluency passages are selected and scaled for teacher that provide multiple versions of grade-level texts (see http://www.progressmonitoring.com).

The teacher tells the student, "When I say 'Begin,' start reading aloud at the top of the page. Do your best reading. If you come to a word that you don't know, I'll tell it to you." If a student does not read a word within 3 seconds, the teacher says the word. The student reads for 1 minute. Following along as the student reads, the teacher marks his or her own copy by putting a slash (/) through words that were read incorrectly. This includes mispronunciations, substitutions, omissions, words pronounced after hesitations of more than 3 seconds, and reversals. Insertions, self-corrections, and repetitions should not be counted. The teacher should also note whether the student is having difficulty with phrasing; is ignoring punctuation; is reading slowly, word by word, or laboriously; and/or has frequent extended pauses, false starts, sound-outs, and repetitions. The teacher notes the last word the student read when the minute is up. If the student is in the middle of a sentence when the time is up, the teacher should have the student finish the sentence but count only the words the student read up to the stop point. If using WCPM infrequently (once every 10 weeks), the teacher should use two passages to ensure accuracy.

The following formula is used to calculate fluency:

$$\frac{\text{Number of words read}}{\text{correctly in 1 minute}} - \text{Number of errors}$$

For example, if a student reads 83 words during a 1-minute sample and makes 6 errors, then the WCPM would be 83 minus 6, which equals 77. The scores are averaged across at least two passages to get a mean rate. For example, if on the second reading of a different passage at the same grade level, the student read 84 words correctly but made 11 errors, the WCPM would be 73. The average of 73 and 77 is 75, so during this period, the student's WCPM is recorded as 75.

Guidelines for fluency rates for grades 1 through 8 were presented in Table 8-1. You can use this table to determine the relative performance of your students. For example, you have a student in the fifth grade and at the beginning of the year she is reading 60 WCPM. You can look at the chart and see that students in fifth grade at the beginning of the year read on average 110 to 139 WCPM—well above the 60 WCPM of your student. Looking at the chart you see that students read about 60 WCPM in the fall of second grade, providing you with a benchmark for necessary improvement.

Teachers should consider several critical points when assessing reading fluency:

- Text passages that are used for assessment should be comparably leveled each time so that when a student's performance is compared over time, the test

is at an appropriate level to compare performance. More difficult texts reduce the rate and accuracy of reading, making comparisons with previous fluency checks invalid.

- Words that are pronounced correctly within the context of a passage are considered read correctly (Shinn, 1989). If a student repeats a word or phrase, it is counted as correct. When students make an error but correct themselves within 3 seconds, it is also counted as correct.
- Words that are read incorrectly are counted as errors. Errors include mispronunciations, substitutions, and omissions.
- When students pause for more than 3 seconds, you should tell them the word and then mark it as an error.

Apply the Concept 8-1 offers commercial fluency measures that provide leveled passages.

Using Oral Reading Fluency Scores to Establish Fluency Goals

Fluency information can be plotted in graphs such as the one shown in Figure 8-1. Having students record their own progress serves as a motivation for reading, provides immediate feedback, and allows the students to set goals and see concrete evidence of their progress. Generally, for students with fluency problems, the goal is to add one or two more WCPM per week, with fluency increasing

Apply the Concept

8-1   Published Fluency Assessments

Teachers can use several sources of passages to compare students' fluency rates over time. Each year there are additional companies and individuals who publish fluency assessments. Following is a brief description of some of the more frequently used fluency measures:

Dynamic Indicators of Basic Early Literacy Skills (DIBELS, Sixth Edition—Good, Kaminski, Laimon, & Dill, 2003; 7th ed. DIBELS Next, 2010). DIBELS has leveled reading passages for assessing fluency for kindergarten through sixth grade. The fluency assessment passages are also available for kindergarten through third grade in Spanish (*Indicadores dinámicos del éxito en*

la lectura—Good, Bank, & Watson, 2004). DIBELS is administered to individual students and takes about 2 to 3 minutes per student.
http://dibels.uoregon.edu
http://sopriswest.com

The Test of Oral Reading Fluency (2005). Like DIBELS, TORF is administered individually and takes about 2 to 3 minutes per student. Curriculum-based measures were developed by Drs. Stan Deno and Doug Marston.

Ed Checkup
http://www.edcheckup.com
AIMSweb. This group provides multiple passages at each grade level to provide extensive text for

monitoring students' progress. They also provide professional development and training as needed. This measure is owned by Pearson publishers.
http://www.AIMSweb.com

Test of Silent Word Reading Fluency (TOSWRF). This group-administered measure is designed to determine whether students can recognize printed words accurately and efficiently and can be administered to students in first grade and above.

PRO-ED
http://www.proedinc.com

more quickly in the earlier grades (Fuchs, Fuchs, Hamlett, Walz, & Germann, 1993). Audiotape recordings of readings allow students not only to graph their progress but also to hear their progress over time. Generally, these reading samples are collected every 1 to 2 months and can be kept across the year.

Jeff's fluency instruction and progress as shown in Figure 8-1 was measured weekly by using beginning second-grade instructional-level reading materials. He was making consistent progress and his WCPM increased substantially from the third to the fourth week (three words), when he began to rely less on sounding out words and to attempt to read the words automatically. This also resulted in better phrasing and reading with more expression.

Teachers and students can establish baseline fluency scores and then target acceptable rates of growth in fluency on a bimonthly basis. For example, a student in third grade who reads 50 words per minute WCPM in a second-grade passage is below grade level in both accuracy (the text is below grade level) and speed (the student is reading too slowly). The teacher and student may decide to establish one word per week as the improvement goal. These goals can motivate to students and provide excellent reporting data to parents. Using fluency data can assist teachers in making instructional decisions, as seen in Apply the Concept 8-2.

▶ **Figure 8-1** Fluency Monitoring

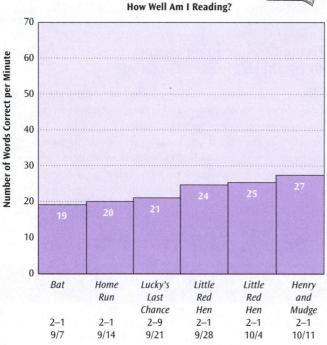

Name __Jeff__

How Well Am I Reading?

Number of Words Correct per Minute

	Bat	Home Run	Lucky's Last Chance	Little Red Hen	Little Red Hen	Henry and Mudge
WCPM	19	20	21	24	25	27
Level	2–1	2–1	2–9	2–1	2–1	2–1
Date	9/7	9/14	9/21	9/28	10/4	10/11

Reading Sessions (Title/Level/Date)

Response to Intervention (RTI) and Fluency

Oral reading fluency is frequently used to monitor students' progress in reading. For this reason, it is also used as a means for determining how students with reading difficulties may be responding to interventions. For example, many schools screen students in first, second, and third grade using oral reading fluency to determine students who are at risk for reading problems. Teachers provided an intervention to these students, four to five times per week for 20–40 minutes per day over an

For a complete description of RTI, see Chapter 3.

● ● ● ● ● ● ● *Apply the Concept* ● ● ● ● ● ●

8-2	**Using Fluency Data**

Student Data Show	Instructional Decisions
Student is making steady progress.	Continue in the same level of text.
Student meets goals on first reading.	Move to higher level of text or raise goal.
Student has difficulty achieving goals.	Alter fluency instruction; move to lower-level text or lower fluency goal.

Source: University of Texas Vaughn Gross Center for Reading and Language Arts (2009). Reprinted by permission.

8- to 12-week period. During this intervention, students typically receive an oral reading fluency test every week or two so that the "slope" of their progress could be charted. Based on students' overall progress and the extent to which they are "closing the gap" between their oral reading fluency prior to intervention and during intervention, a decision is made about participation in subsequent interventions. To illustrate, Jeanine, a second grader, was making adequate progress in reading after she was placed in an intervention (more than two words correct per week gain on average) and appeared to be very close to meeting expected reading performance. Her teachers decided that it would be in her best interest to continue in the intervention for another 10 weeks. Max displayed a different pattern of learning. His overall progress was very low (less than one word correct per week on average) and teachers were concerned that he needed even more intensive intervention. They adjusted his instruction both in the classroom and in the intervention, and provided one-on-one instruction during intervention.

Teaching Fluency

What are effective instructional practices for increasing reading fluency? Fluency instruction is designed to increase automatic word recognition, or the smoothness of the reading; rate, or the pace of reading; and prosody, or expression, appropriate phrasing, and attention to punctuation. According to the theory of automaticity (LaBerge & Samuels, 1974; Samuels, 1997), fluent readers automatically process information at the visual and phonological levels, and are therefore able to focus most of their attention on the meaning of the text, integrating this information into their existing knowledge. The fluent reader's multitask functioning is made possible by the reduced demands on cognitive resources: The reader no longer has to focus on word recognition and other reading processes, thus freeing cognitive resources for comprehension (National Reading Panel, 2000; Stahl & Kuhn, 2002). Because poor readers take much longer and require more exposures to automatically recognize and recall words, it is important that fluency instruction provide multiple opportunities for practice.

However, it is important to note that fluency may be much more important with beginning readers (students who are reading at the first- and second-grade levels) than it is when students become more mature readers. In the beginning stages of reading, being able to read words automatically and effortlessly is associated with comprehension. As students read better (more than 70 WCPM), fluency may be less important (Stahl, 2004). Also, there is little compelling evidence to suggest that fluency practice with the majority of secondary readers—even those with reading difficulties, is valuable (Wexler, Vaughn, Roberts, & Denton, 2010), and additional research that meets rigorous guidelines is needed (Chard, Ketterlin-Geller, Baker, Doabler, & Apichataburtra, 2009).

Fluency instruction and guided practice reading are important parts of any reading program, particularly for students with learning and behavior problems. Good fluency instruction provides students with repeated practice of reading materials at the student's independent or instructional reading level. In the following section, we will examine several proven practices for assisting students in developing fluency in their reading as well as ideas for making difficult text more accessible.

Reading Aloud and Previewing Books

Students develop the concept of fluent reading through listening to and watching others read aloud, through previewing books, and through practice reading materials that are at their instructional to independent reading levels (word recognition from 90% to 100%). There is a growing emphasis on the importance of reading aloud to children and previewing a book as ways not only to develop an enjoyment of literature and books but also to model and build fluent reading (Gunning, 2010; Whitehurst & Lonigan, 2001).

Guided oral reading is recommended practice for enhancing students' fluency (National Reading Panel, 2000). What is guided reading? Guided reading refers to many related approaches of providing support to improve students' fluency. These approaches include reading aloud, modeling fluent reading while students read along, providing opportunities for better readers to serve as models for other students, listening to text read aloud on a tape recorder and then reading aloud, and reading poems and other genres after they have been read aloud by the teacher. Guided oral reading promotes the development of reading fluency in a number of ways.

First, it allows a teacher to model fluent reading. In reading aloud to a group of students who are just learning to read, the use of big books can be helpful because it allows the teacher to make the literacy act more visible and creates interest in the story. If a teacher, family member, or volunteer is reading aloud to one child, then sitting close to the child makes it easy for the child to interact with the print and the teacher. When reading aloud, the teacher or volunteer should read with expression, pointing to the words while reading or sweeping the fingers underneath them.

Second, modeling fluent reading by reading aloud provides background knowledge for students so that they can read a book by themselves, with a partner, or while listening to an audio recording. Reading aloud gives the teacher the opportunity to preview difficult words and unfamiliar concepts. Once students have listened to and previewed a book, they have a wealth of knowledge about the book to assist them in reading. In addition, once children have listened to a book, they are more likely to select it as a book they want to read. In a study of kindergartners, Martinez and Teale (1988) found that children chose familiar books (i.e., those read repeatedly by the teacher) to read during free time three times more frequently than they chose unfamiliar books (books the teacher had not read). Rose (1984) compared the effects of teacher-directed previewing and not previewing texts with six students with learning disabilities, and found that previewing substantially increased oral reading rates. Other studies have investigated the effects of taped previewing (Rose & Beattie, 1986) and peer previewing (Salend & Nowak, 1988). These procedures also increased fluency of the text but not to the degree that teacher-directed previewing did. Apply the Concept 8-3 presents a procedure for teacher-directed previewing.

Third, modeling fluent reading aloud for students exposes them to books that may be too difficult for them to read. Many students with learning and behavior problems have listening comprehension that is several years more advanced than their reading comprehension. Reading a book aloud affords students the opportunity to talk about literature that is at a more advanced level.

> Techniques for building sight words are discussed in Chapter 7.

Fourth, reading aloud can be orchestrated so that older, less adept readers can read books to young children and serve as cross-age tutors. This gives the older students the opportunity to read aloud and to model the role of a good reader, an opportunity that is not often available in the regular or resource classroom.

Reading aloud has the following benefits (Trelease, 2006):

- It provides a positive reading role model.
- It furnishes new information.

- It demonstrates the pleasures of reading.
- It develops vocabulary.
- It provides examples of good sentences and good story grammar.
- It enables students to be exposed to a book to which they might not otherwise be exposed.
- It provides opportunities for discussions concerning the content of the book.

It is important to remember that reading aloud builds vocabulary and comprehension when teachers (Santoro, Chard, Howard, & Baker, 2008): (a) select texts to encourage "text to text" and "text to self" connections, (b) identify target words and teachers then ask students to listen for these key words, (c) promote discussions that link students' responses to the text, (d) and preview text, stop while reading, and summarize after reading in ways that promote comprehension.

Repeated Reading

Have you noticed how young children thoroughly enjoy having the same story read to them over and over again? As the adult sits with the child and reads a familiar book, the child automatically begins to read along. At first, the child joins in on some of the words and phrases. Eventually, the child is reading along for most of the book. With repeated reading of a story, children become so familiar with the text that their memory becomes a great aid to them. Repeated reading as a means of enhancing fluency is based on the idea that as students repeatedly read text, they become fluent and confident in their reading (Chard et al., 2009; Samuels, 1979, 1997). And because they are exposed to the same story several times,

● ● ● ● ● ● ● *Apply the Concept* ● ● ● ● ● ● ●

8-3   Guidelines for Implementing Previewing for Promoting Fluency

1. *Decide on an appropriate book or text* (i.e., one that is of interest to the students and at their independent to instructional reading levels). For longer books, preview only a section of the book at a time. Have student copies of the book or text available.

2. *Introduce the book or text* using the title and looking through the text or section. With the students, make predictions about the content. Introduce

words that may be difficult for the students to automatically recognize or for which the meaning may be unfamiliar. Students may write these words in a personal dictionary or on word cards.

3. *Have students follow along as you read the book or text orally* at a relatively slow conversational rate (approximately 130 words per minute).

4. *Have students partner and take turns reading* a section after you

have read it. Have the stronger partner read first, and as one student reads, have the other student provide support by pronouncing words the student does not know.

5. *Have the students review the difficult words* using techniques for building sight words.

6. *Monitor students' reading fluency* on a regular basis by using the procedures discussed above in the section "Monitoring Student Progress in Fluency."

they have the opportunity to practice identifying unknown words while relying on their memory of the language flow to assist them.

Repeated reading is an empirically based practice that has improved rate of reading in elementary students with reading difficulties (Vadasy & Sanders, 2008). What about the use of repeated reading with secondary students? There are considerably fewer studies examining the effectiveness of repeated reading with older students with disabilities and the studies we have reveal low effects (see Wexler, Vaughn, Edmonds, & Reutebuch, 2008). Another question that teachers may have about repeated reading is whether there are special considerations for students who are English language learners (ELLs). A report on effective instruction for ELLs (Francis, Rivera, Rivera, Lesaux, & Kieffer, 2006) indicates that successful repeated reading includes

- Oral reading, providing opportunities for students to attend to words and opportunities to practice speaking and reading with expression.
- Corrective feedback from adults, drawing students' attention to miscues and pronunciation.
- Discussions and questioning about the text read.
- Increased exposure to print.
- Increased engagement and motivation to read.

 EVIDENCE-BASED PRACTICE

Repeated Reading

PROCEDURES: Repeated reading consists of rereading short, meaningful passages several times (three to five) until a satisfactory level of fluency is reached. The procedure is then repeated with a new passage. Generally, the student repeatedly reads passages that range from 50 to 200 words in length, until he or she reaches a more fluent reading rate (see Table 8-1) and an adequate word-recognition level (e.g., 90% to 100% word recognition). When a student reads under the direct supervision of a teacher, the words a student does not recognize are pronounced by the teacher. To foster comprehension, discussion of the passage follows reading.

A number of researchers have investigated the use of tape-recorded books for this procedure (Hasbrouck, Ihnot, & Rogers, 1999; Dunn & Blake, 2008; Rasinski, 1990a, 1990b). Using audio books, students listen to the stories and read and/or follow along with the written text. They listen to and read the same story until they can read the book by themselves. The teacher then listens to students individually read the story and discusses the story with the students. Guidelines for using recorded books, keeping records of students' reading, and using computers are presented in Apply the Concept 8-4.

COMMENTS: Students reading below grade level who have used repeated reading have consistently demonstrated

gains in both fluency and reading comprehension (Chard, Vaughn, & Tyler, 2002; Meyer & Felton, 1999):

- Consistently using repeated reading with poor readers increases reading speed, accuracy, expression, and comprehension.
- Text materials should be at the students' independent to instructional reading level (90% to 100% word recognition).
- Passages should be read three to five times.
- Multiple reading of phrases may improve fluency.
- Specific strategies should take into account individual student's characteristics. For more impaired readers, provide more adult guidance during reading, use more decodable texts as reading materials, practice on words and phrases from the text before reading the text, practice reading shorter passages, and model expressive reading.
- Short, frequent sessions of fluency practice (generally 10 to 15 minutes) should be used.
- Transfer of fluency is increased when the overlap of words across passages is substantial (Rashotte & Torgesen, 1985).
- Having a way for students to set goals and record their progress should be provided.

Choral Repeated Reading

Choral repeated reading is a technique that combines ideas and procedures from repeated reading and choral reading. We have used the approach with students who have significant reading difficulties in word identification and reading rate.

 EVIDENCE-BASED PRACTICE

Choral Repeated Reading

PROCEDURES: Choral repeated reading is designed for students who can comprehend material that is read to them but, because of difficulties in word identification and reading rate, are unable to read material commensurate with their listening comprehension level. Students should have a sight vocabulary of at least 25 words. We suggest the following procedure:

1. Explain the technique to the student.
2. With the student, select a book of interest that is at a challenging reading level (85% to 90% word recognition) and that has frequent repetition of words and decodable text.
3. Establish a purpose for reading by introducing the book and making predictions. Read the book with the student, using the following three-step process:
   a. *Teacher reads:* Start at the beginning of the book, and read a piece of text to the student, ranging from several sentences to a paragraph. (The length of each section should be short enough

8-4   **Using Tapes and E-Books for Repeated Reading**

Selecting Books and Passages

Select books and passages that are of interest to the students and for which the students' word recognition is from 85% to 95%. For older readers, high-interest, low-vocabulary stories provide another source.

For more impaired readers, select more easily decodable texts (see Chapter 7). Pattern-language books (see Chapter 7) can be another good source of books because they provide students with frequent repetition of language patterns and words.

Tape-Recording the Books

Use a good-quality recording tape and recorder. Audiotape a book speaking at a conversational rate and with expression. Use appropriate phrasing. Provide the students with cues to assist them in keeping their place in the text while listening to the recording.

- Allow 10 seconds of blank tape before recording.
- Remind students of any strategies you want them to use (e.g., "Remember to use your finger or a marker as a guide").
- Use a signal to cue turning the page.
- For a new page announce each page number.
- Direct students to put their finger on the first word on the page.

Record about 10 minutes of reading on each side of the tape so that it will be easy for students to find their place. Label each side of the tape with the title of the book and the page numbers covered. You can instruct parent volunteers to record books. You can also purchase prerecorded taped books, but be aware that they may not provide the same level of cueing.

Store the books with their tapes in clear plastic bags. Inside the bag, place the book and tape. If you have multiple copies of the book with a tape, they can be stored together.

Keeping Student Records

Have each student make a reading folder. Staple forms inside the folder on which the student can record the name of the book, the author, the date, how he or she read the book, and with whom he or she discussed the book. In this way, both the teacher and the student have a record of the student's reading.

Computer-Based Reading Practice

Computer software provides another avenue for children to repeatedly read books using the computer. For example, *Living Book Series* (Discus Books) and *Wiggleworks* (Scholastic) both provide opportunities for students to listen to books being read, to read along with the computer, and in the case of *Wiggleworks*, to record their own reading of the book. Reading software provides flexibility; the text can be read in sentences or phrases, or the students can highlight individual words and have them pronounced. Many of these programs easily switch languages (most commonly between English and Spanish) and have built-in record-keeping systems so that teachers know the number of times students read the books and the type of assistance they use.

Using Taped Books at Home to Support English Language Learners

Taped books can also be integrated into a home-reading component. The advantage is that well-recorded books require minimal reading from parents, making them an ideal resource for parents who do not speak or read English. Students can be taught how to use the taped books, and notes can be sent home with the audiotaped books reminding the children and their parents to read and listen to the books two or three times every day.

Using Voice Mail to Support Summer Reading

Elementary-aged students with learning and behavior problems usually do not choose reading as a recreational activity during the summer. Ann Willman, a reading specialist, used her school's voice mail to promote summer reading (Willman, 1999). She sent home books with the students along with directions on how to use the school voice mail. The students practiced reading a book until they were comfortable. Then she asked the students, with the assistance of their parents, to call her voice mail and read the book to her for 3 minutes or to summarize the book. She called back to compliment the students. Ann also invited parents to leave a message about how the process was going. Parents noted that they liked the summer school-connection that made their "sometimes reluctant reader more amenable to reading during vacation".

Name of Book	Author	Dates	Read with				Discussed with	
			Self	*Tape*	*Student*	*Teacher*	*Student*	*Teacher*

that the student can rely on his or her short-term memory as an aid for reading.) Read at a normal rate, and move your finger smoothly along underneath the words as the student watches, making sure that your reading matches your movement from word to word.

b. *Teacher and student read:* Read the same section together aloud with the student. Continue to point to the words. The two of you may read the section once or several times, rereading until the student feels comfortable reading the section independently.

c. *Student reads:* Have the student read the section independently. Pronounce any unknown words, and note words that the student consistently has difficulty recognizing.

4. Discuss after reading how the story related to your predictions and what you have learned. New predictions and purposes for reading can be set.

5. Repeat the three-step process throughout the book. The length of each section usually increases as the book is read, and the number of times you and the student read together usually decreases. For some students, the first step is discontinued.

6. Write on word cards the words that the student consistently has difficulty identifying automatically. Use a variety of activities, for example, discussing the word meanings or locating the words in the text and rereading the sentences, as a means of increasing practice.

7. Have the student keep records of his or her progress (see Figure 8-1). Check the student's progress at least every third day when initially using the procedure.

In this method most of the 10 to 15 minutes allocated is focused on oral reading. As the student becomes more confident in reading ability, use repeated readings with tape-recorded books or stories as independent reading activities.

COMMENTS: Choral repeated reading allows the teacher and student to attend to word identification skills and comprehension as well as fluency. Using the three-step process also allows the student to read more difficult books. We have found this particularly rewarding for older nonreaders in that the technique quickly gives them success in reading books.

Peer-Supported Reading

One concern for students with learning and behavior problems is that they read substantially less than high-achieving readers and spend less time engaged in academic behaviors (Allington, 1983a, 1983b; Greenwood, Delquadri, & Hall, 1989). How can the amount of time devoted to text reading be increased? One strategy is to use peers to support each other when reading for the purpose of building fluency as well as supporting word

recognition and comprehension. Techniques such as *assisted reading* (Hoskisson & Krohm, 1974), *classwide peer tutoring* or *partner reading* (e.g., Fuchs, Fuchs, & Burish, 2000; Fuchs et al., 1997; Simmons, Fuchs, Fuchs, Hodge, & Mathes, 1994), and *dyad reading* (Eldredge & Quinn, 1988) provide opportunities for students to work in pairs and provide support for each other while reading. For the most part, these techniques have been used in general education classrooms to provide more opportunities for students to actively engage in reading. It is important to note that peer-supported reading is an opportunity for supportive practice and not an alternative to instruction provided by teachers. Research suggests that adult instruction to promote fluency is quite important (Kuhn & Stahl, 2003).

 **EVIDENCE-BASED PRACTICE**

Peer-Supported Reading

PROCEDURES: Peer-supported reading involves matching higher readers with less able readers to practice rereading text and asking and answering questions about text meaning. How to successfully pair students and select appropriate reading materials are important considerations. One way to pair students is to rank-order the class on the basis of reading fluency and reading level. Then split the class in half, and pair the top-ranked high-performing student with the top-ranked low-performing student, the second-ranked high-performing student with the second-ranked low-performing student, and so on. It is important to check whether there are partners who will not work well together socially, and adjust accordingly. Maintain the pairings for 3 to 4 weeks. Reading materials should be at the lower-performing student's independent to instructional reading levels. If peer-supported reading is used three to four times per week, have enough materials selected so that students can work on two new passages per week. As in other fluency techniques, such as repeated reading and repeated choral reading, the reading materials will vary according to the students' needs. At first, it may be advantageous to use short passages or books as students learn the procedures, but high-interest–low-vocabulary chapter books can also be a good source of reading materials.

Teach students how to be both tutors/listeners and tutees/readers, and provide role-play practice and feedback. Give the tutors guidelines for how to correct errors during oral reading (e.g., point out the word, pronounce the word, and have the tutee say the word) and the questions they should ask when the tutee has finished reading (e.g., What is the story about? What is happening in the story now? What do you think will happen next?). Also assist the students in giving positive feedback.

When the students work with their partners, first the stronger reader reads aloud to serve as a model, and then the other reader reads. The teacher should refer to them

Partner Reading Procedures
- First reader reads.
- Second reader reads.
- Students discuss reading with one student asking questions and other student answering.
- Repeat until story is complete.

Tutoring Rules
- Talk only to your partner.
- Talk only about partner reading.
- Be cooperative.

Kinds of Errors
- Saying the word wrong.
- Leaving out a word.
- Adding a word.
- Waiting longer than 4 seconds.

Feedback about Words
- Stop. You missed this word (point to it). Can you figure it out?
- That word is _____. What word? (Reader says word). Good! Read the sentence again.

as *reader one* and *reader two*. Because the lower-performing students read what has just been read by the higher-performing students, the lower-performing students are more likely to read fluently and comfortably. How much material is read before the students switch roles depends on the material and the readers; it usually ranges from a sentence to a page, or each student reads a specified amount of time (e.g., 5 minutes). Partners can take turns reading a book or passage several times, thus adding a repeated reading component. Copies of guidelines for the tutor and reader can be posted, and each pair can rate themselves on their effort (see Figure 8-2).

COMMENTS: Research consistently indicates that peer-supported reading has positive outcomes for the reading fluency and comprehension of students with learning and behavior problems (Mastropieri, Leinart, & Scruggs, 1999; Okilwa & Shelby, 2010) even in first-grade classrooms (Mathes, Grek, Howard, Babyak, & Allen, 1999; Mathes, Torgesen, & Howard, 2001). The research results suggest that the strength of the intervention may be related to the additional instructional time and student reading involvement afforded by peer-supported reading. The effects of peer-pairing for reading fluency need more research with secondary students (Wexler, Vaughn, Edmonds, & Reutebuch, 2008).

Scaffolded Sustained Silent Reading

A frequently used practice in the general education classroom is to allocate time each day for silent reading of student-selected texts—typically 20–30 minutes. There is little

research documenting the effectiveness of this practice for students with learning or behavior probems; however, a modified version of scaffolded sustained silent reading holds promise (Reutzel, Jones, Fawson, & Smith, 2008).

  EVIDENCE-BASED PRACTICE

Scaffolded Sustained Silent Reading

PROCEDURES: Most approaches to sustained silent reading involve little interaction between the teacher and the students during the time allocated for reading. Typically both the teacher and the students read for the designated amount of time. Reutzel et al. (2008) recommend a more instructive role for the teacher that involves:

- Rather than allowing students to select whatever text they want to read, the teacher assists in identifying appropriate books or texts at their independent reading level.
- Promote reading across a variety of genres rather than allowing students to consistently read one or two genres (e.g., poetry, fairy tale, biography, information text).
- Teacher scaffolds learning to read for fluency and comprehension.
- Teacher holds brief conferences (5 minutes) to determine students understanding of text.
- Teachers and students record progress in books, read aloud passages for fluency checks, and answer questions.

Reading Performance

Although Ms. Sadlowski, the special education teacher, and Ms. Martinez, the fifth-grade teacher, were pleased with the progress students with learning and behavior problems were making in fluency through specific fluency-building activities, they wanted the students to have the opportunity to practice reading for purposes other than to build fluency. They decided to use readers' theater and buddy reading as techniques in which students practice reading a selection until they are fluent and then perform the reading, sometimes referred to as *reading performance* (Worthy & Broaddus, 2002).

   EVIDENCE-BASED PRACTICE

Reading Performance

PROCEDURES: In *readers' theater*, students perform a play or a book adapted to script form by reading it aloud to an audience. Because the focus is on reading fluently, students are not expected to memorize the text, and props are minimal. Students with different reading skills can use the same text, since the different parts often vary widely in reading level. Students practice reading their parts with a teacher, tutor, and/or other students who are taking part in the performance. Even simple texts can be adapted to a script form, as Figure 8-3 illustrates.

Original Text	Scripted Text	
One day Mrs. Duck went to the pond. It was hot and she wanted a cool drink. Mr. Fox was sitting by the side of the pond. He told Mrs. Duck that she could not get a drink because he was in a bad mood and did not want anyone near his pond. Mrs. Bird heard Mr. Fox say this and she called down sweetly from her branch. . . .	**Mrs. Duck:**	I have been working so hard and now I am so thirsty. I need to go to the pond for a nice, cool drink.
	Mr. Fox:	Hello, Mrs. Duck. I am in a very bad mood. No one can drink from my pond today.
	Mrs. Bird:	This is not your pond. It belongs to everyone.

Source: Adapted from Texas Center for Reading and Language Arts, *Professional Development Guide: Reading Fluency: Principles of Instruction and Progress Monitoring* (Austin: Texas Center for Reading and Language Arts, University of Texas-Austin, 2000).

Buddy reading consists of the students practicing and reading texts to younger students. This provides opportunities for students with learning and behavior problems to practice reading texts that are not at their grade level but are at their independent reading level without the stigma of reading "easy" books. In using buddy reading, it is important to choose books that the students can read easily and that are appropriate for and interesting to younger children.

COMMENTS: Although techniques such as readers' theater and buddy reading do not provide the level of explicit instruction and support that are used with techniques such as repeated choral reading and peer-supported reading, they do give students who have learning and behavior problems opportunities to transfer their reading fluency to tasks other than practicing fluency. Furthermore, they lend themselves to implementation in general education classrooms.

Making Easy Books Acceptable and Difficult Books Accessible

One key to becoming a fluent reader is to read. Yet students with learning and behavior problems who have difficulty reading generally do not have adequate text sources at their reading level.

Fielding and Roller (1992) and Worthy (1996) discuss several strategies for making difficult books more accessible to older readers with disabilities. These strategies include the following:

- Using tape-recorded books and books on CD-ROM, DVD, or e-books for the computer (see Apply the Concept 8-4).
- Reading aloud to the students.
- Using partner reading, in which less able and more able readers are paired.
- Preceding difficult books with easier books about the same topic or in the same genre (e.g., books about comets, the solar system, or ghosts; fairy tales; mystery books), thereby familiarizing the child with the vocabulary and text structure in books that are easier to read.

- Using series books to increase students' comfort level. Reading books in a series provides benefits that are similar to those of repeated reading of the same text because of the consistent use of characters, language, and content.

Integrating Fluency Building into a Reading Program

Fluency building is an integral part of a reading program for students who have reading difficulties, and generally represents 15–25 minutes of time approximately three times per week (Figure 8-4 describes several fluency-building programs). In teaching fluency, strategies for improving word identification skills and comprehension should also be instructional goals. As we mentioned in the discussions of previewing and repeated choral reading, word recognition and word extension activities can be developed naturally from the text. Although improving fluency can allow students to allocate more attention to comprehension, not all students will automatically acquire the skills associated with effective comprehension. For some students, methods of teaching comprehension may be required.

> The same activities that we recommended for the word cards generated from language experience stories (see Chapter 7) can be used with word cards generated from these fluency techniques.

Helping Families Improve Their Children's Reading Fluency

Perhaps one of the most necessary tools for improving reading outcomes for children with special needs is wide reading. *Wide reading* refers to both the amount and type of reading in which children are engaged. When students read widely, they read often—at least 20 minutes a day—and they read across many genres. This means that they read different types of books, not just narrative or information books but biographies, history, and technical books. How can teachers increase the wide

Peer-Assisted Learning Strategies—Reading (PALS)
(Classwide Peer Tutoring)

PALS Reading was developed for students in kindergarten through high school. It is designed primarily for general education classrooms and as supplements to a teacher's more comprehensive reading program. PALS programs target key reading skills including fluency and, because students work with students on these skills, PALS provides students with intensive practice. Evaluative studies indicate that on average PALS accelerates the reading achievement of students with learning disabilities, low-achieving students, and average- and high-achieving students. PALS Math uses a similar format but focuses on math.

Contact: PALS Outreach
　　　　　Vanderbilt University
　　　　　Peabody Box 328
　　　　　230 Appleton Place
　　　　　Nashville, TN 37203-5701
　　　　　615-343-4782
　　　　　e-mail: PALS@vanderbilt.edu

Read Naturally

Students read along while listening to a tape of leveled, recorded high-interest passages and practice until they can read them at a predetermined rate. Students graph WCPM before and after practicing. Comprehension questions provided.

Contact: Read Naturally
　　　　　750 S. Plaza Dr. #100
　　　　　Saint Paul, MN 55120
　　　　　800-788-4085
　　　　　Web site: http://www.readnaturally.com
　　　　　e-mail: info@readnaturally.com

Great Leaps

Great Leaps addresses fluency at three levels: phonics—students identify sounds and decode simple word patterns; sight phrases—students read phrases with sight words; reading fluency—students read stories. Students graph progress.

Contact: Diarmuid, Inc.
　　　　　Box 357580
　　　　　Gainesville, FL 32635
　　　　　877-GRL-EAPS
　　　　　Web site: http://www.greatleaps.com
　　　　　e-mail: info@greatleaps.com

Carbo Reading Styles Program

The Carbo reading method has children listen to and repeatedly read along with audiotapes of books that have been recorded at a slow pace but with proper phrasing and intonation until they can read fluently. Books can be recorded by the teacher or can be purchased from the National Reading Styles Institute.

Contact: National Reading Styles Institute, Inc.
　　　　　Box 737
　　　　　Syosset, NY 11791
　　　　　800-331-3117
　　　　　Web site: http://www.nrsi.com
　　　　　e-mail: readingstyle@nrsi.com

First Grade PALS (Peer-Assisted Literacy Strategies)

This program contains 48 lessons, enough for teachers to use three times a week for 16 weeks as a supplement to their reading program. The emphasis is on peer-interacted learning that addresses phonemic awareness and fluency tasks. The goal is to improve accuracy through repeated practice.

Contact: Sopris West
　　　　　4093 Specialty Place
　　　　　Longwood, CO 80504-5400
　　　　　800-547-6747
　　　　　Web site: http://www.sopriswest.com
　　　　　e-mail: customerservice@sopriswest.com

The Six-Minute Solution: A Reading Fluency Program

This program has high-interest nonfiction practice passages (approximately 20 for each of the eight levels). The materials include assessment records, charts, word lists, and differentiated instruction through multiple reading levels.

Contact: Sopris West
　　　　　4093 Specialty Place
　　　　　Longwood, CO 80504-5400
　　　　　800-547-6747
　　　　　Web site: http://www.sopriswest.com
　　　　　e-mail: customerservice@sopriswest.com

QuickReads

This series of program books and materials features short, high-interest nonfiction texts at second- through fourth-grade levels. The materials are designed to improve students' fluency, comprehension, and background knowledge. Each grade level sequentially builds across three books and includes increasingly more difficult high-frequency words and phonics elements. The program includes a pre- and posttest for placement, 12 copies each of the three leveled student books per grade level, a teacher's resource manual, and three read-along audio CDs per grade level. Additional comprehension strategies and extension lessons can be used to support ESL (English as a second language)/ELL students (Hiebert, 2002).

Contact: Modern Curriculum Press
　　　　　299 Jefferson Road
　　　　　Parsippany, NJ 07054
　　　　　800-321-3106
　　　　　Web site: http://www.pearsonlearning.com
　　　　　e-mail: technical.support@pearson.com

reading of the students they teach? The best way may be to engage family members in supporting wide reading.

The following are some ideas that teachers can share with families to promote wide reading by their children:

- Establish a time each evening when you read with your child. For beginning readers, this may mean that you take turns reading from a book on his or her level. If your child is a more advanced reader, you may each read different books, but you sit near each other and are engaged in the reading process.
- Determine many ways to access books and print materials. Libraries, bookstores, and online activities are excellent resources to access a wide range of books and print materials. Take advantage of every opportunity to examine and discuss books and other print materials.
- Share what you are reading. Discuss the books and materials that you are reading with your child.
- Ask questions about what your child is reading. The types of questions you ask about what your child is reading can promote continued reading. Children are likely to engage in and extend reading when family members show interest in what children are reading.
- Read different types of print materials and share them with your child. Sources that adults read include recipes, newspapers, magazines, reference books, and leisure books. Share these types of reading materials with your child, and engage your child in reading different sources of text. Remember wide reading is associated with overall improved vocabulary and knowledge.

Assessing Comprehension and Monitoring Progress in Reading Comprehension

What assessments and instructional components should be present in a reading comprehension program? Reading comprehension is the most difficult aspect of reading to assess. Perhaps this is because understanding and interacting with text occurs largely as thinking and is not readily observed. The only access teachers have to knowing whether and how students understand text is to ask students to respond orally or in writing about what they have read. Figure 8-5 lists 12 tests that can assist teachers in making decisions about their students' reading comprehension. These tests can be combined to assess students' comprehension more accurately and completely.

Teachers must consider several critical aspects of a comprehension test before selecting one. First, what is the purpose of the test? Does the teacher want to screen, monitor, diagnose, or evaluate students? Second, what type of information about the students' comprehension is the teacher seeking? Does the teacher want to know

whether they can recall what is in the text? Is the teacher interested in whether the students can tell the main idea or make inferences? Third, does the test require a short or long amount of time, is it difficult or easy to score, and will it provide the type of information that will inform instruction?

When children are at the beginning stages of reading (first- or second-grade-level readers) and read fewer than 80 words correctly per minute, it is possible for teachers to monitor their reading comprehension by monitoring the students' oral reading fluency. For early readers, fluency is a good, though not perfect, predictor of reading comprehension. Oral reading fluency is a feasible means for determining whether students understand what they read and whether they are likely to pass high-stakes reading comprehension tests. However, as students develop more mature reading skills, other practices for monitoring their reading comprehension are needed.

One way to monitor students' comprehension is to ask them to retell the most important parts of a text that they have just read. Story retelling provides an alternative to traditional questioning techniques for evaluating students' reading comprehension because it involves the integration of many skills that are necessary for reading comprehension. It requires students to sequence and reconstruct key information presented in text. It also requires students to rely on their memory for factual details and to relate them in an organized meaningful pattern. One advantage to retelling is that the teacher can learn a great deal about what students understand and can determine what additional comprehension skills need to be taught.

For the purposes of monitoring the progress of comprehension, retelling is administered individually. The following procedures can be applied:

1. Select brief passages (1 to 2 minutes) that are at the students' reading level.
2. Ask younger students to read their passage aloud. Ask older students to read their passage silently.
3. After reading ask students to tell you what it was about or tell you the story.
4. Score the retell on the basis of the depth of information provided. Teachers may want to consider whether students mentioned characters, the story problem, events, problem resolutions, and story quality.
5. You can rate the quality of a students' retell on a 7-point scale with a higher number indicating a better retell and use this to monitor their retelling effectiveness over time.

Another way to monitor students' comprehension is by using maze passages. Maze passages provide text written at a range of grade levels and provide students with opportunities to select words from several options that fulfill the meaning of the text where words have been deleted.

Assessing and Teaching Reading: Fluency and Comprehension   **245**

Spotlight on Diversity
Instructing English-Language Learners Who Are at Risk for Reading Problems

What instructional practices should teachers consider when providing reading instruction to students with reading difficulties who are also ELLs? Teachers might consider the following seven best practices for instruction:

1. *Consider the commonalities between reading instruction in English and the reading instruction that is provided in the student's native language.* These commonalities can be used to build bridges between languages and apply what is known in one language to the other. Many commonalities exist between reading instruction practices in different languages, even though features of the instructional practices may differ (Gersten & Geva, 2003; Linan-Thompson & Vaughn, 2007). For example, oral language instruction, fluency, and reading comprehension are important aspects of learning to read for learners of all languages (Goldenberg, 2008).

2. *Identify procedures for instructing students in all of the critical elements of beginning reading (phonemic awareness, spelling, phonics, vocabulary, language development, fluency, and comprehension).* The following are six instructional practices in reading that are effective for beginning ELLs (Gersten & Geva, 2003; Linan-Thompson & Vaughn, 2007): teaching explicity; promoting learning of the English language; teaching phonemic decoding and phonics; integrating vocabulary development, use, and extension across the curriculum; maximizing student engagement through interactive teaching and student pairs; and scaffolding learners through instruction that provides opportunities to respond with teacher feedback.

The foundation skills of phonemic awareness and phonics are more critical in the very beginning stages of reading and less important as students become readers of connected text. Improving vocabulary is an important part of reading and content learning all along. Improving listening comprehension is initially important, and then transferring these comprehension skills to text understanding becomes important.

3. *Recognize that English is the most difficult language of all alphabetic languages to learn to read, and therefore, many of the foundation skills such as spelling and phonics require more explicit and systematic instruction than they might in other alphabetic languages.* A study across 12 alphabetic languages revealed that many of the foundation skills of reading take twice as long for young children to acquire in English than in other alphabetic languages such as Spanish (Seymour, Aro, & Erskine, 2003). Thus, students who know another alphabetic language such as Spanish or Italian will require more time to learn foundation skills such as phonics and spelling to develop fluency and comprehension.

4. *Make connections between the home language and the language of instruction in school.* There are many benefits when teachers make connections between the home language and English. First, it provides students with a ready connection between what they know and what they need to know. Second, it helps students learn more quickly because much

of what they know can be used as a foundation for learning a new literacy. Third, it honors the students' home language and background, building language concepts and self-esteem.

5. *Capitalize on every opportunity to use and promote language development during instruction, and give opportunities for students to engage in higher-order questions.* ELLs often have limited opportunities to use oral language during instruction and few opportunities to address challenging or higher-order questions. Because students' language development may still be growing, teachers often ask these students questions that allow for one- or two-word responses. These students may have difficulty providing more complex answers, but with structured conversation and opportunities to use academic language, their skills will improve. For example, oral participation can be facilitated by providing scaffolding in the form of sentence stems that offer students a structure for orally responding to challenging questions. To assist students in addressing higher-order questions, teachers may initially model more complex syntactic structures and fade support as students become more proficient in English. Planned discussions can be promoted to encourage academic language, providing small group or paired cooperative learning activities and development of prior knowledge.

6. *Promote all opportunities to teach and engage in vocabulary and concept building.* Vocabulary development is an essential feature of reading, comprehension, and content learning for ELLs. To fully appreciate and interpret what they are reading, students will be required to learn new words to understand expository and narrative texts (e.g., *civil, equity, molecule*) as well as to learn the meaning of descriptive words (e.g., *worried, marvelous, eagerly*). Teachers will add to students' vocabulary knowledge by providing highly organized, focused, and repeated opportunities to learn core words well enough to both understand their meaning in context and to apply them in their own language use. Ulanoff and Pucci (1999) suggest that students benefit from previewing important concepts and vocabulary in their primary language before listening to stories read in English and reviewing key concepts in both languages after the reading.

7. *Peer pairing and cooperative groups can be used to enhance learning.* Peer pairing and structured group activities are effective practices for improving oral language, acquisition of higher-level comprehension skills, and interaction for ELLs (Klingner & Vaughn, 1996, 2000; Saenz, Fuchs, & Fuchs, 2005). Peer pairing or cooperative grouping provides intensive individualized instruction for students from varied literacy backgrounds by increasing the amount of time spent in academic engagement and providing immediate feedback (e.g., reading errors, pacing) from peers. Paired learning in which students have specific tasks and opportunities to discuss what they are learning may be particularly beneficial for ELLs by presenting opportunities for them to use and learn specific vocabulary related to academic language. (August, Branum-Martin, Cardenas-Hagan, & Francis, 2009; Vaughn et al., 2009).

▶ **Figure 8-5**   Reading Comprehension Assessments

Title	Ages/Grade Levels	Estimated Testing Time	Key Elements and Strategies	Administration
Clay Observational Survey (Clay, 2002)	Grades K–3	15 minutes	• Oral reading • Reading vocabulary (i.e., words known in reading)	Individual
Comprehensive Reading Assessment Battery	Grades K–6	30–40 minutes	• Fluency • Oral comprehension • Sentence completion	Individual
Gates-MacGinitie Reading Tests (MacGinitie et al., 2000)	Grades K–12 and adult	55–75 minutes	• Word meanings (levels 1 and 2) • Comprehension (short passages of 1–3 sentences for levels 1 and 2; paragraphs for levels 3 and up)	Group
Gray Diagnostic Reading Tests (Bryant, Wiederholt, Bryant, 2004)	Ages 6–13	45–60 minutes	• Letter/word identification • Phonetic analysis • Reading vocabulary • Meaningful reading	Individual
Gray Oral Reading Test 4 (Wiederholt Bryant, 2001)	Ages 6–19	15–45 minutes	• Comprehension (14 separate stories, each followed by 5 multiple-choice questions)	Individual
Gray Silent Reading Test (Wiederholt Blalock, 2000)	Ages 7–26	15–30 minutes	• Comprehension (13 passages with 5 questions each)	Individual, small groups, or entire class
Qualitative Reading Inventory (Leslie Caldwell, 2001)	Emergent to high school	30–40 minutes	• Comprehension • Oral reading • Silent reading • Listening	
Test of Early Reading Ability 3 (Reid et al., 2001)	Preschool–second grade	20 minutes	• Comprehension of words, sentences, and paragraphs • Vocabulary • Understanding of sentence construction • Paraphrasing	Individual
Test of Reading Comprehension (Brown et al., 1995)	Ages 7–18	30–90 minutes	• General vocabulary • Understanding syntactic similarities • Paragraph reading (6 paragraphs with 5 questions each) • Sentence sequencing (5 randomly ordered sentences that need reordering) • Diagnostic supplement: content area vocabulary in math, social studies, and science • Reading directions	Individual, small groups, or entire class
Standardized Reading Inventory 2 (Newcomer, 1999)	Ages 6–14-and-a-half	30–90 minutes	• Vocabulary in context • Passage comprehension	Individual
Woodcock Reading Mastery (Woodcock, 1998)	Ages 5–75	10–30 minutes	• Word comprehension (i.e., antonyms, synonyms, analogies)	Individual
Woodcock-Johnson III Diagnostic Reading Battery (Woodcock, Mather, & Schrank, 2006)	Ages 2–90	5–10 minutes	• Phonemic awareness • Phonics • Fluency • Vocabulary • Reading comprehension	Individual

Source: S. Vaughn & S. Linan-Thompson, *Research-Based Methods of Reading Instruction, Grades K–3* (Alexandria, VA: Association for Supervision and Curriculum Development, 2004), pp. 102–103. Reprinted by permission.

Response to Intervention and Reading Comprehension

How can teachers use reading comprehension practices to determine students' RTI? Knowing students' comprehension of text is the single most important outcome of interest when determining their RTI. There are several progress-monitoring measures that attempt to gauge comprehension. For example, the maze test provides a means for determining whether students can identify the syntactically and semantically correct word that fits in a passage providing some information about text understanding.

Teaching Comprehension

What is the purpose of comprehension instruction?
Comprehension is the essence of reading and the ultimate goal of reading instruction. Reading comprehension is the process of constructing meaning by integrating the information provided by an author with a reader's background knowledge. It consists of three elements: the reader, the text, and the purpose for reading (RAND Reading Study Group, 2002). It involves complex cognitive skills and strategies with which the reader interacts with the text to construct meaning. There are many reasons why students may have difficulty comprehending what they read.

As a fourth grader reading at second-grade level, Amanda would probably better comprehend what she reads if she did not have to allocate so much attention to word identification. On the other hand, Scott is a word caller. He thinks that reading is "reading the words correctly." Even though he is able to read fluently, he does not attend to the meaning of passages. He frequently has difficulty recalling both the gist and details of a story. Sofia has been diagnosed as having language disabilities, with difficulties in syntax and semantics. These low oral language skills affect her comprehension of what she reads.

Sam can remember what he reads but does not relate it to what he already knows about the topic (schema). Therefore, he has particular difficulty answering questions that require him to use his background knowledge. Paolo, on the other hand, relies too heavily on his background knowledge. This is adversely affecting his reading

comprehension because he uses what he knows rather than what the text says when reading.

Kim fails to monitor her comprehension as she reads. She often reports that everything makes sense. Yet when her teacher asks questions, it becomes obvious that Kim has achieved limited comprehension.

All these students are struggling with reading comprehension, although their problems are very different. For students such as Amanda, word identification difficulties get in the way of comprehension. Focusing on building word identification skills is probably appropriate for her. However, comprehension skills should not be ignored. This may mean building listening comprehension at her current grade level as well as extending her knowledge of word meanings. For Amanda, it is making sure that reading is perceived as understanding and interacting with the text to construct meaning, not just reading the words correctly. Although word identification skill development will be important, it needs to be coupled with teaching comprehension.

For Scott, a considerable amount of emphasis in his reading program should be on comprehension. He requires assistance in changing his definition of the reading process. Helping Scott to set comprehension-oriented purposes for reading and teaching him how to ask questions as he reads should assist him in changing his definition of reading.

Sofia's difficulties relate to a language problem that affects her reading comprehension as well as her receptive language. For students such as Sofia, instruction in reading comprehension often parallels instruction in receptive language. Both reading and listening comprehension can be improved simultaneously. For example, when Sofia either listens to or reads a story, she needs to learn to ask and answer such questions as: "Who is the story about?" "Where did it happen?" "What was the problem in the story?" "What happened to solve the problem?" "How did the story end?"

Some students fail to relate what they are reading to what they already know about a topic. This is the case with Sam. Other students have limited background knowledge to bring to the reading process. Teaching strategies that encourage students to activate their knowledge or activities that provide opportunities for students to enrich their backgrounds before reading can facilitate comprehension.

Although some students do not rely enough on background knowledge, other students rely too much on background knowledge, as is the case with Paolo. Often, these are the same students who tend to overrely on context clues when identifying unknown words. When these students begin reading informational and technical texts that require accurate recall of information, comprehension problems become more evident. Comprehension strategies that encourage self-questioning can encourage such students to pay closer attention to the information presented in the text.

Kim has difficulty monitoring her understanding while reading with the metacognitive skill of comprehension monitoring. Strategies that teach students to ask questions about their comprehension and that require them to paraphrase and summarize what they read should help them to develop metacognitive skills (see Klingner, Vaughn, & Boardman, 2007 for sample reading comprehension practices for students with learning disabilities).

In this section on reading comprehension, we will examine a framework for reading comprehension and then focus on instructional strategies for improving reading comprehension. Finally, we will discuss approaches used for teaching reading and reading comprehension.

A Framework for Reading Comprehension

One way of guiding reading comprehension instruction is to determine the different reasoning and information-processing skills that are required by readers to construct meaning from what they read. Read the passage in Apply the Concept 8-5. Now answer each of the following questions, and think about the processes that were needed for you to arrive at an answer.

1. What did Pat do first to get help?
2. Where did you find the information to answer the question?
   The answer, of course, is in the text. If information is found in the text, then we say that the information is *textually explicit* or *literal* (i.e., taken directly from the text) or that we are *reading the lines* (Dale, 1966).
3. What time of day was it in the story?
4. Where did you find that information?
   You may have automatically answered question 3 as "early in the morning" or "in the morning" without looking back at the text. If you did this, go back and read to find out whether that information is in the text. It is not. Instead, you will find in the first paragraph that Pat "watched the sun come up over the mountains." You may have automatically integrated that information with your background knowledge to conclude that it was in the morning. When information is not in the text but requires you to integrate your background knowledge with text information to generate the answer, then we say the information is *implicit* or *inferential* (i.e., not stated directly in the text). Can we be more specific about this kind of implicit information? Pearson and Johnson (1978) refer to this kind of relationship between the question and the answer as *scriptually implicit*. It requires the reader to use a schema, or *script*, about *morning* to generate the answer. Dale (1966) has referred to this as *reading beyond the lines*.
5. Was Pat successful in using the C.B. radio?
6. Where did you find that information?

It was in the text, but not nearly as clearly as was the case for the first question. In this case, you had to read several sentences and piece the information together. The information was *implicit* in that it was not directly stated in the text, but it did not require you to use your background knowledge in the same way that question 4 did. Pearson and Johnson (1978) refer to this kind of implicit information as *textually implicit*. The relationship between the question and the answer required you to get the information from the text, but the relationship is not directly, or *explicitly*, stated. You had to use your knowledge about language and how ideas related to answer the question. Dale (1966) has referred to this relationship as *reading between the lines*.

Therefore, when teaching reading comprehension, we can divide comprehension into types of reasoning according to how readers have to activate their background

Apply the Concept

8-5

Thinking About Reading Comprehension

The Drive to Big Lake

Pat and her father were driving to Big Lake in the Blue Mountains. They were going to Big Lake to go fishing. As they drove Pat watched her father talk on the C.B. radio and watched the sun come up over the mountains.

When Pat and her father were near Big Lake it became very foggy. Pat's father drove slowly but did not see a sharp bend in the road. The car ran off the road and into a ditch. Pat was OK, but she knew that she needed to get help for her father.

She climbed out of the car and went to the road. She thought maybe a car would come by, but none did.

She walked down the road. She was looking for a house. As she walked, she yelled for help.

Then she remembered the C.B. radio that was in the car. She ran back to the car. She had never used the C.B., but she tried to call for help on it. A fisherman at Big Lake was listening to his C.B. Pat told him where she and her father were. Fifteen minutes later help came.

By this time Pat's father had opened his eyes and was OK. The police helped Pat and her father get the car out of the ditch and back on the road. Everyone was proud of Pat.

Source: C. S. Bos, Inferential Operations in the Reading Comprehension of Educable Mentally Retarded and Average Students, doctoral dissertation (Tucson: University of Arizona, 1979), p. 164.

knowledge to construct the meaning. These three arbitrary categories are as follows:

1. *Textually explicit:* Information is derived directly from the text with minimal input from the readers' background knowledge.
2. *Textually implicit:* Information is derived from the text, but readers are required to use their background knowledge to put together the ideas presented in the text.
3. *Scriptually implicit:* Information is not stated in the text. Readers have to activate and use their background knowledge to obtain the information.

We can also categorize comprehension by the type of information or relationship it represents. For example, the first question, "What did Pat do first to get help?" requires the reader to focus on the sequence of the events in the story. Therefore, it requires a sequencing or temporal relationship. The question "Why was everyone proud of Pat?" requires understanding of a causal relationship. Barrett (1976) has identified a number of types of information or relationships that can be represented in text (e.g., main ideas, details, sequence, cause and effect) as part of his taxonomy of reading. We can combine types of information with processes required (i.e., textually explicit, textually implicit, and scriptually implicit) to form a matrix for reading comprehension (Figure 8-6).

This matrix can be used in planning comprehension instruction, such as planning activities that will encourage students to engage in all the different facets of comprehension (cells in the matrix). For example, to work on

sequencing of ideas, students could retell a story by having each student in the group tell one episode from the story; copy a story onto sentence strips and discuss how to arrange the sentences in a logical order; read an explanation of how to do something and write a list of the steps in order; ask each other sequence questions about a description of how to make something; write a description of how to make something; and then have the other students in the group read the description and make the object. Whereas all of these activities focus on sequencing, both explicit and implicit comprehension are required to complete the various activities.

A matrix rather than a taxonomy is used to depict the various aspects of comprehension because comprehension should not be thought of as a set of hierarchical skills. The comprehension process entails ongoing transactions between a text, the reader, and the author and the active use of comprehension strategies such as predicting, activating background knowledge, asking questions, clarifying, and checking for understanding (Blachowicz & Ogle, 2008; Klingner, Vaughn, & Boardman, 2007).

But comprehension goes further than this. We also read to reflect on and judge the quality of the information. To read critically, students must be able to suspend judgment, consider other viewpoints, and draw logical conclusions. Thus, we engage in *critical reading*, including such skills as the following:

- Recognizing the author's purpose
- Distinguishing between facts and opinions
- Identifying words that signal opinions

▶ **Figure 8-6**   Matrix for Reading Comprehension

Type of Information or Relationship	Type of Reasoning Based on Background Knowledge		
	Textually Explicit	Textually Implicit	Scriptually Implicit
Main idea/summary	X	X	X
Detail	X	X	X
Sequence	X	X	X
Comparative relationship	X	X	X
Cause/effect relationship	X	X	X
Conditional relationship	X	X	X
Vocabulary definition	X	X	X
Vocabulary application	X	X	X
Figurative language definition	X	X	X
Figurative language application	X	X	X
Conclusion	X	X	X
Application		X	X
Analysis		X	X
Synthesis		X	X
Evaluation			X

- Verifying factual statements
- Detecting assumptions
- Judging sources
- Identifying persuasive language
- Detecting propaganda
- Drawing logical conclusions

In *aesthetic reading*, a reader's attention is centered on the literary style of a piece and the feelings that are engendered by reading the piece (Rosenblatt, 1978). Reading aesthetically results in a deeper level of involvement, with the reader identifying with the characters and picturing the story in his or her mind.

Both critical and aesthetic reading involve thinking about the text in relation to the readers' beliefs. For example, when Ms. Andretti, the intermediate-level inclusion teacher, was working on critical and aesthetic reading in a third-grade classroom, she had the students read the passage about Pat and her father (Apply the Concept 8-5). After reading, she asked the students, "Have you ever had an experience that made you feel like Pat?" Figure 8-7 lists sample areas of critical and aesthetic reading and sample teacher comments.

Guidelines for Teaching Reading Comprehension

If comprehension is the essence of reading, how do teachers go about teaching students with learning and behavior problems to be effective comprehenders? Three decades ago, observational research indicated that teachers spent little time teaching children how to comprehend (Duffy, Lanier, & Roehler, 1980; Durkin, 1978–79). For example, in Durkin's observational studies of reading instruction in fourth-grade classrooms, only 20 minutes of comprehension instruction was observed in more than 4,000 minutes of reading instruction. Much of what teachers did to "teach" comprehension was ask questions, have students respond, and provide feedback. Furthermore, they provided a steady diet of literal or textually explicit comprehension questions, a ratio of 4:1 literal to inferential, with lower reading groups getting asked even more literal questions than higher-level groups (Guszak, 1972).

Since then, instructional research and practice have focused on how to teach reading comprehension. Even when students have reading comprehension problems, it is important to first determine the factors that may be contributing to these reading difficulties. Before focusing solely on reading comprehension instruction, teachers should answer the following questions:

- Do students have adequate decoding and phonics skills so that they can read words?
- Do students read within the expected rate of reading for their grade level?
- Do students have adequate knowledge of the meaning of words?

▶ **Figure 8-7** Critical and Aesthetic Reading

Critical Reading

Critical reading: The reader reflects on and makes judgments about the content or information in the piece.

Sample Areas of Reflection or Judgment	Sample Comments
Reality or Fantasy	I don't think the author expected us to think this could really happen.
Fact or Opinion	You really get the idea they are pushing their point of view.
Adequacy and Validity	Some of this information just isn't right.
Worth	This piece really helped me write my report. I think this article could hurt his political campaign.

Aesthetic Reading

Aesthetic reading: The reader reflects on and makes judgments about the literary style of a piece.

Sample Areas of Reflection or Judgment	Sample Comments
Plot	I like the way the author always kept me interested in what was happening.
Characters	I didn't know enough about the witch to really understand why she did it.
Imagery	I could just picture myself being there.
Language	When the author said, "That was one frightened man," I felt a chill in my body.

- Does students' background knowledge adequately prepare them to understand the text?

For any student who does not meet these criteria, a complete reading comprehension program will require additional emphasis on decoding, fluency, vocabulary, and building background knowledge. It is unlikely that comprehension strategies alone will be sufficient for any student with reading difficulties. Apply the Concept 8-6 looks at comprehension issues with students who are ELLs.

One of the keys to teaching reading comprehension, particularly for students with learning and behavior problems, is to teach them to use comprehension and comprehension-monitoring strategies (Block, Morrow, & Parris, 2008; Klingner et al., 2007; RAND Reading Study Group, 2002). This includes such strategies as the following:

- *Activating background knowledge:* Thinking about what one already knows about the topic and how one's knowledge relates to what one is reading.

8-6

Understanding Reading Comprehension with Students Who Are English-Language Learners

For each of the questions below, ask yourself whether you implement the practice: never (1); some of the time, but not enough (2); whenever needed (3). Then, choose several instructional practices that you rated 1 or 2 and begin to implement them more frequently.

Do You

- ask students to make predictions about what they are going to read by using such features of the text as titles, pictures, and key words?
- provide students with opportunities to integrate their background

knowledge with the critical concepts in the text?
- identify the language demands of the text they are reading and preteach related vocabulary and concepts?
- request that students monitor the words and concepts they do not understand while they're reading, make note of them, and then follow up with them?
- ask students questions they can answer and then scaffold responses to meet language needs?
- model and provide opportunities for students to construct mental images that represent text, so they can better remember and understand what they read?

- provide opportunities for students to seek clarification about confusing aspects of what they read?
- plan language-related activities that link with comprehending text and then make these explicit to students?
- give students adequate opportunities to develop questions about what they have read and pose these questions to fellow students?
- give students adequate time and practice responding orally?
- provide practice in summarizing and integrating information from text?

Source: S. Linan-Thompson & S. Vaughn, *Research-Based Methods of Reading Instruction for English Language Learners* (Alexandria, VA: ASCD, 2007). Reprinted with permission.

- *Preteaching critical vocabulary and concepts:* Teaching students to prepare to read a text by preteaching essential vocabulary and concepts that facilitate learning and understanding.
- *Generating questions:* Asking relevant questions that promote understanding, such as *who, what, when, where, why,* and *how* questions.
- *Monitoring comprehension:* Checking for understanding and using fix-up strategies (e.g., rereading, clarifying a concept) to facilitate comprehension.
- *Clarifying:* Clarifying unclear concepts or vocabulary.
- *Using graphic organizers:* Using visual aids that illustrate concepts and relationships among concepts in a text while reading the text.
- *Finding main ideas:* Determining the most important information and explaining this information in one's own words.
- *Summarizing:* Identifying the main ideas, connecting the main ideas, eliminating redundant information, and putting this information in one's own words.
- *Using text structure:* Using knowledge of different text structures (e.g., narrative, expositive) as a framework for comprehension.

In other words, teachers need to teach cognitive strategies that will give students with learning and behavior problems the tools for understanding and constructing meaning from what they are reading.

Knowing what the strategies are is the first step for a teacher, the more difficult one is knowing how to teach them. As is the case with higher-level academic learning, this is particularly challenging because comprehension involves thinking processes that are not nearly as visible as they are in other skills, such as spelling and math calculations. Therefore, instruction in reading comprehension is beneficial when teachers:

- Provide rationales and evidence for the effectiveness of its use.
- Describe and model the strategy using thinking-aloud.
- Provide supported practice and feedback.
- Provide independent practice.
- Teach for generalization (i.e., when and where strategies apply) and maintenance.

Comprehension instruction can be accomplished through more direct explanations and mental modeling associated with cognitive strategy. Based on ideas from schema theories, our instruction assists students in activating their prior knowledge about a topic before they read so that they can apply this knowledge both during and after reading. Students also learn the importance of predicting and questioning as they read.

See Chapter 2 for an overview of schema theory.

Effective comprehension instruction encourages students to engage actively not only in discussions related to the content of the text, but also in instructional conversations about the reading process. These discussions can be prompted by the following steps:

1. *Before reading,* the teacher activates the students' background knowledge for the selected passage and/or provides experiences to enrich their backgrounds. The teacher assists students in thinking about how this text may be related to other texts in terms of content, story line, and text structure. The teacher helps students to set purposes for reading by predicting and asking questions about what they are going to read. It is important that teacher support and scaffolding are used to prevent students from "guessing" without consideration of relevant text cues. It is also valuable for teachers to preteach proper nouns and to give students key ideas about the text prior to reading.

2. *During reading,* the teacher encourages students to self-question and monitor their comprehension as they read.

3. *After reading,* the teacher uses follow-up activities such as

- discussions that focus on the content of the reading as well as evaluation of the content and the writing style.
- discussions that encourage students to generate more questions and ideas for further reading and investigation.
- retellings that assist students in summarizing and organizing what they have read.

Explicit instruction in comprehension strategies yields positive learner outcomes, especially for students with reading difficulties (Klingner et al., 2007; RAND Reading Study Group, 2002). The idea behind explicit instruction of comprehension is that comprehension can be improved by teaching students to use specific cognitive strategies or to reason strategically when they encounter barriers to comprehension while reading. Tech Tips describes how text enhancements and speech feedback provided by a computer can support self-regulated reading.

Previewing, Predicting, and Developing Prior Knowledge

Reading comprehension instruction occurs before reading through previewing, predicting, and activating/developing background knowledge. Prereading activities help students prepare to understand and learn from what they read. Taking time to prepare students before they read can pay big dividends in terms of their understanding and finding reading an enjoyable experience (Graves, Juel, & Graves, 2007). Graves and his colleagues suggest that prereading activities

- set purposes for reading.
- motivate students to read.
- activate and build background knowledge.
- build knowledge of the text features.
- relate reading to students' lives.
- preteach vocabulary and concepts.
- provide opportunities for prequestioning, predicting, and direction setting.

 **Tech** TIPS

USING TECHNOLOGY TO HELP STRUGGLING READERS

The computer is an ideal tool for helping students learn phonological awareness and phonics, build fluency, increase their vocabulary and work recognition, and enhance comprehension. The following programs are designed to help struggling readers achieve these goals.

Lexia by Lexia Learning Systems. Inc.
http://www.lexialearning.com/reserach/3tier.html
This program is used with K–8 students and is used in conjunction with the three-tiered RTI model to support struggling readers. Students practice phonological awareness and phonics to help themselves improve their reading skills.

Reading Assistant by Scientific Learning.
http://www.scilearn.com/products/
reading-assistant/index.php

Reading Assistant is a scientifically based intervention that helps struggling readers of all ages. Using speech recognition technology, this program allows students to practice their reading with the benefit of instant feedback and progress monitoring as the student moves through the program.

Read Naturally by Read Naturally, Inc.
http://www.readnaturally.com/
This program uses reaching strategies such as modeling, repeat reading, and assessment strategies to help students develop phonological awareness, phonics, fluency, word recognition, and reading comprehension.

What instructional techniques can a teacher use that will help students with learning and behavior problems to activate relevant background knowledge (schema), bridge what they know to what they are reading, motivate them to read, assist them in making predictions about what they are going to be reading, preview the reading, and assist them in becoming familiar with difficult vocabulary? Activating prior knowledge is particularly important for students with learning and behavior problems. As with all learners, their prior knowledge is crucial to the successful construction of meaning. Apply the Concept 8-7 presents ideas for facilitating and teaching comprehension.

Brainstorming Brainstorming is a teaching strategy that activates the students' relevant prior knowledge, aids the teacher in determining the extent of the students' prior knowledge, and stimulates interest in the topic.

 EVIDENCE-BASED PRACTICE

Brainstorming

PROCEDURES: Brainstorming works best with groups of students who are reading the same or related selections. Before beginning the activity, determine the major topic or concept presented in the selection(s). Next decide what to use as a stimulus to represent that topic. It might be a single word or phrase, a picture, a poem, or a short excerpt from the reading passage. Before reading, conduct the brainstorming session:

1. Present the stimulus to the students.
2. Ask the students to list as many words or phrases as they can associate with the stimulus. Encourage them to think about everything they know about the topic or concept. Allow several minutes for the students to think and get ready to report or write their ideas.
3. Record the students' associations on the board. Ask for other associations, and add them to the list. While writing ideas on the board, assist students in making connections among these ideas by talking about how they are related.
4. With the students, categorize the associations. Clarify the ideas and discuss what titles to use for the categories. You may want to organize the ideas into a learning map.

> Strategies for organizing story maps are discussed later in this chapter, and strategies for developing content maps are discussed in Chapter 10.

COMMENTS: Brainstorming is a quick and simple way to activate background knowledge. It usually takes 5 to 10 minutes to complete. However, for some students and topic combinations, simple associations without further discussion may not provide enough input to activate and build on students' prior knowledge. The next procedure provides additional activities for further activating knowledge.

Apply the Concept

8-7 Strategies for Promoting Reading Comprehension for Students Who Are Culturally Diverse and/or English-Language Learners

For students from culturally and linguistically diverse backgrounds and for ELLs, a number of strategies can be used to promote reading comprehension.

Making Input More Comprehensible

- Teach new concepts by working from the students' prior knowledge and incorporating the funds of knowledge from the students' communities.
- Use demonstrations and gestures to augment oral and written communication.
- Discuss connections between the concepts being read and the students' home cultures.

- Encourage students to share the new vocabulary in their first language and incorporate the first language into instruction.
- Pair more proficient ELLs with less proficient peers, and encourage students to discuss what they are reading.
- Provide opportunities for students to learn to read and to read in their first language.
- Highlight key words and phrases in text and incorporate them into semantic maps.
- Teach text structures and use visual representations of text structures.
- Ask questions or discuss new ideas or vocabulary, slow the pace.
- Repeat key ideas and write them.

- Use think-alouds to make comprehension strategies more explicit.

Incorporating Multicultural Literature into the Reading Program

- Select literature that reflects various cultures.
- Study authors from various cultures.
- Read literature that incorporates various dialects.
- Select genres that are typical of different cultures.
- Use book lists, directories, Web sites, and textbooks on multicultural education as resources for multicultural literature.
- Provide text written in the students' first languages available to them.

PreReading Plan The PreReading Plan (PReP) is a three-phase instructional-assessment strategy that builds on the activity of brainstorming. Designed by Langer (1981), it assists students in accessing knowledge related to the major concepts presented in a reading selection.

  EVIDENCE-BASED PRACTICE

PreReading Plan

PROCEDURES: Before beginning the activity, provide a phrase or picture to stimulate group discussion about a key concept in the text. For example, if a science selection is about the types and characteristics of mammals, *mammals* might serve as the stimulus word. After introducing the topic, conduct the following three-phase process:

1. *Initial association with the concept.* Cue students by saying something like, "Say what you think are attributes of mammals." Have the students generate a list of ideas, words, and associations. Record the key ideas on the board, noting the student's name by each association.

2. *Reflections on initial associations.* Now ask the students, "What made you think...[the responses given by each of the students during phase 1]?" This phase requires the students to bring to the conscious level their prior knowledge and how it relates to the key concept. It also allows the students to listen to each other's responses.

3. *Reformation of knowledge.* After students have had an opportunity to think and tell about what triggered their ideas, ask, "On the basis of our discussion, do you have any new ideas about mammals?" This question gives the students the opportunity to discuss how they have elaborated or changed their ideas on the basis of the previous discussion. Because the students have had the opportunity to listen to other students, new links between prior knowledge and the key concept are also formed.

On the basis of the information gathered during this three-phase procedure, Langer presents a means of assessing prior knowledge into levels to determine whether further concept building will need to be completed before reading (see Figure 8-8). The three levels and their instructional implications are as follows:

1. *Much knowledge.* Students whose free associations reflect superordinate concepts, definitions, analogies, or a linking of the key concept to other relevant concepts demonstrate *much* integration of the key concept with concepts that are already in accessible memory. Comprehension for these students should be adequate.

2. *Some knowledge.* Students whose free associations are primarily examples, attributes, or defining characteristics have *some* knowledge about the concepts being taught. Comprehension should be adequate, but some instructional activities that assist the students in making

▶ **Figure 8-8** PreReading Plan: Levels of Prior Knowledge

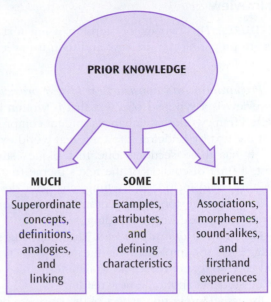

Source: J. A. Langer, Facilitating test processing: The elaboration of prior knowledge, in J. A. Langer & M. T. Smith-Burke (Eds.), *Reader Meets Author/Bridging the Gap* (Newark, DE: International Reading Association, 1982), p. 156. Reprinted by permission of Judith A. Langer and the International Reading Association.

the critical links between existing and new knowledge may be necessary.

3. *Little knowledge.* Students whose free associations reflect morphemes (prefixes, suffixes, root words), rhyming words, or unelaborated or unrelated firsthand experiences demonstrate *little* knowledge of the concept. These students need concept instruction before reading commences, with the reported firsthand experiences serving as a reference point for starting instruction.

COMMENTS: The PReP provides a direct means of activating the students' background knowledge. The authors have frequently used both brainstorming and PReP, particularly with upper-elementary and secondary students with learning and behavior problems. We find that taking the extra time to conduct PReP is worthwhile, since it requires students to bring to the conscious level why they made their associations, and it gives them the opportunity to reflect on what they have learned through the discussion. It is a good idea to have students add to and adjust their lists during reading and after they read.

Text Preview Text previews are designed to increase students' prior knowledge, motivate students to read, and provide a scaffold for text comprehension (Graves et al., 2007). Text previews can be used with students at varying reading and grade levels and with both narrative and expository texts.

Text Preview

PROCEDURES: The two major steps in using text previews are preparing the preview and then using it with the students.

1. *Preparation and construction of text previews.* A text preview is a synopsis of a text that is written in an organized framework that enhances student comprehension of the text by bridging it to their real-world experiences. It has three sections: one that piques student interest, a brief discussion of the text's theme (e.g., for stories this could include the setting, character descriptions, and essential story organization), and questions or directions that guide student reading.

2. *Presentation of text previews.* The following steps are suggested for implementing the text preview and should take no longer than 5 to 10 minutes:

- Cue students about the new reading.
- Discuss an interesting aspect of the story or content that will pique motivation.
- Make connections to the students' lives and world knowledge.
- Present the questions or directions that should guide student reading.
- Have students read the text.

Discussing an interesting aspect of the story or content helps students to delve into reading materials, knowing that there will be new knowledge, discoveries, and/or excitement. These motivational activities often involve hands-on experiences and intrigue that are then tied to the story that is being read. For example, a teacher might say, "Feel these fabrics, and tell me what it makes you think about and how it makes you feel. In the story, Robbie has a special blanket made out of these fabrics—satin and flannel. As you read the story think about what is special about this blanket and how it feels." Making connections to the students' lives and their world knowledge also activates background knowledge and creates motivation. Using a connections chart such as the one in Figure 8-9 helps students think about connections they can make to their own lives and to world knowledge they have about a topic. For example, in reading about dolphins, students can list experiences they have had with dolphins as well as facts they know about dolphins before they read and then add to the list after they read.

COMMENTS: Although text previews take time to prepare, students report that previews enable them to understand texts to a fuller extent (Dole, Valencia, Greer, & Wardrop, 1991; Simmons et al., 2010). When using text previews with expository text, the teacher may want to include important points, vocabulary, and big ideas related to the

▶ **Figure 8-9** Connections Chart About Dolphins

Connection to Dolphins

Connections to Our Experiences	Connections to World Knowledge
Reneé, Maria, Jon, Marcos petted the dolphins at Sea World	Skin is soft and smooth
Peter saw dolphins swim under boat when his family was sailing in Florida	Seem to communicate with one another
Everyone has seen dolphins on TV	Bottlenose dolphin
	Have to come to surface to breathe

text (Simmons et al., 2010). Additionally, teachers can use text previews as potential writing assignments. Students can be assigned to develop text previews for other students' guided reading. Critical thinking about the ideas presented in a text selection will ensue as students create text previews for one another.

K-W-L K-W-L is a strategy that is designed to activate students' background knowledge and to assist students in setting purposes for reading expository text (Bryant, 1998; Ogle, 1986, 1989).

● ● ● **EVIDENCE-BASED PRACTICE**

K-W-L

PROCEDURES: The K-W-L strategy consists of three basic steps representative of the cognitive/metacognitive steps that students employ as they use the strategy:

1. Accessing what I <u>K</u>now
2. Determining what I <u>W</u>ant to learn
3. Recalling what I <u>L</u>earned

To assist the students in using the strategy, Ogle (1986, 1989) developed a simple worksheet for the students to complete during the reading–thinking process (see Figure 8-10).

During the *Know* step, the teacher and students engage in a discussion that is designed to assist students in thinking about what they already know about the topic of the text. For this step, the teacher starts by using a brainstorming procedure (see the section on brainstorming). As in the PReP, students are encouraged to discuss where or how they learned the information so as to provide information about the source and substantiveness of their ideas. After brainstorming, the teachers and students discuss the general categories of information that are likely to be encountered when they read, and how their brainstormed ideas could help them determine the

What I Know	What I Want to Learn	What I Learned	More Questions I Have
Contains water	How does the pond get its water?	Underground springs and rain	Why do ponds die?
Smaller than a lake	Why are ponds green and muddy?	Algae and other plants make it green	What happens to a pond in winter?
Fish			
Ducks	Does the temperature change?	Like the air but temperature is less affected the deeper you go	How does algae help or hurt a pond?
Frogs			
Muddy	What fish live in the pond?	Blue gill, trout, bass, catfish	
Algae	What insects live in the pond?	Dragonflies, mosquitoes, water fleas	
Insect on top			
Birds eat insects	What plants live in the pond?	Algae, cattails, water lilies	

Source: Adapted from P. R. Schmidt (1999), KWLQ: Inquiry and literacy learning in science, *The Reading Teachers*, 52, pp. 789–792.

categories. For example, a teacher might cue students that when they read they should consider one category that addresses "causes of the war" and a second category that considers "consequences of the war." During the *Want to Learn* step, the teacher and students discuss what they want to learn from reading the text. Although most of this step utilizes group discussion, before students begin to read, each student writes down the specific questions in which he or she is most interested.

During the *Learned* step, the students write what they learned from reading. They should also check the questions that they generated in the previous step to find out whether they were addressed in the text.

COMMENTS: K-W-L is a strategy for helping students to actively engage in the reading process and for assisting teachers in teaching reading using an interactive model of reading. Informal evaluation of the strategy indicates that students recalled more information in articles when they used K-W-L and that they enjoyed using the strategy and used it independently (Ogle, 1986). Carr and Ogle (1987) added mapping and summarizing activities to K-W-L to gain the advantage of these powerful comprehension tools. Ogle (1989) added a fourth column "what we still want to learn" and referred to this adaptation as K-W-L Plus. Bryant (1998) referred to it as K-W-W-L to assist students in generating questions and designing scientific experiments, and Schmidt (1999) referred to it as K-W-L-Q, with the *Q* representing more questions. This addition encourages further research and reading.

Questioning Strategies

Asking questions is a major vehicle that teachers use to foster understanding and retention and to check for comprehension. When questions are asked about information in text, that information is remembered better. Asking higher-level questions that require integration of background and text knowledge (see Figure 8-6) will promote deeper

processing and therefore more learning (Vaughn & Edmonds, 2006). Even asking "Why?" and "How?" can significantly increase retention of information.

However, simply asking questions does not ensure that students will develop questioning strategies. Students' answers to questions can give limited insight into their understanding of text. As has already been demonstrated, teacher and student questioning before reading helps to activate prior knowledge and to set purposes for reading. Self-questioning during reading (e.g., Does this make sense? Am I understanding what I am reading? How does this relate to what I already know? What will happen next?) assists students in monitoring comprehension.

The following techniques require teachers to model comprehension questions and comprehension-monitoring questions, teach students to recognize types of questions, and encourage students to self-question before, during, and after they read.

ReQuest or Reciprocal Questioning   The ReQuest procedure is a reciprocal questioning technique that is designed to assist students in formulating their own questions about what they read. The procedure was developed by Manzo (1969; Manzo & Manzo, 1993), who stressed the importance of students' setting their own purposes for reading and asking their own questions as they read.

 **EVIDENCE-BASED PRACTICE**

ReQuest or Reciprocal Questioning

PROCEDURES: This technique relies heavily on modeling, which is a major premise of cognitive strategy instruction. To use ReQuest, select materials at the students' instructional to independent reading levels. You and the students read a sentence or section of the passage and then take turns asking each other questions. Your role is to model good questioning and to provide feedback to students about their questions. In modeling, include higher-level questions that require you to use scriptually and textually implicit information and that require critical and aesthetic reading. Also include monitoring questions (e.g., Does this make sense?).

Manzo suggests that this procedure first be introduced on an individual basis and then used in small groups. The following explanation can be used to introduce ReQuest:

The purpose of this lesson is to improve your understanding of what you read. We will each read silently the first sentence [section]. Then we will take turns asking questions about the sentence [section] and what it means. You will ask questions first, then I will ask questions. Try to ask the kinds of questions a teacher might ask in the way a teacher might ask them.

You may ask me as many questions as you wish. When you are asking me questions, I will close my book (or pass the book to you if there is only one between us). When I ask questions, you close your book (Manzo, 1969, p. 124).

The rules are that the answer "I don't know" is not allowed, unclear questions are to be restated, and uncertain answers are to be justified by reference to the text or other source material if necessary. In addition, you and the students may need to discuss unfamiliar vocabulary.

The procedure itself consists of the following steps:

1. *Silent reading.* You and the students read the sentence or section.
2. *Student questioning.* Close your book while the students ask questions. Model appropriate answers, and reinforce appropriate questioning behavior. The students ask as many questions as possible.
3. *Teacher questioning.* The students close their books, and you ask questions modeling a variety of question types (see Figure 8-6).
4. *Integration of the text.* After completing the procedure with the first sentence or section, repeat the process with subsequent sentences or sections. Integrate the new section with previous sections by asking questions that relate to new and old sections.
5. *Predictive questioning.* When the students have read enough to make a prediction about the rest of the passage, ask predictive questions (e.g., What do you think will happen? Why do you think so?). If the predictions and verification are reasonable, you and the students move to the next step.
6. *Reading.* You and the students read to the end of the passage to verify and discuss your predictions.

COMMENTS: One important aspect of this strategy is the questions that the teacher models, including:

- *Predictable questions:* The typical *who, what, when, where, why,* and *how* questions
- *Mind-opening questions:* Questions that are designed to help the students understand how written and oral language are used to communicate ideas

- *Introspective questions:* Metacognitive questions that are oriented toward self-monitoring and self-evaluation
- *Ponderable questions:* Questions that stimulate discussion and for which no right or wrong answer is apparent
- *Elaborative knowledge questions:* Questions that require students to integrate their background knowledge with the information given in the text

The ReQuest procedure assists students in developing appropriate questions. We have used several variations of these procedures. For instance, we have introduced the ReQuest procedure as a game. The students and teacher take turns asking questions and keeping score of appropriate answers. We also recommend that the text be read in longer, more natural segments rather than individual sentences. Some students benefit from having question starters to help them initiate questions. These question starters could be things like: Why did he . . . ? Why do you think the ending . . . ? What would happen if . . . ?

Question–Answer Relationships Strategy The question–answer relationships strategy (QARs; Raphael, 1982, 1984, 1986) is designed to assist students in labeling the types of questions that are asked and to use this information to help guide them as they develop answers. QARs was developed by Raphael and Pearson (1982) to facilitate correct responses to questions. It helps students to realize they need to consider both the text and their prior knowledge when answering questions and to use strategic behavior to adjust the use of each of these sources.

 **EVIDENCE-BASED PRACTICE**

Question–Answer Relationships Strategy

PROCEDURES: QARs was originally taught by Raphael (1984), using the three categories of information suggested in the matrix for reading comprehension (Figure 8-6). The three categories were renamed for use with students:

1. *Right There:* Words used to create the question and words used for the answer are in the same sentence (textually explicit).
2. *Think and Search:* The answer is in the text, but words used to create the question and those used for an appropriate answer would not be in the same sentence (textually implicit).
3. *On My Own:* The answer is not found in the text but in one's head (scriptually implicit).

On the basis of input from teachers, Raphael (1986) modified these categories to include two major categories—*In the Book* and *In My Head*—and then further divided these categories, as shown in Figure 8-11.

Raphael suggests the following procedure for introducing QARs: The first day, introduce the students to the concept of question–answer relationships (QARs),

► **Figure 8-11**   Cue Card for Question–Answer Relationships (QARs)

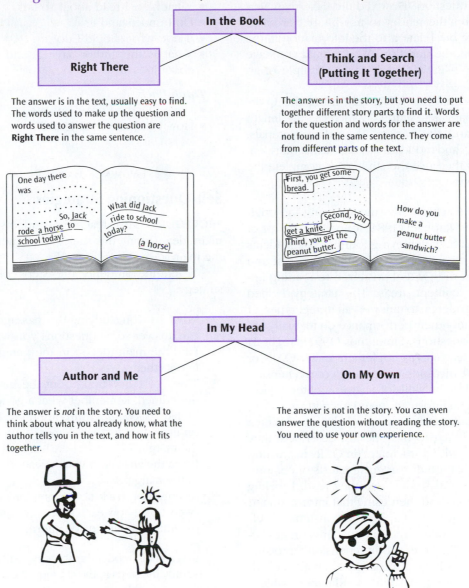

The answer is in the text, usually easy to find. The words used to make up the question and words used to answer the question are **Right There** in the same sentence.

The answer is in the story, but you need to put together different story parts to find it. Words for the question and words for the answer are not found in the same sentence. They come from different parts of the text.

The answer is *not* in the story. You need to think about what you already know, what the author tells you in the text, and how it fits together.

The answer is not in the story. You can even answer the question without reading the story. You need to use your own experience.

Source: Adapted from T. E. Raphael (1986), Teaching question–answer relationships, revisited, *The Reading Teacher, 39* (6), pp. 516–523.

using the two major categories. Use several short passages (from two to five sentences) to demonstrate the relationships. Provide practice by asking students to identify the type of QAR, the answer to the question, and the strategy they used for finding the answer. The progression for teaching should be from highly supportive to independent:

1. Provide the text, questions, answers, QAR label for each question, and reason why the label was appropriate.
2. Provide the text, questions, answers, and QAR label for each question. Have the students supply the reason for the label.

3. Provide the text, questions, and answers, and have the students supply the QAR labels and reasons for the labels.
4. Provide the text and questions, and have the students supply the answers, QAR labels, and reasons for the labels.

When the students have a clear picture of the difference between *In My Head* and *In the Book*, teach the next level of differentiation for each one of the major categories. First, work on *In the Book*, then go to *In My Head*. When the information must come from the reader but in connection with the information presented by the author, then the QAR is *Author and You*. For example, in the story about Pat and her father (Apply the Concept 8-5), the question "How did the fisherman alert the police?" requires the reader to use his or her background knowledge but relate it to the information in the text. In comparison, the question "What would you have done if you were in Pat's shoes?" is an example of an *On My Own* QAR.

Once the students are effectively using the QARs strategy in short passages, gradually increase the length of the passages and the variety of reading materials. Review the strategy, and model its use on the first question. Have the students then use the strategy to complete the rest of the questions.

COMMENTS: After teaching this strategy using the original three categories, Raphael (1984) found that groups of low-, average-, and high-achieving fourth-grade students had higher performance on a comprehension test and gave evidence that the QARs transferred to reading improvement in the content areas. This strategy helped lower-achieving students to answer all three types of questions, particularly their performance on textually explicit and implicit questions. Simmonds (1992) taught 24 special education teachers to implement either QARs or selected traditional methods of reading comprehension instruction, including the skills of answering literal questions (recall of factual information and main ideas), locating supportive details, and drawing conclusions. Using a lesson sequence similar to the one just described, they found that students who participated in QARs instruction performed better than other students on tests of comprehension over the social studies text they read. Labeling the types of questions and then using that information to assist in answering questions appear to constitute an effective strategy for students and one that encourages active involvement in the comprehension process. QAR-type approaches have also been used with secondary students with reading disabilities (Klingner, Vaughn et al., 2001).

Self-Questioning Strategies Self-questioning strategies are a good example of how metacognition assists students in reading. These questions typically have the student focus on activating prior knowledge and setting purposes for reading, asking questions to assist the comprehension process, checking understanding during reading, and reviewing after reading to determine understanding. For example, Alvermann et al. (1989) suggest the following self-questions to foster comprehension:

Think Ahead
- What is this section about?
- What do I already know about the topic?
- What do I want to find out?
- What is my goal?
- How should I go about reading to meet my goal?

Think While Reading
- What have I read about so far?
- Do I understand it?
- If not, what should I do?
- What is the author saying, and what did I think about it?

Think Back
- Have I learned what I wanted to learn?
- How can I use what I read?

● ● ● EVIDENCE-BASED PRACTICE

Self-Questioning Strategies

PROCEDURES: First, teach the students the concept of a main idea. During this stage, teach them how to identify the main idea(s) in paragraphs.

Teach the students the steps of self-questioning strategy:

1. What are you studying this passage for? (So that you can answer some questions you will be given later.)
2. Find the main idea(s) in the paragraph, and underline it (them).
3. Think of a question about the main idea you have underlined. Remember what a good question should be like. (*Good questions* are those that directly focus on important textual elements. Write the question in the margin.)
4. Learn the answer to your question. (Write the answer in the margin.)
5. Always look back at the previous questions and answers to see how each successive question and answer provides you with more information.

In teaching, model the strategy, and then have the students study the steps in the strategy. Next, have the students practice using this strategy on individual paragraphs, and provide them with immediate corrective feedback. Have the students use a cue card like the one in Figure 8-12 to assist them in remembering the steps in the strategy. When the students are successful, switch to multiple-paragraph passages, and gradually fade the use of the cue cards. Give feedback at the end of each passage. At the end of each lesson, discuss the students' progress and the usefulness of the self-questioning strategy.

COMMENTS: Results from the Wong and Jones (1982) study indicate that students with learning disabilities who learned the self-questioning strategy performed significantly higher on comprehension tests than did students who were not taught the strategy.

Another self-questioning strategy, the Kansas University Center for Research on Learning (KU-CRL) self-questioning strategy, was developed at the KU-CRL (Clark, Deshler, Shumaker, Alley, & Warner, 1984). This strategy was used to

► **Figure 8-12** Frame for Answering
Wh- and How Questions

Student Name: _____

Title: _____

Pages: _____

Date: _____

| Who? |
| What? |
| Where? |
| When? |
| Why? |
| How? |

reading, and talk to themselves about the answers by using the mnemonic ASK IT. The ASK IT steps are as follows:

1. Attend to the clues as you read.
2. Say some questions.
3. Keep predictions in mind.
4. Identify the answer.
5. Talk about the answers.

For self-questioning strategies to be effective for students with reading difficulties, it is important that teachers provide modeling, direct coaching, prompting, and guidance (Chan, 1991; Gersten, Williams, Fuchs, & Baker, in press; Mastropieri, Scruggs, Hamilton et al., 1996). Teaching students to stop and question themselves before, during, and/or after reading is another key element of success (Edmonds, Vaughn et al., 2009; Mastropieri & Scruggs, 1997).

Questioning the Author Though not technically a practice designed to teach students to ask themselves questions, Questioning the Author (Beck & McKeown, 2006) provides students with well-scaffolded instruction that supports their interactions with texts and eventually with each other as though the author were available for comment and conversation. The idea is to have students actively engage with a text. With Questioning the Author, the teacher has given distinct goals and several queries that assist students in reaching those goals. First, students and teachers require coherent texts so that understanding and engaging in discussion is a possible enterprise. Second, students need to have some background knowledge of the topic so that they can adequately discuss what they are reading; and third, teachers and students require a logical set of questions to better understand text.

 **EVIDENCE-BASED PRACTICE**

Questioning the Author

PROCEDURES: First, select text that is coherent. The text type selected may be either narrative or expository. Be sure to consider the background knowledge that students require to understand the text. To the extent possible, identify key ideas and concepts and preteach them to students prior to reading the text.

Second, students are taught to "grapple" with ideas while they are reading and to consider what the author means and the extent to which the author may not have communicated very well. In this way, meaning is built "as they read" rather than at the end of the reading. In this way, students share and discuss while reading, enhancing background knowledge and understanding, and increasing understanding of text as they continue reading. The focus is not on the discussion per se but on the understanding of what they are reading.

Third, teachers and students use queries to promote understanding and to place responsibility for understanding

assist secondary-level students with learning disabilities in comprehending and remembering the important information presented in content area textbooks. The KU-CRL self-questioning strategy focuses on teaching students how to generate questions about important information in a passage, predict the answers, search for the answers while text onto the students; for example, What is the author trying to tell us? and Why do you think the author is saying this?

Fourth, the teacher establishes the fallibility of the author with the students so that they learn that a text is simply one person's ideas written down and that these ideas should be considered in light of other knowledge and their own experience. This provides students with an engagement with text and the author that is typically not available.

COMMENTS: Several studies document the effectiveness of Questioning the Author in classwide implementation in general education classrooms with at-risk students (for a review, see Beck & McKeown, 2006). Findings have not been conducted separately for students with learning disabilities. Also, studies have been conducted with fourth-grade students. Consequently, Questioning the Author may be a very valuable way to engage students with learning disabilities—particularly older students.

According to McKeown and Beck (2004), "the development of meaning in [Questioning the Author] focuses on readers' interactions with text as it is being read, situates reader-text interactions in whole-class discussion, and encourages explanatory, evidence-based responses to questions about text" (p. 393). Evidence from their studies in many classrooms suggest that teachers and students who adopted this Questioning the Author perspective also became increasingly engaged with text. In addition, interactions in the classroom changed from the traditional question-and-answer routines, which appear to be much like test questions and answers, to more collaborative discussions that involved both teacher and students in questioning and the development and elaboration of new ideas.

Text Structure and Summarization Strategies

Text structure refers to the organizational features of text that help readers understand and predict how the text will be organized. For example, text structures around fairy tales and text structures around biographies are different. Understanding how they are different can help you with comprehension. Often, teachers divide text into two major types: narrative and expository. *Narrative texts* tell a story and can be organized into components such as setting, problem statement, goals, event sequences or episodes, and ending. Generally, stories are easier for students to comprehend than expository text because the story structure is more consistent and has a linear orientation, making it more predictable. Carnine, Silbert, and Kame'enui (1997) suggest that teachers use the following four story grammar questions:

1. Who is the story about?
2. What is she or he trying to do?
3. What happens when she or he tries to do it?
4. What happens in the end?

Typical questions that focus on story grammar include:

- Where does the story take place (setting)?
- When does the story take place (setting)?

- Who are the main people in the story (characters)?
- What problems does the main character face (problem)?
- What are the main character's goals (goal)?
- What does the main character want to do to solve the problem (goal)?
- What are the main things that happened in the story to solve the problem (plot)?
- How did each thing work out (plot)?
- Is the problem finally resolved? If so, how (outcome/ending)?

Expository texts are also referred to as *information texts* because they are designed to explain phenomena or provide information. These are the informational texts that students encounter not only in school content area subjects such as social studies, science, math, and vocational education, but also in newspapers and magazines and on the Internet. Expository texts can be more difficult to comprehend because there is more variation in their organization (e.g., describing an object, comparing and contrasting two ideas, explaining a cause–effect relationship), the content may be less familiar, and there may be a high proportion of technical terms. Teaching types of expository texts can help students with comprehension problems to understand the more complex scientific style of thinking that is evident in expository text (Williams, 2005). Figure 8-13 presents six types of expository texts with signal words and cohesive ties that note the relationships and sample frameworks that depict the relationships. These text structures can also guide the types of questions that promote comprehension. For example, here are some questions that can be asked to help students understand the process of rusting (cause–effect structure) and how it relates to their lives (Muth, 1987):

- What causes rusting?
- What are some of the effects of rusting?
- What conditions cause rusting?
- What kinds of things rust in your home and why?
- What can be done around your home to prevent rusting? Why would these things work?

The type of text may vary within an expository passage or paragraph, and thinking about the specific type can facilitate comprehension.

More techniques related to expository texts are presented in Chapter 10 in the discussion of content area learning.

Story-Mapping and Story-Retelling Strategies Story-retelling strategies provide students with a framework for retelling the key points of narrative texts. The strategies can be combined with story maps, which provide students with a visual guide to understanding and retelling stories. Figure 8-15 shows a visual framework for a simple story.

Text Type	Cohesive Ties and Signal Words	Sample Frameworks
Descriptive or Enumerative Describes the characteristics, attributes, examples, or a series of facts about a topic	for example, for instance in addition besides to illustrate characteristics are can be described as moreover such as in other words	
Sequential or How To Tell how to do something or a series of events presented in order	first, second, third next last, finally before, after in the past, in the future currently	
Compare–Contrast Two or more topics are compared according to the their likenesses and differences	different from same as, alike however in contrast in comparison, compared to instead of on the other hand whereas similarly	
Cause–Effect Explanation of the reason(s) for something or why something happened and the resulting effect(s)	cause, because therefore, thus as a result of if . . . then consequently for this reason	
Problem–Solution Statement of a problem and possible solutions, sometimes with resulting effects	problem is possible solutions	
Argument or Persuasion Statement of a position on an issue with justification	the point is first, second, next, last reasons major reason consequently therefore	

Sample Frameworks diagrams:
- Descriptive: central circle with Facts, Examples, Characteristics radiating out.
- Sequential: four connected boxes in a chain with arrows.
- Compare–Contrast: Topic branching to Alike and Different.
- Cause–Effect: Cause branching to three Effects.
- Problem–Solution: Problem branching to four Solutions.
- Argument: Position branching to Reason 1, Reason 2, Reason 3, leading to Conclusion.

Teachers have taught students with reading problems how to use story maps and story strategies to aid in comprehending and retelling stories (Bos, 1999; Cain, 1996; Gurney, Gersten, Dimino, & Carnine, 1990; Idol, 1987a, 1987b; Williams, 1998; Williams, Brown, Silverstein, & deCani, 1994). For example, Idol (1987a, 1987b) used a model-lead-test paradigm (Carnine et al., 1997) to teach story mapping to five intermediate-grade students with learning disabilities. Bos (1987) used a story-retelling strategy to assist intermediate students with learning and language disabilities in retelling stories. Whereas these two strategies focus on the components of the story, Williams (1998) has developed an instructional lesson to assist students with severe learning disabilities to identify the themes of stories and relate them to their lives.

  EVIDENCE-BASED PRACTICE

Story Mapping

PROCEDURES: Idol (1987b) used the visual in Figure 8-14 and the following procedure to teach story mapping:

1. During the *model* phase, model how to use the story map by reading the story aloud, stopping at points where information pertaining to one of the story components is presented. Ask the students to label the part, and then demonstrate how to write the information on the story map. Have the students copy the information on their own maps. If the information is implicit in the story, model how to generate the inference.

2. During the *lead* phase, have students read the story independently and complete their maps, prompting when necessary. Encourage the students to review their maps after completing the story, adding details that may have been omitted.

3. During the *test* phase, ask students to read a story, generate their maps, and then answer questions such as "Who were the characters?" "Where did the story take place?" and "What was the main character trying to accomplish?"

Bos (1987) used principles based on cognitive strategy instruction to teach a story-retelling strategy. The procedures are as follows:

1. Motivate the students to learn the strategy by demonstrating how it will help them remember what they have read.
2. Describe the components in a story and the steps used to identify and remember the different components: STORE the Story
   Setting: Who, what, when, where
   Trouble: What is the trouble that the main character(s) needs (need) to solve?
   Order of action: What action(s) does (do) the main character(s) take to solve the problem?

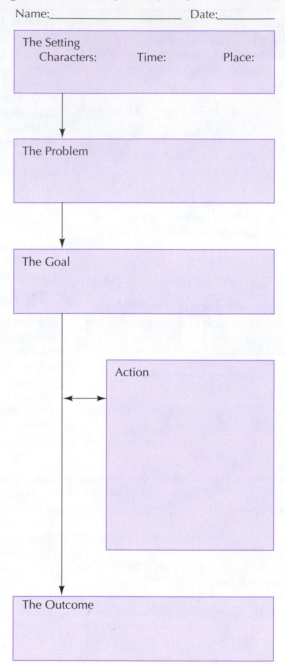

▶ **Figure 8-14** Simple Story Map

Name:_____ Date:_____

Source: L. Idol (1987), Group story mapping: A comprehension strategy for both skilled and unskilled readers, *Journal of Learning Disabilities, 20,* p. 199. Reprinted by permission.

Resolution: What was the outcome (resolution) for each action? How does (do) the main character(s) react and feel?
End: What happened in the end?
Explain how answering these questions will help the students STORE, or remember, the important parts of the story.

3. Practice together reading stories, labeling the components, and retelling the stories. The students can retell their stories to the teacher, retell them to each other, tape-record their retellings, or answer questions about the stories.

4. Have the students independently read stories and retell them by using the STORE the Story strategy.

Williams (1998) developed an instructional program to assist students with learning disabilities to generate themes for stories and relate them to the students' lives. The lesson was organized around a single story and had five parts, as demonstrated for the story "Kate Shelly and the Midnight Limited." This story is about how Kate braved great danger to warn the stationmaster that a railroad bridge had collapsed and thereby averted the wreck of the Midnight Limited. The procedure was as follows:

1. *Prereading discussion about lesson purpose and story topic*. This includes discussion of the importance of identifying and understanding the theme.

2. *Story reading*. The students listen to and/or read the story and discuss the story grammar components and the story (e.g., What do you think will happen next? Do you think Kate was brave? Why?).

3. *Discussion to generate theme*. The teacher and students discuss five questions designed to help generate the theme:
   - Who is the main character? (Kate Shelly.)
   - What did she do? (She ran more than a mile in a terrible storm to warn the stationmaster about a collapsed railroad bridge; she persevered.)
   - What happened? (She reached the station in time to save the train and the passengers.)
   - Was this good or bad? (Good.)
   - Why was this good or bad? (It was good that Kate persevered because she saved lives.)

4. *Writing the theme*. The teachers and students write the theme using the format "Kate should have persevered. We should persevere."

5. *Generalization to real-life experiences*. Discussion is focused around the following questions: "To whom would this theme apply?" "When would it apply?" "In what situations?"

Williams compared this theme discussion framework to more traditional discussions about stories.

COMMENTS: Results from the Idol (1987b) and Bos (1999) studies indicate that students were able to recall substantially more relevant information after learning each strategy. They were also able to answer more explicit and implicit comprehension questions about the stories. Students were also more likely to label the parts of the story in their retellings, thereby providing the listener with a framework for listening. Results from the Williams (1998) study indicate that students were able to generate and apply qualitatively better themes. These same strategies have also been adapted and used to help students plan and write stories.

One aspect that is particularly challenging for students to comprehend is different characters' perspectives and internal reactions as the story progresses (Emery, 1996; Shannon, Kame'enui, & Baumann, 1988). Emery (1996) suggests using story guides in which the story events are outlined in one column and different characters' perspectives are listed in subsequent columns. This assists the students in seeing how different characters react to different events in the story. Using *why* questions about the characters during discussions (e.g., Why did the characters act that way? Why did the characters feel that way?) also promotes comprehension.

Paraphrasing Strategy Getting the main idea(s), paraphrasing, and/or summarizing when reading expository materials are important skills, particularly in content area subjects such as science and social studies. The paraphrasing strategy, developed and validated at KU-CRL (Schumaker, Denton, & Deshler, 1993), instructs students in recalling the main ideas and specific facts of materials they read and has been used successfully with students in middle school and adults (Hagaman & Reid, 2008; Hock & Mellard, 2005).

 EVIDENCE-BASED PRACTICE

Paraphrasing Strategy

PROCEDURES: The steps in the strategy that the students learn are as follows:

1. *Read a paragraph*. As you silently read, think about what the words mean.

2. *Ask yourself, "What were the main ideas and details of this paragraph?"* This question helps you to think about what you just read. To help you, you may need to look quickly back over the paragraph and find the main idea and the details that are related to the main idea.

3. *Put the main idea and details in your own words*. When you put the information into your own words, it helps you to remember the information. Try to give at least two details related to the main idea.

The acronym for the steps in the strategy is RAP. (Paraphrasing is like rapping or talking to yourself.) Students are also given the following two rules for finding the main idea:

1. Look for it in the first sentence of the paragraph.
2. Look for repetitions of the same word or words in the whole paragraph (Schumaker et al., 1993).

The criteria that are used in generating a paraphrase are that it (1) must contain a complete thought and have

Chapter 2 provides a description of cognitive strategy instruction (CSI)

a subject and a verb; (2) must be accurate; (3) must make sense; (4) must contain useful information; (5) must be in one's own words; and (6) must have one general statement per paragraph (Schumaker et al., 1993). Specifics for teaching the strategy, including a scripted lesson, cue cards for learning and generalizing the strategy, record and worksheets, and suggested materials for practicing the strategy, are presented in the instructors' guide, *The Paraphrasing Strategy* (*Learning Strategies Curriculum*) (Schumaker et al., 1993).

COMMENTS: Students with learning disabilities who learned and used the paraphrasing strategy increased their ability to answer comprehension questions about materials written at their grade level from 48% to 84% and middle-grade students improved their comprehension (Schumaker et al., 1993; Hagaman & Reid, 2008).

When using this strategy, students talk their paraphrases into a tape recorder rather than write them. This approach seems particularly advantageous for students with learning and behavior problems because many of them also experience writing problems. However, once students have mastered the skill, it may be helpful for them to write their paraphrases. Students can then use the paraphrases as an overview to integrate the information across the entire passage.

We have had students put their paraphrases for each paragraph or section on sticky notes so that they can then arrange the notes to make a summary of the whole reading selection. You and the students may also want to vary the size of the unit that the students paraphrase. For example, for some books, it may work better to paraphrase each section or subsection rather than each paragraph.

Summarization Strategies Summarization also requires students to generate the main idea and important details from a text. On the basis of analyses of informational or expository texts, Brown and Day (1983) generated five rules for writing summaries:

Summarizing strategies employ many of the principles of cognitive strategy instruction, including explicit explanation of the rules, modeling of the strategy, guided practice in controlled materials, monitoring with corrective feedback, independent practice, and teaching each rule to criterion.

1. Delete irrelevant or trivial information.
2. Delete redundant information.
3. Select topic sentences.
4. Substitute a superordinate term or event for a list of terms or actions.
5. Invent topic sentences when the author has not provided any.

Gajria and Salvia (1992) used these rules to teach sixth- through ninth-grade students with learning disabilities how to summarize expository passages.

Summarization Strategy

PROCEDURES: To teach the summarization strategy, use sets of short paragraphs, each set highlighting a different rule. In this way, the rules can be explained, modeled, and practiced individually. Then apply the rules to informational passages. As the students learn the rules and their application, give the students more responsibility for practicing the rules and checking that each rule has been applied. Figure 8-15 presents a checklist that students can use to judge the quality of their summaries and teachers can use to monitor student progress.

COMMENTS: When Gajria and Salvia (1992) taught the summarization strategy to 15 students with learning disabilities, they found that at the end of instruction, students who were taught the summarization strategy performed better than a comparison group of students with learning disabilities on main idea, inference, and factual questions, and better than a group of average-achieving students on main idea and inference questions. Students who participated in the strategy instruction also improved performance on a reading test.

Malone and Mastropieri (1992) taught middle school students with learning disabilities how to summarize and self-question using two questions:

1. Who or what is the passage about?
2. What is happening (to the characters)?

Using principles of direct instruction and explicit teaching of the summarization and self-questioning, they found that these middle school students outperformed students who had received traditional comprehension instruction on recall of the passage content and that the students could generalize the strategy to new texts. Simmons et al. (2010) taught summarization strategies to middle-grade students to improve their reading comprehension during social studies resulting in overall gains in reading comprehension.

Using Multicomponent Cognitive Strategy Instruction to Teach Comprehension

So far, we have discussed techniques to facilitate the use of specific comprehension skills such as activating prior knowledge, predicting, asking and answering questions, getting the main idea, and summarizing the text. Students with learning and behavior problems often have difficulty with a number of these skills. For example, even when Shamika, an eighth-grade student with decoding and reading comprehension problems, is reading text that is easy for her to decode (about fifth-grade level), she still has difficulty understanding what she reads. Her approach to reading comprehension is to "just begin reading and read to the end." She reads quickly and when finished can answer detailed questions about what she

▶ Figure 8-15 Student Checklist for Monitoring Summaries

How Good Is That Summary?

Student: _____   Date: _____

Title: _____

Pages: _____

Summary:

_____

_____

_____

Rating: 3 = Clear, Concise Summary

2 = Somewhat Clear, Concise Summary

1 = Several Sentences That Do Not Accurately Summarize Information

0 = Not Completed

_____ Does the summary state the **main idea**?

_____ Is the **main idea** stated first?

_____ Does the summary give *only* **the most important information**?

_____ Is the summary brief with **unimportant and redundant information** deleted?

_____ Is the summary written well and clear?

has read if the information is provided in the text. If she is not sure about an idea, Shamika reports, "I usually just skip it." She has difficulty generating a summary and reports that she does not make predictions during reading and does not think about how what she is reading relates to what she already knows. For students like Shamika, it may be more efficient and effective to teach a multicomponent strategy that includes several robust strategies such as predicting, questioning, and summarizing than to teach individual strategies (RAND Reading Study Group, 2002; Klingner, Vaughn, & Boardman, 2007). This section discusses one such multicomponent approach to teaching comprehension—reciprocal teaching (Palincsar & Brown, 1984, 1986; see Rosenshine & Meister, 1994, for a review)—and an adaptation of reciprocal teaching: collaborative strategic reading (CSR; Klingner & Vaughn, 1996; Vaughn & Klingner, 1999)

Both are built on ideas associated with metacognition, schema theory, and the sociocultural theory of learning. From metacognition comes the strong emphasis on comprehension monitoring (e.g., checking to determine whether understanding is adequate, given the purposes for reading). From schema theory, these approaches incorporate activities that encourage students to activate and use relevant background knowledge. From sociocultural theory comes scaffolded instruction in which the teacher and students take turns assuming the leader role.

These instructional techniques build on the idea that successful comprehension and learning are based on six activities:

1. Clarifying the purpose of reading (i.e., understanding the task demands, both explicit and implicit)
2. Activating relevant background knowledge
3. Allocating attention to the major content at the expense of trivia
4. Evaluating content for internal consistency and compatibility with prior knowledge and common sense
5. Monitoring ongoing activities to determine whether comprehension is occurring by engaging in such activities as periodic review and self-questioning
6. Drawing and testing inferences including interpretations, predictions, and conclusions (Brown, Palincsar, & Armbruster, 1984)

Although both approaches build on these activities, reciprocal teaching was developed first; CSR further elaborates on reciprocal teaching.

Reciprocal Teaching In the initial research on reciprocal teaching, Palincsar and Brown (Palincsar, 1982; Palincsar & Brown, 1984) chose four comprehension strategies to teach seventh-grade students who had average decoding skills but had significant difficulty with comprehension. The four strategies were as follows:

1. Predicting
2. Clarifying
3. Questioning
4. Summarizing

They used an interactive mode of teaching that emphasized modeling, feedback, and scaffolded instruction.

Reciprocal Teaching

PROCEDURES: The procedure used to teach the four strategies was *reciprocal teaching*, a technique in which the teacher and students took turns leading a dialogue that covered sections of the text. Palincsar and Brown (1984) described the teaching procedure as follows:

> The basic prsocedure was that an adult teacher, working individually with a seventh-grade poor reader, assigned a segment of the passage to be read and either indicated that it was her turn to be the teacher or assigned the student to teach the segment. The adult teacher and the student then read the assigned segment. After reading the text, the teacher (student or adult) for that segment asked a question that a teacher or test might ask on the segment, summarized the content, discussed and clarified any difficulties, and finally made a prediction about future content. All of these activities were embedded in as natural a dialogue as possible, with the teacher and student giving feedback to each other. (pp. 124–125)

The teacher initially modeled the leader role, and as the students assumed the role, the teacher provided feedback by using the following sequence:

1. *Modeling.* "A question I would have asked would be…"
2. *Prompting.* "What question do you think might be on a test?"
3. *Instruction.* "Remember, a summary is a short version—it doesn't include details."
4. *Modifying the activity.* "If you can't think of a question right now, go ahead and summarize, and then see if you can think of one."
5. *Praise.* "That was a clear question, because I knew what you wanted." "Excellent prediction—let's see if you're right."
6. *Corrective feedback.* "That was interesting information. It was information I would call a detail. Can you find the most important information?"

To ensure a level of competency, each strategy is introduced individually and in a functional manner (e.g., summarize a television show or movie), and opportunities are provided for the students to practice using the strategy. Palincsar (1988) provides a number of suggestions for teaching each comprehension strategy.

Predicting
- Begin a new passage by having students predict on the basis of the title.
- Encourage students to share information they already know about the topic.
- Refer to, and interweave the text with, their predictions and background knowledge as you read.
- Use headings to help students make predictions.
- Use other opportunities to predict, such as when the author asks questions or gives information about what will be covered next.
- Use predictions in an opportunistic and flexible manner.

Questioning
- Encourage students to ask teacherlike questions.
- Fill-in-the-blank questions should be discouraged.
- If the students cannot think of a question, have the students summarize first.
- Provide prompts if needed (e.g., identify the topic, provide a question word).

Summarizing
- Encourage students to identify the main idea and an example of supportive information.
- Encourage students to attempt their summaries without looking at the passage.
- Remind students of the rules for generating summaries:
  Look for a topic sentence.
  Make up a topic sentence if one is not available.
  Give a name to a list of items.
  Delete what is unimportant or redundant.

Clarifying
- Opportunities for clarifying generally occur when referents (e.g., *you, he, it*) are unclear; difficult or unfamiliar vocabulary is presented; text is disorganized or the information is incomplete; or unusual, idiomatic, or metaphorical expressions are used.
- Clarifying will not always be necessary.
- It may be helpful if students are asked to point out something that may be unclear to a younger student.

COMMENTS: Palincsar and Brown studied the effectiveness of reciprocal teaching with poorly comprehending seventh-grade students who were taught individually or in groups of four to seven students (Palincsar, 2007; Palincsar, 1986; Palincsar & Brown, 1984). Even substantial improvements in standardized reading comprehension scores were reported. Lovett et al. (1996) found that reciprocal teaching resulted in significant improvements in the comprehension skills of seventh- and eighth-grade students with reading disabilities compared to control students. Like Palincsar and Brown (1984), they also found that reciprocal teaching transferred to new texts. Lederer (2000) found that reciprocal teaching improved the ability of fourth through sixth graders with learning disabilities to compose summaries of what they read but not their ability to answer comprehension questions. When three student teachers used reciprocal teaching, they reported that marking children's copies of the text with cue pictures, implementing a reward system to maintain focus, and selecting interesting and challenging literature were important for student success (Speece, MacDonald, Kilsheimer, & Krist, 1997). Reciprocal teaching has been implemented effectively with a range of students including middle school ELLs with learning disabilities, including low decoders (Klingner & Vaughn, 1996; Vaughn & Klingner, 2004); high school students in remedial classes (Alfassi, 1998), and average and above-average readers at various grade levels (Rosenshine & Meister, 1994).

Collaborative Strategic Reading CSR is related to reciprocal teaching, but elaborates on its use by focusing on expository text, specifying use of strategies, engaging students in pairs or cooperative groups, and teaching students to record what they are learning through learning (Klingner et al., 2007; Klingner, Vaughn, Dimino, Schumm, & Bryant, 2001; Klingner, Vaughn, & Schumm, 1998; Vaughn, Klingner, & Schumm, 1996; Vaughn, Denton et al., 2010).

  EVIDENCE-BASED PRACTICE

Collaborative Strategic Reading

PROCEDURES: As with reciprocal teaching, students learn four strategies: Previewing (i.e., brainstorming and predicting), Click and Clunk (i.e., comprehension monitoring and clarifying), Get the Gist (i.e., summarization), and Wrap-Up (i.e., self-questioning and summarization). Previewing is used before reading, and Wrap-Up after reading the entire text.

Previewing. The goals of previewing are for students to learn as much about the passage as they can in 2 to 3 minutes, activate their background knowledge about the topic, make predictions about what they will read, and pique their interest in the topic to foster active reading. Using the analogy of a movie preview is a good way to teach previewing. In previewing, students are taught to check out the headings, key words, pictures, tables, graphs, and other key information to identify what they know about the topic and to make predictions. Ms. Royal, who teaches a fifth-grade class that includes a number of students with learning and behavior problems, gives her students 1.5 minutes to write down everything they already know about the topic, 1 minute to share with the group, 1.5 minutes to write down predictions, and 1 minute to share (Klingner & Vaughn, 1998). Figure 8-16 presents the four strategies for CSR with key questions the students can ask as they complete the process.

Click and Clunk. Students "click and clunk" while reading each section of the text. *Clicks* are the portions of the text that make sense, and *clunks* are the portions that aren't clear (e.g., students do not know the meaning of a word). The clicking and clunking strategy is designed to assist students in monitoring their comprehension and to employ fix-up strategies to clarify their understanding. Ms. Royal places the fix-up strategies on clunk cards so that the cooperative groups can use them during reading:

- Reread the sentence and look for ideas that help you to understand the word.
- Reread the sentence leaving out the clunk. What word makes sense?

- Reread the sentences before and after the sentence with the clunk.
- Look for prefixes or suffixes in the word.
- Break the word apart and look for smaller words you know.

Getting the Gist. Students learn to get the gist by reading each section and then asking themselves the following questions:

- Who or what is it about?
- What is most important about information about the who or what?

The goal is to teach the students to restate in their own words the most important point as a way of making sure they understand what they read (Klingner & Vaughn, 1998). Students are taught that a "good" gist does the following:

- Answers the two questions: Who or what is it about? and What is most important about the who or what?
- Is paraphrased in your own words
- Contains 10 words or fewer (Fuchs et al., 1997)

In teaching how to get the gist, we have used the analogy of a sand sieve to demonstrate that the sand (i.e., details) goes through, and all that is left are the rocks (i.e., the main details that answer the two questions). Using the gists from several students or groups to discuss and construct a "best" gist is another technique that can assist students in understanding how to get the gist or main idea. Students repeat the second and third strategies (Clink and Clunk and Getting the Gist) for each paragraph or section of the passage. Having students keep a CSR learning log such as the one in Figure 8-17 can help them to identify information that will assist them in completing the last strategy: Wrap-Up.

Wrap-Up. In the Wrap-Up step, students formulate questions and answers about the key ideas from the entire passage and discuss what they have learned. The goal is to improve their knowledge, understanding, and memory of what they read (Klingner & Vaughn, 1998). For students with learning and language disabilities, it may be necessary to explicitly teach them to ask questions using *what, where, who, when, why,* and *how.* As in reciprocal teaching, students are to think about questions that a teacher might ask. To assist students in generating higher-level questions, it is important to model question stems such as What do you think would happen if…?, How were _____ and _____ the same?, How were they different?, and Why do you think…? Students can use the gists they have generated for the different sections to think about the most important information in the whole passage.

Cooperative Learning Groups. Once they have developed proficiency in applying the comprehension strategies through teacher-led activities, the students learn to use CSR in peer-led cooperative learning groups of about

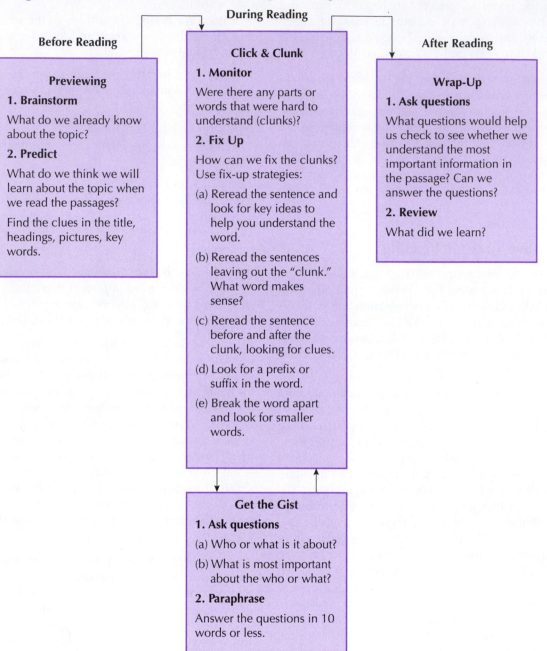

During Reading

Before Reading

After Reading

Previewing

1. Brainstorm

What do we already know about the topic?

2. Predict

What do we think we will learn about the topic when we read the passages?

Find the clues in the title, headings, pictures, key words.

Click & Clunk

1. Monitor

Were there any parts or words that were hard to understand (clunks)?

2. Fix Up

How can we fix the clunks? Use fix-up strategies:

(a) Reread the sentence and look for key ideas to help you understand the word.

(b) Reread the sentences leaving out the "clunk." What word makes sense?

(c) Reread the sentence before and after the clunk, looking for clues.

(d) Look for a prefix or suffix in the word.

(e) Break the word apart and look for smaller words.

Wrap-Up

1. Ask questions

What questions would help us check to see whether we understand the most important information in the passage? Can we answer the questions?

2. Review

What did we learn?

Get the Gist

1. Ask questions

(a) Who or what is it about?

(b) What is most important about the who or what?

2. Paraphrase

Answer the questions in 10 words or less.

Source: Adapted from J. K. Klingner & S. Vaughn (1999), Promoting reading comprehension, content learning, and English acquisition through collaborative strategic reading (CSR), *The Reading Teacher, 52*, pp. 738–747.

four or five students. Typical roles that are used during CSR include the following:

- *Leader:* Leads group by saying what to read and what strategy to use next.
- *Clunk expert:* Reminds students to use clunk strategies to figure out a difficult word or concept.
- *Announcer:* Calls on different members to read and share ideas.
- *Encourager:* Watches the group and gives encouragement and feedback.

- *Reporter:* During the whole-class wrap-up, reports to class the important ideas learned and favorite questions.
- *Timekeeper:* Keeps time and lets the group know when it is time to move on Students should change roles on a regular basis. After wrapping up in their cooperative groups, a whole-class wrap-up is completed to give the teacher and groups the opportunity to report and to discuss the content.

COMMENTS: CSR has been used by a number of classroom teachers who have students with learning and

CSR Learning Log

Name: _____

Title: _____   Date: _____

Pages: _____

Preview

What I already know about the topic: _____

_____

What I predict I will learn: _____

_____

Clicks and Clunks

List your clunks and what they mean.

Getting the Gist

Write/tell the gists for the sections you read.

Wrap-Up

What was the most important thing the entire passage was about? _____

_____

Write questions you may have for your classmates. _____

_____

What I learned. _____

_____

behavior problems and ELLs included in their classrooms (Klingner et al., 1998; Klingner & Vaughn, 1996, 2000; Vaughn, Klingner et al., 2010). For example, seventh- and eighth-grade ELLs with learning disabilities were taught to apply CSR while working on social studies content (Klingner & Vaughn, 1996). Students' reading comprehension scores for the passages they read as well as their scores on standardized tests improved significantly. It has also been a successful practice with upper-elementary and middle school students with reading problems (Bryant, Vaughn et al., 2000; Klingner et al., 1998; Klingner, Vaughn, Arguelles, Hughes, & Ahwee, 2003). CSR has also been used through technology with middle and high school students with reading difficulties or disabilities (Kim, 2002; Kim et al., 2003). The computer program *Computer-Assisted Collaborative Strategic Reading* is designed to provide systematic instruction in comprehension strategies of

CSR along with ample practices to apply those strategies. Students' ability to find main ideas and generate comprehension questions improved significantly, and their scores on standardized comprehension tests also improved to a moderate extent (Kim et al., 2003). Overall, the results demonstrate the effectiveness of explicit instruction of cognitive strategy training and comprehension monitoring in improving a range of reading comprehension skills.

Adapting Approaches to Teaching Reading in Inclusive Classrooms

In this section, we discuss three lesson frameworks or approaches to teaching reading that are often used in general education elementary classrooms and found in basal reading programs. These are approaches that many students with learning and behavior problems encounter;

therefore, practices for adapting them for effective instruction of these students are presented.

► **WEB RESOURCES**
The following Web site provides helpful practices for improving reading instruction in inclusion settings: Reading Rockets
http://www.readingrockets.org.

The first approach, the Directed Reading Activity (DRA; Betts, 1946), has been a standard framework used for organizing the reading lesson in basal readers. The Directed Reading–Thinking Activity (DR–TA; Stauffer, 1969, 1970) is an adaptation of this framework that encourages more active participation on the part of the reader. Literature-based reading (Cullinan, 1992; Holdaway, 1979) and whole language (Goodman, 1986, 1996) emphasize the use of literature as the major medium for teaching reading. The approaches advocate for integrating reading, writing, speaking, and listening, and focus on reading comprehension and implicit code instruction for teaching word recognition. Each of these three approaches is summarized, and modifications for students with reading difficulties are discussed. For more comprehensive discussions of these approaches, see textbooks on methods for teaching reading in elementary schools (e.g., Graves et al., 2007; Gunning, 2010).

Directed Reading Activity The DRA, developed by Betts (1946), is the general framework or lesson plan used in many basal readers (Gunning, 2010; Wilkinson & Anderson, 1995). The DRA is a systematic method for providing instruction in reading, including procedures for teaching word identification as well as comprehension.

 EVIDENCE-BASED PRACTICE

Directed Reading Activity (DRA)

PROCEDURES: This general method for teaching reading is designed to be used with students reading at any level who are reading the same selection. The following outline presents the stages that are usually found in a DRA (Betts, 1946):

1. Readiness
   a. Developing conceptual background
   b. Creating interest
   c. Introducing new vocabulary
   d. Establishing purposes for reading
2. Directed silent reading
   a. Constructing meaning
   b. Monitoring comprehension
3. Discussion and comprehension check
   a. Revisiting purposes for reading
   b. Clarifying concepts and vocabulary

   c. Correcting difficulties in applying word identification and comprehension strategies
   d. Evaluating student performance
4. Rereading
   a. Clarifying information
   b. Obtaining additional information
   c. Enhancing appreciation and understanding
   d. Providing opportunities for purposeful oral reading
5. Follow-up activities
   a. Extending skill development
   b. Enriching and generalizing

COMMENTS: Although the DRA is suggested as a framework for teaching in basal readers, modifications are necessary for students who experience reading difficulties. For example, in both the earlier and later elementary grades, many of these students need more systematic, explicit instruction in phonics and decoding strategies than are usually provided. Incorporating fluency building through repeated and partner reading will also assist in providing the needed practice required of these students. The PRePand previewing could be added to the readiness stage of the DRA to activate and build on prior knowledge. Explicit instruction of comprehension and comprehension-monitoring strategies such as self-questioning and summarizing would also support students with reading difficulties. Finally, it is important that reading materials are at the students' instructional level.

One concern about the DRA is that it is teacher dominated and therefore may not facilitate the development of independent reading skills. Encouraging the students to set their own purposes for reading, to self-question as they read, and to generate their own questions and follow-up activities is emphasized in the next framework: the DR–TA.

Directed Reading–Thinking Activity (DR–TA) Stauffer (1969, 1970, 1976) developed the DR–TA as a framework for teaching reading that stresses students' abilities to read reflectively and to use prediction and preview strategies to set their own purposes for reading (Gunning, 2010). The purpose of the DR–TA is to provide readers with the ability to do the following:

- Determine purposes for reading.
- Extract, comprehend, and assimilate information.
- Use prediction while reading.
- Suspend judgments.
- Make decisions based on evidence gained from reading.

DR–TA is based on the notion that reading is a thinking process that requires students to relate their own experiences to the author's ideas and thereby construct meaning from the text.

In using this approach, the construction of meaning starts with setting purposes for reading and generating hypotheses about meaning. Constructing meaning from text continues as students acquire more information, confirm or disconfirm hypotheses, and establish new hypotheses. It ends when the hypotheses have been confirmed and the purposes for reading have been met.

Stauffer (1969) describes seven distinguishing features about group DR–TA activities:

1. Students of approximately the same reading level are grouped together.
2. The group size ranges from 2 to 10 students to promote interaction and participation.
3. All students in a group read the same material at the same time. This permits each student to compare and contrast predictions, justifications for answers, and evaluations with those of his or her peers.
4. Purposes for reading are declared by students; students ask questions to become active readers and thinkers.
5. Answers to questions are validated. Proof is found and tested, and the group judges whether the offered proof is trustworthy.
6. Immediate feedback helps develop integrity and a regard for authenticity.
7. The teacher serves as a facilitator or moderator, and asks provocative questions that require the students to interpret and make inferences from what they have read.

 EVIDENCE-BASED PRACTICE

DR–TA

PROCEDURES: Adapt the following procedures in using a DR–TA:

1. After each student receives a copy of the material, direct the students to identify a purpose for reading by studying the title, subtitles, pictures, and other elements, to develop a hypothesis about what the passage is about. Following are two questions you might ask to stimulate hypotheses: What do you think a story with this title might be about? What do you think might happen in this story? Have students share these hypotheses, discussing how they arrived at them. Have students use information from their prior knowledge to substantiate their predictions.

2. Once each student has stated his or her hypothesis, encourage the students to adjust their rate of silent reading to their purpose for reading.

3. Teach the students or remind them of the strategies they can use when they come to a word they cannot identify, such as sounding out the word parts and thinking what makes sense and asking for assistance.

4. Select a segment of the text and direct the students to read it to themselves and check their predictions.

5. When the students have finished reading, have them discuss their predictions. Two target questions to ask are as follows: "Were you correct?" "What do you think now?" Have students reread orally the sections of the text that confirm or contradict their hypotheses. Assist the students in determining whether other source materials may be necessary to clarify meaning, and have the students discuss concepts and vocabulary that are critical to the comprehension process.

6. Repeat the procedure (hypothesis setting, silent reading to validate, oral reading to prove, and discussion) with subsequent segments of the text.

7. Once the passage has been completed, use skill activities to teach skill training (Stauffer, 1969). This entails rereading the story, and reexamining selected words, phrases, pictures, and/or diagrams for the purpose of concurrently developing the students' reading–thinking abilities with the other reading-related skills (Tierney & Readence, 2005). These might include word-attack skills and concept clarification and development.

The processing involved in a DR–TA is summarized as follows:

1. Pupil actions
   a. Predict (set purposes)
   b. Read (process ideas)
   c. Prove (test answers)
2. Teacher actions
   a. What do you think? (activate thought)
   b. Why do you think so? (agitate thought)
   c. Prove it! (require evidence) (Stauffer, 1969)

Stauffer (1969) suggests that once the students are comfortable with the DR–TA process, they should be encouraged to use an individualized DR–TA. In other words, students should use this systematic, predictive process as they read individually. Figure 8-18 presents a sample worksheet that students may use to guide themselves as they complete individual DR–TAs.

COMMENTS: The DR–TA provides teachers with a procedure for teaching students to become active thinkers as they read. This is particularly relevant for students with learning and behavior problems, since it requires that students assume responsibility for the reading–learning process. In comparison to the DRA, in which the teacher sets the purpose for reading and preteaches vocabulary, the DR–TA encourages the students to set their own purposes and decide which vocabulary warrants further development.

Two cautions, however, seem relevant to the DR–TA. First, it requires a great deal of self-directiveness on the part of the students, particularly when they use the individualized DR–TA. For students with learning and behavior problems, teachers will need to scaffold instruction so that there is a systematic movement from teacher modeling and control to student control. Second, there is little or no emphasis on teaching word decoding and word

Name: _____

Passage/Book: _____

Pages	Prediction	Outcome

Summary _____

_____

identification or fluency-building skills in a direct or systematic manner. Like DRA, providing direct instruction in these areas and having students work in instructional-level materials will be important modifications to make in inclusive classes.

 EVIDENCE-BASED PRACTICE

Literature-Based Reading

PROCEDURES: The focal points of whole-language and literature-based reading programs center on involving students in lots of reading and writing, creating an environment that accepts and encourages risk taking, and maintaining a focus on meaning (Goodman, 1986, 1996; Weaver, 1990).

In literature-based or whole-language classrooms, the curriculum is often organized around themes and units that integrate oral language, reading, and writing. With the focus on meaning, phonics and word recognition skills are generally not taught in isolation but within the context of connected text, when children are writing during writer's workshop, and according to the students' needs (Dahl & Scharer, 2000; Dahl, Scharer, Lawson, & Grogan, 1999; Stahl, Pagnucco, & Suttles, 1996). Strategies for comprehension are taught within the context of books; teachers and students discuss not only the content

but also the processes that are used in constructing meaning from text (Goodman, Watson, & Burke, 1996; Jewell & Pratt, 1999). Literature circles, literature discussion groups, book clubs, and reader response journals are techniques that have been used to structure discussions about books and to promote critical reading.

Literature circles are often used to structure discussions about books (Short, 1997; Short & Harste, with Burke, 1995). Literature circles facilitate literacy by providing opportunities for students to explore ideas about the content and craft of literacy and to think critically and deeply about what they read. In literature circles, a teacher initially introduces several books for which there are multiple copies, and the group decides which book to read. Students read the book or, if it is too long, chapters or smaller segments of the book, and then meet in the literature circle to discuss the book. The first day the discussion starts with a broad focus (e.g., What was the story about?). In the discussion, the teacher listens to what the students highlight as interesting or challenging, and leads the students to talk about the outstanding characteristics of the book (e.g., character development, plot development, use of dialogue). As the discussions progress across several meetings, the teacher models and guides the students in making connections between the book they read and their personal experiences and other literature they have read or written. Questions focus on character development, authenticity, mood, voice, writing style and genre, text structure, comparison across literature, and tying reader to author (e.g., How is this story like or different from previous ones you've read? What kind of people are the characters in the story?). At the end of each discussion, the group decides what they want to discuss the next time. They prepare for the next discussion by rereading sections of the book or related literature.

In literature-based and whole-language classrooms, writing is reciprocally tied to reading so that the students have opportunities to work in the roles of both reader and author. Literature for reading and topics for writing are often self-selected, giving the students the opportunity to explore topics of interest to them. Students also learn about the authors and illustrators of the books they are reading. With this approach, librarians, annotated bibliographies of children's literature, and teacher resource books are important tools for teaching.

> Process writing and conferencing about books and written pieces allow the teacher to facilitate the students' understanding of the processes.

COMMENTS: Using literature-based reading programs and whole language emphasizes the purposeful reading, writing, discussion, and analyzing of literature in learning to read, critically analyze, and appreciate literature. Research investigating the use of literature-based programs and whole language, primarily using case studies, indicates that there is some evidence that such approaches facilitate reading and positive attitudes toward reading by students with learning and behavior problems (e.g., Allen, Michalove, Shockley, & West, 1991; Mills, O'Keefe, & Stephens, 1992; Morrow, 1992; Stires, 1991). However, there is substantial evidence that students with learning and behavior problems need more direct and intensive instruction than is usually associated with these approaches (National Reading Panel, 2000; Snow, Burns, & Griffin, 1998; Swanson, 1999b).

INSTRUCTIONAL ACTIVITIES

This section provides instructional activities that are related to reading comprehension and fluency. Some of the activities teach new skills; others are best suited for practice and reinforcement of already acquired skills. For each activity, the objective, materials, and teaching procedures are described.

▶ Choral Reading

Objective: To provide students with opportunities to practice reading aloud rapidly, accurately, and expressively with the teacher.

Grades: Kindergarten through primary

Materials: Reading passages

Teaching Procedures:
1. Provide each student with a copy of the reading passage.
2. Model fluent reading of the passage by reading aloud. The teacher reads the passage accurately with prosody and sets the pace.
3. Students read along with the teacher the second time the passage is read. This strategy can be implemented individually, in whole groups, or in small groups.

Source: Adapted from University of Texas Center for Reading and Language Arts (2003b).

▶ Partner Reading

Objective: To improve students' reading accuracy and rate.

Grades: Elementary through secondary

Materials: Reading passages, graph paper, colored pencils, timer for the teacher

Teaching Procedures:
1. Pair students, using the following procedure: (1) Rank the students according to reading ability, (2) split the list in half, (3) pair the top-ranked student in the higher-performing half (partner 1) with the top-ranked student in the lower-performing half (partner 2) and so forth.
2. Give each pair two copies of the reading passage at the instructional level of the less fluent student. (Instructional reading level means that the reader is able to decode about 90% of the words correctly.)
3. Remind students of the procedures for partner reading: (1) read for 4 minutes each; (2) correct errors (omission/addition of words, stopping more than 3 seconds, etc.); (3) do the best 1-minute reading (while timed); (4) calculate the fluency rate; and (5) graph the fluency rate.
4. Have partner 1 model fluent reading for 4 minutes while partner 2 follows along and identifies and corrects errors. Partner 2 should use the following procedure for error correction:
   a. Say, "Sound it out."
   b. Wait 4 seconds.
   c. If the partner figures out the word, say, "Good. Now reread the sentence."
   d. If the partner doesn't figure out the word, say, "That word is . What word?" Wait for the partner to respond _____. Say, "Good. Now reread the sentence."
5. Have the students reread the passage for 1 minute (best reading), with partner 1 reading first. Partner 2 follows along, marks errors, and marks the last word read at the 1-minute mark.

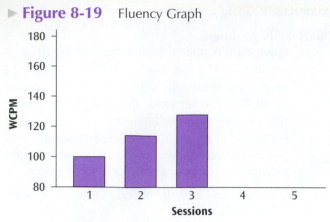

▶ Figure 8-19 Fluency Graph

Source: Adapted from University of Texas Center for Reading and Language Arts (2001a). Reprinted by permission.

6. Have the students calculate their fluency during the 1-minute best reading using WCPM. This is found by subtracting the number of errors from the total number of words read: (Total − errors = fluency).

7. Have the students graph their fluency using colored pencils and graph paper, as shown in Figure 8-19.

▶ Phrase Card Reading

Objective: To help students improve their reading rate and accuracy.

Grades: Elementary through intermediate

Materials: Reading passages, index cards, pens

Teaching Procedures:

1. Pair students, using the procedure described in "Partner Reading."

2. Give each pair two copies of the reading passage at the instructional level of the less fluent student.

3. Have each pair highlight phrases from the passage that include difficult words.

4. Have each pair write these phrases on index cards.

5. Have the more fluent reader in each pair read the phrases from the cards first.

6. Then have the less fluent reader in each pair read the same phrases from the cards. While the less fluent reader reads the phrases, the fluent reader identifies and corrects errors, if any.

Source: Adapted from University of Texas Center for Reading and Language Arts (2002).

▶ Tape-Assisted Reading

Objective: To help students improve their reading rate and accuracy.

Grades: Elementary through secondary

Materials: Reading passages, tape recorder, blank tapes

Teaching Procedures:

1. Before the instruction, select a reading passage at each student's instructional or independent reading level. Record the passage. While recording, read with appropriate rate, accuracy, and expression.

2. Tell the students to listen to the passage on tape and to follow along by running their fingers under the line of the print. (*Note:* Students should not point to each word.)

3. Have the students read the passage aloud three times along with the tape.

4. Have the students read the passage aloud along with the tape while you listen to identify and correct errors.

5. Have the students read the passage aloud without listening to the tape for 1 minute.

6. Have the students calculate and graph their fluency rate (using the procedure described in "Partner Reading").

Source: Adapted from University of Texas Center for Reading and Language Arts (2002).

▶ Chunk Reading

Objective: To help students improve their reading accuracy and rate while reading phrases.

Grades: Elementary

Materials: Reading passages, graph paper, colored pencils, timer for the teacher

Teaching Procedures:

1. Before the instruction, select a reading passage at an instructional level that is appropriate for the less fluent students. Place slash marks between chunks (i.e., phrases) to mark two- to five-word sentence segments and prepositional phrases in each passage.

2. Pair students using the procedure described in "Partner Reading."

3. Give each pair two copies of the reading passages with chunking marks.

4. Tell the students that connected text is divided into meaningful phrases and that paying attention to these phrases while reading will enhance their fluency and comprehension.

5. Tell the students to pause briefly between phrases, exactly as marked. No pauses should be made except at slash marks.

6. Remind students of the procedure for partner reading: (1) 4-minute reading for each, (2) 1-minute best reading for each, (3) calculating fluency, and (4) graphing.

7. Have partner 1 model fluent reading while partner 2 follows along. Partner 1 emphasizes chunking phrases together for meaning. For instance, read the sentence "One day last week my sister and I drove to the lake" like this: "One day last week / my sister and I / drove to the lake." (A slash indicates a pause.) Then partner 2 reads the passage while partner 1 follows along.

8. Tell the students to reread the passage for 1 minute (best reading), with partner 1 reading first. While partner 1 reads, partner 2 follows along, marks errors, and marks the last word read at the 1-minute mark.

9. Ask the students to calculate the fluency using WCPM (see the procedures in "Partner Reading") and to graph their fluency on the graph paper with colored pencils.

Source: Adapted from University of Texas Center for Reading and Language Arts (2001a).

▶ Dramatic Reading

Objective: To help students improve their reading fluency.

Grades: Elementary through secondary

Materials: Copies of a play for each student

Teaching Procedures:
1. Make groups of four, consisting of two more fluent readers and two less fluent readers.

2. Give a copy of the play to each student, and assign each student a role.

3. Tell students that they will practice the play with other group members and will put on the play for the class.

4. Set a performance day and time.

5. Instruct students to practice the play in their group. Have each student practice reading his or her lines while the other group members listen and provide feedback.

6. Next, have students work together to read their parts as if in a play. Encourage students to provide feedback to each other.

7. On the performance day, have each group put on their play for the class.

Source: Adapted from University of Texas Center for Reading and Language Arts (2002).

▶ Critiquing Oral Reading

Objective: To provide students with opportunities to critique their oral reading.

Grades: Primary and intermediate

Materials: Reading passages, tape recorder, a blank tape for each student labeled with the student's name

Teaching Procedures:
1. Explain that the purpose of the activity is to give the students an opportunity to listen to how they read.

2. Let the students know that they are to listen for things they do well and things they want to improve.

3. Model the process by practicing, recording, listening, and critiquing a passage you read.

4. Before the students read into the tape recorder, have them practice the segment. Each student should practice and then read and record a passage of about 100 to 500 words.

5. After the students record, they should listen to their tapes and finish writing the following statements:

   When I read orally, I do a really good job of _____.

   One thing I could do better when I read out loud is _____.

6. Listen to and discuss each tape, and then ask the students to critique each presentation. Have the students record their oral reading every 3 to 6 weeks so that they can compare and hear how they are improving.

Adaptations: Each student can record two passages: one that has been practiced and one that is unpracticed.

▶ Previewing

Objective: To help students activate their prior knowledge and make predictions about what they are going to learn from the passage.

Grades: Elementary through secondary

Materials: Expository reading passage, copies of a preview log (see Figure 8-20)

Teaching Procedures:
1. Pass out a preview log to each student.

2. Introduce the topic of the lesson, and ask students to record it at the top of their preview logs.

3. Divide the class into small groups.

4. Give each group 2 minutes to brainstorm what they already know about the topic, and ask them to record their ideas in their preview logs along with how this topic relates to previous lessons.

5. Ask several groups to share their brainstorming ideas.

6. Introduce and discuss three key vocabulary words. Have students record the words along with the definition in their preview logs.

7. Pass out a reading passage to each student.

► **Figure 8-20**   Preview Log

Topic:
What do I already know about the topic?
How does this topic relate to previous lessons?
Key vocabulary and definitions
1. _____ : _____
2. _____ : _____
3. _____ : _____
Predictions
By looking at the ☐ title ☐ headings ☐ pictures ☐ others: _____
I think that I am going to learn about . . .
By looking at the ☐ title ☐ headings ☐ pictures ☐ others: _____
I think that I am going to learn about . . .

8. Ask the students to scan the passage, looking for clues or physical features, such as the title, subtitle, headings, subheadings, bolded words, graphics, and/or pictures, which could be used to make predictions about the passage.

9. Ask each group to make two predictions about what they think they are going to learn from the passage. Have students record their predictions in their preview logs.

10. Ask several groups to share their predictions.

11. After the lesson, discuss and check students' predictions to see how close their predictions were to what they actually learned from the text.

Source: Adapted from University of Texas Center for Reading and Language Arts (2001a).

► Getting the Gist

Objective: To help students identify the main idea of a paragraph.

Grades: Elementary through secondary

Materials: Expository reading passage, copies of a gist log (see Figure 8-21)

Teaching Procedures:
1. Pass out a reading passage and a gist log to each student.

2. Explain to students that a gist statement represents the main idea of a paragraph. The main idea is the most important information in a paragraph.

3. Tell students that there are three steps to getting the gist: (1) naming the who or what the paragraph is mostly about, (2) telling the most important information about the who or what, and (3) writing a complete sentence about the gist in 10 words or less.

4. Pair the students, and have them take turns reading with a partner.

5. After each paragraph, each pair identifies who or what the paragraph is mostly about.

6. Next, each pair identifies the most important information about the who or what.

7. Then each pair puts the two pieces of information together in a complete sentence of 10 words or less.

8. After all pairs complete getting the gist statements, call on several pairs to share their statements with others.

Source: Adapted from Klingner et al. (2001).

► Self-Monitoring

Objective: To help students monitor their understanding.

Grades: Secondary

Materials: Two different triple-spaced reading passages, two transparencies of both passages, copies of a monitoring symbol cue card, overhead projector, marker

1. Who or what is the paragraph mostly about?

2. What is the most important information about the who or what?

   (Use this information to develop the gist statement.)

3. Write a gist of 10 words or less in a complete sentence.

Monitoring Symbol Cue Card

✓	= Got it!
?	= What Does This Mean?
MBI	= Must Be Important
RR	= Reread
DW	= Difficult Word
LG	= Look at Graphs

Teaching Procedures:

1. Introduce monitoring symbols, and tell students that the use of the symbols will help them to monitor their understanding

2. Present and describe each symbol.

3. Pass out the first triple-spaced passage.

4. Place the first passage on the overhead projector, and model how to use the symbols while reading.

5. Read the passage aloud, and insert the symbols where appropriate to mirror your self-monitoring strategies. Tell why you insert the symbols.

6. Pass out the second reading passage and a monitoring symbol cue card to each student.

7. Ask the students to insert monitoring symbols as they read.

8. Circulate around the class, and provide additional support if necessary.

9. After the students finish the second passage, place the second passage on the overhead projector. Call on several students to share which symbols they used and why.

10. Answer any questions about the passage or difficult words.

Adaptations: This instructional activity can be used with a "click and clunk" activity. A teacher can ask students to use the "click and clunk" strategy when they come across difficult words.

Source: Adapted from University of Texas Center for Reading and Language Arts (2002).

For a description of "click and clunk," see the "Instructional Activities" section in this chapter.

► **Generating Questions**

Objective: To help students generate questions about important information after reading.

Grades: Elementary through secondary

Materials: Two different reading passages, overhead projector, marker, transparency

Teaching Procedures:

1. Pass out the first reading passage to each student.

2. Explain to students that there are three types of questions: "right there" questions (the answer to the question is right in the text), "think and search" questions (the answer to the question is in the text, but students have to read the text and to compose the answer themselves based on what they have read), and "on my own" questions (the answer to the question is not in the text, and students have to integrate their own previous experiences with what they have learned from the text).

3. Read the entire reading passage aloud.

4. Model how to generate questions about the important information by using the key words *how, who, what, when, where,* and *why.*

5. Pass out the second reading passage to each student.

6. Remind students that there are three types of questions.

7. Pair the students, and have them take turns reading with a partner.

8. After reading the entire passage, have each pair generate at least one question for each type.

9. Monitor the students to make sure that they all properly generate questions.

10. After all pairs have finished generating the questions, call on several pairs to share their questions with others.

Source: Adapted from Klingner et al. (2001).

▶ ### Directed Reading–Thinking Activity (DR–TA)

Objective: To help students make and check predictions before, during, and after reading.

Grades: Elementary through secondary

Materials: Reading passage in which a teacher marks several stop points, copies of a DR–TA organizer (see Figure 8-22)

Teaching Procedures:
1. Pass out a reading passage and a DR–TA organizer to each student.

2. Before reading, discuss the topic.

3. Show pictures, graphs, headings, or bolded text in the passage, and ask students what they think the passage topic could be.

4. Call on several students to share their predictions about the passage topic. Discuss with students how to generate the best predictions, and record the predictions on the DR–TA organizer. Have students write predictions on their DR–TA organizers.

5. Have students take turns reading the first part of the passage (before the first stop point).

6. Ask the students to think back about predictions they generated and what evidence is presented to either confirm or disprove their predictions.

7. Ask the students to revise or make new predictions if necessary.

8. Call on several students to share their revised and/or new predictions. Discuss with students how to generate the best predictions, and record the predictions on the DR–TA organizer. Have the students write the predictions on their DR–TA organizers.

9. Repeat the same procedure until the entire passage is read.

10. After finishing the entire passage, ask the students to reflect on their predictions.

11. Call on several students to share their reflections.

Source: Adapted from Blachowicz and Ogle (2001).

▶ ### Expository Text Question Cards

Objective: To teach students to identify different types of expository text structure and to ask comprehension questions appropriate to each text structure while reading text.

Grades: Secondary

Materials: Expository reading passages (two different passages for each text structure type), expository comprehension cards (one card set for each text structure type; see Figure 8-23)

Teaching Procedures:
1. Hand out a passage with a concept/definition type to each student.

2. Tell students that the text is the concept/definition type.

3. Provide the students with the card set for the concept/definition type.

4. Model how the students can use the sample questions on the card to ask and answer specific questions about the content.

▶ **Figure 8-22**   DR–TA Organizer

Title: _____

Predictions based on the topic:

Predictions based on skimming information such as the title, pictures, etc.:

Predictions after reading the first part of the text: Pages _____ to _____

Predictions after reading the second part of the text: Pages _____ to _____

Predictions after reading the third part of the text: Pages _____ to _____

Concept or Definition

1. What topic or concept is described? _____

2. What are some of its characteristics? _____

3. What is its function? _____

4. To what category does it belong? _____

5. What are some related ideas or words? _____

6. What are some examples? _____

7. What do you think is the most unusual or memorable characteristic?
_____

Cause and Effect

1. What happens? _____

2. What causes it to happen? _____

3. What are the important elements or factors that caused it to happen? _____

4. Will the result always happen this way? Why or why not? _____

5. How can elements or factors change? _____

Compare and Contrast

1. What is being compared and contrasted? _____

2. How are things similar? _____

3. How are they different? _____

4. What are the most important qualities that make them the same or different? _____

5. What conclusions can we make? _____

6. How can the things be classified? _____

Position Statement or Support

1. What is the opinion, hypothesis, theory, or argument?
_____

2. Are valid reasons given to accept it? _____

3. Do you agree with the viewpoint, theory, hypothesis presented? Why? Why not? _____

4. What credible evidence and data are presented?
_____

5. Hand out another passage with the concept/definition type to each student.

6. Have the students take turns reading.

7. During reading, periodically stop the students from reading, and ask several students to use the

Green Cards—Use Before Reading

Card 1: What does the title tell me about this story?

Card 2: What do the pictures tell me?

Card 3: What do I already know about?

Yellow Cards—Use During Reading

Card 4: Who? (Tell who the story is about, or name the characters.)

Card 5: What? (State the problem.)

Card 6: When? (Tell the time the story takes place.)

Card 7: Where? (Tell the place of the story.)

Card 8: Why? (Explain why something happened.)

Card 9: How? (Tell how the problem was solved.)

Card 10: What do I think will happen next? (Make predictions.)

Red Cards—Use After Reading

Card 11: Who were the characters?

Card 12: What was the setting? (When and where.)

Card 13: What was the problem?

Card 14: How was the problem solved?

Card 15: Why did . . . ? (Elaborate on why something happened.)

sample questions on the card to ask and answer specific questions about the content.

8. Use the same procedure for expository reading passages with other text structure types (e.g., cause and effect, compare and contrast).

Source: Adapted from University of Texas Center for Reading and Language Arts (2003a).

► **Using Narrative Comprehension Cards**

Objective: To teach students to use narrative comprehension cards while reading text.

Grades: Elementary

Materials: Narrative reading passage, narrative comprehension cards (see Figure 8-24), pocket chart

Teaching Procedures: Before the instruction, set narrative comprehension cards on the left side of the pocket chart in the correct order (1 to 15).

1. Hand out a reading passage to each student.

2. Introduce narrative comprehension cards. Explain to students that each card is color coded. Tell them that green cards are used *before reading*, yellow cards are used *during reading*, and red cards are used *after reading*.

3. Before reading, read the first green card question (card 1) aloud.

4. Call on several students to answer the question. As the first green card question is answered, move the card to the right side of the pocket chart to indicate that the question has been answered.

5. Repeat the same procedure until all green card questions have been answered.

6. Have the students take turns reading.

7. During reading, periodically stop the students from reading, and ask several students to answer the first yellow card question (card 4).

8. As each yellow card question is answered, move the card to the right side of the pocket chart.

9. Repeat the same procedure until all of the yellow card questions have been answered.

10. After reading, ask the students the first red card question.

11. As each red card question is answered, move the card to the right side of the pocket chart.

12. Repeat the same procedure until all red card questions have been answered.

Source: Adapted from University of Texas, Center for Reading and Language Arts (2000a, 2000b).

▶ Story Jumble

Objective: To provide students practice in sequencing a story.

Grades: Primary and intermediate

Materials: Short stories that have been cut into story parts (e.g., setting, episodes, endings), paragraphs, or sentences; index cards with the segments of the story mounted onto them

Teaching Procedures:
1. Present the cards to the students, and have the students read each part and arrange the cards so that the story makes sense.

2. Have students read the story again to determine whether it makes sense. If students disagree about the order, have them explain why they prefer a certain order.

Adaptations: Students can work on this activity in groups of two or three or individually.

▶ Predict the Plot

Objective: To provide students with practice in predicting the events and plots in stories.

Grades: Intermediate and secondary

Materials: Cartoon strips such as *Peanuts, Broom-Hilda,* or *Beetle Bailey*

Teaching Procedures:
1. Select a cartoon strip, and expose one frame at a time for the students to read.

2. Have students predict the plot by asking such questions as these:
   - What do you think is going to be pictured in the next frame? Why?
   - Of the ideas we have generated, which one do you like best? Why?
   - How do you think the cartoonist will end this story? Why?

3. Read the next frame, discussing the previous predictions and making predictions about the next frame.

4. After the story is completed, have students draw and write their own cartoons, using the characters presented in the strip or creating new characters.

5. Have students share their cartoons with others.

Adaptations: Mystery and adventure stories also lend themselves to this type of plot prediction. Segments of the story could be read, and then predictions could be made. Students could also finish this activity by writing a mystery or adventure story.

▶ WH Game

Objective: To provide students with practice in answering *who, what, when, where, why,* and *how* (WH) questions.

Grades: Elementary through secondary

Materials: Generic game board, spinner or die, and markers; WH cards, which are small cards with "WH Game" written on one side and one of the following words written on the other side: Who, What, When, Where, Why, How; sets of Story and Article Cards, which are copies of short stories and articles mounted on cards. There should be one copy for each player. Select topics of interest for the age level of students.

Teaching Procedures:
1. Explain the game to the students.

2. Have students select a set of Story or Article Cards.

3. Have all students read the story or article and place their cards face down.

4. Have students take a turn by throwing the die or spinning and selecting a WH Card.

5. Have the student make up a question using the Wh- word indicated on the card and answer it correctly in order to move his or her marker.

6. If another player questions the validity of a player's question or answer, the players may look at the story or article card. Otherwise, these cards should remain face down during play.

7. After questions have been asked using one Story or Article Card, another set is selected. The students read this card, and then the game continues.

8. The first player to arrive at the finish wins.

Adaptations: Students may also work in pairs, with one person on the team making up the question and the other person answering it.

FOCUS Answers

▶ **FOCUS Question 1. What is reading fluency, and how is progress in fluency monitored?**

Answer: Fluency is the ability to read a text quickly, accurately, and with expression. For assessing fluency, the progress-monitoring practice most frequently used and the one highly associated with comprehension is oral reading fluency. Oral reading fluency can be addressed by determining the number of WCPM and observing phrasing, smoothness and pace using a grade-level appropriate text.

▶ **FOCUS Question 2. What are effective instructional practices for increasing reading fluency?**

Answer: The following techniques have been identified as effective for increasing reading fluency for struggling readers:

- Reading aloud and modeling fluent reading while students read along
- Repeated reading of a text
- Choral repeated reading
- Peer-supported reading
- Reading performance

▶ **FOCUS Question 3. What assessments and instructional components should be present in a reading comprehension program?**

Answer: Comprehension is a difficult task to measure quickly (in less than 5 minutes) although maze procedures are used to assess reading comprehension for progress-monitoring purposes. There are several standardized and norm-referenced measures that take between 25 and 45 minutes to administer (some group administered and some individually administered) that provide reliable and valid information on students' reading comprehension.

▶ **FOCUS Question 4. What is the purpose of comprehension instruction?**

Answer: Comprehension instruction should encourage students to engage actively in discussions related to the content of the text and about how to read for meaning. The components of reading comprehension instruction include preview techniques, questioning strategies and comprehension monitoring, and text structure and summarizing strategies.

9

Assessing and Teaching Writing and Spelling

1. What assessment and instructional practices improve writing outcomes for students with learning and behavior problems?
2. What are the critical features of spelling assessment and instruction for students with learning and behavior problems?
3. What are the characteristics of students with handwriting problems, and what components should be included in an effective handwriting and keyboarding program?

Mike York, a high school teacher of students with learning disabilities (LD), reports, "The adolescents in my program do not want to write. They do not even want to answer questions in writing. Writing a theme for a class is torture." He goes on to describe the students in his class. "You should see the handwriting of the majority of students in my class. It is awful. They print poorly and slowly. So even when they are motivated to write it is painfully difficult for them. Furthermore, most of them have little experience writing before they get to secondary school. Many were identified as learning disabled in the early elementary grades and then were provided with writing assistance as they went through school. Fortunately, some of the students were provided with instruction in how to use a keyboard and this helps with their writing production. However, production is not the only problem. Quality of writing is also extremely poor. This poor writing influences their success in content area classes. For example, several of my students are very interested in science and work hard to understand and participate in the general education classroom. They also know a lot more about science that they can talk about than that they are able to write about. Unfortunately, almost all assessments in the classroom require students to write their answers. Since my students have writing challenges, they frequently write brief and incomplete answers which give an inaccurate portrait of what they really know. I am now working closely with my students to improve their writing production and quality so that they can be more successful in both general education classrooms as well as the world of work."

Most young children love to scribble. They enjoy writing and drawing on paper, sidewalks, chalkboards, and, unfortunately, even walls. On the first day of school, when first graders are asked whether they know how to write, most of them say yes. What happens to the interest and joy in writing from age 3 to age 13?

Many researchers in the field believe that students do not spend enough time on writing as a craft and are given too little choice about what they write. Writing has many negative associations for students because it is often used as a form of punishment, and when their writing is returned to them, it is covered with corrections. There is little question that writing is one of the most difficult tasks that students must perform in school (MacArthur, Graham, & Fitzgerald, 2008).

The good news is that we have made considerable progress on how to effectively teach writing to students with disabilities (Graham & Harris, 2005), including students who are bilingual (Cumming, 2006; Graves, Valles, & Rueda, 2000). When teachers

> **PEARSON myeducationlab**
>
> Visit the MyEducationLab for this course to enhance your understanding of chapter concepts with a personalized Study Plan. You'll also have the opportunity to hone your teaching skills through video-based Assignments and Activities, IRIS Center Resources, and Building Teaching Skills and Dispositions lessons.

implement effective intervention approaches that use both the conventions of teaching writing (e.g., capitalization, punctuation, sentence structure) and strategies for improving written expression (e.g., planning, composing the results), the results are quite positive (Dixon, Isaacson, & Stein, 2002; Gersten & Baker, 2001). The chapter presents background and instructional procedures for using writing strategies and teaching spelling, handwriting, and keyboarding to students who have learning difficulties and provides a table showing the pros and cons of teaching cursive versus manuscript.

Assessing and Teaching the Writing Process

What assessment and instructional practices improve writing outcomes for students with learning and behavior problems? Marynell Schlegel, a resource-room teacher who works with students who have learning and emotional disabilities, disliked teaching writing almost as much as the students disliked doing it. Questioning her students about what made writing "good" revealed that they perceived good writing as spelling words correctly, writing correct sentences, and having good handwriting—the very skills that these students often have the most difficulty developing. None of the students included a purpose for writing in their description of good writing nor using writing as a means of conveying a message.

Ms. Schlegel decided to read about writing and to change her writing instruction. She decided to implement the writing process approach to written expression as part of her overall writing program (Graves, 1983, 1994; MacArthur, Graham, Schwartz, & Schafer, 1995).

The Writing Process for Students with Learning and Behavior Problems

Ms. Schlegel arranged for students with writing difficulties and students with LD to be in the same classroom so that she could coteach with a general education teacher for three 40-minute periods a week (see Apply the

Concept 9-1.). During this time, students were to write and participate in skills groups. Initially, instruction included selecting topics of the student's choice, focusing first on the message and then on the mechanics of writing within each written piece. Skills such as organizing ideas and editing for capitalization, punctuation, and spelling were explicitly taught and linked directly to students' writing. Ms. Schlegel initiated the writing process approach but also retained many of the elements of her old writing program that were effective, such as recognizing the scope and sequence of writer development and teaching writing conventions (e.g., capital letters). She knew that to implement the writing process approach in her instruction she would need to consider setting, scheduling and preparing materials, teaching skills, and the teacher's role as a writer. Furthermore, she was aware that there were many strategic approaches to enhance writing that she wanted to include in her instruction.

Setting According to Graves (1983), the setting should create a working atmosphere similar to that of a studio, one that promotes independence but in which students can easily interact. Figure 9-1 depicts how Ms. Schlegel and the classroom teacher arranged the room to create such an atmosphere. Materials and supplies for writing, and the students' individual writing folders were stored in specific locations in the room. Students knew where materials could be found, so they did not have to rely on the teacher to get them started at the beginning of the

Apply the Concept

9-1	**Knowledge of Writing Strategies**

Students who have been identified as learning disabled differ from other students in their knowledge of strategies related to writing. They are less aware of steps in the writing process (e.g., think of an idea, decide what the purpose will be, organize the key parts sequentially) and ideas and procedures for organizing their written text. Students with LD are also more dependent on external cues, such as how much to write, teacher feedback, and mechanical presentation of the paper. They demonstrate significant difficulties in planning, writing, and revising text. Overall, the writing instruction of students with LD improves with well-organized and specific instruction along with ongoing feedback and encouragement to keep writing.

1. Create a working atmosphere that is similar to a studio.
2. Create an atmosphere in which students can interact easily.
3. Create an atmosphere that encourages independence.

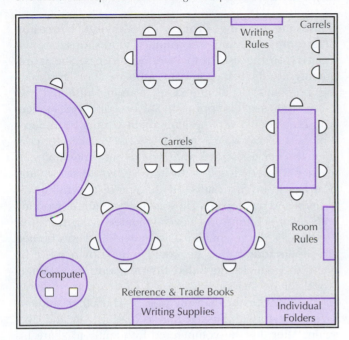

▶ **Figure 9-2** Individual Writing Folder

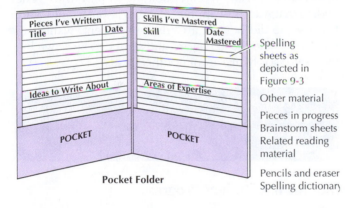

▶ **Figure 9-3** Sample Spelling Form
for the Individual Writing Folder

Student: _____

Words I'm Learning to Spell

Date	Word	Written on Card	Practiced Using Strategy	Learned for Test	Learned in Writing	Date Mastered
3/12	1. mystery	✓	✓	✓		
	2. chasing	✓	✓	✓		
	3. haunted	✓	✓			
	4. wouldn't	✓	✓			
	5. elsewhere	✓	✓	✓		
	6. whatever	✓	✓	✓		
	7. their	✓	✓	✓		
	8. there	✓	✓	✓		
	9.					
	10.					

writing period. The room arrangement facilitated conferencing between small groups of students, teacher and student, and student and student.

Scheduling and Preparing Materials Ms. Schlegel set up individual writing folders, illustrated in Figure 9-2, where students keep unfinished writing, a list of possible writing topics, a list of selected writing pieces they had completed, a list of writing skills they had mastered, a list of skills and topics in which they had expertise, and dates when conferences with the teacher were held. Students also kept mnemonic cues to assist them in practicing writing strategies that they were learning. A list of the words

an individual student was learning to spell, along with a procedure for learning the words and measuring mastery, were also included in the folder (see Figure 9-3).

Ms. Zaragoza is an elementary teacher who organizes skill lessons, 5 to 20 minutes each day, for small groups of students and individual skill lessons for students who have specific difficulties. She also addresses prevailing writing problems by providing approximately 20 minutes of whole-class instruction specifically teaching a target area (e.g., topic sentence, summary) two to three times per week. When she notices that several students are having difficulty with a particular skill (e.g., quotation marks) or thinks that several students are ready to learn a more advanced writing procedure (e.g., the difference between first and third person when writing), she organizes a skill group. She usually teaches one skill group a day and advertises the skill group by writing the name of it on the board. She writes the names of the students whom she has identified as likely to benefit from the skill group on the board but also allows other students to sign up for the skill group. A skill group would last for one day or several, depending on the difficulty of the skill. Ms. Zaragoza also teaches daily skill lessons to individual students. Sometimes these skill lessons are responses to a teachable moment—for example, a student might ask how to develop an ending for a story—and at other times are planned and scheduled. Ms. Zaragoza's viewpoint is that practice in writing is essential to enhancing writing skills, but practice alone is insufficient, and skill groups are an essential way to keep students moving and learning as writers.

Teaching Writing Conventions Students with LD display a wide range of abilities in writing (Berninger et al., 2008; Re, Pedron, & Cornoldi, 2007). They are also very different in terms of the writing skills they need to acquire and the ways in which they respond to instruction. Students who are better able to cope with the demands of schooling are better readers and writers over time, so one of the important tasks is to help students cope effectively with their writing difficulties (Niemi, Poskiparta, Vauras, & Mäki, 2008). In designing effective writing skills programs for students with learning problems, variables such as motivation and attitude must be considered, as well as writing conventions.

Ms. Schlegel taught spelling, capitalization, punctuation, and other writing-related skills during each writing period, and then looked for these skills in students' writing, providing feedback and instructional support when they were not well developed. Much of the time was devoted to small group instruction and individual writing and conferences with classmates and the teacher. Time for sharing ideas and drafts was often scheduled near the end of the period.

Ms. Schlegel conducted short (5- to 15-minute) skill lessons with individuals or small groups of students. The topics and groupings for these lessons were based on the students' needs. Skill lessons were decided on the basis of observations of student writing, requests for help, and data collected from conferences. Students were selected to participate in the skill lessons contingent on their abilities and needs. The same topic with different activities was usually covered for four lessons to help provide sufficient practice. She maintained records on each skill area, carefully monitoring students' progress. Ms. Schlegel realized that teaching the elements of writing as well as teaching writing conventions provided her students with the tools they needed to make progress in their writing.

Remember the following critical points about teaching conventions (Fearn & Farnan, 1998):

- Attention to conventions does not disrupt the flow of writing but is part of the discipline of writing.
- Focus on the conventions of writing does not inhibit growth in writing but facilitates it.
- Teach even young children writing conventions. Very young children can learn simple conventions and perform them automatically (see Figure 9-4).
- Reserve about 20% of the instructional time of students with learning and behavior problems for teaching writing conventions.

Perhaps the most important thing to remember about teaching writing to students with learning and behavior problems is that they require adequate time to write—and

to receive scaffolded instruction with feedback from the teacher. However, they also require explicit and systematic instruction in the critical elements and skills necessary for effective writing.

Using the Writing Process in General Education Classrooms Ms. Zaragoza conducts workshops for other teachers on the use of the writing process. She is frequently asked whether students who are at risk for learning problems or identified as learning disabled can successfully use this approach. She describes one student with LD as being very hesitant about writing for the first 2 months (Zaragoza & Vaughn, 1992). He asked for constant teacher assistance and would not write unless a teacher worked closely with him. He wrote slowly and neatly even on first drafts. His first piece of writing was untitled and incomplete. He was insecure about working with other students and never volunteered to share his writing. His piece, entitled "Disneyworld," demonstrated an understanding that he could write down what he really thought. He included his own dog in a Disney World theme ("Goofy is a dog I like to play with but Goofy is not better than my dog."). The other students loved this story and asked him to read it over and over again. After this, he volunteered frequently to share his writing in front of the class. He had a flair for good endings and became the class expert on developing endings. For example, in "The Spooky Halloween," he ended with this sentence, "Halloween is nothing to play with." The ending that was most appreciated was about a child who, because he did not get a Christmas present, wanted to die. He went to the graveyard and started to lie down but then said, "Holy macaroni not this dead."

> ▶ **WEB RESOURCES**
> For help on teaching writing, see the Web site of the National Council of Teachers of English: http://www.ncte.org.

Monitoring Student Progress

How does a teacher monitor students' progress in writing? When teachers monitor students' progress on critical elements regularly (at least every 2 weeks), students make improved progress (Gunning, 2010). Teachers record students' progress so that they, the students, and parents can see progress, such as the number of words written for younger children and developing a checklist of story elements and their quality for older students.

Teachers monitor students' progress by noting the following:

- Whether students can complete the written project
- How proficient they are at each element of the writing process (e.g., planning, spelling, handwriting, accuracy of letter formation, composing)

Instructional Concept	K	1	2	3	4	5	6	7	8
End Punctuation	*	*	*						
Commas in Dates	*	*	*						
Commas in Series	*	*	*	*					
Commas in Addresses	*	*	*	*					
Apostrophes in Contractions		*	*	*	*				
Periods in Abbreviations		*	*	*	*				
Commas in Compound Sentences			*	*	*				
Punctuation in Dialogue			*	*	*	*			
Apostrophes in Possessives			*	*	*	*			
Commas in Complex Sentences				*	*	*			
Quotation Marks and Underlining in Published Titles				*	*	*			
Commas in Series of Adjectives				*	*	*			
Commas to Set Off Appositives				*	*	*	*		
Commas After Introductory Words				*	*	*	*		
Commas After Introductory Phrases				*	*	*	*		
Commas in Compound-Complex Sentences					*	*	*	*	
Commas to Set Off Parenthetical Expressions					*	*	*		
Dashes and Parentheses to Set Off Parenthetical Expressions					*	*	*	*	
Colons in Sentences					*	*	*	*	
Semicolons in Sentences					*	*	*	*	
Capital Letters to Begin Sentences	*	*	*						
Capital Letters in Names	*	*	*						
Capitalizing	*	*	*						
Capital Letters in Days and Months	*	*	*	*					
Capital Letters in Place Names	*	*	*	*					
Capital Letters in Person's Title		*	*	*	*				
Capital Letters in Published Titles		*	*	*	*				
Capital Letters to Show Nationality, Ethnicity, and Language		*	*	*	*				
Capital Letters in Trade Names, Commercial Products, and Company Names		*	*	*	*				
Capital Letters in Names of Institutions, Associations, and Events		*	*	*	*				

Source: L. Fearn & N. Farnan, *Writing Effectively: Helping Children Master the Conventions of Writing* (Boston: Allyn & Bacon, 1998). Copyright © 1998 by Allyn & Bacon. Reprinted by permission.

- Whether they can apply the skills and knowledge to other contexts (e.g., during classes other than a writing class)
- How they explain the process they are using
- Which elements of writing are proceeding as expected (e.g., capital letters) and which require additional instruction (e.g., too many run-on sentences).

See Apply the Concept 9-2 for questions concerning progress monitoring.

Monitoring students' progress in writing involves evaluating written products and observing the writing process. Teachers can observe students as they write and use conference times to assess and record their progress. By observing and examining writing processes and products, teachers can plan instruction to meet individual needs. Many teachers keep anecdotal records by creating a record sheet to quickly document students' progress on writing projects. They include a summary of what they observe, the date, and context, and they list skills and writing strategies that need to be taught. Collections of students' written work help teachers, families, and students document growth and development over the school year. Journals and writing folders also provide insight into writing growth. Teachers may periodically review and select representative pieces to show writing development and use progress monitoring to establish writing goals for students.

Determining how the teacher will measure writing progress for each student requires consideration. For example, for young students, the teacher may monitor the number of words written, number of words spelled correctly, and use of capital letters and punctuation. As students mature in their writing, the teacher may decide to monitor use of adjectives and vivid verbs, facility in editing and revising, and overall quality of the writing. Also,

9-2

Questions to Consider in Monitoring Student Progress

Assessing Progress

How does the student respond during the activity?

- Can the student complete the task?
- How comfortably and proficiently is the task completed?
- Can the student explain the process used to complete the task?
- Can the student apply the skills and knowledge to other contexts?
- Are there aspects of the task that are causing difficulties?

Adjusting Instruction

Will different approaches, materials, or settings improve student progress?

Different approaches

- Simplify tasks into small steps.
- Do more modeling or demonstration.
- Provide more review.
- Give more guidance.

Different materials

- Decrease difficulty of the material.
- Use different types of writing genres.
- Provide checklists or cue card.

Different settings

- Use peers to assist.
- Change time of day of instruction.
- Change location of task.

Sources: T. G. Gunning, *Assessing and Correcting Reading and Writing Difficulties* (Boston: Allyn & Bacon, 2009); and B. Rosenshine, Advances in research on instruction, in J. W. Lloyd, E. J. Kame'enui, & D. Chard (Eds.), *Issues in Educating Students with Disabilities* (Mahwah, NJ: Erlbaum, 1997).

---

these records of progress monitoring may be kept separately for each type of writing. For example, Mr. Dodge expected students to write an "opinion" piece, a "persuasive" piece, an information report, and a narrative story. He kept separate progress-monitoring forms for each of these genres for each student.

It is important to focus on only one or two things at a time. After students demonstrate progress in the target areas, the teacher can add other elements of writing. This way, progress is recorded, but students are not overwhelmed by the number of writing conventions that they need to monitor.

▶ **WEB RESOURCES**
For a helpful Web site on progress monitoring in writing, see http://www.progressmonitoring.org.

Elements of the Writing Process

The elements of the writing process include prewriting or planning, composing, revising, editing, and publishing. When students learn to write they do not proceed through the process in a linear fashion. In fact, many authors circle back through previous elements and jump ahead to later ones when they are writing their drafts. Also, not all writing leads to publishing. For example, Steven realized after he read his draft to his friend Jacob that he needed to have more information about what submarines look like on the inside. He returned to the prewriting stage and checked out several books on submarines so that he could complete his story. Furthermore, students must learn to

master these elements in a variety of writing styles, including reports, letters, notes, and persuasive writing.

In prewriting, students collect information about a topic through observing, remembering, interviewing, and reading. When composing, students attempt to get ideas on paper in the form of a draft. This process tells students what they know and do not know. During revising, points are explored further, ideas are elaborated, and further connections are made. When students are satisfied with the content, they edit the piece, reviewing it line by line to determine that each word is necessary. Punctuation, spelling, and other mechanical processes are checked. The final element is publication. If the piece is a good one for the student, it is published. Obviously, not all pieces are published.

Many students with LD experience significant problems in editing and writing final copies because they have difficulty with mechanical skills such as spelling, punctuation, and handwriting. These students often produce well-developed stories that are hard to read because of mechanical errors. Other students with LD have difficulty organizing their first drafts and need to rethink sequencing and order during their revisions.

Graham, Harris, and their colleagues (Lane et al., 2008; Graham & Harris, 2005) have successfully taught students with LD and behavior disorders to use self-regulated strategy development when writing:

1. Think: who will read this, and why am I writing it?
2. Plan what to say using TREE:
   T: Topic Sentence
   R: Reasons
   E: Examine Reasons
   E: Ending
3. Write and say more.

Prewriting: Getting Started The first hurdle in starting to write is topic selection. For younger students, they can write about what know and have experienced. For older students, topic choice may be within parameters established by the teacher. For example, they may need to write an information report on a country in the world, but they can pick the country and they can pick the topic. This leaves a lot of room for choice, and for some students with LD, a lot of room for indecision. One of the most important roles the teacher can play is to facilitate decision making about topic selection and sticking with the topic.

For younger students, keeping a list of topics so that they are ready to write is a good idea. Students can also share their topics with the class to spark more ideas for others. Teachers can ask for volunteer students to read their topic lists to the entire group. Now ask the students to expand their ideas for writing and to keep their topic lists in their writing folders. Also tell the students that if they think of new topics they want to write about, they may add them to their lists. Finally, ask the students to select a topic and begin writing. Throughout the school make opportunities for students to identify additional topics for writing. After they become more comfortable writing and more expert in their use of writing conventions, you can work with students to identify, select, and write about an increasing range of genres including information pieces, reports, persuasive writing, and poetry.

Problems in Topic Selection There are two common problems in topic selection: difficulty in finding a topic and persistence in writing about the same topic. Maintaining a supply of writing topics is difficult for some students and rarely a problem for others. During reading of any text, ask students questions to prompt ideas for future writing. If they were going to write the ending of this story, how would they do it? If they were going to continue this story, what would happen? If they were going to add characters to the story, what types of characters would they add? Would they change the setting?

Teachers can also facilitate topic selection by presenting a range of writing styles including stories, factual descriptions, mysteries, persuasive writing, writing that involves comparing and contrasting, reporting on topics, and observing. Students often begin writing by telling personal experiences. Through the writing of other authors, students can be introduced to a wide range of categories that can provide exposure to other genres. Figure 9-5 presents a list of suggestions for students when they are stuck about a topic for writing. One of those suggestions, asking a friend to help, is discussed in Apply the Concept 9-3.

In addition to difficulty in thinking of a topic, immature writers often repeat the same topic. Teachers review students' work and determine whether the stories are changing through vocabulary development, concept development, story development, or character development. It

▶ **Figure 9-5**   Up in the Air for a Topic?

- Check your folder and reread your idea list.
- Ask a friend to help you brainstorm ideas.
- Listen to others' ideas.
- Write about what you know: your experiences.
- Write a make-believe story.
- Write about a special interest or hobby.
- Write about how to do something.
- Think about how you got your last idea.

could be that the student is learning a great deal about writing even though the story content is changing very little. The teacher can provide specific examples of other genres and instructional procedures for how to write in these genres.

Prewriting Strategies Many students with learning and behavior problems begin writing without much planning about what they are going to write. They find that when they read their drafts aloud, others have difficulty understanding the story or following the sequence. Students with LD often have limited text organization skills because they have difficulty categorizing ideas related to a specific topic, providing advanced organizers for the topic, and relating and extending ideas about the topic (Englert & Raphael, 1988). Consequently, we need to teach students prewriting skills so that the writing and rewriting stages will be easier.

In teaching the organization that goes into writing a piece, teachers can model their thinking as they move from topic selection to writing a first draft. Some teachers find it helpful to teach this thinking process by writing their ideas in an organized structure and by asking students to set goals, brainstorm ideas, and sequence their ideas while they are writing (Troia & Graham, 2002). Some teachers use graphic organizers across curriculum areas to organize writing for both narrative and expository texts.

9-3

A Friend Helps with Topic Selection

Ruth Ann returned with a piece of blank paper, which she handed to Cary. Cary wrote Ruth Ann's name on the paper and underlined it. Then she conducted a rather sophisticated interview.

"Think of three ideas. Want to write about your first day of school?"

"I can't remember. That was 5 years ago," answered Ruth Ann.

"How about the first day in the learning lab?" continued Cary.

"I don't remember that either. It was over a year ago."

Looking at her idea sheet, Cary commented, "I'm writing about a talking dishwasher. Do you want to write about that?"

"Not really," replied Ruth Ann.

"Where do you go on vacations?" asked Cary.

"To Iowa, but I've already written about that."

"Well, have you ever been to a circus?" Cary pursued.

"No."

"How about a zoo?"

"The Los Angeles Zoo," Ruth Ann answered.

"Do you want to write about that?" asked Cary.

"Yeah," remarked Ruth Ann, "that's a good idea."

Cary wrote the number 1 on the paper she had labeled with Ruth Ann's name, and wrote, "las angels zoo" beside it. She remarked, "I don't know how to spell Los Angeles."

"Don't worry," Ruth Ann commented. "I can find that out when I start writing about it."

"OK, let's think up another idea. Have you ever ridden a horse?" asked Cary as she continued the interview.

"No," replied Ruth Ann.

"Do you have any pets?" asked Cary.

"Yeah, I have a cat named Pierre."

"Do you want to write about him?" continued Cary.

"Yes, I could do that," replied Ruth Ann enthusiastically.

Cary wrote the number 2 on the paper and beside it wrote, "writing about your cat."

The conversation continued, with Cary explaining that it is helpful to think up three ideas so that you have some choice when you decide what to write about. After more questioning, Ruth Ann decided that it would be okay to write about a talking shoe, so Cary wrote down Ruth Ann's third idea. Then Cary helped Ruth Ann decide that she was first going to write about her cat. Cary wrote this idea at the bottom of the page and starred it to note that Ruth Ann had selected this topic. Cary ended the interview by saying, "Put this paper in your writing folder so that the next time you have to select a topic, we'll already have two ideas thought up."

Graphic organizers that are used to assist in writing are referred to as *brainstorm sheets* or *structured organizers*, *semantic maps*, and *story frames* or *maps*. Although these visual organization devices have been used as aids to reading comprehension, they also serve to facilitate the writing process (Pehrsson & Robinson, 1985; MacArthur, Graham, & Fitzgerald, 2006). Ms. Turk, a resource teacher who works with Ms. Schlegel, used a think-aloud technique to model how to use the brainstorm sheet presented in Apply the Concept 9-4. She drew a large brainstorm sheet on the board and then introduced the brainstorming technique to the students.

Ms. Turk began, "I want to write a story about a time when I was really scared. So I decided to write about the time when I was about 10 years old and my dad and I went for a horseback ride. He got hurt, and I wasn't sure we'd get back to the car. There is so much to remember about this story that I am going to jot down a few ideas so that when I begin to write my story, I can remember them all and put them in order. To help me organize my ideas, I'm going to use a brainstorm sheet."

At this point, Ms. Turk explained the brainstorm sheet and the parts of a story. Through class discussion, the students identified a story they had written recently and each part in their story.

Ms. Turk continued modeling, using the brainstorm sheet. "I am going to call my story 'Horseback Ride' for now. I may want to change the name later, since it's easier for me to think of a title after I write the story. Well, it happened when we were on a trip to Mount Graham. So I'm going to write 'Mt. Graham' by 'Where.' I'm not sure how to spell Mt. Graham, but it doesn't matter that I spell it correctly now. I can find out later. Also, since the brainstorm sheet is for me, I don't have to write sentences—just ideas that will help me remember when I'm writing my first draft of the story." Ms. Turk continued to think aloud as she completed the sheet.

Ms. Turk demonstrated that the students did not have to fill in the brainstorm sheet in a linear fashion. Sometimes it is easier to fill out the ending first. She also demonstrated how, after she listed all the ideas under the action section, she could go back and number them in the order that made the most sense.

In subsequent lessons, Ms. Turk demonstrated how to write a story from the brainstorm sheet. She also worked

Apply the Concept

9-4   Sample Brainstorm Sheet

Name: Mrs. Turk

Date: 2/7

Working Title: Horseback Ride

Setting:

Where: Mt. Graham
start at trash dump

When: When I was ten years old

Who: Dad and I, also mom and brother

Dad and I were riding on trail.
Trail got bad.

Action: Dad's horse stumbled on rock.
Dad fell off + hurt his arm.
Finally he got on horse. I helped.
Rode to top of mt. Mom met us. So
did brother. Went to hospital.

Ending: Dad was OK.

---

individually with students to complete brainstorm sheets and to use them in their writing.

During the year, several different brainstorm sheets were used in Ms. Turk's classroom. Figure 9-6 shows a brainstorm sheet that was developed for expository writing (writing that describes the facts or information about a subject area; often associated with social studies and science). However, the students also used this brainstorm sheet for stories. They wrote the title in the center circle, and information related to the setting, problem, action, and ending in the four other circles and their accompanying lines. Students also developed their own brainstorming sheets. For example, Cary combined topic selection and brainstorming, and developed the brainstorm sheet in Figure 9-7. Graphic organizers can assist students in organizing the key ideas in their writing, remembering the steps in completing a well-written piece, and remembering writing strategies that they need to use.

Teaching students to think about what they are going to say before they write is generally a helpful technique. However, completing a visual representation before writing may not facilitate writing for all students (see Apply the Concept 9-5).

Composing Many students with learning and behavior problems begin the writing process here. They think of a topic and, without much planning, begin to write. They write ideas as they think of them, and each idea they write serves as a stimulus for the next idea. Therefore, students benefit from instruction on how to be more reflective as they write (Graham, Harris, & MacArthur, 1995).

▶ **Figure 9-6**   Brainstorm Sheet

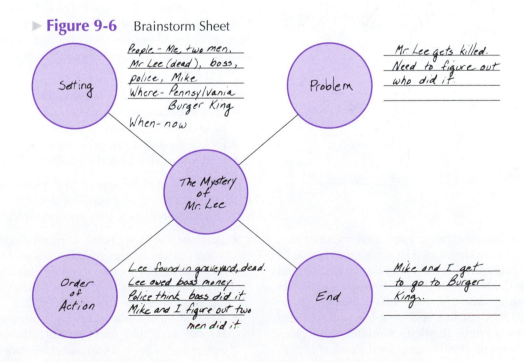

9-5 The Big Picture

A common problem with poor writers is that the surface structure of their writing—the spelling, grammar, and punctuation—prevents them from expressing their ideas in writing and also keeps others from reading them. Many students with learning problems do not focus on thinking about their story. Their stories are often poorly organized, and their ideas are disconnected and/or missing. These same students can *tell* you about the story but have a hard time getting all of the ideas about the story in writing.

Following is the description of a procedure developed by Kucer (1986) to help poor writers focus on the "big picture" of writing:

1. Give students notecards, and allow them to write possible topics on the cards (one topic per card). Students then share ideas about topics and make additions on their topic cards.

2. Students select a writing topic about which they would like to write.

3. Major ideas related to the writing topic are written on notecards. The major ideas may come from the student's knowledge and experience or, if the writing is in a content area, the student may need to seek the assistance of class notes, books, and magazines. Major ideas are written as key concepts or thoughts rather than as complete sentences.

4. Students share their major ideas about the topics with each other. They make any additions or comments about the ideas they feel will be helpful in writing about the topics.

5. Once major ideas have been selected, they are organized in a meaningful sequence.

6. With their cards as a guide, students write their pieces.

▶ **Figure 9-7** Cary's Brainstorm Sheet

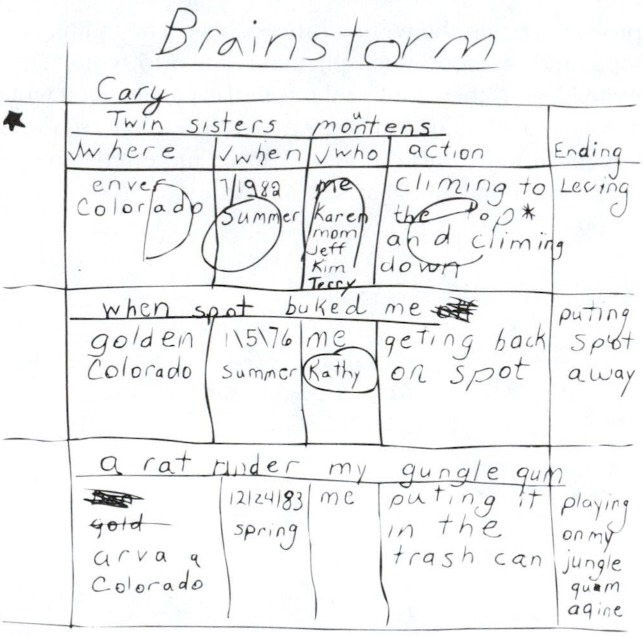

Some authors suggest using cue cards to assist students in writing better-developed stories or essays (De La Paz, 1999). A cue card, used by Montague and Leavell (1994), asks students to consider the following elements when composing: where and when, character (have them think and feel just like real people), problem and plan, and story ending. Englert, Raphael, Anderson, Anthony, and Stevens (1991) developed think sheets to assist students in first planning and then organizing their ideas before writing. Figure 9-8 presents the plan think sheet, and Figure 9-9 presents the organization think sheet for the text structure associated with explanations.

▶ **WEB RESOURCES**

For a helpful Web site on instructional practices in writing for students with LD, see www.ldonline.org.

One of the skills that students must acquire is how to write sentences that are effective and then to organize these effective sentences into meaningful paragraphs. In particular, students with learning problems require instruction in how to

- add vivid words and lively verbs.
- combine short and choppy sentences to make more productive sentences.
- reduce long and run-on sentences.
- read and revise to add meaning.

These skills can be taught and practiced separately and then monitored and supported when students write texts. Instructional principles and examples include:

- Teach students to paint a picture with words by using adjectives and adverbs to show readers what they mean. For example, rather than "I ate lunch," the student can write, "I ate my lunch quickly, shoving large bites into my mouth."
- Teach students to avoid using common verbs such as *was, were,* and *said* and instead use more interesting verbs such as *avoided, clamored, quipped,*

► **Figure 9-8** Plan Think Sheet

PLAN

Name _____ Date _____

TOPIC: _____

WHO: Who am I writing for?

_____

_____

WHY: Why am I writing this?

_____

_____

WHAT: What do I know? (Brainstorm)

1. _____
2. _____
3. _____
4. _____
5. _____
6. _____
7. _____
8. _____

HOW: How can I group my ideas?

☐	☐
_____	_____
_____	_____
☐	☐
_____	_____
_____	_____

How will I organize my ideas?

___ Compare/Contrast   ___ Problem/Solution
___ Explanation   ___ Other

Source: C. S. Englert, T. E. Raphael, & L. M. Anderson, *Cognitive Strategy Instruction in Writing Project* (East Lansing, MI: Institute for Research on Teaching, 1989). Reprinted by permission.

► **Figure 9-9** Organization Think Sheet for Text Structure Associated with Explanations

Explanation Organization Form

What is being explained? [   ]

Materials/things you need? [   ]

Setting? [   ]

What are the steps?

First, [   ]

Next, [   ]

Third, [   ]

Then, [   ]

Last, [   ]

Source: C. S. Englert, T. E. Raphael, & L. M. Anderson, *Cognitive Strategy Instruction in Writing Project* (East Lansing, MI: Institute for Research on Teaching, 1989). Reprinted by permission.

Spotlight on Diversity
Guidelines for Teaching Writing to Students Who Are English-Language Learners

Students' writing is influenced by several factors: their knowledge of the English language, English vocabulary development, understanding of word use, and knowledge of the conventions of writing such as noun–verb agreement. Many of the approaches to writing that are discussed in this chapter are highly appropriate for ELLs. Teachers should ask themselves the following questions when planning writing instruction for ELLs (Haley & Austin, 2004):

• Do they know what they want to write about?
• Do they feel comfortable using their personal, family, and other relevant experiences in their writing?

• Do they use what they know to support their writing?
• What ways are helpful to get them to start thinking about their composition?
• Do they try to use new words in their writing?
• Do they get suggestions for their writing from family and friends?
• Do they use procedures for deciding what is important and not important in their writing?
• Do they choose different ways to express their ideas and feelings in their writing?
• Do they increasingly use more appropriate and effective language in their writing?

barked, existed, and *repeated.* In fact, teachers can make lists of words to substitute for more common words and post the lists in the room as a resource. Students can expand the lists themselves by adding more interesting words.

- Teach students to list ideas and then to sequence them (Troia & Graham, 2002).

▶ **WEB RESOURCES**
For additional Web resources related to ELLs, see http://Colorincolorado.org.

Revising Revising is a difficult task for all authors and especially for students with learning problems. Getting the entire message down on paper the first time is difficult enough; making changes so the piece is at its best and can be understood by others is a most formidable task. Many authors need to go back to prewriting and obtain more information, or they spend time conferring with others to find out what parts of their sentences or ideas require additional work. It is also at this stage that some authors abandon the piece. They believe it can never be really good, and so they start again with a new idea.

Most students with learning and behavior problems have difficulty revising and would like to move straight to publication, with little or no revision. Ms. Takamura finds that students will revise their pieces if teachers show them how through the work of other students or the work of professional authors.

Students with LD, particularly adolescents (Wong, Butler, Ficzere, & Kuperis, 1997), can learn procedures such as diagnosing, comparing, and operating to assist themselves during the revision process (De La Paz, Swanson, & Graham, 1998). When teachers model, demonstrate, and provide feedback using the following procedure, students' revisions and writing improve.

Compare and Diagnose Read your writing and consider the following:

- It ignores the obvious point against my idea.
- There are too few ideas.
- Part of the essay doesn't belong with the rest.
- Part of the essay is not in the right order.

Tactical Operations The listed problems can be fixed by doing the following:

- Rewrite
- Delete
- Add
- Move

Compare Reread the paper, and highlight problems.

Diagnose and Operate Read your writing and determine whether any of the following apply:

- This doesn't sound right.
- This isn't what I intended to say.

- This is an incomplete idea.
- This part is not clear.
- The problem is _____.

Teachers can show students how to use a "box and explode" strategy as a means for selecting the one sentence in their writing that is the most important but may not be adequately expanded (Block, 1997; Gersten & Baker, 2001; Strickland, Ganske, & Monroe, 2002). Students learn to put this sentence in a box and then to use it as a focus for extending the idea and clarifying story events. Students are taught to "explode" the main idea in the box. For example, suppose a student wrote the following paragraph:

> Julia went to her aunt's house on Sunday. After she got there she saw that her aunt's door was open. She walked in the house and saw her uncle on the floor. She didn't know what to do.

Students would be taught to put a box around the sentence "She walked in the house and saw her uncle on the floor." Then they would work to "explode" that sentence so that the reader would learn more about what happened.

Editing In addition to editing their own work, students serve as editors for the work of their peers. Whereas revision focuses mainly on content, editing focuses mainly on mechanics. After the student and teacher are happy with the content, it is time to make corrections for spelling, capitalizing, punctuation, and language. Students are expected to circle words they are unsure how to spell, put boxes in places where they are unsure of the punctuation, and underline the sentences about which they feel the language may not be correct Figure 9-10 provides a poster that can be used in a classroom to remind students of the editing rules. Figure 9-11 depicts a form that can be included inside the students' folders to remind them of editing skills they know how to use. Apply the Concept 9-6 provides guidelines for how teachers and peers might respond to writing.

Although many spelling, punctuation, and language modifications are made during writing and revising, when students edit, they focus solely on mechanical errors. Often, they need to read the text for each type of error. First, they read the text looking for spelling difficulties; next, they read the text looking for punctuation and capitalization difficulties; and finally, they read the text looking for

▶ **Figure 9-10** Editing Rules

(Circle) misspelled words.

Put a [box] around punctuation.

Underline writing that <u>doesn't sound so good.</u>

Add a ^ to insert a word or phrase.

Add a ^① with a number to insert a sentence.

9-6 Ways for Teachers and Peers to Respond to Writing

Suggestions to Compliment Writing

- I like the way your paper began because . . .
- I like the part where . . .
- I like the way you explained . . .
- I like the order you used in your paper because . . .
- I like the details you used to describe . . .
- I like the way you used dialogue to make your story sound real.
- I like the words you used in your writing, such as . . .

- I like the facts you used like . . .
- I like the way the paper ended because . . .
- I like the mood of your writing because it made me feel . . .

Questions and Suggestions to Improve Writing

- I got confused in the part about . . .
- Could you add an example to the part about . . .
- Could you add more to this _____ part because . . .

- Do you think your order would make more sense if you . . .
- Do you think you could leave this part out because . . .
- Could you use a different word for _____ because . . .
- Is this _____ paragraph on one topic?
- Could you write a beginning sentence to "grab" your readers?

▶ **Figure 9-11** Editing Skills I Know

Spelling

1. done
2. was
3. from
4. come
5. girl
6. because
7. what
8. where
9. children
10. playground

Punctuation

1. Put a period at the end of a sentence.
2. Put a question mark at the end of an asking sentence.

Capitalization

1. Capitalize the first letter of a sentence.
2. Capitalize the first letter of a person's name.
3. Capitalize the name of a town.

language problems such as noun–verb agreement. Young students may not know what noun–verb agreement is, so they should simply look for sentences that do not "sound right" when they read them aloud.

The following suggestions are designed to assist students in removing the mechanical errors from their writing (Isaacson & Gleason, 1997):

- Have students dictate their story to improve the flow of their writing.
- Provide students with a list of key words and words that are hard to spell to assist with writing and editing.

- Teach students to use a word book.
- Promote peer collaboration in editing.
- Teach students to use technology to support editing and writing.
- Hold students accountable for using the rules of writing they know, such as punctuation, spelling, and other writing conventions that they have been taught.

Publishing What does it mean to have a piece published? A piece is prepared in some way that it can be read and shared by others. For younger students this may be in the form of books that have cardboard binding decorated with contact paper, scraps of wallpaper, or clip art. Sometimes these books include a picture of the author, a description of the author, and a list of books published by the author.

Older students who spend more time composing and revising are more likely to "publish" or "publicly share" work that is the result of many weeks of effort and several revisions. Why publish? Publishing is a way of confirming a student's hard work and sharing the piece with others. Writing requires an audience, and periodically we need to share what we write. It is important for all students to publish—not just the best authors. Publishing is a way of involving others in the school and home with the students' writing.

What Can Families Do to Promote Children's Writing?

Encourage parents/guardians to play with their children and adolescents using words. Ask them to be sure that the writing they promote and do with their children is fun, interesting, and encourages learning. As children get older, encourage them to use writing as a means of communicating with grandparents or other family members. Suggest that parents/guardians leave notes for their children on their pillows, by their plates, and in other places where the children are likely to find them. Encourage the children to leave notes for family members.

▶ **WEB RESOURCES**
For additional information on writing and spelling practices for teachers and parents, see http://k12reader.com.

Following are some fun and simple activities that children (and their families) will love. Families can make the activities easier or more challenging, depending on the children's ability.

For beginning or reluctant writers:

- Spell with letter blocks or magnetic letters, or write the alphabet on small pieces of paper and store it in an envelope. Give children four or five letters, and ask them to spell simple words. Ask the child to find the letters that spell *bed, bad, bat,* and *bet.* This is "writing" without actually having to write.
- Help children make labels for their room. Use colorful markers and paper to write *chair, desk, bed, window, curtains, computer, fish, floor, closet,* and so on. Tape the labels on the objects.
- Go on a word walk. Go outside with a pad or clipboard. Look in one direction, and write everything you see. Compare notes with the children. Or write down only things that are green, moving, in the sky, or on the ground, and so on.

- Make a list. Children love to help with grocery lists, lists of errands, wish lists, chores, things to do on a rainy Saturday, and so on.
- Make a word collage. Have children cut words out of the newspaper or old magazines and glue them on paper to make a word collage. Help children read the words they found.

For more competent writers:

- Play the "What am I?" game: Take turns writing or giving a description and trying to guess what it is. *You can sit on me. I like to be near tables. I am sometimes made of wood. What am I?* Answer: *A chair.*
- Do a sentence switcheroo. Start by writing a simple sentence. For example, "The man walked down the street." Take turns changing or adding words. The sentence might become "The friendly old man ran up the gigantic mountain."
- Write alliterative sentences with words that start with the same letter. For example, "Six slimy snakes slithered into my salami sandwich."
- Write a letter to a friend or relative, and send it in the mail or use e-mail.
- Write questions. Children have lots of questions. Write them down. For example, "Do dogs dream? What do ladybugs eat? Why can't I eat candy for breakfast?" Help children find answers to their questions at the library or on the Internet.

Promoting Writing

Writing conferences in which teachers use time with students to promote and improve their writing are a critical aspect of promoting successful writing.

 Tech TIPS

WRITTEN EXPRESSION

Computer programs can help learners with written expression in many ways. The following software programs are particularly useful in helping students to master the writing process by giving them tools that help them compose with confidence.

Write: Outloud by Don Johnston Incorporated,
www.donjohnston.com/products/write_outloud/index.html
This program, for students in grades 3 through 12, is a talking word processor that allows students to hear letters, words, sentences, and paragraphs spoken as they type. Other speech features include speaking any selected text and changing voice and speed. Learners who can benefit from hearing what they have typed should have access to a talking word processor.

The Secret Writer's Society from SmartKids Software,
www.smartkidssoftware.com/99v.htm
This program is designed for students in grades 8 and up has levels (missions) of teaching topics such as capitalization, end punctuation, sentence writing, paragraph writing, planning and ordering sentences, and revision and editing. A final level guides the learner through the five-step writing process.

Draft: Builder by Don Johnston Incorporated,
www.donjohnston.com/products/draft_builder/
This word processing and writing program, designed for students in grades 3 though 8, helps students map and organize their written products, it also helps them to edit and revise their work.

9-7 Sample Student Writing

"My best football game"

Football is my favorite game I like to play it even when I was little I played for a good team the bandits and one game we played against Macarther school and it started off with us 0 and them 7 and then the game was tied 7 to 7 and then it was time for me to sit on the bench and the score was 7–14 we was winning soon they told me to go back into the game it was getting close to the end and we wanted to win they said it was my turn to run a play and so I ran fast down the feild after the ball was Mike and I look back and see the ball coming right at me and I thought I was going to miss it but I kept looking at it and after I watched it I reached up and pulled the ball down and I kept on running and we won the game 7 to 21.

The Writing Conference Conferring is the heart of the writing process. Students also know that they will be asked challenging questions about their work. Questions are not asked in a rapid-fire sequence with little time for the student to formulate answers. Instead, questions are carefully selected, and enough time is allowed for the student to respond. Conferences focus on specific areas and are not designed to address all elements of writing. During the conference with the author of "My Best Football Game" (see Apply the Concept 9-7), the teacher realized that the writing had many problems. She was aware of grammatical, spelling, and punctuation errors. She was also aware that the story rambled, lacked sufficient details, and did not reflect the author's voice. However, she was ecstatic that this 14-year-old student with severe emotional problems had produced a piece of writing that he was excited about. Apply the Concept 9-8 presents the conference the teacher had with the student.

Some key points about conferring with students are as follows:

- Do not attempt to get the writer to write about a topic because it is of interest to you or to write the story the way you would write it.
- Ask the student what steps in the writing process were used to develop this piece.
- Ask questions that teach. (Apply the Concept 9-9 illustrates a conference in which the teacher asks questions that teach.)
- Agree on the steps the student will take to improve the paper, and establish a procedure for checking that these activities occur.
- Conferences should be frequent and brief. Although conferences can range from 30 seconds to 10 minutes, most of them last only 2 to 3 minutes with younger children and longer with older students.

Establishing a Writing Community For students to write well within their classroom, an environment of mutual trust and respect is essential. Establishing a writing community requires that you take the following steps:

1. *Write every day for at least 30 minutes.* Students need time to think, write, discuss, rewrite, confer, revise, talk, read, and write some more. Good writing takes time.
2. *Encourage students to develop areas of expertise.* Younger students write about what they know. However, with encouragement, both younger and older students can become experts in a particular area, subject, or writing form.
3. *Keep students' writing in folders.* Folders should include writing as documentation of what each student knows and has accomplished. Students can refer to their work to illustrate their progress, to indicate skills learned, and to demonstrate range of topic.
4. *Monitor students' progress, establish writing goals, and hold students accountable for learning and practicing what they know.* Together, identify the expected goals for each student, discuss what aspects of these goals are achieved and represented in their writing, and guide rewriting and skills lessons to ensure that these goals are met.
5. *Share writing.* Provide training to students and opportunities for them to share and give feedback to each other.
6. *Expand the writing community outside of the classroom.* Place published books by your students in the library for use by other students, and allow students to share their writing with other classes. Encourage authors from other classrooms to visit and read their writings.
7. *Develop children's capacity to evaluate their own work.* Students need to develop their own goals and document their progress toward them.

9-8 **Conferencing with the Author of "My Best Football Game"**

Teacher: "Mark, this football game was a special one for you. I bet you have a lot of feelings about this game. What are some of your feelings about this game?"

Mark: "I felt good."

Teacher: "Did you feel good like when you remember your homework or was it stronger than that?"

Mark: "It was stronger. I felt great. Like I was a hero or something."

Teacher: "Like a hero?"

Mark: "Yeah, like in the movies. I really saved the game. Well, I guess not really saved the game because we were already winning. But it was, like, 'cause I made the last touchdown it really said something."

Teacher: "What do you think it said?"

Mark: "It said, hey, watch out 'cause I'm good. Also, that we won and I scored the final points. It was great."

Teacher: "What could you do so the reader of your piece would know all of the things you just told me?"

Mark: "I guess I could include more about how I felt and all."

Teacher: "How could you do that? Where would it go?"

The teacher decided it was too early to focus on mechanical errors such as spelling and punctuation. Besides being discouraging to Mark, focusing too early on mechanical errors would sidetrack this writer from the story. After the author's story is complete, then work on mechanical errors can begin.

9-9 **Conferencing: Following the Lead of the Student**

During conferences, the teacher listens to what students say, follows the lead of the students, and asks questions that teach:

Teacher: "How's it going, Karin?"

Karin: "Not very good. I don't know what to write about."

Teacher: "You are having trouble with a topic?"

Karin: "I was going to write about how I want to go and live with my real mom again but I don't know what to say. All I do is write that I want to live with my real mom and then the story is over."

Teacher: "It's hard to think of what else might go in the story?"

Karin: "Well, yeah. I guess I could tell why, but I don't know why, I just want to."

Teacher: "Would it be any easier to get started if you told the story as though it were about someone else?"

Karin: "Like I could tell about a kid who wanted to go and live with her real mom. Then I could tell it like a story."

Teacher: "What are some of the things you might write if you told the story this way?"

8. *Facilitate spelling during writing.* Teachers and students can provide instructional feedback to support students in spelling correctly during the writing process. (See Apply the Concept 9-10 for suggestions.)

9. *Assist students who are culturally and linguistically diverse.* With a few adjustments, teachers can create classroom communities that promote their success and learning. See Apply the Concept 9-11 for suggestions.

10. *Remember to teach students specific strategies for writing purposefully* such as compare and contrast, reports, persuasive writing, and interviews.

The writing process approach to instruction of children who have special needs requires time—time to follow the progress of students, confer with students, and teach math skills. Most important, it requires time each day for the students to write. (See Apply the Concept 9-12.)

Using Computers to Facilitate Writing

The use of spell checkers and speech synthesizers to facilitate writing effectiveness for students with LD has been well documented (Graham & Perin, 2007; MacArthur, 1988; McNaughton, Hughes, & Ofiesh, 1997). These tools can be

9-10   Providing Instructional Feedback to Facilitate Spelling Correctly

Prompts to Help Students Notice Errors

- Check to see if that looks/sounds right.
- There is a tricky word on this line.
- You are nearly right.
- Try that again.
- Try it another way.
- You have almost got that. See if you can find what is wrong.

Prompts to Help Students Find Errors

- Find the part that is not right.
- Look carefully to see what's wrong.
- You noticed something was wrong.
- Where is the part that is not right?
- What made you stop?
- Can you find the problem spot?

Prompts to Help Students Fix Errors

- What do you hear first? Next? Last?
- What word starts with those letters?
- Do you think it looks/sounds like ?
- What does an *e* do at the end of a word?
- What do you know that might help?

- What could you try?
- You have only one letter to change.
- That sounds right, but does it look right?
- One more letter will make it right.
- It starts like that. Now check the last part.
- Did you write all the sounds you hear?
- Did you write a vowel for each syllable?
- It starts (ends) like _____.
- There is a silent letter in that word.
- You wrote all the sounds you hear. Now look at what you wrote—think!

Prompts of Encouragement

- I like the way you worked that out.
- The results are worth all your hard work.
- You have come a long way with this one.
- That was some quick thinking.
- That looks like an impressive piece of work.
- You are right on target.
- You are on the right track now.

- Now you have figured it out.
- That is quite an improvement.
- That is quite an accomplishment.
- That is coming along.
- You are really settling down to work.
- You have shown a lot of patience with this.
- You have been paying close attention.
- You have put in a full day today.
- I knew you could finish it.
- You make it look so easy.
- You have really tackled that assignment.
- This shows you have been thinking/working.
- It looks like you have put a lot of work into this.

Source: Adapted from I. C. Fountas & G. S. Pinnell, *Guided Reading: Good First Teaching for All Children* (Portsmouth, NH: Heinemann, 1996); I. C. Fountas & G. S. Pinnell, *Word Matters: Teaching Phonics and Spelling in the Reading/Writing Classroom* (Portsmouth, NH: Heinemann, 1998); and E. B. Fry, J. E. Kress, & D. L. Fountoukidis, *The Reading Teacher's Book of Lists* (New York: Center for Applied Research in Education, 1993).

---

used to assist students whose writing or motor skills interfere with their ability to develop independent writing skills. Displaying writing on a computer monitor facilitates discussion between students and teachers and allows for immediate and easy editing (Zorfass, Corley, & Remz, 1994). When a computer-based speech recognition program was provided to college students with LD, the students performed significantly better on tasks of written expression than did students without the speech recognition program and as well as those who had an assistant (Higgins & Raskind, 1995).

Computers facilitate writing for students with learning problems because they do the following:

- Make revising and editing easier.
- Increase the amount and quality of revision completed.
- Provide spell-checking features.
- Produce neat printed copies that enhance readability.
- Allow for easy error correction (MacArthur et al., 1995).
- Increase the amount of time they spend on the task (Wade-Stein & Kintsch, 2004).
- Improve the quality of writing (Wade-Stein & Kintsch, 2004).

Response to Intervention and Writing

How might response to intervention be used for students with writing difficulties? Students with extreme writing challenges might be provided extra time each day (20 minutes) and extra instruction to determine if their writing improves. Specific research-based strategies like those identified in Graham and Harris (2005) might be implemented. Teachers can maintain copies of students' writing to determine if adequate progress in writing has occurred.

Improving the Writing of Older Students

Most of the practices described above are designed to be used with a broad range of learners. However, the crisis in the overall poor quality of students' writing has provided a push for improving the writing of older students. Recently, the Carnegie Corporation of New York (Graham & Perin, 2007) issued a report on effective writing practices for older students (grades 4–12). They suggest the following research-based practices:

- Teach students writing strategies that include planning, revising, and editing their compositions. Many

Apply the Concept

9-11 Considerations for Students Who Are Culturally and Linguistically Diverse

Creating a learning community in the classroom that provides opportunities for all students to succeed is essential to promoting effective written expression. A few guidelines follow:

- Have high expectations for all students. Teachers demonstrate respect and provide opportunities when they treat each student as an able writer and provide the support necessary to ensure their success.
- Allow students to write about topics they know and have experienced. Students with diverse backgrounds and experiences should be viewed as having a rich source of material for writing. Students benefit when they are encouraged to tap into their backgrounds and experiences and to share them with others.
- Allow students to teach all of us about their backgrounds and

experiences through their writing. Students' writing can be viewed as an opportunity for them to better inform us about themselves, their families and communities, and their interpretations of them. Students will want to write when they perceive that their writing has a purpose and is instructive to others.

- Encourage family involvement in writing. Parents and/or family members often have a rich bank of stories and experiences that they are willing to share with the class if encouraged to do so. These experiences and stories can provide background for students' writing or can be used to prompt stories and ideas.
- Create a classroom setting that is culturally compatible. The social

organization of the classroom can facilitate or impair the written expression of students from diverse cultures. Whole-class instructional formats with high expectations for students to volunteer to answer questions may not be compatible with their cultural backgrounds. Read and ask questions about the cultures of the students in your classroom so that you can establish a writing lab that is responsive to their learning styles.

- Use materials, stories, and books that are culturally relevant. Read stories about a range of cultures to students. Encourage students to exchange stories that are culturally familiar. Provide examples of cultures that are similar and different from the ones represented in your classroom.

---

of the writing strategies discussed previously were developed to meet this recommendation.

- Help students combine sentences to achieve more complex sentence types and to summarize texts.
- Provide opportunities for students to work together in pairs and groups toward cooperative written products to facilitate quality of composition.
- Establish goals for students' writing to improve outcomes.
- Give students access to and instruction in word processing to facilitate writing.
- Assist students in developing prewriting practices that help generate or organize ideas for writing.
- Use inquiry activities to analyze data related to writing reports.
- Provide extended time for writing and revision.
- Provide students with good models of writing to study and to compare with their own writing.
- Use writing as a tool to enhance content knowledge.

Assessing and Teaching Spelling

What are the critical features of spelling assessment and instruction for students with learning and behavior problems? Most students with learning and behavior disorders need specific instruction in spelling and

handwriting largely as a function of their phonological awareness problems. The core phonological deficit is associated with not just reading problems but also spelling problems.

Chapter 7 discusses phonological awareness.

Manuel hates spelling and finds it the most frustrating part of writing. He is an eighth-grade student who is adjusting to the transition from a self-contained classroom for students with emotional disabilities to a resource room in a middle school setting. He has learned to use writing to express his feelings, convey information, and create stories. Manuel is proud of the way his writing has improved, and he often shares his stories with others. But he has difficulty with spelling. Manuel has learned to use inventive spelling (spelling words the way they sound or the way he thinks they are spelled) to aid in getting his ideas on paper, but he has difficulty editing because he is unable to detect or correct most of his spelling errors. Like many students with learning and behavior disorders, Manuel needs specialized instruction in spelling to be a successful writer.

Spelling is an important tool in our society. Many people measure one's intelligence or education by their ability to spell. Spelling is particularly difficult in the English language because there is not a one-to-one correspondence between the individual sounds of spoken

Apply the Concept

9-12 Ten Pointers for Teaching Writing to Students with Special Learning Needs

1. *Allocate adequate time for writing.* Adequate time is a necessary but not sufficient criterion for improving the writing skills of special learners. Students who merely spend 10 to 15 minutes a day practicing the craft of writing are not spending adequate time to improve their skills. Students need a minimum of 30 minutes of time for writing every day.

2. *Provide a range of writing tasks.* Writing about what students know best—self-selected topics—is the first step in writing. After students' skills improve, the range of writing tasks should broaden to include problem solving, writing games, and a variety of writing tasks.

3. *Create a social climate that promotes and encourages writing.* Teachers set the tone through an accepting, encouraging manner. Conferences between students, students and teachers, and students and other persons in the school are conducted to provide constructive feedback on their writing and to provide an audience to share what is written.

4. *Integrate writing with other academic subjects.* Writing can be integrated with almost every

subject that is taught. This includes using writing as a means of expression in content area subjects such as social studies and science as well as part of an instructional activity with reading and language arts.

5. *Focus on the processes central to writing.* These processes include prewriting activities, writing, and rewriting activities.

6. *During the writing phase, focus on the higher-order task of composing, and attend to the basic elements of spelling and punctuation after the writing is complete.* Some students' mechanics of writing are so poor that they interfere with the students' ability to get ideas down on paper successfully. With these students, focus first on some of the basic elements so that the writing process can be facilitated.

7. *Teach explicit knowledge about characteristics of good writing.* The implicit knowledge about writing needs to be made explicit. For example, different genres and their characteristics need to be discussed and practiced.

8. *Teach skills that aid higher-level composing.* These skills include conferencing with teachers and

peers, and strategy instruction. Strategy instruction may provide guidelines for brainstorming, sentence composition, or evaluating the effectiveness of the written piece.

9. *Ask students to identify goals for improving their writing.* Students can set realistic goals regarding their progress in writing. These goals can focus on prewriting, writing, and/or rewriting. Both the students and the teacher can provide feedback as to how successful the students have been in realizing their goals.

10. *Use instructional practices that are associated with improved writing for students.* Several examples of instructional practice not associated with improved writing are grammar instruction, diagramming sentences, and overemphasis on students' errors.

Source: Adapted from S. Graham & K. Harris (2006), Preventing writing difficulties: Providing additional handwriting and spelling instruction to at-risk students in 1st grade, *Teaching Exceptional Children,* 38(5), pp. 64–66; and S. Graham & K. R. Harris (1988), Instructional recommendations for teaching writing to exceptional students, *Exceptional Children, 54* (6), pp. 506–512.

words and the letters of the written words. We learn to spell many words by remembering the unique combination or order of letters that produce the correct spelling of that word. Spelling facilitates the writing process by freeing the writer to concentrate on content. Although many students with LD have spelling difficulties, spelling is often difficult even for those without an LD. Most beginning writers identify spelling as the key problem they need to solve in writing. Many good readers are poor spellers, and almost all poor readers are poor spellers. The spelling of older students with reading disabilities is similar to the spelling of average readers who are much younger (Bourassa, Treiman, & Kessler, 2006).

Error Analysis

The first step in developing an appropriate spelling program is to determine the type and pattern of the students' spelling errors. After completion of an error analysis, a spelling approach based on students' needs can be implemented.

Error analysis should be done by using both dictated spelling tests and a student's written work. Random errors do not occur in the spelling of most students with LD. They are consistent in the types of misspellings to which they are prone (DeMaster, Crossland, & Hasselbring, 1986).

When Manuel and his teacher, Laurie Redwing, attempted to develop Manuel's spelling program, they

Assessing and Teaching Writing and Spelling **303**

began by selecting samples of his written work, which included writing he had created and work written from dictation. Ms. Redwing examined these pieces to determine whether there was a pattern to his spelling errors. Ms. Redwing asked herself the following questions about Manuel's spelling:

- Is he applying mistaken rules?
- Is he applying rules that assist him in remembering spellings?
- Is he making careless errors on words he knows how to spell?
- Is he spelling words correctly in isolation but not in context?
- Are there frequently used words that he is consistently misspelling?

After examining the written work and answering these questions, Ms. Redwing discovered the following:

- Manuel did not apply the -ing rule appropriately. For example, *run* became *runing*.
- Manuel did not use the spelling rule "*i* before *e* except after *c*." For example, he spelled *believe* as *beleive* and *piece* as *peice*.
- He was inconsistent in spelling words. He would spell them correctly in one piece of written work but not in another.
- He spelled several words correctly on spelling tests but not in context.
- He misspelled many frequently used words, such as *there, was, because, somewhere, very*, and *would*.

After answering the questions, Ms. Redwing examined Manuel's work to look for the following error patterns:

- Additions of unneeded letters (e.g., *boxxes*)
- Omissions of letters (e.g., *som*)
- Reflections of mispronunciations (e.g., *ruf* for *roof*)
- Reflections of dialect (e.g., *sodar* for *soda*)
- Reversals of whole words (e.g., *eno* for *one*)
- Reversals of consonant order (e.g., *cobm* for *comb*)
- Reversals of consonant or vowel directionality (e.g., *Thrusday* for *Thursday*)
- Phonetic spellings of nonphonetic word parts (e.g., *site* for *sight*)
- Neographisms, which are spellings that don't resemble the word (e.g., *sumfin* for *something*)
- Combinations of error patterns

In addition to examining Manuel's work, Ms. Redwing interviewed and observed Manuel to determine what strategies he used when he was unable to spell a word and whether he used any corrective or proofreading strategies after he wrote. Ms. Redwing observed Manuel's writing and then asked him the following two questions:

1. *When you finish writing a piece, what do you do?* (Ms. Redwing was attempting to determine whether Manuel rereads for spelling errors.)

2. *If you are writing and do not know how to spell a word, what do you do?* (Ms. Redwing was attempting to determine what, if any, strategies he used. Did he use invented spelling to facilitate the writing process and underline the word so that he could check the spelling later? Did he stop and try to visualize the word or look for how it was spelled in another location? Did he continue writing and go back later to check the spelling?)

Ms. Redwing discovered that Manuel used few strategies to check or recall spelling when he was writing. In addition to teaching and rehearsing spelling rules, Manuel needed to learn and apply strategies for improving his spelling. After error analysis, intervention included discussing with Manuel the types of errors he was making, teaching him proofreading skills, teaching him techniques for remembering the correct spelling of words, and teaching him one of the spelling approaches discussed in the following subsections. Before looking at specialized approaches to teaching spelling to students with learning and behavior disorders, we will first examine traditional approaches to spelling instruction.

Traditional Spelling Instruction

Spelling is taught in most classrooms through an integrated reading and writing approach or the use of spelling basal programs. Typical spelling basals include a prescribed list of weekly words to be mastered by all students (Fresch, 2007). In the usual procedure, a pretest occurs on Monday, followed on Tuesday by a description of the spelling theme (e.g., long *e* words, homophones, *au* words). Wednesday and Thursday typically involve assignments from the text that students work on independently that involve practice spelling the key words or using them in sentences. These assignments usually include dictionary activities; sentence or paragraph writing using the spelling words; writing the words a designated number of times; and using the words in sentences, stories, or crossword puzzles. Friday is usually designated for the posttest in spelling. Although variations on this format occur, such as when the teacher attempts to individualize the spelling program, most classrooms follow a procedure similar to this.

How effective is this procedure for teaching spelling to students with LD? What other procedures might need to be considered in developing effective spelling strategies for these students? The spelling practices used in most classrooms are based more on tradition than on research (Fresch, 2007). For most students with learning difficulties, the introduction of all the words at once, often words that are not in the students' reading vocabularies, and the lack of systematic practice and specific feedback make spelling difficult if not impossible. Students with LD acquire proficiency as spellers when they know the meaning of the word and are asked to learn to spell fewer words at a time.

Phonics Rules for Spelling

How much emphasis should be placed on teaching phonics rules to improve spelling? Evidence suggests that students who are taught spelling alongside code-based (phonics) reading instruction improve in both spelling and word reading (O'Connor & Jenkins, 1995; Snow, Burns, & Griffin, 1998). At least for young children, a code-based approach to reading and spelling is likely to be both necessary and helpful. Students with learning problems require systematic and explicit instruction in phonics rules and how these rules relate to writing words. Thus, students need to be taught the clear connection between phonics rules in reading and spelling.

Because there is a lack of consistency in phonics rules, primary emphasis should be given to basic spelling vocabulary with supplemented instruction in basic phonics rules (Graham & Miller, 1979). According to Graham and Miller (1979), the phonetic skills that should be taught include base words, prefixes, suffixes, consonants, consonant blends, digraphs, and vowel sound–symbol associations.

Principles for Teaching Spelling to Students with Learning Difficulties

Several principles should be included in any spelling approach that is used in teaching students who have learning problems.

Teach in Small Units Teach 3 words a day rather than 4 or 5 (or 15 at the beginning of the week). In a study (Bryant, Drabin, & Gettinger, 1981) in which the number of spelling words allocated each day to students with LD was controlled, higher performance, less distractibility, and less variance in overall performance were obtained from the group with LD assigned 3 words a day, when compared with groups assigned 4 and 5 words a day.

Teach Spelling Patterns If the spelling lists each week are based on spelling patterns (Bloodgood, 1991; Carrekar, 1999), students have a better chance of learning and remembering them. Several sample word lists based on patterned spelling follow:

List 1	List 2	List 3
cat	am	aim
bat	slam	claim
rat	clam	chain
fat	tram	rain
sat	tam	train
can	Pam	gain
fan	same	regain
ran	fame	brain
man	tame	pain
tan	blame	afraid
	flame	braid
	frame	

Zutell (1993) and Graham, Harris, and Loynachan (1996) recommend the use of contrast words to assist in identifying and teaching spelling patterns. Thus, the spelling patterns that are taught in the sample word lists 1–3 would be supplemented with several words that do not fit the pattern. Students would then be encouraged to identify the pattern and sort the words that do not fit.

Provide Sufficient Practice and Feedback Give students opportunities to practice the words each day and provide feedback. Many teachers do this by having students work with spelling partners who ask them their words and provide immediate feedback. The following method can be used for self-correction and practice. Fold a paper into five columns. Write the correctly spelled words in the first column. The student studies one word, folds the column back, and writes the word in the second column. The student then checks his or her spelling with the correctly spelled word in the first column. After folding the column back, the student writes the word in the third column. The student continues writing the word until it has been spelled correctly three times. The student then moves to the next word and continues until the word is spelled correctly three times in a row. This procedure should not be confused with spelling assignments that require the student to write the assigned spelling words a designated number of times. Those procedures are often ineffective because the student does not attend to the details of the spelling word as a whole, often writes the word in segments, and usually copies rather than writing from memory. The student also fails to check words each time they write them, sometimes resulting in words being practiced incorrectly. Adding peer tutoring can help to alleviate these problems (see Apply the Concept 9-13).

Select Appropriate Words The most important strategy for teaching spelling is that the students already should be able to read the word and know its meaning. Spelling should not focus on teaching the students to read and know the meaning of words. Selection of spelling words should be based on the students' reading and meaning vocabularies. Ideally, high-frequency words should be used (Graham & Voth, 1990).

Teach Spelling Through Direct Instruction Incidental learning in spelling is reserved primarily for good spellers. Spelling words can be selected from the students' reading or written words or can be part of a programmed text, such as lists provided in basal readers. Direct instruction includes mastery of specific words each day, individualized instruction, and continual review.

Use Instructional Language The language of instruction, or the dialogue between teachers and students, is critical to success in spelling, particularly for youngsters

9-13   **Peer Tutoring and Spelling**

Use of peer tutors to teach spelling can be helpful in improving spelling for the tutors and the tutees. When a peer-tutoring system was used with students with LD and a good speller from the same classroom, the spelling performance of the student with LD improved and both students rated the peer-tutoring system favorably (Mandoli, Mandoli, & McLaughlin, 1982). To increase effectiveness, peer tutors should be trained to implement the spelling approach that is most suitable for the target student.

---

with learning and behavior problems. Gerber and Hall (1989) indicate that a teacher's language provides a structure that calls attention to critical relationships within and between words and also isolates critical letter sequences. For example, "You wrote 'nife'; however, the word *knife* starts with a silent letter. It is very unusual, and you just have to remember that it is there. Think about the letter *k* as looking like an open jackknife, and remember that the word *knife* starts with a *k*."

Maintain Previously Learned Words Maintenance of spelling words requires that previously learned words be assigned as review words and interspersed with the learning of new spelling words. Previously learned words need to be reviewed frequently to be maintained. Gettinger, Bryant, and Fayne (1982) conducted a study of students with LD to determine the efficacy of a spelling procedure that was designed to practice the principles of teaching smaller units, sufficient and distributed practice, and maintenance of words learned. Students were able to reach an 80% criterion on more of the spelling words and were able to spell 75% of the transfer words when compared with a control group that was involved in a spelling program that did not emphasize these principles. After spelling words have been mastered, provide opportunities for students to see and use spelling words in context.

Motivate Students to Spell Correctly Using games and activities, selecting meaningful words, and providing examples of the use and need for correct spelling are strategies that help to motivate students and give them a positive attitude about spelling.

Include Dictionary Training As part of the spelling program, dictionary training should be developed, which includes alphabetizing, identifying target words, and locating the correct definition when several are provided. Some students can develop a personal spelling dictionary to assist with their writing (Scheuremann & Jacobs, 1994).

Spelling Approaches

There are many approaches to teaching spelling. No one approach has been proven to be superior to others for all students with LD. Some students learn effectively with a multisensory approach, such as the Fernald method; others learn best with a combination of several approaches. A synthesis of spelling interventions (Wanzek, Vaughn, Wexler, Swanson, & Edmonds, 2006) indicated that spelling practices that provide students with spelling strategies or systematic study and word practice methods yield the highest rates of spelling improvement. Other approaches, including sensorimotor activities and technology supports for spelling, resulted in a slight advantage for students over students in comparison conditions. Following are several approaches to teaching spelling, all of which make use of the principles discussed in the previous section.

Test-Study-Test Method This method of learning spelling words is superior to the study-test method (Fitzsimmons & Loomer, 1978; Yee, 1969). In using the test-study-test method, students are first tested on a list of words and then instructed to study the missed words. Strategies are taught for recalling the correct spelling of these words. These strategies often include verbal mediation—saying the word while writing it or spelling it aloud to a partner. After instruction and study, students are then retested. Using this process, students then correct their own spelling test, which is an important factor in learning to spell.

Several word study techniques that can be applied in using the test-study-test method are presented in Figure 9-12

Visualization Approach This approach to spelling teaches students to visualize the correct spelling as a means to recall. The visualization approach uses the following procedures:

1. On the board or on a piece of paper, the teacher writes a word that the children can read but cannot spell.
2. Students read the word aloud.

► Figure 9-12 Effective Word Study Procedures

Kinesthetic Method (Graham and Freeman, 1986)

1. Say the word.
2. Write and say the word.
3. Check the word and correct if needed.
4. Trace and say the word.
5. Write the word from memory, check it, and correct if needed.
6. Repeat steps one through five.

Copy-Cover-Compare (Murphy et al., 1990)

1. Examine the spelling of the word closely.
2. Copy the word.
3. Cover the word and write from memory.
4. Check the word and correct if needed.
5. If spelled correctly, go to next word.
6. If spelled incorrectly, repeat steps one through four.

Connections Approach (Berninger et al., 1998)

1. Teacher says word, points to each letter, and names it.
2. Child names word and letters.
3. Child shown a copy of the word with the onset and rime printed in different colors.

4. Teacher says the sound and simultaneously points to the onset and rime in order.
5. Child looks at, points to, and says the sound of the onset and rime in order.

Simultaneous Oral Spelling (Bradley, 1981)

1. Teacher reads the word.
2. Child reads the word.
3. Child writes the word saying the name of each letter.
4. Child says word again.
5. Teacher examines correctness of written response; child corrects if needed.
6. Repeat steps one through five two times.

Visual Imagery (Berninger et al., 1995)

1. Look at word and say its name.
2. Close your eyes and imagine the word in your mind's eye.
3. Name letters with your inside voice.
4. Open eyes and write word.
5. Check spelling and repeat steps one through four if the word is not spelled correctly.

Source: S. Graham (1999), Handwriting and spelling instruction for students with learning disabilities: A review, *Learning Disability Quarterly, 22* (2), pp. 78–98. Reprinted with permission.

3. Students read the letters in the word.
4. Students write the word on paper.
5. The teacher asks the students to look at the word and "take a picture of it" as if the students' eyes were a camera.
6. The teacher asks the students to close their eyes and spell the word aloud, visualizing the letters while spelling it.
7. The teacher asks the students to write the word and check the model for accuracy.

The Five-Step Word Study Strategy This strategy requires students to learn and rehearse the following five steps and practice them with the teacher and then alone. The steps are as follows:

1. Say the word.
2. Write and say the word.
3. Check the word.
4. Trace and say the word.
5. Write the word from memory and check.
6. Repeat the first five steps.

When students learn this technique, the teacher models the procedure, then the students practice the procedure with assistance from the teacher, and finally the students demonstrate proficiency in the application of the procedure without teacher assistance (Graham & Freeman, 1986).

Johnson and Myklebust Technique Johnson and Myklebust (1967) suggest working from recognition to partial recall to total recall when teaching new spelling words.

Recognition can be taught by showing students a word and then writing the word with several unrelated words, asking the students to circle the word they previously saw. The task can gradually be made more difficult by writing distracting words that more closely resemble the target word. In teaching partial recall, the correct word can be written with missing spaces for completing the spelling under it. For example:

with
w _____ th
wit _____
_____ ith
wi _____ _____
w _____ _____ _____
_____ _____ _____ _____

Total recall requires the students to write the word after it is pronounced by another or write the word in a sentence. This approach gives repeated practice and focuses students on the relevant details of the word. Johnson and Myklebust (1967) also suggest that when initial spelling tests are given, the teacher may need to say the word very slowly, emphasizing each syllable. As students learn to spell the words correctly, the test is given in a normal voice and at a normal rate.

Cloze Spelling Approach This is referred to as the cloze spelling approach because students need to supply missing letters systematically in much the same way that students supply words in the cloze reading procedure. The cloze spelling approach uses a four-step process for teaching students to spell words.

Assessing and Teaching Writing and Spelling **307**

1. *Look-study*. Students are shown the word on a card. Students look at the word and study the letters and their order.
2. *Write missing vowels*. Students are shown the same word on a card with blanks where the vowels usually appear. Students write the entire word, supplying the missing vowel(s).
3. *Write missing consonants*. Students are shown the word with blanks where the consonants usually appear. Students write the entire word, supplying the missing consonant(s).
4. *Write the word*. Students write the word without the model.

Fernald Method Fernald (1943) believed that most spelling approaches were useful for the extremely visual student but not for students who need auditory and kinesthetic input for learning. Because poor spellers are characterized as having poor visual imagery, many may need to be taught through multisensory approaches such as the Fernald method.

According to Fernald (1943), specific school techniques that tend to produce poor spellers include the following:

- Formal spelling periods in which children move through a series of practice lessons, writing and taking dictation with little time to think about how the word is spelled before writing it
- A focus on misspellings and spelling errors, which builds a negative attitude toward spelling

A brief description of the Fernald approach to teaching spelling includes the following procedures:

1. The teacher writes the word to be learned on the chalkboard or paper. The word can be selected from the spelling book or by the children.
2. The teacher pronounces the word clearly. The students repeat the pronunciation of the word while looking at the word. This is done several times for each word.
3. The teacher allows time for students to study the word for later recall. If a student is a kinesthetic learner, the teacher writes the word in crayon and has the student trace the letters of the word with his or her finger. Fernald found that tracing is necessary in learning to spell only when the spelling difficulty is coupled with a reading disability.
4. The teacher removes the word and has the students write it from memory.
5. The students turn the paper over and write the word a second time.
6. The teacher creates opportunities for students to use the word in their writing.
7. The teacher gives written, not oral, spelling drills.

In contrast with Fernald's approach, which recommends not focusing on the student's errors and suggests

blocking out errors immediately, other researchers have found some support for a spelling strategy that emphasizes imitation of students' errors plus modeling (Kauffman, Hallahan, Haas, Brame, & Boren, 1978; Nulman & Gerber, 1984). Using the imitation plus modeling strategy, the teacher erases the misspelled word and imitates the child's error by writing it on the board. The teacher then writes it correctly with the student and asks the student to compare what he or she wrote with the correct spelling of the word.

Gillingham and Stillman Approach According to Gillingham and Stillman (1973), spelling is taught by using the following procedures:

1. The teacher says the word very slowly and distinctly, and students repeat the word after the teacher. This is referred to as *echo speech*.
2. Students are asked what sound is heard first. This process continues with all of the letters in the words. This is referred to as *oral spelling*.
3. The students are asked to locate the letter card with the first letter of the word on it and then to write the letter. Students continue with this process until the card for each letter is found, placed in order, and written. This is referred to as *written spelling*.
4. Students read the word.

When writing the word, students orally spell the word letter by letter. This establishes visual-auditory-kinesthetic association.

Correctional procedures in the Gillingham and Stillman approach include the following:

1. Students check their own written words and find errors.
2. If a word is read incorrectly, the students should spell what they said and match it with the original word.
3. If a word is misspelled orally, the teacher writes what the students spelled and asks them to read it, or the teacher may repeat the pronunciation of the original word.

Constant Time-Delay Procedure The time-delay procedure is designed to reduce errors in instruction. Stevens and Schuster (1987) applied the procedure this way:

1. The verbal cue "Spell _____ (target word)" is immediately followed with a printed model of the target word to be copied by students.
2. After several trials in which there is no time delay between asking students to spell a word and providing a model of the word, a five-second delay is introduced. This allows children to write the word, or part of the word, if they know it but does not require them to wait very long if they are unable to correctly write the word.
3. The amount of time between the request to spell the word and the presentation of the model can be increased after several more trials.

The time-delay procedure has been effective with students with LD and has several advantages as a spelling instructional method. It is a simple procedure that is easy to implement. Also, it is fun for students because it provides for nearly errorless instruction.

Self-Questioning Strategy for Teaching Spelling Wong (1986) describes the following self-questioning strategy for teaching spelling:

1. Do I know this word?
2. How many syllables do I hear in this word?
3. Write the word the way I think it is spelled.
4. Do I have the right number of syllables?
5. Underline any part of the word that I am not sure how to spell.
6. Check to see whether it is correct. If it is not correct, underline the part of the word that is not correct, and write it again.
7. When I have finished, tell myself I have been a good worker.

Morphographic Spelling Morphographic spelling provides a highly structured and sequenced approach to teaching remedial spelling (Dixon & Engelmann, 2001). This teacher-directed approach assumes that students have some spelling skills and begins with teaching small units of meaningful writing (morphographs). Students are taught to spell morphographs in isolation, then to combine them to make words. Critical components of this instructional approach to spelling include: error correction and feedback (including positive feedback), cumulative review, distributed practice, and highly sequenced lessons.

> ▶ *WEB RESOURCES*
> For a helpful Web site on instructional practices related to writing and spelling, see http://www.readingrockets.org.

Instructional Practices in Spelling

Most students with LD have problems with spelling. Yet students with LD have been the focus of relatively few research studies on spelling acquisition. Findings from two syntheses on effective spelling practices for students with LD (Gordon, Vaughn, & Schumm, 1993; Wanzek et al., 2006) yield the following instructional practices:

1. *Providing a weekly list of words.* Students benefit when teachers provide a weekly list of words that are taught. This procedure allows students to practice words throughout the week. Monitoring correct use of these words in writing and then following up on accuracy in spelling with these words is valuable. See instructional practice #3 for the number of words taught and how they should be distributed.

2. *Error imitation and modeling.* Students with LD need to compare each of their incorrectly spelled words

with the correct spellings. The teacher imitates the students' incorrect spelling and, beside it, writes the word correctly. The teacher then calls attention to features in the word that will help students remember the correct spelling.

3. *Allocate three spelling words per day.* Students with LD learn to spell fewer words correctly and experience greater frustration when they are required to study a long list of words. Reduce the number of words assigned at any one time to approximately three words per day and provide effective instruction for those words.

4. *Modality.* It has long been thought that students with LD learn to spell most easily when their modality preferences are considered. An investigation of the usefulness of a spelling study by writing the words, arranging and tracing letter shapes or tiles, and typing the words at a computer revealed that students with LD learned equally well when studying words by any of these procedures. Of significance, however, was the fact that most of the students preferred to practice their spelling words at a computer. Because students' preferences are likely to affect their motivation to practice, teachers are wise to consider students' personal preferences.

5. *Computer-assisted instruction.* Computer-assisted instruction (CAI) has been shown to be effective in improving the spelling skills of students with LD. CAI software programs for spelling improvement often incorporate procedures that emphasize awareness of word structure and spelling strategies, and make use of time delay, voice simulation, and sound effects. Such capabilities make the computer an instructional tool with much potential to aid and motivate students with LD in learning to spell.

6. *Peer tutoring.* A teacher's individual help is preferable, but the realities of the classroom frequently make individualized instruction difficult to offer. Structured peer tutoring can be a viable alternative. Delquadri, Greenwood, Stretton, and Hall (1983) have demonstrated efficacy of the "Peer Tutoring Spelling Game" useful at all grade levels. The game takes about 15 minutes and includes the following procedures:

   a. Tell the students that they will be playing a new game that is like basketball only it will help them learn to spell words. In this game, they will make "baskets" (2 points) and "foul shots" (1 point).
   b. On Monday of each week, teach the list of new words.
   c. Assign students to "tutor" pairs: one is speller #1 and one is speller #2.
   d. Speller #1 says a word while speller #2 writes it on his or her paper. Speller #2 then orally spells the written word.
   e. If the word is correct, Speller #1 says, "Correct! Give yourself two points!" and Speller #2 marks a "2" on his or her list. If the word is incorrect, Speller #1 points to, pronounces, and spells the missed word orally. Speller #2 then writes the word correctly 3 times before moving to the next word.

f. When completed, Speller #1 becomes Speller #2 and vice-versa.

g. Ask each student report his or her points and record them on the individual score chart.

h. Announce the team winner for the week, and post the winner on the team chart.

7. *Study techniques.* Study techniques help students with LD to organize their spelling study by providing a format. As the students approach the study of a new word, they know exactly how to go about studying. This is in contrast to the haphazard, unproductive study used by students who follow no such strategy.

8. *Explicit and systematic instruction in spelling.* Interventions in spelling that systematically and explicitly taught students common patterns and strategies for spelling words were associated with the highest outcomes in spelling.

Most of the research investigating the effectiveness of spelling interventions for students with learning and behavior problems has involved the use of teaching single words from lists rather than spelling in context (Fulk & Stormont-Spurgin, 1995). Nevertheless, spelling instruction for students with learning problems is best conducted explicitly and directly rather than through indirect methods (Wanzek et al., 2006).

Teaching Handwriting and Keyboarding

What are the characteristics of students with handwriting problems, and what components should be included in an effective handwriting and keyboarding program? Often described as the most poorly taught subject in the elementary curriculum, handwriting is usually thought of as the least important. However, handwriting difficulties create barriers to efficient work production and negatively influence academic success and self-esteem (Feder & Majnemer, 2007). Many students dislike the entire writing process because they find the motor skill involved in handwriting so laborious. *Dysgraphia* refers to students with extreme difficulties with handwriting.

Despite the use of word processors, handheld computers, and other devices that can facilitate the writing process, handwriting remains an important skill. Taking notes in class, filling out forms, and success on the job often require legible, fluent writing.

Handwriting Problems

Students with dysgraphia have severe problems learning to write and may exhibit any or all of the following characteristics:

- Poor letter formation
- Letters that are too large, too small, or inconsistent in size

- Incorrect use of capital and lowercase letters
- Letters that are crowded and cramped
- Inconsistent spacing between letters
- Incorrect alignment (letters do not rest on a baseline)
- Incorrect or inconsistent slant of cursive letters
- Lack of fluency in writing
- Incomplete words or missing words
- Slow writing even when asked to write as quickly as possible

Fortunately, with direct instruction and specific practice, many of these problems can be alleviated (Berninger et al., 2006). It is important to alleviate handwriting problems for several reasons: They are associated with reduced interest in writing and thus influence written expression, and students with handwriting difficulties spell worse than those without handwriting problems even when spelling interventions are provided (Berninger, Abbott, Whitaker, Sylvester, & Nolen, 1995).

Manuscript and Cursive Writing

Traditionally, most students learn manuscript writing first and then, generally in second or third grade, make the transition to cursive writing. Although this procedure seems to be effective for most students, many students with LD have difficulty transitioning from one writing form to another. Many LD specialists advocate the use of instruction in only one form of handwriting, either manuscript or cursive. Some argue that manuscript is easier to learn, is more like book print, is more legible, and requires less difficulty in motoric movement. Others believe that cursive is faster, is continuous and connected, makes it more difficult to reverse letters, teaches students to perceive whole words, and is easier to write. (See Table 9-1 for a summary of arguments for manuscript versus cursive.) Some critics maintain that time could be better spent in teaching students to use a keyboard. Students should be able to use one form (print or cursive) to communicate effectively, and

Table 9-1 Manuscript versus Cursive

Manuscript	Cursive
1. It more closely resembles print and facilitates learning to read.	1. Many students want to learn to write cursive.
2. It is easier for young children to learn.	2. Many students write cursive faster.
3. Manuscript is more legible than cursive.	3. Many adults object to students using manuscript beyond the primary grades.
4. Many students write manuscript at the same rate as cursive and this rate can be significantly influenced through direct instruction.	
5. It is better for students with LD to learn one writing process well than to attempt to learn two.	

there are some advantages to learning early and well to print because it corresponds more obviously with the print students read (Spear-Swerling, 2006).

The bulk of evidence appears to support teaching students with LD to use manuscript effectively and neatly, with the exception of learning to write their name in cursive. For most students with LD and handwriting difficulties, manuscript should be taught in the early years and maintained throughout the educational program. Some students with LD can and want to make the transition to cursive and benefit from its instruction. On some occasions, students who have struggled with manuscript writing feel that learning cursive is "grown up" and therefore respond well to the introduction of a new writing form.

Reversals

When 5-year-old Abe signed his name on notes to his grandmother, he often reversed the direction of the *b* in his name. He would often write other letters backward or upside down. His mother worried that this might be an indication that Abe was dyslexic or having reading problems. Many parents/guardians are concerned when their children make reversals, and often their alarmed response frightens their children. Most children, aged 5 and younger, make reversals when writing letters and numbers. Reversals made by students before the age of 6 or 7 are not an indication that the student has LD or is dyslexic and are rarely cause for concern.

Teachers should recognize the following:

- Reversals are common before the age of 6 or 7. Teachers should provide correctional procedures for school-age students who are reversing letters and numbers but should not become overly concerned.
- A few students continue to reverse numbers and letters after the age of 7 and may need direct intervention techniques.

For students who persist in reversing letters and numbers, the following two direct instructional techniques may be helpful:

1. The teacher traces the letter and talks aloud about the characteristics of the letter, asking the students to model the teacher's procedure. For example, while tracing the letter *d*, the teacher says, "First I make a stick starting at the top of the page and going down, and then I put a ball in front of the stick." Students are asked to follow the same procedure and to talk aloud while tracing the letter. Next, the students are asked to do the same procedure, this time drawing the letter. Finally, the students are asked to draw the letter and say the process to themselves.

2. The teacher and students can develop a mnemonic picture device that helps the students recall the direction of the letter. For example, with a student who is reversing the direction of the letter *p*, the teacher might say, "What letter does the word *pie* begin with? That's right, *pie*

begins with the letter *p*. Now watch me draw *p*." Drawing the straight line, the teacher says, "This is my straight line before I eat pie, then after I eat pie my stomach swells in front of me. Whenever you make *p* you can think of pie and how your stomach gets big after you eat it, and that will help you make a *p* the right way." This procedure can be repeated several times, with the student drawing the letter and talking through the mnemonic device. Different mnemonic devices can be developed to correspond with the specific letter or number reversal(s) of the child. Berninger et al. (2006) reported that direct instruction with visual cues and memory delays with additional practice checks lead to reduced reversals.

Components of Handwriting

Teaching handwriting requires the teacher to assess, model, and teach letter formation, spacing, and fluency as well as posture, pencil grip, and position of the paper.

Legibility Legibility is the most important goal of handwriting instruction, and incorrect letter formation is the most frequent interference.

The following six letters account for many of the errors (48%) that students make when forming letters: *q, j, z, u, n,* and *k* (Graham, Berninger, & Weintraub, 1998). Spacing between letters, words, and margins; connecting lines; and closing and crossing of letters (e.g., *t, x*) also influence legibility.

Fluent Writing How does fluency relate to handwriting? Just as not knowing how to read words fluently impairs reading comprehension, inadequate fluency in writing letters and words impairs written expression and the quality of written responses (Spear-Swerling, 2006). Nine-year-old Nguyen's handwriting has improved considerably during the past year. She and her teacher have identified letters that were not formed correctly, and Nguyen has learned to write these letters so that they are legible. Now that her handwriting is easier to read, the teacher realizes that Nguyen has another handwriting problem. In the regular classroom, Nguyen has difficulty taking notes and writing down assignments that are given orally, because she is a very slow writer. She needs to learn writing fluency, which is the ability to write quickly and with ease, without undue attention to letter formation.

Nguyen's teacher decides to teach fluency by gradually increasing expectations about the speed at which letter formation occurs. Nguyen selects two paragraphs and is told to write them as quickly as she can while still maintaining good letter formation. The teacher times her in this procedure. They decide to keep a graph of Nguyen's progress by indicating the time it takes her each day to write the two paragraphs legibly. Nguyen finds that graphing her progress is very reinforcing (see Figure 9-13 and Apply the Concept 9-14). Because Nguyen's fluency problems were not just for copying but

Obtaining a Handwriting Fluency Sample

The following procedures can be used to obtain a fluency sample:

1. Have the student become familiar with the test sentence.
2. Tell the student to write the test sentence a designated number of times at his or her usual rate (2- to 3-minute sample).
3. After relaxing, have the student write the sentence as well and as neatly as he or she can.
4. After relaxing, have the student write the sentence as quickly and as many times as he or she can in 3 minutes.
5. After relaxing, the student and the teacher repeat this process with the same sentence.

▶ **Figure 9-13** Nguyen's Fluency

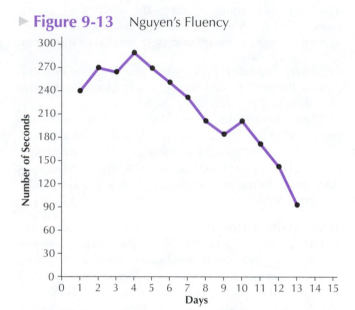

also for writing from dictation, her teacher implemented the same program, this time requiring Nguyen to time herself on oral dictations. Nguyen's time for completion of the passage decreased considerably over a 3-week period.

Instructional Principles for Teaching Handwriting

The following instructional principles are suggested for any effective handwriting program:

- Teach handwriting explicitly including letter formation.
- Provide modeling and feedback to ensure correct letter formation. It may be necessary to guide the stroke of the pencil by providing manual assistance.
- Initially focus on the motor pattern and then increasingly focus on legibility.
- Teach handwriting frequently, several times a week.

- In addition to separate mini lessons on handwriting and letter formation, provide short handwriting lessons in the context of the students' writing assignment.
- Handwriting skills should be overlearned in isolation, then applied in context and periodically checked.
- Ask students to evaluate their own handwriting and, when appropriate, the handwriting of others.
- The teacher's handwriting should be a model for the students to follow.
- In the beginning stages of letter formation, teachers can integrate letter writing with letter naming, letter sounds, or spelling words.
- After students acquire proficiency in letter formation, provide opportunities for them to improve fluency through speed and accuracy of letter writing.

A self-instructional strategy such as the following was used in the Graham (1983) study and was associated with improved handwriting with students. The six-step procedure is as follows:

1. The teacher models the writing of the target letter and describes the formation of the letter. Students then describe the formation of the letter. This step is repeated three times.
2. The teacher writes the letter while describing the process. This continues until the students can recite the process for writing the letter.
3. Students trace the letter, and the teacher and students recite the process of the letter formation together.
4. The teacher writes the letter, traces it, and then verbally discusses the process, including corrections (e.g., "My letter is too slanted"), then provides self-reinforcement (e.g., "Now, that looks a lot better"). The procedure continues with and without errors until the students can model the process.
5. The teacher writes the letter, and the students copy it while defining the process and providing self-correction. Students need to complete this process successfully three times before moving to step 6.
6. Students write the letter from memory.

Following are two methods that have been devised for teaching students who have handwriting difficulties.

Hanover Cursive Writing Method

Hanover's (1983) method of teaching cursive writing is founded on a single principle: the grouping of letters based on similar strokes into letter families. The letter families include the following:

e, l, h, f, b, k	This is the e family and is taught first.
b, o, v, w	This family has a handle to which the next letter is attached.
n, s, y	This family is grouped together to emphasize the correct formation of hump-shaped letters.
c, a, d, o, q, g	This is the c family.
n, m, v, y, x	This is the hump family.
f, q	This family has tails in the back.
g, p, y, z	This family has tails in the front.

Some letters are included in more than one group. This approach is based on the idea that cursive letters are learned faster and more easily when they are taught in their grouped families because of the similar strokes within the groups.

Teaching Handwriting at the High School Level

Handwriting often becomes important later in school because of the emphasis on taking notes and submitting written assignments. Many students have found that although the content of their assignment is correct, they have lost points or were given a lower grade because their handwriting was difficult to read. Teaching handwriting to older students is difficult because the immediate needs of most older students are content related, and it is often difficult for teachers to justify instructional time for handwriting. Also, most materials for handwriting instruction were developed for younger students and can seem insulting to older students. Teachers need to carefully evaluate students' handwriting problems to determine whether handwriting instruction could be helpful in a relatively short period of time or the students should learn compensatory methods, such as typing. The two most important criteria for evaluating handwriting of older students are legibility and fluency.

Corrective feedback, short trace and copy exercises, and content exercises that require little thinking and allow the students to concentrate on letter formation and fluency should be emphasized in teaching handwriting to older students (Ruedy, 1983).

Teaching Keyboarding

Since many students with LD exhibit difficulties in handwriting, what additional options are there for improving their communication through writing? The most obvious solution is one that students will be expected to know in almost any job situation, familiar and fluent use of the computer keyboard. How and when can students learn keyboarding skills? Most students are at least somewhat familiar with keyboards as early as kindergarten and first grade, and they are able to enter their first name into the computer to log onto programs. Keyboarding skills continue to improve as students proceed through early elementary grades; however, formal instruction in keyboarding usually begins in third or fourth grade. As many teachers and employers note, the "hunt-and-peck" method of keyboarding is no longer acceptable and students who are keyboard familiar are better advantaged in both school and work settings.

One of the first things that students should learn is the correct hand position on the keys and how to develop the motor memory skills for using the keyboard while reading or writing a report. In other words, effective keyboarding skills require not looking at the keys. Following are some tips for improving keyboarding skills in students:

- Be sure students are using the correct hand position on the keys.
- Give students opportunities to practice their technique by keyboarding their own writing or assignments so that there is personal benefit from acquiring keyboarding skills.
- Provide students with ample opportunities to practice.
- Assure students that even though they are slow when first learning to keyboard without looking at the keys, they will ultimately become much faster and successful.
- Provide demonstrations to students so that they can observe good technique and facile keyboard use.
- Initially, emphasize proper form and not speed.
- Students should have their fingers on the key and their thumbs on the space bar.
- As students' technique improves, then increasing speed is a reasonable goal.
- Develop procedures in school so that all teachers encourage and support keyboarding.
- Involve families in reinforcing good form and keyboarding at home.

Keyboarding is an important skill that will improve students' success as writers and also make writing a less laborious process. Further benefits are that students can use a printer to demonstrate what they've written in ways that are easily read and reviewed, making revision and editing more successful. There is much to be gained by teaching students to keyboard.

INSTRUCTIONAL ACTIVITIES

This section provides instructional activities that are related to written expression, including spelling and handwriting. Some of the activities teach new skills; others are best suited for practice and reinforcement of already acquired skills. For each activity, the objective, materials, and teaching procedures are described.

▶ Cubing

Objective: To help students develop preliminary ideas about the topic during the prewriting phase.

Grades: Elementary through secondary

Materials: A cube-shaped outline, glue, scissors

Teaching Procedures:

1. Explain to students that the topic is like a cube that contains different information on each side. Topics can be explored from different angles.

2. Introduce six different ways in which the topic can be explored.
   a. *Describe:* What does it look like?
   b. *Compare:* What is it similar to? What is it different from?
   c. *Associate:* What does it remind you of?
   d. *Analyze:* What are the parts?
   e. *Apply:* What can you do with it?
   f. *Argue for or against:* Take a stand about your topic. Why is it good or why is it not good?

3. Pass out a cube-shaped outline to each student.

4. Have students write their ideas down on the cube-shaped outline. Students work through each side of the cube: describe, compare, associate, analyze, apply, and argue for or against the topic. (Depending on the topic, questions for each dimension will need to be adjusted.)

5. Have the students cut out the outline and glue it together to make a cube.

Extended Activity: The cube can be used as a resource in writing the essay.

Source: Adapted from University of Texas Center for Reading and Language Arts (2000a, 2000b).

▶ Writing Warm-Up

Objective: To help students, especially reluctant writers, gain writing experiences.

Materials: Graph paper, colored pencils, timer for the teacher

Grades: Elementary through secondary

Teaching Procedures:

1. Explain to students that writing is like exercising. Tell them that writing practice can help them improve their writing and make the writing easier.

2. Choose a topic that will be easy for students to write about. Have students do writing warm-up once or twice a week.

3. Introduce the day's topic (e.g., homework).

4. Ask students to write as much as they can about the topic for 3 minutes. Tell the students that they do not need to worry about spelling, grammar, or punctuation.

5. Set a timer for 3 minutes. When time is up, have the students put their pencils down and count the number of words they have written.

6. Have students graph the number of words they have written, using colored pencils and graph paper.

7. When students feel comfortable writing their ideas about the topic, introduce the next writing process (e.g, organizing their ideas, revising, editing).

Source: Adapted from University of Texas Center for Reading and Language Arts (2000a, 2000b).

▶ Writing Reports

Objective: To help students prepare for a research report by providing guidelines for gathering information necessary for writing a research report.

Grades: Secondary

Materials: Report planning sheet (see Figure 9-14)

Teaching Procedures:

1. Explain to students that a report planning sheet will help them to prepare for writing a research report. After filling out the planning sheet, they can use the information on the planning sheet to write their report.

2. Introduce the day's topic (e.g., volcanoes).

3. Pass out a planning sheet to each student.

4. Have students brainstorm a list of everything they know about the topic and write it down in the first column (i.e., What I Know).

5. Have the students examine their brainstorming ideas carefully to identify the areas in need of further research. For instance, if a student knows names of active volcanoes but not much about how a volcano is formed, the student may want to study that. Have students identify what they want to study and write that down in the second column.

6. In the third column, have students write down why they want to study the subtopic they selected.

7. Have students think about a variety of sources where they can find information (e.g., science textbook, Web sites, etc.) on the subtopic and list those sources in the fourth column.

Topic: _____				
What I Know	What I Want to Find Out	Why I Want to Find Out	How I Will Find Out	What I Learned

8. Have students conduct their research and write down what they learn in the fifth column.

9. After the students have completed the planning sheet, have them use that information to write the report.

Source: Adapted from Macrorie (1980) and Ogle (1986).

▶ The Use of Graphic Organizers for Writing

Objective: To help students organize their ideas when writing first drafts.

Grades: Elementary through secondary

Materials: Copies of a graphic organizer (see Figure 9-15)

Teaching Procedures:

1. Explain to students that graphic organizers can help them write their draft. (*Note:* Different types of graphic organizers are used depending on type of text.)

▶ **Figure 9-15**   Graphic Organizer

Topic: _____

Sentence describing the topic:

1. _____

2. _____

3. _____

2. Model how to use graphic organizers. For instance, write the topic in the center and supporting details on the branches on the graphic organizer. Then create sentences describing the topic by using ideas written on the graphic.

3. Introduce the topic, and pass out copies of a graphic organizer to each student.

4. Have students use the graphic organizer as they write their draft with a partner, in a small group, or independently.

5. After students finish filling out the graphic organizer and creating sentences, call on several students to share their drafts. Provide feedback on their drafts.

Source: Adapted from Nancy and Dill (1997).

▶ Peer Editing

Objective: To provide students with opportunities to edit a revised draft as one part of the editing process.

Grades: Elementary

Materials: Student-generated revised draft, peer-editing checklist (see Figure 9-16)

Teaching Procedures:

1. Explain to students that editing focuses on correcting technical aspects of writing.

2. Introduce each of the five editing points on the checklist:
   a. End punctuation
   b. Beginning capitalization
   c. Complete sentences
   d. Indented paragraphs
   e. Spelling check

3. Pair students, making sure that each pair consists of a good writer and a poor writer.

4. Pass out peer-editing checklists to each pair, and ask students in pairs to exchange their revised drafts.

5. Have the good writer in each pair edit his or her partner's draft by following editing steps, which

▶ **Figure 9-16** Peer-Editing Checklist

	Yes	No	Edits Made
1. Does each sentence end with a period, question mark, or exclamation point?			
2. Does each sentence start with a capital letter?			
3. Is each sentence a complete sentence?			
4. Is the first sentence of each paragraph indented?			
5. Did my partner check my spelling (by using dictionary and/or thesaurus)?			

are outlined on the peer-editing checklist. If a step is followed, a check mark should be placed in the Yes column after that step. If a step is not followed, then a check should be placed in the No column.

6. While the student is completing the checklist, have his or her partner correct errors, if any, and record what corrections were made in the Edits Made column.

7. Repeat the procedure, this time with the poor writer editing his or her partner's draft by following the editing steps.

Source: Adapted from University of Texas Center for Reading and Language Arts (2001b).

▶ Peer Revision

Objective: To give students an opportunity to work together in pairs to elaborate on their writing as one part of the revision process.

Grades: Elementary through secondary

Materials: Student-generated rough draft, sticky notes

Teaching Procedures:

1. Explain to students that good writers get help from their friends and colleagues to improve their writing. One way to do this is to get ideas for elaborating or expanding on what you have already written. Each student needs a rough draft that is ready to be revised (and is neat enough to be read by another student and checked by the teacher).

2. Students work in pairs to complete the following revision steps:
   a. Have a student read his or her rough draft out loud to his or her partner. While the student is reading, he or she may catch a few mistakes. Encourage the student to correct them.
   b. Have the partner read through the rough draft, focusing on the content. The partner makes three sticky-note comments and puts them on the rough draft. One comment is positive (e.g., "I really liked the part where . . ."). The other two comments are helpful (e.g., "Tell me more about . . ." and "I don't understand the part where . . .").
   c. Repeat the process with the second partner.
   d. Have each student work individually to elaborate on his or her draft by addressing the peer sticky-note comments.

▶ Acrostic Writing in the Content Areas

Objective: To help students improve their understanding of content through acrostic writing.

Grades: Secondary

Materials: Content area textbook

Teaching Procedures:

1. Explain to students that they will write a poem about what they have read (e.g., the unit on Native Americans in social studies).

2. Review important information on the previously studied unit (e.g., Native Americans), and create a semantic map by writing the name of the tribe they read about (e.g., Apache) on the blackboard, asking the students to share what they have read about this tribe (prompt the students if necessary), and recording the students' responses on the blackboard.

3. Have students write a poem to describe important characteristics of the Apache by using each letter in it to create one sentence. For instance,

   Amazing hunters who once enjoyed a nomadic style of life

    Powerful nation of warriors

    Adaptable people who learned to tend fields of maize, beans, pumpkins, and watermelons when buffalo became scarce

    Courageous Indians known for their resistance to the U.S. government

    Hut building, farming, trading, and horse riding were necessary for survival of this proud nation

    Epidemics of smallpox and other European diseases almost decimated the once large tribe

4. Call on several students to share their poems. Provide feedback on their poems in terms of the writing styles and the content.

Source: Adapted from Bromley (1999).

▶ Proofreading with SCOPE

Objective: To teach students a mnemonic strategy (SCOPE) to help with proofreading their writing.

Grades: Upper elementary through secondary

Materials: Student-generated writing piece that needs to be edited

Teaching Procedures:

1. Discuss with students how they can get into difficulty if they are not sufficiently skilled at proofreading their papers before they submit them and therefore get low grades because their papers have many errors.

2. Teach the students SCOPE, a mnemonic strategy that will assist them in proofreading their work before they submit it:

    Spelling: Is the spelling correct?

    Capitalization: Are the first words of sentences, proper names, and proper nouns capitalized?

    Order of words: Is the syntax correct?

    Punctuation: Are there appropriate marks for punctuation where necessary?

    Express complete thought: Does the sentence contain a noun and a verb, or is it only a phrase?

3. Next, demonstrate using SCOPE with a sample piece of writing on an overhead projector.

4. Give the students ample practice and opportunity to apply SCOPE to their own work.

▶ Interview a Classmate

Objective: To give students practice in developing and using questions to obtain more information for the piece they are writing.

Grades: Upper elementary through secondary

Materials: Writing materials and a writing topic, a list of possible questions, a tape recorder (optional)

Teaching Procedures:

1. Using the format of a radio or television interview, demonstrate and role-play mock interviews with sports, movie, music, and political celebrities. (*Note:* Give students opportunities to play both roles.)

2. Discuss what types of questions allow the interviewee to give elaborate responses (e.g., open questions) and what types of questions do not allow the interviewee to give an expanded answer (e.g., closed questions). Practice asking open questions.

3. Use a piece that you are writing as an example, and discuss whom you might interview to obtain more information. For example, "In writing a piece about what it might have been like to go to the New York World's Fair in 1964, I might interview my grandfather, who was there, to obtain more information."

4. Ask students to select an appropriate person to interview for their writing piece and write possible questions.

5. In pairs, have students refine their questions for the actual interview.

6. Have students then conduct interviews and later discuss how information from the interview assisted them in writing their piece.

▶ What Would You Do If . . . ?

By Alison Gould Boardman

Objective: To give students experience developing ideas for narrative writing and following simple story structure.

Grades: Upper elementary and middle school

Materials: Pencil, drawing paper, writing paper

Teaching Procedures:

1. Have students fold a piece of drawing paper so that there are four squares.

2. Ask students what they would do if they were invisible for 24 hours. Share ideas, and probe students to add details (e.g., "You would go to the moon. Great, how would you get there? Would you take anyone with you?"). Tell students that now that they have some ideas, they are going to make a rough drawing of four possible things they would do if they were invisible for 24 hours.

3. Students should use pencil or one color to draw pictures of their ideas, one in each box. Pictures can be rough drawings or sketches. The purpose of the drawings is to help students generate interest in

and remember what they want to write about without the pressure of having to write it down.

4. Begin with the introduction. Students write about how they become invisible. For the body of the story, students choose three of their four ideas to expand on. They use their pictures and build from there. The ending of the story details what happens when they become visible again and concludes their invisible day.

Adaptations: This assignment can be repeated with topics (from the teacher or students) such as, What would you do if you could fly, run 50 miles an hour, drive a car, etc.? Depending on students' skill levels, the length and content requirements can be adjusted.

▶ **Step-by-Step Cartoon Writing**

By Alison Gould Boardman

Objective: To give beginning or reluctant writers experience sequencing steps, using transition words, and writing a paragraph.

Grades: Elementary

Materials: Index cards without lines, colored pencils, tape, writing materials

Teaching Procedures:

1. Discuss as a group the types of things students do to get ready for school in the morning.

2. Tell students that they will be drawing a comic strip about what they do when they get up in the morning.

3. Have students draw one event on each index card (e.g., waking up, getting dressed, eating breakfast). Encourage the students to add detail to their pictures to help them remember exactly what happens.

4. Have students put their ideas in order and tape the cards together like a comic strip.

5. Before the students begin writing, have them use their comic strip as a guide to help them tell the story out loud. Encourage students to use transition words such as *first, next, later,* and *finally.* Teachers can post a list of transition words for students to use while telling and writing their paragraphs.

6. Have students write one descriptive sentence about each frame of their comic strip to form a paragraph.

7. Attach the final copy of the paragraph to the comic strip and display in the classroom.

Adaptations: Students can use this procedure to write any sequenced or how-to paragraph, such as how to bake a cake, make a peanut-butter-and-jelly sandwich, play checkers, or make a bed.

FOCUS Answers

▶ **FOCUS Question 1. What assessment and instructional practices improve writing outcomes for students with learning and behavior problems?**

Answer: For many students with learning and behavior problems, writing is one of the most difficult things that they do, asking them to use skills they have not mastered well, such as spelling and handwriting. Teachers need to consider these negative associations when they set up a writing program that encourages students to explore and expand their writing ability while practicing the writing conventions that students will need to express themselves effectively. Assessment practices that include ongoing progress monitoring of the accuracy of letter formation, speed of writing, and quality of writing provide important feedback to teachers as they

alter their writing instruction. The physical environment, or setting, is an important feature that sets the tone for writing.

▶ **FOCUS Question 2. What are the critical features of spelling assessment and instruction for students with learning and behavior problems?**

Answer: Many students with learning and behavior problems do not benefit from traditional approaches to spelling (e.g., weekly word lists) and need instruction in phonics rules and how these rules relate to writing words. The first step is to conduct a spelling error analysis to identify which spelling patterns students understand and which are misunderstood. Through ongoing instruction in these spelling patterns and progress monitoring to determine learning, teachers can integrate assessment and instruction for improving spelling outcomes for their students. Teachers should teach in small units, and cluster new words according to spelling patterns. They should allow time for students to practice new words, provide feedback, and maintain previously learned words through frequent reviews. Finally, they can motivate students by making spelling fun.

▶ **FOCUS Question 3. What are the effects of poor handwriting and what components should be included in an effective handwriting program?**

Answer: Handwriting difficulties often result in spelling difficulties, low motivation to write as well as poor academic performance, low work production, and reduced self-esteem.

Weaknesses in handwriting can be assessed by examining legibility, fluency, and hand position and can usually be remediated with direct instruction and specific practice. Principles of instruction include using a variety of techniques to provide direct instruction that is specific to a student's individual handwriting needs. Provide short, frequent instruction in handwriting skills and many opportunities to practice. Skills should be thoroughly learned in isolation and then applied in the context of the student's writing assignment. Students should evaluate their own handwriting and use the teacher as a model. Handwriting should also be taught as a combined visual–motor task. For each student, teachers must assess, model, and teach the needed skills as well as provide opportunities for practice and feedback.

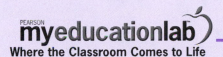

PEARSON
myeducationlab
Where the Classroom Comes to Life

The MyEducationLab for this course can help you solidify your comprehension of Chapter 9 concepts.

- Gauge and further develop your understanding of chapter concepts by taking the quizzes and examining the enrichment materials in the Chapter 9 Study Plan.
- Visit Topic 4, Assessing and Teaching Literacy and Language, to connect with challenge-based interactive modules, case study units, and podcasts that provide research-validated information about working with

students in inclusive settings, by visiting the IRIS Center Resources.

- Explore Assignments and Activities, assignable exercises showing concepts in action through video, cases, and student and teacher artifacts.
- Practice and strengthen skills essential to quality teaching through the Building Teaching Skills and Dispositions lessons.

10

Assessing and Teaching Content Area Learning and Vocabulary Instruction

FOCUS Questions

1. How can teachers use specific word instruction and word-learning strategies to teach vocabulary?

2. What is content enhancement, and how can teachers use it to teach content area reading?

3. How do teachers adapt textbooks, lectures, assignments, homework, and tests to meet the needs of students with learning and behavior problems?

4. What are the three types of study skills, and why are they important to learning?

When Ms. Cho moved from her position as a special education teacher at the elementary school to one at a high school, her experience and education in teaching reading, writing, and math served her well for part of the school day. However, in addition to the two English periods she teaches daily, she is expected to teach sections of American history and American government to students with learning and behavior problems. Although she minored in political science and history in college, she was concerned that her content knowledge was weak in these areas and that she lacked adequate instructional procedures for teaching content to students with learning and behavior problems. She has also been asked to teach a section of general science; she has chosen to team-teach the class with a science teacher because of her limited content knowledge and her desire to integrate the special education students into general education classes.

Juan, a fourth grader with a reading disability, moved to the United States when he was in the first grade. With the help of his special education teacher, Juan has made considerable progress in reading and understanding texts that have stories. Since entering fourth grade, however, he has been challenged by vocabulary words in expository texts (his math and social studies texts). The vocabulary words that he is encountering in these texts are more complex and abstract than the words in narrative texts, for example, *exponent, ecosystem, matriculate, fibrosis*. As a result, Juan is having significant difficulty understanding what he reads in his math and social studies classes and he is failing to learn the content from these texts.

When Desmond entered Bailey Middle School, he had been receiving help in a special education resource room since second grade. During that time, Ms. Jackson, the resource room teacher, had been working with Desmond on word identification and basic comprehension skills as well as spelling and writing compositions. In elementary school, Desmond went to the resource room for 45 minutes every afternoon. He consistently missed either social studies or science in the general education classroom while he was receiving special assistance in the resource room.

Desmond attends resource English and reading, but he has social studies, science, and home economics classes in general education classes. All of these classes require him to listen to lectures in class and take notes, read textbooks and answer the questions at the end of each section, take timed tests, write reports, and keep track of assignments and turn them in on time. Textbooks for these classes are information driven and contain

PEARSON
myeducationlab

Visit the MyEducationLab for this course to enhance your understanding of chapter concepts with a personalized Study Plan. You'll also have the opportunity to hone your teaching skills through video-based Assignments and Activities, IRIS Center Resources, and Building Teaching Skills and Dispositions lessons.

unfamiliar technical vocabulary. It is challenging for Desmond to learn from textbooks because he does not know the meaning of many of the vocabulary words that are crucial to understanding the content. By the end of the first 9 weeks, Desmond has received failing slips in all three classes. He is frustrated by his classes and is becoming disruptive.

Doreen worked hard in high school and, despite her reading and writing disabilities, is a senior in high school with a high-enough grade point average to enter college. However, she is feeling overwhelmed by the demands of her classes. Doreen can't seem to get organized. She has difficulty estimating how long it will take her to complete an assignment, and she is unable to keep up with the reading assignments. Doreen is a bright student with good potential to succeed as an architect or engineer, but she may never get through the basic liberal arts courses required for her degree.

Both Desmond and Doreen need strategies to assist them in being more effective learners. They need skills in managing time, organizing notebooks, taking notes, studying for tests, taking tests, reading textbooks, learning new vocabulary, and writing reports and essays. Desmond and Doreen have mastered many of the basics of reading and writing, but they are having difficulty applying them in content area classes.

Both Juan and Desmond need systematic vocabulary instruction that introduces important vocabulary words and word-building strategies. Preteaching specific vocabulary words that are crucial to understanding the texts should improve their comprehension. Also, word-building strategies they can apply to figure out the meanings of a variety of words would help improve their vocabulary acquisition.

Ms. Cho, Juan, Desmond, and Doreen are experiencing difficulties functioning in the upper-elementary, secondary, postsecondary school, and professional environments. In these environments, the task demands for teachers and students change dramatically. Special education teachers often coteach, teach content subjects, or need to provide content area teachers with learning and teaching strategies to support students so that they can access the general education curriculum. Students are asked to apply learning strategies and study skills as well as skills in listening, reading, writing, and math to learn content area subjects such as biology, American history, art history, welding, computer programming, and home economics.

This chapter focuses on instructional practices for teaching vocabulary and content area information, making adaptations, and teaching learning strategies and study skills.

> Many of the reading comprehension and writing strategies highlighted in Chapters 8 and 9 are effective in promoting content area learning and effective studying and learning. In addition, the Strategies Intervention Model presented in Chapter 2 can be used to teach many of the study skills and learning strategies suggested in this chapter.

Teaching Content Area Information and Vocabulary

How can teachers use specific word instruction and word-learning strategies to teach vocabulary? How important is knowing the meaning of words, or having an adequate vocabulary, to reading and content learning? According to Rupley, Logan, and Nichols (1998), "vocabulary is the glue that holds stories, ideas, and content . . . making comprehension accessible for children" (p. 339). Limited vocabulary has been viewed as both a cause and an effect of poor reading achievements (Gunning, 2010). Students with a low vocabulary have a difficult time understanding what they read. Think about it this way: You can probably read the words in a book about quantum physics, but you may not be able to answer questions very well afterwards. Why? One of the important ingredients to reading is having adequate background knowledge and knowing the meaning of words. Not only

do students with limited vocabulary know fewer words, but their knowledge of the words may also lack depth. After third grade, when content area texts contain more unfamiliar technical and abstract vocabulary words than primary-grade texts do, the cumulative vocabulary differences between students who are good readers and students who are poor readers gets larger. In fact, good readers know about twice as many words as do poor readers in the first grade, and as these students go through the grades, the gap widens. Stanovich (1986) described this phenomenon as the Matthew Effect—the rich get richer and the poor get poorer. By the end of high school, good readers know four times as many words as do their counterparts with limited reading skills (Smith, 1941). This growing gap means that when students with a rich vocabulary read or hear new words, they are more likely to figure out the meaning of unknown words on the basis of words they already know. Students with limited vocabulary are more likely to miss the opportunities to learn unknown words. Closing the gap is challenging; however, systematic, explicit vocabulary instruction holds promise.

Types of Vocabulary and Vocabulary Instruction

In general, there are two types of vocabulary: oral and reading. *Oral vocabulary* refers to words that a reader recognizes in listening and uses in speaking. *Reading vocabulary* refers to words that a reader recognizes or uses in print (National Reading Panel, 2000). If the word is in a reader's oral vocabulary, the reader can understand what the word means as long as he or she can decode it. However, if the word is not in the reader's oral vocabulary, the reader must learn its meaning. As students read more complex content area texts, they usually encounter more unfamiliar words that are not part of their oral vocabulary. This relationship between oral and reading vocabulary provides insight into vocabulary learning and instruction (see Apply the Concept 10-1).

There are two main approaches to teaching vocabulary: the indirect approach and the direct approach (Graves, 2009; National Reading Panel, 2000). Students can learn vocabulary words indirectly when they hear and see words through conversations with other people, especially adults; through listening to adults read aloud; and through reading extensively on their own. Because not all the words in a text can be taught directly, it is important that teachers promote students' indirect learning of vocabulary by teaching them to be "word detectives" who recognize knew words and try to find their meaning.

Many students with learning and behavior problems are less likely to learn words indirectly than are their average-achieving peers. Because of this, directly teaching vocabulary is recommended as an effective approach to improving vocabulary knowledge for poor readers or at-risk students (Beck, McKeown, & Kukan, 2002). In the direct approach to vocabulary instruction, students learn difficult words that are not usually part of their everyday experiences through systematic, explicit instruction of individual words and word-learning strategies. Directly teaching vocabulary provides access to learning new words that students, especially those with reading difficulties, may not pick up incidentally.

Teaching Vocabulary Through Specific Word Instruction

Specific word instruction, or teaching individual words, helps students to build in-depth understanding not just of word meaning but of text reading. For both of the specific word instruction approaches we describe, instruction starts with teachers' careful selection of a few vocabulary words (about 7 to 10 per week) that are critical for understanding the text and difficult for students. Students should have multiple interactions with selected vocabulary words. Students need approximately 12 exposures to a word before they will be able to use the word to aid their comprehension (Beck et al., 1985). Exposures should allow students to interact with the words in a variety of formats, such as classroom discussions, multiple texts, and writing exercises.

Using Oral Language For young students, a teacher can teach words from texts that are read aloud to students (Hickman, Pollard-Durodola, & Vaughn, 2004; Swanson et al., in press). Regular read-alouds provide students with opportunities to be exposed to new words that may be difficult for them to read. Remember, it is valuable to select text that is slightly above the level of students so that new information, concepts, and vocabulary can be acquired. The teacher identifies about three key vocabulary words (high-utility words) in a reading passage for direct teaching. High-utility words are words that students will encounter in a variety of contexts, and are necessary for understanding the main idea of a particular text. After a story is read aloud to students, the teacher discusses the passage with students to provide a context in which to

●●●●●● *Apply the Concept* ●●●●●●

10-1	Word Learning and Instruction

Kind of Word Learning	Instruction
Knows a word when hears it but does not recognize its meaning	Teach the word in printed form
Knows the concept but does not know the particular word for that concept	Teach the word and relate it to the concept that the reader knows
Recognizes the word but does not know the concept	Develop the concept
Does not know the word and the concept	Develop the word and the concept

Source: Adapted from National Reading Panel (2000); Ruddell (1994).

begin the vocabulary instruction. Then the teacher provides systematic vocabulary instruction:

1. Contextualize the word in the story. (Teacher: "In the story, the leaders of the Cherokee Nation were *amazed* by characters developed by Sequoyah.")

2. Ask students to repeat the word (e.g., *amazed*) so that they know how to pronounce it. (Teacher: "Say the word with me.")

3. Provide a simple definition so that students can easily understand its meaning. (Teacher: "When people are *amazed,* they are very surprised.")

4. Provide other examples to further facilitate students' understanding of word meaning. (Teacher: "Someone might be *amazed* by the number of stars in our galaxy, or someone might be *amazed* by how big a bear is.")

5. Ask students to use their own examples, to promote their active involvement. (Teacher: "Tell about something you would be *amazed* by. Try to use *amazed* when you tell about it. You could say 'I would be *amazed* _____.'")

Using Preteaching Before Reading Preteaching vocabulary before reading is an effective strategy to enhance students' knowledge of word meanings (Graves, 2009). Preteaching vocabulary is especially helpful for students with learning problems because it provides them with background knowledge on the text that they will be reading. To increase the effectiveness of preteaching vocabulary, it is important for teachers to appropriately select words that are critical to understanding the passage and are challenging for their students.

Preteaching key words and concepts is effective for older readers when teaching reading, social studies, science, and math (Vaughn, Martinez et al., 2009). Preteaching such key words as *freedom, abolitionist, advocate, decimal, galaxy,* and *incubate* helps all readers prepare to read with meaning. These words can be considered as high-utility words as students may encounter them in a variety of contexts.

Using synonyms, examples, and/or readily understood definitions can be an effective way to enhance students' understanding of a word. First, interact with students to develop a list of synonyms for the new word. Second, teachers can provide examples when few words are available to appropriately define the concept (e.g., *feeling*). Third, teachers can use definitions when introducing new words that are complex. As students progress through the grades and words become more complex, teachers may increasingly use definitions to introduce new words. Teachers should provide student-friendly definitions consisting of words that students know:

- Introduce a vocabulary word (e.g., *immigrant*), and ask students to repeat the word so that they know how to pronounce the word.

- Discuss the meaning of the word using synonyms, examples, pictures, and/or definitions (e.g., *immigrant* means "someone who comes from abroad to live permanently in another country"). Most of us have relatives who were immigrants—for example, my grandfather came from Germany and he was an immigrant to the United States.

- Check with students on their understanding of the word by asking students to figure out positive or incorrect examples and to explain why. (Positive example of the word *immigrant:* "Tom's grandparents came to the United States from England in 1912. They lived in the United States until they passed away." Ask the students, "Are Tom's grandparents immigrants? Why or why not?" An example of an incorrect use of the word *immigrant:* "Recently, many international students came to the United States to study." Ask the students, "Are the international students immigrants? Why or why not?")

Give students an opportunity to interact with the word either verbally or in writing with either a partner or a group of three. Using the word orally or in writing ensures that the word will retain meaning.

> ▶ **WEB RESOURCES**
> For a helpful Web site on vocabulary instruction, see http://www.literacymatters.org/content/readandwrite/vocab.htm.

Teaching Vocabulary Through Word-Learning Strategies

In addition to specific word instruction, it is critical to teach students word-learning strategies that are supported by research, including using contextual analysis, morphemic analysis, and dictionaries and other reference aids.

Using Contextual Analysis *Contextual analysis* involves using the context, or text that surrounds an unknown word, to find clues to reveal a word's meaning (Blachowicz & Ogle, 2001). Contextual analysis may be a useful word-building strategy for students to use during their independent reading. In text writers often provide the definition, synonym, description, or examples of a word that may be difficult for the reader (Carnine, Silbert, & Kame'enui, 1997). Writers provide several types of context clues in their text:

- *Definition.* The word is defined in the sentence. (Example: The *surplus*—that is, an amount left over—was so great that the office was full and desks and chairs were lying on the floor.)
- *Synonym.* The word is compared to another word with a similar meaning. (Example: When Tom went to the parking garage and his car was not there, he was *furious.* Tom was *very mad.*)

- *Description*. The word is described by the context. (Example: After taking a spill on her bike, she was able to stand up, get back on the bike, and pedal away on her own *volition.*)
- *Contrast*. The word is contrasted with some other word, like an antonym. (Example: Kim was *lethargic,* yet her sister was very energetic.)
- *Comparison*. The word is compared with some other word or phrase to illustrate the similarities between them. (Example: John was exhausted after the *interview,* which was more work than mowing grass all day in the neighborhood.)

Regardless of types of context clues, the first step in teaching contextual analysis is to provide explicit modeling in looking at the words surrounding an unknown word and finding possible clues that may help students figure out its meaning. Then a teacher gives students ample opportunities to practice how to use contextual analysis and engage them in lively discussions. Teachers should introduce a few types of context clues (about two) at one time and sequence types of context clues from easy (e.g., definition) to difficult (e.g., comparison).

The following activity helps students understand the supporting role of context in understanding word meanings:

1. Prepare a series of passages in which context is used to define a difficult word.
2. Present the difficult word in isolation.
3. Ask students for the definition of the word.
4. Present the difficult word in context, and point out the word.
5. Have students reread the sentence before, with, and after the one with the difficult word, to look for context clues.
6. Ask students for the definition of the word and how the definition is derived.
7. Have students compare the definition of the word from context with that of the word in isolation.
8. Present other vocabulary words in context. Pair students, and ask them to analyze the context to figure out the meaning of each vocabulary word and record the definition for each word.
9. Have students look up the definitions for the vocabulary words in a dictionary (University of Texas Center for Reading and Language Arts, 2002).

It is valuable to prepare students for text that does not provide sufficient information to help them understand words and concepts. They will undoubtedly encounter text in content areas as well as narrative that provides little information or perhaps even misleading information about words and concepts. It is necessary to help students distinguish words that are not defined in text and how to use other resources to gain meaning.

Using Morphemic Analysis Morphemic analysis in vocabulary instruction involves breaking a word into morphemes, the smallest linguistic units that have meaning, and using their meanings to figure out the meaning of the whole word (Reed, 2008). There are two types of morphemes: free, which can stand alone (e.g., *some*), and bound, which must be linked to words or other morphemes (i.e., prefixes and suffixes). Because Greek and Latin morphemes are found commonly in content area textbooks, teaching morphemes and their meanings helps students to independently figure out the meanings of the words. Figure 10-1 provides common Greek and Latin roots and their meanings. Having students break words into small parts based on meaning can help them to figure out the meaning of words on the basis of what they know about the meanings of the smaller parts (Denton et al., 2007). For instance, a student can break the word *unchangeable* into the word parts *un, change,* and *able*. If the student knows the meanings of these word parts (*un* meaning "not," *change,* and *able* meaning "able to"), the student can determine that *unchangeable* means "not able to change." Figure 10-2 presents common prefixes and suffixes and their meanings.

> ▶ **WEB RESOURCES**
>
> For a helpful Web site and resource for teaching older students vocabulary instruction, see http://www.meadowscenter.org/vgc/ and click on **MATERIALS** and then click on **Secondary,** looking for the document entitled "Effective Instruction for Middle School Students with Reading Difficulties: The Reading Teacher's Sourcebook."

▶ **Figure 10-1**   Common Greek and Latin Roots

Root	Meaning	Sample Words
astro	star	astrology, astronaut, asteroid
aud	hear	auditorium, audition
bio	life	biography, biology
dict	speak	dictate, dictator
geo	earth	geography, geology
meter	measure	thermometer
mit, mis	send	transmit, mission, missile
ped	foot	pedal, pedestrian
phon	sound	microphone, phonograph
port	carry	portable, transport
scrib, script	write	manuscript, scribble
spect	see	inspect, spectator
struct	build	construction, destruction

Source: Adapted from University of Texas Center for Reading and Language Arts (2009). Reprinted by permission.

Prefix	Meaning	Sample Words	Suffix	Meaning/Function	Sample Words
ante-	before, front	antechamber	-able, -ible	can be done	comfortable, changeable
anti-	against	antislavery, antisocial	-al, -ial	characteristic of	natural, remedial
bi-	two	bicycle	-ance, -ence	state of	importance
co-	with, together	coworker	-ation, -ition,	act, process	tension, attention,
de-	opposite of,	deactivate, devalue,	-tion, -ion, -sion		imagination
	down, remove,	dethrone	-ant	person connected	accountant
	reduce			with	
dis-	not, opposite of	dishonest, disagree	-en	noting action from	harden, loosen, wooden
en-, em-	cause to	enable, embrace		an adjective made of	
ex-	out, out of	exterior, exhaust,	-er, -or	person connected	painter, director
		expose		with	
fore-	before	foreground	-ful	full of	fearful, beautiful, hopeful
in-	in or into	inside, interior	-fy	make	clarify
in-, im-,	not	inactive, immature,	-ic	having of	poetic
ir-, il-		irregular, illegal	-ish	characteristic of	greenish
inter-	between	international,	-ity, -ty	state of	necessity, honesty
		intersection	-ive, -ative,	noting action from	active, affirmative
intra-	inside	intrastate	-itive	an adjective	
mid-	middle	midnight	-less	without	fearless, tireless, hopeless
mis-	wrongly	misbehave,	-ly	characteristic of	gladly, happily
		mispronounce	-ment	result of an action	entertainment, excitement
non-	not	nonfiction	-ness	state of, condition of	kindness, happiness
over-	too much	overdue, oversleep	-ous, -eous,	having of	joyous, gracious
pre-	before	preheat, preschool	-ious		
re-	again	reread, redo	-y	characterized by	rainy
semi-	half	semicircle			
sub-	under	submarine, subway			
super-	above	supernatural			
trans-	across	transport			
tri-	three	tricycle			
un-	not, opposite of	unable, unchangeable			
under-	too little	underpaid			

Source: Adapted from University of Texas Center for Reading and Language Arts (2009). Reprinted by permission.

Learning prefixes is relatively easy in comparison to learning suffixes (National Reading Panel, 2000). Prefixes generally have clearer meanings and are spelled more regularly than suffixes. For instance, the prefixes un- and re- have clear meanings of "not" and "again," respectively, and are spelled as *un* and *re* all the time. In contrast, the suffixes -tion and -ness have more abstract meanings of "the act or process of" and "the state or condition of," respectively. Some suffixes can also be spelled differently depending on the base words (e.g., -tion, -ion, -sion). However, not all suffixes have abstract meanings (e.g., -less meaning "without" and -ful meaning "full of").

Morphemic analysis instruction involves presenting new morphemes and their meanings in several specific steps:

1. Introduce a new morpheme and its meaning.
2. Introduce words containing that morpheme.
3. Provide practice for determining the meaning of words that contain that morpheme.
4. Test students on the meaning of several words that contain that morpheme.
5. Provide practice for the meaning of the new morpheme and previously taught morphemes.

Although morphemic analysis can help students build their vocabulary, several cautions should be considered when planning morphemic analysis instruction. First, this strategy works with a limited set of words; therefore, morphemic analysis instruction should not be too long. Second, only one or two prefixes or suffixes should be introduced at a time, with an emphasis on their applications to unfamiliar words. Teachers can utilize small groups to promote student discussion of the meanings of word parts and the new words.

Using Dictionaries and Other Reference Aids
It is important for students to learn how to use dictionaries, glossaries, and thesauruses to help broaden and deepen their word knowledge (National Institute for Literacy, 2001). Using dictionaries and other reference aids can be a difficult task for young students for several reasons:

- Definitions often contain words that students do not understand. Therefore, when possible, teachers should select dictionaries that are written at the appropriate reading level. Second, many words have more than one definition listed in the dictionary (e.g., the word *parcel* can mean something wrapped up or packaged, or a portion or plot of. Teachers should teach students how to decide on the most appropriate meaning. For example, a teacher may present a word having several meanings in sentences. The teacher then asks students to look up the word, examine the definitions listed in the dictionary, read the sentence substituting each definition in the dictionary to see whether it makes sense, and select the definition that is most appropriate for the sentence.
- Although using dictionaries and other reference aids is an important word-building strategy students can use while reading, students should not look up every unknown word. Teachers should encourage students to use contextual analysis and morphemic analysis to assist in determining word meanings. Teachers should encourage students to decide whether a word is important to understanding the passage. When students fail to figure out the meaning of important words through contextual analysis and morphemic analysis, they can look up the word in a dictionary or other reference aid.

Assessing Vocabulary

Determining whether students know the meaning of a single word is not difficult. However, knowing how many words students know, which words they know and don't know, and whether they know one or more meanings and can use them orally and in writing—well, that is all more than a little overwhelming. Vocabulary is perhaps one of the most difficult areas of reading and content learning to assess. Vocabulary is also difficult to assess because there are many different levels of knowing what a word means.

We can recognize the word when we see or hear it, we can know what the word means when someone else uses it, and/or we can use the word adeptly in conversation and writing. For the purposes of instruction, teachers can monitor the words and concepts related to understanding text or learning from their content area instruction.

Progress Monitoring What can teachers do to monitor their students' vocabulary and concept learning? The first step is to identify the words and concepts that students most need to know and understand for the text or unit to make sense to them. Although it is tempting to select a lot of words for instruction, the most important goal is to select words that have high impact on learning and comprehension. For example, Mr. O'Malley, a middle school social studies teacher, was concerned that many of his students would not understand many of the most important words in his unit on how money works. He realized that he couldn't teach every word at a deep-enough level that students would be able to use them orally and in their writing. He selected eight words for the first week of his unit. He decided to teach two new words each day for the first 4 days and then briefly review the words that he had previously taught. He monitored the progress of students' understanding of these words in two ways. First, he did daily checks with selected students to determine whether they knew what the words meant. Second, he asked students to document in their notebook if they saw or heard any of the key words either during the day at school or at home. Third, he provided a paper-and-pencil assessment of all eight words at the end of the week so that he would know which words required further review during the second week of the unit.

Families and Vocabulary Acquisition

The essence of vocabulary learning begins with language learning. To support their children's efforts to build vocabulary, families should have fun with words during reading at home, at the dinner table, when they are watching a movie, and throughout the day. For example, whenever anyone hears or sees a new or unusual use of a word, asking questions about it and extending its meaning should be a family goal.

Teachers can suggest the following activities:

- Play with words by rhyming, finding synonyms and antonyms, or categorizing words (things that are hot, different ways to say "good").
- Select a family word of the day—a difficult word that you or your child chooses. Define the word, and see how many times you and your child can use the new word during the day. At the end of the day, discuss how and when you used the word.
- Read and discuss the vocabulary you see in the community on billboards, signs, at the grocery store, and so on. For example, when you are at the Department

of Motor Vehicles renewing your driver's license, talk about what you are doing using relevant words such as *application, license, examination,* and *renew.*

Teachers can also suggest ways to improve reading at home through the following activities:

- Choose books that your child is interested in reading. You may want to select a short passage or read just a few pages each day, depending on the length of the book.
- Before reading a story aloud or listening to your child read, select a few difficult words and give simple definitions using familiar language. Write down the words and definitions (for example, *flee: to run away*).
- During reading, tell your child to listen for the vocabulary words, and encourage the child to use clues in the story to find out what they mean.
- After reading, ask questions to help your child *explain* and *describe* what has been read. Listen for use of one or more of the vocabulary words in your child's retelling of the story (Hickman, Pollard-Durodola, & Vaughn, 2004; Swanson et al., in press).

Games that encourage vocabulary development can also be played at home. For example, word games such as Scrabble, Scattegories, Balderdash, and Taboo expose children to new words and encourage them to use a wide range of vocabulary.

Teaching Content Area Reading Through Content Enhancement

What is content enhancement, and how can teachers use it to teach content area reading? To teach content area information in any subject, a teacher must teach the important concepts and vocabulary and their relationships. The goal is to enhance the content and teach related vocabulary so that the "critical features of the content are selected, organized, manipulated, and complemented in a manner that promotes effective and efficient information processing" (Lenz, Bulgren, & Hudson, 1990, p. 132).

Content enhancements are techniques to help students identify, organize, and comprehend important content information (Bulgren et al., 2006, Bulgren, Marquis, Lenz, Shumaker, & Deshler, 2009). In addition, content enhancements inform students of the purpose of instruction and increase student motivation (Mastropieri & Scruggs, 2000). According to Bulgren, Deschler, and Lenz (2007), content enhancement routines ensure that students possess the prerequisite background knowledge or provide scaffolded instruction so students can obtain this knowledge; assist students in working with related concepts; and give students the skills to predict, solve problems, infer, and synthesize information in a variety of settings. Several types of content enhancements

have been developed and recommended: advance organizers, concept diagrams, comparison tables, semantic feature analysis (SFA), or semantic maps, concept mastery, anchoring, and comparison routines.

What is a concept? A concept is a key word or limited number of words that is essential for understanding content. For example, the following concept might be used in a science course:

Bacteria are a class of microscopic plants that help people, other animals, and plants; however, bacteria also do things that hurt people, other animals, and plants.

Several related ideas that elaborate on the concept of *bacteria* are as follows:

Bacteria are small; you use a microscope to see them; bacteria multiply; bacteria live in soil, water, organic matter, plants, or animals; bacteria can make you ill; bacteria can spoil food.

The vocabulary associated with the general concept and its related concepts is the *conceptual vocabulary.* These are the words that are necessary for understanding the general idea and are associated with it. Examples of the conceptual vocabulary for a unit on bacteria in a science text are *bacteria, microscope, colony, multiply, reproduce,* and *decay*. These words and their meanings facilitate understanding of the general concept.

A six-step process or teaching routine can be used to teach concepts through content enhancement (Anders, Bos, & Filip, 1984; Lenz & Bulgren, 1995). Admittedly, some concepts and vocabulary are more important than others. Deciding what concepts to teach is a crucial part of content area teaching. The process for teaching concepts is presented in Apply the Concept 10-2 and discussed in more detail in the following sections.

> ▶ **WEB RESOURCES**
> For further description of content enhancement routines and a video discussing them, see http://www.KU-CRL.org.

Selecting the Big Idea of Content Learning

Before proceeding with selecting content vocabulary and teaching it, teachers must decide what the "big ideas" are they want every student to learn. One way to do this is for the teacher to ask, "What do I want every student to know about this content unit when I finish teaching it?" The answer to this question provides the big ideas for learning and guides the teacher in selecting key concepts and related vocabulary. A teacher needs to determine the conceptual framework for the unit so that the information can be presented in an organized fashion on the basis of this framework. During this step, the teacher should focus on the critical information or knowledge all students need to understand about a particular unit (Bulgren et al., 2007).

10-2   **Process for Teaching Concepts**

The following steps can be used to identify and teach key concepts within content area (e.g., science and social studies) instruction:

1. Identify the "big idea" of what you want students to learn.
2. Decide what concepts and related vocabulary to teach.
3. Evaluate the instructional materials to be used for reader-friendliness or considerateness—alter and supplement as needed.
4. Assess the students on their background knowledge for the concepts and related vocabulary.
5. Use prelearning or prereading activities to facilitate and support learning.
6. Conduct the learning or reading activity.
7. Provide postlearning activities that further reinforce and extend the concepts and information learned.
8. Assess students' learning and reteach if necessary.

Selecting Concepts and Related Vocabulary

Selecting the major concepts and related vocabulary to be taught in a unit, a chapter, a section of a book, or a lecture is best completed before students interact with the material.

The process that a teacher uses for determining the major concepts depends on his or her expertise and knowledge in the content area, knowledge of the structure of the textbook information, and knowledge about the students' background for the content and their study/reading skills (Bulgren et al., 2006). A teacher who has specialized in a given content area can probably generate concepts from expert knowledge and experiences and use the assigned textbook along with key resource books and Web sites as the primary resources for verifying the appropriateness of those concepts. A teacher with limited background knowledge could use a variety of resources, such as the assigned textbooks, trade books, state or local curriculum guides, Web sites and other computer-based resources, and other teachers or experts in the field. Some texts—especially those written for students with reading problems—tend to provide too much detail and fail to explain the overall concept or to relate the concepts.

After articulating the major concepts to be learned, the teacher next generates and organizes the related vocabulary. To do this, the teacher studies the assigned text and instructional materials and compiles a list of relevant related words and phrases. In doing this, the teacher might realize that some important vocabulary is missing from the text; if so, it can be added to the list.

To organize the vocabulary list, a teacher can group words that are related and then create a semantic or content map to visually represent the relationships among these terms (Scanlon, Duran, Reyes, & Gallego, 1992). Figure 10-3 depicts a map that was developed with the conceptual vocabulary a teacher generated from a chapter in a biology text. The map highlights the critical vocabulary and the organization and relationships of the concepts (Anders & Bos, 1984; Lenz & Bulgren, 1995). The map helps to solve an all-too-common problem that confronts content area teachers: deciding what concepts and related vocabulary to teach in a content lesson.

Evaluating Instructional Materials

Before teaching concepts and related vocabulary, teachers need to evaluate the instructional materials they intend to use in teaching the unit to make adaptations so that students with learning disabilities can access the content. Although the breadth of instructional materials has increased with the use of the Internet and other media, textbooks still continue to serve as a key resource in instruction. How concepts are presented in a text, whether it is the class textbook, a resource book, or on the Internet, will affect how easily the students comprehend and learn the concepts (McKeown, Beck, Sinatra, & Loxterman, 1992). The manner in which the text is organized (e.g., use of headings and subheadings, highlighted words, marginal notes) will also affect the comprehensibility of the text.

Readability Traditionally, evaluations of content area texts emphasized readability as determined by readability formulas (e.g., Dale & Chall, 1948; Fry, 1977). Most readability formulas, including the Fry readability formula presented in Figure 10-4, are based on two factors: sentence complexity as measured by sentence length, and word difficulty as indexed by word length or frequency. One of the most frequently used procedures for determining the reading level of text is by assessing the Lexile level of the text (http://www.lexile.com).

Readability formulas should be used as only one aspect of evaluating a text since they often have a large range of grade levels and do not reveal how difficult the text is for a particular student. For example, a text whose readability formula is predicted to be at grade 7 can range by chance from grade 6.0 to grade 9.0. Readability formulas do not

▶ **Figure 10-3**   Content Map of a Biology Chapter on Mollusks

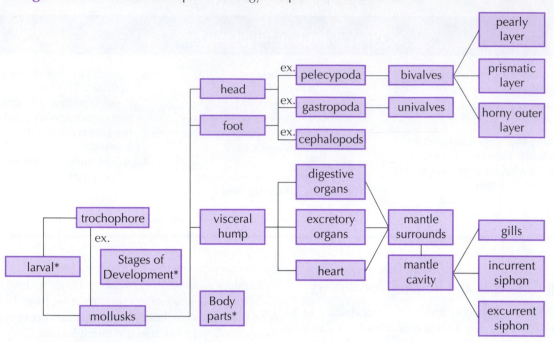

*Note: There seem to be two concepts being developed (apologies to the biologists among us):

1. When classifying animals, biologists look for relationships between animals during the various stages of development from birth to adulthood.

2. Biologists describe the body parts of animals and the functions of each part.

Source: P. L. Anders & C. S. Bos (1984), In the beginning: Vocabulary instruction in content classes, *Topics in Learning and Learning Disabilities, 3* (4), p. 56. Reprinted with permission of PRO-ED.

take into account many characteristics of text that are important in comprehension and learning. For example, to reduce the reading level or difficulty as measured by readability formulas, textbooks—particularly adapted textbooks that are designed for students with learning and behavior problems—are written in short sentences. Often this means that important relational words such as *and, or, because,* and *if . . . then* have been eliminated to shorten the length of the sentences and thus lower the readability level as predicted by the formula. Although the readability level according to the formula may be lower, the text is actually more difficult to understand. Students' prior knowledge of the content and the concepts and technical vocabulary associated with the content can dramatically affect how easy a text is to comprehend. Lastly, readability formulas neglect to consider other reader characteristics that affect comprehension, such as interest, purpose, and perseverance.

Considerate or User-Friendly Text   What characteristics should be considered in evaluating how considerate or user-friendly a text is? Criteria for developing considerate text that students can read to understand (Armbruster & Anderson, 1988) fall into three broad categories:

   1. *Structure* refers to the manner in which a text is organized and how the text signals its structure. Use of

titles, headings, subheadings, introductions, and summary statements; informative and relevant pictures, charts, and graphs; highlighted key concepts; marginal notes; and signaling words (e.g., *first, second, then, therefore*) can facilitate comprehension. In evaluating a text, it is important to check not only whether such structural features are used, but also whether they match the content. For example, sometimes headings will not relate well to the text that follows the headings. In this case, the structural features may serve more as a source of confusion than as an aid. Also, the teacher should check whether the highlighted words in the text represent the important concepts or simply the words that are difficult to decode.

   The teacher should also consider whether the format and the table of contents help readers to draw relationships between the various chapters by using such devices as sections and subsections. Do introductions to each section or chapter encourage readers to make connections between previous ideas and concepts already discussed and the new ideas to be presented? Some key features to consider in assessing text structure include:

- The introduction is clearly identified.
- The introduction provides purpose, relevance, and overview.
- Titles, headings, and subheadings reflect main ideas of content.

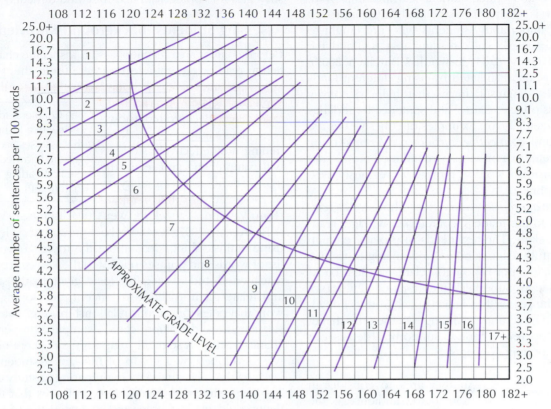

▶ Figure 10-4 Fry Readability Graph for Estimating Readability—Extended

1. Randomly select three text samples of exactly 100 words, beginning with the beginning of a sentence. Count proper nouns, numerals, and initializations as words.

2. Count the number of sentences in each 100-word sample, estimating the length of the last sentence to the nearest one-tenth.

3. Count the total number of syllables in each 100-word sample. Count one syllable for each numeral or initial or symbol; for example, 1990 is one word and four syllables, LD is one word and two syllables, and "&" is one word and one syllable.

4. Average the number of sentences and number of syllables across the three samples.

5. Enter the average sentence length and average number of syllables on the graph. Put a dot where the two lines intersect. The area in which the dot is plotted will give you an approximate estimated readability.

6. If there is a great deal of variability in the syllable or sentence count across the three samples, more samples can be added.

Source: E. Fry (1977), Fry's readability graph: Clarifications, validity, and extension to level 17, *Journal of Reading, 21*, pp. 242–252.

- Key vocabulary words are highlighted and reflect important concepts.
- Definitions of key terms are provided.
- Signal words or headings are provided.
- Margin notes provide summaries or expand on information.
- Illustrations and pictures enhance important information.
- The summary is clearly identified.
- The summary reviews goals and the most important concepts.

- Review questions require students to think about key concepts and ideas.
- The questions have good balance among main concepts, fact/detail, and critical thinking (application, analysis, reactions).

2. *Coherence* refers to how well the ideas in a text are organized and make sense. Particularly in content area texts it is the way in which the text is able to instruct and make sense to the reader. With coherent text, the relationships among concepts are clear. For example, when Herman, Anderson, Pearson, and Nagy (1987) rewrote a text about the circulatory system and made explicit the connections between motive and action, form and function, and cause and effect, student learning improved. Also, text that is clearer is associated with improved learning, and, importantly, students who are taught to use "self-explanation" while reading text retained the most about what they read (Ainsworth & Burcham, 2007).

Coherence is also facilitated by using different kinds of *cohesive ties*—linguistic forms that help to convey meaning across phrase, clause, and sentence boundaries (Anders & Guzzetti, 1996). Examples of cohesive ties are *conjunctions* and *connectives, pronoun referents* (using a pronoun to refer to a previously mentioned noun), and *substitutions* (using a word to replace a previously used noun or verb phrase).

3. *Audience appropriateness* refers to how well a textbook is suited to the readers' content knowledge, reading, and study skills. The text needs to provide enough explanation, attributes, examples, and analogies to give readers adequate information to relate to their background knowledge. Superficial mentions of new topics about which the reader has limited background knowledge do little to build understanding. On the other hand, too many or too few technical supporting details can obscure the important concepts.

> Chapter 8 discusses how to teach strategies for understanding the main ideas to students with learning and behavior difficulties.

Another area to consider in relation to the audience is the explicitness of main ideas. Text in which the main ideas are explicit and are regularly placed at the beginning of paragraphs and sections facilitates learning. Part of the process of preparing to teach content knowledge is evaluating instructional materials for readability and friendliness. By considering the structure, cohesion, and audience appropriateness when evaluating text or other types of instructional materials (e.g., films, lectures, demonstrations), teachers develop a good idea of how considerate or user-friendly the materials are. Based on this evaluation, teachers may decide to modify, augment, or adapt the instructional materials (see the section on adapting textbooks later in this chapter).

The ultimate judge of the readability and friendliness of a textbook is the reader. The FLIP chart strategy helps students learn to evaluate text on their own (Schumm & Mangrum, 1991). FLIP stands for Friendliness, Language, Interest, and Prior knowledge. By filling out charts like the one shown in Figure 10-5, students learn what is comfortable for them individually as readers. After students have completed the FLIP chart, you can learn (through class discussions and individual conferences) what is difficult for them in terms of text friendliness, language, interest, and prior knowledge. Students with reading and learning problems especially need to learn how to talk about the textbook and any problems they have with it.

Classroom discussions based on the FLIP chart strategy also help students to think as a group about effective strategies for coping with text they find difficult.

Assessing Students' Background Knowledge

Before content area teachers assign a specific chapter or text to read or present a lecture on a topic, they need to assess the students' background knowledge for the concepts and related vocabulary to be covered. Background knowledge plays a critical role in determining how effectively students will comprehend and retain the information and vocabulary to be presented. Semantic mapping (Kim, Vaughn, Wanzek, & Wei, 2004; Klingner, Vaughn, & Boardman, 2007) develops background knowledge by using brainstorming ideas about the topic to generate a list of words and phrases related to the key concept. The teacher and students take the ideas given by the students and relate them to the key concept, developing a network that notes the various relationships (e.g., categories, subcategories, definition, class, examples, properties, or characteristics). A semantic map for the concept of *desert* was developed by a group of fifth-grade students with learning disabilities who were preparing to study deserts. The map, shown in Figure 10-6, indicates that the students could give examples and characteristics of a desert. However, the students did not produce a superordinate class (landform) or a definition ("What is it?"). Additionally, the property and example relations that were generated lacked technical vocabulary, despite further probing on the part of the teacher. The semantic map in Figure 10-6 serves not only as a visual representation of the students' current understanding of the concept of *desert,* but also as an initial blueprint for teaching (Reyes & Bos, 1998).

> See Chapter 8 for a review of a technique that assesses background knowledge, the PreReading Plan (PReP).

Using activities such as semantic mapping and PReP not only provides teachers with valuable information about their students' knowledge, but also activates the students' knowledge. We have found that promoting discussions during these activities and encouraging students to relate firsthand experiences helps both students and teachers make connections and clarifies concepts.

Using Prelearning Activities

Limited background knowledge signals the teacher that students need more instruction to learn the information that will be presented in a text or lecture. Teachers can present any number of prelearning activities—such as advance organizers, SFA, semantic mapping, and concept diagrams—that students can use before reading an assigned text or listening to a lecture. All these activities enhance the content and have been referred to as *content*

Title of assignment: _____

Number of pages: _____

General directions: Rate each of the four FLIP categories on a 1–5 scale (5 = high). Then determine your purpose for reading and appropriate reading rate, and budget your reading/study time.

Friendliness: How friendly is my reading assignment?

Directions: Examine your assignment to see if it includes the friendly elements listed below.

Friendly text features

Table of contents	Index	Glossary
Chapter introductions	Headings	Subheadings
Margin notes	Study questions	Chapter summary
Key terms highlighted	Graphs	Charts
Pictures	Signal words	Lists of key facts

1 —————————— 2 —————————— 3 —————————— 4 —————————5

No friendly text features   Some friendly text features   Many friendly text features

Friendliness rating _____

Language: How difficult is the language in my reading assignment?

Directions: Skim the chapter quickly to determine the number of new terms. Read 3 random paragraphs to get a feel for the vocabulary level and number of long, complicated sentences.

1 —————————— 2 —————————— 3 —————————— 4 —————————5

Many new words;   Some new words: No new words;
complicated sentences   somewhat complicated sentences   clear sentences

Language rating _____

Interest: How interesting is my reading assignment?

Directions: Read the title, introduction, headings/subheadings, and summary. Examine the pictures and graphics included.

1 —————————— 2 —————————— 3 —————————— 4 —————————5

Boring   Somewhat interesting   Very interesting

Interest rating _____

Prior knowledge: What do I already know about the material covered in my reading assignment?

Directions: Think about the title, introduction, headings/subheadings, and summary.

1 —————————— 2 —————————— 3 —————————— 4 —————————5

Mostly new information   Some new information   Mostly familiar information

Prior knowledge rating _____

Overall, this reading assignment appears to be at:

❑ a comfortable reading level for me
❑ a somewhat comfortable reading level for me
❑ an uncomfortable reading level for me

Source: J. S. Schumm & C. T. Magnum (1991), FLIP: A framework for textbook thinking, *Journal of Reading, 35*, pp. 120–124. Copyright by the International Reading Association.

enhancement devices (Bulgren et al., 2007; Walther-Thomas & Brownell, 2000).

Advance Organizers Advance organizers are activities that orient students to the material before reading or class presentation (Slavin, 2000). They provide students with an overview or preview of the content they will be learning. Use of advance organizers is based on schema theory and the notion that students profit from having a framework for the material to be learned to help them assimilate the new information into their current schemas or cognitive structure. Advance organizers should inform students of the purpose of instruction, identify topics and subtopics, supply background information, introduce new vocabulary, provide an organizational structure, and state the intended student outcomes. Reviews of studies that have explored the effectiveness of advance organizers on learning have drawn the following conclusions (Corkill, 1992; Preiss & Gayle, 2006):

• Groups that are given advance organizers consistently perform better than control groups that do not

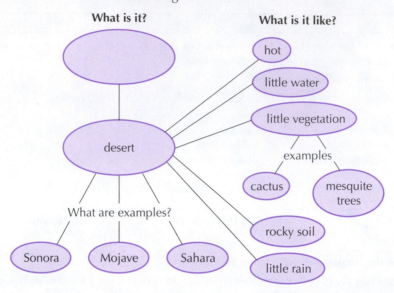

► **Figure 10-6** Concept Map of Fifth-Grade Students'
Knowledge of Deserts

receive them. This advantage diminishes when the material is familiar, when the learners have an extensive background of knowledge about the area, when the learners have high IQs, and when tests fail to measure the breadth of transfer ability.

- Advance organizers particularly aid students of lower ability and/or limited background knowledge.
- Advance organizers are more effective when presented before a learning task than when presented after the task.

 **EVIDENCE-BASED PRACTICE**

Advance Organizers

PROCEDURES: Lenz (1983) identified 10 steps for teachers to follow in using an advance organizer (see Apply the Concept 10-3). The resource teacher trained the students in the resource classroom to use advance organizers by giving the students a worksheet with each of the 10 steps as headings. The students then practiced listening to advance organizers given by the resource teacher and completing the worksheets. Next, the students used the advance organizer worksheet in inclusive content area classes, and the resource teacher and students met afterward to discuss the success of the worksheets. They discussed how the advance organizer information could be used to organize notes and how the worksheet could be modified to assist the students to cue in on the most common organizing principles used by particular teachers.

In giving an advance organizer, the teacher provides an organizational framework for the information to be learned (see step 3 in Apply the Concept 10-3). This

framework might be an outline, a diagram in which the parts are labeled, or a picture semantic map, as discussed earlier. Townsend and Clarihew (1989) found that a pictorial component in a verbal advance organizer was necessary to improve the comprehension of eight-year-old students with limited background knowledge. The use of visual representations or pictures is particularly salient for students with learning and behavior problems (Schwartz, Ellsworth, Graham, & Knight, 1998).

COMMENTS: Lenz, Alley, and Schumaker (1987) found that regular content area teachers are able to implement advance organizers with minimal teacher training (45 minutes). Teachers who used advance organizers expressed satisfaction with the students' response to the instruction as well as the improvement in the overall quality of their own instruction. However, Lenz did find that teacher use of an advance organizer alone was not enough to facilitate student learning. "Learning disabled students had to be made aware that advance organizers were being presented and then had to be trained in the types of information presented in the advance organizer and ways in which that information could be made useful" (Lenz, 1983, p. 12).

Concept Diagrams and Comparison Tables The concept diagram as part of the *Concept Mastery Routine* (Bulgren et al., 2007; Bulgren, Schumaker, & Deshler, 1988, 1996) is a content enhancement tool that can be used to assist students in understanding important key concepts in the reading or lecture; it also works well as a prelearning activity. Research revealed that the Concept Mastery Routine led to gains in students' knowledge in concept and expression of information. The concept diagram is a visual

10-3 | **Steps in Using an Advance Organizer**

1. Inform the students of advance organizers.
   a. Announce the advance organizer.
   b. State the benefits of the advance organizer.
   c. Suggest that students take notes on the advance organizer.
2. Clarify the action to be taken.
   a. State the teacher's actions.
   b. State the students' actions.
3. Identify the topics or tasks.
   a. Identify major topics or activities.
   b. Identify subtopics or component activities.
4. Provide background information.
   a. Relate the topic to the course or previous lesson.
   b. Relate the topic to new information.

5. State the concepts to be learned.
   a. State specific concepts/ideas from the lesson.
   b. State general concepts/ideas that are broader than the lesson's content.
6. Clarify the concepts to be learned.
   a. Clarify by examples or analogies.
   b. Clarify by nonexamples.
   c. Caution students of possible misunderstandings.
7. Motivate the students to learn.
   a. Point out the relevance to students.
   b. Be specific, short-term, personalized, and believable.

8. Introduce vocabulary.
   a. Identify the new terms and define them.
   b. Repeat difficult terms and define them.
9. Provide an organizational framework.
   a. Present an outline, list, or narrative of the lesson's content.
10. State the general outcome desired.
    a. State the objectives of the instruction/learning.
    b. Relate the outcomes to test performance.

Source: Adapted from B. K. Lenz (1983), Promoting active learning through effective instruction, *Pointer, 27* (2), p. 12.

---

tool that supports students as they delineate a concept by doing the following:

- Exploring their prior knowledge of the concept
- Understanding the relationship of the concept to the overall concept class to which it belongs
- Classifying characteristics of the concept
- Generating examples and nonexamples
- Constructing a content-related definition of the concept

 **EVIDENCE-BASED PRACTICE**

Concept Diagrams and Comparison Tables

PROCEDURES: In using a concept diagram (see Figure 10-7), the first step is to prepare the diagram. The teacher identifies major and related concepts of which the students need a deeper or more technical understanding. In a science chapter on fossils, Mr. Bello felt that it was important that the students develop a more technical understanding of the concept of fossils, so this became the concept to diagram. Second, Mr. Bello used the instructional materials and his knowledge to list important characteristics of fossils. He also thought about whether each characteristic is "always present," "sometimes present," or "never present." Third, he located examples and nonexamples of the concepts in the instructional materials. In reviewing the chapter he found that nonexamples

were not provided, so he decided to show the students fossils and nonfossils to help them to start thinking about examples and nonexamples. Finally, Mr. Bello constructed a definition.

After preparing the concept diagram, the next step is using it with the students to develop their understanding of the concept. After giving an advance organizer to explain its purpose, how the diagram works, and the expectations, the teacher can use the linking steps to teach the concept (Bulgren et al., 1988):

Convey the concept name and why it is the focus of study.

Offer the overall or overarching concept.

Note the key words by having the students brainstorm words related to the concept.

Classify the characteristics by using the key words and other ideas to generate characteristics that are always, sometimes, and never present.

Explore and list examples and nonexamples.

Practice with the examples by having students discuss how the examples relate to the characteristics.

Tie down a definition by generating a content-related definition that includes the concept, the overall concepts, and the characteristics that are always present.

COMMENTS: Concept diagrams help not just students with learning disabilities but all learners in the classroom,

CONCEPT DIAGRAM

Concept	fossils
Overall Concept	past geologic age

Classifying Characteristics

Always Present	Sometimes Present	Never Present
remains or prints	frozen in ice	still alive
plants or animals	trapped in tar	still decaying
thousands of years old	crushed by water	
preserved in the earth	in volcanic ash	

Example:

(tigers in La Brea tar pits)

(Siberian mammoth)

(petrified forest in Arizona)

(fish skeleton in limestone layers)

Nonexample:

(your pet cat)

(elephant in Africa today)

(tree limbs and leaves in your yard)

(fish in supermarket)

Definition: Fossils are remains or prints of plants or animals who lived thousands of years ago that have been preserved in the earth.

making them ideal for inclusion settings. Figure 10-8 presents a sample comparison table and includes the steps that are used in generating the table (see the steps in the upper-right-hand corner, which use the acrostic COMPARING). An important part of this table and the steps in generating it is outlining the similar and dissimilar characteristics.

Bulgren and her colleagues note that both the concept diagram and the comparison table as shown in Figures 10-7 and 10-8 are "instructional tools developed and researched at the University of Kansas Center for Research on Learning. They represent a number of organizing and teaching devices designed for teachers to use as they teach content information to classes containing diverse student populations. They are data-based teaching instruments that have been found effective when used in instructional routines that combine cues about the instruction, specialized delivery of the content, involvement of the students in the cognitive processes, and a review of the learning process and content materials." (Bulgren, Lenz, Schumaker, & Deshler, 1995).

Semantic Feature Analysis/Relationship Charts Like an advance organizer, SFA is a prelearning activity that serves to organize the major concepts and related vocabulary to be taught in a unit, chapter, or lecture. Whereas the concept diagram can be used to clarify a concept that is difficult for the students, this activity helps students to see the relationships between the major concepts, the related vocabulary, and their current knowledge of the topic. Since knowledge is hierarchically organized, relating the new concepts to students' prior knowledge will help students learn these new concepts, that teaching attributes of a concept as well as teaching examples and nonexamples are important to concept learning, and that principles of scaffolded instruction and interactive dialogues will promote learning.

COMPARISON TABLE

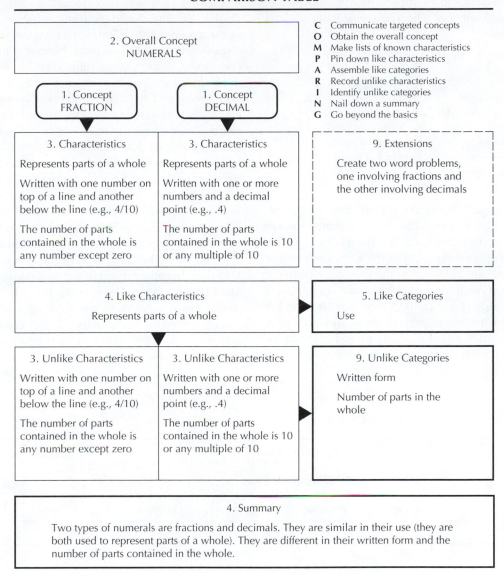

C   Communicate targeted concepts
O   Obtain the overall concept
M   Make lists of known characteristics
P   Pin down like characteristics
A   Assemble like categories
R   Record unlike characteristics
I   Identify unlike categories
N   Nail down a summary
G   Go beyond the basics

Source: J. A. Bulgren, B. Lenz, D. D. Deshler, & J. B. Schumaker, *The Concept Comparison Routine* (Lawrence, KS: Edge Enterprises, Inc., 1995), p. 55. Reprinted with permission.

 **EVIDENCE-BASED PRACTICE**

Semantic Feature Analysis and Relationship Charts

PROCEDURES: The first step in preparing for an SFA activity is to develop a relationship chart. This chart is based on the idea that ideas or concepts are related to one another in terms of a hierarchy of abstractness. The most inclusive or abstract ideas are called *superordinate concepts;* the most concrete or narrow ideas are identified as *subordinate concepts.* Ideas or concepts that fall in between the superordinate and subordinate concepts are referred to as *coordinate concepts* (Frayer, Frederick, &

Klausmeier, 1969). These ideas are then organized into a relationship chart, and the students and teacher discuss the relationship between the various levels of concepts and their own background knowledge. This SFA activity was originally developed for use in teaching a specific concept, such as is used with concept diagrams (Johnson & Pearson, 1984). In their interactive teaching research, Bos and her colleagues have adapted this strategy to text (Anders & Bos, 1986; Bos & Anders, 1992; Reyes & Bos, 1998).

When Ms. Cho, the teacher described at the beginning of the chapter, used this technique in her American government class, she first read the assigned American government chapter on contracts. As she read, she listed the important concepts or vocabulary and then arranged them according to superordinate, coordinate, and subordinate concepts. She used words as well as relevant phrases:

Contract	Counteroffer
Promise	Holding good
Contracting parties	Conditions
Buyer	Acceptance
Seller	Consideration
Written contracts	Statute of frauds
Verbal contracts	Legal obligation
Contractual offer	Legal action

Next, she organized the vocabulary into a relationship chart (see Figure 10-9). The superordinate concept "Contracts" is used as the name for the chart. The five coordinate concepts (main ideas in the text) serve as the column headings and are listed as the important or major ideas. The related vocabulary or subordinate concepts are listed down the side of the chart. Notice that Ms. Cho left blank spaces for adding important ideas and important vocabulary. She encourages students to add relevant information from their background knowledge.

The relationship chart became Ms. Cho's instructional tool. She made a copy for each student and a transparency so that the class could complete the chart as a group. To do this, she introduced the topic (superordinate concept) of the assignment. The students then discussed what they already knew about contracts. Next, she introduced each coordinate concept (important idea) by assisting the students in generating meanings. During this introduction and throughout the activity, she encouraged students to add their personal experiences or understandings of the terms. For example, when Ms. Cho presented the major idea of *contract*, Joe inquired whether a contract had to be written to be legal. This led to Anya's conveying a first-hand experience of her father's making a verbal contract and having the contract honored in court even though it was not written. The discussion ended with one of the purposes for reading being the clarification of what was needed for a verbal contract to be considered legal.

Following the discussion of the coordinate concepts, Ms. Cho introduced each subordinate concept. Again Ms. Cho and her students predicted what the meanings would be in relation to the topic of contracts. For the more technical vocabulary (e.g., *contractual offer, statute of frauds*), Ms. Cho sometimes provided the meaning, or the students decided to read to clarify the

▶ **Figure 10-9**   Relationship Chart: Contracts

CONTRACTS					Name: _____ Period: _____
Important Ideas					
	Contract	Promise	Written Contracts	Verbal Contracts	Conditions
Legal action					
Consideration					
Legal obligation					
Holding good					
Contractual offer					
Counteroffer					
Acceptance					
Statute of frauds					
Contracting parties					

+ = positive relationship
– = negative relationship
0 = no relationship
? = unknown relationship

concept. After introducing each concept, she and the students discussed the relationship between each coordinate concept or phrase and each subordinate term or phrase. They used a plus sign (+) to represent a positive relationship, a minus sign (−) to represent a negative relationship, a zero (0) to signify no relationship, and a question mark (?) to indicate that no consensus could be reached without further information.

Ms. Cho found that student involvement during the discussion was important to the success of the SFA strategy. One key to a fruitful discussion was encouraging students to ask each other why they had reached a certain relationship rating. This seemed to encourage students to use their prior knowledge about the topic and seemed to encourage other students to activate what they already knew about the vocabulary.

After completing the relationship chart, Ms. Cho guided the students in setting purposes for reading. These purposes, for the most part, focused on the chart, reading to confirm their predictions and to determine the relationships between the terms for which no agreement could be reached. After completing the reading, Ms. Cho and the students reviewed the relationship chart. They discussed changes to any of the relationships if necessary and reached consensus on those that were previously unknown.

Sometimes when Ms. Cho and her students used a relationship chart, they found that some information was still unclear after reading the text. Then they checked other sources, such as experts in the field, technical and trade books, the Internet, and other media. Ms. Cho also taught the students how to use the relationship chart to study for chapter tests by asking each other questions based on the meanings of the concepts and vocabulary and on their relationships (e.g., What is a contractual offer? What are the conditions necessary to have a contract?). She also taught how the chart could be used to write a report about the concepts.

COMMENTS: Findings from a synthesis on graphic organizers (Kim et al., 2004) confirmed that SFA was consistently associated with gains in comprehension. One of the most important questions that is asked during discussion is, Why? (e.g., Why is *evidence* positively related to *evidence in court*?) Students need to justify their reasoning. By answering *why* questions, students think through concepts, reaching a deeper understanding and more effectively relating new information to old.

Semantic and Curriculum Maps Semantic and curriculum maps (Klingner et al., 2007; Lenz, Adams, Bulgren, Pouloit, & Laraux, 2007; Scanlon et al., 1992) are ways of visually representing the concepts and important vocabulary to be taught (see Figure 10-6). These content enhancement devices can be used as prelearning activities that assist students in activating their prior knowledge

and in seeing the relationships between new concepts and related vocabulary.

 EVIDENCE-BASED PRACTICE

Semantic Maps

PROCEDURES: In using semantic maps, the teacher can begin by putting the major concept for a lecture or text on the board and then ask students to generate a list of related vocabulary from their background knowledge. However, when presenting more technical vocabulary, the teacher could begin by writing on the board the list of important vocabulary he or she generated in reviewing the text chapter or developing the lecture. After the words have been listed, the teacher discusses the meanings of the words, using a procedure similar to the one just presented in the section on SFA. Next, the teacher arranges and rearranges the vocabulary with the students until the class has a map that shows the relationships that exist among the ideas.

For example, when presenting the following words for a chapter on fossils, the students and teacher first grouped the animals together.

Trilobites	Small horses
Crinoids	Winged insects
Ferns	Geography of the present
Dinosaurs	Land masses
Lakes	Brachiopods
Bodies of water	Saber-toothed tigers
Animals	Guide fossils
Geography	Rivers of the past
Trees	Plants
Oceans	Continents

Next, they grouped the plants together. In the case of guide fossils and several other types of fossils with which the students were not familiar (e.g., crinoids, trilobites), they decided to wait until they had read before placing the concepts on the map. Finally, they grouped together the geography terms.

After the map is completed, the teacher instructs the students to refer to the map while reading and/or listening to the lecture. Like the relationship chart, the semantic map can provide a framework for setting purposes for reading. The students read to confirm and clarify their understanding in relation to the map and make changes to it during discussions held as they read or after completing a chapter. The map can also serve as a blueprint for studying and for writing reports.

COMMENTS: A number of researchers have investigated the use of semantic mapping with students who are low achievers or have learning disabilities (see for review, Kim et al., 2004). In some cases, the students generated

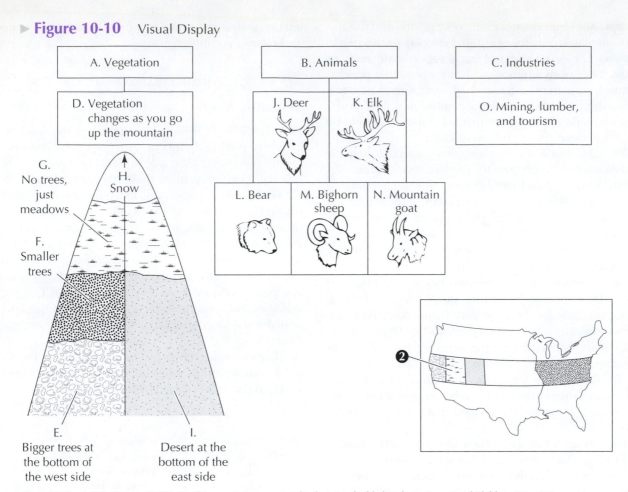

► **Figure 10-10** Visual Display

Source: C. Darch & D. Carnine (1986), Teaching content area material to learning disabled students, *Exceptional Children, 53*, p. 243. Copyright © 1986 by the Council for Exceptional Children. Reprinted with permission.

the maps and in other studies the framework for the map was already developed by the teacher and the student completed them. Some studies provided a map or visual display (see Figure 10-10) to the students in completed form, and systematic direct instruction (Carnine, 1989) was used to assist the students in learning the information contained in the display (Bergerud, Lovitt, & Horton, 1988; Darch & Carnine, 1986). The research has been consistently encouraging in this area: The use of semantic maps or visual representations of information improves the learning performance of students with learning and behavior problems.

Reinforcing Concept Learning During and After Learning

Whether using an advance organizer, SFA, semantic map, concept diagram, or comparison table, these frameworks can be used to guide students as they read a text or listen to a lecture and as they react to their learning. For example, a semantic map can be used before, during, and after a lesson—students can add new vocabulary to the existing map during the lesson and can revise the map after the lesson. Also, the list of major ideas that is obtained from the advance organizer can serve as the framework in which students can take notes when listening to a lecture. After the lecture, students can meet in small groups and share their notes to create one overview that can serve as a study guide for the test. Students can be instructed on how to develop questions based on a concept diagram or semantic map. These questions can serve as self-questions to be asked when reading and when studying for a test.

Students generally require considerable practice in using these content enhancement devices.

► **WEB RESOURCES**
For helpful Web sites on content area learning, see:
• National Science Teachers Association (NSTA) Web site, http://www.nsta.org;
• National Council for the Social Studies, http://www.socialstudies.org.

Making Adaptations

How do teachers adapt textbooks, lectures, assignments, homework, and tests to meet the needs of students with learning and behavior problems? Why do classroom teachers make relatively few instructional adaptations for students with disabilities? First, adapting instructional materials takes time, and teachers' time for planning and preparing for instruction is already limited. Second, adaptations often slow down instruction, and teachers cannot cover as much material as they would like. Third, some teachers think that making adaptations for the few students who need them is not fair to the higher-achieving students who are ready to work at a faster pace. When asked to make specific modifications for a student with learning disabilities in her high school French class, a teacher commented, "I have a number of students in my class who would benefit from the modifications you are asking me to make for Mia. I'm not sure it would be fair to the other students for me to do these things for Mia and not offer the other students the same opportunities."

How do students' respond when teachers make adaptations for individual students within the regular classroom? Which of these adaptations do students view as acceptable? Both elementary and secondary students overwhelmingly preferred teachers who made adaptations for students who need more help. They reported learning better when teachers use flexible grouping for learning, meet with and assist students who have special needs, and vary instruction to meet those needs. They liked mixed-ability grouping and working in pairs with mixed ability. They also preferred teachers who gave all students the same homework assignments. Elementary students did not mind if some students were given different tests as long as the tests were the same length and took the same amount of time. Secondary students, however, preferred teachers who gave all students the same tests and textbooks because they were concerned that they would be embarrassed if friends recognized that they took different tests or read different textbooks. Similarly, some low-achieving students preferred a teacher who made no adaptations for students with special needs. Two possible reasons that they felt negatively about teacher adaptations were because they were concerned about fitting in socially and did not wish to have their deficiencies revealed to their peers.

An especially interesting finding was that high-achieving students not only were aware that certain students in their classrooms needed extra help, but also preferred a teacher who made adaptations to help all the students learn. No high-achieving student in these studies expressed concern that instructional time would be taken away from him or her if the teacher took the time to give extra help to those who needed it. The following comment by one high-achieving high school student illustrates the altruism that was typical: "Even though I am smart enough to deal with any method of teaching, I realize not everyone else is. I like to see a diversified method of teaching in which the individual needs of students are met. Often students who do not perform as well are overlooked as ignorant and stupid, unable to learn. But these students are the ones that must be concentrated on so that they can develop better" (Vaughn, Schumm, Niarhos, & Daugherty, 1993).

Adapting Textbooks

Despite the concerns about making adaptations described previously, research indicates that students at all achievement levels need textbook adaptations (Schumm et al., 1992, 2009). Text adaptation is a technique that involves making changes to or adding to an existing text to make it more comprehensible for students with and without special needs. Apply the Concept 10-4 lists textbook adaptations that teachers may consider, three of which are discussed here in greater depth.

Study Guides Study guides are tools teachers can use to lead students through a reading assignment. A typical study guide is a series of questions or activities that emphasize important content information. Students complete study guides while they read a selection. Study guides help direct students to the key points to be learned. The study guide also provides an organizational structure for students to reflect about what they are reading and to engage in higher-order thinking. In short, study guides help to "tutor" a student through a chapter.

Commercially prepared study guides can be purchased or obtained through the Internet as supplements to some textbooks. The advantage of commercial study guides is that they are already prepared, so they are real time-savers. The disadvantage is that the publisher does not know a given teacher's style of teaching, emphasis, or school district's requirements. Moreover, the publisher does not know the students. For these reasons, many teachers construct their own study guides.

Many types of study guides exist. Some are designed to help students activate prior knowledge, others to help students understand literal or inferential information in the textbook, others to foster peer interaction and discussion, and still others to help students recognize meaning patterns in text (e.g., cause and effect, compare and contrast). Consider the following when developing a study guide:

- *Decide how a guide will assist the students with special needs.* Is the textbook information difficult for the students to access and understand? Are there particular sources of information (e.g., graphs and figures) that need to be interpreted? Will students with special needs require support and guidance to get through the chapter and to grasp the most important ideas?

10-4   Guidelines for Adapting Content Area Textbooks

Substitute the textbook for students who have severe word-recognition problems:

- Audiotape textbook content.
- Read textbook aloud to students.
- Pair students to master textbook content.
- Use direct experiences, films, videotapes, tape recorders, and computer programs as substitutes for textbook reading.
- Work with students individually or in small groups to master textbook material.

Simplify the textbook for students whose reading level is far below that of the textbook used in class:

- Construct abridged versions of the textbook content, or use the publisher's abridged version.
- Provide students with chapter outlines or summaries.
- Use a multilevel, multimaterial approach.

Highlight key concepts for students who have difficulty comprehending textbook material:

- Preview reading assignments with students to orient them to the topic and provide guidelines for budgeting reading and study time.
- Provide students with a purpose for reading.
- Provide an overview of an assignment before reading.
- Structure opportunities for students to activate prior knowledge before starting a reading assignment.
- Introduce key vocabulary before assigning reading.
- Develop a study guide to direct learning.
- Summarize or reduce textbook information to guide classroom discussions and independent reading.
- Color-code or highlight textbooks.
- Reduce the length of assignments.
- Slow down the pace of reading assignments.
- Provide assistance in answering text-based questions.

- Demonstrate or model effective reading strategies.
- Place students in cooperative learning groups to master textbook content.
- Teach comprehension-monitoring techniques to improve ongoing understanding of text material.
- Teach students to use graphic aids to understand textbook information.

Increase idea retention for students who have difficulty with long-term memory:

- Structure postreading activities to improve retention of content.
- Teach reading strategies to improve retention.
- Teach students to record key concepts and terms for study purposes.
- Teach memory strategies to improve retention of text material.

Source: Adapted from J. S. Schumm & K. Strickler (1991), Guidelines for adapting content area textbooks: Keeping teachers and students content, *Intervention in School and Clinic, 27* (2), pp. 79–84.

- *Analyze the chapter organization and content.* Can some parts be omitted? Are some parts easier to understand than others? What skills will students need to read and understand this material?
- *Decide how you want to structure your study guide.* Create one that includes the suggested components:
  - Specific information about the reading assignment (page numbers, title)
  - Learning objectives of the assignment
  - Purpose statement for the assignment
  - Introduction of key terms or vocabulary
  - Activities for students to complete
  - Questions for students to answer as they read
  - Sources and Web sites that might provide further information
  - Suggestions about how and when parents and other students can provide assistance

Text Highlighting Students with comprehension problems have difficulty sifting out important information. Underlining or highlighting key points in textbooks can

help students attend to the most salient information. Teachers can highlight the information in a textbook that they think is most important. Then students or adult volunteers can use this book as a guide to highlight the same information in books for students with reading and learning disabilities. Keep in mind that the teacher will also want to teach students this and other textbook study skills (see the section "Study Skills and Learning Strategies").

Using Alternative Reading Materials For students with very low reading skills who are able to learn by listening, the teacher can do the following:

- *Audiotape textbook chapters.* Some publishers provide cassettes or CDs with their textbooks. If the textbook you are using is not accompanied by an audio version, adult and/or student volunteers can read the chapters on audiotape. Students can then listen to the tapes at home or in their resource classes. Tech Tips provides ideas for using technology to aid in content area learning.

- *Read text aloud to students.* Encourage students to follow along, reading silently. Pause frequently to assess student learning from the reading.
- *Pair a good reader with a poor reader.* The good reader reads the textbook material aloud and, together, the two students learn the content. Both students should use self-monitoring comprehension strategies to ensure that both readers comprehend the text.
  - *Identify Web sites that teach.* Most students are comfortable using Web sites to acquire information, including video sites.

Sometimes teachers find it necessary to use alternative materials that present similar content, such as films, videotapes, and trade books. Computer software programs in which the text can be read by the computer, such as encyclopedias on CD-ROM, are other resources.

Teachers may also supplement textbooks with informational trade books (both fiction and nonfiction) and other reading materials (such as magazines and journals). By providing additional reading material that covers similar content to the textbook, teachers enable students who cannot read the textbook to access the content. People today discuss software programs in terms of their user-friendliness. Is the program easy to understand? Does the program use familiar language or at least define unfamiliar terms? Does the program give the user cue words or icons to signal the important ideas and processes? If the user does not understand something, does the program allow the user to ask questions? Does the program have more than one way to explain a difficult concept or process? If the program has these features, then one might consider it user-friendly.

Now take a minute to reread the previous paragraph, but substitute the word *lecture* for the word *program* and the word *listener* for the word *user.* Just as using considerate or user-friendly text assists students in learning the critical information, a well-organized lecture makes the students' work easier in that it assists them in seeing relationships among concepts and distinguishing important from supplementary information. It also helps them relate new information to old.

As teachers plan their teaching, the following guidelines can make lectures "listener-friendly":

- Use advance organizers.
- Preteach important vocabulary.
- Use cue words or phrases to let students know what information is important (e.g., "It is important that you know. . .," "The key information to remember is. . .," "In summary . . .").
- Repeat important information.
- Write important information on the board, a transparency, and/or a handout.
- Stress key points by varying the tone and quality of your voice.
- Number ideas or points (e.g., first, second, next, then, finally).
- Write technical words or words that are difficult to spell.
- Use a study guide that lists the major concepts, with space for students to add other information.
- Use pictures, concept diagrams, and content maps to show relationships among ideas.
- Provide examples and nonexamples of the concepts you are discussing.

 Tech TIPS

USING TECHNOLOGY TO SUPPORT LEARNING IN CONTENT AREAS

Learners with difficulties in reading and comprehending written text often experience failure in content area classes such as social studies and science. Although learners may be receiving support in their reading and writing skills, they also need support in their content area classes. There are many programs online that you can use in the classroom or that students can use on their own. Consider some of the following:

On-line science museum by the Smithsonian at
www.smithsonian.org/.
The Smithsonian Institution home page, with extensive links to art, design, history, culture, science, and technology collections, is a treasure trove of information for students looking to learn about content areas that will enrich their knowledge base.

Cast e-reader by CAST, Inc. at
www.cast.org.
This Web site uses the universal design framework for accommodating all learners. Using a wide array of technologies and media, this site allows educators to assess all students accurately and to provide instruction that will meet students' needs.

Bookshare by Benetech at
http://www.bookshare.org/.
For students with visual, learning, or physical disabilities, this site is an online library that provides access to online books, periodicals, newspapers, and textbooks. Once students provide proof of their disability, they may become eligible to become members of Bookshare.

- Ask questions and encourage discussion that requires students to relate the new information to ideas they already know (from their own background or your previous lectures).
- Stop frequently and have students discuss what they have learned with partners.
- Allow time at the end of a lecture for students to look over their notes, summarize, and ask questions.

Apply the Concept 10-5 provides cues that can assist students in "seeing" the key information. By using these guidelines, teachers will naturally incorporate cues that indicate what information is important.

One technique that has been effective for students with learning and behavior problems in enhancing their understanding and recall of information presented through lectures is the pause procedure (e.g., Dyson, 2008; Ruhl, 1996). This procedure consists of pausing during natural breaks in lectures and having students work as partners for about two minutes to discuss what they are learning and review their notes. Another way to implement the pause procedure is to give students a chance to write one thing they learned and to write one question. At the end of the two minutes, the teacher asks students whether they have

any questions or concepts that need further discussion or clarification. The teacher then resumes lecturing.

Adapting Class Assignments and Homework

One area in which students with learning and behavior problems often struggle is the completion of assignments and homework. In a survey of students with and without learning disabilities in grades 6–8, the students with learning disabilities had greater difficulty completing homework assignments because of problems with attention, motivation, and study skills (Gajria & Salend, 1995). Furthermore, students with special learning needs spend more time completing homework assignments than average-achieving students (Harniss, Epstein, Bursuck, Nelson, & Jayanthi, 2001). At the same time, homework has become a significant part of schooling. In the 1996 National Assessment of Educational Progress in math and science, more than half of all eighth and twelfth graders and nearly half of the fourth graders reported having at least 1 hour of homework every night (Bursuck et al., 1999), accounting for more than 20% of the time students spend on academic tasks (Cooper & Nye, 1994). In one survey, middle school students indicated that they preferred

●●●●●● *Apply the Concept* ●●●●●●

10-5	Cues to Listen and Watch for in Lectures

Type of Cue	Examples
Organizational cues	Today, we will be discussing . . .
	The topic I want to cover today . . .
	There are [number] points I want you to be sure to learn . . .
	The important relationship is . . .
	The main point of this discussion is . . .
	Any statement that signals a number or position (e.g., first, last, next, then).
	To review/summarize/recap . . .
Emphasis cues	
Verbal	You need to know/understand/remember . . .
	This is important/key/basic/critical . . .
	Let me repeat this . . .
	Let me check, now do you understand . . .
	Any statement is repeated.
	Words or terms are emphasized.
	Teacher speaks more slowly, more loudly, or with more emphasis.
	Teacher stresses certain words.
	Teacher spells words.
	Teacher asks rhetorical question.
Nonverbal	Information written on overhead/board.
	Information handed out in study guide.
	Teacher emphasizes the point using gestures.

Source: Adapted from S. K. Suritsky & C. A. Hughes, Note-taking strategy instruction, in D. D. Deshler, E. S. Ellis, & B. K. Lenz, *Teaching Adolescents with Learning Disabilities*, 2nd ed. (Denver, CO: Love, 1996), p. 275.

adaptations in which assignments are finished at school, extra credit is allowed, assignments are graded according to effort, and assignments are begun and checked for understanding in class (Nelson, Epstein, Bursuck, Jayanthi, & Sawyer, 1998). These same students were least supportive of adaptations in which shorter or different assignments were given to students with learning problems or these students' assignments were graded more easily.

After conducting a comprehensive review of the literature, Cooper and Nye (1994; Cooper, 2007) concluded that homework assignments for students with disabilities should be brief, focused on reinforcement rather than new material, monitored carefully, and supported through parental involvement. Especially for students with special needs, we do not want homework to result in a "battle" between parents and students. One way to prevent this is to is to give complete information for assignments. Having complete information helps to motivate students, as does giving them real-life assignments (i.e., assignments that connect homework to events or activities in the home) plus reinforcement, using homework planners, and graphing homework completion (Bryan & Sullivan-Burstein, 1998). The tips in Apply the Concept 10-6 can help teachers to provide students with a complete set of directions.

Class assignments and homework can be adapted for special learners so that they can experience success without undue attention being brought to their learning difficulties. The key to success is to make assignments appropriate in content, length, time required to complete, and skill level needed to accomplish the task. It is also important to explain the assignments, model several problems if appropriate, and check for understanding (Bender, 2008; Sawyer, Nelson, Jayanthi, Bursuck, & Epstein, 1996). Students should know how and where to get help if they get stuck.

Constructing and Adapting Tests

The best way to discover what students have learned is to construct student-friendly tests, adapt test administration and scoring as necessary, consider alternatives to testing (such as assessment portfolios), and teach test-taking skills. Student-friendly tests are considerate to the test taker in both content and format. The content has been covered in class or assigned readings, and students have been told explicitly that they are responsible for learning it. The format is clear and easy to understand.

To construct student-friendly tests, a teacher must first decide what skills and concepts to include. In the test format, directions should be clear and unambiguous, and items should be legible and properly spaced. Attention to format is important for all students, but particularly for those who have difficulty reading and taking tests and who are overly anxious about taking tests. Perhaps one of the most important things to consider with testing is time. Particularly for students with disabilities, most will need additional time to show what they know in a testing situation.

Even with student-friendly tests, students with learning and behavior problems may have difficulty reading tests, working within time constraints, or resisting distractions during a test. Poor or laborious writing can cause them to tire easily and can inhibit performance on a test. Apply the Concept 10-7 suggests accommodations for test administration and scoring. Nelson, Jayanthi, Epstein, and Bursuck (2000) examined student preferences for test adaptations in general education classrooms. Results revealed that the most preferred test adaptations involved providing assistive materials during a test (e.g., open-notes tests, open-book tests, dictionaries and calculators, extra answer space). In contrast, the least-preferred test adaptations involved differential assistance for students with

● ● ● ● ● ● *Apply the Concept* ● ● ● ● ● ●

10-6 — Tips for Giving Assignments

1. Explain the purpose of the assignment. Stress what you expect students to learn and why learning the skill or concept is important. Connect the skill or concept to real-life applications.
2. Explain in detail the procedures for completing the assignment. To check for understanding, ask one or two students to summarize the procedures.
3. Get students started by modeling one or two problems or by providing an example.
4. Describe the equipment and materials needed to complete the assignment.
5. Anticipate trouble spots, and ask students how they might tackle difficult parts in the assignment.
6. Explain when the assignment is due.
7. Explain how the assignment will be graded and how it will affect students' grades.
8. Describe appropriate ways to get help or support in completing the assignment.
9. For an in-class assignment, explain your expectations for student behavior while they complete the assignment and what students who finish early should do.
10. Address students' questions.

special needs (e.g., teacher reading of questions to students, tests with fewer questions, tests covering less material). More important, as teachers decide which, if any, adaptations to use, they should consider the material to be covered by the test, the test's task requirements

(e.g., reading, taking dictation), and the particular needs of special learners.

In addition to or instead of tests, teachers may use portfolios as an assessment tool. Apply the Concept 10-8 presents ideas for developing and using portfolios.

● ● ● ● ● ● ● *Apply the Concept* ● ● ● ● ● ●

10-7   Testing Accommodations

- Teach students test-taking skills.
- Give frequent quizzes rather than only exams.
- Give take-home tests.
- Test on less content than the rest of the class.
- Change types of questions (e.g., from essay to multiple choice).
- Give extended time to finish tests.
- Read test questions to students.
- Use tests with enlarged print.
- Highlight key words in questions.
- Provide extra space on tests for answering.

- Simplify wording of test questions.
- Allow students to answer fewer questions.
- Give extra help in preparing for tests.
- Give practice questions as a study guide.
- Give open-book and note tests.
- Give tests to small groups.
- Allow the use of learning aids during tests (e.g., calculators).
- Give individual help with directions during tests.

- Allow oral instead of written answers (e.g., tape recorders).
- Allow answers in outline format.
- Allow word processors.
- Grade for content, not for spelling and writing mechanics.
- Give feedback to individual students during tests.

Source: Adapted from M. Jayanthi, M. H. Epstein, E. A. Polloway, & W. D. Bursuck (1981), Testing adaptations: A national survey of the testing practices of general education teachers, *Journal of Special Education, 30,* pp. 99–115.

● ● ● ● ● ● ● *Apply the Concept* ● ● ● ● ● ●

10-8   Using Portfolios to Monitor Student Progress

Assessment portfolios are collections of work samples that document a student's progress in a content area. You can use portfolios to provide tangible evidence of student performance over a period of time. Portfolios can include writing samples of all stages of the writing process in all genres. Suggestions for developing assessment portfolios include the following:

- Develop a portfolio plan that is consistent with your purposes for the assignment.
- Clarify what work will go into portfolios.
- Start with only a couple of different kinds of entries, and expand gradually.
- Compare notes with other teachers as you experiment with portfolios.
- Make it a long-term goal to include a variety of assessments that address content, process, and attitude goals across the curriculum.

- Make portfolios accessible in the classroom. Students and teachers should be able to add to the collection quickly and easily.
- Develop summary sheets or graphs that help to describe a body of information (e.g., "I can do" lists, lists of books read, or pieces of writing completed). Let students record these data when possible.
- Work with students to choose a few representative samples that demonstrate the student's progress.
- Review portfolios with students periodically (at least four times during the school year). The review should be a time to celebrate progress and to set future goals.
- Encourage students to review portfolios with a classmate before reviewing with the teacher. Students should help to make decisions about what to keep.
- In preparation for a family conference, have students develop

a table of contents for the portfolio (Radencich, Beers, & Schumm, 1993, pp. 119–120).
Examples of items that can be included in a portfolio are as follows:

- Student assignments and work samples
- Student interviews
- Self-assessments
- Audiotapes
- Videotapes
- Diagnostic tests
- Achievement tests
- Teacher-made tests
- Pages from writing journals
- Awards
- Personal reading and writing records
- Interest and attitude inventories
- Photographs
- Copies of passages read fluently
- Contributions from parents
- Report cards
- List of accomplishments
- Observation checklists

Study Skills and Learning Strategies

What are the three types of study skills, and why are they important to learning? Even when teachers plan user-friendly lectures and make adaptations, students will still need to develop study skills and learning strategies. Particularly as students move into secondary and postsecondary settings, their tasks increasingly require time management, self-monitoring and feedback, listening and note taking, studying from textbooks, and test-taking skills. These study skills are particularly important in secondary settings since students' grades are often reliant on written products such as papers, reports, and tests.

Study skills are the competencies associated with acquiring, recording, organizing, synthesizing, remembering, and using information and ideas (Pauk, 2001). Study skills are the key to independent learning, and they help students gain and use information effectively. Study skills are particularly important in postsecondary settings, where students with dyslexia report that their greatest needs are in learning how to organize coursework, learning in lectures, and academic writing (Mortimer & Crozier, 2006).

Students with effective study skills can be characterized as executive learners (Schumm & Post, 1997; Olson, Platt, & Dieker, 2008) in that they

- are knowledgeable about personal learning strengths and challenges.
- have a clear understanding about tasks to be accomplished.
- have a repertoire of learning strategies that can be applied in independent learning situations.
- have developed a set of help-seeking behaviors to activate when additional assistance is needed.
- have independent note-taking skills for class lectures as well as for text reading.
- can organize and plan for the completion of assignments.

Study skills can be divided into three areas:

1. *Personal development skills:* personal discipline, management and organizational skills, self-monitoring and reinforcement, and positive attitudes toward studying
2. *Process skills:* technical methods of studying such as note taking, outlining, learning information from a text, and library reference skills
3. *Expression skills:* retrieval skills, test-taking skills, and using oral and/or written expression to demonstrate understanding

As one would expect, these are the very skills and strategies that students with learning and behavior problems have difficulty developing. This may be because they require explicit and ongoing instruction in how to use study skills practices during class, for independent assignments, and for class planning.

Personal Development Skills

Personal development skills include personal discipline, goal setting, management and organizational skills, self-monitoring and reinforcement, and positive attitudes toward studying. Many of the personal development skills related to school focus on time management, scheduling, organization, self-monitoring, and reinforcement.

Time Management and Scheduling Jon's mother is concerned because Jon, who has learning disabilities, falls asleep while trying to finish book reports the night before they are due. Even if she gets him up early in the morning, there is little chance that he will have time to finish. Even though he knows about the assignments in advance, he waits until they are due to start reading, despite his mom's queries about homework. Granted, it takes Jon longer than the other students to complete assignments, but his teacher gives him the assignments early. He has the skills to get a B or a C if he would just start working on assignments earlier.

Many families and teachers can identify with this scenario. Jon has the skills to complete assignments successfully, but he lacks personal management skills, particularly time management. Teaching a unit on time management at the beginning of the year and then reinforcing students during the year for the effective use of time can be well worth the effort.

Building a Rationale The first step in getting students to schedule and manage their time is to build a rationale for its importance to success in school and later life. Discuss the following ideas with your students to build a rationale for effective time management:

- Parents/guardians will get off your back when they see that you are getting your work done on time.
- If you write down what you have to do, you don't have to try to remember everything.
- If you set a time to begin, it is easier to get started and not procrastinate.
- When you set a time frame to complete an assignment, it helps you work for a goal and concentrate.
- When you have a schedule, you're less likely to let a short break become a long break.
- Being in control of time makes you feel that you have more control of your life.
- When you get assignments and jobs done on time, then you can really enjoy your free time.
- Scheduling your time helps you to get jobs done and have more time for fun and your friends.

Determining How the Time Is Spent Before students can decide how to schedule their time, they need to determine how they are currently spending it. Using a schedule, have students keep track of their activities for 1 or 2 weeks. Also have them list the school assignments they have for the time period and whether they have "too little," "enough," or "too much" time to complete them.

Estimating Time As part of the time management process, have students determine how long it takes them to complete regularly scheduled tasks such as meals, going to and from school, reading assignments in their various textbooks, writing a paragraph on a topic, and completing a 10-problem math assignment. Although there will probably be considerable variability in the time taken to complete a task, most students with learning and behavior problems underestimate the time it takes. Having students get an idea of the time required can be helpful in planning a schedule. This step will also help students identify and prioritize tasks that need to be completed.

Scheduling If students do not have enough time to get their tasks completed or if they do not have regular times for studying, encourage them to set up a schedule. Some suggestions that students might want to use when setting up their schedules are as follows:

1. Plan regular study times.
2. Plan at least 1-hour blocks of time in which to study.
3. Plan which assignments you are going to work on during study time.
4. Take the first 5 minutes of each study activity to review what you have done already and what you have learned, and to plan what you are going to accomplish today. This helps to promote long-term learning and a sense of accomplishment.
5. When studying longer than 1 hour, plan breaks and stick to the time allowed for the breaks.
6. Use daytime or early evening for study if possible. Most people work less efficiently at night.
7. Work on your most difficult subjects when you are most alert.
8. Distribute your studying for a test over several days rather than cramming the night before the test.
9. Balance your time between studying and other activities. Allow time for recreational activities.
10. Reward yourself by marking through your schedule each time you meet a scheduled commitment and by crossing off items you complete on your to-do list.

Not only should regular times for studying be listed on the schedule, but due dates for assignments and dates for other events should also be noted so that the schedule serves as a calendar. Students should be encouraged to set aside some time they can use as they please if they accomplish their tasks on schedule during the day or week. This type of self-determined reinforcer can serve as an extra motivation for some students.

Monitoring and Using a To-Do List Setting up a schedule does little good unless students follow and monitor their schedules. Teachers can have students fill in the activities they feel are important to monitor on a weekly schedule. Figure 10-11 presents a schedule and to-do list for Jon. His study time, time spent working out, and recreational time were the most important tasks for him to monitor, so he scheduled them in each week. He also noted when the next book report was due and used his to-do list to schedule other assignments and chores, crossing off tasks as they were accomplished.

Jon developed a contract with himself. If he studied at least 80% of the time he had scheduled during the week, then he could work out at the gym or goof off 2 extra hours on Saturday. In this way, Jon was not only monitoring his schedule, but also setting goals and providing rewards for meeting his goals. After 2 weeks, Jon's teacher encouraged him to review his deadlines and adjust his schedule based on how he had done over the past 2 weeks. While Jon had met his goal of studying 80% of the scheduled time, he still did not complete all his tasks. He had to adjust his goal in order to complete all of this work on time. Although Jon realized that schedules need to be flexible, he found that planning, even when plans change, helped him to get more work accomplished in a timely manner.

Self-Monitoring and Reinforcement Students with learning and behavior problems have difficulty setting goals and self-monitoring, whether it be in the areas of attention and memory, reading comprehension, or personal and management skills (Schumm & Avalos, 2009). Van Reusen and Bos (1990) developed a strategy that students can use to assist them in setting goals and keeping track of their progress. The strategy uses the acrostic MARKER (it gives students a *mark* to work toward and is a *marker* of their progress) and includes the following steps:

Make a list of goals, set the order, set the date.
Arrange a plan for each goal and predict your success.
Run your plan for each goal and adjust if necessary.
Keep records of your progress.
Evaluate your progress toward each goal.
Reward yourself when you reach a goal, and set a new goal.

For each goal, students use a goal-planning sheet (see Figure 10-12) to answer the following questions:

- Can I describe my goal?
- What is the reason or purpose for the goal?
- What am I going to do first, second, and third to complete this goal?
- How much time do I have to complete the goal?
- What materials do I need to complete the goal?
- Can I divide the goal into steps or parts? If so, in what order should I complete each step or part?

NAME: ___Jon___

WEEK OF: ___Oct 14___

	MON.	TUES.	WEDS.	THURS.	FRI.	SAT.	SUN.	
6:00 a.m.	get up and eat ——————→							6:00 a.m.
7:00	ride bus —————————→					sleep	sleep	7:00
8:00								8:00
9:00	History					house & yard chores		9:00
10:00	English PE	*Some every day*					go to church	10:00
11:00	Welding							11:00
12:00	Lunch						eat	12:00
1:00 p.m.	Algebra					eat	read for fun	1:00 p.m.
2:00	General Science					go to gym		2:00
3:00	ride bus						goof off and eat	3:00
4:00								4:00
5:00	recreational activity		study		eat have fun	eat and have fun		5:00
6:00	eat ————————————→							6:00
7:00	study	study	study	study			study	7:00
8:00								8:00
9:00				↓			↓	9:00
10:00	sleep ——————————→						sleep	10:00
11:00	↓				sleep ——→		↓	11:00

TO-DO LIST						
history paper due math assign finish book	math assign	math assign book report due	math assign welding project due	science test math test	chores mow grass pull weeds fix cooler	start English paper

---

- How am I going to keep records of my progress?
- How will I reward myself for reaching my goal?

___For more on the Strategies Intervention Model, see Chapter 2.___

The teacher can use the steps in the Strategies Intervention Model to teach the students the MARKER strategy. After learning the strategy, students usually work on one to three goals at a time, keeping progress data on each goal.

When Van Reusen and Bos (1992) used this strategy with middle and high school students with learning disabilities and behavior disorders, they found that students accomplished more goals and gained a more informed perspective of their educational and personal goals.

Hughes and his colleagues (Hughes, Ruhl, Deshler, & Schumaker, 1995) developed an assignment completion strategy for the Strategies Intervention Model that is similar. The steps in this learning strategy are as follows:

*P*sych up. Prepare your assignment-monitoring form and your mind.
*R*ecord and ask. Record the assignment, think about it, and ask questions.

► **Figure 10-12** Goal-Planning and -Monitoring Sheet

Name: _____ Class: _____ Date: _____

1. Goal: _____

2. Reason(s) for working on goal: _____

3. Goal will be worked on at: _____

4. Date to reach goal (due date): _____

5. Materials needed: _____

_____

6. Steps used to reach the goal: _____

_____

_____

7. Progress toward the goal: Record in each box the date and progress rating.

   3—Goal reached   2—Good progress made   1—Some progress made   0—No progress made

Date / Rating					

8. Reward for reaching goal: _____

Source: Adapted from A. K. Van Reusen & C. S. Bos, *Use of the Goal-Regulation Strategy to Improve the Goal Attainment of Students with Learning Disabilities* (Final Report) (Tucson: University of Arizona, 1992).

Organize. Break the assignment into parts, estimate and schedule the number of study sessions, and organize your materials.

Jump to it. Survey the assignment, and set goals and a reward.

Engage in the work. Follow the instructions, note questions, and get help if you need it.

Check the work. Check for requirements and quality, store the assignment, and reward yourself.

Turn it in. Take it to class, turn it in, record the date, and praise yourself.

Set your course. Record your grade, evaluate your assignment, and think about future assignments.

Classroom Participation Students who actively participate in class tend to be more successful academically than their quieter, less attentive peers. Students with learning and behavior problems may benefit from specific strategies to enhance their classroom participation. The SLANT strategy is part of the Strategies Intervention Model and was designed to increase active participation in class. The acrostic SLANT stands for the following:

Sit up.
Lean forward.
Activate your thinking.
Name key information.
Track the talker.

Examples of activating your thinking include asking yourself questions (What is this about? What do I need to remember?), answering your questions (This is about _____. I need to remember _____.), and asking the teacher a question when you do not understand. Examples of naming key information include answering the teacher's questions, sharing your ideas, and additions to other's comments (Ellis, 1991). This general set of activities can be used in any learning situation to improve students' active participation.

An important part of assignment completion and class participation in inclusive classrooms is recruiting positive teacher attention. Students with learning and behavior problems often get the teacher's attention for their negative behaviors rather than their positive behaviors in class. Using instruction, role play, and reinforcement, one special education teacher taught four middle school students with learning disabilities to recruit positive teacher attention in their general education classrooms (Alber, Heward, & Hippler, 1999). Students were taught to raise their hands and wait quietly or at an appropriate time to ask such questions as "How am I doing?" or "I don't understand" or "Would you please look at my work?" Observations in the general education classrooms demonstrated that students increased their amount of positive teacher recruiting and teachers increased their rate of student praise. Teaching students strategies for self-monitoring, self-reinforcement, and classroom participation is an important part of the special education curriculum in that these skills, like study skills, support student success in the general education classroom and curriculum.

Process Skills

Process skills include the technical methods of studying such as note taking, outlining, learning information from text, and research and library skills.

Listening and Taking Notes In school, students spend more time listening than reading, speaking, or writing. On the average, teachers in secondary settings spend at least half of their class time presenting information through lectures (Putnam, Deshler, & Schumaker, 1993). Furthermore, teachers rely on information presented in class discussion and lectures as the basis for a significant number of items on tests (Putnam et al., 1993). Note taking is one of the most efficient ways to record this information and retrieve it in one's own words. It has several important functions:

- Note taking increases students' attention.
- Note taking, as opposed to simply listening, requires a deeper level of cognitive processing in that students must make sense of the information to write the ideas.
- Because the information has been processed more deeply, note taking helps students learn and remember the information more easily.

Even if students do not go back and review their notes, just the act of taking notes results in greater recall of information on tests.

Students with learning and behavior problems often have difficulties with listening and taking notes. For some students with severe writing disabilities, it will be important that they have a note taker. Lightweight laptop computers or devices designed specifically for taking notes are also very beneficial if students are instructed in how to use them. Students with learning disabilities may have difficulty with the following:

- Paying attention
- Writing fast and legibly
- Deciding what information to write
- Spelling
- Making sense of notes after the lecture

Given the importance of taking notes and the difficulty some students encounter with this skill, teachers will want to teach students how to take notes and consider using listener-friendly lectures to make note taking easier.

Teaching Students to Take Notes Note taking is a procedure that requires students to listen, interpret, organize, and record information. Therefore, students with limited reading and study skills often feel overwhelmed when they must take notes. Numerous formats for note taking have been suggested (see for review; Kobayashi, 2006). One aspect that these systems have in common is the focus on making note taking and reviewing an interactive learning process (Schumm et al., 2009). To facilitate this interactive process, two- and three-column note-taking systems have been developed. Figure 10-13 gives an example of each system. Students take class notes in the second column in both systems, using only the front side of the paper. Modified outlining is the format that is most often suggested for taking these notes. In both systems, students note the key concepts in the left-hand column, sometimes referred to as *triggers,* since they are meant to trigger the ideas noted in the class-notes column. Later, in reviewing, students should be able to cover the second column and use their personal triggers to help them remember the ideas covered in the class notes. In three-column systems, the additional column generally serves as a space to write textbook notes so that they can be integrated with class notes. This is most helpful when the teacher's lectures make frequent, direct ties to the textbook. It is also important to teach some students note-taking subskills such as using abbreviations, diagrams to related ideas, or visual markers and editing notes.

The following list gives several hints for helping students to develop efficient note-taking skills:

- Take notes using a two- or three-column system.
- Take notes on only one side of the paper.
- Date and label the topic of the notes.
- Generally use a modified outline format, indenting subordinate ideas and numbering ideas when possible.
- Skip lines to note changes in ideas.
- Don't worry about punctuation or grammar.
- Write ideas or key phrases, not complete sentences.
- Don't write down every word the teacher says.
- Use pictures and diagrams to relate ideas.

▶ **Figure 10-13** Formats for Note Taking

Sample Two-Column System	
Topic: _____ Date: _____	
Triggers or Key Concepts	Class Notes

Sample Three-Column System		
Topic: _____ Date: _____		
Triggers or Key Concepts	Class Notes	Text Notes

- Use consistent abbreviations (e.g., w/ = with, & = and).
- Put question marks by any points you don't understand. Check them later with the teacher.
- Underline or asterisk information that the lecturer stresses as important.
- Write down information that the lecturer writes on the board or transparency.
- If you miss an idea you want to include, draw a blank (_____) so that you can go back and fill it in.
- If you cannot automatically remember how to spell a word, spell it the way it sounds or the way you think it looks.
- If possible, review the previous sessions' notes right before the lecture.
- If the lecture is about an assigned reading topic, read the information before listening to the lecture.
- As soon as possible after the lecture, go over your notes, filling in the Key Concepts column and listing any questions you still have.
- After going over your notes, try to summarize the major points presented during the lecture.
- Listen actively. In other words, think about what you already know about the topic being presented and how it relates.
- Review your notes before a test.

Direct Instruction in Note Taking Regardless of the note-taking format chosen, a teacher should provide direct instruction in note taking. Direct instruction should include explicit demonstrations of the note-taking process and ample opportunities for students to practice with guidance and feedback. For many students with learning and behavior problems, telling them how to take notes is insufficient; note-taking practice is key. Teachers may want to develop and conduct a unit on listening and note taking. The following is a list of teaching ideas for developing such a unit:

1. *Have students evaluate the effectiveness of their current note-taking skills and determine whether they will profit from instruction.* Generally, this can be assessed in two ways. First, have students bring to class current examples of notes, and have them evaluate the notes for completeness, format, ease of use for review, and legibility. Apply the Concept 10-9 presents one way that students can evaluate their own notes. Second, present a simulated 10- to 15-minute lecture or a videotape of a lecture, and ask the students to take notes. Give a test covering the information on the following day. Have the students again evaluate their notes and their test results.

2. *Use videotaped lectures when teaching students to listen effectively and to take notes.* The use of videotaped lectures is particularly helpful because it allows the students to replay the tape so that they can watch or listen for main ideas. For example, you may be teaching students to watch and listen for cues the lecturer gives to note the important information. After listening to a short segment of videotape, have the students list the cues and then discuss why they are important. Then replay the segment so that students can verify their list of cues and add other cues.

3. *Control the difficulty of the lectures.* When first introducing new listening or note-taking skills such as listening for cues or using a two-column system, begin with short, well-organized lectures with ample use of advance organizers and visual aids, covering fairly simple, relatively familiar materials. As students reach proficiency, gradually increase the length of the lectures, reduce the use of organizers and visual

Apply the Concept

10-9 — Note-Taking Inventory

From time to time, it's smart to check the quality of your notes to see how you're doing. Then you'll know if you need to make any changes or improvements. Use this Note-Taking Inventory whenever you feel the need. Simply check it against that day's class notes.

You'll need a piece of paper something to write with. Number the paper from 1–10. Give yourself one point for each item you find in your notes.

1. Date of lecture
2. Title of lecture
3. Writing neat enough for you to read (that's all that counts)
4. No more than one idea per line
5. Plenty of blank space to add extra ideas later
6. All main ideas brought up during class
7. All important details mentioned during class
8. All key terms and definitions given during class
9. Abbreviations used where necessary
10. No unnecessary words

Scoring: Add up your points.

9–10 points: You're a great note taker!
7–8 points: You're a good note taker!
5–6 points: You need to take better notes.
4 points or less: Make a note of this—practice, practice, practice.

Source: J. S. Schumm (2001), *School Power: Study Skill Strategies for Succeeding in School*, (Minneapolis, MN: Free Spirit Publishing, Inc).

aids, and increase the difficulty and novelty levels of the materials.

4. *Have students learn how to review their notes for tests*. Although students may learn to take more effective notes, they may fail to use the notes to study for tests. Teach students how to review their notes and ask themselves questions, using the Triggers column to develop questions about the material in the Class Notes column.

5. *Have students monitor the use and effectiveness of note taking in other classes*. To increase the probability that students will generalize the note-taking skills to other classes, have them discuss in which classes the skills would be helpful and then have them monitor and discuss their effectiveness in those classes.

6. *Have students determine the effects that note taking has on learning*. Students need to know that there is a payoff for their increased effort. Have students rate how well they feel they have taken notes over a unit or lecture, and have them monitor their performance on tests of the material. This will aid them in determining whether better note taking leads to better learning.

Overall, note taking and reviewing notes is associated with better performance and more learning (Kobayashi, 2006).

Learning from Text Probably the best-known technique for learning information from text is SQ3R, developed by Robinson (1946). This acronym stands for the five steps in this study skill: Survey, Question, Read, Recite, Review. The purpose of this technique is to provide students with a systematic approach to studying text. The following is a brief description of each one of the five steps in the process (Robinson, 1946):

> *Survey*. Read through the headings quickly to learn what is to be studied.
> *Question*. Change each heading into a question (to have in mind what is to be learned from the reading).
> *Read*. Read to answer the question.
> *Recite*. At the end of each heading, either write brief notes about the highlights of the reading or engage in self-recitation.
> *Review*. After completing the above steps on the entire selection, review the main points of the notes by self-recitation. Check to see if the information is correct.

One of the major difficulties associated with the SQ3R method is the complexity of the process, particularly for students who are experiencing reading problems. In content area classes, these students are often attempting to read and learn information from textbooks that are written above their instructional reading levels. A modified version that uses only read, recite, and review has been implemented with effective results with secondary students and may hold promise with older readers (McDaniel, Howard, & Einstein, 2009).

Multipass Schumaker, Deshler, Alley, Warner, and Denton (1982) developed a strategy based on SQ3R that incorporates the learning acquisition and generalization stages from the Strategies Intervention Model for students who experience problems learning information from textbooks. This strategy is referred to as Multipass because students make three passes through a text while carrying out the process. Each pass through the text (i.e., Survey, Size-Up, and Sort-Out) entails the use of a different substrategy. Because each substrategy represents a fairly complex set of behaviors, each of the substrategies is taught as a unit, with students reaching proficiency in the first substrategy before learning the next substrategy. Prerequisite skills include the ability to paraphrase and a reading level of fourth grade or above. Research conducted with eight high school students with learning disabilities indicated that the students were able to master the strategy in instructional-level materials and were able to use the strategy in grade-level materials without further training or practice. The students' grade on content tests improved—from barely passing to a grade of C or better.

  EVIDENCE-BASED PRACTICE

Multipass

PROCEDURES: During the Survey Pass, students become familiar with the main ideas and organization of the chapter (Deshler, Schumaker, & McKnight, 1997; Hock & Mellard, 2005). In completing the Survey Pass, students complete the following steps:

1. *Title*. Read the chapter title. Think about how it fits with what you have already studied. Predict what the chapter will be about.

2. *Introduction*. Read the introduction, and make a statement about the main idea of the chapter. If there is no introduction, read the first paragraph, which is usually the introduction.

3. *Summary*. Turn to the last page of the chapter, read the summary, and make a summary statement. If there is no summary, check the last paragraph to see whether it is a summary. If it is not a summary, make a mental note so that you can summarize later.

4. *Organization*. Look through the chapter to see how the chapter is organized. Use the major headings to make a written outline. Paraphrase each heading.

5. *Pictures, maps, charts*. Look at the illustrations. Think about why they might have been included.

6. *Table of Contents*. Determine how this chapter fits in with the other information in the book by perusing the table of contents. Decide what relationships this chapter has with the others, especially the chapters immediately preceding and following it. For example, in a history book, chapters are often related because of chronological sequence. Chapters might also have

a causal relationship (e.g., perhaps Chapter 6 talks about the causes of the Depression and Chapter 7 talks about its effects). Other types of frequently occurring relationships include general/specific, compare/contrast, and related concepts.

After completing this process, close the book, and think about what the chapter is going to be about and what you already know about the topic.

Using the strategies intervention model, the teacher first describes and then models this survey process. Students should practice with guidance and feedback in materials at their reading instructional level until they are effective and efficient at surveying a chapter.

During the Size-Up Pass, students gain more specific information from the chapter without reading the chapter from beginning to end. Whereas the Survey Pass provides a general framework for the chapter, the Size-Up Pass allows the students to look for the information that fits into that general framework using textual cues. In learning the Size-Up Pass, students complete the following steps:

1. *Illustrations.* Again look over the pictures, maps, and charts, and read the captions. Think about why they are included.
2. *Questions.* Read the questions, including those found at the beginning or interspersed in the chapter. If you can already answer a study question, put a check mark by it.
3. *Words.* Read over the vocabulary words, including any vocabulary list and words highlighted in the chapter.
4. *Headings.* Read a heading. Ask yourself a question that you think will be answered in the section. Scan for the answer. When you find the answer, paraphrase it orally, or state something that you have learned from the information under the heading. Note on your outline what information you have learned from the section.

As with the Survey Pass, the teacher needs to describe the Size-Up process, and the students should practice in instructional-level material until they are proficient.

During the third and final pass, the Sort-Out Pass, students test themselves on the material in the chapter. This pass assists them in determining what they have learned and on what information they should still concentrate. In the final pass, the students read and answer each question at the end of the chapter, using the following process:

1. *Read.* Read the study question at the end of the chapter or each question provided by the teacher.
2. *Answer.* Answer the question if you can.
3. *Mark.* If you can answer a question, put a check by it; if you cannot answer it, put a box in front of it. If you do not know the answer, scan the headings on your outline to determine in which section it most likely will be answered. When you find the likely

section, look for the answer. If you find the answer, paraphrase it and check the box. If you do not find the answer, scan the headings a second time for another likely place to find the answer. Again, look for the answer, and paraphrase it if you find it. If you do not find the answer after trying twice, circle the box so that you know you need to come back to it later and possibly get help.

As in the other two steps, the students should practice with materials at their instructional level until they are effective and efficient at answering questions about the material presented in the chapter.

COMMENTS: From the description of Multipass, it should be clear that when students use this strategy, they do not have to read a text in its entirety. Instead, they study the text to determine the main ideas, its overall framework, and related details and to answer the study questions. In this way, students can use this strategy with textbooks that are written above their instructional level. However, several cautionary notes are in order. First, remember to have the students reach proficiency on each substrategy before they begin learning the next substrategy. Second, when the difference between the students' instructional reading level and reading level of the textbook is greater than 1 to 2 years, students may have difficulty moving from instructional-level materials to grade-level materials. Teachers will generally need to provide graduated instructional materials. (For example, Hector's instructional reading level is fifth grade, and he is a ninth grader. Hector will probably need to practice using the strategy in seventh-grade material as an intermediary step.) Third, do not expect students with learning and behavior problems to transfer this study strategy automatically to various content area textbooks. You will need to instruct for generalization.

Expression Skills

Expression skills include memory, retrieval, and test-taking skills, as well as other oral and/or written expression skills that are used to demonstrate understanding and application of knowledge.

Remembering Information Have you ever arrived at the grocery store without your grocery list? What strategies do you use to help you remember what was on the list? Maybe you know how many items were on the list, and now you just need to find out how many of them you can recall. Or maybe you read the list over several times, almost rehearsing it, so it was easier to recall. Or you might use association by thinking of the meals that you were planning for the next few days and trying to associate the needed items with the meals. Or you might visualize your kitchen and quickly think about the refrigerator and each cabinet and the items needed for each. Finally, you might categorize the items on the basis of the sections in the grocery store (e.g., produce, cereal, dairy products, frozen foods). Clearly, there are many strategies for remembering information.

In many ways, remembering information for a test is similar to remembering the items on a grocery list. Often we are asked to remember a list of things (e.g., the major exports of the United Kingdom, the different kinds of flour and their uses, the names of the cranial nerves). During tests, we may be asked to take this information and apply it to specific situations (e.g., to explain why the U.K. economy is struggling), but we still need to remember the basic information.

Students with disabilities often have difficulty memorizing information, whether it be for tests, presentations, or written work. Sometimes the students do not understand the information to be learned, but in other cases poor performance may be due to difficulties with retrieval of the information, failure to use deliberate memory strategies, and/or poor motivation for school tasks (Swanson, Howard, & Saez, 2006). Research suggests that these students also have difficulty with metamemory (i.e., awareness of memory strategies and the ability to use and monitor these strategies) in that they have trouble with one or more of the following:

- Knowing, selecting, and using appropriate strategies
- Estimating their own memory capacity for specific tasks
- Predicting accuracy on a memory task
- Allotting appropriate time to study
- Deciding when they have studied enough

Consequently, it is important to teach students memory strategies and tricks for remembering. Because teachers regularly ask students to remember information (e.g., for tests, class discussions), it is relatively easy to incorporate teaching memory strategies into the content curriculum. Incorporating the general teaching principles presented in Apply the Concept 10-10 makes the information more memorable and encourages learning and remembering the information.

Many content area learning strategies such as semantic mapping, advance organizers, and SFA can be thought of as teaching procedures that facilitate memory. In addition to these kinds of activities, a number of formal strategies have been deliberately designed to improve memory. These are often referred to as *mnemonics*.

Mnemonics are strategies for improving memorization. The word *mnemonics* literally means "aids memory." Mnemonics aid memory and retrieval by forming associations that do not exist naturally in the content (Eggen & Kauchak, 1992). To use mnemonics, the information needs to be distilled so that the students are learning conceptual lists or frameworks. The students then operate on this information by using mnemonics. Mnemonic strategies can be grouped into three types: organization and association, visualization, and verbal rehearsal.

Organization and Association Organizing and associating information refers to arranging the information or associating it with other information in such a way that it is easier to remember. Study the following list of terms in order to remember them:

Democracy	Mammals
Socket wrench	Judiciary
Biology	Anatomy
Photosynthesis	Drill press
Lathe	Blowtorch
Freedom of speech	Constitution

Chances are that you categorized the words according to three superordinate categories, possibly labeled *tools, science concepts,* and *social studies concepts.* Now, instead of learning 12 unrelated words, you are learning three sets of 4 related words. Research shows that the second task is considerably easier. Research and practice have also demonstrated that students experiencing learning problems do not tend to make these associations spontaneously (Mastropieri, Scruggs, & Marshak, 2008). Therefore, one mnemonic strategy to teach students when they are trying to remember lists of information is to associate or categorize related ideas.

●●●●●●● *Apply the Concept* ●●●●●●●

10-10 General Teaching Principles for Increasing Students' Memory of Information

- Orient student attention before presenting information, and emphasize important vocabulary and concepts when they occur.
- Activate prior knowledge, and help students to make connections between old and new knowledge.
- Use visual aids such as graphic organizers to highlight the important information and make it more memorable.
- Control the amount of information presented; group related ideas.
- Control the rate at which the information is presented.
- Provide time to review, rehearse, and elaborate on the information.
- Teach the students how to use and apply memory strategies and devices.
- Provide time and guidance in developing associations and mnemonics such as acronyms and acrostics.
- Provide opportunities for distributed review of information and encourage mastery.

Another type of association is the use of acrostics and acronyms. *Acrostics* are sentences made of words that begin with the first letters of a series of words. For examples of acrostics, see SLANT, MARKER, and COMPARING in this chapter.

Acronyms are words or abbreviations that are created by joining the first letters of a series of words (or just the major words in a series). Examples are *radar* (radio detecting and ranging), *scuba* (self-contained underwater breathing apparatus), *laser* (light amplification by stimulated emission of radiation); and *FBI* (Federal Bureau of Investigation). If needed, extra letters can be inserted, or the letters can be rearranged. This technique has been used extensively in the development of learning strategies for students with learning and behavior problems (Deshler, Ellis, & Lenz, 1996). By teaching students to construct acronyms and acrostics, sharing them in class, and then cueing students to use them when they study and take tests, you help them to learn and retrieve information.

The FIRST-letter mnemonic strategy (Nagel, Schumaker, & Deshler, 1994) is one way to help students construct lists of information to memorize and develop an acronym or acrostic for learning and remembering the information. The strategy includes an overall strategy (LISTS) and a substrategy for making the mnemonic device (FIRST). The steps in the overall strategy include the following:

*L*ook *for clues*. In the class notes and textbooks, look for lists of information that are important to learn. Name or give a heading to each list.
*I*nvestigate the items. Decide which items should be included in the list.
*S*elect a mnemonic device, using FIRST. Use the FIRST substrategy, explained next, to construct a mnemonic.
*T*ransfer the information to a card. Write the mnemonic and the list on one side of a card and the name of the list on the other side of the card.
*S*elf-test. Study by looking at the heading using the mnemonic to recall the list.

To complete the Select step, students use the FIRST strategy to design an acronym or acrostic:

*F*orm a word. Using uppercase letters, write the first letter of each word in the list; see whether an acronym—a recognizable word or nonsense word—can be made.
*I*nsert a letter or letters. Insert one or more letters to see whether a word can be made. (Be sure to use lowercase letters so that you know they do not represent an item on the list—BACk, for example.)
*R*earrange the letters. Rearrange the letters to see whether a word can be made.
*S*hape a sentence. Using the first letter of each word in the list, try to construct a sentence (an acrostic).

*T*ry combinations. Try combinations of these steps to generate the mnemonic.

This strategy is taught by using the Strategies Intervention Model. It can be used with most content but is particularly effective with science and social studies, in which lists of information are to be learned. The strategy provides a systematic method for students to review text and class notes, construct lists, and develop acronyms and acrostics that help them to remember and retrieve information.

Visualization and Key-Word Method Another strategy that is helpful in remembering information is visualization. Visualization is making a mental image of what you want to remember. Sometimes the visual image is simply the information that needs to be remembered. For example, it is not unusual to notice students closing their eyes when they are trying to remember how to spell a word. They may be using visualization to recall "what the word looks like."

If the information is complex, however, it may be helpful for the students to change the image of what they want to remember into a picture that will trigger or cue the information. One strategy used to do this is the *key-word method* (e.g., Mastropieri, Sweda, & Scruggs, 2000; Scruggs, Mastropieri, Berkeley, & Graetz, 2009). Using this visualization strategy, students construct a picture that represents an interactive relationship between a concept and its definition. Figure 10-14 shows a key-word picture generated for the concept of *allegro* and its definition (i.e., to move quickly). This picture is used to link the vocabulary word with the definition using key words that together sound like the vocabulary word. In Figure 10-14, *leg* and *row* are the key words used to construct a picture that triggers the definition of *allegro*.

▶ **Figure 10-14** Key-Word Picture Generated for the Concept *Allegro*

Source: C. A. Hughes, Memory and test-taking strategies, in D. D. Deshler, E. S. Ellis, & B. K. Lenz, *Teaching Adolescents with Learning Disabilities*, 2nd ed. (Denver, CO: Love, 1996), p. 223. Reprinted with permission.

The following steps are suggested for creating the key-word picture (King-Sears, Mercer, & Sindelar, 1992) and use the acrostic IT FITS:

Identify the word or term.
Tell the definition or answer information.
Find a key word that sounds like the new word or the word you need to remember.
Imagine an interaction, that is, something that the key word and the answer information can do together. If you draw a sketch of the interaction, you may review it later for improved memory.
Think about the key word and the interaction.
Study your vocabulary and the information, using your key word to help you remember. Review by asking for each item: What was my key word for [word]? What was happening in my picture [or image]? What is the information I am supposed to remember?

The key-word method is most effective in increasing the recall of information by students with learning disabilities when the key-word relationships are presented to the students rather than having individual students generate them (Fulk, Mastropieri, & Scruggs, 1992). Students should have ample opportunities to create key-word associations as a class or in cooperative groups before having students work individually.

Verbal Rehearsal Repeating the information aloud or to yourself can help to facilitate memory. Verbal rehearsal is the major cognitive strategy that is used to enhance short-term memory (Hughes, 1996; Loomes, Rasmussen, Pei, Manji, & Andrew, 2008). Rehearsal is most effective if there is limited interference between the time of the rehearsal and the time of recall, the number of items to be remembered is limited, and the information is clustered or chunked.

General Memory Strategies Often several mnemonics are used simultaneously. For example, after you have categorized the words in a list, you can use acronyms and acrostics within each category to help you remember the specific words and then use rehearsal to practice, review, and test your memory. Teaching students with learning and behavior problems which strategies to use for which types of information and how to combine strategies is generally necessary. In addition to teaching students how to use the various memory strategies, it is also important to teach students to use periodic review to minimize forgetting.

Studying and Taking Tests

Studying and taking tests are important aspects of secondary schools. Tests are the primary means that teachers use to determine whether students have learned new concepts and can apply them. For example, Putnam (1992a) surveyed 120 English, science, social studies, and mathematics teachers of grades 7 to 12 to determine how frequently they used tests. In a 9-week grading period, students were expected to take an average of 11 tests in each content area. On the average, teachers used scores on tests to determine approximately half of a grade for a course. Although a great deal of effort is placed on tests to measure learning, only 25% of the teachers surveyed indicated that they taught strategies for taking tests. Yet research on students with disabilities and at-risk students indicates that they have limited study and test-taking strategies to employ (Hughes & Schumaker, 1991; Scruggs & Mastropieri, 1988). For example, the only strategy college students with learning disabilities regularly reported using when taking objective tests was skipping over difficult or unknown items. For essay questions, only half the students reported rereading questions or proofreading their responses.

Studying for Tests Studying for tests means that students should be reviewing information on a regular basis so they are not left cramming the day before the test. To help promote positive study habits, Teri Martinez, a middle school resource social studies teacher, taught the following guidelines for studying:

1. *Manage your study time.* Keep up with assignments, and do daily and weekly reviews. Ms. Martinez planned 5 minutes each day at the end of her social studies class for students to review the material. On Monday, she took an extra 5 minutes and had the students review the previous week's work. She used individual, small group, and whole-class discussion to review.

2. *Create study aids.* Create a semantic map or other graphic organizer to help students remember key information. Ms. Martinez often used an ongoing map during review sessions, and the students added to the map each day. Ms. Martinez also taught the students how to create and use flash cards for key concepts and vocabulary. She taught the students the following procedures:

- When learning vocabulary, put the word on one side and the definition and an example on the other side.
- When learning other information, put the question on one side and the answer on the other side.
- When learning a formula, put the formula on one side and examples of how it is used on the other side.
- Review the flash cards in random order or after sorting the cards into categories or making a semantic map.
- Keep index cards in notebooks and on desks during class.
- Make a card when learning about a key concept or idea.

3. *Learn about the test.* The more information students learn about the format, type, and time allotted for the test, the more effectively they can prepare for it. Rather than telling the students about the test, Ms. Martinez would start the discussion by saying, "Let's talk about the test.

What do you want to ask me?" She used the following checklist to guide the students' questioning:

- Format of test, types of questions
- How much test is worth
- Date of test
- Time allotted for test
- Whether books or notes are allowed
- Information covered
- Teacher recommendations for how to study
- Teacher recommendations for what to study

4. *Predict questions.* Ms. Martinez also demonstrated how the students can predict the questions that will be asked. The students can use what they know about the teacher's testing style, their class notes, their maps, and other study aids to predict questions. Two days before a test, Ms. Martinez had the students work in cooperative groups and write what they thought would be the most important questions on the test and then answer them.

5. *Think positive.* An important part of doing well on a test is having a positive attitude and believing that one is going to do well. Ms. Martinez finds that she enjoys working with the students on having positive attitudes. Each day during their review, she asks the students about the following:

- What they learned today
- How it relates to what they already know
- What they will be working on tomorrow
- How well they have learned the information

She also has them rate how well they think they will do on the test and think about what they could do to improve their ratings. Just before a test, Ms. Martinez takes several minutes to review test-taking strategies and to have the students visualize themselves being successful as they take the test.

Test-Taking Strategies In a 2005 study, Carter and colleagues taught 38 high school students with disabilities the following test-taking strategies in a series of six lessons:

- Bubble-sheet completion and pacing
- Sorting problems: identifying which items are the easiest and solving those problems first
- Estimating: solving math problems by rounding
- Substitution and backsolving: substituting the given answers in a multiple choice test into the question to find the correct answer
- Recopying problems: rewriting problems in a more familiar form
- Underlining and reading all answers
- Elimination of redundant or off-the-wall answers

While students in the study did demonstrate small increases in their test scores after learning the strategies, Carter et al. (2005) feel that in order to see larger gains, students with disabilities need to learn test-taking strategies within the content instruction. In other words, in

order to best prepare students with disabilities to take multiple-choice tests, you should integrate test-taking instruction into content instruction on a regular basis.

Other test-taking strategies and hints that can help students perform better on tests include:

- Survey the test.
- Read the directions carefully. Underline key words in the directions that tell you what to do.
- Be sure you understand the scoring system (e.g., is guessing penalized?).
- If you have memorized specific outlines, formulas, mnemonics, and the like, write down that information before you forget it.
- When answering questions, place a mark in the margin for those questions about which you are unsure and/or want to review.
- Place the questions in the context of what has been discussed in class and what you have read.
- Avoid changing answers arbitrarily.
- Review your answers.

Taking Objective Tests For students with learning and behavior problems, it may be beneficial to teach specific test-taking strategies. The PIRATES strategy can be used for taking objective tests (Hughes, Deshler, Ruhl, & Schumaker, 1993) and uses the Strategies Intervention Model. Research indicates that students with learning disabilities can increase their performance by 20–40 percentage points by learning and applying this strategy. The steps in the strategy are as follows:

Prepare to succeed.
  - Put your name and PIRATES on the test.
  - Allot time and order the sections.
  - Say affirmations.
  - Start within 2 minutes.
Inspect the instructions.
  - Read instructions carefully.
  - Underline what to do and where to respond.
  - Notice special requirements.
Read, remember, reduce.
  - Read the whole question.
  - Remember what you studied.
  - Reduce your choices.
Answer or abandon.
  - Answer the question.
  - Abandon the question for the moment.
Turn back.
Estimate your answer.
  - Avoid absolutes.
  - Choose the longest or most detailed choice.
  - Eliminate similar choices.
Survey.
  - Survey to ensure that all questions have been answered.
  - Switch an answer only if you are sure.

When using this strategy, a student repeats, for each section of the test, the second, third, and fourth steps (i.e., inspect the instructions; read, remember, reduce; answer or abandon).

In addition to this strategy, there are a number of hints for taking objective tests. Apply the Concept 10-11 presents information that is helpful in answering objective questions (e.g., true-false, multiple-choice, matching, and completion).

Taking Essay Tests Essays tests are not used as frequently as objective tests, but when essay questions are incorporated into a test, they make up a sizable portion of the test grade (Hughes, 1996). This type of test can be particularly difficult for students with disabilities. Not only do the test-takers have to recall information, they have to write clearly in terms of organization, legibility, spelling, and grammar. Students with difficulties in written expression may be able to orally express the answer to the question, but their writing skills may make it difficult for them to communicate that knowledge. You may want to record the student's answers on audiotape. For some students, it may be advantageous to teach a strategy for answering essay questions so that the students organize the information and communicate it effectively. One strategy that has been developed to assist students in organizing better responses to essay questions is called ANSWER (Hughes, Schumaker, & Deshler, 2001). The steps include the following:

Analyze the situation.
- Read the question carefully.
- Underline key words.
- Gauge the time you need.

Notice requirements.
- Scan for and mark the parts of the question.
- Ask and say what is required.
- Tell yourself that you will write a high-quality answer.

Apply the Concept

10-11 — Tips for Answering Objective Questions

True-False Questions

- Remember, *everything* in a true statement must be true. One false detail makes it false.
- Look for qualifying words that tend to make statements false, such as *all, always, everyone, everybody, never, no, none, no one, only*.
- Look for qualifying words that tend to make statements true, such as *generally, most, often, probably, some, sometimes, usually*.
- Simplify questions that contain double negatives by crossing out both negatives and then determining whether the statement is true or false.
- Don't change an answer unless you have a good reason to. Usually, your first impression is correct.

Matching Questions

- Read directions carefully. Determine whether each column contains an equal number of items and whether items can be used more than once.
- Read both columns before you start matching, to get a sense of the items.

- Focus on each item in one column and look for its match in the other column.
- If you can use items only once, cross out each item as you use it.

Multiple-Choice Questions

- Determine whether you are penalized for guessing.
- Answer the questions you know, putting a check mark in the margin next to items you want to return to later.
- Read all possible options, even when you are pretty sure of the right answer.
- See whether multiple options are available (e.g., c. A and B; d. All of the above).
- Minimize the risk of guessing by reading the stem with each option to see which option is most logical.
- Use a process of elimination, crossing out options you know are wrong.
- When you do not know the answer and you are not penalized for guessing, use the following signals to help you select the right option:
- The longest option is often correct.

- The most complete answer is often correct.
- The first time the option "all of the above" or "none of the above" is used, it is usually correct.
- The option in the middle, particularly if it is the longest, is often correct.
- Answers with qualifiers such as *generally, probably, sometimes*, and *usually* are frequently correct.

Completion Questions

- Determine whether more than one word can be put in one blank.
- If blanks are of different lengths, use length as a clue for the length of the answer.
- Read the question to yourself so that you can hear what is being asked.
- If more than one answer comes to mind, write them down; then reread the question with each answer to see which one fits best.
- Make sure that the answer you provide fits grammatically and logically.

Source: Selected ideas adapted from J. Langan, *Reading and Study Skills*, 8th ed. (New York: McGraw-Hill, 2007).

Set up an outline.
- Set up the main ideas.
- Assess whether they match the question.
- Make changes if necessary.

Work in details.
- Remember what you learned.
- Add details to the main ideas using abbreviations.
- Indicate the order.
- Decide whether you are ready to write.

Engineer your answer.
- Write an introductory paragraph.
- Refer to your outline.
- Include topic sentences.
- Tell about details for each topic sentence.
- Use examples.

Review your answer.
- Look to see whether you answered all parts of the question.
- Inspect to see whether you included all main ideas and details.
- Touch up your answer.

In her social studies class, Ms. Martinez taught the ANSWER strategy because essay questions were one format she used in her tests. She also gave students a list of direction words for essay questions (see Figure 10-15). She demonstrated how taking one concept such as *democracy* and using different direction words would change the response. In her daily reviews, she frequently discussed one of the cue words in relation to the content that had been covered that day. She provided examples of how to write an answer to a question using that cue word.

Providing appropriate content instruction for students with special needs in general education classrooms is challenging but potentially beneficial to all learners. Effective teachers implement the following practices associated with improved outcomes in content area learning (Scruggs et al., 2009):

- Hands-on activities
- Computer-assisted learning
- Peer mediation
- Spatial or graphic organization
- Study aids
- Classroom learning strategies
- Mnemonic strategies
- Explicit instruction

INSTRUCTIONAL ACTIVITIES

This section provides instructional activities that are related to content area learning and study skills. Some of the activities teach new skills; others are best suited for practice and reinforcement of already acquired skills. For each activity, the objective, materials, and teaching procedures are described.

▶ Word Association Map

Objectives: To teach students a strategy for learning vocabulary words.

Grades: Secondary

▶ **Figure 10-15**   Direction Words for Answering Essay Questions

Cue	Meaning	Cue	Meaning
Analyze	Break into parts, and examine each part.	Interpret	Explain, and share your own judgment.
Apply	Discuss how the principles would apply to a situation.	Justify	Provide reasons for your statements or conclusion.
Compare	Discuss differences and similarities.	List	Provide a numbered list of items or points.
Contrast	Discuss differences and similarities, stressing the differences.	Outline	Organize your answer into main points and supporting details. If appropriate, use outline format.
Critique	Analyze and evaluate, using criteria.	Prove	Provide factual evidence to support your logic or position.
Define	Provide a clear, concise statement that explains the concept.	Relate	Show the connection among ideas.
Describe	Give a detailed account, listing characteristics, qualities, and components as appropriate.	Review	Provide a critical summary in which you summarize and present your comments.
Diagram	Provide a drawing.	State	Explain precisely.
Discuss	Provide an in-depth explanation. Be analytical.	Summarize	Provide a synopsis that does not include your comments.
Explain	Give a logical development that discusses reasons or causes.	Trace	Describe the development or progress of the idea.
Illustrate	Use examples or, when appropriate, provide a diagram or picture.		

Add your own direction words and definitions!

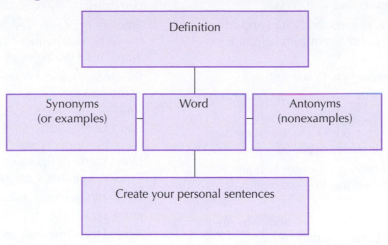

Materials: Textbook chapter, word association map worksheet (see Figure 10-16)

Teaching Procedures:
1. Introduce a key vocabulary word (e.g., *wicked*), and write it on the map.
2. Ask students to brainstorm what the word means.
3. With student input, come up with a good definition, and write it on the map. If necessary, provide examples to help students understand the meaning of the word.
4. Test students on several examples and nonexamples (e.g., example: "The witch in the children's story is mean for no reason and is wicked"; nonexample: "Diana is a considerate boss who is always willing to listen").
5. Ask the students to identify synonyms and antonyms of the word and write them on their word maps (e.g., synonyms: *unkind, bad;* antonyms: *good, considerate*).
6. Finally, ask the students to create their own personal sentences with the word.

Source: Adapted from University of Texas Center for Reading and Language Arts (2001a).

► Add-a-Part: Prefixes and Suffixes

Objective: To give students practice in creating words with prefixes and suffixes.

Grades: Fourth through secondary

Materials: Cards with prefixes (e.g., *dis-*), cards with suffixes (e.g., *-able*), cards with root words (e.g., *honest, comfort*) that can be combined with these prefixes and suffixes, two plastic bags

Teaching Procedures:
1. Have students sit in a circle.
2. Place the plastic bag of cards with prefixes and suffixes and the other bag with root words in the middle of the circle within reach of everyone.
3. Model playing the "add-a-part" game by drawing one card out of each bag, saying the affix (e.g., *-less*) and the root word (e.g., *care*) on the cards, and creating a new word with the affix (e.g., *careless*). Say the new word and its meaning, and tell whether the word is real or not.
4. Have the students take turns playing the game.

Source: Adapted from University of Texas Center for Reading and Language Arts (2001b).

► VOCAB

Objective: To teach students the VOCAB strategy and enhance their vocabulary.

Grades: Secondary

Materials: A list of vocabulary terms that are generally related (e.g., federal government, legislative branch, executive branch, judicial branch); index cards or pieces of paper

Teaching Procedures:
1. Discuss the components of the VOCAB strategy, and introduce the strategy step by step:

   Verify the key vocabulary terms and concepts to be learned, and put them on individual vocabulary cards or pieces of paper.

   Organize the vocabulary word cards into a diagram that shows the relationship of the words to each other as you understand them in the context of what is being learned.

Communicate your reasoning, and share your diagram with a partner and vice versa.

Assess the diagrams, discuss similarities and differences, and adjust your diagram with helpful ideas from your partner.

Build your understanding with self-testing.

2. Identify and provide for students a list of vocabulary words.

3. Have the students write one of the words on each of the index cards or pieces of paper.

4. Ask the students to organize the words in any way that they think shows the correct relationships among the words.

5. Have the students explain how and why they organized the words the way they did.

6. On the basis of the discussion, have the students reorganize their words if they think they have a different understanding of the meaning of the words.

7. Circulate among the pairs, and monitor students' discussions to make sure that they are building their understanding of the words through self-testing.

8. As a whole class, have several pairs of students share how and why they arranged their words.

Source: Adapted from University of Texas Center for Reading and Language Arts (1999).

▶ Click and Clunk

Objective: To help students monitor their understanding as they read and apply fix-up strategies to determine the meanings of unfamiliar words.

Grades: Elementary through secondary

Materials: Reading passage, clunk cards, paper

Teaching Procedures:
1. Introduce clunk cards. Explain to students that *click* means words or ideas they understand and *clunk* means the words or ideas that they do not know. The students continue to read until they have a clunk. Tell the students that they can use the clunk cards when they have a clunk to figure out the meaning of a word.

2. Model each of the fix-up strategies on the clunk cue cards.

3. Provide opportunities for guided practice, followed by independent practice in which students apply these strategies as they read.

4. Pair students, and ask them to read each paragraph of the passage.

5. After reading each paragraph, have the students find clunks and write them on the paper. Then, have the students use the fix-up strategies on the clunk cards to figure out what the clunks mean. Provide supports if necessary.

6. Have the students record the definition of the clunk on the paper.

7. Repeat the same procedure until the entire selection has been read.

8. When the entire selection has been read, have several pairs of students share their clunks and the fix-up strategies they used to help them determine meaning.

Source: Adapted from Klingner, Vaughn, Dimino, Schumm, and Bryant (2001).

▶ Contextual Searching

Objective: To help students use various context clues to identify the meaning of the words.

Grades: Secondary

Materials: Ten vocabulary words; contextual sentences for each vocabulary word using the five types of context clues (i.e., definition, description, contrast, comparison, synonym); sentence strips; list of possible definitions; dictionary

Teaching Procedures: Before the instruction,
1. Identify 10 vocabulary words.

2. Develop one context clue for each word. Be sure to use different types of context clues.

3. Write a sentence with a vocabulary word containing one context-clue type (definition, description, contrast, comparison, or synonym) on each sentence strip.

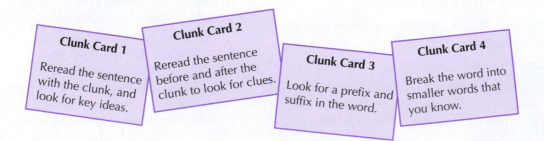

Clunk Card 1

Reread the sentence with the clunk, and look for key ideas.

Clunk Card 2

Reread the sentence before and after the clunk to look for clues.

Clunk Card 3

Look for a prefix and suffix in the word.

Clunk Card 4

Break the word into smaller words that you know.

► **Figure 10-17** Using Context Clues

Context Clue Type	Example
Definition: The word is defined in the sentence.	If disease reaches your bronchial tubes, *cilia*—tiny hairlike structures—are another barrier to prevent infection.
Description: The word is described by the context.	After taking a spill on her bike, she was able to stand up, get back on the bike, and pedal away on her own *volition*.
Contrast: The word is compared with some other word as an antonym.	Kim was *lethargic*, yet her sister was very energetic.
Comparison: The word is compared with some other word or phrase to illustrate the similarities between them.	Birgit was exhausted after the *inquisition*, which was like being in a boat on rough seas.
Synonym: The word is compared to another word with a similar meaning.	Tom interpreted the message *literally*; that is, he believed the message as though every word were real.

During the instruction,

4. Present the first five vocabulary words in isolation (e.g., *cilia, volition, lethargic, inquisition,* and *literally*).

5. Ask the students for definitions of the words.

6. Write the words and the students' definitions on the chalkboard or overhead.

7. Present the vocabulary words in context.

8. Model how to use the type of context clue to figure out the meaning of the unfamiliar words (see Figure 10-17).

9. Have the students compare the definitions from context to their definitions in isolation.

10. Present the other five vocabulary words in isolation.

11. Ask the students for definitions of the words.

12. Write the words and the students' definitions on the chalkboard or overhead.

13. Present the vocabulary words in context.

14. Pair students, and ask them to analyze the context to figure out the meaning of each vocabulary word and record their definitions for each word.

15. Ask the students to identify which type of context clue they used for each vocabulary word.

16. Ask the students to compare their definitions from context clues to their definitions in isolation.

17. Have students look up the definitions for the vocabulary words in the dictionary.

18. Call on several pairs of students to share how the dictionary definition fits with their definition from context clues.

Source: Adapted from University of Texas Center for Reading and Language Arts (2002).

► **Jeopardy!**

Objective: To give students practice in using reference and trade books to obtain information and to generate questions.

Grades: Secondary

Materials: Reference and trade books, Jeopardy! board with four categories and five answers per category, index cards to fit in the Jeopardy! board

Teaching Procedures:

1. Divide the students into three teams of two to four students. Explain that each team is going to make a Jeopardy!-style game for the other students to play.

JEOPARDY!

Pop Music	Presidents	Football	Southwest
20	20	20	20
40	40	40	40
60	60	60	60
80	80	80	80
100	100	100	100

2. To make the game, each team needs to select four categories. Then have the students use reference books, trade books, and other sources to generate five questions and answers for each category that other students could possibly answer. Have them write the questions and answers on separate index cards and order the questions and answers from easy to difficult.

3. Each team then takes a turn directing its Jeopardy! game. First, the team inserts their category names and answer cards into the Jeopardy! board. Then they direct the game as the two other teams compete against each other. To direct the game, one student should serve as master of ceremonies, another as timekeeper, and the rest as judges.

4. To play, each team takes a turn selecting a category and a level underneath the category. The answer is then exposed, and the team members have 15 seconds to give the question. If the question is correct, they get the number of points indicated and are allowed to make another selection. If the answer is incorrect, the other team has 15 seconds to give an answer.

▶ Study Groups

Objective: To provide students with the opportunity to work in groups when studying a textbook for a test.

Grades: Secondary

Materials: Content area textbook chapter or sections on which the students are going to be tested, index cards

Teaching Procedures:

1. Have students who are studying for tests that cover the same material work in groups of two to three students. (*Note:* When students first do this activity, the teacher will generally need to demonstrate and guide the students through the process.)

2. Have the students read the assigned materials together, stopping at the end of each paragraph or section to discuss the main ideas and the important vocabulary. Each main idea and important vocabulary for each section should be written on an index card.

3. After the students finish reading the assignment using this technique, they should take all the main idea cards and arrange them in logical groupings or in a logical order.

4. Have the students take each important vocabulary card and write a simple definition that makes sense according to the text. Then have them arrange the important vocabulary next to the related main idea.

5. Next, have each student copy onto paper the arrangement that was organized for the main ideas and vocabulary (with definitions).

6. Finally, the students should study the paper and then take turns quizzing each other on the information.

▶ Learn Those Words!

Objective: To teach students a simple strategy for memorizing vocabulary words—either English words or those of a foreign language.

Grades: Fifth through secondary

Materials: Index cards used whole or cut in half or in thirds, a pen, a paper cutter or scissors

Teaching Procedures:

1. Have students write a word on one side of an index card and its definition or translation on the reverse side.

2. Have students study the words and then test themselves. Have them form two piles of cards as they work: a pile for the words they know and another for those they do not know. Students continue to study the words they don't know until there are no more cards in the unknown pile.

3. Tell the students that they should always keep a set of words with them. While they are waiting in line or waiting for class to begin, they can test themselves on their words.

4. Have students make new sets of words and continuously review the old sets.

▶ **FOCUS Question 1. How can teachers use specific word instruction and word-learning strategies to teach vocabulary?**

Answer: In specific word instruction, teachers select a few vocabulary words that are critical for understanding a text and are difficult for students. Words can be selected from a text that the teacher will read aloud or from a text that students will read themselves. Teachers can highlight selected words after reading or preteach the vocabulary words. Students also need word-learning strategies that they can use independently while reading. Effective word-learning strategies include using contextual analysis, morphemic analysis, and reference aids.

▶ **FOCUS Question 2. What is content enhancement, and how can teachers use it to teach content area reading?**

Answer: Content enhancement is used to help students identify, organize, and comprehend important content. First, teachers select important concepts and related vocabulary. Next, teachers evaluate materials. Reviewing texts before reading helps teachers to identify the difficulty of the ideas or concepts. Teachers then assess students' prior knowledge through the use of activities. Next, teachers can implement appropriate prelearning activities that students can use before reading an assigned text or listening to a lecture. Finally, the semantic map, concept diagram, or other activity becomes a learning tool that can be used as a guide during and after reading.

▶ **FOCUS Question 3. How do teachers adapt textbooks, lectures, assignments, homework, and tests to meet the needs of students with learning and behavior problems?**

Answer: Text adaptation involves changing an existing text to make it more comprehensible for students. Methods for adapting textbooks include using study guides, highlighting important points, or using alternatives to reading such as audiotaping text chapters or reading aloud. Lectures can be adapted by making their organization and key points clear to students through aids such as advance organizers, vocal cues, or visual aids. Teachers who are aware of students' abilities and needs construct assignments and homework that are appropriate in content, length, time required to complete, and skill level. Teachers should always communicate why an assignment is important, when it is due, what support is available, and what steps are involved. Teachers should tell students explicitly what they will be responsible for knowing, should design tests that are clear and easy to understand, and should provide accommodations during testing situations.

▶ **FOCUS Question 4. What are the three types of study skills, and why are they important to learning?**

Answer: Personal development skills, process skills, and expression skills are the three types of study skills. They are important because they help students to manage their time; use strategies to organize, synthesize, and remember new information; and communicate what they have learned to others. Study skills are critical to independent and efficient learning.

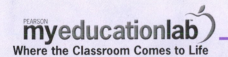

Where the Classroom Comes to Life

The MyEducationLab for this course can help you solidify your comprehension of Chapter 10 concepts.

- Gauge and further develop your understanding of chapter concepts by taking the quizzes and examining the enrichment materials in the Chapter 10 Study Plan.
- Visit Topic 6, Assessing and Teaching Other Content Areas, to
  - connect with challenge-based interactive modules, case study units, and podcasts that provide

  research-validated information about working with students in inclusive settings, by visiting the IRIS Center Resources.
- explore Assignments and Activities, assignable exercises showing concepts in action through video, cases, and student and teacher artifacts.
- practice and strengthen skills essential to quality teaching through the Building Teaching Skills and Dispositions lessons.

11

Assessing and Teaching Mathematics*

Contributed by Terry L. Weaver, Union University

FOCUS Questions

1. What factors influence math ability?
2. How is mathematics performance assessed and progress monitored?
3. What are the prenumber skills students need to progress in arithmetic?
4. What are several numeration concepts?
5. What factors contribute to difficulties with problem solving, and how can teachers assist students in learning problem-solving strategies?
6. How can math interventions be used to improve math performance?

Sanjay, a third-grade student who has behavior disorders, spends most of his day in the general education third-grade classroom. He is in the top math group and is proud of this achievement. His special education teacher is pleased that he is fulfilling his behavior contract and has not had any serious disturbances since he has been included in the general education classroom.

Claudia, a seventh-grade student who spends part of her day in a classroom for students with learning disabilities, is not nearly as successful in math. In fact, when asked what her favorite academic time is during the day, she says, "I love to write. In fact, I think I will be an author. I have already written several books for the classroom, and one was even selected for the library." When asked what she thinks of math, she looks away and says, "No way! Don't even mention it. I can't do math. We don't get along."

Claudia has had difficulty with mathematics since she was in the primary grades. Her first-grade teacher thought that she simply was not interested in math and suggested that her parents obtain special tutoring help during the following summer. Her parents found that the special help did little good, and when Claudia continued to have serious difficulty with math in second grade, the teacher referred her for assessment for possible learning disabilities. The assessment results suggested that she had difficulty with spatial relations and using memory to recall rote math facts. She has received special help in math for the past four years, and though she seems to have made progress, her math skills are still her weakest academic area.

Some students with learning and behavior problems have difficulty with language arts (reading, writing, and spelling), some have difficulty with mathematics, and some have difficulty with both. Compared with students who only have math problems, students who have both math and reading problems are far more likely to continue to have math problems in later grades (Jordan & Hanich, 2003). However, despite the number of students who have math problems, by far the skill that has received the most attention from researchers, writers, and even clinicians is reading. Reading is often viewed as an essential skill for survival in our society, whereas math is often considered less important. With an increased need for students to understand problem solving for success in the workplace, the inferior status of mathematics instruction may need to change.

Factors Influencing Math Ability

What factors influence math ability? Kosc (1981) identified four variables that significantly influence mathematics ability:

1. *Psychological factors* such as intelligence/cognitive ability, distractibility, and cognitive learning strategies
2. *Education factors* such as the quality and amount of instructional intervention across the range of areas of mathematics (e.g., computation, measurement, time, and problem solving)
3. *Personality factors* such as persistence, self-concept, and attitudes toward mathematics
4. *Neuropsychological patterns* such as perception and neurological trauma

Considering these four factors, it is not surprising that many students with learning and behavior problems have difficulty in math. Interestingly, though students with learning disabilities demonstrate significant difficulties with math, they do not report lower self-perceptions of their math skills than those of average-achieving students (Montague & van Garderen, 2003). Because much of their educational intervention has focused on computation, they often have limited exposure to other elements of math, including measurement, time, and practical problem solving. Many students with learning and behavior problems struggle with applying computation skills to everyday math problems. Persistence and motivation to succeed are associated with good math performance and many students with learning and behavior problems lack these qualities. The fourth factor that was identified, unique neuropsychological patterns, characterizes many students with learning and behavior problems.

Language development also plays an important role in learning mathematics. Reduced vocabulary levels and difficulties with reasoning and conceptual abstractions interfere with learning. The language of teacher directions, curricular materials, and mathematics does not aid students with learning and behavior problems to understand and learn the concepts and skills needed to be successful in mathematics. This is especially applicable to students with lower cognitive abilities and those with difficulties in understanding English (i.e., English-language learners; ELLs). Teachers can simplify the vocabulary that is used within a lesson since students with lower cognitive abilities and who are ELLs may have difficulty understanding oral and written concepts (Tucker, Singleton, & Weaver, 2006). The teacher can use the more readily understood vocabulary and follow it with a less complex term meaning the same thing (e.g., "Show me the fraction that equals one-half" becomes "Show me the fraction or part that equals or is the same as one half"). The teacher can also use an example that is visually easy to image (e.g., "parallel lines" or "like railroad tracks running side by side"). Teachers can make revisions to the directions provided in texts, thereby allowing better understanding. However, if a difficult word is essential, then a marginal note (a simpler word written in the margin and tied to the difficult word by a line) can be provided to increase the understanding of the directions (Leverett & Diefendorf, 1992).

Moreover, students can benefit from developmental activities wherein students are provided opportunities to develop mathematical experiences that will become the basis for generalizations of mathematical concepts and skills. These activities provide opportunities for students to develop connections to what they already know and can more readily help the student "to see" how new learning is related to learning that is already understood (Tucker, Singleton, & Weaver, 2006). Mental imagery is built by developmental activities allowing the student to have a better picture of what the teacher is saying (they can see that the real world is this way). As a teacher builds mental imagery, concrete thinking is facilitated. The use of developmental activities increases memory of skills learning, the practice needed is reduced, and the overall time to master skills is decreased (Tucker, Singleton, & Weaver, 2006).

When mathematics material is organized into smaller, more manageable amounts rather than larger amounts of new material, successful learning occurs more easily (Tucker, Singleton, & Weaver, 2006). The student may then know he or she is able to learn, which leads to an attitude of wanting to learn more. The following six difficulties may interfere with the mathematics performance of a student with learning disabilities (Ginsburg, 1997):

1. *Perceptual skills.* Students with learning disabilities often have difficulties with spatial relationships, distances, size relationships, and sequencing, which interfere with such math skills as measurement, estimation, problem solving, and geometry. Students with weak perceptual skills will need practice in estimating size and distance and then in verifying their estimates with direct measurement. Students with weak spatial awareness may have difficulty with positional relationships between themselves and real objects or among real objects or those on printed materials (Tucker, Singleton, & Weaver, 2006). Opportunities to explore objects of similar sizes and shapes and different sizes and shapes will help students to identify positional relationships that can aid in strengthening their understanding of themselves and their connection to the world around them.

2. *Perseveration.* Some students may have difficulty in mentally shifting from one task or operation to the next. This can interfere with their performance on problems that require multiple operations or on applied mathematics problems that generally require several steps. Teachers can provide cues to illustrate the number of steps that are involved in each operation. After the students have mastered the skills for two operations (e.g., addition and

subtraction), teachers can provide opportunities to practice both types of problems. Visual cues can be added to problems to alert students to a change (e.g., plus signs for addition, subtraction signs for take away). The visual cues will help to draw the student's attention to the need to change the operation. An arrow pointed at the subtraction sign will trigger the need for the shift in the operation. Colored operation signs or highlighting the sign can also be visual cues for an operation change.

3. *Language.* Students may have difficulty understanding such mathematical concepts as *first, last, next, greater than,* and *less than* when learning arithmetic, so instructions should be precise. Presenting unnecessary concepts and rules can confuse students and distract them from concentrating on the concept being presented. Demonstrating how to perform problems and guiding students in completing the work independently are effective instructional practices. Give plenty of examples, and allow students to provide examples to demonstrate their understanding of the concepts.

4. *Reasoning.* Reasoning is often difficult because it requires a great deal of abstract thinking. Teachers should use concrete materials and real-life application whenever possible. After students understand a mathematical concept at an automatic level, the teacher can introduce tasks that ask students to think through the process, explain the rationale, and apply reason. Some students acquire "bugs" (Ginsburg, 1997) in their thinking that lead them to develop faulty ideas about how practices in mathematics work. These bugs need to be "reprogrammed" so that the students can understand the correct operation. Such reprogramming may include more developmental activities wherein opportunities to handle real-world, concrete, or representational materials will help to make new connections to what the students already know. These developmental activities encourage the students' mental imagery for mathematical ideas. The mental imagery also provides opportunities for the students to make sense of mathematics because they can "see" what the teacher is talking about (Tucker, Singleton, & Weaver, 2006).

5. *Memory.* Many students with learning and behavior problems have difficulty remembering information. Teachers can assist students who have memory problems by reducing the amount of new information they are required to learn, increasing the number of exposures to new material, and giving the students opportunities to verbalize and demonstrate their ability with new material. Teachers can also provide strategies for moving information into and out of long-term memory. Procedures can be developed into a mnemonic that can be helpful in remembering what to do (e.g., FOIL—first, outer, inner, and last—the order of algebraic operations). A list of procedural steps may also be developed and taped to the student's desk to remind the student what to do.

6. *Symbolism difficulty.* Many students with learning disabilities have a difficult time understanding mathematics symbols. These students may know the rote behavior for what they are supposed to do but cannot tell you the meaning or use of such symbols as equals, subtract, and multiply. Developmental activities can aid the student in developing experiences that will aid in an understanding of mathematical symbols as part of the real world: "the way the world works" (Tucker, Singleton, & Weaver, 2006). Connections between symbols and the concepts behind the symbols are enhanced with consolidating developmental activities that allow students opportunities to identify mathematical patterns and relationships in the process of hypothesizing and testing mathematical relationships. Through developmental activities the students are aided in understanding concepts, developing procedures, and learning mathematical terminology and symbols (Tucker, Singleton, & Weaver, 2006).

To enhance opportunities for peer support, pair students or have them work in small groups to identify mathematical patterns and relationships, test mathematical relationships, or solve mathematical problems with manipulatives. This type of grouping encourages social interaction as it builds skills in arithmetic.

Barnes et al. (2006) reported that students with math disabilities are likely to have problems with both math facts and math procedures. Also, in a study by Badian and Ghublikian (1983), students with significantly lower math than reading skills (low math) were compared with two other groups: students with significantly higher math skills than reading skills and students who had similar math and reading skills. The results indicated that the low math group demonstrated lower scores overall on the following abilities:

- Paying sustained attention
- Working in a careful and organized manner
- Accepting responsibility

These findings partially explain why students with learning and behavior problems have difficulty with mathematics. Students with learning disabilities often have difficulty applying learning strategies and are frequently characterized as having perceptual and neurological complications. Students with emotional disturbances may have greater difficulties with mathematics than with other subjects because it requires persistence and concentration. Students with mild cognitive difficulties have more difficulty with mathematics than students with learning disabilities do (Parmar, Cawley, & Miller, 1994). Furthermore, adolescents with learning disabilities perform in many areas of mathematics, such as multiplication, in ways that are similar to those of much younger non-learning-disabled students (Barrouillet, Fayol, & Lathuliere, 1997), sometimes referred to as delayed selective attention. Moreover, problems with memory, difficulty in considering math problems from a "reasonable" perspective, poor calculation skills, number reversals, and difficulty understanding operation signs have been suggested (Bryant, Bryant, & Hammill, 2000; Bryant, Hartman, & Kim, 2003).

Remember that students with math disabilities, besides having difficulties within the area of mathematics, often have other related difficulties that cause interference in learning mathematics. Students with math disabilities only are less at risk than are students with both math and reading disabilities. Yet when looking at math disabilities, as with any disability, there is a lot of diversity among the various students. This requires much attention to and development of instructional interventions to meet specific needs.

Teaching Considerations

Teachers need to consider a number of factors when developing math programs for students with special needs, regardless of the students' ages or the curricular program being used.

Comprehensive Programming Mr. Noppe was not happy with his math program. He taught students in special education at an elementary school, and 90% of his math program consisted of teaching math computation. In discussing his math program with a coteacher, he said, "I know I need to include more than just computation, but I'm not sure what else I should be teaching. I guess I should ask the students to apply some of their math computation. Next year, I want to concentrate on my math program and make it more comprehensive."

Students need to be taught and be involved in a full range of mathematics skills, including basic facts, operations, algebra, word problems, mathematical reasoning, time, measurement, fractions, and math application. Teachers should not focus their entire mathematics program on math facts and the four basic operations of addition, subtraction, multiplication, and division. The National Council of Teachers of Mathematics (NCTM) has issued standards for a comprehensive mathematics program. Many special education teachers of students with learning and behavior problems report that they have very little knowledge of the NCTM standards (Maccini & Gagnon, 2002). These standards (listed in Apply the Concept 11-1) can be useful to teachers as they design curriculum and instruction for students with special needs. Having students work on the developmental and conceptual foundations of mathematics will aid them in understanding the big ideas underlying mathematics (e.g., the use of like units in their computations and problem solving) that will be needed in their learning of new skills and their practice of the skills. Building the foundational scaffold onto which new skills and concepts may be fused is a key element to success in mathematics learning.

Remember that a relevant feature of a comprehensive math program is to teach concepts and vocabulary—to make sure that students understand the language of mathematics. Students with disabilities are less likely to know the relevant concepts and specific vocabulary related to mathematics learning. Thus, when they are participating in problem solving in real-life contexts, they may not understand key words such as *perimeter* or *diameter;* younger students may not understand words like *minus, half,* or *percentage.* Pairing the difficult concept with lots of examples and nonexamples and the difficult vocabulary with simpler words aids in understanding.

Individualization Sanjay and Claudia, the two students described at the beginning of this chapter, have very different needs in math. Individualization in math programming refers not just to the task but also to the way in which the task is learned (Carnine, 1991). Some students learn math facts through rote drill, whereas other students learn math facts by associating them with known facts. We often assume that an individualized program means that a student works alone; but individualization actually means that the program is designed to meet the individual needs of the student. It is often beneficial for the students to work in small groups to explore and develop patterns and relationships, and hypothesize and test those hypotheses in the process of learning new skills and rehearsing and practicing problems. In addition, small groups that focus on solving the same problem can include students of different abilities, particularly when the teacher creates a cooperative environment for solving the problems and allowing the students to learn from each other.

Correction and Feedback Receiving immediate feedback about performance is particularly important in mathematics. If students are performing an operation incorrectly, they should be told which parts are correct and which parts are incorrect. Showing students patterns in their errors is an important source of feedback. Students also need to learn to check their own work and monitor their errors. Working in pairs can help in this process of checking and monitoring because students benefit from a peer's help when they may not from the teacher. Remember, feedback includes pointing out improvements as well as needed changes.

Students in Ms. Wong's math class were given a worksheet to practice their new skill of using dollar signs and decimal points in their subtraction problems. Ms. Wong told the students to do only the first problem. After they completed the problem, they were to check it and make any necessary changes. If they thought that their answer to the problem was correct, they were to write a small *c* next to their answer; if not, they were to write a small *i* for incorrect next to the answer. They were also to indicate with a check mark where they thought they had

11-1

NCTM Standards 2000

Instructional programs from prekindergarten through grade 12 in the following areas should enable all students to use the following concepts:

1. Number and operations
   - Understand numbers, ways of representing numbers, relationships among numbers, and number systems
   - Understand meanings of operations and how they relate to one another
   - Compute fluently and make reasonable estimates
2. Algebra
   - Understand patterns, relations, and functions
   - Represent and analyze mathematical solutions and structures using algebraic symbols
   - Use mathematical models to represent and understand quantitative relationships
   - Analyze change in various contexts
3. Geometry
   - Analyze characteristics and properties of two- and three-dimensional geometric shapes, and develop mathematical arguments about geometric relationships
   - Specify locations and describe spatial relationships using coordinate geometry and other representational systems
   - Apply transformations and use symmetry to analyze mathematical situations
   - Use visualization, spatial reasoning, and geometric modeling to solve problems

4. Measurement
   - Understand measurable attributes of objects and the units, systems, and processes of measurement
   - Apply appropriate techniques, tools, and formulas to determine measurements
5. Data analysis and probability
   - Formulate questions that can be addressed with data, and collect, organize, and display relevant data to answer them
   - Select and use appropriate statistical methods to analyze data
   - Develop and evaluate inferences and predictions that are based on data
   - Understand and apply basic concepts of probability
6. Problem solving
   - Build new mathematical knowledge through problem solving
   - Solve problems that arise in mathematics and in other contexts
   - Apply and adapt a variety of appropriate strategies to solve problems
   - Monitor and reflect on the process of mathematical problem solving
7. Reasoning and proof
   - Recognize reasoning and proof as fundamental aspects of mathematics
   - Make and investigate mathematical conjectures
   - Develop and evaluate mathematical arguments and proofs

   - Select and use various types of reasoning and methods of proof
8. Communication
   - Organize and consolidate their mathematical thinking through communication
   - Communicate their mathematical thinking coherently and clearly to peers, teachers, and others
   - Analyze and evaluate the mathematical thinking and strategies of others
   - Use the language of mathematics to express mathematical ideas precisely
9. Connections
   - Recognize and use connections among mathematical ideas
   - Understand how mathematical ideas interconnect and build on one another to produce a coherent whole
   - Recognize and apply mathematics in contexts outside of mathematics
10. Representation
    - Create and use representations to organize, record, and communicate mathematical ideas
    - Select, apply, and translate among mathematical representations to solve problems
    - Use representations to model and interpret physical, social, and mathematical phenomena

Source: National Council of Teachers of Mathematics, *Principles and Standards for School Mathematics* (2000). Available online at http://www.nctm.org/standards.

made a mistake. Ms. Wong moved quickly from student to student, checking their work. Students who had the first problem correct were given task-specific praise and directions for the rest of the problems: "Good for you. You got the first problem correct, and you had the confidence, after checking it, to call it correct. I see you remembered to use the dollar sign and decimal points where they were needed. After you finish the first row, including checking your problems, meet with another student to see how your answers compare. Do you know what to do if there is a discrepancy in your answers? That's right. You'll need to check each other's problem to locate the error." For the students who had solved the problem incorrectly, Ms. Wong stopped by each student's desk and said, "Tell aloud how you did this. Start from the beginning, and as you think of what you're doing, say it aloud so I can follow." Ms. Wong finds that students often notice their own errors, or she will identify some faulty thinking by the students that keeps them from correctly solving the problem. Once the error has been found and corrected Ms. Wong asks the student to do the next problem, again saying what is being done aloud. If correct, Ms. Wong gives task-specific praise and directions for the rest of the problems.

Alternative Approaches to Instruction If a student is not succeeding with one instructional approach or program, the teacher should not hesitate to make a change. Despite years of research, no single method of mathematics instruction has been proven to be significantly better than others. This includes using a range of formats such as textbooks, workbooks, math stations, and manipulatives.

Applied Mathematics Concrete and representational materials and real-life applications of math problems make math relevant and increase the likelihood that students will transfer skills to applied settings such as home and work. Students can continue to make progress in mathematics throughout their school years when they have the underlying foundational scaffold from which to build their skills and problem solving. The emphasis needs to be on problem solving rather than on rote drill and practice activities (Cawley & Miller, 1989).

The term *situated cognition* refers to the principle that students will learn complex ideas and concepts in the contexts in which they occur in day-to-day life (real-world application). Students need many opportunities to practice what they learn in the ways in which they will eventually use what they learn. This is a critical way to promote the generalization of mathematical skills. For example, when teaching measurement, a teacher can give students real-world application opportunities to use the mathematics they are learning, such as measuring rooms for carpet, determining the mileage to specific locations, and so on.

When Ms. Wong's students were able to successfully use dollar signs and decimals in subtraction, she gave each of them a mock checkbook, which included checks and a ledger for keeping the balance. In each of their checkbooks she wrote the amount of $100.00. During math class for the rest of the month, she gave students "money" for their checkbook when their assignments were completed and their behavior was appropriate. She asked them to write her checks when they wanted supplies (pencils, erasers, chalk) or privileges (going to the bathroom, free time, meeting briefly with a friend). Students were asked to maintain the balances in their checkbooks. Students were penalized $5.00 for each mistake the "bank" located in the checkbook ledgers at the end of the week, much like a charge a real bank would make for an overdrawn account.

Generalization Generalization, or transfer of learning, needs to be taught. As most experienced teachers know, students often can perform skills in the special education room but are unable to perform them in a regular classroom. To facilitate the transfer of learning between settings, teachers must provide opportunities to practice skills by using a wide range of materials such as textbooks, workbooks, manipulatives (e.g., blocks, rods, tokens, real money), and word problems. For example, the teacher could have students measure different objects with things (unsharpened pencils, sheets of construction paper, or newspaper pages) rather than rulers or yardsticks. Teachers also need to systematically reduce the amount of help they provide students in solving problems. When students are first learning a math concept or operation, teachers provide a lot of assistance in performing it correctly. As students become more skillful, they need less assistance. Teachers must remember that generalization or transfer of learning must be planned for rather than "teach and hope" that it will occur.

When Ms. Wong's students were able to correctly apply subtraction with dollars and decimals in their checkbooks, she asked students to perform similar problems for homework. Ms. Wong realized that before she could be satisfied that the students had mastered the skill, they needed to perform it outside of her classroom and without her assistance.

Participation in Goal Selection Allowing students to participate in setting their own goals for mathematics is likely to increase their commitment to achieving goals. Students who selected their own mathematics goals improved their performance on math tasks over time more than did those students whose mathematics goals were assigned to them by a teacher (Fuchs, Bahr, & Rieth, 1989). Even very young children can participate in selecting their overall mathematics goals and can keep progress charts on how well they are performing.

Instructional Approaches Given that the students in the United States have scored well below others (Taiwan, South Korea, Singapore, Hong Kong, Japan) on the *Trends in International Mathematics and Science Study* (TIMSS; National Center for Educational Statistics, 2007), an international assessment of mathematics, in their mathematics proficiency in grades 4 and 8, there is a need for examining how we teach. The teaching techniques (more time in the development of fewer important mathematics topics and less time spent on computation skills) used in other countries may need to be considered (Ginsburg, Cooke, Leinwand, Noell, & Pollock, 2005) if we are to help our students become more proficient in mathematics and more competitive worldwide in general.

Furthermore, the National Research Council (NRC) has examined U.S. mathematics education from kindergarten through graduate study (National Research Council, 1989). This study was conducted jointly with the Mathematical Sciences Education Board, the Board on Mathematical Sciences, and the Committee on the Mathematical Sciences in the Year 2000. Their extensive report not only outlines problems in mathematics education but also charts a course for remedying them. The suggestions that relate to students with learning and behavior problems include:

- Do not alter curricular goals to differentiate students; instead, change the type and speed of instruction.
- Make mathematics education student-centered, not an authoritarian model that is teacher focused.
- Encourage students to explore, verbalize ideas, and understand that mathematics is part of their life.
- Provide daily opportunities for students to apply mathematics to work problems that are related to their daily lives. Instill in students the importance and need for mathematics.
- Teach mathematics so that students understand when an exact answer is necessary and when an estimate is sufficient.
- Teach problem solving, computer applications, and use of calculators to all students.
- Teach students to understand probability, data analysis, and statistics as they relate to daily decision making, model building, operations research, and applications of computers.
- Shift from performing primarily paper-and-pencil activities to use of calculators, computers, and other applied materials.

The National Research Council (2001) indicates that "mathematical proficiency" is the essential goal of instruction. What is mathematical proficiency? It is what any student needs in order to acquire mathematical understanding. The NRC describes five interwoven strands that compose proficiency. Consider how you are integrating these strands into your instruction. Also consider how you might determine whether the students you teach are making progress along each of these strands.

1. *Conceptual understanding* refers to understanding mathematic concepts and operations.
2. *Procedural fluency* is being able to accurately and efficiently conduct operations and mathematics practices.
3. *Strategic competence* is the ability to formulate and conduct mathematical problems.
4. *Adaptive reasoning* refers to thinking about, explaining, and justifying mathematical work.
5. *Productive disposition* is appreciating the useful and positive influences of understanding mathematics and how ones disposition toward mathematics influences success.

See Apply the Concept 11-2 for suggested instructional practices.

It is particularly important for teachers to design mathematics programs that enhance learning for all students, especially those with diverse cultural or linguistic backgrounds. See the next section for suggestions on how to do this.

Considerations for Students Who Are Culturally and Linguistically Diverse: Enhancing Skills in Mathematics

An essential part of successful mathematics learning is to provide instructional practices and assignments that facilitate the learning of mathematics for all students. An important caution when dealing with students with diverse backgrounds is that their prior experiences will also be diverse (Tucker, Singleton, & Weaver, 2006). To build on particular prior experiences you must ensure that all students have had those same experiences. To take for granted that they have them is a common error of many teachers. To accomplish successful learning, one must consider the needs of students from diverse cultures and language backgrounds; suggestions to consider include:

- Assign individuals from different backgrounds to work in pairs or small groups, providing opportunities in mathematical problem solving that will ensure similarity of prior learning experiences and social interaction, with infrequent failure.
- Use manipulatives to provide common first hand experiences to concretely explore the meaning of mathematical symbols and problems. Manipulatives enhance learning, increase social interaction, and provide an easy means of crossing potential language barriers.
- Model an enthusiastic and positive attitude about appreciating and learning more about the cultures and languages of other groups.
- Consider ways to infuse aspects of the various cultures of the students in your classroom and of students not represented into the mathematics curriculum provided by your school. Students will appreciate the inclusiveness you develop, feel accepted, be more engaged, and learn a great deal about each other and other cultures when cultural diversity is a part of their daily learning routines.
- Infuse aspects of mathematics and story problems that reflect names and events from diverse cultures. Encourage students to design mathematics and story problems that are reflective of other cultures. Books and newspaper or magazine articles or stories about individuals, families, groups, and data from other cultures can be incorporated to design mathematically based story problems.
- Link students' accomplishments to their hard work and effort. Remind students that they performed a task well because they worked hard, persisted,

On the basis of several syntheses of mathematics instruction for students with learning and behavior problems (Baker, Gersten, & Lee, 2002; Cawley, Parmar, Yan, & Miller, 1998; Dixon, Carnine, Lee, Wallin, & Chard, 1998; Gersten et al., 2009; Rivera, Smith, Goodwin, & Bryant, 1998; Xin & Jitendra, 1999), we recommend the following 10 instructional practices:

1. *Use data to make decisions about instruction and progress.* Teachers and/or students should use data to determine if instructional changes are needed. The links to changes in instruction are central to the use of data-based decision making.

2. *Involve peers* in working together to develop understandings and a foundational scaffold from which to engage the learning of mathematics skills and practice computation and word problems. In addition to developing a foundational scaffold, practicing computations, and problem solving, peers can provide support by teaching each other self-monitoring, correcting answers, and charting data for progress monitoring.

3. *Inform parents* about students' progress and success in mathematics *and involve parents in their student's learning* so that they can enhance interest and practice of mathematics at home. Provide parents with information about students' success in mathematics so that they can recognize those accomplishments at home. Have students demonstrate (teach) the mathematics that they are learning at school to their parents rather than having parents just help with homework. Many times, the parents' mathematics knowledge is based on rote memorization that is not helpful to their child's learning and understanding.

4. *Use instructional routines* that focus on developmental and cognitive behavioral techniques benefits students with learning and behavior problems and engages them in the learning process.

5. *Instructional design features* are effective ways to teach students to develop a foundational scaffold onto which to infuse additional learning, differentiate problem types, use a wide range of examples, and separate confusing elements, and provide opportunities for students to reach performance levels before introducing more new principles.

6. *Teach students the principles of mathematics to mastery* and then move to more advanced principles. Many students with special needs are given the same instructional mathematics curriculum (e.g., subtraction with regrouping) from second through ninth grades. Upper-level students need to learn mathematics at levels beyond, this including prealgebra and algebra. Some may need to focus on functional mathematics.

7. *Establish realistic goals* for progress in mathematics with students by providing information to students about their present performance and what they need to learn and how to learn best (e.g., paired with peers, or use of manipulatives, number lines, or calculators).

8. *Monitor progress* on a weekly basis through graphing or visual display so that students can chart and see how they are performing. Make adjustments in teaching, materials, grouping, or other features of instruction if students are not making adequate progress.

9. *Provide evidence* that hard work and effort yield good outcomes and progress. Students can also learn to reinforce themselves for setting and meeting goals in mathematics.

10. *Utilize computer-assisted instruction* as an effective way to learn and practice arithmetic computation and mathematical problem solving.

reread, rethought, revisualized, modeled, and so forth (Mercer & Mercer, 2005).
- Use culturally relevant materials as a springboard for mathematics learning. The ways in which mathematics is practiced in various cultures, mathematical games that are played, and the use of mathematics cross-culturally can be embedded into mathematics instruction.
- Use the students' languages within the instruction. Ask students to provide the mathematical word that means the same as "_____" and then use both words when referring to the term. Encourage students in the room to learn the term, use and apply the terms that represent the languages of the students in the class. Communicate to students that you value their home language and culture.
- Use technology to enhance learning and understanding of mathematical principles (Woodward, 1995). Computers provide language that typically is available to most students. Encourage expertise on the computer and provide multiple opportunities to practice skills.

Assessing and Progress-Monitoring Mathematics Performance

How is mathematics performance assessed and how is progress monitored? Mr. Sebeny is a first-year special education teacher. He is fortunate to work in a middle school with three other special education teachers who have been at the school for several years and are used to team teaching. They've asked Mr. Sebeny whether he would be comfortable teaching mathematics to all of the special education students. He quickly realized that his first task would be to determine the mathematics performance level of all of his students. Mr. Sebeny knows that he needs to select a measure that will tell him what students know and don't know and how they compare with other students in their grade.

There are many ways in which Mr. Sebeny could obtain the information he needs to develop instructional programs for his students. One of the first questions Mr. Sebeny needs to address is whether he has the time to use an individually administered assessment or whether he needs to use a group-administered measure. For students with special needs, individually administered measures yield the most information.

Second, Mr. Sebeny needs to determine whether the measure is designed for students in the age range of the students he is teaching. Figure 11-1 provides a list of mathematics measures, states whether they are administered to groups or individuals, and lists the age range for which they are appropriate. Figure 11-2 provides a list of progress-monitoring measures for math.

Yet how can teachers best make decisions about whether students are learning mathematics effectively? How can teachers monitor the progress of their students so that they can document the rate of progress they are making in mathematics? Bryant and Rivera (1997) have stated that "one would be hard-pressed to find a more effective technique than curriculum-based measurement (CBM) for directing, monitoring, and redirecting remedial efforts" (p. 63). There is considerable and growing evidence that when teachers use CBM to monitor their students' progress and to adjust their instruction accordingly, students make gains at much more rapid rates than when CBM is not used.

What is CBM for math? Simply stated, it is a way of documenting the extent to which the student is learning the critical elements in the curriculum that you have targeted. To illustrate, let's consider the case of Ricky, a fifth-grade boy with learning and attention problems, who has been struggling with math. His goals for the next 10 weeks are to know all subtraction facts up to 100 automatically and quickly, to be able to do addition

▶ **Figure 11-1**   Measures to Assess Mathematics Performance Progress Monitoring

Test Name	How Administered	Age/Grade Appropriate	Other Information
Comprehensive Math Assessment	Group	Grades 2–8	Based largely on the NCTM'S critical elements in mathematics instruction
Diagnostic Achievement Battery	Individual	Most grade levels	Provides normative data on student performance but not specific information for designing strengths and weaknesses
Wide Range Achievement Test	Individual or group	Most grade levels	Provides normative data on student performance but difficult to identify students' needs for instruction
Woodcock Johnson III Tests of Achievement	Individual	Most grade levels	Provides normative data on student performance but may not provide adequate information for designing instruction
Test of Early Mathematics Ability	Individual	Ages 3–9	Provides information to assist with designing and monitoring instruction
BRIGANCE Diagnostic Comprehensive Inventory of Basic Skills—Revised	Individual	Prekindergarten–grade 9	Provides information to assist with designing and monitoring instruction
Comprehensive Mathematical Ability Test	Individual	Grades 1–12	Provides information to assist with designing instruction
Key Math—Revised	Individual	Grades 1–12	Provides information to assist with designing instruction
Test of Mathematical Abilities	Individual	Grades 3–12	Provides information to assist with designing instruction
Math—Level Indicator: A Quick Group Math Placement Test	Group	Grades 4–12	Takes approximately 30 minutes, and because it is group administered, it quickly determines the performance levels of a large group of students. The problems are based on the NCTM standards.

Test Name	Concepts Addressed	Grade	Website	Forms
Monitoring Basic	Math computation	Grade 1 and above	http://www.proedinc.com	30 forms per grade
Skills Progress	Math concepts			
PASeries Math	Numbers	Grades 3–12	http://www.paseries.com	6 forms per grade
	Operations			
	Geometry			
	Algebra			
	Data analysis			
	Measurement			
Star Math	Computation	Grades 1–12	http://www.renlearn.com	Unlimited forms
	Application			
	Concepts			
Yearly ProgressPro	Curriculum-based measurement	Grade 1 and above	http://Mhdigitallearning.com	13 forms per grade
AIMSweb Systems	Oral counting	Grades K–8	http://www.aimsweb.com	33–50 forms for each construct
	Number identification			
	Quantity discrimination			
	Missing number			
	Basic skill areas			

with regrouping word problems, and to be able to appropriately use basic measurement terms such as *inches, feet*, and *yards*. Here is how Ricky and his teacher use CBM.

Ricky's teacher pretested on all 100 subtraction facts in random order, timing him while he completed the worksheet. She then showed Ricky how to graph his performance in two ways: by graphing how long it took him to complete the worksheet and by graphing the number of correct problems. Together, they agreed that Ricky would take a version of this test once every week to determine whether he could decrease the amount of time he needed to complete the test and increase the number of problems he got correct. Together, they established a schedule of work assignments and practice sessions. Figure 11-3 shows the graph that Ricky kept.

Ricky's teacher followed a similar procedure with measurement and problem solving to determine what Ricky knew and what he needed to know. Then the teacher established a simple graph that Ricky could complete to monitor his progress. Ricky and his teacher frequently discussed Ricky's progress and modified assignments and instruction to facilitate his learning.

Computerized applications of CBM procedures are available for mathematics as well as spelling and reading (Fuchs, Hamlett, & Fuchs, 1990).

Assessing Number Sense

Assessing number sense can be an effective way to monitor the progress of young children in mathematics and determine who has mathematics difficulties. *Number sense* refers to whether a student's understanding of a number and of its use and meaning is flexible and fully developed. One definition of number sense is "a child's fluidity and flexibility with numbers, the sense of what numbers mean, and an ability to perform mental mathematics and to look at the world and make comparisons" (Gersten & Chard, 1999, p. 19). In terms of assessment, number sense is particularly important because it assists teachers in determining which students currently have mathematical difficulty and even serves as a predictor for students who may have learning difficulties in the future.

Clarke and Shinn (in press) and Fuchs, Fuchs, Compton et al. (2007) describe measures that can be used to quickly determine students' understanding of number sense. Each of these measures can easily be constructed and changed

Ricky's teacher developed three versions of a subtraction fact sheet that had 30 problems representing the 100 subtraction facts he was learning. Once a week, Ricky was timed on one version of the test and the number of problems correct were counted. Ricky kept the following two charts to demonstrate his progress.

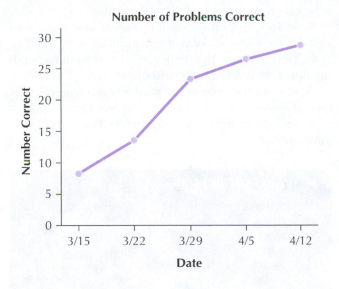

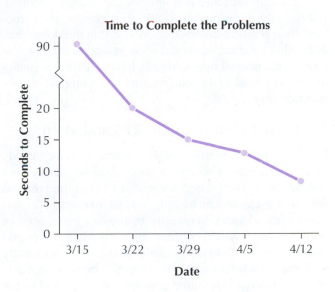

by the teacher to determine what a student knows. These include the following five:

1. *Number identification.* In this task, students must orally identify numbers between 0 and 20 when these are presented randomly on a piece of paper.

2. *Number writing.* Students are asked to write the number when given a number orally between 1 and 20.

3. *Quantity discrimination.* This task requires students to name which of two numbers is the larger (or smaller).

4. *Missing number.* Students are provided with a string of numbers and are asked to identify which number is missing.

5. *Computation.* Students are asked to complete computations that are representative of their grade level. Students have 2 minutes to complete as many problems as possible.

In addition, several counting measures can be used as effective screening tools for students with mathematical difficulties or to monitor students' progress in this area (Clarke & Shinn, 2004):

1. *Count to 20.* This is a beginning-level skill requiring students to count to 20 while the teacher records which numbers were in the correct sequence and which ones were not.

2. *Count by 3 and 6.* This skill requires students to count from a predetermined number, such as from 5, in increments of 3 or 6. The teacher records the accuracy and speed with which the students perform this task.

3. *Count by 2, 5, or 10.* This skill requires student to count by the designated number—2, 5, or 10—in increments up to a specified number, such as 20 for 2s, 50 for 5s, or 100 for 10s. The teacher records the accuracy with which students perform this task.

How Effective Are Test Accommodations in Mathematics for Students with Disabilities?

Assessment is an important part of the instructional routine. Teachers use assessment to assist them in determining what students know and can do and what they need to know and do. Appropriate assessments allow teachers to monitor students' progress and to make effective instructional decisions that will improve the students' performances. Having the results of daily, weekly, and monthly progress assessments long with more long-term assessments (e.g., state-mandated tests) makes planning effective instruction easier. Assessments can also tell teachers how students compare to others at their same age or grade level.

The idea behind test accommodations is that they are more responsive to the individual needs of students with disabilities. Elbaum (2007) reports that when mathematics tests are read aloud to students with disabilities and their performance on these tests are compared with students without disabilities, the read-aloud condition is more helpful to elementary students with disabilities than elementary students without disabilities. However, the reverse is true for secondary students with disabilities whose improved performance with accommodations is overall lower than for students without disabilities. Keep in mind that a teacher is bound by the student's individualized education program (IEP) to make the accommodations and modifications that are stated in the document. Many times the accommodation is extended time (1.5 or 2 times the normal time allotted), having the mathematics assessment read to the student, and spreading the assessment over several days.

Response to Intervention (RTI) and Math

Response to intervention (RTI) is a way to more quickly identify students who are in need of additional instruction and provide the necessary instructional intervention within the classroom to help ensure mastery. RTI has been applied most frequently to the academic area of early reading. However, there are currently schools and districts using RTI in mathematics at both the elementary and middle school levels. How can RTI be used in math? Initially, many of the same principles that applied to the use of RTI in reading also can be applied to math. These include:

- *Screening.* Students can be screened to determine if they have math problems in numeracy, math calculations, and/or problem solving.
- *Evidence-based math.* Schools and districts can ensure that math instruction for all students is based on the best research available.
- *Interventions.* When students have difficulties that are not adequately addressed through the evidence-based math program in the classroom, additional instruction through short-term interventions (10–20 weeks) can be implemented.
- *Progress monitoring.* Students' progress in the classroom and in interventions can be documented to ensure that they are staying on track and meeting curriculum benchmarks.

More recently, Gersten et al. (2009) provided a set of recommendations to aid teachers, principals, and others in their use of RTI for early identification of students who need help in mathematics and for focused mathematics intervention in elementary and middle schools. These recommendations include:

1. Screen all students to identify those at risk for potential mathematics difficulties and provide interventions to students identified as at risk.

2. Focus instructional materials for students receiving interventions on in-depth treatment of whole numbers in kindergarten through grade 5 and on rational numbers in grades 4 through 8. These materials should be selected by committee.

3. Provide explicit and systematic instruction during intervention. This includes providing models of proficient problem solving, verbalization of thought processes, guided practice, corrective feedback, and frequent cumulative review.

4. Provide instruction on solving word problems that is based on common underlying structures.

5. Include opportunities for students to work with visual representations of mathematical ideas.

6. Devote about 10 minutes in each session to building fluent retrieval of basic arithmetic facts.

7. Monitor the progress of students receiving supplemental instruction and other students who are at risk.

8. Include motivational strategies in Tier 2 and Tier 3 interventions.

> ▶ **WEB RESOURCES**
> A Web site located at http://superkids.com/aweb/ tools/math/ can be used to generate worksheets that can be used by teachers who want to provide additional practice to aid students' proficiency in mathematics. Topics available are addition, subtraction, multiplication, division, fractions, telling time, and many others.

Prenumber Skills

What are the prenumber skills students need to progress in arithmetic? Many students come to school with few experiences that allow them to develop important prenumber skills, such as one-to-one correspondence, classification, and seriation. These skills are essential to success in learning other mathematics concepts and skills.

One-to-One Correspondence

Matching one object with another is a core skill in any mathematics curriculum. It eventually leads the student to a better understanding of numeration and representation. One-to-one correspondence is used in life when we set a table, one place setting for each person; go to the theater, one ticket and seat for each person; and distribute paper in the classroom, one piece for each student. Activities for teaching one-to-one correspondence include the following:

- Use every opportunity to teach students the relationship between number words (e.g., *one, two, three, four*) and objects. For example, "Here are two paintbrushes: one for you and one for Madju." "There are five students in our group, and we need one chair for each student."
- Use familiar objects such as toy cars or blocks, and give a designated number (e.g., three) to each student. Pointing to the objects, ask students to place one block next to each of the objects. "You have

one block here, and you placed one block next to it. You have a second block here, and you placed a block next to it. And you have a third block here, and you placed a block next to it."

- Give the student a set of cards with numbers that the student recognizes. Ask the student to put the correct number of blocks on top of each number card. Reverse the task by giving objects to students and asking them to put the correct number card next to the objects.

Classification

Classification is the ability to group or sort objects on the basis of one or more common properties. For example, classification can be done by size, color, shape, texture, or design. Classification is an important prenumber skill because it focuses on common properties of objects and requires students to reduce large numbers of objects to smaller groups. Most students are naturally interested in sorting, ordering, and classifying. Activities for teaching classification include the following:

- Ask students to sort different-colored, -shaped, and -sized objects into groups. Ask them which rule they used for sorting their objects.
- Give each student an empty egg carton and a box of small objects. Ask the students to sort the objects according to one property (e.g., color). Now ask them to think of another way in which they can sort the objects (e.g., size, texture).
- Using an assortment of objects, ask a student to classify several of the objects into one group. Other students then try to guess the property or properties that qualify the objects for the group.
- Students can use pictures for sorting tasks. Animals, foods, plants, toys, and people can all be sorted by different properties.
- Board games and bingo games can be played by sorting or classifying shapes, colors, or pictures.

Seriation

Seriation is similar to classification in that it depends on the recognition of common attributes or properties of objects. With seriation, ordering depends on the degree to which the object possesses the attribute. For example, seriation can occur by length, height, color, or weight. Activities for teaching seriation include the following:

- Give students some objects of varied length, like sharpened pencils or used crayons, and ask the students to put the objects in order from shortest to longest.
- Ask students to stack their books from largest, on the bottom, to smallest, on the top.

- Using a peg and some rings of varied sizes, ask students to put the rings on the peg, from largest to smallest.
- Fill jars of the same size with varied amounts of sand, rice, water, or marbles, and ask students to put them in order.

Algebraic Principles

Most teachers think that algebra is a subject taught in secondary schools. Yet the algebra standard (National Council of Teachers of Mathematics, 2000) indicates that all students should understand the foundations of algebra. Students should understand mathematical patterns, relationships, and functions. Students should also be able to view mathematical structures and situations and represent and analyze them using algebraic symbols. Moreover, students should be able to represent and understand quantitative relationships through the use of mathematical models in their problem solving. The foundations of algebra and its basic principles can be learned at many different ages and within many math topics.

You might not point out to young students that they are solving algebraic problems when they are presented with fill-in the symbol that completes a pattern (e.g., XX OO XX O_) or provide a number that creates an equality (e.g., 2 + [_] = 3). However, just thinking that they can do algebra could be that great motivator that jump-starts their learning of more mathematics.

Math Concepts and Computation

Numeration and Place Value

What are several numeration concepts? Teachers and parents often assume that children understand numbers because they can count or name them. Understanding numbers is an essential basic concept; many children who have trouble with computation and word problems are missing numeral concepts. For example, Nadia's beginning experiences with math were positive. She had learned to read and write numbers and even to perform basic addition and subtraction facts. However, when Nadia was asked to perform problems that involved addition with regrouping, she demonstrated that she had very little knowledge of numbers and their meaning (her errors as shown here) and thus quickly fell behind her peers in math.

$$
\begin{array}{r} 48 \\ +26 \\ \hline 614 \end{array}
\qquad
\begin{array}{r} 37 \\ +55 \\ \hline 812 \end{array}
\qquad
\begin{array}{r} 68 \\ +17 \\ \hline 715 \end{array}
$$

Her computations are correct but she lacks the understanding of the concepts *numeration* and *place value* and what to do when the result exceeds the place value (tens and ones). The use of manipulatives would aid her understanding. She could use bundled and loose sticks to represent the problem; she could take 10 of the 14 (8 + 6) loose sticks and make a new bundle of ten to be placed with the other bundled tens (4 and 2). This would aid her in her understanding of numeration and place value.

Understanding numeration and place value is necessary in the following areas of mathematics:

- *Progress in computation.* Like Nadia, many students fail to make adequate progress in math because they lack understanding of numbers and place value.
- *Estimation* (i.e., "number sense"). Many students with learning difficulties in math do not have a sense of how much $1.00 is, what it means to have 35 eggs, or "about" how much 24 and 35 equals. They cannot check their answers by looking at problems and determining which answers could not be correct because the answer doesn't make "sense."
- *Reducing conceptual errors.* Students who understand the meaning of the numbers 43 and 25 would be less likely to make the following error:

$$\begin{array}{r} 43 \\ -25 \\ \hline 22 \end{array}$$

- *Understanding place value.* Students who know the meaning of the number 28 are going to have far less difficulty understanding the value of the 2 and the 8. Students need to understand that the 2 in 28 represents two 10s and the 8 represents eight 1s.
- *Understanding regrouping.* Regrouping errors, such as those below, are less likely to occur if a student understands numeration.

$$\begin{array}{r} 39 \\ +27 \\ \hline 516 \end{array} \qquad \begin{array}{r} 56 \\ -18 \\ \hline 42 \end{array} \qquad \begin{array}{r} 41 \\ -24 \\ \hline 23 \end{array}$$

- *Application of math computation to everyday problems.* Students who do not understand the real meaning of numbers have difficulty applying computation to everyday problems.
- *Understanding zero.* Students need to understand that 0 (zero) has more meaning than just "nothing." For example, in the number 40, they need to understand the meaning of the 0 as a place holder (zero ones).

Readiness for Numeration: Eighteen Concepts

Engelhardt, Ashlock, and Wiebe (1984) identified 18 numeration readiness concepts that can be assessed through paper-and-pencil assessment and interview.

A list of the behaviors that correspond to each concept, along with examples of how each concept can be assessed, follows.

Concept 1: Cardinality The face value of each of the 10 digits (0 through 9) tells how many. It is a good idea to get students to learn that zero is a number and is the empty set.

1. Identify sets with like numerousness (1 through 9). Circle the groups with the same number of *x*s.

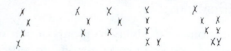

2. Represent and name the numerousness of the empty set (zero). "The box has 2 hats in it. Make 0 hats in the circle." Zero can be illustrated as [ ] or the empty set.
3. Identify, write, and name the numeral that corresponds to the numerousness of a set (1 through 9). Circle the numeral showing how many mice there are. How many mice are there?

3   2   6   4   9

4. Construct sets with a given numerousness (1 through 9). "Draw five dots." Remember to include zero set in these examples.
5. Recognize sets of one to five without counting. Place from one to five objects behind a book. Say to the students, "As soon as I move this book, I want you to tell me how many objects there are." Without counting, the students should tell you how many objects are in the group. Remember to include the zero set in these examples.

Concept 2: Grouping Pattern When representing quantity, objects are grouped into sets of a specified size (base) and sets of sets.

1. Form sets of 10 from a random set of objects or marks. Circle the *x*s to make as many groups of 10

as possible. Now circle the *o*s, *A*s, and the *s to make as many groups of 10 as possible.

```
xxxxxxxxxxxxx      xxxxxx      xxxxxxx
ooooooooooooooo    ooooooo     ooooooooo
AAAAAAAAAAA        AAAAA       AAAAAAA
***************    *******     *********
```

2. Construct appropriate groups to show how many. Give students about 125 Popsicle sticks and rubber bands. Say, "Bundle these sticks so that it will be easy to tell how many there are." Ask the students what was the basis (the number in each set) they used for their bundling the sticks together.

Concept 3: Place Value The position of a digit in a multidigit number determines its value (places are assigned values).

1. Given two multidigit numbers with the same digits but in different orders, identify the position of the digits as distinguishing the two numbers. How are 145 and 154 alike? How are they different?
2. Explain that the value of a digit in a multidigit number is dependent on its position. Using the numeral 5, place it in each column and ask, "How does the number change? How much is it worth?" Repeat with several other numerals (e.g., 3; 8) and then with other multidigit numbers (e.g., 125; 372).

100s	10s	1s

Concept 4: Place Value (Base 10) A power of 10 is assigned to each position or place (the place values). It is a good idea to provide the position or place names: thousands, hundreds, tens, and ones. Furthermore, it is a good idea to build from single-digit numbers to double-, then triple-, and four-digit numbers. With middle school students who have mastery of the base 10 concept, other base numbers (e.g., base 5 or 2) can be introduced.

1. Identify, name, and show the values for each place in a multidigit number. Show the number 1,829 and say, "What is the name of the place the numeral 8 is in?"
2. Select the place having a given value. Show the number 6,243 and say, "Circle or point to the numeral in the thousands place."

Concept 5: One Digit per Place Only one digit is written in a position or place.

1. Identify and name which numerals (digits) can be assigned to a place. Say to the students, "Tell me the numerals that can be written in the tens place."
2. State that no more than one digit should be written in a place or position. Then ask, "What's wrong with these problems?"

$$
\begin{array}{r} 85 \\ +39 \\ \hline 1114 \end{array} \qquad
\begin{array}{r} 27 \\ +35 \\ \hline 512 \end{array} \qquad
\begin{array}{r} 13 \\ +48 \\ \hline 511 \end{array}
$$

3. Rewrite or restate a nonstandard multidigit numeral (or its representation) as a numeral with only one digit in each place or position. Say to the students, "Write the numeral for this:"

10s	1s
5	4
7	8

Bundled and loose straws or ten blocks and unit blocks could also be used to help gain this understanding of one digit per place.

Concept 6: Places—Linear/Ordered The places (and their values) in a multidigit (whole-number) number are linearly arranged and ordered from right to left.

1. Identify the smaller-to-larger ordering of place values in a multidigit number. Show the number 6,666 to the students and say, "Underline the 6 that is worth the most, and circle the 6 that is worth the least."
2. Describe how the place values are ordered. Show the number 8,888 to the students, and say, "Point to the 8 which is 8 hundreds; point to the 8 which is 8 tens." Then ask, "Which of these 8s is worth more?"
3. State or demonstrate that the places in a multidigit number are linearly arranged. Say to the students, "Rewrite this problem correctly."

$$
\begin{array}{r} 7 \qquad 1 \\ 2 \qquad 4 \\ 6 \quad 3 \qquad 8 \\ + \qquad\quad 0 \\ \hline \end{array}
$$

Concept 7: Decimal Point The decimal point in a decimal fraction indicates the location of the units (ones) and tenths and hundredths places. Use the table to illustrate where this occurs so that a link to prior knowledge is made. Have the students place the numerals in the correct place. Start with the number 13, then 13.5, and several more numbers with tenths; once the tenths are understood use numbers with hundredths, like 26.34, 57.92, and 10.01. Ask the students to tell you the value of different numbers.

10s	1s	tenths	hundredths

1. Given a decimal fraction, identify the digit in the units (ones) place. Show the number 29.64 to the students, and say, "Circle the numeral in the ones place." Repeat this with several other numbers like 45.72, 26.89, and 19.03.
2. Given juxtaposed digits and a digit's value, identify and place the decimal point to show the appropriate multidigit number. Show the number 284 to the students, and say, "Place the decimal in the correct place to show 2 tens, 8 ones, and 4 tenths." After tenths then numbers that include hundredths can be used. As students get more proficient with this you can show a number like 3201 and say, "Place the decimal in the correct place to show 3 tens, 2 ones, and 1 hundredth."
3. State the meaning (function) of the decimal point.

Concept 8: Place Relation/Regrouping Each place in a multidigit number has a value 10 times greater than that of the place to its right and one-tenth the value of the place to its left (place relationships and regrouping).

1. Describe the relationships between the values of two adjacent places in a multidigit number. Show the number 222 to the students, and say, "How does the first 2 in the number compare with the second 2?"
2. Express the value of a multidigit number in several ways. Give the following problem to the students: 1 hundred, 8 tens, and 6 ones can also be expressed as _____ tens and _____ ones.

Concept 9: Implied Zeros All numbers have an infinite number of juxtaposed places, each occupied by an expressed or implied digit. In places to the left of nonzero digits in whole numbers written as numerals, zeros are understood; in places to the right of nonzero digits and the decimal point in decimal fractions, zeros are understood.

1. Name the digit in any given place for any multidigit number. Tell the students to rewrite each number and show a digit in each place.

1000s	100s	10s	1s	tenths	hundredths
683					
27					
79					
4.3					
351.84					

2. Rewrite a given number with as few digits as needed. Tell the students to cross out the zeros that are not needed.

0301	004	01.30
1010	105	0246.080

3. State a rule for writing zeros in a multidigit number. Ask the students, "When do we need to write zeros in a number?"

Concept 10: Face Times Place The value of any digit in a multidigit number is determined by the product of its face and place values (implied multiplication).

1. Show, name, and identify the value of a specified digit within a multidigit number. Show the number 1,468 to the students and ask, "How much is the 6 worth: 0, 6, 10, 60, or 16?" Ask, "What is the 4 is worth: 4, 40, 400, or 4,000?" Then use more examples. Also, include a decimal number, like 25.79, and ask, "How much is the 7 worth: 70, 7, 7 tenths or 7 hundredths?
2. Name and identify the operation that is used to determine the value of a digit in a multidigit number. Ask the students, "In 1,468 how do we find that 6 is worth 60? Do we add, subtract, multiply, or divide?"
3. State a rule for finding the value of a specified digit in a multidigit number. Ask the students, "How do you know that 6 is worth 60 in the number 1,468?"

Concept 11: Implied Addition The value of a multidigit number is determined by the sum of the values of each digit (implied addition).

1. Express any multidigit number as the sum of the values of each digit.
294 = _____ ones + _____ tens + _____ hundreds
Also use a decimal number, like 38.4. 38.4 = _____ tenths + _____ ones + _____ tens.
2. Express the sum of digit values as a multidigit number.
4 ones + 3 tens + 6 hundreds = _____
Also use a decimal number, 2 tenths, 4 ones, 5 tens, _____ (remind students who may forget the decimal point).
3. Identify the operation that is used to determine the value of a multidigit number. Ask the students, "To know the value of 287, do we add, subtract, multiply, or divide the value of each numeral?"

Concept 12: Order Multidigit numbers are ordered.

1. Order multidigit numbers. Say to the students, "Put these numbers in the correct order from smallest to largest: 1689, 1001, 421, 1421." Remember to use multidigit decimal numbers too (e.g., 32.4, 101.45, 7.1, 78.23, 45.34, 45.23, 45.31, 45.07).
2. Describe a procedure for determining which of two unequal multidigit numbers is larger. Show the numbers 984 and 849 to the students and ask, "How do

you know which is larger?" Also use unequal multi-digit decimal numbers like 3.45 and 3.06 and ask, "How do you know which is larger?"

Concept 13: Verbal Names (0 through 9) In English, the verbal names for the numbers 0 through 9 are unique.

1. Identify the oral/written names of the 10 digits. Ask the students to write the name next to each digit:

   0 _____   4 _____   7 _____
   1 _____   5 _____   8 _____
   2 _____   6 _____   9 _____
   3 _____

2. State the names for the 10 digits.

Concept 14: Verbal Names with Places In English, the verbal names for multidigit numbers (except 10 through 12) are closely associated with the written numbers (i.e., combining face and place names).

1. Give a multidigit number, identify the verbal name for one of the digits that includes both a face and place name. Show the number 2,847 and ask the students, "How is the 8 read?"
   a. eight   c. eighty
   b. eight hundred   d. eighteen
2. Identify the digit in a multidigit number that is stated first in giving the verbal name. Say to the students, "Write the numeral that is said first in reading the number."

   44 _____   6,186 _____
   284 _____   37 _____

3. Select two-digit numbers whose naming pattern is different from most. Ask the students to circle the numbers that when read aloud are different from the others: 17, 43, 126, 11, 281.

Concept 15: Periods and Names Beginning with the ones place, clusters of three (whole numbers) adjacent places are called *periods* and are named by the place value of the rightmost member of the number triad (e.g., ones, thousands, millions).

1. Given a multidigit number, insert commas to form periods. Ask the students to put commas in the correct places: 28146, 682, 7810, 192642.
2. Name the periods of a given multidigit number. Ask the students, "Which number represents the periods?"

   284,000,163_____

   (ones, hundreds, thousands, millions)

Concept 16: Naming in the Ones Period Numerals in the ones period are named by stating, from left to right, each digit's name (except zero) followed by its place

name (ones being omitted; special rules exist for naming tens).

1. Name three-digit numbers (tens digit not being a 1 or 0). Tell the students to write the name for 683.
2. Name three-digit numbers (tens digit being 1). Tell the students to write the name for 718.
3. Name three-digit numbers (tens digit being 0). Tell the students to write the name for 502.

Concept 17: Naming Multidigit Numbers In naming a multidigit number, the digits in each period are read as if they were in the ones period, followed by the period name (ones period name being omitted).

1. Name multidigit numbers up to six digits. Tell the students to write the name for 284,163.
2. Name multidigit numbers over six digits. Ask the students to read the following numbers:

   1,846,283   27,219,143
   103,600,101   3,078,420

Concept 18: Decimal Places and Their Verbal Names Beginning with the decimal, the first place to the right is the tenths place. The adjacent places (to the right) are hundredths, thousandths, ten thousandths, hundred thousandths. In reading the decimal numbers they are named by the place value of the rightmost member of the decimal number (e.g., 25.6 is twenty-five and six tenths; 65.39 is sixty-five and thirty-nine hundredths).

1. Give a decimal number, identify the verbal name for the decimal digits place. Show the number 43.7 and ask the students, "How is the 7 read?"
   a. seven hundredths
   b. seven tenths
   c. seventy
   d. seventeen
2. Identify the decimal digit name in a multidigit decimal number that is stated by giving the verbal name. Say to the students, "Write the decimal verbal name that is said in reading the number."

   4.63 _____   6.18 _____
   28.41 _____   1.373 _____

Teaching Place Value Place value is directly related to the students' understanding of numeration. Students need to be able to do the following:

- *Group by ones and tens.* Using manipulatives, pictures, and then numerals, students need practice and instruction in grouping by ones and tens. Students can sort manipulatives such as buttons or sticks in groups of 10. Students can also use a table grid to record their answers.

Assessing and Teaching Mathematics   **383**

	Ones	Answer
2	3	23
6	2	62
4	7	47

Source: J. M. Engelhardt, R. B. Ashlock, & J. H. G. Wiebe, *Helping Children Understand and Use Numerals* (Boston: Allyn & Bacon, 1984), pp. 89–149. Copyright 1984 by Allyn & Bacon. Adapted by permission.

Use "tens blocks" and "single blocks" to represent numbers. For example, 24 can be represented as follows:

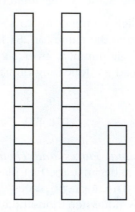

Flannel boards can also be used to group tens and ones.

• *Naming tens.* Teach students to identify numbers by the number of tens. For example, 6 tens is 60, 4 tens is 40, 8 tens is 80, and so on. Give students opportunities to count by tens and then name the number. For example, "Count by tens 3 times." "Ten, twenty, thirty." "Count by tens 7 times." "Ten, twenty, thirty, forty, fifty, sixty, seventy." Also give students opportunities to draw picture diagrams that represent the place values of tens and ones and to identify the number from diagrams.

• *Place value beyond two digits.* Once students can accurately group and identify numbers at the two-digit level, introduce them to three- and four-digit numbers. It is a good idea to be certain students have mastered the concept of *two-digit place value* before the teacher introduces numbers and place values greater than two digits. Many of the principles that students have learned in terms of two-digit place value will generalize to three digits and beyond. Give students plenty of opportunity to group, orally name, and sequence three- and four-digit place values.

• *Place value with older students.* Because place value is a concept that is taught during the primary grades, students who have not adequately learned the skill will likely have problems with computation and word problems. Students need opportunities to learn place value. Many of the games and activities that have been designed to teach place value focus on young children and are less appropriate for older students.

Following are five sources of numbers that may be useful for teaching place value to older students:

1. An odometer
2. Numbers from students' science or social studies texts
3. Numbers from the population of your school (e.g., number of freshmen, sophomores, juniors, seniors)
4. Population data from your town, county, state, or country
5. The financial data page from a newspaper

Addition, Subtraction, Multiplication, and Division

Most of students' time in math instruction is spent on computation: memorizing facts and practicing addition, subtraction, multiplication, and division problems; and completing math sheets, workbook pages, and problems copied from books that require the continued practice and application of math computation principles. It is probably for this reason that many students find math boring and miss its applicability to everyday life. Providing appropriate instruction and instructional activities is important to turning the learning of computation into a more desirable process for students.

Teachers can help to make computation exercises and fact learning more engaging by using computer-assisted instruction, which is equally effective for teaching basic arithmetic facts as the conventional drill and practice (Okolo, 1992). Students are likely to be more persistent in solving math problems and have a better attitude toward math when they participate in computer-assisted instruction (Cawley, Foley, & Doan, 2003).

Teachers can also improve students' understanding of computation as they improve students' conceptual knowledge and understanding of mathematics. One intervention for third-grade students with math disabilities addressed conceptual knowledge (Kaufmann, Handl, & Thony, 2003). Students were taught counting principles, the use of arithmetic symbols, memorization of numerals that equaled 10, strategies for memorizing facts, complex multistep calculations, and procedural language for using memorized facts. Students who participated in the intervention made significant gains.

▶ **WEB RESOURCES**

There is a Web site that may be useful to you to locate sources of information and lesson plans for teaching a wide variety of mathematics. There are links to almost every math topic at http://www.awesomelibrary.org/Classroom/Mathematics/Elementary_School_Math/Elementary_School_Math.html.

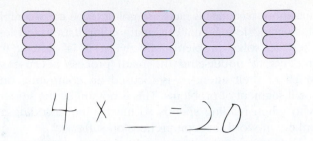

Computing math problems is much easier for students if they understand numeration and place value and if they are given frequent practical application of the math problems. When students are having difficulty performing math computation, it may be for the following three reasons:

1. They do not have an understanding of numeration and/or place value.
2. They do not understand the operation they are performing.
3. They do not know basic math facts and their application to more complicated computation. Students with attention deficit disorder often demonstrate difficulty in computation because they fail to automatize computational skills at an appropriate age (Ackerman, Anhalt, & Dykman, 1986). By *automatize*, we mean learning computational facts so that they are automatic, quickly done in one's head. Students with attention deficit disorder require more time for computation.

Understanding the Operation Students should be able to demonstrate their understanding of an operation by drawing picture diagrams and illustrating it with manipulatives. For example, Sara was able to write the correct answer to the multiplication fact 3 × 2 = 6. However, when asked to draw a picture to represent the problem, she drew three flowers and two flowers. She seemed totally undisturbed that the number of flowers she drew was different from the answer she wrote. When asked why she had drawn the number of flowers she did, Sara said, "I drew three flowers for the 3 and two flowers for the 2." When the teacher questioned her further, she discovered that Sara had no understanding of multiplication. By rote, she had memorized the answers to some of the elementary multiplication facts. The teacher used manipulatives such as chips and buttons to illustrate multiplication.

The following activities can be helpful in teaching students to understand mathematical operations:

- The following drawing illustrates how chips in rows can be used to illustrate multiplication. For example, ask, "How many 4s make 20? Fours are placed on the board _____ times."

- Have students talk aloud about what is involved in solving a problem. Do not let them merely *read* the problem; ask them to *explain* what it means. For example, "63 – 27 means that someone had 63 jelly beans and gave 27 of them to a friend."
- Have students explain the process to another student by using block manipulatives. For example, "24 + 31 is the same as adding 4 one-block pieces to 1 one-block piece and 2 ten-block pieces to 3 ten-block pieces."
- Have students close their eyes and use noises to illustrate operations. For example, to illustrate multiplication, the teacher can tap in groups of six and ask, "How many times did I tap a group of 6?"

> tap-tap-tap-tap-tap-tap
> tap-tap-tap-tap-tap-tap
> tap-tap-tap-tap-tap-tap

"Yes, I tapped a group of 6 three times. Now I am going to tap a group of 6 three times again and I want you to tell me how many taps there are altogether. Yes, when you tap a group of 6 three times there are 18 total taps." This same process can be used for addition and subtraction (Bley & Thornton, 1981).

In addition, for a student who is more visual in his or her learning or has a hearing impairment, you could show the 3 rows of 6 stars and ask similar questions. "How many rows of 6 stars are there? Now count the rows by sixes. Six, twelve, eighteen; that is correct." For the more kinesthetic learners the teacher could have the students stand in three groups of six students each, and ask the questions and count off.

Knowing Basic Math Facts Two of the reasons students may have difficulty with computation have been discussed: They do not understand numeration and/or place value, and they do not understand the computation process. A third reason students may have difficulty with computation is they do not know basic math facts. A common instructional misconception is that if students learn basic arithmetic facts they will no longer have difficulties with other arithmetic operations and problems. Arithmetic facts do not help students in analyzing or understanding the application of arithmetic operations; however, they do aid in the acquisition and speed of performing arithmetic operations. Students who do not know basic math facts are going to be considerably slower and less accurate in math computation and less likely to solve problems effectively. It is difficult for students to understand the math process because so much of their attention is focused on computing one small segment of problems. This is not unlike the student who when reading spends so much time decoding an unknown word that comprehension suffers.

Using thinking strategies assists in the acquisition and retention of basic math facts (Thornton & Toohey, 1985). Without direct instruction, students with learning disabilities often do not discover and use these strategies and relationships for learning and retaining math facts (Thornton, 1978). Some thinking strategies that are used by students who are successful at solving basic math facts (Thornton & Toohey, 1985; Thornton, Tucker, Dossey, & Bazik, 1983) can be taught to students who are having difficulties:

- *Using doubles.* Students can learn to use doubles to solve basic math facts. If a student knows 6 + 6 = 12, then the student can easily compute 6 + 7.
- *Counting-on.* Students do not need to resort to counting from one to solve math facts. They can learn to count on from the largest number in an addition fact. For example:

$$7 + 2 = \_\_\_\_\_$$

The student counts on two more from 7: "seven, eight, nine." Students can use this same principle when subtracting, only they count backwards. For example:

$$7 - 2 = \_\_\_\_\_$$

The student counts backward two from 7: "seven, six, five." Students can be taught counting-on before operations, and then they will only need to learn to apply the principle.

- *Using the commutative idea.* The commutative property means that adding or multiplying any two numbers always yields the same answer regardless of their order. Students can be taught that with addition and multiplication, if they know it one way, they know it the other. For example:

$$3 + 5 = 8$$
$$5 + 3 = 8$$
$$2 \times 9 = 18$$
$$9 \times 2 = 18$$

- *Thinking one more or less than a known fact.* Rasheed knew most of the easy math facts and several of the basic math facts but had trouble with the more difficult ones. When his teacher taught him how to use the math facts he knew to solve the more difficult ones, his math performance improved. For example, Rasheed knew 5 + 5 = 10, but when he was presented with 5 + 6, he began counting on his fingers. His teacher taught him to

think of 5 + 6 as one more than 5 + 5, and 5 + 4 as one less than 5 + 5. Pictures such as the following can help to illustrate the principle:

$$
\begin{array}{ccccc}
 & & ** & & ** \\
5 + 5 = 10 & & ** & + & ** & = \\
 & & * & & * \\
 & & & & \\
 & & ** & & ** \\
5 + 6 = & & ** & + & ** & = \\
 & & * & & ** \\
 & & & & \\
 & & ** & & ** \\
5 + 4 = & & ** & + & ** & = \\
 & & ** & & ** \\
 & & * & & * \\
\end{array}
$$

- *Using tens.* Students can learn that 10 + any single-digit number merely changes the 0 in the 10 to the number they are adding to it.
- *Using nines.* There are two strategies that students can apply to addition facts that involve nines. First, they can think of the 9 as a 10 and then subtract 1 from the answer. As illustrated here, the student is taught to think of the 9 as a 10:

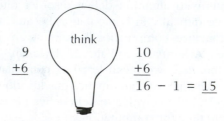

$$
\begin{array}{cc}
9 & \quad\quad 10 \\
+6 & \quad\quad +6 \\
\hline
 & \quad\quad \overline{16} - 1 = \underline{15}
\end{array}
$$

- *Counting by twos, threes, and fours.* Being able to count by multiples helps in addition, multiplication, and division. Multiplication facts can be taught by interpreting 3 × 4 as counting by threes 4 times. Division facts, such as 8 ÷ 2, can be interpreted as, "How many times do you count by twos before you reach 8?"
- *Relationships between addition and subtraction, between multiplication and division.* After students learn addition facts, you can show them the relationship between the addition fact and subtraction. For example, if students know 7 + 6 = 13, they can learn the relationships between the known addition fact and the subtraction fact, 13 − 7 = _____. Whenever possible, reinforce this principle as students are working, "You know 8 + 4 = 12, so 12 − 4 = must be _____." Give students known addition facts and ask them to form subtraction problems. These sample relationships can be used to teach multiplication and division facts (see Figure 11-4).

Van Luit and Naglieri (1999) have been successful in teaching students to compute multiplication and division by ensuring that they learn the following six concepts:

1. Multiplication is repeated addition.
2. Reversibility means that 4 × 7 is the same as 7 × 4.

► **Figure 11-4** Relationships between
Addition and Subtraction;
Multiplication and Division

Known Addition Facts	Made-Up Subtraction Facts
5 + 5 = 10	$10 - 5 = 5$
3 + 2 = 5	_____
8 + 8 = 16	_____
6 + 4 = 10	_____

Known Multiplication Facts	Made-Up Division Facts
7 × 4 = 28	$28 \div 4 = 7$
8 × 8 = 64	_____
5 × 9 = 45	_____
5 × 10 = 50	_____

3. The need to memorize the basic multiplication facts below 100.
4. Division is repeated subtraction.
5. The need to memorize the basic division facts below 100.
6. Ways to apply multiplication and division in real-life problems.

If you think these strategies for assisting students in learning math facts seem logical and automatic, you are right. For most students, they are. However, students with learning difficulties in math do not automatically use these strategies, and this prevents them from acquiring the math facts they need for accurate and speedy computation.

When these strategies are taught directly, students' math performance improves. When Ms. Pappas taught strategies to students who were having difficulty in addition, she used the strategies summarized in Apply the Concept 11-3, and she enlisted the help of other students who were performing the math skill accurately. She interviewed students who knew how to perform the skill and asked them to talk aloud while they solved the problems so that she could learn what strategies they used. She then taught these strategies to students who were having problems.

Peer-Assisted Instructional Practices Perhaps one of the most effective procedures for teaching math facts to students with learning and behavior problems is the use of cross-age tutors. Cross-age tutors are older students, often students who do not have learning or behavior problems, who serve as tutors for younger students with learning difficulties. Cross-age tutors are particularly effective in teaching math facts because the skills they need to be effective can be acquired quickly, in as little as two 45-minute periods. In a study that successfully used cross-age tutors to teach addition facts to students with learning disabilities (Beirne-Smith, 1991), tutors were trained to do the following:

- Use contingent reinforcement.
- Use task and error correction procedures.

- Use procedures for counting-on.
- Use procedures for rote memorization of facts.
- Repeat skills and instruction until mastery.

Cooperative learning groups, usually small groups of students (three to five per group), can be used to have students work together to solve problems. Maheady, Harper, and Sacca (1988) conducted a cooperative learning math instruction program for ninth- and tenth-grade students with mild disabilities. Students who participated in the cooperative teams performed better in mathematics and received higher grades than those who did not.

Constant Time-Delay Procedure Constant time delay is a procedure for teaching math facts that provides for systematic assistance from the teacher through near errorless control of the prompt to ensure the successful performance of the student (Gast, Ault, Wolery, Doyle, & Belanger, 1988; Schuster, Stevens, & Doak, 1990; Stevens & Schuster, 1988; Wolery, Cybriwsky, Gast, & Boyle-Gast, 1991). Students are presented with a math problem and are allowed a specific amount of time to give the correct answer. If students do not respond within the allotted time, a controlling prompt, typically the teacher modeling the correct response, is provided. Students then repeat the model. Correct responses before and after the prompt are reinforced; however, only correct responses that are provided before the prompt are counted toward criterion.

Math Computation Errors How could students make the errors in Figure 11-5? It appears as though all the students did was guess. Yet each of the students who computed the problems can tell you what he or she did to get the answer. Most errors that students make are rule governed. Although the rule they are applying is not always obvious, the students are using some rule to tell them how to compute a problem. In problem A in Figure 11-5, Erika said, "I took 1 away from 7 to get 6 and took 0 away from 5 to get 5." In problem B, Jeff added across, adding the 3 and 1 to get 4 and adding the 2 and 3 to get 5. In problem C, Yolanda said, "I knew this wasn't right, but it was the best I knew how to do. I multiplied 3 × 4 to get 12, and then 6 × 4 to get 24." In

► **Figure 11-5** Math Computational Errors

(A)	15	(B)	15	(C)	63
	− 7		+ 23		× 23
	65		45		2412

(D)	37	(E)	13
	27		+ 4
	17		53
	72		

Assessing and Teaching Mathematics **387**

11-3 Strategies for Teaching Addition Facts

Addition Facts Groups by Strategy for Recall

Fact Group	Examples	Most Popular Strategy for Working Out Unknown Answers
Count-Ons	(+1, +2, +3, facts)	"Feel" the count
Zero Facts	(6 + 0, 0 + 4)	Show it
Doubles	(4 + 4, 7 + 7)	Use pictures (e.g., 7 + 7 is the 2-week fact; 7 + 7 = 14)
10 Sums	(especially 6 + 4)	Use 10-frame

No fingers needed! (applies to the four groups above)

9s	(4 + 9, 9 + 6)	Use pattern
Near Doubles	(4 + 5, 7 + 8)	Relate to doubles (via pictures)
Four Last Facts	(7 + 5, 8 + 4, 8 + 5, 8 + 6)	Make 10, add extra

Note: Turnarounds (commutatives of facts within each group) would be learned before moving to a different group of facts.

Verbal Prompts Used in the Addition Program

Fact Group	Sample	Facts	Sentence Patterns (Verbal Prompts)
Count-Ons	8 $+2$	3 $+7$	Start BIG and count on.
Zeros	6 $+0$	0 $+3$	Plus zero stays the same.
Doubles	5 $+5$	7 $+7$	Think of the picture.
Near Doubles	5 $+6$	7 $+8$	Think doubles to help.
9s	4 $+9$	9 $+7$	What's the pattern?
Near 10s	7 $+5$	6 $+8$	Use 10 to help.

Source: C. A. Thornton & M. A. Toohey (1985), Basic math facts: Guidelines for teaching and learning, *Learning Disabilities Focus, 1* (1), pp. 50, 51. Reprinted with permission of the Division for Learning Disabilities.

problem D, Shawn knew that 7 plus 7 plus 7 was 21, but he was operating under the faulty rule that you always carry the smaller number, so he wrote the 2 in the ones column and carried the 1. In problem E, Jae said, "I added 4 plus 1 because it was easier than adding 4 plus 3." When given several similar problems, she had no concerns about placing the number in the ones or tens column, depending on where it was easier for her to add. All of these students applied faulty rules as they performed math computations. Once the teacher discovered the faulty rules they were applying, she was able to teach them the underlying concepts and the correct rule for completing computations.

Teachers can learn a great deal about students' thinking in mathematics through an oral diagnostic interview (Lankford, 1974). Such an interview will provide information about what each student is doing and why he or she is doing it that way. For the diagnostic interview to yield accurate, helpful information, the teacher must ask the student questions about math computation in a nonthreatening way. For example, "I am interested in learning what you say to yourself while you do this problem. Say aloud what you are thinking." It is often most effective to use a problem that is different from the one the student has performed incorrectly. The assumption behind this interview is

Apply the Concept

11-4   Errors in Computation

1. *Wrong operation.* The student attempts to solve the problem by using the wrong process. In this example the student subtracted instead of adding.

$$\begin{array}{r} 24 \\ +\ 11 \\ \hline 13 \end{array}$$

2. *Computational error.* The student uses the correct operation but makes an error recalling a basic number fact.

$$\begin{array}{r} 24 \\ +\ 11 \\ \hline 58 \end{array}$$

3. *Defective algorithm.* The student attempts to use the correct operation but uses a wrong procedure for solving the problem. The error is not due to computation.

$$\begin{array}{r} 24 \\ -\ 17 \\ \hline 13 \end{array}$$

4. *Random response.* The student has little or no idea how to solve the problem, and writes numbers randomly.

$$\begin{array}{r} 304 \\ -\ 196 \\ \hline 396 \end{array}$$

Source: Adapted from G. H. Roberts (1968), The failure strategies of third-grade arithmetic pupils, *The Arithmetic Teacher, 15*, pp. 442–446.

that there is an underlying reason behind the mistakes, and understanding why a student is making errors provides valuable diagnostic information that leads directly to instruction. Roberts (1968) identified four common failure strategies in computation, which are summarized in Apply the Concept 11-4.

Students with learning problems are slower but not necessarily less accurate when it comes to doing computation and learning math facts. When teaching mathematics in your classroom, teachers should consider that students with learning problems may need additional practice to learn math facts and more time to perform mathematics computations because they often lack the skill in automatization to perform math computation effectively and efficiently.

Language of Math Computation "What do you mean by 'find the difference'?" a student might ask. "Am I supposed to add or subtract? Why don't you just say it in plain English?" Many students with learning and behavior problems have difficulty with the language of computation. However, understanding the vocabulary is important for success in the regular classroom, application to math story problems, and communication with others. Understanding the terminology of the four basic operations as well as the symbols associated with the processes is important. Students also need to understand the vocabulary that is associated with the answer derived from each of these processes. Table 11-1 illustrates the relationship between the process, symbol, answer, and problem.

After teaching the information on the chart, the teacher can use the following three activities:

1. Cover one column (e.g., the symbols), and ask the student to write the answer.

2. Place each of the symbols, answers, and problems on a separate index card, and ask the student to sort them by process.

3. Play concentration with two columns. Two columns of index cards (e.g., the symbol cards and answer cards) are laid answer down, and the students take turns searching for matching pairs by selecting two cards. When a student picks up a corresponding pair, he or she keeps the pair and takes another turn.

Use of Calculators Many students with learning and behavior problems let computation interfere with their ability to learn problem solving. They spend so much time learning to compute the problem accurately that they miss the more important aspects of mathematics, such as concept development and practical application.

Many teachers do not use calculators because they believe that the use of calculators threatens the acquisition of basic skills. Mr. Coffland, a third-grade teacher, put it this way: "If I let my students use calculators to solve problems, they will not have adequate practice in

Table 11-1   Relationship of Process, Symbol, Answer, and Problem

Process	Symbol	Answer	Problem
Addition	+	Sum	$6 + 4 =$
Subtraction	−	Difference	$5 - 3 =$
Multiplication	×	Product	$8 \times 5 =$
Division	÷	Quotient	$12 \div 6 =$

Apply the Concept

11-5 Sequence for Teaching Fractional Concepts

The student

1. manipulates concrete models (e.g., manipulating fractional blocks and pegs).
2. matches fractional models (e.g., matching halves, thirds, fourths).
3. points to fractional model when name is stated by another (e.g., the teacher says "half" and the student selects a model of "half" from several distractors).
4. names fractional units when selected by another (e.g., the teacher points to a fractional unit such as a "fourth" and the student names it).
5. draws diagrams or uses manipulatives to represent fractional units (e.g., the teacher says or writes fractional units such as "whole," "half," and "third," and the student uses manipulatives or drawings to represent these units).
6. writes fraction names when given fractional drawings (e.g., next to the student writes "half").
7. uses fractions to solve problems (e.g., place $1\frac{1}{2}$ cups of sugar in a bowl).
8. uses the concept of like units to help solve computations with fractions.

basic skills. They will become too dependent on using the calculator." Research suggests that Mr. Coffland has little to fear. The results of a summary of 79 studies (Hembree, 1986) on the use of calculators suggest the following:

- The use of calculators does not interfere with basic mathematics skill acquisition. In fact, calculator use can improve skill acquisition.
- Only in fourth grade does sustained calculator use interfere with skill development.
- The use of calculators in testing situations results in much higher achievement scores, particularly when students are low in problem-solving ability.
- The use of calculators improves students' attitudes toward mathematics.
- Calculators can be introduced at the same time that paper-and-pencil practice exercises are introduced.
- Students can use calculators to solve complex problems that they construct. This also provides support for improved self-concept with math skills.

In summary, as long as students get basic skills instruction, the use of calculators is a positive aid to mathematics instruction. There are several ways in which students who are having difficulty with mathematics instruction can use calculators:

1. *To develop a positive attitude.* Using a calculator removes the drudgery associated with solving computations and makes problem solving fun.
2. *To improve self-concept.* Being able to compute extremely complex problems on a calculator gives students confidence in their mathematics abilities.
3. *To improve practice in problem solving.* Students are willing to tackle difficult problem-solving tasks when they have a calculator to help solve the problem. Students still have to decide what numbers are used, what operation is involved, and whether additional operations are necessary. Using a calculator can free students from the burden of computation and allow more focus on thinking about the problem.
4. *To develop their own problems.* Using a calculator lets students develop their own problems. They can then exchange their problems with each other and use their calculators to solve them.

Fractions

The National Mathematics Advisory Panel (2008) states that a conceptual understanding of fractions and decimals, as with learning whole numbers, and the operational procedures for using them are mutually reinforcing, however, the concept of fractions is one of the most difficult math concepts for children and adults (Hecht, Vagi, & Torgeson, 2007). Moreover, the difficulties with fractions (including decimals and percents) is a great obstacle to further progress in mathematics (National Mathematics Advisory Panel, 2008). Teachers, through the use of their instructional materials, ensure the learning of conceptual and procedural knowledge of fractions and of proportional reasoning. Even though many teachers think the concept of fractions is difficult to teach, the concept of a fraction can be introduced before the actual fractions are even discussed. For example, Figure 11-6 shows the relationship between common fractional terminology and represented units. Moreover, through the availability of calculators, teachers can now place less emphasis on being able to compute fractions and more emphasis on understanding the meaning and use of fractions.

Figure 11-6 Unit Representation of Fractions

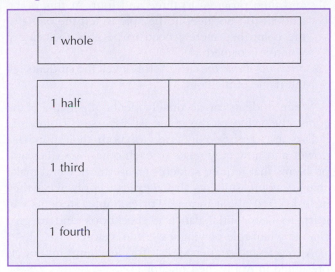

Children as young as 3, 4, and 5 are introduced to the concept of fractions as they receive halves or quarters of apples as part of lunch. They also help a parent in food preparation and cooking. "We use one cup of milk and one-half cup of flour." "You'll need to share the cookie with your brother. You each may have half of the cookie." When children enter school teachers often use cooking activities to enhance students' understanding of fractions. Many manipulative aids can be used to teach fractions: colored rods, cardboard strips and squares, blocks, fractional circle wheels, cooking utensils such as measuring cups, and any unit dividers such as egg cartons and muffin pans.

Teaching fractions, like teaching most concepts, proceeds from concrete to abstract. Apply the Concept 11-5 demonstrates the teaching sequence.

However, the use of intuitive procedures for the acquisition of knowledge in fractions is unlikely to be successful with low achievers (Kelly, Gersten, & Carnine, 1990). Success in understanding fractions is likely to occur when the following three variables are presented (Kelly et al., 1990):

1. *Systematic practice in discriminating among different problem types.* Students with learning and behavior problems often confuse algorithms when computing fractions. For example, they learn to compute denominators and then use this procedure when adding, subtracting, multiplying, and dividing.
2. *Separation of confusing elements and terminology.* Much of the language of learning fractions is unfamiliar and confusing to youngsters. If the language is well explained and the concepts are well illustrated,

students are more likely to be successful in learning fractions.
3. *Use a wide range of examples to illustrate each concept.* Students have a difficult time generalizing beyond the number of examples provided by the teacher; a wide range and large number of examples facilitate understanding.

Measurement

Measurement includes weight, distance, quantity, length, money, and time. Measurement can be taught almost entirely with applied problems. For example, students learn time by using the clock in the classroom or by manipulating a toy clock; they learn money by making purchases with real or toy money; and they learn measures such as pint, liter, and teaspoon through following recipes. With each measurement unit that is taught (e.g., weight, distance, money), students need to learn the vocabulary and concepts for that unit. Only after students understand the terminology and concepts and have had experience applying the concepts in real measurement problems should they be exposed to measurement instruction through the use of less applied procedures such as textbooks and worksheets.

In addition, an instructional activity has been provided for you to help illustrate the use of a real-world problem to help in the teaching of the concept of fractions (see Cake for Four—No, Make that Six! in the "Instructional Activities" section later in the chapter). Another instructional activity has been provided for you to help illustrate the use of lots of examples to teach the concept of use of like units with fractions (see Finding Like Units in the "Instructional Activities" section later in the chapter).

Time Even before coming to school, most children can tell time by the hour or know when the clock says that it is time to go to bed or time for dinner. The following teaching sequence assists students in understanding time:

1. *Teach students to sequence events.* Younger students can sequence the normal routine of the school day. For instance, "First we have a group story, then reading, then we go to recess." Additional practice in sequencing events can occur with story cards, events that occur at home, field trips, and so on.
2. *Ask students to identify which events take longer.* Name two events (e.g., math time and lining up for recess), and ask students to identify which event takes longer. Name several events, and ask students to put them in order from the event that takes the longest to the one that is quickest to complete.

1:25

one twenty-five

A scope-and-sequence list of skills for teaching time is presented in Apply the Concept 11-6.

Money Students with learning disabilities often have difficulty applying money concepts because they have not mastered many of the earlier concepts, such as the value of coins, how coins compare (e.g., a quarter is more than two times as much as a dime), and how the value of the coins relates to what can be purchased. One parent reported that her child was frequently taken advantage of because he would trade coins of high value for coins of less value. Students with learning difficulties often do not know the price of common goods. Although they may not need to know the exact price of a loaf of bread or a television set, they should be able to estimate what these items cost.

When initially teaching students to identify money, start with real coins. After they learn to recognize real coins, switch to play money and then to representations of money on workbook pages. The following sequence is useful in teaching money identification:

1. *Teach students to match the same coins.* Give students several different coins, and ask them to place all of the same coins in the same group.
2. *Ask students to point to the coin when you name it.* Depending on the students' skill level, you may want to start with two coins (e.g., a penny and a nickel) and then progress to three and four. At this point, students do not need to be able to tell the name of the coin; they merely need to be able to locate it when it is named.
3. *Students name the coin.* At this level, the students tell the name of the coin.

When students can accurately identify the name of the coins, the value of the coins is discussed. Coins and dollars are discussed in terms of both their purchase power and how they relate to each other. Activities and problems that require students to use money and make change assure students that they can apply what they have learned about money. For example, students can learn to keep and balance a checkbook and to give change when role-playing a clerk in a store.

A scope-and-sequence list for teaching money is presented in Apply the Concept 11-7.

Problem Solving

What factors contribute to difficulties with problem solving, and how can teachers assist students in learning problem-solving strategies? "I can read the arithmetic all right; I just can't read the writing" (Barney, 1973, p. 57). Many students with learning problems have trouble with traditional story problems in mathematics because their difficulty in reading makes understanding the math problem almost impossible. In addition, students with learning problems often have difficulty with logical reasoning, which is the basis of many story problems. It is also common that their mathematics education has focused primarily on operations and not on understanding the reasons for operations or even a thorough understanding of the numbers that are involved in operations. Because of their difficulties with reading and logical reasoning and perhaps because of insufficient

● ● ● ● ● ● *Apply the Concept* ● ● ● ● ● ●

11-6 **Time: Scope and Sequence of Skills**

The student

- Sequences events—first, and then next.
- Identifies duration of events—what takes longer and what is quicker to do.
- Tells time to the hour.
- Tells time to the half hour.
- Knows the days of the week.

- Knows the names of the months.
- Tells time to the quarter hour.
- Knows the number of days in a week.
- Knows the number of months in a year.
- Can use a calendar to answer questions about the date, the day, and the month.

- Writes time to the hour.
- Writes time to the half hour.
- Writes time using 5-minute increments.
- Writes time accurately.
- Can solve story problems using time.

11-7 Money: Scope and Sequence of Skills

The student

- Correctly identifies penny, nickel, dime, and quarter.
- Knows how many cents are in a penny, nickel, dime, and quarter.
- Can add to the correct amount when shown combinations of pennies, nickels, dimes, and quarters.

- Can describe items that can be purchased with combinations of pennies, nickels, dimes, and quarters.
- Can solve simple word problems involving pennies, nickels, dimes, and quarters.
- Can identify a dollar bill, a $5 bill, a $10 bill, and a $20 bill.

- Can identify the value of combinations of coins and various dollar bills.
- Can solve verbal math problems involving combinations of coins and various dollar bills.

instruction in mathematics, students with learning problems often find problem solving the most difficult aspect of mathematics.

Despite its difficulties, problem solving may be the most important skill we teach students who have learning and behavior problems. Whereas most other students are able to apply the operations they learn to real-life problems with little direct instruction, students with learning problems will be less able to apply these skills without instruction, rehearsal, and practice. Students with learning disabilities lack metacognitive knowledge about strategies for math problem solving. Poor math performance is not solely a function of math computation difficulties (Montague & Bos, 1990). Students who are taught strategies for problem solving are more likely to be successful than are students who are taught the sequence for solving problems (Wilson & Sindelar, 1991).

Students need to know when and how to add, subtract, multiply, and divide. Knowing *when* involves understanding the operation and applying it in the appropriate situation. Knowing *how* is the accurate performance of the operation. Most students are better at *how* than at *when;* problem solving gives students practice at these skills.

Factors Affecting Successful Verbal Problem Solving

Teachers need to consider the factors that affect successful story problem solving (Carnine, 1997; Goodstein, 1981; Jitendra, Hoff, & Beck, 1999) when writing and selecting story problems and instructing students. Use the following strategies:

- *Teach big ideas.* When students understand the big idea or principle, all of the subordinate concepts around that big idea make more sense and are easier to learn and remember (Carnine, 1997). An example of a big idea is

volume. You can teach students the principle of volume and then provide examples of real-life problems that students can solve by applying the big-idea principles they learn about volume.

- *Sameness analysis.* Carnine and colleagues determined the importance of sameness in mathematical problem solving through a series of research investigations (Engelmann, Carnine, & Steely, 1991). The idea is to connect math concepts so that students see the ways in which aspects of mathematical problem solving are the same. Identify types of word problems, and then explicitly teach students the ways in which these word problems are alike.

- *Cue words.* The presence or absence of cue words can significantly affect students' abilities to solve verbal word problems. The cue word *altogether* is illustrated in the following example: Maria has 4 erasers. Joe has 7 erasers. How many erasers do they have *altogether?* The cue word *left* is illustrated in the following example: Jasmine has 9 pieces of candy. She gave 3 pieces to Lin. How many does she have *left?* Students need to be taught to look for cue words that will guide them in solving problems.

- *Reasoning.* Ask students to think about the idea behind the story problem. Does it appear that the person in the problem will get more or less? Why? What operation will help to solve this? What numbers in the story do we have to use? Are there numbers that we do not have and need to compute? Ask students to explain the way in which they set up and calculated the problem so that they can justify what they've done and why they've done it that way.

- *Syntactic complexity.* The sentence structure within the story problem needs to be kept simple. Learner performance can be significantly impaired when the sentence contains a complex interrogative sentence structure (Larsen, Parker, & Trenholme, 1978). The sentence length and vocabulary can also affect verbal problem solving.

• *Extraneous information.* Extraneous information in word problems causes difficulties because the majority of students attempt to use all of the information in solving the problem. For example: "Mary's mother baked 10 cookies. Mary's sister baked 8 cookies. Mary's brother baked 3 cupcakes. How many *cookies* were baked?" The information regarding Mary's brother baking three cupcakes is extraneous, yet many students will use the information in attempting to solve the problem. Extraneous information in story problems is associated with decreases in accuracy and computation speed with students. Blankenship and Lovitt (1976) explain students' difficulties with extraneous information by suggesting that the difficulties are based not on reading the entire story problem but merely on knowing which numbers are needed to solve the problem. Students will construct the problem using the numbers available in the story problem, disregarding the question and the content available in the story problem. When students are able to complete story problems successfully without extraneous information, teach them to complete story problems with extraneous information.

• *Content load.* The content load refers to the number of ideas contained within a story problem. The story problem should not be overloaded with concepts (West, 1978). Students need to be taught to discriminate between relevant and irrelevant concepts.

• *Suitable content.* Story problems should contain content that is interesting and appealing to students and relevant to the types of real problems that students have or are likely to encounter.

• *Monitor progress.* Use weekly tests of word-problem solving to monitor study progress on each type of word problem students have mastered and/or are learning. Reteach when necessary.

• *Provide guided practice.* Use diagrams to demonstrate how to solve the problem, and guide students through the development and use of these diagrams. As students demonstrate increasing proficiency with independent use of diagrams and strategies for effective problem solving, reduce the amount of support provided.

• *Use computer-assisted instruction.* Computer-assisted instruction gives students opportunities to practice computation and problem solving independently, and provides correction and feedback. Many students prefer to do mathematics with the computer. *My Math* (Cawley, 2002) is an example of a computer software program that incorporates three mathematical components: computation problems, arithmetic word problems, and arithmetic story problems. See Tech Tips for additional information about using software to enhance mathematics instruction.

Methods of Teaching Story Problem Solving

There are three important considerations in preparing students for success in solving story problems: (1) providing anchored instruction that relates to a real-life problem the students might encounter (Goldman, Hasselbring, & the Cognition and Technology Group at Vanderbilt, 1997); (2) providing story problems in an appropriate sequence; and (3) making students aware of common types of errors. Students also need to learn specific strategies that will assist them in using a successful process for mastering story problems in class and applying those principles to the mathematics of everyday life.

A step-by-step strategy for teaching sixth-grade students to solve story problems is illustrated in Apply the Concept 11-8 (Smith & Alley, 1981). Students first need to learn the strategies, then practice them with support from a teacher, and finally practice them independently until they can apply the principles with success. After continued success, students make adaptations in or condense the steps they use.

The section on cognitive strategy instruction in Chapter 2 discusses how to teach students learning strategies.

Fleischner, Nuzum, and Marzola (1987, p. 216) devised the following instructional program to teach arithmetic problem solving to students with learning disabilities:

READ	What is the question?
REREAD	What is the necessary information?
THINK	Putting together = addition
	Taking apart = subtraction
	Do I need all the information?
	Is it a two-step problem?
SOLVE	Write the equation
CHECK	Recalculate
	Label
	Compare

Montague and Bos (1986a, 1986b) demonstrated the efficacy of the learning-strategy approach, described in Apply the Concept 11-9, with high school adolescents with learning disabilities.

TECHNOLOGY THAT HELPS STUDENTS SOLVE MATH PROBLEMS

Many educational software programs, with varying foci, are designed to enhance mathematics instruction. As a tool or utility, programs that offer students and teachers ease of use can be extremely helpful in accommodating all learners in your class.

MathPad and MathPad plus and Number Concepts by Cabmium LearningTechnologies, Inc. at http://store.cambiumlearning.com/Search ResultsHP.aspx?searchtype=Subject&sorttype= Subject&Query=Mathematics&site=itc
These programs, designed for students K-8, enable learners to do arithmetic directly on the computer. These programs are ideal for learners who need help organizing or navigating through math problems or who need help organizing or navigating through math problems or who have difficulty using pencil and paper with math.

AAA Math at
   www.aaamath.com
This Web resource for math activities is loaded with explanations, interactive practice, and games, along with teacher resources.

Ten Tricky Tiles by Sunburst Technologies at http://store.sunburst.com/Category.aspx? MODE=RESULTS&CATID=3360
This program is for young children who are developing their arithmetic and number skills. Sunburst Technologies offers numerous math programs for all ages and skill levels.

In summary, when teaching story problems to students with learning and behavior problems, teachers should keep the following guidelines in mind:

- Be certain the students can perform the arithmetic computation before introducing the computation in story problems.
- Develop a range of story problems that contain the type of problem you want the student to learn to solve.
- Instruct with one type of problem until mastery is attained.
- Teach the students to read through a word problem and visualize the situation. Ask them to read the story aloud and tell what it is about.
- Ask the students to reread the story—this time to get the facts.
- Identify the key question. In the beginning stages of problem solving, the students should write the key question so that they can refer to it when the computation is complete.
- Identify extraneous information.
- Reread the story problem, and attempt to state the situation in a mathematical sentence. The teacher plays an important role in this step by asking the students questions and guiding them in formulating the arithmetic problem.
- Tell the students to write the arithmetic problem and compute the answer. (Students can compute some problems in their heads without completing this step.)
- Tell the students to reread the key question and be sure that they have completed the problem correctly.
- Ask the students whether their answer is likely, based on their estimate.

Apply the Concept

11-8 · Steps for Teaching Students to Solve Story Problems

Story Problem: Mark had $1.47 to spend. He spent $0.34 on gum. How much money does he have left?

I. Read the problem
   A. Find unknown words
   B. Find cue words
      (e.g., *left*)

II. Reread the problem
   A. Identify what is given
      1. Is renaming needed?
      2. Are there unit changes?
   B. Decide what is asked for
      1. What process is needed?

   2. What unit or category is asked for? (e.g., seconds, pounds, money)
III. Use objects to show the problem
   A. Decide what operation to use
IV. Write the problem
V. Work the problem

11-9   Teaching Adolescents to Solve Story Problems

The eight steps in the verbal math problem-solving strategy are described below:

1. *Read the problem aloud.* Ask the teacher to pronounce or define any word you do not know. (The teacher will pronounce and provide meanings for any words if the student asks.)

   Example: In a high school there are 2,878 male and 1,943 female students enrolled. By how many students must the enrollment increase to make the enrollment 5,000?

2. *Paraphrase the problem aloud.* State important information, giving close attention to the numbers in the problem. Repeat the question part aloud. A self-questioning technique such as "What is asked?" or "What am I looking for?" is used to provide focus on the outcome.

   Example: Altogether there are a certain number of kids in high school. There are 2,878 boys and 1,943 girls. The question is by how many students must the enrollment increase to make the total enrollment 5,000. What is asked? How many more students are needed to total 5,000 in the school?

3. *Visualize.* Graphically display the information. Draw a representation of the problem.

4. *State the problem.* Complete the following statements aloud: "I have . . ." "I want to find . . ." Underline the important information in the problem.

   Example: I have the number of boys and the number of girls who go to the school now. I want to find how many more kids are needed to total 5,000.

5. *Hypothesize.* Complete the following statements aloud: "If I . . ." "Then . . ." "How many steps will I use to find the answer?" Write the operation signs.

   Example: If I add 2,878 boys and 1,943 girls, I'll get the number of kids now. Then I must subtract that number from 5,000 to find out how many more must enroll. First add, then subtract. + −. This is a two-step problem.

6. *Estimate.* Write the estimate. My answer should be around . . . or about . . . (The skills of rounding and estimating answers should be reinforced at this step.) Underline the estimate.

   Example: 2,800 and 2,000 are 4,800. 4,800 from 5,000

is 200. My answer should be around 200.

7. *Calculate.* Show the calculation and label the answer. Circle the answer. Use a self-questioning technique such as, "Is this answer in the correct form?" (Change from cent sign to dollar sign and decimal point should be reinforced when solving money problems.) Correct labels for the problems should be reinforced.

   Example:

   $$\begin{array}{r} 2,878 \\ +1,943 \\ \hline 4,821 \end{array} \qquad \begin{array}{r} 5,000 \\ -4,821 \\ \hline 179 \text{ students} \end{array}$$

8. *Self-check.* Refer to the problem and check every step to determine accuracy of operation(s) selected and correctness of response and solution. Check computation for accuracy. (Checking skills will be reinforced at this step.) Use the self-questioning technique by asking whether the answer makes sense.

Source: M. Montague & C. S. Bos (1986), The effect of cognitive strategy training on verbal math problem-solving performance of learning disabled adolescents, *Journal of Learning Disabilities, 19,* pp. 26–33. Copyright © 1986 by PRO-ED, Inc. Reprinted by permission.

Teaching math story problems does not have to be limited to the content area of math. Cawley (1984) discusses how story problems can be integrated with instruction in reading so that reading level does not interfere with understanding the math problems. At the same time, story problems can enhance and support what the student is doing in reading. For example, a story about a mother duck and her babies was part of a student's reading lesson. During mathematics, the teacher made minor changes in the story and used it for instruction in story problems in mathematics (see Figure 11-7).

This same procedure can be used with junior high and high school students' content area textbooks. Math

▶ **Figure 11-7**   Example of Teacher-Altered Story for Use in Story-Problem Instruction

The mother duck went to the pond with her *eight* babies. They looked for their new friend. *Two* more baby ducks joined them. How many baby ducks were there?

story problems can be taken from social studies and science tests; Cawley and Miller (1986) refer to these as knowledge-based problems. Usually, these problems require specific knowledge in the content area. Cawley (1984) identifies the integration of math into other content areas as an important means of promoting generalization of math concepts.

Pictures can be used to facilitate processing information in solving mathematical word problems. For example, using Figure 11-8, a teacher could say, "The small monkeys have four bananas, and the large monkeys have six bananas. How many bananas would they have if they put them all together?"

Instructional manipulatives can also be used to assist students with learning problems in solving mathematical word problems. Cuisenaire rods can be used to represent the numerical values in the problem and assist students in better understanding and solving mathematical word problems (Marsh & Cooke, 1996).

Improving Math Performance

How can math interventions be used to improve math performance? There are three types of interventions for mathematics instruction for individuals with learning disabilities (for review, see Mastropieri, Scruggs, & Shiah, 1991; Parmar & Cawley, 1997). One type of intervention is cognitive, one is behavioral, and the third is alternative instructional delivery systems, which includes cooperative learning, computer-assisted instruction, and interactive video games.

Cognitive Approaches

Cognitive behavior modification (CBM) can be used with instructional procedures in mathematics. CBM often takes the form of self-instruction, which relies on using internalized language to facilitate the problem-solving process. Based largely on the work of Meichenbaum (1977, 1985), CBM is receiving attention as an alternative strategy for teaching arithmetic to students

with learning difficulties. When self-talk is said aloud these verbalizations are beneficial to the arithmetic process. Either by naming the sign before proceeding (Parsons, 1972) or verbalizing the steps in the arithmetic process while solving the problem (Grimm, Bijou, & Parsons, 1973), there is a significant improvement in performance.

Leon and Pepe (1983) taught a five-step self-instructional sequence to special education teachers. Students receiving arithmetic instruction from these teachers who were trained in the sequence improved greatly both in arithmetic computation and in generalizing the skills they acquired. Second-grade students with learning disabilities became more proficient at learning addition through strategy instruction than through drill and practice. This study demonstrated that even very young children with learning disabilities can benefit from cognitive approaches to math instruction (Tournaki, 2003). The following sequence for using self-instruction in mathematics is a modification of the approach used by Leon and Pepe (1983):

1. *Modeling.* The teacher demonstrates how to compute a problem by using overt self-instruction. This overt self-instruction, or talking aloud about the process, assists students who have learning problems in knowing what they should say to themselves and what questions they should ask to keep themselves focused on the process.
2. *Coparticipation.* The teacher and students compute the problem together by using overt self-instruction. This step helps the students to put the procedure in their own words, yet supplies the support of the teacher while the students are still learning the process.
3. *Student demonstration.* The students compute the problem alone by using overt self-instruction, and the teacher monitors the students' performance. The students are more independent in this step; however, the teacher is still available to give correction and feedback.
4. *Fading overt self-instruction.* The students continue to demonstrate the computation of the problem with internal self-instruction. Often students have a check sheet of symbols or key words to cue them to the key points.
5. *Feedback.* The students complete the problem independently by using covert self-instruction and providing self-reinforcement for a job well done.

Behavioral Approaches

Cues Behavioral techniques are also available to improve students' math performance. As you know, stimulus cues precede responses and often control or provide information to control responses. In arithmetic instruction, teachers need to identify relevant cues and determine whether

▶ Figure 11-9 Math Problems Enlisting Various Cues

(1)
```
   37
   24
 + 89
```

(2) *[clock showing approximately 6:30]*

What time is it?_____

(3) How long is this line?_____

the students are aware of these cues and are using them appropriately. In Figure 11-9, three different problems are presented; there are many different cues that a student must understand and attend to before accurately performing these problems. For example, in problem 1 of Figure 11-9, the student must know what "+" means, what the numbers represent, and what procedure to follow to perform the problem. In problem 2, the student must know what the picture represents, the difference between the short and long hands of the clock, and what each of the numbers represents. Problem 3 requires the student to understand the cue *long* and to know what type of tool is needed to address the problem. Math provides many stimulus cues, and teachers need to be certain that students recognize and understand the cues and attend to them.

Teachers can also provide cues to assist students in learning new skills. For example, the following list illustrates cues a teacher provided when students were first learning long division:

$\div$ (divide) $6\sqrt{478}$ $8\sqrt{521}$
$\times$ (multiply)
$-$ (subtract)
$\downarrow$ (bring down)

Corrective Feedback Providing corrective feedback reinforces student performance. Corrective feedback involves telling the students what they are doing well, including procedures, accuracy of responses, and work style. It also involves identifying areas in which a student needs further assistance. Corrective feedback should be given frequently. Teachers should not wait until students have completed tasks but should give feedback while they are working on the task. Feedback should also be precise. Rather than saying, "You are doing a good job," a teacher should say, "You remembered to carry. All of the answers in the first row are correct. Good job."

Task Analysis Task analysis is a process of specifying the behaviors needed for a particular task that can help to shape student responses. Students are taught behaviors

from the simple to the more complex until they can perform the target behavior. For example, a teacher's goal may be for a student to complete two-place addition with carrying by solving a verbal math problem. The student's present level of performance is knowledge of math facts when adding numbers between 0 and 9. Through task analysis, the teacher identifies the prerequisite concepts that need to be known and the many problem-solving skills that need to be shaped through instruction and practice before the student is performing the target behavior, in this case a verbal math problem with two-place addition:

- Number concepts for 0–9
- Number concepts for 10–100
- Place value
- Simple oral word problems, requiring addition knowledge for 0–9
- Simple written word problems, requiring addition knowledge for 0–9
- Two-place addition problems
- Oral-addition word problems requiring knowledge of two-place addition
- Written-addition word problems requiring knowledge of two-place addition

The teacher decided that it would take approximately three months to reach the goal. He knew that his mathematics program would focus on other skills during that period (e.g., time, measurements, and graphs). Apply the Concept 11-10 lists several things teachers can do to improve their students' math performance.

Focus on Real-World Mathematics

Many students with learning and behavior problems manage to graduate despite having only a minimal understanding of mathematics skills. Many, relieved to escape formal education in mathematics, have the unfortunate misconception that they are finished with mathematics. Soon they find that functioning as an adult requires managing money, checkbooks, interest on loans, and credit cards as well as filing taxes, completing employment forms for deductions, and using basic math skills in their jobs. Apply the Concept 11-11 lists the mathematics skills all students need to acquire because they are essential for survival in the real world.

Mathematics instruction for students with learning disabilities needs to focus on teaching functional skills necessary for independent living (Patton, Cronin, Bassett, & Koppel, 1997). Many of the skills that are most important for students with learning disabilities are not part of general mathematics curricula because they do not need to be taught through direct instruction to non-learning-disabled students. Halpern (1981) suggests that students with learning disabilities learn the realistic prices of products, how to estimate, and how to tell time and estimate

11-10   Ways to Improve Math Performance

Baker, Gersten, and Lee (2002) conducted a synthesis of all of the empirical research on teaching mathematics to students with math difficulties. They reported several themes from these studies that teachers should consider in their instructional routines:

- Use ongoing progress-monitoring data in mathematics. These data allow teachers to determine how students are progressing, adjust instruction, and give feedback to students on their performance.
- Use peer-assisted learning to provide support for mathematical learning. When peers work together on organized practices of computing and problem solving, both peers benefit.
- Use explicit and systematic instruction in the elements of mathematics, which is associated with improved outcomes in math for students. This type of instruction guides students through problems and calculations rather than relying on students to figure it out independently.
- Provide families with information on how their students are performing, and engage families as the supporters and motivators for their children's progress in mathematics.

---

time intervals. According to Halpern (1981), most arithmetic that is done in the real world is done orally, yet arithmetic done in classrooms is largely done with pencil and paper. More attention to oral practice in the classroom is needed.

Math instruction for students with disabilities requires teachers to consider the functional math skills that students need. Apply the Concept 11-12 presents an outline of content for teaching functional math.

Furthermore, Schwartz and Budd (1981) recommend an eight-step sequence for teaching a functional math curriculum. This approach appears to be particularly useful with junior high and high school students.

1. *Become motivated.* Students need to feel that there is a valid reason for learning to solve mathematics problems. This may include identifying how math is used at home and on the job. Students can interview their parents to determine all of the ways in which they use functional math. Former students or speakers can be invited to discuss the need for math when they joined the work world.

2. *Choose the operation.* When students are able to identify the question being asked, they find it much easier to identify the appropriate operation for resolving the question. Students must understand how an operation is performed before they use the operation in functional mathematics.

3. *Understand the problem.* Students need to understand the type of question being asked in verbal problem solving. They need to understand such terms as *fewer, greater, more, altogether*, and *in addition to* in order to be successful in doing functional math. The teacher should present realistic problem situations and discuss the questions being asked. The teacher then asks students to focus on key words and discuss their meaning and assists students in identifying unnecessary information.

4. *Estimate the answer.* This step encourages students to check to determine whether their selected operation is reasonable. For example, a teacher may give the following problem: After Lee lends half of his total savings of $8.40 to his sister, how much money will he have left? A student selects multiplication as the operation for solving the problem. The student estimates the answer and has a second opportunity to check whether the correct operation was chosen. Questions such as the following should be asked of the student: "After multiplying, will Lee have more money or less? When we lend money to people, do we usually have more money or less? Is multiplying the correct operation?"

5. *Do the operation.* Students should be able to perform the operation, but a review of skills may be necessary.

6. *Check the answer.* Students check to be sure that numbers were copied correctly and the problem was performed correctly. Students are encouraged to answer the question: Is this a reasonable answer to the problem?

7. *Understand the answer.* After determining the answer, students should be able to interpret it. The teacher may ask additional questions that allow students to demonstrate more fully that they understand the answer and the problem.

8. *Apply the skill.* The application of the first seven steps is discussed in relation to problems generated by the students and the teacher.

Curricula and Materials

Traditional math curricula have provided problems for students with learning disabilities. These problems have been summarized by Blankenship (1984):

- The reading vocabulary is difficult, and the reading level is too high.

11-11

Mathematical Concepts for the Everyday World

More and more science and technology are permeating our society, and with this, the need for more mathematics to understand the scientific and technological concepts is increasing. The new level of mathematical competencies, skills, and attitudes toward mathematics required of modern citizenry is much higher than what was expected 25 years ago. The following represent the skills and competencies considered necessary for adults to participate effectively in contemporary society:

1. Numbers and numerals
   - Express a rational number using a decimal notation.
   - List the first ten multiples of 2 through 12.
   - Use the whole numbers (four basic operations) in problem solving.
   - Recognize the digit, its place value, and the number represented, through billions.
   - Describe a given positive rational number using decimal, percent, or fractional notation.
   - Convert to roman numerals from decimal numerals and conversely (e.g., data translation).
   - Represent very large and very small numbers using scientific notation.

2. Operations and properties
   - Write equivalent fractions for given fractions such as $\frac{1}{2}$, $\frac{2}{3}$, $\frac{3}{4}$, and $\frac{7}{8}$.
   - Use the standard algorithms for the operations of arithmetic of positive rational numbers.
   - Solve addition, subtraction, multiplication, and division problems involving fractions.
   - Solve problems involving percentages.
   - Perform arithmetic operations with measures.
   - Estimate results.
   - Judge the reasonableness of answers to computational problems.

3. Mathematical sentences
   - Construct a mathematical sentence from a given verbal problem.
   - Solve simple equations.

4. Geometry and measurement
   - Recognize horizontal lines, vertical lines, parallel lines, perpendicular lines, and intersecting lines.
   - Recognize different shapes.
   - Compute areas, surfaces, volumes, densities.
   - Understand similarities and congruence.
   - Use measurement devices.

5. Relations and functions
   - Interpret information from a graphical representation.
   - Understand and apply ratio and proportion.
   - Construct scales.

6. Probability and statistics
   - Determine mean, average, mode, median.
   - Understand simple probability.

7. Mathematical reasoning
   - Produce counterexamples to test validity of a statement.
   - Detect and describe flaws and fallacies in advertising and propaganda where statistical data and inferences are employed.
   - Gather and present data to support an inference or argument.

8. General skills
   - Maintain personal bank records.
   - Plan a budget and keep personal records.
   - Apply simple interest formula to calculate interest.
   - Estimate the real cost of an item.
   - Compute taxes and investment returns.
   - Appraise insurance and retirement benefits.

Source: M. C. Sharma, "Mathematics in the Real World," in J. F. Cawley (Ed.), *Developmental Teaching of Mathematics for the Learning Disabled* (Austin, TX: PRO-ED, 1984), pp. 224–225. Reprinted with permission of PRO-ED, Inc.

- The sequencing of material presented is poor, multiple concepts are introduced, and focus skips from one concept to another.
- There is an insufficient number of problems covering each concept.
- There are insufficient opportunities and problems focusing on application.
- There is too much variance in the formatting of the pages.
- Students often do not have the prerequisite skills that the text assumes they possess.

Teachers who attempt to use traditional curricula with students who have learning difficulties will need to control for these factors in their teaching. This means that the teacher may have to carefully and thoughtfully select the concepts, skills, and problems as well as the instructional explanations from the traditional math curricula materials or choose alternative math materials.

A number of curricula have been developed that focus on teaching math skills to students with learning difficulties. Some of these curricula are described in Apply the Concept 11-13.

11-12 · Content for Teaching Functional Math

Consumer Skills

Making change
Determining cost of sale items utilizing
    percentages (e.g., "25% off")
Determining tax amounts
Doing cost comparisons
Buying on "time"
Balancing a checkbook
Determining total cost of purchases

Homemaking Skills

Measuring ingredients
Budgeting for household expenses
Calculating length of cooking and
    baking time when there are
    options (e.g., for a cake using
    two 9" round pans vs. two
    8" round pans)
Measuring material for clothing
    construction
Doing cost comparisons

Health Care

Weighing oneself and others
Calculating caloric intake
Determining when to take medication

Auto Care

Calculating cost of auto parts
Measuring spark plug gaps
Determining if tire pressure is correct
Figuring gas mileage

Home Care

Determining amount of supplies (paint,
    rug shampoo) to buy
Determining time needed to do projects
Measuring rods and drapes
Finding cost of supplies
Finding cost of repairs

Vocational Needs

Calculating payroll deductions
Determining money owed
Knowing when to be at work
Doing actual math for various jobs

Leisure Activities

Comparing travel expenses
Magazine and newspaper costs
Membership fees
Entertainment: movies, video rentals,
    sporting and artistic events

Home Management

Determining where to live
Moving expenses
Move-in expenses
Utilities
Insurance
Furniture
Additional expense

Transportation

Public or automobile
Maintenance
Insurance

Source: Adapted from J. R. Patton, M. E. Cronin,
D. S. Bassett, & A. E. Koppel (1997), A life skills
approach to mathematics instruction: Preparing
students with learning disabilities for the real-life
demands of adulthood, *Journal of Learning
Disabilities, 30* (2), pp. 178–187; and
S. E. Schwartz & D. Budd (1981), Mathematics
for handicapped learners: A functional approach
for adolescents, *Focus on Exceptional Children,
13* (7), pp. 7–8. Reproduced by permission
of Love Publishing Company.

INSTRUCTIONAL ACTIVITIES

This section provides instructional activities related
to mathematics. Some of the activities teach new
skills; others are best suited for practice and reinforcement of already acquired skills. For each activity, the
objective, materials, and teaching procedures are
described.

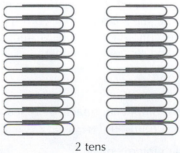

2 tens   3 ones

▶ Two-Digit Numbers: Focus on Reversals

Objective: To help students understand and use two-digit
numbers successfully (for use with students who write 23
for 32, 41 for 14, etc.).

Grades: Primary

Materials: Objects that can be grouped by tens (e.g.,
pencils, paper, chips, sticks)

Teaching Procedures: Four steps are recommended: First,
tell the students to group objects such as popsicle sticks or
chips in tens and then to tell the number of tens and the
number of ones left over. Next, the students count orally by
tens and use objects to show the count (e.g., 2 tens is 20,
6 tens is 60, and so on). When multiples of ten are established, extra ones are included (e.g., 2 tens and 3 is 23).
Because of naming irregularities, teens are dealt with last.

11-13   Sources of Curricula and Materials

- *Connecting Math Concepts* (Bernadette, Carnine, Engelmann, & Engelmann, 2003) is designed to provide explicit instruction and explanations of basic math concepts and the relationships between concepts for students in grades K–8. Mastered concepts are then used to build problem-solving skills. The lessons proceed in small, incremental steps with continuous review. Materials include teacher's guides, student textbooks and workbooks, and fact and independent worksheets for additional practice. All lessons are scripted for teachers and provide systematic instruction in story problems.

- *Math Exploration and Applications*, developed by Bereiter, Hilton, Rubinstein, and Willoughby (1998), provides instruction, games, and manipulatives for building fluency in math skills. It is also available in Spanish.

- The *Corrective Mathematics Program*, by Engelmann, Carnine, and Steely (2005), provides remedial basic math for students in grades 3 through 12, addressing seven areas: addition, subtraction, multiplication, division, basic fractions, decimals and percentages, and rational numbers and equations.

- *Structural Arithmetic*, by Stern, Stern, and Gould (1998), involves students in prekindergarten through third grade in making, discovering, and learning math concepts and facts. Colorful blocks are used to assist students in discovering math concepts.

- Cuisenaire rods, developed by M. Georges Cuisenaire, help impart conceptual knowledge of the basic structure of mathematics.

- *Real-Life Math* (Ellen McPeek Glisam) provides an imaginary town (Willow, USA) where students learn math by learning to live on a paycheck. Students learn to budget money and pay expenses. Activity book and materials are available from PRO-ED publishers (http://www.proedinc.com).

- *Key Math Teach and Practice*, by Connolly (1988), was developed to provide diagnosis of math difficulties and remedial practice. Materials include a teacher's guide, student progress charts, and sequence charts. Activities and worksheets are also provided.

- *Saxon Math* for kindergarten through secondary grades was developed to provide math instruction that continuously builds on previous instruction while increasing the complexity to learn math concepts in depth. Math concepts, problem solving, and applications are sequential.

- *Progress in Math*, developed by William H. Sadlier (Sadlier Oxford, 2006) for students in kindergarten through sixth grade, teaches math concepts with an emphasis on strategies for solving math problems. Step-by-step problem-solving strategies are taught, and the use of specific strategies is scaffolded throughout the lessons.

The students then group objects by tens and write to describe the grouping. The tens–ones labels, used in early stages, are gradually eliminated. On separate sheets of paper, the students write the number that corresponds with the grouping. The children use objects (tens and ones) to help compare and sequence numbers.

▶ Two Up

Objective: To practice multiplication facts by rehearsing counting by twos, threes, fours, and so on.

Grades: Primary through intermediate

Prerequisite Behaviors: Counting by twos, threes, and so on

Materials: A set of 48 cards made by printing the multiples of 2 from 1 to 12, using a different color of pen for each set (e.g., 2, 4, . . . , 12 in red, blue, green, and brown)

Teaching Procedures: Directions for playing the game are as follows: The cards are shuffled and dealt, giving an equal number of cards to each player. The player who has the red 2 starts the game by placing the red 2 in the middle of the table. The next player must place a red 4 on top of the red 2 or pass. Next a red 6 is needed, and so on. Each of the players plays in a similar manner. A player can play only one card each turn.

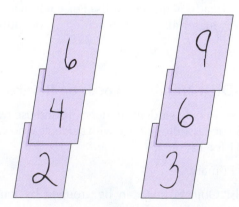

The object of the game is to play the cards from 2 on up. The first player to play all of his or her cards is the winner.

Adaptations: This game can be played with decks of threes, fours, sixes, and so on, called "Three Up," "Four Up," and so on. A different deck of cards must be made for each multiple.

▶ Clock-Reading Bingo

Objective: To give students practice in associating the time on a clock face to its written and spoken form.

Grades: Primary

three o'clock	seven o'clock	fifteen minutes after four	twenty minutes after twelve
fifteen minutes after six	twenty minutes after twelve	twenty minutes to eleven	twenty minutes after eleven
five minutes after five	fifteen minutes after ten	twenty-five minutes after one	twenty-five minutes to eleven
nine thirty	five minutes to seven	twenty-five minutes after twelve	ten o'clock

Materials: Cards that show times on a standard clock, large game boards with 16 squares and with times written at the bottom of each square, 16 "clock" chips (made by placing gummed labels on cardboard chips and drawing a clock on the face of the label), markers

Teaching Procedures: A caller holds up a clock face. The players must decide whether the time shown by that clock is on their game board. If it is, the player places a marker in the square that contains the written form. The winner is the first person who correctly completes a row

in any direction and reads the time in each winning square.

▶ Coin Concentration

Objective: To practice reading money amounts in four different notations and to reinforce coin recognition.

Grades: Primary, intermediate to high school (see "Adaptations" for older students)

Prerequisite Behaviors: Coin value, value placement, coin recognition of dollars and cents

Materials: Money picture card, money word card, money decimal card, money cents card

Teaching Procedures: The game of Coin Concentration can be played at several levels of difficulty, with varying skill emphasis depending on specific classroom needs. At the simplest level, use only one kind of money card. (Make two copies of the card, and cut it apart on the solid lines so students play with a total of 20 cards.) Decide on the number and type of cards to be used, and place them face down on the table.

The first player turns over two cards, one at a time, trying to match values. If the cards match, the player keeps them. If not, the player turns them back over on the table in their original location. Then the next player tries to make a match by turning over two more cards and so on, until all the cards are matched with their pair.

The winner is the player with the most matched cards. For variety, ask the students to add the total value of their cards and the player with the highest value wins. To add variety and increase difficulty, put different type cards down, and players can match 4¢ to $.04 or to *four cents*.

Adaptations: This activity can be used with older students by increasing the difficulty of the coin values represented and by adding a fifth card. On the fifth card is the name of an object that costs the corresponding amount. For example, if the money value is $329.00, the fifth card may have "Videocassette Recorder" written on it.

▶ Shopping Spree

Objective: To give students practice using money and understanding the concept of addition and subtraction with money.

Grades: Elementary-age students who are having difficulty with the money concepts (see "Adaptations" for use with older students)

Materials: Coins (and dollar bills when teaching the more advanced concepts), pictures of items

Teaching Procedures: Cut out magazine pictures of things children would like to buy, and put a price on each picture. Start with easy amounts, such as 5¢, 10¢, 25¢; then in future lessons, increase the complexity of the amounts to such things as 63¢ and 51¢. For higher grades, use dollar amounts. Have the class divide into two groups, with half the students serving as store clerks and the other half as shoppers. The shoppers buy picture items from the clerks. The shoppers are responsible for giving the correct amount of money. The clerks are responsible for giving the correct change. Then have students trade roles.

At a later date, distribute specific amounts of money and ask students to select several items without going over their designated amount. Or, ask students to show two or three different items and tell which item they can afford with their amount of money.

Adaptations: For older students, you can distribute pretend checkbooks. Each student gets a specified amount in his or her checkbook and must make appropriate deductions as he or she makes purchases.

▶ **99**

Objective: To generalize and practice adding numbers in one's head or on paper.

Grades: Intermediate to high school

Materials: Playing cards, paper, and pencils

Teaching Procedures: Explain that the objective of this game is to add cards up to a score of 99. Establish the following rules:

Jacks and queens = 10

Kings = 99

Nines = free-turn pass—to be used anytime

Fours = pass

Aces = 1

Other cards = face value

Each player is dealt three cards. The rest of the cards go face down on a draw pile. The players take turns discarding one card from their hand face up on a discard pile and drawing one card from the draw pile to put back into their hand. As a player discards his or her card, the player must add the number from the card to any previous score acquired up to that point in the game and say the new score out loud. Note the exceptions: If a player plays a nine, he or she receives a free-turn pass. If a player plays a four, he or she has to pass a turn with no score. The first player to score higher than 99 loses the game.

▶ **Shopping**

Objective: To provide practice in addition, subtraction, and comparing prices (problem solving).

Grades: Junior high

Materials: Supermarket sale ads that include the price per item (optionally mounted individually on cardboard and covered with clear plastic), made-up shopping lists to hand out to the class, pencil, and paper

Teaching Procedures: Divide the class into small groups. Tell the students that their shopping list contains the items that they will need this week. Assign each group a designated amount for groceries (e.g., $30.00). The object is to buy everything on the list while spending the least amount of money. Place on each desk the supermarket sale ads, each with the name of its store. After students buy an item, they record its price and the store where they bought it. (It's easier if one student in each group buys the meats, one buys the dairy products, and so on.) When the students have bought all the items on the list, tell them to total their bills and be ready to present the results.

▶ Cake for Four—No, Make That Six!

By Sandra Stroud

Objective: Developing students' concept of fractions by having them partition an object into equal parts.

Grades: Second through fourth grades (possibly higher)

Materials: For each student, a 6-inch paper circle; five strips construction paper, 1 inch wide by 8 inches long, in a color contrasting to that of the paper circle; eight small cookies, placed in a small sandwich bag

Teaching Procedures: Students move desks together so that each student has a partner with whom to compare his or her work. Materials are distributed. The teacher introduces the lesson by telling the students that they are going to take part in a "Let's Pretend" activity that will help them to learn that when they eat a piece of cake that has been divided into equal parts, they are actually eating a fraction of that cake.

The students are asked to imagine that they have just helped to bake a cake. It is their favorite kind of cake, and because there are four people in their pretend family, they are planning to divide it into four equal pieces. They are asked to think of the paper circle on their desk as the top of the cake and to show the teacher—and their partners—how they would use the strips of paper to divide the cake into four equal parts. When each child has successfully demonstrated this first partitioning task, they are asked what fraction of the whole cake each piece is and how that fraction is written.

Next, they are asked to imagine that their grandmother and grandfather have arrived unexpectedly and that the grandparents have accepted the family's invitation to stay for supper. The family certainly wants to share the cake with their grandparents, so into how many pieces will they now divide their cake? The teacher makes sure that each student shows six equal portions and that they understand that each piece of cake is now 1/6 of the whole—just enough for the six people at the dinner table. However, before that cake is served, Uncle Bob and Aunt Doris arrive! Now the cake will be divided into how many equal pieces? Finally, the time comes to decorate the cake with the cookies and to cut and serve the cake. (As a reward for all their good thinking, the students now get to eat the decorations—1/8 at a time!)

Students enjoy the story associated with this activity, and they enjoy comparing their partitioned cakes with those of their peers. This is a good example of cooperative learning. Students especially enjoy eating their cookies at the end of this activity.

▶ The Values of Coins

By Ae-Hwa Kim

Objective: To help students learn the relative values of coins (for example, students will determine that a quarter is worth 25 times as much as one cent).

Grades: Primary

Materials: Models with real coins for each step

Teaching Procedures: For the initial instruction, the teacher shows all models and coins and addresses the objective of the lesson. During the lesson, the teacher models and verbally explains each step, provides students with guided and independent practice, and gives them feedback.

1. Show students proportionate models to represent the values of coins.

1	1	1	1	1	1	1	1	1	1
1	1	1	1	1	1	1	1	1	1
1	1	1	1	1	1	1	1	1	1
1	1	1	1	1	1	1	1	1	1
1	1	1	1	1	1	1	1	1	1
1	1	1	1	1	1	1	1	1	1
1	1	1	1	1	1	1	1	1	1
1	1	1	1	1	1	1	1	1	1
1	1	1	1	1	1	1	1	1	1
1	1	1	1	1	1	1	1	1	1

2. Teach the values of coins and their relative values with models, which visually represent the values of coins and their relative worth. For example, one nickel is worth five pennies and so takes up the space of five pennies.

⑤	1	1	1	1	1	1	1	1	1
	1	1	1	1	1	1	1	1	1
	1	1	1	1	1	1	1	1	1
	1	1	1	1	1	1	1	1	1
	1	1	1	1	1	1	1	1	1
1	1	1	1	1	1	1	1	1	1
1	1	1	1	1	1	1	1	1	1
1	1	1	1	1	1	1	1	1	1
1	1	1	1	1	1	1	1	1	1
1	1	1	1	1	1	1	1	1	1

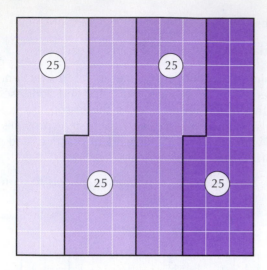

3. Teach the value of a set of coins with models, which visually represent the value of a set of coins.

4. Teach the students to compare the values of sets of coins with models.

5. Teach the students to use models to create a set of coins with a given value. Allow the students to use different combinations of coins to make the given value.

6. Teach the students to create a set of coins with a given value by using the fewest coins with models.

Source: Based on an activity by R. L. Drum & W. G. Petty (1997), Teaching the value of coins, *Teaching Children Mathematics, 5* (5), pp. 264–268.

▶ Learning Addition

By Ae-Hwa Kim

Objective: To help students understand how to do addition with three-digit numbers and provide practice in addition through activities.

Grades: Primary

Materials: Pictures of three different types of animals; three lengths of bricks (short, medium, and long); scratch paper

Teaching Procedures:

1. Seat three volunteer "animals" (e.g., zebra, giraffe, and deer) on chairs side by side in front of a chalkboard. Hang a sign with a picture of each animal around the neck of the student who acts as that animal. The sign on the right (deer) also has the word *ones* or *1s*, signifying the units place of the number. The middle sign (giraffe) shows the word *tens* or *10s*, signifying the tens place of the number. The sign on the left (zebra) has the word *hundreds* or *100s*, signifying the hundreds place of the number. Throughout the activity, the place-value words are visible.

2. Give each animal a supply of bricks. Long bricks signify hundreds; medium bricks signify tens; and short bricks signify single units. Give two long bricks to the hundreds zebra, five medium bricks to the tens giraffe, and eight short bricks to the ones deer. (First number = 258.)

3. Ask each animal to tell what he or she has been given as the teacher writes the combined number on the chalkboard.

4. Teach students the rules to this activity:
   • All business exchanges begin with the ones deer, then the tens giraffe, and finally the hundreds zebra. The animals receive their shipments in turn and take inventory of their bricks as they are received.
   • The inventory process ensures that the ones deer never has 10 ones bricks (short), the tens giraffe never has 10 tens bricks (medium), and the hundreds zebra never has 10 hundreds bricks (i.e., each animal's total is nine or less). If any animal has more than 10 bricks, he or she must trade 10 bricks for 1 brick of the next greater value.

5. The brick suppliers will arrive to deliver more bricks to each animal. For example, the supplier may bring 4 hundreds bricks, 7 tens bricks, and 3 ones bricks. (Second number = 473.)

6. When the ones deer inventories 11 bricks, a teacher reminds him or her of the rules and establishes that the ones deer must deliver a stack of 10 short bricks back to the supplier in exchange for 1 medium brick, which must then be given to the tens giraffe. The single short brick that remains is recorded on the chalkboard. When the 7 newly delivered medium bricks are added to the original 5 medium bricks and the medium brick passed from the ones deer, the tens giraffe then has 13 medium bricks. Therefore, he or she delivers one set of 10 bricks to the supplier in exchange for 1 long brick, which is then given to the hundreds zebra. The tens giraffe then reports an inventory of 3 medium bricks remaining. Our hundreds zebra then reports a total inventory of 7 long bricks, or hundreds. (Final answer: 258 + 473 = 731.)

Source: Based on an activity by M. M. Bartek (1997), Hands-on addition and subtraction with the Three Pigs, *Teaching Children Mathematics, 4* (2), pp. 68–71.

▶ Addition and America

By Ae-Hwa Kim

Objective: To motivate students to solve addition problems as well as to increase their accuracy of solving problems.

Grades: Second through fourth grades (possibly higher)

Materials: Map of the United States, tickets made of cards on which math addition facts are printed

Teaching Procedures:

1. Show students the map of the United States to get their attention.

2. Explain the rules of game:
   - The students try to move from their home state to another state across the nation.
   - Students have to have their ticket to travel from state to state.
   - Students must solve the addition problem printed on the ticket and read the name of the state. (The name of the state will be printed on the map, so students just need to read the word.)
   - Only when students get the right answer are they allowed to move to the next state. If students miss the problem, they have to stay in their current state until their next trial time.

3. Let the students play a game. During the game, the teacher assists them and also records the speed and accuracy of their answers.

Note: This game can be extended to subtraction, multiplication, and division.
Source: Based on an activity by D. E. Miller (1997), Math across America, *Teaching Exceptional Children, 24* (2), pp. 47–49.

▶ The Value of Numbers

By Ae-Hwa Kim

Objective: To help students understand the value of numbers (ones value, tens value, and hundreds value).

Grades: Primary

Materials: Popsicle sticks; rubber bands to group the popsicle sticks; a sign; number cards; three boxes to hold ones, tens, and hundreds of popsicle sticks

Teaching Procedures:
Practice

1. Count the number of popsicle sticks.

2. Model putting a rubber band around a group of 10 sticks; then ask students to put a rubber band around each new group of 10 sticks.

3. Model putting 1s in the ones box, 10s in the tens box, and so on. Ask students to put 1s in the ones box, 10s in the tens box, and so on.

Activity

1. Show the students a sign that says "Thank you for the _____ popsicle sticks" (e.g., 157).

2. Model putting that number of popsicle sticks in the boxes; then ask students to put the number of popsicle sticks in the boxes.

3. Change the numbers on the sign repeatedly, and allow students to practice grouping Popsicle sticks according to the sign.

Source: Based on an activity by C. Paddock (1997). Ice cream stick math. *Teaching Exceptional Children, 24* (2), pp. 50–51.

▶ Finding Like Units

Objective: To help students understand the need to use like units in working with fractions (common denominator for addition, subtraction, multiplication, and division of fractions).

Grades: Middle and upper grades

Materials: Whiteboard (chalkboard), dry-erase markers (chalk), overhead projector (document camera/projector), and transparencies

Teaching Procedures:

1. Write on the whiteboard the terms "8 feet" and "98 inches". Then below those write "12 yards" and "24 yards". Point to the top two lengths and ask, "Which is longer?" Then point to the bottom two lengths and repeat the question, "Which is longer?" Ask, "Why was the second group easier to compare?" [Students should indicate that the same units were used.]

2. Now write "48 eggs" and "60 eggs" on the whiteboard. Next, below that write "51 eggs" and "5 dozen eggs" and then point to top two amounts and ask, "Which is more?" Now point to the bottom amounts and ask, "Which is more?" Ask, "Why are the first two egg amounts easier to compare?" [Students should indicate that the same units were used.] Next, explain that when comparing quantities, it is always easier when like units are compared.

3. Write two fractions on the whiteboard (4/7 and 2/7). Below these write two other fractions with different denominators (1/3 and 3/8). Point to the top pair of fractions and ask, "Which is greater?" Then point to the bottom pair of fractions and ask, "Which is greater?" Ask why the first pair of fractions is easier to compare. [Students should indicate that the same units were used.] Repeat to the students, "It is always easier to compare quantities if the units are the same."

4. Next, write "13 inches" and "1 foot" on the whiteboard. Ask the students, "How many inches are there in a foot?" Next mark out the "1 foot" and write "12 inches" above it. Tell the students how much easier it is to compare two lengths when we rewrite them using the same units.

5. Write the fractions, "2/3" and "3/4" on the whiteboard. Tell the students that you are going to show

them how to rewrite these two fractions so that they will have the same units. Next, get two transparencies. One should be lined horizontally with four equal segments and the other should be lined with three equal segments that look like the illustration below.

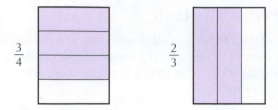

$\frac{3}{4}$ $\frac{2}{3}$

6. Next, tell the students that you want them to cut the pieces so that you will have the same size pieces in both of the fractions. Show them that you can cut the first fraction vertically into three equal parts and then you can cut the second fraction horizontally into four equal parts. Do this with each transparency (see the illustration below). After doing this write the new names for each of the fractions.

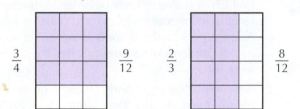

$\frac{3}{4}$ $\frac{9}{12}$ $\frac{2}{3}$ $\frac{8}{12}$

Now ask the students to look at the new fractions' names and decide which is greater.

[The students should say 3/4 is greater than 2/3 because 9/12 is greater than 8/12.]

7. Now show the students that in a multiplication problem involving two fractions they can get the new names for the two fractions by multiplying the numerator and the denominator by the other fractions denominator.

$$\frac{3 \times 3}{4 \times 3} = \frac{9}{12} \qquad \frac{2 \times 4}{3 \times 4} = \frac{8}{12}$$

Activity

1. Show the students two new fractions and ask them which is greater. Then give two more new ones and ask which is the lesser one.

2. Pair the students and have them create two fractions for each other and have them ask which one is greater or lesser.

3. Have the students generate multiplication of two fractions for each to solve using multiplication of the numerator and the denominator by the other fraction's denominator.

Source: Based on an activity by B. F. Tucker, A. H. Singleton, & T. L. Weaver (2006), *Teaching Mathematics to All Children: Designing and Adapting Instruction to Meet the Needs of Diverse Learners* (Upper Saddle River, NJ: Pearson Education, Inc.).

FOCUS Answers

▶ FOCUS Question 1. What factors influence math ability?

Answer: Deficits in math skills are commonly seen in perceptual skills, such as spatial relationships and sequencing; perseveration, making it difficult to shift from one task to another; language ability, impacting understanding of math concepts and vocabulary; reasoning, or dealing with abstract concepts that prevail in math; poor memory, making it difficult to remember new concepts; and symbolism difficulties, interfering with learning what symbols refer to. Many students with learning disabilities and behavior problems also have difficulty in paying and sustaining attention, working carefully, and accepting responsibility. Furthermore, because of their difficulty with math, many of these students have received an overabundance of instruction in basic skills but have not been exposed to essential math concepts and problem-solving strategies. In planning curricula for these students, teachers should consider such factors as comprehensive yet individualized programming, providing correction and feedback, generalizing examples to real-life situations, allowing students to participate in goal selection, and using discovery instead of didactic instruction.

▶ FOCUS Question 2. How is mathematics performance assessed and progress monitored?

Answer: Assessment helps teachers determine what students know and need to know as well as how students compare to others of the same age or grade level. In addition, appropriate assessments allow teachers to monitor students' progress and make effective instructional decisions based on the information they have gathered. When curriculum-based measurement is used to monitor students' progress and adjust instruction accordingly, students make gains at much more rapid rates. Assessments that measure number sense include counting measures, number identification measures, and number writing.

▶ **FOCUS Question 3. What are the prenumber skills students need to progress in arithmetic?**

Answer: Prenumber skills that facilitate students' growth in math include one-to-one correspondence, classification, and seriation.

▶ **FOCUS Question 4. What are several numeration concepts?**

Answer: Numeration concepts include: cardinality; grouping patterns; place value; one digit per place; linear order; decimal point; place relation; implied zeros; implied addition; order; name of numbers; periods and names; and understanding "zero."

▶ **FOCUS Question 5. What factors contribute to difficulties with problem solving, and how can teachers assist students in learning problem-solving strategies?**

Answer: Reading problems, poorly developed logical reasoning skills, and instruction that focuses primarily on computation contribute to difficulty with mathematical problem solving. Teachers can increase students' problem-solving abilities by teaching big ideas, using sameness analysis, teaching cue words, teaching reasoning strategies, simplifying the sentence structure of word problems, eliminating extraneous information, and monitoring the number of concepts presented as well as the interest level. Computer-assisted instruction is a motivational way to provide practice in problem solving and feedback on performance.

▶ **FOCUS Question 6. How can math interventions be used to improve math performance?**

Answer: Cognitive approaches to math instruction rely on verbalizing or making explicit steps or strategies in solving math problems. Behavioral approaches use the idea of stimulus-response learning to focus on the cues that students need to know in order to be successful in math. Alternative ways to deliver math instruction include cooperative learning, computer-assisted instruction, and interactive video. The best approach to teaching math is one that combines a variety of techniques that are appropriate for the student and the skills that need to be developed. New curricula have been developed specifically for teaching math skills to students with learning and behavior problems.

myeducationlab

Where the Classroom Comes to Life

The MyEducationLab for this course can help you solidify your comprehension of Chapter 11 concepts.

- Gauge and further develop your understanding of chapter concepts by taking the quizzes and examining the enrichment materials in the Chapter 11 Study Plan.
- Visit Topic 4, Assessing and Teaching Literacy and Language, to
  - connect with challenge-based interactive modules, case study units, and podcasts that provide

research-validated information about working with students in inclusive settings, by visiting the IRIS Center Resources.

- explore Assignments and Activities, assignable exercises showing concepts in action through video, cases, and student and teacher artifacts.
- practice and strengthen skills essential to quality teaching through the Building Teaching Skills and Dispositions lessons.

Abudarham, S. (2002). Assessment and appraisal of communication needs. In S. Abudarham and A. Hurd (Eds.), *Management of communication needs in people with learning disability* (pp. 33–81). London: Whurr.

Ackerman, P. T., Anhalt, J. M., and Dykman, R. A. (1986). Arithmetic automatization failure in children with attention and reading disorders: Associations and sequelae. *Journal of Learning Disabilities, 19,* 222–232.

Adams, M. J. (1990). *Beginning to read: Thinking and learning about print.* Cambridge, MA: MIT Press.

Ainsworth, S., and Burcham, S. (2007). The impact of text coherence on learning by self-explanation. *Learning and Instruction, 17*(3), 286–303.

Al Otaiba, S., and Fuchs, D. (2006). Who are the young children for whom best practices in reading are ineffective? *Journal of Learning Disabilities, 39,* 414–431.

Alber, S. R., Heward, W. L., and Hippler, B. J. (1999). Teaching middle school students with learning disabilities to recruit positive teacher attention. *Exceptional Children, 65,* 253–270.

Alberto, P. A., and Troutman, A. C. (2006). *Applied behavior analysis for teachers.* Upper Saddle River, NJ: Merrill/Prentice Hall.

Alfassi, M. (1998). Reading for meaning: The efficacy of reciprocal teaching in fostering reading comprehension in high school students in remedial classes. *American Educational Research Journal, 35*(2), 309–332.

Allen, J., Michalove, B., Shockley, B., and West, M. (1991). I'm really worried about Joseph: Reducing the risks of literacy learning. *The Reading Teacher, 44,* 458–472.

Allen, R. V. (1976). *Language experiences in communication.* Boston: Houghton Mifflin.

Allen, R. V., and Allen, C. (1966–68). *Language experiences in reading* (Levels I, II, and III). Chicago: Encyclopedia Britannica.

Allen, R. V., and Allen, C. (1982). *Language experience activities* (2nd ed.). Boston: Houghton Mifflin.

Alley, G. R., and Deshler, D. D. (1979). *Teaching the learning disabled adolescent: Strategies and methods.* Denver: Love.

Allington, R. L. (1983a). Fluency: The neglected reading goal. *The Reading Teacher, 36,* 556–561.

Allington, R. L. (1983b). The reading instruction provided readers of differing reading abilities. *The Elementary School Journal, 83,* 548–559.

Alvermann, D., Bridge, C., Schmidt, R., Seafoss, L., Winograd, P., Paris, S., et al. (1989). *Health reading.* Lexington, MA: D. C. Heath.

Al-Yagon, M., and Mikulincer, M. (2004). Patterns of close relationships and socioemotional and academic adjustment among school-age children with learning disabilities. *Learning Disabilities Research and Practice, 19*(1), 12–19.

American Academy of Child and Adolescent Psychology. (2009). *FAQs on child and adolescent depression.* Retrieved from http://www.aacap.org/cs/child_and_adolescent_depression_resource_center/faqs

American Foundation for Suicide Prevention. (2009). *Warning signs of suicide.* Retrieved from http://www.afsp.org/index.cfm?/page_id=0519EC1A-D73A-8D90-7D2E9E2456182D66

American Psychiatric Association. (1994). *Diagnostic and statistical manual of mental disorders* (4th ed.). Washington, DC: Author.

Amish, P. L., Gesten, E. L., Smith, J. K., Clark, H. B., and Stark, C. (1988). Social problem-solving training for severely emotionally and behaviorally disturbed children. *Behavioral Disorders, 13*(3), 175–186.

Anders, P. L., and Bos, C. S. (1984). In the beginning: Vocabulary instruction in content classroom. *Topics in Learning and Learning Disabilities, 3*(4), 53–65.

Anders, P. L., and Bos, C. S. (1986). Semantic feature analysis: An interactive strategy for vocabulary development and text comprehension. *Journal of Reading, 29*(7), 610–616.

Anders, P. L., and Guzzetti, B. J. (1996). *Literacy instruction in the content areas.* Fort Worth, TX: Harcourt Brace College.

Anderson, D. H., Fisher, A., Marchant, M., Young, K. R., and Smith, J. A. (2006). The cool card intervention: A positive support strategy for managing anger. *Beyond Behavior, 16,* 3–5.

Anderson, J. R. (1995). *Cognitive psychology and its implications* (3rd ed.). San Francisco: Freeman & Company.

Arguelles, M. E., Vaughn, S., and Schumm, J. S. (1996). *Executive summaries of 69 schools throughout the state of Florida participating in the ESE/FEFP 1995–1996 pilot program.*

Armbruster, B. B., and Anderson, T. H. (1988). On selecting "considerate" content area textbooks. *Remedial and Special Education, 9*(1), 47–52.

Arndt, S. A., Konrad, M., and Test, D. W. (2006). Effects of the self-directed IEP on student participation in planning meetings. *Remedial and Special Education, 27*(4), 194–207.

Ashbaker, B. Y., and Morgan, J. (2005). *Paraprofessionals in the classroom.* Boston: Pearson.

Ashton-Warner, S. (1958). *Spinster.* New York: Simon and Schuster.

Ashton-Warner, S. (1963). *Teacher.* New York: Simon and Schuster.

Ashton-Warner, S. (1972). *Spearpoint.* New York: Knopf.

August, D., Branum-Martin, L., Cardenas-Hagan, E., and Francis, D. J. (2009). The impact of an instructional intervention on the science and language learning of middle grade English language learners. *Journal for Research on Educational Effectiveness, 2*(4), 345–376.

August, D., and Shanahan, T. (2006). *Developing literacy in second-language learners: Report of the National Literacy Panel on language-minority children and youth.* Mahwah, NJ: Erlbaum.

Axelrod, S. (1998). *How to use group contingencies.* Austin, TX: PRO-ED.

Badian, N. A., and Ghublikian, M. (1983). The personal-social characteristics of children with poor mathematical computation skills. *Journal of Learning Disabilities, 16*(3), 154–157.

Baker, S., Gersten, R., and Lee, D. (2002). A synthesis of empirical research on teaching mathematics to low-achieving students. *The Elementary School Journal, 103*(1), 51–73.

Bandura, A. (1977). *Social learning theory.* Englewood Cliffs, NJ: Prentice Hall.

Bandura, A. (1986). *Social foundations of thought and action: A social cognitive theory.* Englewood Cliffs, NJ: Prentice Hall.

Barnes, M. A., Wilkinson, M., Khemani, E., Boudousquie, A., Dennis, M., and Fletcher, J. M. (2006). Arithmetic processing in children with spina bifida: Calculation accuracy, strategy use, and fact retrieval fluency. *Journal of Learning Disabilities, 39,* 174–187.

Barney, L. (1973). The first and third R's. *Today's Education, 62,* 57–58.

Barrett, T. (1976). Taxonomy of reading comprehension. In R. Smith and T. Barrett (Eds.), *Teaching reading in the middle grades.* Reading, MA: Addison-Wesley.

Barrouillet, P., Fayol, M., and Lathuliere, E. (1997). Selecting between competitors in multiplication tasks: An explanation of the errors produced by adolescents with learning difficulties. *International Journal of Behavioral Development, 21*(2), 253–275.

Batsche, G., Elliott J., Graden, J. L., Grimes, J., Kovaleski. J. F., Prasse, D., et al. (2005). *Response to intervention: Policy considerations and implementation.* Alexandria, VA: National Association of State Directors of Special Education.

Bay, M., Bryan, T., and O'Connor, R. (1994). Teachers assisting teachers: A prereferral model for urban educators. *Teacher Education and Special Education, 17*(1), 10–21.

Bear, D. R., Invernizzi, M., Templeton, S., and Johnston, F. (2000). *Words their way: Word study for phonics, vocabulary, and spelling instruction* (2nd ed.). Columbus, OH: Merrill.

Bear, G. C., Clever, A., and Proctor, W. A. (1991). Self-perceptions of nonhandicapped children and children with learning disabilities in integrated classes. *Journal of Special Education, 24,* 409–426.

Beck, I. L. (2006). *Making sense of phonics.* New York: Guilford.

Beck, I. L., and McKeown, M. G. (2006). *Improving comprehension with questioning the author.* New York: Scholastic.

Beck, I. L., McKeown, M. G., and Kucan, L. (2002). *Bringing words to life: Robust vocabulary instruction.* New York: Guilford.

Becker, W. C. (1977). Teaching reading and language to the disadvantaged: What we have learned from field research. *Harvard Educational Review, 44*(4), 518–543.

Beirne-Smith, M. (1991). Peer tutoring in arithmetic for children with learning disabilities. *Exceptional Children, 57,* 330–337.

Bell, A. C., and D'Zurilla, T. J. (2009). Problem-solving therapy for depression: A meta-analysis. *Clinical Psychology Review, 29*(4), 348–353.

Bender, W. N. (2008). *Differentiating instruction for students with learning disabilities: Best teaching practices for general and special educators* (2nd ed.). Thousand Oaks, CA: Corwin Press.

Bereiter, C., Hilton, P., Rubinstein, J., and Willoughby, S. (1998). *Math exploration and applications.* Chicago: Science Research Associates.

Bergerud, D., Lovitt, T. C., and Horton, S. (1988). The effectiveness of textbook adaptations in life science for high school students with learning disabilities. *Journal of Learning Disabilities, 21,* 70–76.

Berkeley, S., Bender, W. N., Peaster, L. G., and Saunders, L. (2009). Implementation of response to intervention. *Journal of Learning Disabilities, 42*(1), 85–95.

Bernadette, K., Carnine, D., Engelmann, S., and Engelmann, O. (2003). *Connecting math concepts.* Chicago: Science Research Associates.

Berninger, V. W., Abbott, R. D., Whitaker, D., Sylvester, L., and Nolen, S. B. (1995). Integrating low- and high-level skills in instructional protocols for writing disabilities. *Learning Disability Quarterly, 18,* 293–310.

Berninger, V. W., Nielsen, K. H., Abbott, R. D., Wijsman, E., and Raskind, W. (2008). Writing problems in developmental dyslexia: Under-recognized and under-treated. *Journal of School Psychology, 46*(1), 1–21.

Berninger, V. W., Rutberg, J. E., Abbott, R. D., Noelia, G., Anderson-Youngstrom, M., Brooks, A., et al. (2006). Tier 1 and Tier 2 early intervention for handwriting and composing. *Journal of School Psychology, 44*(1), 3–30.

Bernstein, D. K. (1986). The development of humor: Implications for assessment and intervention. *Topics in Language Disorders, 6*(4), 65–71.

Berres, F., and Eyer, J. T. (1970). In A. J. Harris (Ed.), *Casebook on reading disability* (pp. 25–47). New York: David McKay.

Betts, E. A. (1946). *Foundations of reading instruction.* New York: American Book.

Bishop, D., and Norbury, C. (2002). Exploring the borderlands of autistic disorder and specific language impairment: A study using standardised diagnostic instruments. *Journal of Child Psychology and Psychiatry, and Allied Disciplines, 43*(7), 917–929.

Blachman, B. A. (2000). Phonological awareness. In M. L. Kamil, P. B. Mosenthal, P. D. Pearson, and R. Barr (Eds.), *Handbook of reading research.* (Vol. 3, pp. 483–502). Mahwah, NJ: Erlbaum.

Blachowicz, C., and Ogle, D. (2001). *Reading comprehension: Strategies for independent learners.* New York: Guilford.

Blachowicz, D. O., and Ogle, D. (2008). *Reading comprehension: Strategies for independent learners.* New York: Guilford.

Blair, K. S. (1996). *Context-based functional assessment and intervention for preschool age children with problem behaviors in childcare.* Unpublished dissertation, University of Arizona, Tucson.

Blankenship, C. S. (1984). Curriculum and instruction: An examination of models in special and regular education. In J. F. Cawley (Ed.), *Developmental teaching of mathematics for the learning disabled.* Rockville, MD: Aspen.

Blankenship, C. S., and Lovitt, T. C. (1976). Story problems: Merely confusing or downright befuddling. *Journal for Research in Mathematics Education, 7,* 290–298.

Bley, N. S., and Thornton, C. A. (1981). *Teaching mathematics to the learning disabled*. Rockville, MD: Aspen.

Block, C. C. (1997). *Literacy difficulties: Diagnosis and instruction*. Orlando, FL: Harcourt Brace.

Block, C. C., Morrow, L. M., and Parris, S. R. (2008). *Comprehension instruction: research-based best practices*. New York: Guilford.

Bloodgood, J. (1991). A new approach to spelling instruction in language arts programs. *Elementary School Journal, 92,* 203–211.

Boatner, M. T., Gates, J. E., and Makkai, A. (1975). *A dictionary of American idioms* (Rev. ed.). Woodbury, NJ: Barron's.

Boegler, S., and Abruzzini, D. (1996). *Scissors, glue, and grammar too!* East Moline, IL: LinguiSystems.

Bos, C. S. (1987, October). *Promoting story comprehension using a story retelling strategy*. Paper presented at the Teachers Applying Whole Language Conference, Tucson, AZ.

Bos, C. S. (1999). Informed, flexible teaching: Promoting student advocacy and action. In P. Westwood and W. Scott (Eds.), *Learning disabilities: Advocacy and action* (pp. 9–19). Melbourne: Australian Resource Educators Association.

Bos, C. S., and Anders, P. L. (1990). Effects of interactive vocabulary instruction on the vocabulary learning and reading comprehension of junior-high learning disabled students. *Learning Disability Quarterly, 13,* 31–42.

Bos, C. S., and Anders, P. L. (1992). A theory-driven interactive instructional model for text comprehension and content learning. In B. Y. L. Wong (Ed.), *Contemporary intervention research in learning disabilities: An international perspective* (pp. 81–95). New York: Springer-Verlag.

Bos, C. S., and Filip, D. (1984). Comprehension monitoring in learning disabled and average students. *Journal of Learning Disabilities, 17*(4), 229–233.

Bos, C. S., and Van Reusen, A. K. (1986). *Effects of teaching a strategy for facilitating student and parent participation in the IEP process* (Partner Project Final Report G008400643). Tucson: University of Arizona, Department of Special Education.

Bourassa, D. C., Treiman, R., and Kessler, B. (2006). Use of morphology in spelling by children with dyslexia and typically developing children. *Memory and Cognition, 34*(3), 703–714.

Bowers, L., Huisingh, R., LoGiudice, C., Orman, J., and Johnson, P. F. (2000). *125 vocabulary builders*. East Moline, IL: LinguiSystems.

Bowers, R., and Bowers, L. (1998). *Grammar scramble: A grammar and sentence-building game*. East Moline, IL: LinguiSystems.

Bradley, J. M. (1975). *Sight word association procedure*. Unpublished manuscript, College of Education, University of Arizona, Tucson.

Bradley, L. (1981). The organization of motor patterns for spelling: An effective remedial strategy for backward readers. *Developmental Medicine and Child Neurology, 23,* 83–91.

Bradley, R., Danielson, L., and Hallahan, D. P. (2002). *Identification of learning disabilities: Research to practice*. Mahwah, NJ: Erlbaum.

Brent, D., Melhem, N., Donohoe, B., and Walker, M. (2009). The incidence and course of depression in bereaved youth 21 months after the loss of a parent to suicide, accident, or sudden natural death. *American Journal of Psychiatry, 166,* 786–794.

Brice, A., and Montgomery, J. (1996). Adolescent pragmatic skills: A comparison of Latino students in English as a second language and speech and language programs. *Language, Speech, and Hearing Services in Schools, 27,* 68–81.

Briggs, A., Austin, R., and Underwood, G. (1984). Phonological coding in good and poor readers. *Reading Research Quarterly, 20,* 54–66.

Brinton, B., Fujiki, M., and McKee, L. (1998). Negotiation skills of children with specific language impairment. *Journal of Speech, Language, and Hearing Research, 41,* 927–940.

Bromley, K. (1999). Key components of sound writing instruction. In L. B. Gambrell, L. M. Morrow, S. B. Neuman, and M. Pressley (Eds.), *Best practices in literacy instruction* (pp. 152–174). New York: Guilford.

Brophy, J. (1988). Educating teachers about managing classrooms and students. *Teacher and Teacher Education, 4,* 1–18.

Brown, A. L., and Day, J. D. (1983). Macrorules for summarizing texts: The development of expertise. *Journal of Verbal Learning and Verbal Behavior, 22,* 1–14.

Brown, A. L., Palincsar, A. S., and Armbruster, B. B. (1984). Instructing comprehension-fostering activities in interactive learning situations. In H. Mandl, N. L. Stein, and T. Trabasso (Eds.), *Learning and comprehension of text* (pp. 255–286). Hillsdale, NJ: Erlbaum.

Bryan, T. H. (1986). Self-concept and attributions of the learning disabled. *Learning Disabilities Focus, 1*(2), 82–89.

Bryan, T., Pearl, R., and Fallon, P. (1989). Conformity to peer pressure by students with learning disabilities: A replication. *Journal of Learning Disabilities, 22*(7), 458–459.

Bryan, T., and Sullivan-Burstein, K. (1998). Teacher-selected strategies for improving homework completion. *Remedial and Special Education, 19,* 263–275.

Bryant, B. R., and Rivera, D. P. (1997). Educational assessment of mathematics skills and abilities. *Journal of Learning Disabilities, 30*(1), 57–68.

Bryant, D. P., Bryant, B., and Hammill, D. (2000). Characteristic behaviors of students with LD who have teacher-identified math weaknesses. *Journal of Learning Disabilities, 33,* 168–177, 199.

Bryant, D. P., Hartman, P., and Kim, S. A. (2003). Using explicit and systematic instruction to teach division skills to students with learning disabilities. *Exceptionality, 11*(3), 151–164.

Bryant, D., Vaughn S., Linan-Thompson, S., Ugel, N., Hamff, A., and Hougen, M. (2000). Reading outcomes for students with and without reading disabilities in general education middle school content area classes. *Learning Disability Quarterly, 23,* 238–252.

Bryant, J. (1998). K-W-W-L: Questioning the known. *The Reading Teacher, 51,* 618–620.

Bryant, N. D., Drabin, I. R., and Gettinger, M. (1981). Effects of varying unit size on spell-ing achievement in learning disabled chil-dren. *Journal of Learning Disabilities, 14*(4), 200–203.

Bulgren, J., Deshler, D. D., and Lenz, B. K. (2007). Engaging adolescents with LD in higher order thinking about history concepts using integrated content enhancement routines. *Journal of Learning Disabilities, 40*(2), 121–133.

Bulgren, J., Schumaker, J. B., and Deshler, D. D. (1988). Effectiveness of a concept teaching routine in enhancing the performance of LD students in secondary-level mainstream classes. *Learning Disability Quarterly, 11,* 3–17.

Bulgren, J., Schumaker, J. B., and Deshler, D. D. (1996). *The content enhancement series: The concept mastery routine.* Lawrence, KS: Edge Enterprises.

Bulgren, J. A. (2006). Integrated content enhancement routines: Responding to the needs of adolescents with disabilities in rigorous inclusive secondary content classes. *Teaching Exceptional Children, 38*(6), 54–58.

Bulgren, J. A., Lenz, B. K., Schumaker, J. B., and Deshler, D. D. (1995). *The content enhancement series: The concept comparison routine.* Lawrence, KS: Edge Enterprises.

Bulgren, J. A., Marquis, J. G., Lenz, B. K., Shumaker, J. B., and Deshler, D. D. (2009). Effectiveness of question exploration to enhance students' written expression of content knowledge and comprehension. *Reading and Writing Quarterly, 25*(4), 271–289.

Burns, M. K., and Ysseldyke, J. E. (2005). Questions about response-to-intervention implementations: Seeking answers from existing models. *California School Psychologist, 10,* 9–20.

Bursuck, W. D., Harniss, M. K., Epstein, M. H., Polloway, E. A., Jayanthi, M., and Wissinger, L. M. (1999). Solving communication problems about homework: Recommendations of special education teachers. *Learning Disabilities Research and Practice, 14*(3), 149–158.

Byrnes, J. P. (1996). *Cognitive development and learning in instructional contexts.* Boston: Allyn & Bacon.

Cain, K. (1996). Story knowledge and comprehension skill. In C. Cornoldi and J. Oakhill (Eds.), *Reading comprehension difficulties* (pp. 167–192). Hillsdale, NJ: Erlbaum.

Calhoon, M. B., and Fuchs, L. S. (2003). The effects of peer-assisted learning strategies and curriculum-based measurement on the mathematics performance of secondary students with disabilities. *Remedial and Special Education, 24*(4), 235–245.

Camp, B. W., Blom, G. E., Herbert, F., and Van Doorninck, W. J. (1977). "Think around": A program for developing self-control in young aggressive boys. *Journal of Abnormal Child Psychology, 5,* 157–169.

Cangelosi, J. S. (2004). *Classroom management strategies: Gaining and maintaining students' cooperation.* Hoboken, NJ: Wiley.

Canter, A. (2006). Problem solving and RTI: New roles for school psychologists. NASP *Communiqué, 34*(5). Retrieved December 14, 2007, from http://www.nasponline.org/publications/cq/cq345rti.aspx.

Carnine, D. (1989). Teaching complex content to learning disabled students: The role of technology. *Exceptional Children, 55,* 524–533.

Carnine, D. (1991). Curricular interventions for teaching higher order thinking to all students: Introduction to the special series. *Journal of Learning Disabilities, 24,* 261–269.

Carnine, D. (1997). Instructional design in mathematics for students with learning disabilities. *Journal of Learning Disabilities, 30*(2), 130–141.

Carnine, D., Silbert, J., and Kame'enui, E. J. (1997). *Direct instruction reading* (3rd ed.). Columbus, OH: Merrill.

Carr, E., and Ogle, D. (1987). K-W-L plus: A strategy for comprehension and summarization. *Journal of Reading, 30,* 626–631.

Carr, E. G., Dunlap, G., Horner, R. H., Koegel, R. L., Turnbull, A. P., Sailor, W., et al. (2002). Positive behavior support: Evolution of an applied science. *Journal of Positive Behavior Interventions, 4,* 4–16.

Carrekar, S. (1999). Teaching spelling. In J. R. Birsh (Ed.), *Multisensory teaching of basic language skills* (pp. 217–256). Baltimore: Brookes.

Carroll, J. (1964). *Language and thought.* Englewood Cliffs, NJ: Prentice Hall.

Carrow, E. (1973). *Test of auditory comprehension of language.* Austin, TX: Urban Research Group.

Carter, E. W., and Kennedy, C. H. (2006). Promoting access to the general curriculum using peer support strategies. *Research and Prac-tice for Persons with Severe Disabilities, 31,* 284–292.

Catts, H. W., Fey, M. E., Tomblin, J. B., and Zhang, X. (2002). A longitudinal investigation of reading outcomes in children with language impairments. *Journal of Speech, Language, and Hearing Research, 45*(6), 1142–1157.

Catts, H., and Kahmi, A. (Eds.). (2005). *The connection between language and reading disabilities.* Mahwah, NJ: Erlbaum.

Cavanaugh, C. L., Kim, A., Wanzek, J., and Vaughn, S. (2004). Kindergarten reading interventions for at-risk students: Twenty years of research. *Learning Disabilities: A Contemporary Journal, 2*(1), 9–21.

Cawley, J. (2002). My Math [Unpublished computer software]. Storrs, CT.

Cawley, J. F. (1984). An integrative approach to needs of learning disabled children: Expanded use of mathematics. In J. F. Cawley (Ed.), *Developmental teaching of mathematics for the learning disabled.* Rockville, MD: Aspen.

Cawley, J. F., Foley, T. F., and Doan, T. (2003). Giving students a voice in selecting arithmetical context. *Teaching Exceptional Children, 36,* 8–17.

Cawley, J. F., and Miller, J. H. (1986). Selected views on metacognition, arithmetic problem solving, and learning disabilities. *Learning Disabilities Focus, 2*(1), 36–48.

Cawley, J. F., and Miller, J. H. (1989). Cross-sectional comparisons of the mathematical performance of children with learning disabilities: Are we on the right track toward comprehensive programming? *Journal of Learning Disabilities, 22,* 250–254, 259.

Cawley, J. F., Parmar, R. S., Yan, W., and Miller, J. H. (1998). Arithmetic computation performance of students with learning disabilities: Implications for curriculum. *Learning Disabilities Research and Practice, 13*(2), 68–74.

Chalfant, J. C., and Pysh, M. V. (1989). Teacher assistance teams: Five descriptive studies on 96 teams. *Remedial and Special Education, 10*(6), 49–58.

Chalfant, J. C., and Pysh, M. V. (1993). Teacher assistance teams: Implications for the gifted. In C. J. Maker (Ed.), *Critical issues in gifted education: Vol. 3. Gifted students in the regular classroom* (pp. 32–48). Austin, TX: PRO-ED.

Chan, L. K. S. (1991). Promoting strategy generalization through self-instructional training in students with reading disabilities. *Journal of Learning Disabilities, 24,* 427–433.

Chapman, J. W., and Boersman, F. J. (1980). *Affective correlates of learning disabilities.* Lisse, Netherlands: Swets & Zeitlinger.

Chard, D. J., Ketterlin-Geller, L. R., Baker, S. K., Doabler, C., and Apichatabutra, C. (2009). Repeated reading intervention for students with learning disabilities: Status for the evidence. *Exceptional Children, 75*(3), 263–281.

Chard, D. J., Vaughn, S., and Tyler, B. (2002). A synthesis of research on effective intervention for building reading fluency with elementary students with learning disabilities. *Journal of Learning Disabilities, 35*(5), 386–406.

Chomsky, C. (1969). *The acquisition of syntax in children from 5 to 10.* Cambridge, MA: MIT Press.

Christ, T. J., and Ardoin, S. P. (2009). Curriculum-based measurement of oral reading: Passage equivalence and probe-set development. *Journal of School Psychology, 47*(1), 55–75.

Christ, T. J., Burns, M. K., and Ysseldyke, J. E. (2005). Conceptual confusion within response-to-intervention vernacular: Clarifying meaningful differences. NASP *Communiqué, 34*(3). Retrieved December 14, 2007, from http://www.nasponline.org/publications/cq/cq343rti.aspx

Cimbolic, P. and Jobes, D. A. (1990). Youth suicide: The scope of the problem. In P. Cimbolic and D. A. Jobes (Eds.), *Youth suicide: Issues, assessment, and intervention* (pp. 3–32). Springfield, IL: Charles C. Thomas.

Clark, F. L., Deshler, D. D., Schumaker, J. B., Alley, G. R., and Warner, M. M. (1984). Visual imagery and self-questioning: Strategies to improve comprehension of written materials. *Journal of Learning Disabilities, 17*(3), 145–149.

Clark, G. M., Patton, J. R., and Moulton, R. (2001). *Informal assessments in transition planning.* Austin, TX: PRO-ED.

Clark, J. O. (1990). *Harrup's dictionary of English idioms.* London: Harrup.

Clarke, B., and Shinn, M. R. 2004. A preliminary investigation into the identification and development of early mathematics curriculum-based measurement. *School Psychology Review, 33*(2), 234–248.

Cole, J. (2000). *Gram's cracker: A grammar game.* East Moline, IL: LinguiSystems.

Conderman, G., Bresnahan, V., and Pedersen, T. (2009). *Purposeful co-teaching: Real cases and effective strategies.* Thousand Oaks, CA: Corwin Press.

Connolly, A. J. (1998). *Key math–revised: A diagnostic inventory of essential mathematics.* Circle Pines, MN: American Guidance Service.

Cooper, D. H., Roth, F. P., Schatschneider, C., and Speece, D. L. (2002). The contribution of oral language skills to the development of phonological awareness. *Applied Psycholinguistics, 23,* 399–416.

Cooper, H., and Nye, B. (1994). Homework for students with learning disabilities: The implications of research for policy and practice. *Journal of Learning Disabilities, 27,* 470–479.

Cooper, H. M. (2007). *The battle over homework: Common ground for administrators, teachers, and parents* (3rd ed.). Thousand Oaks, CA: Corwin Press.

Cooper, P., and Bilton, K. M. (2002). *Attention deficit/hyperactivity disorder: A practical guide for teachers* (2nd ed.). Great Britain: David Fulton Publishers Ltd.

Corkill, A. J. (1992). Advance organizers: Facilitators of recall. *Educational Psychology Review, 4,* 33–67.

Cortiella, C. (2006). *A parent's guide to response to intervention.* National Center for Learning Disabilities. Retrieved December 14, 2007, from www.ncld.org/images/stories/downloads/parent_center/rti_final.pdf.

Coterell, G. (1972). A case of severe learning disability. *Remedial Education, 7,* 5–9.

Cox, A. R. (1992). *Foundations for literacy: Structures and techniques for multisensory teaching of basic written English language skills (Alphabetic phonics).* Cambridge, MA: Educators Publishing Service.

Coyne, M. D., Kame'enui, E. J., Simmons, D. C. (2001). Prevention and intervention in beginning reading: Two complex systems. *Learning Disabilities: Research and Practice, 16,* 62–73.

Cromley, J. G., and Azevedo, R. (2007). Testing and refining the direct and inferential mediation model of reading comprehension. *Journal of Educational Psychology, 99*(2), 311–325.

Cullinan, B. E. (Ed.). (1992). *Invitation to read: More children's literature in the reading program.* Newark, DE: International Reading Association.

Culp, A. M., Clyman, M. M., and Culp, R. E. (1995). Adolescent depressed mood, reports of suicide attempts, and asking for help. *Adolescence, 30,* 827–837.

Cumming, A., (Ed.). (2006). *ESL students and their instructors.* Philadelphia, PA: John Benjamins North America

Cummins, J. (1981). *Bilingualism and minority language children.* Ontario: Ontario Institute for Students in Education.

Cunningham, P. M. (1991). *Phonics they use: Words for reading and writing.* New York: HarperCollins.

Cunningham, P. M. (2008). *Phonics they use: Words for reading and writing as an author.* Boston: Allyn & Bacon.

Cunningham, P. M., and Hall, D. P. (1994a). *Making words.* Parsippany, NJ: Good Apple.

Cunningham, P. M., and Hall, D. P. (1994b). *Making big words.* Parsippany, NJ: Good Apple.

Dahl, K., Scharer, P., Lawson, L., and Grogan, P. (1999). Phonics teaching and student achievement in whole language first grades. *Reading Research Quarterly, 34*(3), 312–341.

Dahl, K. L., and Scharer, P. L. (2000). Phonics teaching and learning in whole language classrooms: New evidence from research. *The Reading Teacher, 53,* 584–594.

Dale, E., and Chall, J. S. (1948). A formula for predicting readability. *Educational Research Bulletin, 27,* 37–54.

Dale, P. S. (1996). Parent–child book reading as an intervention technique for young children with language delays. *Topics in Early Childhood Special Education, 16,* 213–235.

Daniel, S. S., Walsh, A. K., Goldston, D. B., Arnold, E. M., Reboussin, B. A., and Wood, F. B. (2007). Suicidality, school dropout, and reading problems among adolescents. *Journal of Learning Disabilities, 39*(6), 507–514.

Darch, C., and Carnine, D. (1986). Approaches to teaching learning-disabled students literal comprehension during content area instruction. *Exceptional Children, 53*(3), 240–246.

De La Paz, S. (1999). Teaching writing strategies and self-regulation procedures to middle school students with learning disabilities. *Focus on Exceptional Children, 31*(5), 1–16.

De La Paz, S., Swanson, P., and Graham, S. (1998). Contribution of executive control to the revising problems of students with writing and learning difficulties. *Journal of Educational Psychology, 90,* 448–460.

Delquadri, J. C., Greenwood, C. R., Stretton, K., and Hall, R. V. (1983). The peer tutoring spelling game: A classroom procedure for increasing opportunity to respond and spelling performance. *Education and Treatment of Children, 6*(3), 225–239.

DeMaster, V. K., Crossland, C. L., and Hasselbring, T. S. (1986). Consistency of learning disabled students' spelling performance. *Learning Disability Quarterly, 9*(1), 89–96.

Dembinski, R. J., and Mauser, A. J. (1977). What parents of the learning disabled really want from professionals. *Journal of Learning Disabilities, 10,* 578–584.

Deno, S. L., Fuchs, L. S., Marston, D., and Shin, J. (2001). Using curriculum-based measurement to establish growth standards for students with learning disabilities. *School Psychology Review, 30,* 507–524.

Denton, C. A., Anthony, J. L., Parker, R., and Hasbrouck, J. (2004). The effects of two tutoring programs on the English reading development of Spanish-English bilingual students. *The Elementary School Journal, 104,* 289–305.

Deshler, D. D., Ellis, E. S., and Lenz, B. K. (1996). *Teaching adolescents with learning disabilities: Strategies and methods* (2nd ed.). Denver: Love.

Deshler, D. D., Schumaker, J. B., and McKnight, P. C. (1997). *The survey routine.* Lawrence: University of Kansas Press.

Dettmer, P., Thurston, L. P., and Selberg, N. J. (2004). *Consultation, collaboration, and teamwork for students with special needs* (5th ed.). Boston: Allyn & Bacon.

Dieker, L. A. (2001). What are the characteristics of "effective" middle and high school co-taught teams for students with disabilities? *Preventing School Failure, 48*(1), 14–23.

Dixon, R. C., Carnine, D. W., Lee, D. S., Wallin, J., and Chard, D. (1998). Report to the California State Board of Education and addendum to principal report: Review of high-quality experimental mathematics research. Retrieved from http://idea.uoregon.edu/∼ncite/documents/math/math.html

Dixon, R. C., and Engelmann, S. (2001). *Spelling through morphographs.* Columbus, OH: SRA/McGraw-Hill.

Dixon, R. C., Isaacson, S., and Stein, M. (2002). Effective strategies for teaching writing. In E. J. Kame'enui, D. W. Carnine, R. C. Dixon, D. C. Simmons, and M. D. Coyne (Eds.), *Effective teaching strategies that accommodate diverse learners.* Upper Saddle River, NJ: Merrill Prentice Hall.

Dole, J. A., Valencia, S. W., Greer, E. A., and Wardrop, J. L. (1991). Effects of two types of reading instruction on the comprehension of narrative and expository text. *Reading Research Quarterly, 26,* 142–159.

Donovan, M. S., and Cross, C. T. (2002). *Minority students in special and gifted education.* Washington, DC: National Academy Press.

Duffy, G., Lanier, J. E., and Roehler, L. R. (1980). *On the need to consider instructional practice when looking for instruction implications.* Paper presented at the Reading Expository Materials. University of Wisconsin–Madison.

Duling, W. P. (1999). Literacy development of second language learners with technology and LEA. In O. G. Nelson and W. M. Linek (Eds.), *Practical classroom applications of language experience: Looking back, looking forward* (pp. 248–256). Boston: Allyn & Bacon.

Dunn, R., and Blake, B. R. (2008). *Teaching every child to read: Innovative and practical strategies for K–8 educators and caretakers.* Lanham, MD: Rowman & Littlefield Education.

Dunst, C. J. (2002). Family-centered practices: Birth through high school. *Journal of Special Education, 36,* 139–147.

Durkin, D. D. (1978–79). What classroom observations reveal about reading comprehension instruction. *Reading Research Quarterly, 14*(4), 481–533.

Dweck, C. S., and Kamins, M. L. (1999). Person versus process praise and criticism: Implications for contingent self-worth and coping. *Developmental Psychology, 35*(3), 835–847.

Dyson, B. J. (2008). Assessing small-scale interventions in large-scale teaching: A general methodology and preliminary data. *Active Learning in Higher Education, 9*(3), 265–282.

Echevarria, J., Vogt, D., and Short, D. (2009). *Making content comprehensible for elementary English learners: The SIOP model.* Boston: Allyn & Bacon.

Edmonds, M. S., Vaughn, S., Wexler, J., Reutebuch, C. K., Cable, A., Tackett, K., et. al. 2009. A synthesis of reading interventions and effects on reading outcomes for older struggling readers. *Review of Educational Research, 79,* 262–300.

Eggen, P. D., and Kauchak, D. (1992). *Educational psychology: Classroom connections.* New York: Macmillan.

Ehren, B. J., Montgomery, J., Rudebusch, J., and Whitmire, K. (2006). *Responsiveness to intervention: New roles for speech-language pathologists.* Retrieved from http://www.asha.org/members/slp/schools/prof-consult/NewRolesSLP.htm

Ehri, L. (2004). Teaching phonemic awareness and phonics: An explanation of the National Reading Panel Meta-Analyses. In P. McCardle and V. Chhabra (Eds.), *The voice of evidence in reading research* (pp. 153–186). Baltimore: Paul H. Brookes.

Elam, S. M., and Gallup, A. M. (1989). The 21st annual Gallup poll of the public's attitudes toward the public schools. *Phi Delta Kappan, 71,* 41–54.

Elbaum, B. (2007). Effects of an oral testing accommodation on the mathematics performance of secondary students with and without learning disabilities. *Journal of Special Education, 40*(4), 218–229.

Elbaum, B., and Vaughn, S. (2001). School-based interventions to enhance the self-concept of students with learning disabilities: A meta-analysis. *The Elementary School Journal, 101,* 303–329.

Elbaum, B., Vaughn, S., Hughes, M., and Moody, S. W. (1999). Grouping practices and reading outcomes for students with disabilities. *Exceptional Children, 65*(3), 399–415.

Eldredge, J. L., and Quinn, D. W. (1988). Increasing reading performance of low-achieving second graders with dyad reading groups. *Journal of Educational Research, 82*(1), 40–46.

Elkonin, D. B. (1973). U.S.S.R. In J. Downing (Ed.), *Comparative reading* (pp. 551–579). New York: Macmillan.

Elleman, A. M., Lindo, E. J., Morphy, P., and Compton, D. L. (2009). The impact of vocabulary instruction on passage-level comprehension of school-age children: A meta-analysis. *Journal of Research on Educational Effectiveness, 2*(1), 1–44.

Ellis, E. (1991). *SLANT: A starter strategy for participation.* Lawrence, KS: Edge Enterprises.

Ellis, R. (2005). *Analyzing learner language.* New York: Oxford University Press.

Emery, D. W. (1996). Helping readers comprehend stories from the characters' perspectives. *The Reading Teacher, 49,* 534–541.

Emmer, E. T., Evertson, C. M., Sanford, J. P., Clements, B. S., and Worsham, M. E. (1989). *Classroom management for secondary teachers* (2nd ed.). Englewood Cliffs, NJ: Prentice Hall.

Engelhardt, J. M., Ashlock, R. B., and Wiebe, J. H. (1984). *Helping children understand and use numerals* (pp. 89–149). Boston: Allyn & Bacon.

Engelmann, S., Bruner, E. C., Hanner, S., Osborn, J., Osborn, S., and Zoref, L. (1995). *Reading mastery: Rainbow edition.* Columbus, OH: SRA/McGraw-Hill.

Engelmann, S., Carnine, D., and Steely, D. G. (1991). Making connections in mathematics. *Journal of Learning Disabilities, 24*(5), 292–303.

Engelmann, S., Meyer, L., Carnine, L., Becker, W., Eisele, J., and Johnson, G. (1999). *Corrective reading program*. Columbus, OH: SRA/McGraw-Hill.

Englert, C. S., Garmon, A., Mariage, T., Rozendal, M., Tarrant, K., and Urba, J. (1995). The early literacy project: Connecting across the literacy curriculum. *Learning Disability Quarterly, 18,* 253–277.

Englert, C. S., and Raphael, T. E. (1988). Constructive well-formed prose: Process, structure, and metacognitive knowledge. *Exceptional Children, 54,* 513–520.

Englert, C. S., Raphael, T. E., Anderson, L. M., Anthony, H. M., and Stevens, D. D. (1991). Making strategies and self-talk visible: Writing instruction in regular and special education classrooms. *American Educational Research Journal, 23,* 337–372.

Englert, C. S., Rozendal, M. S., and Mariage, M. (1994). Fostering the search for understanding: A teacher's strategies for leading cognitive development in "zones of proximal development." *Learning Disability Quarterly, 17,* 187–204.

Ericson, K. A., and Kintsch, W. (1995). Long-term working memory. *Psychological Review, 102,* 211–245.

Erickson, R., and Schultz, J. (1981). When is a context? Some issues and methods in the analysis of social competence. In J. L. Green and C. Wallat (Eds.), *Ethnography and language in educational settings.* Norwood, NJ: Ablex.

Espin, C., Wallace, T., Campbell, H., Lembke, E., Long, J. D., and Ticha, R. (2008). Curriculum-based measurement in writing: Predicting the success of high-school students on state standards tests. *Exceptional Children, 74*(2), 174–193.

Exceptional Parent. (1984, March). Parent advocacy. *Exceptional Parent, 14*(2), 41–45.

Fairbanks, S., Sugai, G., Guardino, D., and Lathrop, M. (2007). Response to intervention: Examining classroom behavior support in second grade. *Exceptional Children, 73*(3), 288–310.

Farmer, T. W., Pearl, R., and Van Acker, R. M. (1996). Expanding the social skills deficit framework: A developmental synthesis perspective, classroom social networks, and implications for the social growth of students with disabilities. *Journal of Special Education, 30*(3), 232–256.

Fearn, L., and Farnan, N. (1998). *Writing effectively: Helping children master the conventions of writing.* Boston: Allyn & Bacon.

Ferguson, P. M. (2002). A place in the family: An historical interpretation of research on parental reactions to having a child with a disability. *The Journal of Special Education, 36,* 124–130.

Fernald, G. M. (1943). *Remedial techniques in basic school subjects.* New York: McGraw-Hill.

Fernald, G. M. (1988). *Remedial techniques in basic school subjects.* (L. Idol, Ed.). Austin, TX: PRO-ED (original edition 1943).

Fielding, L., and Roller, C. (1992). Making difficult books accessible and easy books acceptable. *The Reading Teacher, 45,* 678–682.

Fitzsimmons, R. J., and Loomer, B. M. (1978). *Spelling: Learning and instruction.* (Report No. CS 205 117). Des Moines: Iowa State Department of Public Instruction. (ERIC Document Reproduction Service No. ED 176 285).

Flavell, J. H. (1976). Metacognitive aspects of problem solving. In L. B. Resnick (Ed.), *The nature of intelligence.* Hillsdale, NJ: Erlbaum.

Fleischner, J. E., Nuzum, M. G., and Marzola, E. S. (1987). Devising an instructional program to teach arithmetic problem-solving skills to students with learning disabilities. *Journal of Learning Disabilities, 20*(4), 214–217.

Fletcher, J. M. (1989). Nonverbal learning disabilities and suicide: Classification leads to prevention. *Journal of Learning Disabilities, 22,* 176–179.

Fletcher, J. M., Lyon, G. R., Fuchs, L. S, and Barnes, M. A. (2007). *Learning Disabilities.* New York: Guilford.

Florian, L. (2007). *The SAGE handbook of special education.* London: Sage Publications.

Florian, L., and Rouse, M. (2009). The inclusive practice project in Scotland: Teacher education for inclusive education. *Teaching and Teacher Education, 25*(4), 583–587.

Foorman, B. R. (2007). Primary prevention in classroom reading instruction. *Teaching Exceptional Children, 39*(5), 24–30.

Foorman, B. R., and Ciancio, D. J. (2005). Screening for secondary intervention: Concept and context. *Journal of Learning Disabilities, 38*(6), 494–499.

Forness, S. R. (1973). The reinforcement hierarchy. *Psychology in the Schools, 19,* 168–177.

Francis, D., Rivera, M., Lesaux, N., Kieffer, M., and Rivera, H. (2006a). *Practical guidelines for the education of English language learners: Research-based recommendations for serving adolescent newcomers* (under cooperative agreement grant S283B050034 for U.S. Department of Education). Portsmouth, NH: RMC Research Corporation, Center on Instruction. (Available online at http://www.centeroninstruction.org/files/ELL2-Newcomers.pdf)

Francis, D., Rivera, M., Lesaux, N., Kieffer, M., and Rivera, H. (2006b). *Practical guidelines for the education of English language learners: Research-based recommendations for instruction and academic interventions.* (under cooperative agreement grant S283B050034 for U.S. Department of Education). Portsmouth, NH: RMC Research Corporation, Center on Instruction. (Available online at http://www.centeroninstruction.org/files/ELL1-Interventions.pdf)

Francis, D., Rivera, M., Lesaux, N., Kieffer, M., and Rivera, H. (2006c). *Practical guidelines for the education of English language learners: Research-based recommendations for the use of accommodations in large-scale assessments.* (under cooperative agreement grant S283B050034 for U.S. Department of Education). Portsmouth, NH: RMC Research Corporation, Center on Instruction. (Available online at http://www.centeroninstruction.org/files/ELL3-Assessments.pdf)

Francis, D. J., Rivera, M., Rivera, H., Lesaux, N., and Kieffer, M. (2006). Research-based recommendations for instruction and academic interventions. Retrieved from Center on Instruction Web site: http://www.centeroninstruction.org

Frayer, D. A., Frederick, W. C., and Klausmeier, H. J. (1969). *A schema for testing the level of concept mastery* (Working Paper No. 16). Madison: University of Wisconsin, Wisconsin Research and Development Center for Cognitive Learning.

Frederickson, N., and Turner, J. (2003). Utilizing the classroom peer group to address children's social needs: An evaluation of the Circle of Friends intervention approach. *Journal of Special Education, 36,* 234–246.

Fresch, M. J. (2007). Teachers' concerns about spelling instruction: A national survey. *Reading Psychology, 28*(4), 301–330.

Friend, M. (2000). Perspectives: Collaboration in the twenty-first century. *Remedial and Special Education, 20,* 130–132, 160.

Friend, M., Hurley-Chamberlain, D., and Cook, L. (2006, April). *NCLD and IDEA: Disaster or golden opportunity for co-teaching?* Paper presented at the 84th Annual Convention of the Council for Exceptional Children, Salt Lake City, UT.

Fromkin, V., and Rodman, R. (1998). *An instruction to language* (6th ed.). Orlando, FL: Harcourt Brace.

Fry, E. B. (1977). Fry's readability graph: Clarifications, validity, and extension to level 17. *Journal of Reading, 21,* 242–252.

Fry, E. B., Fountoukidis, D. L., and Polk, J. K. (1985). *The new reading teacher's book of lists.* Englewood Cliffs, NJ: Prentice Hall.

Fuchs, D., Fuchs, L. S., and Burish, P. (2000). Peer-assisted learning strategies: An evidence-based practice to promote reading achievement. *Learning Disabilities Research and Practice, 15,* 85–91.

Fuchs, D., Fuchs, L. S., Mathes, P. G., and Simmons, D. C. (1997). Peer-assisted learning strategies: Making classrooms more responsive to diversity. *American Educational Research Journal, 34,* 174–206.

Fuchs, D., Fuchs, L. S., Thompson, A., Al Otaiba, S., Yen, L., Yang, N. J., et al. (2003). Exploring the importance of reading programs for kindergartners with disabilities in mainstream classrooms. *Exceptional Children, 68,* 295–311.

Fuchs, L. S., Bahr, C. M., and Rieth, H. J. (1989). Effects of goal structures and performance contingencies on the math performance of adolescents with learning disabilities. *Journal of Learning Disabilities, 22,* 554–560.

Fuchs, L. S., and Deno, S. L. (1991). Paradigmatic distinctions between instructionally relevant measurement models. *Exceptional Children, 57,* 488–500.

Fuchs, L. S., Fuchs, D., Compton, D. L., Bryant, J. D., Hamlett, C. L., and Seethaler, P. M. (2007). Mathematics screening and progress monitoring at first grade: Implications for responsiveness to intervention. *Exceptional Children, 73*(3), 311–330.

Fuchs, L. S., Fuchs, D., and Hamlett, C. L. (1989). Effects of instrumental use of curriculum-based measurement to enhance instructional programs. *Remedial and Special Education 10*(2), 43–52.

Fuchs, L. S., Fuchs, D., Hamlett, C. L., Phillips, N. B., and Karns, K. (1995). General educators' specialized adaptation for students with learning disabilities. *Exceptional Children, 61*(5), 440–459.

Fuchs, L. S., Fuchs, D., Hamlett, C. L., Phillips, N. B., Karns, K., and Dutka, S. (1997). Enhancing students' helping behavior during peer-mediated instruction with conceptual mathematical explanations. *The Elementary School Journal, 97,* 223–249.

Fuchs, L. S., Fuchs, D., Hamlett, C. L., Walz, L., and Germann, G. (1993). Formative evaluation of academic progress: How much growth can we expect? *School Psychology Review, 22*(1), 27–48.

Fuchs, L. S., Fuchs, D., and Speece, D. L. (2002). Treatment validity as a unifying construct for identifying learning disabilities. *Learning Disability Quarterly, 25,* 33–45.

Fuchs, L. S., Hamlett, C., and Fuchs, D. (1990). *Monitoring basic skills progress: Basic math.* Austin, TX: PRO-ED.

Fujiki, M., Brinton, B., and Todd, C. M. (1996). Social skills of children with specific language impairment. *Language, Speech, and Hearing Services in Schools, 27,* 195–202.

Fulk, B. J. M., Mastropieri, M. A., and Scruggs, T. E. (1992). Mnemonic generalization training with learning disabled adolescents. *Learning Disabilities Research and Practice, 7,* 2–10.

Fulk, B. M., and Stormont-Spurgin, M. (1995). Spelling interventions for students with disabilities: A review. *Journal of Special Education, 28,* 488–513.

Gajria, M., and Salend, S. J. (1995). Homework practices of students with and without learning disabilities: A comparison. *Journal of Learning Disabilities, 28,* 291–296.

Gajria, M., and Salvia, J. (1992). The effects of summarization instruction on text comprehension of students with learning disabilities. *Exceptional Children, 58,* 508–516.

Gallagher, P. A., Powell, T. H., and Rhodes, C. A. (2006). *Brothers & sisters: A special part of exceptional families.* Baltimore: Brookes.

Ganske, K. (2000). *Word journeys: Assessment-guided phonics, spelling, and vocabulary instruction.* New York: Guilford Press.

Gaskins, I. W. with Cress, C., O'Hara, C., and Donnelly, K. (1998). *Word detectives: Benchmark extended word identification program for beginning readers.* Media, PA: Benchmark Press.

Gast, D., Ault, M., Wolery, M., Doyle, P., and Belanger, S. (1988). Comparison of constant time delay and the system of least prompts in teaching sight word reading to students with moderate retardation. *Education and Training in Mental Retardation, 23,* 117–128.

Gately, S. E., and Gately, F. J. (2001). Understanding co-teaching components. *Teaching Exceptional Children, 33*(4), 1–16.

Gerber, M. M., and Hall, R. J. (1989). Cognitive-behavioral training in spelling for learning handicapped students. *Learning Disabilities Quarterly, 12,* 159–171.

German, D. J. (1992). Word-finding intervention for children and adolescents. *Topics in Language Disorders, 13*(1), 33–50.

Gersten, R., and Baker, S. (2001). Teaching expressive writing to students with learning disabilities: A meta-analysis. *Elementary School Journal, 101*(3), 251–272.

Gersten, R., Baker, S. K., Shanahan, T., Linan-Thompson, S., Collins, P., and Scarcella, R. (2007). *Effective literacy and English language instruction for English learners in the elementary grades: A practice guide* (NCEE 2007-4011). Washington, DC: National Center for Education Evaluation and Regional Assistance, Institute of Educational Sciences, U.S. Department of Education. Retrieved from http://ies.ed.gov/ncee/wwc/publications/practiceguides

Gersten, R., Beckmann, S., Clarke, B., Foegen, A., Marsh, L., Star, J. R., and Witzel, B. (2009). *Assisting students struggling with mathematics: Response to Intervention (RtI) for elementary and middle schools* (NCEE 2009-4060). Washington, DC: National Center for Education Evaluation and Regional Assistance, Institute of Education Sciences, U.S. Department of Education. Retrieved from http://ies.ed.gov/ncee/wwc/publications/practiceguides/

Gersten, R., Carnine, D., and Woodward, J. (1987). Direct Instruction research: The third decade. *Remedial and Special Education, 8*(6), 48–56.

Gersten, R., and Chard, D. (1999). Number sense: Rethinking arithmetic instruction for students with mathematical disabilities. *Journal of Special Education, 33*(1), 18–28.

Gersten, R., and Geva, E. (2003). Teaching reading to early language learners. *Educational Leadership, 60*(7), 44–49.

Gersten, R., Fuchs, L. S., Williams, J. P., and Baker, S. (2011). Teaching reading comprehension strategies to students with learning disabilities: A review of research. *Review of Educational Research, 71*(2), 279–320.

Gersten, R., Schiller, E. P., and Vaughn, S. (2000). *Contemporary special education research: Syntheses of knowledge bases in critical instructional issues.* Mahwah, NJ: Erlbaum.

Gettinger, M., Bryant, M. D., and Fayne, H. R. (1982). Designing spelling instruction for learning disabled children: An emphasis on unit size, distributed practice, and training for transfer. *Journal of Special Education, 16*(4), 439–448.

Gibb, G. S., and Dyches, T. T. (2000). *Guide to writing quality individualized educational programs: What's best for students with disabilities?* Boston: Allyn & Bacon.

Gibbs, R. W. (1987). Linguistic factors in children's understanding of idioms. *Journal of Speech and Hearing Research, 54,* 613–620.

Gillingham, A., and Stillman, B. W. (1973). *Remedial training for children with specific disability in reading, spelling, and penmanship.* Cambridge, MA: Educators Publishing Service.

Ginsburg, H. P. (1997). Mathematics learning disabilities: A view from developmental psychology. *Journal of Learning Disabilities, 30*(1), 20–33.

Ginsburg, A., Cooke, G., Leinwand, S., Noell, J., and Pollock, E. (2005). *Reassessing U.S. international mathematics performance: New findings from the 2003 TIMSS and PISA.* Washington, DC: American Institutes for Research.

Ginsburg-Block, M. D., Rohrbeck, C. A., and Fantuzzo, J. W. (2006). A meta-analytic review of social, self-concept, and behavioral outcomes of peer-assisted learning. *Journal of Educational Psychology, 98*(4), 732–749.

Glick, B., and Goldstein, A. P. (1987). Aggression replacement training. *Journal of Counseling and Development, 65*(7), 356–362.

Glover, T. A., and Vaughn, S. (2010). *The promise of response to intervention: Evaluating current science and practice.* New York: Guilford.

Goldenberg, C. (2008). Teaching English language learners: What the teacher does—and does not—say. *American Educator, 32*(2), 1–19.

Goldman, S. R., Hasselbring, T. S., and the Cognition and Technology Group at Vanderbilt (1997). Achieving meaningful mathematics literacy for students with learning disabilities. *Journal of Learning Disabilities, 30*(2), 198–208.

Goldstein, A. P., Sprafkin, R. P., Gershaw, N. J., and Klein, P. (1980). *Skillstreaming the adolescent.* Champaign, IL: Research Press.

Goldstein, A. P., and McGinnis, E. (1995). *Skillstreaming the adolescent: New strategies and perspectives for teaching prosocial skills.* Champaign, IL: Research Press.

Good, R. H., Bank, J., and Watson, J. (2004). *IDEL: Indicadores dinámicos del éxito en la lectura.* Longmont, CO: Sopris West.

Good, T. L., and Brophy, J. E. (1997). *Looking in classrooms* (7th ed.). New York: Addison-Wesley, Longman.

Goodman, K. (1986). *What's whole in whole language?* Portsmouth, NH: Heinemann.

Goodman, K. S. (1996). *On reading.* Portsmouth, NH: Heinemann.

Goodman, Y. M., Watson, D. J., and Burke, C. L. (1996). *Reading strategies: Focus on comprehension* (2nd ed.). Katonah, NY: Richard C. Owens.

Goodstein, H. A. (1981). Are the errors we see the true errors? Error analysis in verbal problem solving. *Topics in Learning and Learning Disabilities, 1*(3), 31–45.

Gordon, J., Vaughn, S., and Schumm, J. S. (1993). Spelling intervention: A review of literature and implications for instruction for students with learning disabilities. *Learning Disabilities Research and Practice, 8,* 175–181.

Goswami, U. (1998). Rime-based coding in early reading development in English: Orthographic analogies and rime neighborhoods. In D. Hulme and R. M. Joshi, (Eds.), *Reading and spelling: Development and disorders* (pp. 69–86). Mahwah, NJ: Erlbaum.

Gould, A., and Vaughn, S. (2000). Planning for the inclusive classroom: Meeting the needs of diverse learners. *Catholic Education: A Journal of Inquiry and Practice, 3*(3), 363–374.

Graham, S. (1983). The effect of self-instructional procedures on LD students' handwriting performance. *Learning Disability Quarterly, 6*(2), 231–244.

Graham, S. (1999). Handwriting and spelling instruction for students with learning disabilities: A review. *Learning Disability Quarterly, 22*(2), 78–98.

Graham, S., Berninger, V., and Weintraub, N. (1998). The relationship between handwriting style and speed and legibility. *Journal of Educational Research, 91,* 290–297.

Graham, S., and Freeman, S. (1986). Strategy training and teacher- vs. student-controlled study conditions: Effects on LD students' spelling performance. *Learning Disability Quarterly, 9,* 15–22.

Graham, S., and Harris, K. (2005). *Writing better: Effective strategies for teaching students with learning difficulties.* Baltimore: Brookes.

Graham, S., Harris, K. R., and Loynachan, C. (1996). The directed spelling thinking activity: Application with high-frequency words. *Learning Disabilities Research and Practice, 1,* 34–40.

Graham, S., Harris, K. R., and MacArthur, C. A. (1995). Introduction to special issue: Research on writing and literacy. *Learning Disability Quarterly, 18,* 250–252.

Graham, S., Harris, K., and Troia, G. (1998). Writing and self-regulation: Cases from the self-regulated strategy development model. In D. Schunk and B. Zimmerman (Eds.), *Self-regulated learning: From teaching to self-reflective practice* (pp. 20–41). New York: Guilford.

Graham, S., and Miller, L. (1979). Spelling research and practice: A unified approach. *Focus on Exceptional Children, 12*(2), 1–16.

Graham, S., and Perin, D. (2007). *Writing next: Effective strategies to improve writing of adolescents in middle and high schools: A report to Carnegie Corporation of New York.* Washington, DC: Alliance for Excellent Education.

Graham, S., and Voth, V. (1990). Spelling instruction: Making modifications for students with learning disabilities. *Academic Therapy, 25,* 447–457.

Graves, A. W., Valles, E. C., and Rueda, R. (2000). Variations in interactive writing instruction: A study in four bilingual special education settings. *Learning Disabilities Research and Practice, 15*(3), 1–9.

Graves, D. (1994). *A fresh look at writing.* Portsmouth, NH: Heinemann.

Graves, D. H. (1983). *Writing: Teachers and children at work.* Portsmouth, NH: Heinemann.

Graves, M. F. (2006). *The vocabulary book: Learning and instruction*. New York: Teachers College Press.

Graves, M. F. (2009). *Essential readings on vocabulary instruction*. Newark, DE: International Reading Association.

Greene, J. R. (1996). Language: The effects of an individualized structured language curriculum for middle and high school students. *Annals of Dyslexia, 38,* 258–275.

Greenham, S. (1999). Learning disabilities and psychosocial adjustment: A critical review. *Child Neuropsychology, 5,* 171–196.

Greenwood, C. R., Delquadri, J. C., and Hall, R. V. (1989). Longitudinal effects of classwide peer tutoring. *Journal of Educational Psychology, 81,* 371–383.

Gregory, R. P., Hackney, C., and Gregory, N. M. (1982). Corrective reading programme: An evaluation. *British Journal of Educational Psychology, 52,* 33–50.

Gresham, F. M. (1982). Misguided mainstreaming: The case for social skills training with handicapped children. *Exceptional Children, 48,* 422–433.

Grimm, J. A., Bijou, S. W., and Parsons, J. A. (1973). A problem solving model for teaching remedial arithmetic to handicapped children. *Journal of Abnormal Child Psychology, 1,* 26–39.

Grossen, B. (1999). *The research base for corrective reading*. Columbus, OH: SRA/McGraw-Hill.

Gunn, B., Biglan, A., Smolkowski, K., and Ary, D. (2000). The efficacy of supplemental instruction in decoding skills for Hispanic and non-Hispanic students in early elementary school. *The Journal of Special Education, 34*(2), 90–103.

Gunning, T. G. (2001). *Building words: A resource manual for teaching word analysis and spelling patterns*. Boston: Allyn & Bacon.

Gunning, T. G. (2010). *Assessing and correcting reading and writing difficulties* (4th ed.). Boston, MA: Allyn & Bacon.

Gunning, T. G. (2010). *Creating literacy instruction for all students* (7 ed.). Boston: Allyn & Bacon.

Gurney, D., Gersten, R., Dimino, J., and Carnine, D. (1990). Story grammar: Effective literature instruction for high school students with learning disabilities. *Journal of Learning Disabilities, 23,* 335–342.

Guszak, F. J. (1972). *Diagnostic reading instruction in the elementary school*. New York: Harper & Row.

Haager, D., and Mahdavi, J. (2007). Teacher roles in implementing intervention (pp. 245–264). In D. Haager, J. Klingner, and S. Vaughn (Eds.), *Evidence-based reading practices for response to intervention*. Baltimore: Brookes.

Hacker, D. J., Dunlosky, J., and Graesser, A. C. (1998). *Metacognition in educational theory and practice*. Mahwah, NJ: Erlbaum.

Hagaman, J. L., and Reid, R. (2008). The effects of the paraphrasing strategy on the reading comprehension of middle school students at risk for failure in reading. *Remedial and Special Education, 29*(4), 222–234.

Haley, M. H., and Austin, T. Y. (2004). *Content-based second language teaching and learning: An interactive approach*. Boston: Allyn & Bacon.

Hall, R. V., and Hall, M. L. (1998). *How to use planned ignoring (Extinction)* (2nd ed.). Austin, TX: PRO-ED.

Hallowell, E. M., and Ratey, J. J. (1995). *Driven to distraction: Recognizing and coping with attention deficit disorder from childhood through adulthood*. New York: Touchstone.

Halpern, N. (1981). Mathematics for the learning disabled. *Journal of Learning Disabilities, 14*(9), 505–506.

Hanover, S. (1983). Handwriting comes naturally? *Academic Therapy, 18,* 407–412.

Harbort, G., Gunter, P. L., Hull, K., Brown, Q., Venn, M. L., Wiley, L. P., et al. (2007). Behaviors of teachers in co-taught classes in a secondary school. *Teacher Education and Special Education, 30*(1), 13–23.

Hardman, M. L. (2009). Redesigning the preparation of all teachers within the framework of an integrated program model. *Teaching and Teacher Education, 25*(4), 583–587.

Harniss, M. K., Epstein, M. H., Bursuck, W. D., Nelson, J., and Jayanthi, M. (2001). Resolving homework-related communication problems: Recommendations of parents of children with and without disabilities. *Reading & Writing Quarterly, 17,* 205–225.

Harris, K. R. (1985). Conceptual, methodological, and clinical issues in cognitive behavior assessment. *Journal of Abnormal Child Psychology, 13,* 373–390.

Harry, B. (2008). Collaboration with culturally and linguistically diverse families: Ideal versus reality. *Exceptional Children, 74*(3), 372–388.

Harry, B., Allen, N., and McLaughlin, M. (1995). Communication versus compliance: African-American parents' involvement in special education. *Exceptional Children, 6*(4), 364–377.

Harry, B., and Klingner, J. K. (2006). *Why are so many minority students in special education? Understanding race and disability in schools*. New York: Teachers College Press.

Hartas, D., and Donahue, L. M. (1997). Conversational and social problem-solving skills in adolescents with learning disabilities. *Learning Disabilities Research and Practice, 12*(4), 213–220.

Hasbrouck, J. E., Ihnot, C., and Rogers, G. H. (1999). "Read naturally": A strategy to increase oral reading fluency. *Reading Research and Instruction, 39*(1), 27–38.

Hastings, R. P., Daley, D., Burns, C., and Beck, A. (2006). Maternal distress and expressed emotion: Cross-sectional and longitudinal relationships with behavior problems of children with intellectual disabilities. *American Journal on Mental Retardation, 111*(1), 48–61.

Hazel, J. S., Schumaker, J. B., Sherman, J. A., and Sheldon, J. (1982). Application of a group training program in social skills and problem solving to learning disabled and non-learning disabled youth. *Learning Disability Quarterly, 5,* 398–409.

Hazel, J. S., Schumaker, J. B., Sherman, J. A., and Sheldon-Wildgen, J. (1981). *ASSET: A social skills program for adolescents*. Champaign, IL: Research Press.

Heath, N. L., and Wiener, J. (1996). Depression and nonacademic self-perceptions in children with and without learning disabilities. *Learning Disability Quarterly, 19,* 34–44.

Hecht, S. A., Vagi, K. J., and Torgesen, J. K. (2007). Fraction skills and proportional reasoning. In D. B. Berch and M. M. M. Mazzocco (Eds.), *Why is math so hard for some children? The nature and origins of mathematical learning difficulties and disabilities* (pp. 121–132). Baltimore: Brookes.

Hembree, R. (1986). Research gives calculators a green light. *Arithmetic Teacher, 34*(1), 18–21.

Hengst, J. A., Frame, S. R., Neuman-Stritzel, T., and Gannaway, R. (2005). Conversational use of reported speech by individuals with aphasia and their communication partners. *Journal of Speech, Language, and Hearing Research, 48*(1), 137–156.

Henry, C. S., Stephenson, A. L., Hanson, M. F., and Hargett, W. (1993). Adolescent suicide and families: An ecological approach. *Adolescence, 28,* 291–308.

Henry, M. (1996). *Patterns for success in reading and spelling: A multisensory approach to teaching phonics and word analysis.* Austin, TX: PRO-ED.

Henry, M. (1997). The decoding/spelling curriculum: Integrated decoding and spelling instruction from pre-school to early secondary school. *Dyslexia, 3,* 178–189.

Herman, P. A., Anderson, R. C., Pearson, P. D., and Nagy, W. E. (1987). Incidental acquisition of word meaning from expositions with varied text features. *Reading Research Quarterly, 22,* 263–284.

Heron, T. E., Welsch, R. G., and Goddard, Y. L. (2003). Applications of tutoring systems in specialized subject areas. *Remedial and Special Education, 24*(5), 288–300.

Herzog, P. R. (1998). *PhonicsQ: The complete cueing system.* Available from http://www.phonicsq.com

Heward, W. L. (2003). Ten faulty notions about teaching and learning that hinder the effectiveness of special education. *Journal of Special Education, 36,* 186–205.

Hickman, P., Pollard-Durodola, S., and Vaughn, S. (2004). Storybook reading: Improving vocabulary and comprehension for English language learners. *The Reading Teacher, 57*(8), 720.

Hiebert, E. H. (2002). *Quickreads: A research-based fluency program.* Parsippany, NJ: Modern Curriculum Press.

Higgins, E. L., and Raskind, M. H. (1995). An investigation of the compensatory effectiveness of speech recognition on the written composition performance of postsecondary students with learning disabilities. *Learning Disability Quarterly, 18,* 159–174.

Hock, M., and Mellard, D. (2005). Reading comprehension strategies for adult literacy outcomes. *Journal of Adolescent and Adult Literacy, 49*(3), 192–200.

Holdaway, D. (1979). *The foundations of literacy.* Portsmouth, NH: Heinemann.

Hoover, J., and Stenhjem, P. (2003). Bullying and teasing of youth with disabilities: Creating positive school environments for effective inclusion. *Issue Brief: Examining current challenges in secondary education and transition, 2*(3), 1–6.

Hoover, J. H., and Salk, J. (2003). *Bullying: Bigger concerns.* St. Cloud, MN: St. Cloud State University, Department of Special Education.

Hoover, J. J., and Patton, J. R. (2008). The role of special educators in a multitiered instructional system. *Intervention in School and Clinic, 43*(4), 195–202.

Hoskisson, K., and Krohm, B. (1974). Reading by immersion: Assisted reading. *Elementary English, 5,* 831–836.

Howard, K. A., and Tryon, G. S. (2002). Depressive symptoms in and type of classroom placement for adolescents with LD. *Journal of Learning Disabilities, 35*(2), 185–190.

Hughes, C. A. (1996). Memory and test-taking strategies. In D. D. Deshler, E. S. Ellis, and B. K. Lenz (Eds.), *Teaching adolescents with learning disabilities: Strategies and methods* (2nd ed., pp. 209–266). Denver: Love.

Hughes, C. A., Ruhl, K. L., Deshler, D. D., and Schumaker, J. B. (1995). *The assignment completion strategy.* Lawrence, KS: Edge Enterprises.

Hughes, C. A., and Schumaker, J. B. (1991). Test-taking strategy instruction for adolescents with learning disabilities. *Exceptionality, 2,* 205–221.

Hughes, C. A., Schumaker, J. B., and Deshler, D. D. (2001). *The essay test-taking strategy.* Lawrence, KS: Edge Enterprises.

Hughes, C. A., Schumaker, J. B., Deshler, D. D., and Mercer, C. D. (1993). *The test-taking strategy* (Rev. ed.). Lawrence, KS: Edge Enterprises.

Idol, L. (1987a). A critical thinking map to improve content area comprehension of poor readers. *Remedial and Special Education, 8*(4), 28–40.

Idol, L. (1987b). Group story mapping: A comprehension strategy for both skilled and unskilled readers. *Journal of Learning Disabilities, 20*(4), 196–205.

Idol, L., Nevin, A., and Paolucci-Whitcomb, P. (2000). *Collaborative consultation* (3rd ed.). Austin, TX: PRO-ED.

Imber, S. C., Imber, S. C., and Rothstein, C. (1979). Modifying independent work habits: An effective teacher-parent communication program. *Exceptional Children, 46,* 218–221.

Isaacson, S., and Gleason, M. M. (1997). Mechanical obstacles to writing: What can teachers do to help students with learning problems? *Learning Disabilities Research Practice, 12*(3), 188–194.

Isherwood, R. S., and Barger-Anderson , R. (2007). Factors affecting the adoption of co-teaching models in inclusive classrooms: One school's journey from mainstreaming to inclusion. *Journal of Ethnographic & Qualitative Research, 2,* 121–128.

Janney, R., and Snell, M. E. (2000). *Behavioral support.* Baltimore: Brookes.

Jarvis, P. A., and Justin, E. M. (1992). Social sensitivity in adolescents and adults with learning disabilities. *Adolescence, 27*(108), 977–988.

Jenkins, J. R., Antil, L. R., Wayne, S. K., and Vadasy, P. F. (2003). How cooperative learning works for special education and remedial students. *Exceptional Children, 69,* 279–292.

Jewell, T. A., and Pratt, D. (1999). Literature discussions in the primary grades: Children's thoughtful discourse about books and what teachers can do to make it happen. *The Reading Teacher, 52,* 842–850.

Jitendra, A. K., Hoff, K., and Beck, M. M. (1999). Teaching middle school students with learning disabilities to solve word problems using a schema-based approach. *Remedial and Special Education, 20*(1), 50–64.

Johns, B. H., Crowley, E. P., and Guetzloe, E. (2002). Planning the IEP for students with emotional and behavioral disorders. *Focus on Exceptional Children, 32*(9), 1–12.

Johnson, C. J., Beitchman, J. H., Young, A., Escobar, M., Atkinson, L., Wilson, B., et al. (1999). Fourteen-year follow-up of children with and without speech/language impairments: Speech/language stability and outcomes. *Journal of Speech, Language, and Hearing Research, 42,* 744–760.

Johnson, D. D., and Pearson, P. D. (1984). *Teaching reading vocabulary* (2nd ed.). New York: Holt, Rinehart and Winston.

Johnson, D. J., and Myklebust, H. R. (1967). *Learning disabilities: Educational principles and practices.* New York: Grune & Stratton.

Johnson, D. W., and Johnson, R. T. (1975). *Learning together & alone.* Englewood Cliffs, NJ: Prentice Hall.

Johnson, D. W., and Johnson, R. T. (1984a). Classroom learning structure and attitudes toward handicapped students in mainstream settings: A theoretical model and research evidence. In R. Jones (Ed.), *Special education in transition: Attitudes toward the handicapped*. Reston, VA.: ERIC Clearinghouse on Handicapped and Gifted Children, Council for Exceptional Children.

Johnson, D. W., Johnson, R. T., and Smith, K. (2007). The state of cooperative learning in postsecondary and professional settings. *Educational Psychology Review, 19*(1), 15–29.

Johnson, R. T., and Johnson, D. W. (1986). Action research: Cooperative learning in the science classroom. *Science and Children, 24,* 31–32.

Johnson Santamaria, L., Fletcher, T. V., and Bos, C. S. (2002). Scaffolded instruction: Promoting biliteracy for second language learners with language/learning disabilities. In A. Artiles and A. Ortiz (Eds.), *English language learners with special education needs: Identification, assessment, and instruction*. Washington, DC: Center for Applied Linguistics.

Jordan, N. C., and Hanich, L. B. (2003). Characteristics of children with moderate mathematics deficiencies: A longitudinal perspective. *Learning Disabilities Research and Practice, 18*(4), 213–221.

Juel, C., and Deffes, R. (2004). Making words stick. *Educational Leadership, 61*(6), 30–34. Retrieved from http://www.montebello.k12.ca.us/k8/ELP/Vocabulary_Development/Making_Words_Stick.pdf

Juel, C., and Minden-Cupp, C. (2000). Learning to read words: Linguistic units and instructional strategies. *Reading Research Quarterly, 35*(4), 458–492.

Juvonen, J., and Bear, G. (1992). Social adjustment of children with and without learning disabilities in integrated classrooms. *Journal of Educational Psychology, 84*(3), 322–330.

Kail, R., and Leonard, L. B. (1986). *Word-finding abilities in language-impaired children* (ASHA Monograph Number 25). Rockville, MD: American Speech-Language-Hearing Association.

Kame'enui, E. J., and Carnine, D. W. (1998). *Effective teaching strategies that accommodate diverse learners*. Upper Saddle River, NJ: Prentice Hall.

Kame'enui, E. J., Simmons, D. C., Baker, S., Chard, D., Dickson, S., Gunn, B. et al. (1998). Effective strategies for teaching beginning reading. In E. J. Kame'enui and D. W. Carnine (Eds.), *Effective teaching strategies that accommodate diverse learners* (pp. 45–70). Columbus, OH: Merrill.

Kaminski, R. A., and Good, R. H. (1996). Toward a technology for assessing basic early literacy skills. *School Psychology Review, 25*(2), 215–227.

Kauffman, J., Hallahan, D., Haas, K., Brame, T., and Boren, R. (1978). Imitating children's errors to improve spelling performance. *Journal of Learning Disabilities, 11,* 33–38.

Kauffman, J. M. (2001). *Characteristics of children's behavior disorders* (7th ed.). Columbus, OH: Merrill.

Kaufmann, L., Handl, P., and Thony, B. (2003). Evaluation of a numeracy intervention program focusing on basic numerical knowledge and conceptual knowledge: A pilot study. *Journal of Learning Disabilities, 36,* 564–573.

Keller-Marulis, M. A., Shapiro, E. S., and Hintze, J. M. (2008). Long-term diagnostic accuracy of curriculum-based measures in reading and mathematics. *School Psychology Review, 37*(3), 374–390.

Kelly, B., Gersten, R., and Carnine, D. (1990). Student error patterns as a function of curriculum design: Teaching fractions to remedial high school students and high school students with learning disabilities. *Journal of Learning Disabilities, 23,* 23–29.

Kim, A. (2002). *Effects of Computer-Assisted Collaborative Strategic Reading (CACSR) on reading comprehension for students with learning disabilities*. Unpublished doctoral dissertation, University of Texas, Austin.

Kim, A., Vaughn, S., Klingner, J. K., Woodruff, A. L., Klein, C., and Kouzekanani, K. (2003). *Improving the reading comprehension of middle school students with reading disabilities through Computer-Assisted -Collaborative Strategic Reading*. Manuscript submitted for publication.

Kim, A., Vaughn, S., Wanzek, J., and Wei, S. (2004). Graphic organizers and their effects on the reading comprehension of students with LD: A synthesis of research. *Journal of Learning Disabilities, 37*(2), 105–118.

King-Sears, M. E., Mercer, C. D., and Sindelar, P. T. (1992). Toward independence with key word mnemonics: A strategy for science vocabulary instruction. *Remedial and Special Education, 13*(5), 22–33.

Kirk, S. A., Kirk, W. D., and Minskoff, E. H. (1985). *Phonic remedial reading lessons*. Novato, CA: Academic Therapy Publications.

Kirkpatrick, E. M., and Schwarz, C. M. (Eds.). (1982). *Chambers idioms*. Edinburgh, Scotland: Chambers.

Kistner, J., and Osborne, M. (1987). A longitudinal study of LD children's self-evaluations. *Learning Disability Quarterly, 10,* 258–266.

Klingner, J. K., and Edwards, P. (2006). Cultural considerations with response-to-intervention models. *Reading Research Quarterly, 41,* 108–117.

Klingner, J. K., and Solano-Flores, G. (2007). Cultural responsiveness in response-to-intervention models. In *Accommodating students with disabilities: What works?* Educational Testing Service.

Klingner, J. K., and Vaughn, S. (1996). Reciprocal teaching of reading comprehension strategies for students with learning disabilities who use English as a second language. *Elementary School Journal, 96,* 275–293.

Klingner, J. K., and Vaughn, S. (1998). Using collaborative strategic reading. *Teaching Exceptional Children, 30*(6), 32–37.

Klingner, J. K., and Vaughn, S. (1999a). Promoting reading comprehension, content learning, and English acquisition through collaborative strategic reading (CSR). *The Reading Teacher, 52*(7), 738–747.

Klingner, J. K., and Vaughn, S. (1999b). Students' perceptions of instructional practice. *Exceptional Children, 66,* 23–37.

Klingner, J. K., and Vaughn, S. (2000). The helping behaviors of fifth graders while using collaborative strategic reading during ESL content classes. *TESOL Quarterly, 34*(1), 69–98.

Klingner, J. K., and Vaughn, S. (2002). Joyce: The changing roles and responsibilities of an LD specialist. *Learning Disability Quarterly, 25,* 19–32.

Klingner, J. K., Vaughn, S., Argüelles, M. E., Hughes, M. T., and Ahwee, S. (2003). Collaborative strategic reading: "Real world" lessons from classroom teachers. *Remedial and Special Education*.

Klingner, J. K., Vaughn, S., and Boardman, A. (2007). *Teaching reading comprehension to students with learning difficulties*. New York: Guilford.

Klingner, J. K., Vaughn, S., Dimino, J., Schumm, J. S., and Bryant, D.P. (2001). *From clunk to click: Collaborative strategic reading*. Longmont, CO: Sopris West.

Klingner, J. K., Vaughn, S., and Schumm, J. S. (1998). Collaborative strategic reading during social studies in heterogeneous fourth-grade classrooms. *Elementary School Journal, 99,* 3–22.

Klingner, J. K., Vaughn, S., Schumm, J. S., Cohen, P., and Forgan, J. W. (1998). Inclusion or pull-out: Which do students prefer? *Journal of Learning Disabilities, 32*(2), 148–158.

Kloo, A., and Zigmond, N. (2008). Co-teaching revisited: Redrawing the blueprint. *Preventing School Failure, 52*(2), 12–20.

Kloomok, S., and Cosden, M. (1994). Self-concept in children with learning disabilities: The relationship between global self-concept, academic discounting, nonacademic self-concept, and perceived social support. *Learning Disability Quarterly, 17*(2), 140–153.

Knoff, H. M. (2003). *The stop & think social skills program*. Longmont, CO: Sopris West.

Kobayashi, K. (2006). Combined effects of note-taking/reviewing on learning and the enhancement through interventions: A meta-analytic review. *Educational Psychology, 26*(3), 459–477.

Kosc, L. (1981). Neuropsychological implications of diagnosis and treatment of mathematical learning disabilities. *Topics in Learning and Learning Disabilities, 1*(3), 19–30.

Kozulin, A., and Presseisen, B. Z. (1995). Mediated learning experience and psychological tools: Vygotsky's and Feuerstein's perspectives in a study of student learning. *Educational Psychologists, 30,* 67–75.

Kress, R. A., and Johnson, M. S. (1970). Martin. In A. J. Harris (Ed.), *Casebook on reading disability* (pp. 1–24). New York: David McKay.

Kucer, S. B. (1986). Helping writers get the "big picture." *Journal of Reading, 30*(1), 18–25.

Kuhn, M. R., and Stahl, S. (2003). Fluency: A review of developmental and remedial practices. *Journal of Educational Psychology, 95,* 3–21.

Kuhne, M., and Wiener, J. (2000). Stability of social status of children with and without learning disabilities. *Learning Disability Quarterly, 23*(1), 64–75.

LaBerge, D., and Samuels, S. J. (1974). Toward a theory of automatic information processing in reading. *Cognitive Psychology, 6,* 293–323.

Lancelotta, G. X., and Vaughn, S. (1989). Relation between types of aggression and sociometric status: Peer and teacher perceptions. *Journal of Educational Psychology, 81*(1), 86–90. In W. R. Borg. (1993). *Applying educational research.* New York: Longman.

Landrum, T. J., Tankersley, M., and Kauffman, J. M. (2003). What is special about special education for students with emotional or behavioral disorders? *Journal of Special Education, 37,* 148–156.

Lane, K. L, Harris, K. R., Graham, S., Weisenbach, J. L., Brindle, M., and Morphy, P. (2008). The effects of self-regulated strategy development on the writing performance of second-grade students with behavioral and writing difficulties. *The Journal of Special Education, 41*(4), 234–253.

Langer, J. A. (1981). From theory to practice: A prereading plan. *Journal of Reading, 25*(2), 152–156.

Lankford, F. G. (1974). *Some computational strategies in seventh grade pupils*. Unpublished manuscript, University of Virginia.

Lardieri, L. A., Blacher, J., and Swanson, H. L. (2000). Sibling relationships and parent stress in families of children with and without learning disabilities. *Learning Disability Quarterly, 23*(2), 105–116.

Larsen, S. C., Parker, R., and Trenholme, B. (1978). The effects of syntactic complexity upon arithmetic performance. *Learning Disability Quarterly, 1*(4), 80–85.

Lazar, R. T., Warr-Leeper, G. A., Nicholson, C. B., and Johnson, S. (1989). Use of figurative language in classrooms. *ELT Journal, 50,* 43–51.

Leadholm, B., and Miller, J. (1992). *Language sample analysis: The Wisconsin guide*. Madison, WI: Bureau for Exceptional Children, Wisconsin Department of Public Education.

Lederer, J. M. (2000). Reciprocal teaching of social studies in inclusive elementary classrooms. *Journal of Learning Disabilities, 33,* 51–106.

LeMare, L., and de la Ronde, M. (2000). Links among social status, service delivery mode, and service delivery preference in LD, low-achieving, and normally achieving elementary-aged children. *Learning Disability Quarterly, 23*(1), 52–62.

Lenz, B. K. (1983). Promoting active learning through effective instruction: Using advance organizers. *Pointer, 27*(2), 11–13.

Lenz, B. K., Adams, G. L., Bulgren, J. A., Pouloit, N., and Laraux, M. (2007). Effects of curriculum maps and guiding questions on the test performance of adolescents with learning disabilities. *Learning Disability Quarterly, 30*(4), 235–244.

Lenz, B. K., Alley, G. R., and Schumaker, J. B. (1987). Activating the inactive learner: Advance organizers in the secondary content classroom. *Learning Disability Quarterly, 10*(10), 53–67.

Lenz, B. K., and Bulgren, J. A. (1995). Promoting learning in content classes. In P. A. Cegleka and W. H. Berdine (Eds.), *Effective instruction for students with learning problems* (pp. 385–417). Boston: Allyn & Bacon.

Lenz, B. K., Bulgren, J. A., and Hudson, P. (1990). Content enhancement: A model for promoting the acquisition of content by individuals with learning disabilities. In T. E. Scruggs and B. L. Y. Wong (Eds.), *Intervention research in learning disabilities* (pp. 122–165). New York: Springer-Verlag.

Lenz, B. K., Schumaker, J., Deshler, D., and Beals, V. (1993). *The word identification strategy*. Lawrence: University of Kansas.

Leon, J. A., and Pepe, H. J. (1983). Self-instructional training: Cognitive behavior modification for remediating arithmetic deficits. *Exceptional Children, 50*(1), 54–60.

Lerner, J. W. (2000). *Learning disabilities: Theories, diagnosis, and teaching strategies* (8th ed.). Boston: Houghton Mifflin.

Lessenbery, B. M., and Rehfeldt, R. A. (2004). Evaluating stress levels of parents with disabilities. *Exceptional Children, 70*(2), 231–233.

Linan-Thompson, S., Cirino, P. T., and Vaughn, S. (2007). Determining English language learners' response to intervention: Questions and some answers. *Learning Disabilities Quarterly, 30*(3), 185–196.

Linan-Thompson, S, and Vaughn, S. (2007). *Research-based methods of reading instruction for English language learners*. Alexandria, VA: ASCD.

Linan-Thompson, S., Vaughn, S., Hickman-Davis, P., and Kouzekanani, K. (2003). Effectiveness of supplemental reading instruction for second-grade English language learners with reading difficulties. *Elementary School Journal, 103*(3), 221–238.

Linan-Thompson, S., Vaughn, S., Prater, K., and Cirino, P. T. (2006). Response to intervention for English language learners. *Journal of Learning Disabilities, 39,* 390–398.

Lindamood, P. A., and Lindamood, P. (1998). *The Lindamood phoneme sequencing program for reading, spelling, and speech: The LiPS program*. Austin, TX: PRO-ED.

LoGiudice, M., and LoGiudice, C. (1997). *100% grammar*. East Moline, IL: LinguiSystems.

Loomes, C., Rasmussen, C., Pei, J., Manji, S., and Andrew, G. (2008). The effect of rehearsal training on working memory span of children with fetal alcohol spectrum disorder. *Research in Developmental Disabilities, 29*(2), 113–124.

Lovett, M. W., Borden, S. L., Warren-Chaplin, P. M., Lacerenza, L., DeLuca, T., and Giovinazzo, R. (1996). Text comprehension training for disabled readers: An evaluation of reciprocal teaching and text analysis training programs. *Brain and Language, 54,* 477–480.

Lucyshyn, J. M., Dunlap, G., and Albin, R. W. (Eds.) (2002). *Families and positive behavior support*. Baltimore: Brookes.

Lucyshyn, J. M., Horner, R. H., Dunlap, G., Albin, R. W., and Ben, K. R. (2002). Positive behavior support with families. In J. M. Lucyshyn, G. Dunlap, and R. W. Albin (Eds.), *Families and positive behavior support* (pp. 3–43). Baltimore: Brookes.

Lyerla, K. D., Schumaker, J. B., and Deshler, D. D. (1994). *The paragraph writing strategy* (Rev. ed.). Lawrence, KS: Edge Enterprises.

MacArthur, C., Graham, S., and Schwartz, S. (1991). Knowledge of revision and revising behavior among learning disabled students. *Learning Disability Quarterly, 14,* 61–73.

MacArthur, C., Graham, S., Schwartz, S., and Schafer, W. D. (1995). Evaluation of a writing instruction model that integrated a process approach, strategy instruction, and word processing. *Learning Disability Quarterly, 18,* 278–291.

MacArthur, C. A. (Winter 1988). Computers and writing instruction. *Teaching Exceptional Children,* 37–39.

MacArthur, C. A., Graham, S., and Fitzgerald, J. (2008). *Handbook of writing research*. New York: Guilford.

Maccini, P., and Gagnon, J. C. (2002). Perceptions and application of NCTM standards by special and general education teachers. *Exceptional Children, 68,* 325–344.

Macrorie, K. (1980). *The I search paper*. Portsmouth, NH: Heinemann.

MacWilliams, L. J. (1978). Mobility board games: Not only for rainy days. *Teaching Exceptional Children, 11*(1), 22–25.

Maheady, L., Harper, G. F., and Mallette, B. (2001). Peer-mediated instruction and interventions and students with mild disabilities. *Remedial and Special Education, 22,* 4–14.

Maheady, L., Harper, G. F., and Sacca, M. K. (1988). Peer mediated instruction: A promising approach to meeting the needs of learning disabled adolescents. *Learning Disability Quarterly, 11,* 108–113.

Malone, L. D., and Mastropieri, M. A. (1992). Reading comprehension instruction: Summarization and self-monitoring training for students with learning disabilities. *Exceptional Children, 58,* 270–279.

Mandoli, M., Mandoli, P., and McLaughlin, T. F. (1982). Effects of same-age peer tutoring on the spelling performance of a mainstreamed elementary learning disabled student. *Learning Disability Quarterly, 5*(2), 185–189.

Manyak, P. C. (2008). Phonemes in use: Multiple activities for a critical process. *The Reading Teacher, 61*(8), 659–662.

Manzo, A. V. (1969). The request procedure. *Journal of Reading, 13,* 123–126.

Manzo, A. V., and Manzo, U. C. (1993). *Literacy disorders: Holistic diagnosis and remediation*. Fort Worth, TX: Harcourt Brace Jovanovich.

Mariage, T. V. (2000). Constructing educational possibilities: A sociolinguistic examination of meaning-making in "sharing chair." *Learning Disability Quarterly, 23,* 79–103.

Marsh, L. G., and Cooke, N. L. (1996). The effects of using manipulatives in teaching math problem solving to students with learning disabilities. *Learning Disabilities Research and Practice, 11,* 58–65.

Marston, D., Muyskens, P., Lau, M., and Canter, H. (2003). Problem solving model for decision-making with high-incidence disabilities: The Minneapolis experience. *Learning Disabilities Research and Practice, 18*(3), 187–200.

Martin, J. H., and Friedberg, A. (1986). *Writing to read. A parent's guide to the new, early learning program for young children*. New York: Warner.

Martinez, M., and Teale, W. H. (February 1988). Reading in a kindergarten classroom library. *The Reading Teacher,* 568–572.

Mastropieri, M., Scruggs, T. E., and Marshak, L. (2008). Training teachers, parents, and peers to implement effective teaching strategies for content area learning. In T. E. Scruggs and M. A. Mastropieri (Eds.), *Personnel preparation: Advances in learning and behavioral disabilities* (Vol. 21, pp. 309–327). Bingley, UK: Emerald.

Mastropieri, M. A., Leinart, A., and Scruggs, T. E. (1999). Strategies to increase reading fluency. *Intervention in School and Clinic, 34*(5), 278–283.

Mastropieri, M. A., and Scruggs, T. E. (1997). Best practices in promoting reading comprehension in students with learning disabilities: 1976–1996. *Remedial and Special Education, 18,* 197–213.

Mastropieri, M. A., and Scruggs, T. E. (1998). Constructing more meaningful relationships in the classroom: Mnemonic research into practice. *Learning Disabilities Research and Practice, 13*(3), 138–145.

Mastropieri, M. A., Scruggs, T. E., Hamilton, S. L., Wolfe, S., Whedon, C., and Canevaro, A. (1996). Promoting thinking skills of students with learning disabilities: Effects on recall and comprehension of expository prose. *Exceptionality, 6,* 1–11.

Mastropieri, M. A., Scruggs, T. E., Norland, J. J., Berkely, S., McDuffie, K., Tornquist, E. H., et al. (2006). Differentiated curriculum enhancement in inclusive middle school science. *The Journal of Special Education, 40*(3), 130–137.

Mastropieri, M. A., Scruggs, T. E., and Shiah, S. (1991). Mathematics instruction for learning disabled students: A review of research. *Learning Disabilities Research and Practice, 6,* 89–98.

Mastropieri, M. A., Scruggs, T. E., Spencer, V., and Fontana, J. (2003). Promoting success in high school world history: Peer tutoring versus guided notes. *Learning Disabilities Research and Practice, 19*(1), 52–65.

Mastropieri, M. A., Sweda, J., and Scruggs, T. E. (2000). Putting mnemonic strategies to work in an inclusive classroom. *Learning Disabilities Research and Practice, 15*(2), 69–74.

Mathes, P. G., Denton, C. A., Fletcher, J. M., Anthony, J. L., Francis, D. J., and Schatschneider, C. (2005). The effects of theoretically different instruction and student characteristics on the skills of struggling readers. *Reading Research Quarterly, 40*(2), 148–182.

Mathes, P. G., Grek, M. L., Howard, J. K., Babyak, A. E., and Allen, S. H. (1999). Peer-assisted learning strategies for first-grade readers: A tool for preventing early reading failure. *Learning Disabilities Research and Practice, 14,* 50–60.

Mathes, P. G., Torgesen, J. K., and Howard, A. J. (2001). The effects of peer-assisted literacy strategies for first-grade readers with and without additional computer-assisted instruction in phonological awareness. *American Educational Research Journal, 38*(2), 371–410.

Mathinos, D. A. (1987). *Communicative abilities of disabled and nondisabled children*. Paper presented at the biennial meeting of the Society for Research in Child Development, Baltimore, MD.

Matuszny, R. M., Banda, D. R., and Coleman, T. J. (2007, Mar./Apr.). A progressive plan for building collaborative relationships with parents from diverse backgrounds. *Teaching Exceptional Children,* 24–31.

McCardle, P., and Chahabra, V. (2004). *The voice of evidence in reading research*. Baltimore: Brookes.

McDaniel, M. A., Howard, D. C., and Einstein, G. O. (2009). The read-recite-review study strategy: Effective and portable. *Psychological Science, 20*(4), 516–522.

McGinnis, E., and Goldstein, A. (1997). *Skillstreaming the elementary school child: New strategies and perspectives for teaching prosocial skills*. Champaign, IL: Research Press.

McGinnis, E., and Goldstein, A. (2003). *Skillstreaming in early childhood: New strategies and perspectives for teaching prosocial skills*. Champaign, IL: Research Press.

McIntosh, R., Vaughn, S., and Bennerson, D. (1995). FAST social skills training for students with learning disabilities. *Teaching Exceptional Children, 28,* 37–41.

McIntosh, R., Vaughn, S., Schumm, J., Haager, D., and Lee, O. (1993). Observations of students with learning disabilities in general education classrooms: You don't bother me and I won't bother you. *Exceptional Children, 60,* 249–261.

McIntyre, C. W., and Pickering, J. S. (1995). *Clinical studies of multisensory structured language education for students with dyslexia and related disorders*. Poughkeepsie, NY: Hamco.

McKeown, M. G., and Beck, I. L. (2004). Transforming knowledge into professional development resources: Six teachers implement a model of teaching for understanding text. *The Elementary School Journal, 104,* 391–408.

McKeown, M. G., Beck, I. S., Sinatra, G. M., and Loxterman, J. A. (1992). The contribution of prior knowledge and coherent text to comprehension. *Reading Research Quarterly, 27,* 78–93.

McLeskey, J. (Ed.). (2007). *Reflections on inclusion: Classic articles that shaped our thinking*. Arlington, VA: Council for Exceptional Children.

McNaughton, D., Hughes, C., and Ofiesh, N. (1997). Proofreading for students with learning disabilities: Integrating computer and strategy use. *Learning Disabilities Research and Practice, 12*(1), 16–28.

Meichenbaum, D. (1977). *Cognitive-behavior modification: An integrative approach*. New York: Plenum.

Meichenbaum, D. (1985). *Stress inoculation training: A clinical guidebook*. Elmsford, NY: Pergamon.

Meichenbaum, D., and Biemiller, A. (1998). *Nurturing independent learners: Helping students take change of their learning*. Cambridge, MA: Brookline.

Meltzer, L., Ranjini, R., Sales Pollica, L., Roditi, B., Sayer, J., and Theokas, C. (2004). Positive and negative self-perceptions: Is there a cyclical relationship between teachers' and students' perceptions of effort, strategy use, and academic performance? *Learning Disabilities Research and Practice, 19*(1), 33–44.

Mercer, C. D., and Mercer, A. R. (2005). *Teaching students with learning problems*. Upper Saddle River, NJ: Merrill/Prentice-Hall.

Mercer, C. D., Mercer, A. R., and Bott, D. A. (1984). *Self-correcting learning materials for the classroom*. Columbus, OH: Merrill.

Meyer, M. S., and Felton, R. H. (1999). Repeated reading to enhance fluency: Old approaches and new directions. *Annals of Dyslexia, 49,* 283–306.

Michaelsen, L. K., and Sweet, M. (2008). The essential elements of team-based learning. *New Directions for Teaching and Learning, 2008*(116), 7–27.

Mills, H., O'Keefe, T., and Stephens, D. (1992). *Looking closely: Exploring the role of phonics in one whole language classroom*. Urbana, IL: National Council of Teachers of English.

Moats, L. C. (1995). *Spelling: Development, disability, and instruction*. Baltimore: York.

Moats, L. C. (2000). *Speech to print: Language essentials for teachers*. Baltimore: Brookes.

Moll, L. C. (1990). Introduction. In L. C. Moll (Ed.), *Vygotsky and education: Instructional implications and applications of sociohistorical psychology* (pp. 1–27). Cambridge: Cambridge University Press.

Moll, L. C., and Greenberg, J. (1990). Creating zones of possibilities: Combining social contexts for instruction. In L. C. Moll (Ed.), *Vygotsky and education* (pp. 319–348). Cambridge: Cambridge University Press.

Montague, M., and Bos, C. S. (1986a). The effect of cognitive strategy training on verbal math problem-solving performance of learning-disabled adolescents. *Journal of Learning Disabilities, 19,* 26–33.

Montague, M., and Bos, C. S. (1986b). Verbal math problem solving and learning disabilities: A review. *Focus on Learning Problems in Math, 8*(2), 7–21.

Montague, M., and Bos, C. S. (1990). Cognitive and metacognitive characteristics of eighth-grade students' mathematical problem solving. *Learning and Individual Differences, 2,* 371–388.

Montague, M., and Leavell, A. G. (1994). Improving the narrative writing of students with learning disabilities. *Remedial and Special Education, 15,* 21–33.

Montague, M., and Rinaldi, C. (2001). Classroom dynamics and children at risk: A follow-up. *Learning Disability Quarterly, 24*(2), 75–83.

Montague, M., and van Garderen, D. (2003). A cross-sectional study of mathematics achievement, estimation skills, and academic self-perception in students of varying ability. *Journal of Learning Disabilities, 36,* 437–447.

Morgan, S. R., and Reinhart, J. A. (1991). *Interventions for students with emotional disorders*. Austin, TX: PRO-ED.

Morrison, G. M. (1985). Differences in teacher perceptions and student self-perceptions for learning disabled and nonhandicapped learners in regular and special education settings. *Learning Disabilities Research, 1,* 32–41.

Morrison, G. M., Walker, D., Wakefield, P., and Solberg, S. (1994). Teacher preferences for collaborative relationships: Relationship to efficacy for teaching in prevention-related domains. *Psychology in the Schools, 31,* 221–231.

Morrow, L. M. (1992). The impact of a literature-based program on literacy achievement, use of literature, and attitudes of children from minority backgrounds. *Reading Research Quarterly, 25,* 251–275.

Mortimore, T., and Crozier, W. R. (2006). Dyslexia and difficulties with study skills in higher education. *Studies in Higher Education, 31*(2), 235–251.

Murphy, J., Hern, C., Williams, R., and McLaughlin, T. (1990). The effects of the copy, cover, compare approach in increasing spelling accuracy with learning disabled students. *Contemporary Educational Psychology, 15,* 378–386.

Muth, K. D. (1987). Teachers' connection questions: Prompting student to organize text idea. *Journal of Reading, 31,* 254–259.

Nagel, B. R., Schumaker, J. B., and Deshler, D. D. (1994). *The FIRST-letter mnemonic strategy* (Rev. ed.). Lawrence, KS: Edge Enterprises.

Nagy, W. E., and Scott, J. E. (2000). Vocabulary processes. In Kamil, M. L., Mosenthal, P. B., Pearson, D. P., and Barr, R. (Eds.), *The handbook of reading research* (Vol. 3). Mahwah, NJ: New York: Longman.

Nancy, A., and Dill, M. (1997). *Let's write.* New York: Scholastic.

National Assessment of Educational Progress. (1990–2007). *The nation's report card.* Retrieved on September 1, 2007 from http://nces.ed.gov/nationsreportcard/

National Association of State Directors of Special Education. (2006). *Response to intervention: Policy considerations and implementation.* Retrieved from http://www.nasdse.org

National Center for Education Evaluation and Regional Assistance, Institute of Education Sciences, U.S. Department of Education. Retrieved from http://ies.ed.gov/ncee/wwc/publications/practiceguides/

National Center for Educational Statistics. *Trends in International Mathematics and Science Study (TIMSS)* (2007 Results). Retrieved June 1, 2009 from http://nces.ed.gov/timss/figure07_2.asp

National Council of Teachers of Mathematics. (2000). *Principles and standards for school mathematics.* Reston, VA: Author.

National Council of Teachers of Mathematics. (2006). *Curriculum focal points for prekindergarten through grade 8 mathematics: A quest for coherence.* Reston, VA: Author.

National Institute for Literacy. (2001). *Put reading first: The research building blocks for teaching children to read.* Washington, DC: U.S. Government Printing Office.

National Mathematics Advisory Panel. (2008). *Foundations for success: The final report of the national mathematics advisory panel.* Washington, DC: U.S. Department of Education.

National Mental Health Association. (2003). *Adolescent depression: Helping depressed teens.* Washington, DC: Author.

National Reading Panel. (2000). *Teaching children to read: An evidence-based assessment of the scientific research literature on reading and its implications for reading instruction.*

Bethesda, MD: National Institute of Child Health and Human Development, National Institutes of Health.

National Research Council. (1989). *Everybody counts: A report to the nation on the future of mathematics education.* Washington, DC: National Academy Press.

National Research Council. (2001). *Adding it up: Helping children learn mathematics.* Washington, DC: National Academy Press.

Nelson, A. (1998). *A long hard day on the ranch.* Buffalo, NY: Firefly Books Limited.

Nelson, J. R., Babyak, A., Gonzalez, J., and Benner, G. J. (2003). An investigation of the types of behavior problems exhibited by K–12 students with emotional or behavioral disorders in public school settings. *Behavioral Disorders, 28*(4), 348–359.

Nelson, J. R., Smith, D. J., Young, R. K., and Dodd, J. M. (1991). A review of self-management outcome research conducted with students who exhibit behavioral disorders. *Behavioral Disorders, 16,* 169–179.

Nelson, J. S., Jayanthi, M., Epstein, M. H., and Bursuck, W. D. (2000). Student preferences for adaptations in classroom testing. *Remedial and Special Education, 21*(1), 41–52.

Nelson, N. W. (1998). *Childhood language disorders in context: Infancy through adolescence* (2nd ed.). Boston: Allyn & Bacon.

Niemi, P., Poskiparta, E. Vauras, M., and Mäki, H. (1998). Reading and writing difficulties do not always occur as the researcher expects. *Scandinavian Journal of Psychology, 39*(3), 159–169.

Nippold, M. A. (1992). The nature of normal and disordered word finding in children and adolescents. *Topics in Language Disorders, 13*(1), 1–14.

Nippold, M. A. (1993). Adolescents language developmental markers in adolescent language: Syntax, semantics, and pragmatics. *Language, Speech, and Hearing Services in Schools, 24,* 21–28.

Nippold, M. A. (1998). *Later language development: The school-age and adolescent years.* Austin, TX: PRO-ED.

Nippold, M. A., and Sun, L. (2008). Knowledge of morphologicaly complex words: A developmental study of older children and young adolescents. *Language, Speech, and Hearing Services in Schools, 39*(3), 365–373.

Nulman, J. H., and Gerber, M. M. (1984). Improving spelling performance by imitating a child's errors. *Journal of Learning Disabilities, 17,* 328–333.

O'Connor, R. E., and Jenkins, J. R. (1995). Improving the generalization of sound/symbol knowledge: Teaching spelling to kindergarten children with disabilities. *Journal of Special Education, 29,* 255–275.

Ogle, D. M. (1986). K-W-L: A teaching model that develops active reading of expository text. *The Reading Teacher, 39,* 564–570.

Ogle, D. M. (1989). The know, want to know, learn strategy. In K. D. Muth (Ed.), *Children's comprehension of text: Research into practice* (pp. 205–233). Newark, DE: International Reading Association.

Okilwa, N. S. A., and Shelby, L. (2010). The effects of peer tutoring on academic performance of students with disabilities in grades 6 through 12: A synthesis of the literature. *Remedial and Special Education* published online 5 January 2010 (DOI: 10.1177/0741932509355991)

Okolo, C. M. (1992). The effects of computer-based attribution retraining on the attributions, persistence, and mathematics computation of students with learning disabilities. *Journal of Learning Disabilities, 25,* 327–334.

Okrainec, J. A., and Hughes, M. J. (1996, July). *Conversational interactions between intellectually disabled and normal progress adolescents during a problem-solving task.* Paper presented at the meeting of the World Congress of IASSD, Helsinki, Finland.

Olson, J. L., Platt, J. M., and Dieker, L. (2008). *Teaching children and adolescents with special needs.* Upper Saddle River, NJ: Prentice Hall.

Olweus, D. (1993). *Bullying at school: What we know and what we can do.* Cambridge, MA: Blackwell.

Orsmond, G. I., Seltzer, M. M., Greenberg, J. S., and Krauss, M. W. (2006). Mother-child relationship quality among adolescents and adults with autism. *American Journal on Mental Retardation, 111*(2), 121–137.

Orton, S. T. (1937). *Reading, writing, and speech problems in children.* New York: W. W. Norton.

OSEP Technical Assistance Center on Positive Behavioral Interventions and Supports. (2009). Reducing behavior problems in the elementary school. Retrieved from http://www.pbis.org/

Ovander, C. J., and Collier, V. P. (1998). *Bilingual and ESL classrooms: Teaching in multicultural contexts.* Boston: McGraw-Hill.

Owens, R. E., Jr. (2005). *Language development: An introduction* (6th ed.). Boston: Allyn & Bacon.

Owens, R. E. (2010). *Language disorders: A functional approach to assessment and intervention* (5th ed.). Boston: Pearson/Allyn & Bacon.

Palincsar, A. S. (1982). *Improving the reading comprehension of junior high students through the reciprocal teaching of comprehension-monitoring.* Unpublished doctoral dissertation, University of Illinois, Urbana.

Palincsar, A. S. (1986). The role of dialogue in providing scaffolded instruction. *Educational Psychologist, 21*(1–2), 73–98.

Palincsar, A. S. (1988). *Reciprocal teaching instructional materials packet.* East Lansing: Michigan State University.

Palincsar, A. S. (2007). Reciprocal teaching 1982 to 2006: The role of research, theory, and representation in the transformation of instructional research. In D. W. Rowe and R. T. Jimenez (Eds.), *56th Yearbook of the national reading conference* (pp. 38–49). Oak Creek, WI: National Reading Conference.

Palincsar, A. S., and Brown, A. L. (1984). Reciprocal teaching of comprehension fostering and comprehension monitoring activities. *Cognition and Instruction, 1*(2), 117–175.

Palincsar, A. S., and Brown, A. L. (1986). Interactive teaching to promote independent learning from text. *The Reading Teacher, 39*(8), 771–777.

Palincsar, A. S., and Duke, N. K. (2004). The role of text and text-reader interactions in young children's reading development and achievement. *The Elementary School Journal, 105*(2), 183–197.

Palmatier, R. A., and Ray, H. L. (1989). *Sports talk: A dictionary of sports metaphors.* New York: Greenwood.

Parker, R., Hasbrouck, J. E., and Denton, C. (2002). How to tutor students with reading problems. *Preventing School Failure, 47,* 42–44.

Parmar, R. S., and Cawley, J. F. (1997). Preparing teachers to teach mathematics to students with learning disabilities. *Journal of Learning Disabilities, 30*(2), 188–197.

Parmar, R. S., Cawley, J. F., and Miller, J. H. (1994). Differences in mathematics performance between students with learning disabilities and students with mild retardation. *Exceptional Children, 60,* 549–563.

Parsons, J. A. (1972). The reciprocal modification of arithmetic behavior and program development. In G. Semb (Ed.), *Behavior analysis and education.* Lawrence: University of Kansas, Department of Human Development.

Paterson, K. (1978). *The great Gilly Hopkins.* New York: Crowell.

Patton, J. R., Cronin, M. E., Bassett, D. S., and Koppel, A. E. (1997). A life skills approach to mathematics instruction: Preparing students with learning disabilities for the real-life math demands of adulthood. *Journal of Learning Disabilities, 30*(2), 178–187.

Patton, J. R., and Dunn, C. (1998). *Transition from school to young adulthood: Basic concepts and recommended practices.* Austin, TX: PRO-ED.

Pauk, W. (2001). *Essential study strategies.* Columbus, OH: Prentice Hall.

Paul, R. (2007). *Language disorders from infancy through adolescence.* St. Louis, MO: Mosby.

Pavri, S., and Monda-Amaya, L. (2000). Loneliness and students with learning disabilities in inclusive classrooms: Self-perceptions, coping strategies, and preferred interventions. *Learning Disabilities Research and Practice, 15*(1), 22–33.

Pearson, P. D., and Johnson, D. D. (1978). *Teaching reading comprehension.* New York: Holt, Rinehart and Winston.

Pecyna-Rhyner, P., Lehr, D., and Pudlas, K. (1990). An analysis of teacher responsiveness to communicative initiations of children with handicaps. *Language, Speech, and Hearing Services in Schools, 21,* 91–97.

Pehrsson, R. S., and Robinson, H. A. (1985). *The semantic organizer approach to writing and reading instruction.* Rockville, MD: Aspen.

Pfeffer, C. R. (1986). *The suicidal child.* New York: Guilford Press.

Polloway, E., Epstein, M., Polloway, C., Patton, J., and Ball, D. (1986). Corrective reading program: An analysis of effectiveness with learning disabled and mentally retarded students. *Remedial and Special Education, 7,* 41–47.

Popenhagen, M. P., and Qualley, R. M. (1998). Adolescent suicide: Detection, intervention, and prevention. *Professional School Counseling, 1*(4), 30–35.

Preiss, R. W., and Gayle, B. M. (2006). A meta-analysis of the educational benefits of employing advanced organizers. In B. M. Gayle, R. W. Preiss, N. Burrell, and M. Allen (Eds.), *Classroom communication and instructional processes: Advances through meta-analysis* (pp. 329–344). Mahwah, N.J.: Lawrence Erlbaum Associates.

Premack, D. (1959). Toward empirical behavior laws. *Psychological Review, 66*(4), 219–233.

President's Commission on Excellence in Special Education. (2002). *A new era: Revitalizing special education.* Washington, DC: U.S. Department of Education.

Pressley, M. (1998). *Reading instruction that works: The case for balanced teaching.* New York: Guilford.

Putnam, M. L. (1992). The testing practices of mainstream secondary classroom teachers. *Remedial and Special Education, 13*(5), 11–21.

Putnam, M. L., Deshler, D. D., and Schumaker, J. S. (1993). The investigation of setting demands: A missing link in learning strategy instruction. In L. S. Meltzer (Ed.), *Strategy assessment and instruction for students with learning disabilities* (pp. 325–354). Austin, TX: PRO-ED.

Radencich, M. C., Beers, P. C., and Schumm, J. S. (1993). *A handbook for the K–12 reading resource specialist*. Boston: Allyn & Bacon.

RAND. (2002). *Reading for understanding: Toward an R&D program in reading comprehension*. Santa Monica, CA: Author.

RAND Reading Study Group (2002). *Reading for Understanding: Toward an R&D Program in Reading Comprehension*. Washington, DC: RAND.

Raphael, T. E. (1982). Question-answering strategies for children. *The Reading Teacher, 36,* 188.

Raphael, T. E. (1984). Teaching learners about sources of information for answering comprehension questions. *Journal of Reading, 27,* 303–311.

Raphael, T. E. (1986). Teaching question-answer relationships revisited. *The Reading Teacher, 39*(6), 516–523.

Raphael, T. E., and Pearson, P. D. (1982). *The effect of metacognitive awareness training on children's question-answering behavior.* (Tech. Rep. No. 238). Urbana: University of Illinois, Center for Study of Reading.

Rashotte, C. A., and Torgesen, J. K. (1985). Repeated reading and reading fluency in learning disabled children. *Reading Research Quarterly, 20*(2), 180–188.

Rasinski, T. V. (1990a). Effects of repeated reading and listening-while-reading on reading fluency. *Journal of Education Research, 83,* 147–150.

Rasinski, T. V. (1990b). Investigating measures of reading fluency. *Educational Research Quarterly, 14*(3), 37–44.

Rasinski, T. V. (Ed.). (2009). *Essential readings on fluency.* Newark, DE: International Reading Association.

Rathvon, N. (2004). *Early reading assessment: A practitioner's handbook.* New York: Guilford.

Rayner, K., Foorman, B. R., Perfetti, C. A., Pesetsky, D., and Seidenberg, M. S. (2001). How psychological science informs the teaching of reading. *Psychological Science in the Public Interest, 2*(2), 31–73.

Re, A. M., Pedron, M., and Cornoldi, C. (2007). Expressive writing difficulties in children described as exhibiting ADHD symptoms. *Journal of Learning Disabilities, 40*(3), 244–255.

Reed, Deborah K. (2008). A synthesis of morphology interventions and effects on reading outcomes for students in grades K–12. *Learning Disabilities Research and Practice, 23*(1), 36–49.

Renik, M. J. (April 1987). *Measuring the relationship between academic self-perceptions and global self-worth: The self-perception profile for learning disabled students.* Presented at the Society for Research in Child Development, Baltimore, MD.

Reutzel, D. R., Jones, C. D., Fawson, P. C., and Smith, J. A. (2008). Scaffolded silent reading: A complement to guided repeated oral reading that works! *The Reading Teacher, 62*(3), 194–207.

Reyes, E. I., and Bos, C. S. (1998). Interactive semantic mapping and charting: Enhancing content area learning for language minority students. In R. Gersten and R. Jimenez (Eds.), *Innovative practices for language minority students* (pp. 133–150). Pacific Grove, CA: Brooks/Cole.

Ritchey, K. D., and Goeke, J. L. (2006). Orton-Gillingham and Orton-Gillinham-based reading instruction: A review of the literature. *The Journal of Special Education, 40*(3), 171–183.

Rivera, D. P., and Smith, D. D. (1997). *Teaching students with learning and behavior problems* (3rd ed.). Boston: Allyn & Bacon.

Rivera, D. P., Smith, R. G., Goodwin, M. W., and Bryant, D. P. (1998). Mathematical word problem solving: A synthesis of intervention research for students with learning disabilities. In T. E. Scruggs and M. A. Mastropieri (Eds.), *Advances in learning and behavioral disabilities* (vol. 12, pp. 245–285). Greenwich, CT: JAI Press.

Roberts, G. H. (1968). The failure strategies of third grade arithmetic pupils. *The Arithmetic Teacher, 15,* 442–446.

Robertson, H. M. (1999). LEA and students with special needs. In O. G. Nelson and W. M. Linek (Eds.), *Practical classroom applications of language experience: Looking back, looking forward* (pp. 221–223). Boston: Allyn & Bacon.

Robinson, F. P. (1946). *Effective study.* New York: Harper and Brothers.

Roehring, A. D., Duggar, S. W., Moats, L., Glover, M., and Nincey, B. (2008). When teachers work to use progress monitoring data to inform literacy instruction. *Remedial and Special Education, 29*(6), 364–368.

Rogers, B. (2002). *Classroom Behaviour: A practical guide to effective teaching, behaviour management, and colleague support.* Thousand Oaks, CA: Sage.

Roller, C. M. (2002). Accommodating variability in reading instruction. *Reading and Writing Quarterly, 18,* 17–38.

Rooney, K. J., and Hallahan, D. P. (1985). Future directions for cognitive behavior modification research: The quest for cognitive change. *Remedial and Special Education, 6*(2), 46–51.

Rose, T. L. (1984). The effect of two prepractice procedures on oral reading. *Journal of Learning Disabilities, 17,* 544–548.

Rose, T. L., and Beattie, J. R. (1986). Relative effects of teacher-directed and taped previewing on oral reading. *Learning Disability Quarterly, 9,* 193–199.

Rosenblatt, L. (1978). *The reader, the text, the poem: The transactional theory of the literary work.* Carbondale: Southern Illinois University Press.

Rosenshine, B. (1997). Advances in research in instruction. In J. W. Lloyd, E. J. Kame'enui, and D. Chard (Eds.), *Issues in educating students with disabilities.* Mahwah, NJ: Erlbaum.

Rosenshine, B., and Meister, C. (1994). Reciprocal teaching: A review of the research. *Review of Education Research, 64,* 479–530.

Rourke, B. P., Young, G. C., and Leenaars, A. A. (1989). A childhood learning disability that predisposes those afflicted to adolescent and adult depression and suicide risk. *Journal of Learning Disabilities, 22*(3), 169–175.

Routh, D. K. (1979). Activity, attention, and aggression in learning disabled children. *Journal of Clinical Child Psychology, 8,* 183–187.

Ruddell, M. R. (1994). Vocabulary knowledge and comprehension: A comprehension process view of complex literacy relationship. In R. B. Ruddell, M. R. Ruddell, and H. Singer (Eds.), *Theoretical models and processes of reading* (4th ed., pp. 414–447). Newark, DE: International Reading Association.

Ruedy, L. R. (1983). Handwriting instruction: It can be part of the high school curriculum. *Academic Therapy, 18*(4), 421–429.

Ruhl, K. L. (1996). Does nature of student activity during lecture pauses affect notes and immediate recall of college students with learning disabilities? *Journal of Postsecondary Education and Disability, 12*(2), 16–27.

Ruhl, K. L., Hughes, C. A., and Gajar, A. H. (1990). Efficacy of the pause procedure for enhancing learning disabled and nondisabled college students' long- and short-term recall of facts presented through lecture. *Learning Disability Quarterly, 13,* 55–64.

Rumelhart, D. E. (1980). Schemata: The building blocks of cognition. In R. J. Spiro, B. C. Bruce, and W. F. Brewer (Eds.), *Theoretical issues in reading comprehension* (pp. 33–58). Hillsdale, NJ: Erlbaum.

Rumelhart, D. E. (1985). Toward an interactive model of reading. In H. Singer and R. B. Ruddell (Eds.), *Theoretical models and processes of reading* (3rd ed.). Newark, DE: International Reading Association.

Rupley, W. H., Logan, J. W., and Nichols, W. D. (1998). Vocabulary instruction in a balanced reading program. *The Reading Teacher, 52,* 338–346.

Ryan, J. B., Sanders, S., Katsiyannis, A., and Yell, M. L. (2007). Using time-out effectively in the classroom. *Teaching Exceptional Children, 39*(4), 60–67.

Saenz, L. M., Fuchs, L. S., and Fuchs, D. (2005). Peer-assisted learning strategies for English language learners with learning disabilities. *Exceptional Children, 71,* 231–247.

Salend, S. J., Gordon, J., and Lopez-Vona, K. (2002). Evaluating cooperative teaching teams. *Intervention in School and Clinic, 37,* 195–200.

Salend, S. J., and Lutz, J. G. (1984). Mainstreaming or mainlining: A competency based approach to mainstreaming. *Journal of Learning Disabilities, 17*(1), 27–29.

Salend, S. J., and Nowak, M. R. (1988). Effects of peer-previewing on LD students' oral reading skills. *Learning Disability Quarterly, 11,* 47–53.

Samuels, S. J. (1979). The method of repeated readings. *The Reading Teacher, 32,* 403–408.

Samuels, S. J. (1997). The method of repeated reading. *The Reading Teacher, 50,* 376–381. Originally published in *The Reading Teacher* in January 1979 (vol. 32).

Santoro, L., Chard, D. J., Howard, L., and Baker, S. K. (2008). Making the very most of classroom read-alouds to promote comprehension and vocabulary. *The Reading Teacher, 61*(5), 396–408.

Sawyer, V., Nelson, J. S., Jayanthi, M., Bursuck, W., and Epstein, M. H. (1996). Views of students with learning disabilities of their homework in general education classes: Student interviews. *Learning Disability Quarterly, 19,* 70–85.

Scammaca, N., Roberts, G., Vaughn, S., Edmonds, M., Wexler, J., Reutebuch, C. K., et al. (2007). Interventions for adolescent struggling readers: A meta-analysis with implications for practice. Portsmouth, NH: RMC Research Corporation. Retrieved from http://www.centeroninstruction.org/files/COI%20Struggling%20Readers.pdf

Scammacca, N., Vaughn, S., Roberts, G., Wanzek, J., and Torgesen, J. K. (2007). Extensive reading interventions in grades K–3: From research to practice. Portsmouth, NH: RMC Research Corporation, Center on Instruction. Retrieved from http://www.centeroninstruction.org/files/Extensive%20Reading%20Interventions.pdf

Scanlon, D. J., Duran, G. Z., Reyes, E. I., and Gallego, M. A. (1992). Interactive semantic mapping: An interactive approach to enhancing LD students' content area comprehension. *Learning Disabilities Research and Practice, 7,* 142–146.

Schank, R. C., and Abelson, R. (1977). *Scripts, plans, goals, and understanding.* Hillsdale, NJ: Erlbaum.

Schatschneider, C., Fletcher, J. M., Francis, D. J., Carlson, C. D., and Foorman, B. R. (2004). Kindergarten predictions of reading skills: A longitudinal comparative analysis. *Journal of Educational Psychology, 96*(2), 583–610.

Scheuermann, B., Jacobs, W. R., McCall, C., and Knies, W. C. (1994). The personal spelling dictionary: An adaptive approach to reducing the spelling hurdle in written language. *Intervention in School and Clinic, 29,* 292–299.

Schmidt, P. R. (1999). KWLQ: Inquiry and literacy learning in science. *The Reading Teacher, 52,* 789–792.

Schumaker, J. B., Denton, P. H., and Deshler, D. D. (1993). *The paraphrasing strategy* (Rev. ed.) (Learning Strategies Curriculum). Lawrence: University of Kansas.

Schumaker, J. B., Deshler, D. D., Alley, G. R., Warner, M. M., and Denton, P. H. (1982). Multipass: A learning strategy for improving reading comprehension. *Learning Disability Quarterly, 5*(3), 295–304.

Schumaker, J. B., Nolan, S. M., and Deshler, D. D. (1994). *The error monitoring strategy* (Rev. ed.). Lawrence: Center for Research on Learning Disabilities, University of Kansas.

Schumm, J. S. (2001). *School power: Study skill strategies for succeeding in school.* Minneapolis, MN: Free Spirit.

Schumm, J. S., and Mangrum, C. T. (1991). FLIP: A framework for textbook thinking. *Journal of Reading, 35,* 120–124.

Schumm, J. S., and Post, S. A. (1997). *Executive learning: Successful strategies for college reading and studying.* Columbus, OH: Prentice Hall.

Schumm, J. S., and Strickler, K. (1991). Guidelines for adapting content area textbooks: Keeping teachers and students content. *Intervention in School and Clinic, 27,* 79–84.

Schumm, J. S., and Vaughn, S. (1991). Making adaptations for mainstreamed students: General classroom teachers' perspectives. *Remedial and Special Education, 12*(4), 18–27.

Schumm, J. S., and Vaughn, S. (1992a). Planning for mainstreamed special education students: Perceptions of general classroom teachers. *Exceptionality, 3,* 81–98.

Schumm, J. S., and Vaughn, S. (1992b). Reflections on planning for mainstreamed special education students. *Exceptionality, 3,* 121–126.

Schumm, J. S., and Vaughn, S. (1995). *Using Making Words in heterogeneous classrooms.* Unpublished manuscript, University of Miami (FL), School Based Research.

Schumm, J. S., Vaughn, S., Haager, D., McDowell, J., Rothlein, L., and Saumell, L. (1995a). General education teacher planning: What can students with learning disabilities expect? *Exceptional Children, 61*(4), 335–352.

Schumm, J. S., Vaughn, S., Haager, D., McDowell, J., Rothlein, L., and Saumell, L. (1995b). Teacher planning for individual student needs: What can mainstreamed special education students expect? *Exceptional Children, 61,* 335–352.

Schumm, J. S., Vaughn, S., and Harris, J. (1997). Pyramid power for collaborative planning. *Teaching Exceptional Children, 29*(6), 62–66.

Schuster, J. W., Stevens, K. B., and Doak, P. K. (1990). Using constant time delay to teach word definitions. *Journal of Special Education, 24,* 306–318.

Schwartz, N. H., Ellsworth, L. S., Graham, L., and Knight, B. (1998). Assessing prior knowledge to remember text: A comparison of advance organizers and maps. *Contemporary Educational Psychology, 23*(1), 65–89.

Schwartz, S. E., and Budd, D. (1981). Mathematics for handicapped learners: A functional approach for adolescents. *Focus on Exceptional Children, 13*(7), 1–12.

Scott, C. M., and Stokes, S. L. (1995). Measures of syntax in school-age children and adolescents. *Language, Speech, and Hearing Services in Schools, 26,* 309–319.

Scruggs, T. E., and Mastropieri, M. A. (1988). Are learning disabled students "test-wise"? A review of recent research. *Learning Disabilities Focus, 3,* 87–97.

Scruggs, T. E., Mastropieri, M. A., Berkeley, S., and Graetz, J. E. (2009). Do special education interventions improve learning of secondary content? A meta-analysis. *Remedial and Special Education.* http://rse.sagepub.com/content/early/2009/02/27/0741932508327465.

Scruggs, T. E., Mastropieri, M. A., and McDuffie, K. A. (2007). Co-teaching in inclusive classrooms: A metasynthesis of qualitative research. *Exceptional Children, 73*(4), 392–416.

Seidel, J. F., and Vaughn, S. (1991). Social alienation and the LD school dropout. *Learning Disabilities Research and Practice, 6*(3), 152–157.

Seligman, M., and Darling, R. B. (2007). *Ordinary families, special children* (3rd ed.). New York: Guilford.

Seymour, P. H. K., Aro, M., and Erskine, J. (2003). Foundation literacy acquisition in European orthographies. *British Journal of Psychology, 94,* 143–174.

Shannon, P., Kame'enui, E., and Baumann, J. (1988). An investigation of children's ability to comprehend character motives. *American Educational Research Journal, 25,* 441–462.

Share, D. L., and Stanovich, K. E. (1995). Cognitive processes in early reading development: A model of acquisition and individual differences. *Issues in Education: Contributions from Education Psychology, 1,* 1–57.

Shaywitz, S. (2003). *Overcoming dyslexia: A new and complete science-based program for reading problems at any level.* New York: Knopf.

Shaywitz, S. E., Morris, R., and Shaywitz, B. A. (2008). The education of dyslexic children from childhood to young adulthood. *Annual Review of Psychology, 59,* 451–475.

Sheras, P. L. (1983). Suicide in adolescence. In E. Walker and M. Roberts (Eds.), *Handbook of clinical child psychology.* New York: Wiley.

Shinn, M. R. (Ed.). (1989). *Curriculum-based measurement: Assessing special children.* New York: Guilford.

Shippen, M. E., Simpson, R. G., and Crites, S. A. (2003). A practical guide to functional behavioral assessment. *Teaching Exceptional Children, 35,* 36–44.

Shore, K. (2003). *Elementary teacher's discipline problem solver: A practical A–Z guide for managing classroom behavior problems.* San Francisco: Jossey-Bass.

Short, K. (1997). *Literature as a way of knowing.* York, ME: Stenhouse.

Short, K. G., Harste, J. C., with Burke, C. (1995). *Creating classrooms for authors and inquirers.* Portsmouth, NH: Heinemann.

Silver, A. A., and Hagin, R. A. (2002). *Disorders of learning in childhood* (2nd ed.). New York: Wiley.

Simmons, D., Fuchs, D., Fuchs, L. S., Hodge, J. P., and Mathes, P. G. (1994). Importance of instructional complexity and role reciprocity to classwide peer tutoring. *Learning Disabilities Research and Practice, 9,* 203–212.

Simmons, D., Hairrell, A., Edmonds, M., Vaughn, S., Larsen, R. Willson, V., et al. (2010). A comparison of multiple-strategy methods: Effects on fourth-grade students' general and content-specific reading comprehension and vocabulary development. *Journal of Research on Educational Effectiveness, 3*(2), 121–156.

Simmons, D. C., Kame'enui, E. J., Stoolmiller, M., Coyne, M. D., and Harn, B. (2003). Accelerating growth and maintaining proficiency: A two-year intervention study of kindergarten and first-grade children at risk for reading difficulties. In B. F. Foorman (Ed.), *Preventing and remediating reading difficulties: Bringing science to scale* (pp. 199–228). Baltimore: York.

Slavin, R. E. (2000). *Educational psychology: Theory and practice.* Boston: Allyn & Bacon.

Slavin, R. E., Madden, N. A., Karweit, N. L., Dolan, L., and Wasik, B. A. (1992). *Success for all: A relentless approach to prevention and early intervention in elementary schools.* Arlington, VA: Educational Research Service.

Smith, E. M., and Alley, G. R. (1981). *The effect of teaching sixth graders with learning difficulties a strategy for solving verbal math problems* (Research Report No. 39). Institute for Research in Learning Disabilities.

Smith, M. K. (1941). Measurement of the size of general English vocabulary through the elementary grades and high school. *Genetic Psychological Monographs, 24,* 311–345.

Smith, T. J., and Adams, G. (2006). The effect of comorbid AD/HD and learning disabilities on parent-reported behavioral and academic outcomes of children. *Learning Disability Quarterly, 29,* 101–112.

Snow, C. E., Burns, M. S., and Griffin, P. (Eds.). (1998). *Preventing reading difficulties in young children.* Washington, DC: National Academy Press.

Soukup, J. H., Wehmeyer, M. L., Bashinski, S. M., and Bovaird, J. A. (2007). Classroom variables and access to the general education curriculum for students with disabilities. *Exceptional Children, 74*(1), 101–120.

Spear-Swerling, L. (2006). *The importance of teaching handwriting.* Retrieved August 10, 2006, from http://www.ldonline.org/spearswerling/10521.

Speece, D. L., MacDonald, V., Kilsheimer, L., and Krist, J. (1997). Research to practice: Preservice teachers reflect on reciprocal teaching. *Learning Disabilities Research and Practice, 12,* 177–187.

Stahl, S. A. (2004). What do we know about fluency? In P. McCardle and V. Chhabra, *The voice of evidence in reading research* (pp. 187–211). Baltimore: Brookes.

Stahl, S. A., and Kuhn, M. R. (2002). Making it sound like language: Developing fluency. *Reading Teacher, 55*(6), 582–584.

Stahl, S. A., Pagnucco, J. R., and Suttles, C. W. (1996). First graders' reading and writing instruction in traditional and process-oriented classes. *The Journal of Educational Research, 89,* 131–144.

Stallings, J. (1975). *Relationships between classroom instructional practices and child development* (Rep. No. PLEDE-C-75). Menlo Park, CA: Stanford Research Institute. (ERIC Document Reproduction Service No. ED 110 200).

Stanovich, K. (1986). Cognitive processes and the reading problems of learning-disabled children: Evaluating the assumption of specificity. In J. K. Torgesen and B. Y. L. Wong (Eds.),

Psychological and educational perspectives on learning disabilities (pp. 85–131). Orlando, FL: Academic Press.

Stauffer, R. G. (1969). *Directing reading maturity as a cognitive process*. New York: Harper & Row.

Stauffer, R. G. (1970). *The language-experience approach to the teaching of reading*. New York: Harper & Row.

Stauffer, R. G. (1976). *Teaching reading as a thinking process*. New York: Harper & Row.

Stern, C., Stern, M. B., and Gould, T. S. (1998). *Structural arithmetic*. Cambridge, MA: Educators Publishing Service.

Stevens, K. B., and Schuster, J. W. (1987). Effects of a constant time delay procedure on the written spelling performance of a learning disabled student. *Learning Disability Quarterly, 10*, 9–16.

Stevens, K. B., and Schuster, J. W. (1988). Time delay: Systematic instruction for academic tasks. *Remedial and Special Education, 9*(5), 16–21.

Stires, S. (Ed.). (1991). *With promise: Redefining reading and writing for "special students."* Portsmouth, NH: Heinemann.

Stivers, J. (2008). Strengthen your coteaching relationship. *Intervention in School and Clinic, 44*(2), 121–125.

Stone, W. L., and LaGreca, A. M. (1990). The social status of children with learning disabilities: A reexamination. *Journal of Learning Disabilities, 23*(1), 32–37.

Stratton, B. D., Grindler, M. C., and Postell, C. M. (1992). Discovering oneself. *Middle School Journal, 24*, 42–43.

Strickland, D. S., Ganske, K., and Monroe, J. (2002). *Supporting struggling readers and writers: Strategies for classroom intervention, 3–6*. Portland, ME: Stenhouse.

Strickland, D. S., and Schickedanz, J. A. (2009). *Learning about print in preschool: Working with letters, words, and beginning links with phonemic awareness*. Newark, DE: International Reading Association.

Stuart, M. (1999). Getting ready for reading: Early phoneme awareness and phonics training improves reading and spelling in inner-city second language learners. *British Journal of Educational Psychology, 69*(4), 587–605.

Stuebing, K. K., Fletcher, J. M., LeDoux, J. M., Lyon, G. R., Shaywitz, S. E., and Shaywitz, B. A. (2002). Validity of IQ-discrepancy classifications of reading difficulties: A meta-analysis. *American Educational Research Journal, 39*, 469–518.

Sugai, G., Horner, R. H., Dunlap, G., Hieneman, M., Lewis, T. J., Nelson, C. M., et al. (2000). Applying positive behavior support and functional assessment in schools. *Journal of Positive Behavior Interventions, 2*, 131–143.

Sugai, G., Horner, R., and Gresham, F. M. (2002). Behaviorally effective school environments. In M. Shinn, H. Walker, and G. Stoner (Eds.), *Interventions for achievement and behavior problems II: Preventive and remedial approaches* (pp. 315–350). Bethesda, MD: National Association of School Psychologists. (ERIC Document Reproduction Service No. ED 462 655).

Suritsky, S. K., and Hughes, C. A. (1996). Notetaking strategy instruction. In D. D. Deshler, E. S. Ellis, and B. K. Lenz (Eds.), *Teaching adolescents with learning disabilities* (2nd ed., pp. 267–312). Denver: Love.

Swafford, K. M., and Reed, V. A. (1986). Language and learning-disabled children. In V. A. Reed (Ed.), *An introduction to children with language disorders* (pp. 105–128). New York: Macmillan.

Swanson, E. A., Wanzek, J., Petscher, Y., Vaughn, S., Cavanaugh, D., Klinger, K., et al. (in press). A synthesis of read-aloud interventions on early reading outcomes among preschool through third graders. *Journal of Learning Disabilities*.

Swanson, H. L. (1999a). Reading research for students with LD: A meta-analysis of intervention outcomes. *Journal of Learning Disabilities, 32*, 504–532.

Swanson, H. L. (1999b). Instructional components that predict treatment outcomes for students with learning disabilities: Support for a combined strategy and direct instruction model. *Learning Disabilities Research and Practice, 14*(3), 129–140.

Swanson, H. L., Howard, C. B., and Saez, L. (2006). Do different components of working memory underlie different subgroups of reading disabilities? *Journal of Learning Disabilities, 39*(3), 252–269.

Swanson, M., McBurnett, K., Wigal, T., Pfiffner, L., Lerner, M., Williams, L., et al. (1993). Effect of stimulant medication on children with attention deficit disorder: A "review of reviews." *Exceptional Children, 60*, 154–162.

Talbott, E., and Fleming, J. (2003). The role of social contexts and special education mental health problems of urban adolescents. *The Journal of Special Education, 37*(2), 111–123.

Teicher, J. D. (1973). A solution to the chronic problem of living: Adolescent attempted suicide. In J. C. Schoolar (Ed.), *Current issues in adolescent psychiatry* (pp. 129–147). New York: Brunner/Mazel.

Tharp, R. G., and Gallimore, R. (1988). *Rousing minds to life: Teaching, learning, and schooling in social context*. New York: Cambridge University Press.

Tharp, R., Estrada, P., Dolton, S. S., and Yamauchi, L. (1999). *Teaching transformed: Achieving excellence, fairness, inclusion, and harmony*. Boulder, CO: Westview Press.

Thorne, M. T. (1978). "Payment for reading": The use of the *Corrective Reading* scheme with junior high maladjusted boys. *Remedial Education, 13*(2), 87–90.

Thornton, C. A. (1978). Emphasizing thinking strategies in basic fact instruction. *Journal for Research in Mathematics Education, 215–227.*

Thornton, C. A., and Toohey, M. A. (1985). Basic math facts: Guidelines for teaching and learning. *Learning Disabilities Focus, 1*(1), 44–57.

Thornton, C. A., Tucker, B. F., Dossey, J. A., and Bazik, E. F. (1983). *Teaching mathematics to children with special needs*. Menlo Park, CA: Addison-Wesley.

Thorpe, H. W., and Borden, K. F. (1985). The effect of multisensory instruction upon the on-task behavior and word reading accuracy of learning disabled students. *Journal of Learning Disabilities, 18*, 279–286.

Tierney, R. J., and Readence, J. E. (2000). *Reading strategies and practices: A compendium* (5th ed.). Boston: Allyn & Bacon.

Tierney, R. J., and Readence, J. E. (2005). *Reading strategies and practices: A compendium* (6th ed.). Boston: Allyn & Bacon.

Toolan, J. M. (1981). Depression and suicide in children: An overview. *American Journal of Psychotherapy, 35*(3), 311–323.

Topping, K., and Eli, S. (1998). *Peer-assisted learning*. Mahwah, NJ: Erlbaum.

Torgesen, J. K. (1999). Assessment and instruction for phonemic awareness and word recognition skills. In H. W. Catts and A. G. Kamhi (Eds.), *Language and reading disabilities* (pp. 128–153). Boston: Allyn & Bacon.

Torgesen, J. K. (2000). Individual differences in response to early interventions in reading: The lingering problem of treatment resisters. *Learning Disabilities Research and Practice, 15,* 55–64.

Torgesen, J. K. (2002). The prevention of reading difficulties. *Journal of School Psychology, 40,* 7–26.

Torgesen, J. K., Wagner, R. K., and Rahsotte, C. A. (1994). Longitudinal studies of phonological processing and reading. *Journal of Learning Disabilities 19,* 623–630.

Torgesen, J. K., Wagner, R. K., and Rashotte, C. A. (1997). Approaches to the prevention and remediation of phonologically based reading disabilities. In B. Blachman (Ed.), *Foundations of reading acquisition and dyslexia: Implications for early intervention.* Mahwah, NJ: Erlbaum.

Torgesen, J. K., Wagner, R. K., Rashotte, C. A., Alexander, A. W., and Conway, T. (1997). Preventive and remedial interventions for children with severe reading disabilities. *Learning Disabilities: A Multidisciplinary Journal, 8*(1), 51–61.

Torgesen, J. K., Alexander, A. W., Wagner, R. K., Rashotte, C. A., Voeller, K., Conway, T., et al. (2001). Intensive remedial instruction for children with severe reading disabilities: Immediate and long-term outcomes from two instructional approaches. *Journal of Learning Disabilities, 34*(1), 33–58.

Tournaki, N. (2003). The differential effects of teaching addition through strategy instruction versus drill and practice to students with and without learning disabilities. *Journal of Learning Disabilities, 36,* 449–458.

Townsend, M. A. R., and Clarihew, A. (1989). Facilitating children's comprehension through the use of advance organizers. *Journal of Reading Behavior, 21,* 15–36.

Trelease, J. (2006). *The read-aloud handbook.* (6th ed.). New York: Penguin.

Troia, G. A., and Graham, S. (2002). The effectiveness of a highly explicit, teacher-directed strategy instruction routine: Changing the writing performance of students with learning disabilities. *Journal of Learning Disabilities, 35,* 290–305.

Troia, G. A., Graham, S., and Harris, K. R. (1999). Teaching students with learning disabilities to mindfully plan when writing. *Exceptional Children, 65*(2), 235–252.

Tucker, B. F., Singleton, A. H., and Weaver, T. L. (2006). *Teaching mathematics to all children: Designing and adapting instruction to meet the needs of diverse learners.* Upper Saddle River, NJ: Pearson.

Tur-Kaspa, H. (2004). Social-information-processing skills of kindergarten children with developmental learning disabilities. *Learning Disabilities Research and Practice, 19*(1), 3–11.

Turnbull, A. P., and Turnbull, H. R. (1990). *Families, professionals, and exceptionality: A special partnership* (2nd ed.). Columbus, OH: Merrill.

U.S. Department of Education. (2006a). "Assistance to states for the education of children with disabilities and preschool grants for children with disabilities: Final rule," 34 CRF Parts 300 and 301, *Federal Register* 71: 156 (Aug. 14, 2006): 46540–46845. Retrieved February 14, 2007, from www.idea.ed.gov/download/final-regulations.pdr.

U.S. Department of Education. (2006b, April). *Twenty-sixth annual report to congress on the implementation of the Individuals with Disabilities Education Act.* Washington, DC: U.S. Department of Education.

U.S. Department of Education. (2007). *Individuals with Disabilities Education Act (IDEA) data* (Table 1-3). Washington, DC: Author. (Available online at https://www.ideadata.org/arc_toc9.asp#partbCC)

U.S. Department of Education, Office of Special Education and Rehabilitative Services, Office of Special Education Programs. (2003). *Identifying and Treating Attention Deficit Hyperactivity Disorder: A Resource for School and Home.* Washington, DC: U.S. Department of Education.

Ulanoff, S. H., and Pucci, S. L. (1999). Learning words from books: The effects of read aloud on second language vocabulary acquisition. *Bilingual Research Journal, 23,* 319–332.

University of Texas Center for Reading and Language Arts. (1999). *Enhancing vocabulary instruction for secondary students.* Austin, TX: UT System/Texas Education Agency.

University of Texas Center for Reading and Language Arts. (2000a). *Establishing an intensive reading and writing program for secondary students.* Austin, TX: UT System/Texas Education Agency.

University of Texas Center for Reading and Language Arts. (2000b). *First grade teacher reading academy.* Austin, TX: UT System/Texas Education Agency.

University of Texas Center for Reading and Language Arts. (2001a). *Effective instruction for elementary struggling readers: Research-based practices.* Austin, TX: UT System/Texas Education Agency.

University of Texas Center for Reading and Language Arts. (2001b). *Second grade teacher reading academy.* Austin, TX: UT System/Texas Education Agency.

University of Texas Center for Reading and Language Arts. (2002). *Effective instruction for secondary struggling readers: Research-based practices.* Austin, TX: UT System/Texas Education Agency.

University of Texas Center for Reading and Language Arts. (2003a). *Fourth grade teacher reading academy.* Austin, TX: UT System/Texas Education Agency.

University of Texas Center for Reading and Language Arts. (2003b). *Third grade teacher reading academy.* Austin, TX: UT System/Texas Education Agency.

Vadasy, P. F., and Sanders, E. A. (2008). Repeated reading intervention: Outcomes and interactions with readers' skills and classroom instruction. *Journal of Educational Psychology, 100*(2), 272–290.

Van Luit, J. E. H., and Naglieri, J. A. (1999). Effectiveness of the MASTER program for teaching children multiplication and division. *Journal of Learning Disabilities, 32,* 98–107.

Van Reusen, A. K., and Bos, C. S. (1990). I PLAN: Helping students communicate in planning conferences. *Teaching Exceptional Children, 22,* 30–32.

Van Reusen, A. K., Bos, C. S., Schumaker, J. B., and Deshler, D. D. (1994). *The self-advocacy strategy for education and transition planning.* Lawrence, KS: Edge Enterprises.

Van Wagenen, M. A., Williams, R. L., and McLaughlin, T. F. (1994). Use of assisted reading to improve reading rate, word accuracy, and comprehension with ESL Spanish-speaking students. *Perceptual and Motor Skills, 79,* 227–230.

Vaughn, S. (1987). TLC—Teaching, learning, and caring: Teaching interpersonal problem solving skills to emotionally disturbed adolescents. *Pointer, 31,* 25–30.

Vaughn, S., and Bos, C. S. (1987). Knowledge and perception of the resource room: The students' perspective. *Journal of Learning Disabilities, 20,* 218–223.

Vaughn, S., Cirino, P. T., Linan-Thompson, S., Mathes, P. G., Carlson, C. D., Cardenas-Hagan, E., et al. (2006). Effectiveness of a Spanish intervention and an English intervention for English language learners at risk for reading problems. *American Educational Research Journal, 43*(3), 449–487.

Vaughn, S., Elbaum, B. E., and Schumm, J. S. (1996). The effects of inclusion on the social functioning of students with learning disabilities. *Journal of Learning Disabilities, 29,* 598–608.

Vaughn, S., Elbaum, B. E., Schumm, J. S., and Hughes, M. T. (1998). Social outcomes for students with and without learning disabilities in inclusive classrooms. *Journal of Learning Disabilities, 31*(5), 428–436.

Vaughn, S., and Fuchs, L. S. (2003). Redefining learning disabilities as inadequate response to treatment: The promise and potential problems. *Learning Disabilities Research and Practice, 18*(3), 137–146.

Vaughn, S., and Fuchs, L. S. (2006). A response to "Competing views: A dialogue on response to intervention": Why response to intervention is necessary but not sufficient for identifying students with learning disabilities. *Assessment for Effective Intervention, 32*(1), 58–61.

Vaughn, S., Gersten, R., and Chard, D. J. (2000). The underlying message in LD intervention research: Findings from research syntheses. *Exceptional Children, 67*(1), 99–114.

Vaughn, S., Hogan, A., Kouzekanani, K., and Shapiro, S. (1990). Peer acceptance, self-perceptions, and social skills of LD students prior to identification. *Journal of Educational Psychology, 82*(1), 1–6.

Vaughn, S., and Klingner, J. (1999). Teaching reading comprehension through collaborative strategic reading. *Intervention in School and Clinic, 34*(5), 284–292.

Vaughn, S., and Klingner, J. K. (2004). Teaching reading comprehension to students with learning disabilities. In K. Apel, B. J. Ehren, E. R. Silliman, and C. A. Stone (Series Eds.); C. A. Stone, E. R. Silliman, B. J. Ehren, and K. Apel (Vol. Eds.), *Challenges in language and literacy; Handbook of language and literacy: Development and disorders* (pp. 541–555). New York: Guilford Press.

Vaughn, S., and Klingner, J. K. (2007). Response to Intervention (RtI): A new era in identifying students with learning disabilities. In D. Haager, J. Klingner, and S. Vaughn (Eds.), *Validated reading practices for three tiers of intervention* (pp. 3–9). Baltimore: Brookes.

Vaughn, S., Klingner, J. K., and Schumm, J. S. (1996). *Collaborative strategic reading.* Miami, FL: School-Based Research, University of Miami.

Vaughn, S., and LaGreca, A. M. (1992). Beyond greetings and making friends: Social skills from a broader perspective. In B. Y. L. Wong (Ed.), *Contemporary intervention research in learning disabilities: An international perspective* (pp. 96–114). New York: Springer-Verlag.

Vaughn, S., and Lancelotta, G. X. (1990). Teaching interpersonal skills to poorly accepted students: Peer-pairing versus non-peer-pairing. *Journal of School Psychology, 28,* 181–188.

Vaughn, S., Lancelotta, G. X., and Minnis, S. (1988). Social strategy training and peer involvement: Increasing peer acceptance of a female LD student. *Learning Disabilities Focus, 4*(1), 32–37.

Vaughn, S., Levine, L., and Ridley, C. A. (1986). *PALS: Problem solving and affective learning strategies.* Chicago: Science Research Associates.

Vaughn, S., and Linan-Thompson, S. (2003). What is special about special education for students with learning disabilities? *Journal of Special Education, 37,* 140–147.

Vaughn, S., and Linan-Thompson, S. (2004). *Research-based methods of reading instruction.* Alexandria, VA: ASCD.

Vaughn, S., Linan-Thompson, S., and Hickman, P. (2003). Response to instruction as a means of identifying students with reading/learning disabilities. *Exceptional Children, 69*(4), 391–409.

Vaughn, S., Linan-Thompson, S., Mathes, P. G., Cirino, P. T., Carlson, C. D., Pollard-Durodola, S. D., et al. (2006). Effectiveness of Spanish intervention for first-grade English language learners at risk for reading difficulties. *Journal of Learning Disabilities, 39*(1), 56–73.

Vaughn, S., Martinez, L. R., Linan-Thompson, S., Reutebuch, C. K., Carlson, C. D., and Francis, D. J. (2009). Enhancing social studies vocabulary and comprehension for seventh-grade English language learners: Findings from two experimental studies. *Journal of Research on Educational Effectiveness, 2*(4), 297–324.

Vaughn, S., Mathes, P. G., Linan-Thompson, S., Cirino, P. T., Carlson, C. D., Pollard-Durodola, S. D., et al. (2006). First-grade English language learners at-risk for reading problems: Effectiveness of an English intervention. *Elementary School Journal, 107*(2), 153–180.

Vaughn, S., McIntosh, R., Schumm, J. S., Haager, D., and Callwood, D. (1993). Social status and peer acceptance revisited. *Learning Disabilities Research and Practice, 8,* 82–88.

Vaughn, S., McIntosh, R., and Spencer-Rowe, J. (1991). Peer rejection is a stubborn thing: Increasing peer acceptance of rejected students with learning disabilities. *Learning Disabilities Research and Practice, 6*(2), 83–88, 152–157.

Vaughn, S., and Schumm, J. S. (1996). Classroom ecologies: Classroom interactions and implications for inclusion of students with learning disabilities. In D. L. Speece and B. Keogh (Eds.), *Research on classroom ecologies: Implications for inclusion of children with learning disabilities* (pp. 107–124). Mahwah, NJ: Erlbaum.

Vaughn, S., Schumm, J. S., and Arguelles, M. E. (1997). The ABCDE's of co-teaching. *Teaching Exceptional Children, 30*(2), 4–10.

Vaughn, S., Schumm, J. S., Jallad, B., Slusher, J., and Saumell, L. (1996). Teachers' views of inclusion. *Learning Disabilities Research and Practice, 11*(2), 96–106.

Vaughn, S., Schumm, J. S., Niarhos, F., and Daugherty, T. (1993). What do students think when teachers make adaptations? *Teaching and Teacher Education, 9,* 107–118.

Vellutino, F. R., Scanlon, D. M., Small, S. G., Fanuele, D. P., and Sweeney, J. (2007). Preventing early reading difficulties through kindergarten and first grade intervention: A variant of the three-tier model. In D. Haager, J. Klingner, and S. Vaughn (Eds.), *Validated reading practices for three tiers of intervention.* Baltimore: Brookes.

Villa, R. A., Thousand, J. S., and Nevin, A. I. (2008). *A guide to co-teaching: Practical tips for facilitating student learning* (2nd ed.). Thousand Oaks, CA: Corwin Press.

Vitale, M., Medland, M., Romance, N., and Weaver, H. P. (1993). Accelerating reading and thinking skills of low-achieving elementary students: Implications for curricular change. *Effective School Practices, 12*(1), 26–31.

Vygotsky, L. S. (1978). *Mind in society: The development of higher psychological processes*. Cambridge, MA: Harvard University Press.

Wade-Stein, D., and Kintsch, E. (2004). Summary street: Interactive computer support for writing. *Cognition and Instruction, 22*(3), 333–362.

Wallace, T., Shin, J., Bartholomay, T., and Stahl, B. J. (2001). Knowledge and skills for teachers supervising the work of paraprofessionals. *Exceptional Children, 67,* 520–534.

Walther-Thomas, C., and Brownell, M. (2000). An interview with Dr. Janice Bulgren. *Intervention in School and Clinic, 35,* 232–236.

Wannan, G., and Fombonne, E. (1998). Gender differences in rates and correlates of suicidal behavior amongst child psychiatric outpatients. *Journal of Adolescence, 21*(4), 371–381.

Wanzek, J., and Vaughn, S. (2009). Students demonstrating persistent low response to reading intervention: Three case studies. *Learning Disabilities Research and Practice, 24*(3), 151–163.

Wanzek, J., Vaughn, S., Wexler, J., Swanson, E. A., and Edmonds, M. (2006). A synthesis of spelling and reading outcomes for students with learning disabilities. *Journal of Learning Disabilities, 39*(6), 528–543.

Weaver, C. (1990). *Understanding whole language: Principles and practices*. Portsmouth, NH: Heinemann.

Weiss, M. P., and Lloyd, J. (2003). Conditions for co-teaching: Lessons from a case study. *Teacher Education and Special Education, 26*(1), 27–41.

Weiss, M. P., and Lloyd, J. W. (2002). Congruence between roles and actions of secondary special educators in co-taught and special education settings. *The Journal of Special Education, 36,* 58–68.

Wells, G. (1999). Language and education: Reconceptualizing education as dialogue. *Annual Review of Applied Linguistics, 19,* 135–155.

West, G. F. (1978). *Teaching reading skills in content areas: A practical guide to the construction of student exercises*. Oviedo, FL: Sandpiper.

Westwood, P. (2003). *Commonsense methods for children with special educational needs* (4th ed.). New York: Routledge Falmer.

Wexler, J., Vaughn, S., Edmonds, M., and Reutebuch, C. K. (2008). A synthesis of fluency interventions for secondary struggling readers. *Reading and Writing: An Interdisciplinary Journal, 21*(4), 317–347.

Wexler, J., Vaughn, S., Roberts, G., and Denton, C. A. (2010). The efficacy of repeated reading and wide reading practice for high school students with severe reading disabilities. *Learning Disabilities Research and Practice, 25*(1), 2–10.

White, T. G., Sowell, J., and Yanagihara A. (1989). Teaching elementary students to use word-part clues. *The Reading Teacher, 42*(4), 302–308.

Whitehurst, G. J., and Lonigan, C. J. (2001). Emergent literacy: Development from pre-readers. In S. B. Neuman and D. K. Dickinson (Eds.), *Handbook of early literacy research* (pp. 11–29). New York: Guilford Press.

Wicks-Nelson, R., and Israel, A. L. (1984). *Behavior disorders of childhood*. Englewood Cliffs, NJ: Prentice Hall.

Wiener, J. (2002). Friendship and social adjustment of children with learning disabilities. In B. Y. L. Wong and M. L. Donahue (Eds.), *The social dimensions of learning disabilities: Essays in honor of Janis Bryan* (pp. 93–114). Mahwah, NJ: Erlbaum.

Wiener, J., and Tardif, C. Y. (2004). Social and emotional functioning of children with learning disabilities: Does special education placement make a difference? *Learning Disabilities Research and Practice, 19*(1), 20–32.

Wiig, E. H., and Semel, E. M. (1984). *Language assessment and intervention for the learning disabled* (2nd ed.). Columbus, OH: Merrill.

Wilkinson, I. A. G., and Anderson, R. C. (1995). Sociocognitive processes in guided silent reading: A microanalysis of small-group lessons. *Reading Research Quarterly, 30*(4), 710–740.

Williams, J. P. (1998). Improving the comprehension of disabled readers. *Annals of Dyslexia, 48,* 213–238.

Williams, J. P. (2005). Instruction in reading comprehension for primary-grade students. *The Journal of Special Education, 39*(1), 6–18.

Williams, J. P., Brown, L. G., Silverstein, A. K., and deCani, J. S. (1994). An instructional program in comprehension of narrative themes for adolescents with learning disabilities. *Learning Disability Quarterly, 17,* 205–221.

Williamson, G. V., and Shields, S. S. (1999). *Rocky's mountain: A word-finding game*. East Moline, IL: LinguiSystems.

Willman, A. T. (1999). "Hello, Mrs. Willman, it's me!" Keep kids reading over the summer by using voice mail. *The Reading Teacher, 52,* 788–789.

Wilson, C. L., and Sindelar, P. T. (1991). Direct instruction in math word problems: Students with learning disabilities. *Journal of Learning Disabilities, 23*(1), 23–29.

Wilson, G. L. (2008). Be an active co-teacher. *Intervention in School and Clinic, 43*(4), 240–243.

Wolery, M., Cybriwsky, C. A., Gast, D. L., and Boyle-Gast, K. (1991). Use of constant time delay and attentional responses with adolescents. *Exceptional Children, 57,* 462–474.

Wolford, P. L., Heward, W. L., and Alber, S. H. (2001). Teaching middle school students with learning disabilities to recruit peer assistance during cooperative learning group activities. *Learning Disabilities Research and Practice, 16*(3), 161–173.

Wong, B. Y. L. (1986). A cognitive approach to teaching spelling. *Exceptional Children, 53,* 169–173.

Wong, B. Y. L., Butler, D. L., Ficzere, S. A., and Kuperis, S. (1997). Teaching adolescents with learning disabilities and low achievers to plan, write, and revise compare-and-contrast essays. *Learning Disabilities Research and Practice, 12*(1), 2–15.

Wong, B. Y. L., and Jones, W. (1982). Increasing metacomprehension in learning disabled and normally achieving students through self-questioning training. *Learning Disability Quarterly, 5,* 228–240.

Wong, B. Y. L., Wong, R., Perry, N., and Sawatsky, D. (1986). The efficacy of a self-questioning summarization strategy for use by underachievers and learning disabled adolescents in social studies. *Learning Disabilities Focus, 2*(1), 20–35.

Woodward, J. (1995). Technology-based research in mathematics for special education. *Focus on Learning Problems in Mathematics, 17*(2), 3–23.

Worthy, J. (1996). A matter of interest: Literature that hooks reluctant readers and keeps them reading. *The Reading Teacher, 50,* 204–212.

Worthy, J., and Broaddus, K. (2002). Fluency beyond the primary grades: From group performance to silent, independent reading. *Reading Teacher, 55*(4), 334–343.

Wylie, R. E., and Durrell, D. D. (1970). Teaching vowels through phonograms. *Elementary English, 47,* 787–791.

Xin, Y. P., and Jitendra, A. K. (1999). The effects of instruction in solving mathematical word problems for students with learning problems: A meta-analysis. *The Journal of Special Education, 32*(4), 207–225.

Yee, A. (1969). Is the phonetic generalization hypothesis in spelling valid? *Journal of Experimental Education, 37,* 82–91.

Yopp, H. K. (1995). A test for assessing phonemic awareness in young children. *The Reading Teacher, 49*(1), 20–29.

Yopp, H. K., and Yopp, R. H. (2009). Phonological awareness is child's play. *Young, 64,* 1–9. Retrieved from http://www.naeyc.org/files/yc/file/200901/BTJPhonologicalAwareness.pdf

Zaragoza, N., and Vaughn, S. (1992). The effects of process writing instruction on three second-grade students with different achievement profiles. *Learning Disabilities Research and Practice, 7*(4), 184–193.

Zeno, S. M., Ivens, S. H., Millard, R. T., and Duvvuri, R. (1995). *The educator's word frequency guide.* Brewster, NY: Touchstone Applied Science Associates.

Zigmond, N. (2001). Special education at a crossroads. *Preventing School Failure, 45*(2), 70–74.

Zigmond, N. (2003). Where should students with disabilities receive special education services? Is one place better than another? *The Journal of Special Education, 37,* 193–199.

Zigmond, N., and Magiera, K. (2002). Co-teaching. *Current Practice Alerts, 6,* 1–4.

Zorfass, J., Corley, P., and Remz, A. (1994). Helping students with disabilities become writers. *Educational Leadership, 51*(5), 62–66.

Zutell, J. (1993). *Directed spelling thinking activity: A developmental, conceptual approach to advance spelling word knowledge.* Paper presented at the First International and 19th National Conference of the Australian Reading Association, Melbourne, Australia.

Cognitive approaches to math performance improvement, 397
Cognitive strategy instruction (CSI), 40–44, 43
  application in the learning strategies curriculum, 46f–47f
  assessing strategy effectiveness, 45f
  generalization strategies, 40, 41–42f
  modeling, 42
  peer editing strategy, 43
  progress monitoring, 43
  reflective thinking, 43–44
  self-regulation, 43, 44f
  strategy steps, 42
  teaching implications of, 44
  verbalization, 43
Collaboration, 126–141
  benefits and misuses of, 129f
  and consultation, 126
  content versus accommodation, 129
  defined, 126
  with families, 140
  with general education teachers, 126–127
  individual versus class focus, 128
  issues and dilemmas in, 128–131
  with paraprofessionals, 138–140, 139f
  problem-solving models, 130
  real world versus the student's world, 129–130
  resources needed for, 128
  in the response to intervention (RTI) model, 127–128, 140–141
  student ownership, 128
  teacher assistance team (TAT), 131
  see also Coteaching
Collaboration among teachers, 6
Collaborative strategic reading, 269–271, 270f, 271f
Communication, 141–145
  difficulties with, 106
  with general education teachers, 144–145
  interviewing skills, 142–143
  principles of, 141–142
  with professionals and families, 143–145, 143f
Composing, 293–296
Comprehension. See Reading comprehension
Comprehension and production in oral language, 164
Comprehension monitoring, 52f
Comprehensive or receptive oral language, 154
Comprehensive Test of Phonological Processing (CTOPP), 198
Computation errors, 387–389, 389f
Concept diagrams and comparison tables, 334–336, 334f, 336f
Concept teaching process, 329
Concrete objects, 172
Conferences with families, 148
Consequences of behavior, 33–39
Consonant diagraphs and clusters, 199–200, 200t
Consonants, 198–200, 199t, 200t

Constant time-delay procedure, 308–309
Consultant teaching, 127
Consultation, 126. See also Collaboration
Content area reading, 328–340
  advanced organizers, 333–334, 335
  alternative reading materials, 342–344
  audiotape textbook chapters, 342–343
  background knowledge of students, 332
  big ideas in content, 328
  class assignments and homework, 344–345
  computer programs for, 343
  concept diagrams and comparison tables, 334–336, 334f, 336f
  concept teaching process, 329
  content enhancement, 328
  content map, 330f
  evaluating instructional materials, 329–332
  FLIP chart, 333f
  Fry readability graph, 331
  instructional activities, 360–364
  lecture adaptations, 343, 344
  portfolios to monitor student progress, 346
  prelearning activities, 332–333
  readability, 329–330
  reinforcing concept learning, 340
  related vocabulary, 329
  semantic and curriculum maps, 339–340
  semantic feature analysis/relationship charts, 336–339, 337f, 338f
  study guides, 341–342
  test construction and adaptation, 345–346
  testing accommodations, 346
  text highlighting, 342
  textbook adaptations, 341–344
  user-friendly text, 330
  visual display, 340f
Content enhancement, 328
Content in teaching oral language, 168–172
Content map, 330f
Content (semantics) in language, 155–156
Content versus accommodation in collaboration, 129
Contextual analysis, vocabulary, 324–325
Contingency contracting in applied behavior analysis, 36, 37f
Conventional code in language, 154
Conversation in teaching oral language, 173–174
Cooperative learning, 116, 81–83, 82f
Coordinating student services, 93
Coplanning, and coteaching, 134–135, 136f, 137f
Corrective feedback in math performance improvement, 398

Coteaching, 92f, 127, 131–138, 138
  classroom management rules, 137–138
  and coplanning, 134–135, 136f, 137f
  core issues in, 137–138
  description of, 132
  evaluation of, 138
  grades, 137
  guidelines for, 135f
  lesson plan, 137f
  models of, 133–134
  parity between teachers, 138
  perceptions in, 132f
  with secondary students, 134
  time to coplan and coordinate, 138
  see also Collaboration
Council for Exceptional Children (CEC), ethical reponsibilities of paraprofessionals, 140
Counseling, 6
Critical reading, 250–251, 251f
Culturally and linguistically diverse families, 149
Culture, community/family/language, 45
Curriculum-based measurement (CBM), 375, 376

Decision-making teams, 64–65, 65f
Decoding strategies for identifying words, 191, 204–211, 206f
  automatic word recognition, 209–210, 210f
  onset-rime, 206–207, 206f, 207f
  phonic analysis, 204–206
  structural analysis, 207–208
  syllabication, 208–209, 209t
  syntax and semantics, 211
  synthetic and analytic phonics, 207
  see also Word identification
Delivering instruction, 27–28
  choral and individual responding, 27
  evaluating, 27
  feedback, 28
  flexible grouping, 28
  limiting teacher talk, 27
  quick pacing, 27
  rate and manner of presentation, 27
  student response opportunities, 27–28
  see also Instruction
Designing instruction, 24–27
  adaptations, 24–25
  for English language learners (ELLs), 28
  flexible grouping, 24
  goal setting, 24
  scaffolding, 25–26
  time management, 26
  see also Instruction; Progress monitoring
Dialogue, interactive, 45–46
Dialogue journals, 23f
Dictionaries, 327
Differential reinforcement in applied behavior analysis, 37–38
  of incompatible behaviors (DRI), 37–38
  of other behaviors, (DRO), 38
Directed reading activity (DRA), 272
Directed reading-thinking activity (DR-TA), 272–274, 274f